Psalms

Volume 1

TEACH THE TEXT COMMENTARY SERIES

John H. Walton
Old Testament General Editor

Mark L. Strauss
New Testament General Editor

When complete, the TEACH THE TEXT COMMENTARY SERIES will include the following volumes:

Old Testament Volumes

Genesis .... Richard S. Hess

Exodus .... T. Desmond Alexander

Leviticus and Numbers .... Joe M. Sprinkle

Deuteronomy .... Michael A. Grisanti

Joshua .... Kenneth A. Mathews

Judges and Ruth .... Kenneth C. Way

1 & 2 Samuel .... Robert B. Chisholm Jr.

1 & 2 Kings .... David W. Baker

1 & 2 Chronicles .... Robert R. Duke

Ezra, Nehemiah, and Esther .... Douglas J. E. Nykolaishen and Andrew J. Schmutzer

Job .... Daniel J. Estes

Psalms, two volumes .... C. Hassell Bullock

Proverbs .... Richard L. Schultz

Ecclesiastes and
   Song of Songs ....Edward M. Curtis

Isaiah ....Frederick J. Mabie

Jeremiah and Lamentations .. J. Daniel Hays

Ezekiel ....John W. Hilber

Daniel ....Ronald W. Pierce

The Minor Prophets .... Douglas Stuart

New Testament Volumes

Matthew .... Jeannine K. Brown

Mark ....Grant R. Osborne

Luke .... R. T. France

John and 1–3 John ....David L. Turner

Acts ....David E. Garland

Romans .... C. Marvin Pate

1 Corinthians .... Preben Vang

2 Corinthians .... Moyer V. Hubbard

Galatians and Ephesians ...... Roy E. Ciampa

Philippians, Colossians, and
   Philemon ....Linda L. Belleville

1 & 2 Thessalonians, 1 & 2 Timothy,
   and Titus .... Philip H. Towner

Hebrews .... Jon C. Laansma

James, 1 & 2 Peter, and Jude .... Jim Samra

1–3 John .... (see *John*)

Revelation .... J. Scott Duvall

To see which titles are available, visit the series website at www.teachthetextseries.com.

TEACH THE TEXT
COMMENTARY SERIES

Psalms

Volume 1
Psalms 1–72

C. Hassell Bullock

Mark L. Strauss and John H. Walton
GENERAL EDITORS

ILLUSTRATING THE TEXT

Kevin and Sherry Harney
ASSOCIATE EDITORS

Donald C. Porter
CONTRIBUTING AUTHOR

BakerBooks

a division of Baker Publishing Group
Grand Rapids, Michigan

Published by Baker Books
a division of Baker Publishing Group
P.O. Box 6287, Grand Rapids, MI 49516-6287
www.bakerbooks.com

Printed in the United States of America

                    Library of Congress Cataloging-in-Publication Data
Bullock, C. Hassell.
    Psalms / C. Hassell Bullock ; Mark L. Strauss and John H. Walton, general
  editors ; illustrating the text, Kevin and Sherry Harney, associate editors ;
  Donald C. Porter, contributing author.
        pages cm. — (Teach the text commentary)
    Includes bibliographical references and index.
    ISBN 978-0-8010-9197-1 (cloth)
    1. Bible. Psalms—Commentaries. I. Strauss, Mark L., 1959– editor. II.
  Walton, John H., 1952– editor. III. Title.
    BS1430.53.P725 2015
    223'.207—dc23   2014044252

15   16   17   18   19   20   21   7   6   5   4   3   2   1

To my children,
Scott—and Britta, Ellen, Klara, and Lukas
Rebecca—and Michael and Hannah

Contents

List of Sidebars

Welcome to the Teach the Text Commentary Series

Why another commentary series? That was the question the general editors posed when Baker Books asked us to produce this series. Is there something that we can offer to pastors and teachers that is not currently being offered by other commentary series, or that can be offered in a more helpful way? After carefully researching the needs of pastors who teach the text on a weekly basis, we concluded that yes, more can be done; this commentary is carefully designed to fill an important gap.

The technicality of modern commentaries often overwhelms readers with details that are tangential to the main purpose of the text. Discussions of source and redaction criticism, as well as detailed surveys of secondary literature, seem far removed from preaching and teaching the Word. Rather than wade through technical discussions, pastors often turn to devotional commentaries, which may contain exegetical weaknesses, misuse the Greek and Hebrew languages, and lack hermeneutical sophistication. There is a need for a commentary that utilizes the best of biblical scholarship

but also presents the material in a clear, concise, attractive, and user-friendly format.

This commentary is designed for that purpose—to provide a ready reference for the exposition of the biblical text, giving easy access to information that a pastor needs to communicate the text effectively. Each passage begins with a concise summary of the central message, or "Big Idea," of the passage and a list of its main themes. This is followed by a more detailed interpretation of the text, including the literary context of the passage, historical background material, and interpretive insights. While drawing on the best of biblical scholarship, this material is clear, concise, and to the point. Technical material is kept to a minimum, with endnotes pointing the reader to more detailed discussion and additional resources.

A second major focus of this commentary is on the preaching and teaching process itself. Few commentaries today help the pastor/teacher move from the meaning of the text to its effective communication. Our goal is to bridge this gap. In addition to interpreting the text in the "Understanding the Text" section, each unit contains a "Teaching the Text" section and an "Illustrating the Text" section. The teaching section points to the key theological themes of the passage and ways to communicate these themes to today's audiences. The illustration section provides ideas and examples for retaining the interest of hearers and connecting the message to daily life.

The creative format of this commentary arises from our belief that the Bible is not just a record of God's dealings in the past but is the living Word of God, "alive and active" and "sharper than any double-edged sword" (Heb. 4:12). Our prayer is that this commentary will help to unleash that transforming power for the glory of God.

The General Editors

Introduction to the Teach the Text Commentary Series

This series is designed to provide a ready reference for teaching the biblical text, giving easy access to information that is needed to communicate a passage effectively. To that end, the commentary is carefully divided into units that are faithful to the biblical authors' ideas and of an appropriate length for teaching or preaching.

The following standard sections are offered in each unit.

1. *Big Idea*. For each unit the commentary identifies the primary theme, or "Big Idea," that drives both the passage and the commentary.
2. *Key Themes*. Together with the Big Idea, the commentary addresses in bullet-point fashion the key ideas presented in the passage.
3. *Understanding the Text*. This section focuses on the exegesis of the text and includes several sections.
   a. The Text in Context. Here the author gives a brief explanation of how the unit fits into the flow of the text around it, including reference to the rhetorical strategy of the book and the unit's contribution to the purpose of the book.
   b. Outline/Structure. For some literary genres (e.g., epistles), a brief exegetical outline may be provided to guide the reader through the structure and flow of the passage.
   c. Historical and Cultural Background. This section addresses historical and cultural background information that may illuminate a verse or passage.
   d. Interpretive Insights. This section provides information needed for a clear understanding of the passage. The intention of the author is to be highly selective and concise rather than exhaustive and expansive.
   e. Theological Insights. In this very brief section the commentary identifies a few carefully selected theological insights about the passage.

4. *Teaching the Text*. Under this second main heading the commentary offers guidance for teaching the text. In this section the author lays out the main themes and applications of the passage. These are linked carefully to the Big Idea and are represented in the Key Themes.

5. *Illustrating the Text*. At this point in the commentary the writers partner with a team of pastor/teachers to provide suggestions for relevant and contemporary illustrations from current culture, entertainment, history, the Bible, news, literature, ethics, biography, daily life, medicine, and over forty other categories. They are designed to spark creative thinking for preachers and teachers and to help them design illustrations that bring alive the passage's key themes and message.

Preface

No book of the Old Testament has touched this writer as deeply as the Psalms. There are many reasons, some too deep for words. This book scans the depths of faith, illuminating the foundations of belief and revealing the cavernous hollows of unbelief. The sinful plight of humanity is left exposed to the scrutiny of time but is redeemed by love when the light of faith dawns, "and that right early" (Ps. 46:5 KJV). The emotional range of the Psalms is wide and deep, and because of that, worshipers throughout the centuries have been borne more freely to the throne of grace on their wings of prayer. Saints, sages, and sinners alike have read and sung the Psalms in life's best and worst moments and have found this book to contain the words they could not draw out of their own souls.

This is the first of two volumes on Psalms that will appear in the Teach the Text Commentary Series. I will refer to discussions in that forthcoming volume occasionally—particularly to sidebars in which I give more detail on a topic or make comparisons among psalms.

In the thanksgiving mode of the Psalter, there are so many people I need to thank as "my heart overflows with a pleasing theme" (Ps. 45:1 ESV). First, I give thanks to God for the gift of the Psalms so full of comfort, admonition, hope, and joy. Second, I give thanks for the Franklin S. Dyrness Chair of Biblical Studies, and the revered man of God for whom it is named, now a member of the Church Triumphant. I began this commentary just before my eligibility for the generous research funds of this endowed chair receded into my retirement, and this project was a new beginning for me as a forty-year teaching career was coming to a close, thirty-six of them at Wheaton College. Third, I give thanks for the staff and the resources of Tyndale House, Cambridge, England, that have made the summer portion of my writing more delightful and efficient. Fourth, I give thanks for my friend and former student Dr. Brian Janeway, who has generously provided travel assistance for most of our summers at Tyndale House. Fifth, I give thanks for the editors of the Teach the Text

Commentary Series and Baker Books, who invited me to write this commentary and have offered their insightful enhancements, for it has been a labor of love. Sixth, I give thanks for the Warren Park Presbyterian Church (Cicero, IL), where I have served as pastor for the past twelve and a half years. Their generosity of study leave, and their attentive listening to my sermons on the Psalms, which have taken me already through half the book, are expressions of God's grace. Seventh, I give thanks for my former graduate assistant, Dr. Stefanos Mihalios, now a faculty member of the Greek Bible College (Athens, Greece), who kindly and expertly took on the task of reading this manuscript and, with his keen insight,

offered many improvements. Eighth, I give thanks for my wife, Rhonda, who shares my love for the Psalms, and whose patient "waiting" with me as I have worked on this project is part of that spiritual legacy about which the Psalms have so much to say. Ninth, I give thanks for my children, Scott, Britta, Ellen, Klara, and Lukas, and for Rebecca, Michael, and Hannah, who continue to affirm to me the lesson of the Psalms that "children are a heritage from the LORD" (Ps. 127:3). To this heritage I dedicate this book. *Soli Deo gloria.*

C. Hassell Bullock
Wheaton, Illinois
September 10, 2014

Abbreviations

Old Testament

Gen.	Genesis	2 Chron.	2 Chronicles	Dan.	Daniel
Exod.	Exodus	Ezra	Ezra	Hosea	Hosea
Lev.	Leviticus	Neh.	Nehemiah	Joel	Joel
Num.	Numbers	Esther	Esther	Amos	Amos
Deut.	Deuteronomy	Job	Job	Obad.	Obadiah
Josh.	Joshua	Ps(s).	Psalm(s)	Jon.	Jonah
Judg.	Judges	Prov.	Proverbs	Mic.	Micah
Ruth	Ruth	Eccles.	Ecclesiastes	Nah.	Nahum
1 Sam.	1 Samuel	Song	Song of Songs	Hab.	Habakkuk
2 Sam.	2 Samuel	Isa.	Isaiah	Zeph.	Zephaniah
1 Kings	1 Kings	Jer.	Jeremiah	Hag.	Haggai
2 Kings	2 Kings	Lam.	Lamentations	Zech.	Zechariah
1 Chron.	1 Chronicles	Ezek.	Ezekiel	Mal.	Malachi

New Testament

Matt.	Matthew	Eph.	Ephesians	Heb.	Hebrews
Mark	Mark	Phil.	Philippians	James	James
Luke	Luke	Col.	Colossians	1 Pet.	1 Peter
John	John	1 Thess.	1 Thessalonians	2 Pet.	2 Peter
Acts	Acts	2 Thess.	2 Thessalonians	1 John	1 John
Rom.	Romans	1 Tim.	1 Timothy	2 John	2 John
1 Cor.	1 Corinthians	2 Tim.	2 Timothy	3 John	3 John
2 Cor.	2 Corinthians	Titus	Titus	Jude	Jude
Gal.	Galatians	Philem.	Philemon	Rev.	Revelation

General

cf.	confer, compare		Eng.	English
chap(s).	chapter(s)		esp.	especially
e.g.	for example		et al.	and others

etc.	and the rest		NLT	New Living Translation
fem.	feminine		NRSV	New Revised Standard Version
Heb.	Hebrew		RSV	Revised Standard Version
i.e.	that is			
lit.	literally			
masc.	masculine			

etc.   and the rest
fem.   feminine
Heb.   Hebrew
i.e.   that is
lit.   literally
masc.   masculine
no(s).   number(s)
NT   New Testament
OT   Old Testament
p(p).   page(s)
par(s).   parallel(s)
pl.   plural
pres.   present (tense)
ptc.   participle
sg.   singular
trans.   translation
v(v).   verse(s)

Ancient Versions

LXX   Septuagint
MT   Masoretic Text

Modern Versions

ASV   American Standard Version
ESV   English Standard Version
HCSB   Holman Christian Standard Bible
JB   Jerusalem Bible
JPS   *The Tanakh: The Holy Scriptures* (1917)
KJV   King James Version
NASB   New American Standard Bible
NEB   The New English Bible
NIV   New International Version
NJPS   *The Tanakh: The Holy Scriptures; The New JPS Translation according to the Traditional Hebrew Text* (2nd ed.; 2000)
NKJV   New King James Version

NLT   New Living Translation
NRSV   New Revised Standard Version
RSV   Revised Standard Version

Apocrypha and Septuagint

1–2 Macc.   1–2 Maccabees
Tob.   Tobit

Mishnah and Talmud

b.   Babylonian Talmud
m.   Mishnah
y.   Jerusalem Talmud

Secondary Sources

ANEP   J. B. Pritchard, ed. *The Ancient Near East in Pictures Relating to the Old Testament*. Princeton: Princeton University Press, 1954.
GKC   E. Kautzsch, ed. *Gesenius' Hebrew Grammar*. Translated by A. E. Cowley. 2nd ed. Oxford: Clarendon, 1910.
NIDB   Katharine Doob Sakenfeld, ed. *The New Interpreter's Dictionary of the Bible*. 5 vols. Nashville: Abingdon, 2009.
NIDOTTE   Willem VanGemeren, ed. *New International Dictionary of Old Testament Theology and Exegesis*. 5 vols. Grand Rapids: Zondervan, 1997.
TLOT   Ernst Jenni and Claus Westermann, eds. *Theological Lexicon of the Old Testament*. Translated by Mark E. Biddle. 3 vols. Peabody, MA: Hendrickson, 1997.

Introduction to the Psalms

The Name of the Book

The Hebrew title of the book of Psalms is *Tehillim* ("praises"), encapsulating praise as one of the central features of the book. We get our English title from the Greek translation of the book, *Psalmoi*; the singular, *psalmos*, is the translation of the Hebrew word *mizmor*, found in many of the psalm titles. The New Testament knows the book by this title (Luke 20:42; Acts 1:20). The Greek translation in the manuscript Alexandrinus (fifth century AD) titles the book *Psalterion*, a term that occurs several times in the book and means "stringed instrument." From this term comes the often-used English name *Psalter*.

The Nature of the Book

The book of Psalms is an anthology written and collected over several centuries.

The earliest named composer is Moses (Ps. 90), and David is the most frequent contributor to the book, with seventy-three psalms attributed or dedicated to him. The normal way of referencing David is *le dawid* ("to," "for" = "by" or "dedicated to"), and in some of those instances, perhaps a majority, the psalm is written by David, but in others it is merely written in honor of him, sometimes using other Davidic psalms as the substance of the psalm (e.g., Ps. 86). Two psalms are connected with Solomon (72; 127). In addition to these authors, twelve psalms are attributed to Asaph (50; 73–83), and eleven to the "sons of Korah," (42–49; 84; 85; 87;

The book of Psalms includes seventy-three psalms attributed or dedicated to David. This ivory bookbinding plaque is from the Dagulf Psalter (eighth century AD). The top register shows David directing the writing of the psalms, and the lower register depicts him singing them.

and 88, considering 42 and 43 a single psalm), both Levitical families in the time of David. One is attributed to Heman the Ezrahite (Ps. 88), and one to Ethan the Ezrahite (Ps. 89), both persons of obscurity (see the discussion on these psalms in volume 2).

Thirteen psalms have titles that provide some historical information, and all of these are attributed to David (3; 7; 18; 34; 51; 52; 54; 56; 57; 59; 60; 63; 142). While these historical titles often connect the psalm to some incident in David's life, the connection between the content and the title is sometimes difficult to detect. Yet the very fact that thirteen psalms have titles that connect them to David shows how strongly the Davidic connection of the book is, and how important history is to this collection and its interpretation. Therefore, in this commentary I will take a combination of interpretive approaches, the historical and the form-critical, both of which will produce a more robust understanding of these religious poems.

The titles also contain literary and musical terms that probably are intended to inform the readers about their performance, and we will deal with these terms as they occur in the psalms.

Categories of Psalms

There is some latitude in current Psalms studies regarding the categories (genres) of classification for the Psalms. Because the psalms of praise and psalms of lament are so basic to the collection, I will discuss those two categories here and then discuss the other categories at the appropriate places in the commentary (see the list of sidebars). The following is a list of the principal genres in the Psalter:

1. Psalms of praise
2. Psalms of lament
3. Psalms of thanksgiving
4. Psalms of trust
5. Psalms of the earthly king
6. Psalms of the heavenly King
7. Wisdom psalms
8. Torah psalms
9. Imprecatory psalms[1]

The Anatomy of Praise

The book of Psalms has been a source of inspiration and spiritual refuge for believers, both Jewish and Christian, for thousands of years. The emotional and spiritual appeal of the Psalms to readers is partly explained by the wide emotional range, from praise to lament, with numerous degrees in between. The Westminster Shorter Catechism verifies the notion, itself taken in part from the Psalter, that humankind's chief end is "to glorify God, and to enjoy him forever."[2] That is to say, our vocation as Christians, our mode of existence, is "to glorify [or "praise"] God." Praise, like obedience (1 Sam. 15:22), is better than sacrifice (Ps. 69:30–31). Indeed, God has created the universe in such a way that it serves his purposes, whatever design we may impose upon it. He rules and overrules, and he turns evil into good. This is what the psalmist means by declaring, "Surely the wrath of man shall praise you" (76:10 ESV).

While praise can be a very private matter, it often—if not most often—carries a cohortative force, inviting others to join in:

Let everything that has breath praise
     the LORD.
Praise the LORD. (Ps. 150:6)

Lewis comments on this aspect of praise even in our common life: "I had not noticed either that just as men spontaneously praise whatever they value, so they spontaneously urge us to join them in praising it: 'Isn't she lovely? Wasn't it glorious? Don't you think that magnificent?' The Psalmists in telling everyone to praise God are doing what all men do when they speak of what they care about."[3] Lewis further comments on the summative nature of praise: "If it were possible for a created soul fully (I mean, up to the full measure conceivable in a finite being) to 'appreciate,' that is to love and delight in, the worthiest object of all, and simultaneously at every moment to give this delight perfect expression, then that soul would be in supreme beatitude."[4]

It should not, therefore, surprise us that at the culmination of the history of redemption, the whole creation joins in consummate praise of God: "Then I heard what sounded like a great multitude, like the roar of rushing waters and like loud peals of thunder, shouting: 'Hallelujah! For our Lord God Almighty reigns. Let us rejoice and be glad and give him glory!'" (Rev. 19:6–7a).

The Anatomy of Lament

The psalms of lament constitute the opposite category from praise. The mood of the psalms gravitates between these

Psalms of Praise

The two extreme moods of the Psalter are *praise* and *lament*, which are also the substance of the two major categories of psalms.[a] The two modes of prayer, however, are *praise* and *petition*,[b] and they are interspersed in the prayers of the Psalter.

"Psalms of praise" is a general category—roughly synonymous to Gunkel's "hymns"[c]—whose fundamental moods are enthusiasm, adoration, reverence, praise, and exaltation, especially lauding God's wonderful deeds in Israel's history. Some of these may also be simultaneously classified in other genres.[d]

Psalms of Praise				
8	66A	99	113	145
19A[e]	68	100	114	146
29	93	104	117	147
33	96	105	134	148
47	97	106	135	149
65	98	111	136	150

[a] Westermann, *Praise and Lament*, 18.
[b] Westermann, *Praise and Lament*, 152.
[c] Gunkel, *Introduction to Psalms*, 22–65.
[d] This is Hans-Joachim Kraus's list of psalms of praise, *Psalms*, 1:43, following F. Crüssemann.
[e] "A" denotes the first part of a psalm that is considered by many to be two psalms in one.

two poles, each of which merits a genre of psalm as its expression. They are the opposite poles of life, with many degrees in between. Laments arise out of difficult and trying circumstances, and they, like praises, provide an index to the spiritual personalities of the psalmists.[5] For some reason, buried in our subconscious mind, we do not seem to be as comfortable with lament as we are with praise, especially

The psalms of lament were responses to difficult circumstances such as the situation illustrated in this Assyrian relief, where five women watch from their city wall and raise their arms in submission while the victorious Assyrian army parades past (Nimrud palace relief, 865–860 BC).

Psalms of Lament

Like psalms of praise, laments may sometimes be simultaneously classified in another category. They fall into individual laments and community laments.

Psalms of Lament				
Individual Laments			Community Laments	
3	23	63	44	85
4	27	69	60	90
5	30	71	74	94
6	31	91	77	123
7	32	102	79	126
11	35	103	80	137
13	39	130	83	
17	51			
22	57			

in worship. Yet, as Witvliet reminds us, "when practiced as an act of faith, lament can be a powerfully healing experience."[6] In the Psalms some occasions for lament are sin, defeat in battle, persecution, criticism, abandonment, illness, and doubt. Just looking at the list, we can easily see how therapeutic a service of lament, uninhibited by social constraints, could be.[7]

Claus Westermann capitalizes on the emotional states of praise and lament for his classification of the Psalms. He further subdivides the psalms of lament into laments of the people and laments of the individual.[8] The essential elements of lament, according to our definition, are two: the lament and the reason for lamenting. The lament of the individual generally will include one or a combination of three complaints: against one's enemies, against God, or against oneself.

Hebrew Poetry

One does not have to read many of the psalms to recognize that they are poetry. Modern English translations render them in verse form (but the KJV does not). Hebrew poetry is different from the classical poetry of the Western world that employs rhyme, rhythm, and meter. In contrast, there is no identifiable effort to give rhyme to Hebrew poetry. And since Hebrew poetry was basically intended to be sung or to be accompanied by musical instruments, there is a natural rhythm involved, especially dependent upon stressed and unstressed syllables, but even that does not produce the kind of strict rhythm that classical Western poetry is known for. Nor are we much better informed about meter in Hebrew poetry. However, counting the stressed syllables in a line of Hebrew poetry has become the favored way of measuring meter. Although the ancient language had no way of indicating stress, the Masoretes, a group of Jewish scholars between the seventh and eleventh centuries AD, studied the Hebrew text and gave it a system of vowels and punctuation that the ancient written language did not have. These additions, while facilitating the reading of the text, indirectly contribute to our understanding of the text as well. The punctuation marks divide a verse into thought units, which would be equivalent to our phrases and clauses, and the number of stressed syllables in each unit becomes the measuring stick. But even that standard of measurement is often dubious. By that system, a line is known by the Latin term *colon* (pl. *cola*; Greek *stichos*, pl. *stichoi*). When cola combine to form the larger units, these are named by a Latin prefix, giving us *bicola* (two units) and *tricola* (three units). Since the reader needs to have a knowledge of Hebrew to understand this division and utilize it as an interpretive tool, I have chosen to use these terms only rarely. Instead I will refer to half verses to indicate the middle of the thought unit as the Masoretes have marked them.[9]

In modern times attention has been drawn to the feature of *parallelism* that distinguishes Hebrew poetry. That simply means that lines of text occur in parallel, and this sets up a certain kind of relationship between the lines. When one line is followed by another line that essentially restates the thought of the first line, it is called *synonymous parallelism*. In the strict sense, there is no genuine synonymous parallelism, however, because each new line adds another nuance to the thought, even though it may be slight. Some call this second phenomenon *focusing*. When the first line expresses a thought and the parallel line introduces a contrary or diverse thought, it is called *antithetic parallelism*.

Synonymous Parallelism

A The One enthroned
   B in heaven
      C laughs;
A′ the Lord
      C′ scoffs at them. (Ps. 2:4)

The Masoretes have divided the verse into halves, indicated in the English translation by the semicolon. The first line (colon) of Psalm 2:4 is made up of three word units, and the second line is composed of two word units (the latter unit indicated by the *maqef*, one of the punctuation marks used to combine two or more words). The scanning pattern would then be indicated as 3:2 (three word units + two word units). Note that the second part of

C′ in the second line has no correspondent in the first line. Obviously, however, C′ provides the object for both verbs ("laughs" and "scoffs").

Antithetic Parallelism

Psalm 1:6 is scanned similarly:

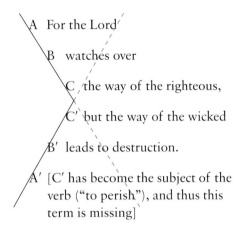

A For the Lord
  B watches over
    C the way of the righteous,
    C′ but the way of the wicked
  B′ leads to destruction.
A′ [C′ has become the subject of the verb ("to perish"), and thus this term is missing]

There are two features we should be aware of in Psalm 1:6. One is parallelism, the two units being parallel: B/B′ and C/C′. Interestingly, the subject "Lord" in A is not paralleled in the second line, but a new subject, "the way of the wicked," is introduced. The second feature is that C has changed places in the verse for the purpose of emphasizing "the way of the wicked"; C′ has been placed first in the second line, putting C and C′ in juxtaposition for a sharp contrast. This is a partial *chiasm*, which, if full, would put the important terms at the points of the left side of the Greek letter *chi* (X).

The Place of Psalms in the Biblical Canon

The placement of the book of Psalms in our English translations follows the order of the Greek Septuagint (LXX) and puts the book second in order of a series of poetic books: Job, Psalms, Proverbs, Ecclesiastes, and the Song of Songs. A chronological sequence probably underlies this order, since Job was considered to have lived in the patriarchal era and to predate David, and then the book associated with David (Psalms) comes next on the timeline, followed by those books associated with David's son Solomon (Proverbs, Ecclesiastes, and the Song of Songs).

However, the Hebrew Bible has three major divisions: Torah (Law or Pentateuch), Prophets, and Writings. The book of Psalms is first in order in the third division, very likely answering to a theological scheme. Since the Torah is the foundational division, and the Prophets, in second position, were considered in Jewish tradition to be interpreters of the Torah, Psalms heads up the third division because it was thought to be a collection of poems describing the Torah life. Psalm 1 is the first indication of this perspective on the book. Luke refers to the third division by the name "Psalms" in Luke 24:44: "Everything must be fulfilled that is written about me in the Law of Moses, the Prophets and the Psalms."

Trends in Psalms Studies

The book of Psalms has exercised a power in Judaism and Christianity that exceeds the communicative power of words. Calvin calls the book an "anatomy of all parts of the soul,"[10] because Psalms touches every surface of life as well as the inner recesses of the heart. Luther, using a different metaphor, calls it the "little Bible,"[11] because it is a compendium of Old Testament faith, history, and theology. There is no doubt that both of these Reformation commentators saw the book as an anthology of biblical theology. And it can be said with some confidence that this view of the Psalms continues into the twenty-first century, even though the way of looking at the Psalms has changed tremendously since the sixteenth century.

Calvin and Luther, in fact, viewed Psalms as having been written in the crucible of history, and in order to understand the book's message, they sought to discover the historical circumstances that produced it, when, of course, those circumstances could be discerned. In the twentieth century the form-critical method, developed particularly at the hand of Gunkel,[12] shifted the context of Psalms composition from history to liturgy. The Psalms, he insisted, were written for temple worship, and he sought to interpret them in this framework, searching

In the Hebrew Bible, Psalms was the first book in the section known as Writings. Shown here is a portion of the Psalms Scroll, one of the Dead Sea Scrolls found in Cave 11 at Qumran. It includes psalms not found in the Bible as well as forty-one canonical psalms.

for worship occasions and specific liturgies when the Psalms would have been used in temple services. Of course, it should be noted that this approach was not alien to the "historical" method, but form criticism made temple worship the primary focus, and history took a backseat to liturgy.

In recent years scholarly attention made another shift intended to enhance the form-critical approach, not replace it. Wilson is largely responsible for this new perspective, which he has developed in his watershed dissertation, *The Editing of the Hebrew Psalter*.[13] His focus aims at understanding the editorial process that brought together the Hebrew Psalter, which was edited over several centuries. The underlying assumption of Wilson's *canonical* approach is that the editors of the book had a shaping purpose in mind as they put the book together.

While we do not know when the book of Psalms was divided into five component books, we must assume that it was early, judging from the doxologies that conclude each book. While some believe these doxologies were appended to each book sometime near the final editing of the Psalter, there are those who insist that some of the doxologies, particularly the one at the end of Book 2 (72:18–19), belonged to the original psalm. In any event, they certainly belonged to the book at an early period of its history, for they are included in the Septuagint and the earliest Hebrew manuscripts. Thus they represent editorial lines that should be taken into account. One might even wonder if the editor of Book 1 set the precedent by closing the first Davidic collection of psalms with a doxology, and the subsequent editors followed this pattern. I am obviously assuming that

the books were edited seriatim and were, for the most part, kept together as a collection, most likely by the Levites. Later additions were enhancements, although it is possible that some adjustments were made to already established macrocollections. (See comments on Psalm 106:47–48.)

The Structure and Composition of the Psalter

The Psalter is the final product of a complex history of composition and editing that extended over several centuries. We have already noted that the book was divided into five books at an early stage, which was done perhaps to reflect the five books of the Torah, but there is no evidence that the Torah and the Psalms were ever coordinated in the synagogue readings as were the Torah and the Prophets. There are strong indications that these five books were edited with a view to Israel's history, as we will explain below. While we do not find references to the five books until the *Midrash on the Psalms*, which was edited around the tenth century AD (but contains materials that originated much earlier), the Septuagint contains the doxological conclusions to each of the five books as they are found in the Hebrew Psalter. That dates the five-fold division at least to the early Christian era, and we can safely assume it was earlier than that, and likely belonged to the era(s) of the editorial process.[14]

It has been the general practice to discuss the composition of the book in terms of Books 1–3 and 4–5. However, the first macrostructure seems to have been Psalms 3–41, with Psalms 1–2 constituting an introduction to the collection.[15] I suggest that this collection came together earlier rather

The Five Books of the Psalter

- Book 1: Psalms 1–41
- Book 2: Psalms 42–72
- Book 3: Psalms 73–89
- Book 4: Psalms 90–106
- Book 5: Psalms 107–50

than later because of the strong interest in the life of David and his dynasty and anything Davidic. We can probably speak about a literary renaissance during or soon after Solomon's reign, and this first macrostructure may belong to that era. The division of the kingdom (931 BC) was a time when the northern tribes seceded from the southern kingdom (Judah and Benjamin) for the purpose of distancing themselves both politically and religiously (1 Kings 12:25–33). It would be surprising if literary activity was not part of that political and religious complex, particularly in view of David's and Solomon's literary legacies in the books of Kings.

The architectural design of the first three books (Pss. 1–41; 42–72; 73–89; see the sidebar "The Five Books of the Psalter") puts a royal seal on this macrocollection (Pss. 2–89) by installing psalms of the earthly king, or royal

psalms, in initial and final positions of the collection (Pss. 2 and 89). When the editor (likely the final editor) installed Psalm 1 in its lead position, Psalm 2 was probably already in place as the preface to an early edition of the Psalter that consisted of Psalms 2–89, or Books 1, 2, and 3. Psalm 2 celebrates the Lord's triumph over the enemies of his kingdom, while Psalm 89 ponders the humiliation that David's dynasty had suffered and asks how long God would permit Israel's enemies to taunt them (89:49–51).[16]

Book 1, with the exception of Psalms 1 and 2, is largely held together by the name and reputation of David, with all psalms attributed to him, except Psalms 1, 2, 10, and 33. Psalms 40–41 form a conclusion to the collection. Psalm 40 appropriately profiles David as the righteous man whose "delight" (*hapatsti*; NIV: "desire"; 40:8) is to do God's will, just as Psalm 1 describes him as the one whose "delight [*heptso*] is in the law of the Lord" (1:2). The use of the term "blessed" (*'ashre*) occurs in 40:4 and 41:1, corresponding to the same term that introduces the book (1:1) and concludes the introduction at 2:12. But Psalms 1 and 2 likely picked the term up from Psalms 40 and 41, rather than vice versa, because these first two psalms were added much later in the editorial process, perhaps with the completion of the second macrostructure (Pss. 3–72) or the third (Pss. 3–89), and some would say even the final edition of the book.[17]

The collection of literary pieces that make up the book of Psalms may have come together because of the strong interest in the life of David and his dynasty. Shown here is an Aramaic inscription from 840 BC that refers to "the house of David." It is the only ancient text outside the Bible that mentions David and his dynasty.

The editing that produced Book 2 (Psalms 42–72) probably took place during the Babylonian exile, providing hope to the Israelite community far from home in Babylon. From 10 to 25 percent of the population of Judah was deported. This Assyrian palace relief shows families being deported after their city was conquered by the armies of Tiglath-pileser III (Nimrud, eighth century BC).

Book 2 (Pss. 42–72) contains several minicollections of psalms that have been preempted for this expanded edition of psalmody, the largest being the Korah psalms (42–49) and Davidic psalms (51–65; 68–70). Included are two other author-attributed psalms, an Asaph psalm (Ps. 50) and a psalm "Of Solomon" (Ps. 72 title). Other clusters of psalms in Book 2 have terms in their titles that connect them: Psalms 52–55 (*maskil*), Psalms 56–59 (*miktam*), Psalms 62–68 (*mizmor*), Psalms 65–68 (*shir*).[18] Since some of these overlap with the Davidic psalms, it is difficult to know whether they were independent collections outside the Davidic psalms. It certainly appears, however, that the David collections form the heart of the first two books (see "The Editing of Book 2" in the unit on Ps. 70).

Judging from the portrait of the "poor and needy" in Psalm 70 (see v. 5), picked up from Psalm 40:13–17, and the allusion to "his [God's] prisoners" (69:33; NIV: "captive people"), the editing of Book 2 likely took place during the Babylonian exile. In that historical context, David has become the paradigm of the "poor and needy," identifying with the exiled community and speaking words of assurance and hope.

The first psalm of Book 3 (Ps. 73) forms a companion to Psalm 72 in the sense that Psalm 72 prays that God may endow the king with justice (see 72:1). Psalm 73 puts the problem in the practical context of the prosperity of the wicked. While Psalm 73 may have been composed as a personal lament, in the larger structure of Book 3 it is given a national setting. The community laments of this collection bring the exile into focus again (Pss. 74; 79; 80; 83; 85:1–8; 89:38–51),[19] while Psalm 89 reveals most clearly the time frame for the editing of Book 3 as the exile, since it deals with the failed Davidic covenant. The earliest possible date for the completion of this collection therefore would be soon after the fall of Jerusalem to the Babylonians in 586 BC. It may be of significance that Book 3 contains only one Davidic psalm (Ps. 86). The inclusion of Psalm 86 would mean that an editor at some point thought it inappropriate to have a macrocollection that was David-less, and he put this psalm together to fill that void—it is made up of short quotes from other Davidic psalms. Perhaps the low David profile of this book is due to the waning confidence in the Davidic covenant or, at least, the confusion over its seeming failure, as reflected in Psalm 89.

Wilson has drawn attention to the placement of three royal psalms: at the beginning of the macrocollection of Psalms 2–89 (Ps. 2), at the end of Book 2 (Ps. 72), and the end of Book 3 (Ps. 89);[20] the placement of these royal psalms makes all the more sense in view of the hopes that the monarchy would revive. Looking ahead, Hossfeld and Zenger see those hopes as the anchor of Book 4 (e.g., Ps. 102:18–22), suggesting that Book 4 is, in an oversimplified way, the "proclamation of YHWH's universal royal rule."[21]

Book 4 (Pss. 90–106) opens with Israel confessing their sins in the voice of Moses "the man of God," affirming God as Israel's refuge, and setting God's vengeance in the context of history, even if it takes a thousand years.[22] While no other psalms are attributed to Moses, his name does appear seven times in Book 4 (Pss. 90 title; 99:6; 103:7; 105:26; 106:16, 23, 32), recalling Moses's role in the exodus from Egypt (esp. 105:26–42). Moses's career was not unconnected to Abraham's, for the exodus and the possession of the land of Canaan were the divine fulfillment of God's promise to Abraham (105:42). Psalm 92, "For the Sabbath day" (title), follows the confession of sin in Psalm 90, with its prayer that God's favor will rest upon Israel (90:17), and Psalm 91, a psalm of trust, that reaffirms Israel's trust in Yahweh, who has ostensibly failed them in the defunct covenant of David (Ps. 89). But with Book 4 a new confidence in the kingdom of God begins to build, and Psalm 92 celebrates not only the weekly Sabbath but the Sabbath day of history, or the eschatological kingdom of God, when the Lord will reign (Pss. 93–100).

The "Yahweh reigns" (or "Yahweh is King") psalms, Psalms 93–100, constitute one of the smaller collections of psalms that make up Book 4. Hossfeld and Zenger speculate that this particular collection was the conclusion of a macrocollection of the Psalms (2–100) at one point in the editorial process.[23] While Psalm 100 does sound the climactic theme of entering the Lord's courts, I would prefer to see this minicollection as a theological reaffirmation of Yahweh's kingship over against the failed Davidic dynasty, putting the former in the light of the latter, thus having the potential for changing the exiles' perspective—the Lord reigns even though other monarchs have momentarily preempted his kingdom. Moreover, the figures of Abraham, Moses, and Aaron shine the spotlight on the Mosaic (Ps. 105:45) and Abrahamic covenants (105:8–11), underscoring the promises of God that have ostensibly failed. Book 4 closes as it began (90:8) with Israel's confession of sin (106:6–7), and with the prayer that God may gather them from among the nations (106:47).

Book 5 (Pss. 107–50) then is poised to reaffirm God's enduring love (*hesed*) and to call the "redeemed of the LORD" (107:2) to praise God. With Hossfeld and Zenger, we may consider Psalms 107–36 as a "thanksgiving liturgy for the restoration and renewal of Israel."[24] It contains the hopes of Israel fulfilled in the restoration of the nation and the return of the exiles (e.g., Ps. 126). The restoration was more than a return to the land. It was, more important, a restoration of worship in Zion. Thus Psalms 135–36 form a liturgical conclusion to the collection made up largely of the Passover Hallel (113–18) and

the "Pilgrim Psalter" (120–34). These are historical psalms in praise of the God of Israel's history, the kind that are called for by Psalm 134:1.[25] It was a history that grew out of God's "love" (*hesed*), and "his love endures forever." In the middle of this collection is Psalm 119, celebrating the Torah, which was God's instrument of making Israel his people. Another Davidic collection (Pss. 138–45) forms the penultimate conclusion to Book 5 and balances the final collection of Davidic psalms against the beginning David collection. These psalms are prayers to God, ending with a call to "all flesh" (NIV: "every creature") to praise the Lord (145:21).

The five concluding psalms (Pss. 146–50) are "Hallelujah" ("Praise the LORD") psalms that begin and end with this command of praise, Psalm 150 ending with a double "Hallelujah." David is absent from these psalms, and the praise of God has become the pure praise of the eschatological kingdom, including Israel and the nations. A date for Book 5 is difficult, but obviously it is the latest installment to the Psalter, and it postdates the return of the exiles. Perhaps the time of Nehemiah in the middle of the fifth century BC would be plausible, although it could be a bit later.

When the preacher and teacher engage the Psalms in the pulpit or at the lectern, they need to keep in mind that this book is not merely a "list" of poems that have no relationship to each other. Rather, these

Book 5 of Psalms contains the praises of Israel as the nation is restored and the exiles return after the conquest of Babylon by the Persian king Cyrus. The cuneiform cylinder shown here records the reforms of Cyrus, which included the return of captive peoples to their homeland and the restoration of their temples (539–530 BC).

timeless compositions are intended to be viewed in the "neighborhood" where the particular psalm stands, studied in the larger context of the book in which they are collected (compare Pss. 14 and 53), and interpreted in the broadest terms of the purpose of the book as set out in the introductory psalm, to instruct the reader in the spiritual life of Torah. The commentary will attempt to prompt the reader in that exercise.

Reading between the Lines

The five books of the Psalter have been collected with the subsidiary purpose of highlighting certain theological concepts and historical eras. With our discussion of the psalms in each book, these thematic emphases will become clearer (for the historical setting, see "The Structure and Composition of the Psalter" above). The individual psalms are often connected by common themes and shared vocabulary, and in other instances, one psalm may answer a question or respond to a query raised by a previous psalm. For example, Psalm 14, in its God-denying world, describes Yahweh looking down from heaven to see if there is anyone who seeks after God (14:2), and Psalm 15 provides a description of those who may enter the Lord's house, affirming that there are still those who seek God and satisfy his demands for entering his presence. Representing a slightly different relationship, the second half of Psalm 19 describes the redeeming qualities of the Torah, and Psalm 20:7 follows with a formula of faith that shows David, rather indirectly, to be a keeper of the Torah (see "The Text in Context" in the unit on Ps. 20). These subtle and implicit connections are built into the editorial plan. Thus the individual psalms constitute the infrastructure, and the way they are put together produces a rhetorical voice that we hear between the lines of the psalm. This is called the *associate reading* of the text, because we are dealing not so much with the historical David, especially with his moral and personal flaws, but with the rhetorical David who arises out of the editorial plan of the book. In fact, the editor(s) is not interested in wiping David's palette clean and starting a new personality sketch, but leaves the moral flaws in place—they often emerge (e.g., Ps. 51)—and shines the editorial light on the David who both is and seeks to become the righteous man. It involves both a selective use of the content of the Psalms and a delicate arrangement of the poems in the larger framework. These observations are often discussed in the commentary. See also the Additional Insights section

The psalmist uses the language of the Torah and may be addressing how a life lived according to the Torah would look. Here modern Jews read from a Torah scroll at the Western Wall of the Temple Mount in Jerusalem.

"David as the Prototype of the 'Poor and Needy'" following the unit on Psalm 86.

A second observation on the between-the-lines readings is the use of the language of the Torah (also other OT books) in the Psalms. The Psalms teach the Torah life (see Ps. 1) by allusions to heroes and events and by using the language of the Torah. That is to say, the psalmists' knowledge of the personalities and language of the Torah becomes the dialect with which they describe and prescribe the spiritual posture of the community they belong to and speak to, as well as their own spiritual direction.[26] For example, Psalm 17:8 employs two metaphors from the Song of Moses (Deut. 32:10–11): "the apple of your eye" and "the shadow of your wings."[27] Applied by Moses to the nation in Deuteronomy, these metaphors are applied to the psalmist in Psalm 17 (a prayer of David), which amounts to a transfer of God's special affection and tender care of Israel to the individual psalmist. Further, Psalm 17:13 recalls the words of Moses when the ark set out on its journey: "Rise up, LORD" (see Num. 10:35). These were combative words, calling Yahweh to rise up and scatter his enemies. These words in this context (other occurrences are Pss. 3:7; 7:6; 9:19; 10:12; 74:22; 82:8; 132:8) summon Yahweh to David's rescue from his enemies and apply the corporate prayer of Numbers 10:35 to the personal situation of David, clarified in 17:14: "By your hand save me from such people, LORD." Framing the psalmist's dilemma in those Torah texts made his relationship to God all the more intimate and engaging and further intimated the psalmist's connection to ancient Israel, especially placing him theologically in covenant community. It is part of

the power of the Psalms, and the kind of application that we ourselves make when we read them in light of our own personal circumstances. John Calvin's commentary is an excellent illustration of this hermeneutical principle, already validated by the psalmists themselves.

The Psalms in Worship

Quite obviously the Psalms were written to be sung or chanted to the accompaniment of musical instruments. The Jewish tradition, of course, is the primary example of the use of the Psalms in worship, both in the temple and in the synagogue. In general, Christians have followed this tradition and as a rule have used this spiritual resource in their receptor languages without alteration. The Roman Catholic and Eastern Orthodox traditions are the lead examples of the Christian use of the Psalms in worship, and Protestants have adopted this book as their book of prayer,

led by Martin Luther and John Calvin and their associates. The practice of paraphrasing the Psalms and setting them to Western metrical form for singing was the practice in the Geneva community, and Calvin's colleague Theodore Beza produced the *Genevan Psalter* with all 150 psalms in 1562, the end product of several editions of that style. Its sibling and the forerunner of the *Scottish Psalter* was the revision of the 1562 edition by two Edinburgh ministers, Robert Pont and John Craig, published in 1564.

These traditions have been transferred to America and in the modern era have taken their form in such examples as the Christian Reformed Church's *Psalter Hymnal* (1959) and the Reformed Presbyterian Church of North America's *Book of Psalms for Singing* (1973), and more recently, *Psalms for All Seasons: A Complete Psalter for Worship*, produced by the Calvin Institute of Christian Worship at Calvin College.[28] Both the musical nature and the potent theological and spiritual resources of the Psalter are hopefully undergoing a rediscovery in the churches of America, as instruments of both praise and lament, and all the degrees of worship expression in between.

"The LORD Watches over the Way of the Righteous"

Big Idea *We begin the spiritual story of Israel, and ours as well, with the psalmist's search for and delight in God's Word.*

Understanding the Text

Psalm 1 is often viewed as a wisdom psalm because it puts forth the merits of the moral life as two "ways," the "way of the righteous" and the "way of the wicked" (1:6), which is characteristic of wisdom thought. For the psalmist the matter was very simple: one must choose between the two ways.

The Text in Context

When the final edition of the book of Psalms was forming, Psalm 1 was installed as an introduction to the Psalter. The book is an anthology that has come into existence over several centuries. Most likely the composition and placement of Psalm 1 was one of the last strokes of the book's editor(s), and it may have been written by the editor(s), or at least chosen for its appropriateness as an introduction to the whole book. By the time of the Psalter's final editing, the Torah (Law) had become the basis of religious study and the source of religious piety. In light of that, the "Torah" meant the Pentateuch in essentially the form that has come down to us. Further, we may understand this mention of the Torah to suggest that this entire collection of poems should be taken as a meditation upon the Torah, and in that sense, a sourcebook for communal and personal piety. The book of Psalms is not, of course, the Torah itself but a reflection upon it, upon its ideas, its ethics, its history, and its faith in general.

Outline/Structure

Psalm 1 is a description of the way of the righteous and the way of the wicked, in that order, concluding with a comparison of the two ways from the Lord's perspective:

1. Description of the way of the righteous (1:1–3)
2. Description of the way of the wicked (1:4)
3. Comparison of the two ways from Yahweh's perspective (1:5–6)

Historical and Cultural Background

This psalm has been viewed both as an early and as a later poem. Based on the content, it is difficult to make this call, especially due to the wisdom language, since wisdom thought and literature are ancient, both in Israel and the ancient Near East. Most likely, it is a later poem composed for its introductory function.

Psalm 1 has no historical memory, making no mention of specific persons or events of Israel's history. Rather, it has a timeless quality, which is quite appropriate for an introduction to the book.

Metaphorically the terms "tree," "streams of water," and "chaff" open a window into Israel's world. The "chaff that the wind blows away" (1:4) is a picture of winnowing, which involves throwing the grain into the air after it has been crushed, with the result that the heavier grain falls to the ground while the lighter hull is blown away by the wind. Still today that custom can be observed in the Middle East.

The clue to its date, however, is found in the interfacing characteristics with Psalm 2 (see the sidebar).

Key Themes of Psalm 1

- The life of the righteous is compared to the life of the wicked.
- Meditation upon the Word (Torah/Law) is the key to a fulfilled life.
- The ethics of association with sinners is spelled out for our instruction.

Interpretive Insights

1:1 *Blessed is the one who does not walk in step with the wicked . . . sinners . . . mockers.* The word "blessed" is a better translation of *'ashre* than "happy," which carries much lighter baggage than "blessed," since the life of the righteous is a life over which the Lord watches. The nouns "wicked," "sinners," and "mockers" are essentially synonyms, but the fact that the final term describes those who not merely reject God's law but "mock" it may suggest some progression in meaning.

1:2 *whose delight is in the law of the* LORD. The noun "law" (or Torah) comes from a verb (*yrh*) that means "to teach." (1) Thus *torah* sometimes means "teaching" (Isa. 8:16; NIV: "instruction"). (2) Closely related to this is the general sense of the will of God (Ps. 19:7). (3) In other instances it refers to the obligations and precepts of the law, indicating certain law codes (Gen. 26:5). (4) In this instance, given the assumed late date of this psalm, it likely refers to the collection of Scriptures that we know as the Pentateuch (or Torah). *and who meditates.* The noun form of the verb "to meditate"

Psalm 1 compares the wicked to the chaff that is blown away by the wind during the winnowing process. These Middle Eastern farmers are winnowing their grain (1940).

The Relationship between Psalms 1 and 2

As for the microcontext, the relationship of Psalms 1 and 2 is quite intimate. The editor of the book, or the psalmist, composed Psalm 1 with Psalm 2 in view and, like a tailor, stitched them together with verbal threads, providing an interpretive code. That code consists, first, in the fact that Psalm 1:1 begins with the first letter of the Hebrew alphabet, *aleph*, and the last word in the final verse, 1:6, begins with the last letter of the alphabet, *taw*.[a] This kind of artistic balance was probably intentional, hinting that Psalm 1 was to be seen as inclusive, coding the entire book in its verbal confines. The second feature of the code involves the inclusiveness of Psalms 1 and 2. Psalm 1 begins with the word *'ashre* ("blessed"), and the final line of Psalm 2 begins with the same word (2:12), thus forming an *inclusio*, linking the two poems together. So the study of the Torah (Ps. 1) and the coming of the kingdom of God (Ps. 2) are linked to give a dual theme for the entire Psalter. The third feature of the code is that Psalm 1 (1:2) employs the verb *hgh* ("meditates"), and so does Psalm 2 (2:1), but with the negative sense of "plot." This verb, in the context of the Torah, is a claim to the good life, but when the context changes to that of political defiance, the verb is a claim to spiritual insolence. Again, this word, by its divergent meanings, provides a window into the reign of the Torah in the human heart and the forces to be overcome by the "anointed one." The fourth item of the code is that our writer reinforces the contrast between the two ways of life, the "way of the righteous" and the "way of the wicked" (1:6), using the same term in 2:12 ("way"). Fifth, the verb "perish" (*'bd*) occurs in both psalms to describe the judgment of the wicked. The way of the righteous will have the Lord's watchful attention, whereas the way of the wicked "leads to destruction" (*'bd*, 1:6). Moreover, from the universal perspective, the kings who do not submit to the son ("kiss his son") "will perish in the way" (2:12 RSV). While "righteous" and "wicked" are shorthand terms for the two ethical poles in Psalm 1, Psalm 2 spells these concepts out in clauses: "blessed are all who take refuge in him" (righteous), "or he will be angry, and your way will lead to your destruction" (*'bd*). So the editor(s) has, by an artful balancing of lexical and thematic features, provided an introduction that lays out the shape of the two aspects of the kingdom of God, the personal (Ps. 1) and the national/universal (Ps. 2).

[a] Schaefer, *Psalms*, 3–4.

is *higgayon*, found in other psalms (9:16; 19:14; 92:3). Perhaps it is the singing of a text in a meditative style. In any event, the activity causes the psalmist to rejoice (19:8; 112:1; 119:92). Joshua's description of this activity produces the same results (Josh. 1:8; note the word "prosperous," from the same Hebrew verb as "prospers" in Ps. 1:3).

1:4 *chaff.* This is the husk that is lighter than the grain, so when the grain is threshed out, usually by beating or crushing, the wind blows the husk away (see "Historical and Cultural Background").

1:5 *Therefore . . . in the judgment . . . in the assembly.* The adverb "therefore" (*'al-ken*, 1:5), the conjunction "but" (*ki 'im*, 1:2, 4), and the conjunction "for" (*ki*, 1:6) serve as grammatical hinges to turn from the positive to the negative perspective, emphasizing the "two ways" that influence the choices one makes. For example, the "blessed" person (*'ashre*) is described in terms of what they do not do (collude with the wicked) and then the first hinge (1:2a, "but," *ki 'im*) swings the thought to the other side to emphasize delight in the Lord's law. The second hinge (1:4b, same Hebrew conjunction, *ki 'im*, but left untranslated by the NIV) swings the thought pattern in the opposite direction to depict the impermanence of the wicked, "[but] they are like chaff that the wind blows away." The third hinge (1:5a, "therefore," *'al-ken*) has a centering effect, centering the thought on the "wicked" and the "sinners," to contrast the two categories (the righteous and the wicked). That centering effect, covering both categories, but this time under the rubrics of the two ways, continues in the final verse, announcing the final pronouncement on the two ways from the Lord's perspective, introduced by the fourth hinge (1:6, "for," *ki*).

The term "judgment" is a reference to the court of law where one's deeds are put on trial, and some would give it an eschatological meaning, the final day of judgment. Parallel to "judgment," the word "assembly" likely refers also to the court where righteous judgment is rendered.

1:6 *righteous.* Parallel to the "wicked," the "righteous" are those whose lives measure up to the standard of God's Word.

Theological Insights

Psalm 1 starts with the idea that life is a relationship with God and that relationship is nurtured by the study of God's Word. This psalm lacks, for the most part, the language of creation, but it definitely has similarities to Genesis 1 and sums up the biblical story: the human search for God, and God's care for humanity. In Genesis, God brings the world into being by his word ("And God said, 'Let there be light,' and there was light," 1:3), while Psalm 1 zooms in on the power of the word of God as the instrument of life—in the case of Psalm 1, spiritual life. So Psalm 1—like Genesis 1, the beginning of the Bible—highlights the power of God's life-giving word. It even carries over the imagery of "day" and "night" of Genesis 1:3–5a. The psalmist, reflecting on the power of God's word, implies that the design of the universe provides the structure of our meditation, "day and night" (1:2).

In fact, Psalm 1 anticipates the portrait of the "righteous person" (who, rhetorically speaking, is David; see "Reading between the Lines" in the introduction) set forth in Book 1 by means of the individual and collective psalms—it is that portrait painted from the palette of colors included in Psalms 3–41.

In ancient Israel, judicial cases were heard at the city gate. At the ancient city of Dan, the excavations shown here reveal a raised platform between the outer and inner gates with pillar bases that may have supported a canopy. This structure may have provided a place for the king or judge to sit while making legal rulings or pronouncing judgment.

Teaching the Text

As we are preparing a sermon or lesson on Psalm 1, we should observe that the structure of Psalms 1 and 2 indicates that they should be interpreted as a single piece. That is indicated by the word "blessed" (*'ashre*) that occurs both in 1:1 and 2:12 (an *inclusio*), stitching the two psalms together. If this is a sermon, then the preacher will need to judge whether this is appropriate to the audience. If we choose to deal with both psalms in one sermon/lesson, we may focus on the two perspectives of these psalms, the individual and the national/universal (see sidebar "The Relationship between Psalms 1 and 2"). The two are complementary, for in the biblical perspective, the spiritual life of the individual is completed by the spiritual life of the world God made (universal kingdom of God). (See "Theological Insights" in the unit on Psalm 106.)

1. If we decide to separate the two psalms, we might first make the point that there are two corresponding terms that draw together the human and divine initiatives. The human is *delighting* "in the law of the LORD" (1:2), and the divine is the Lord's *watching* "over the way of the righteous" (1:6). It is a balance between God-consciousness and self-consciousness, an ongoing struggle of the Christian life. It is not intended to be so much a theological dogma as it is a description of the divine-human relationship seen from both God's and humanity's perspectives.

2. The terms of collusion with the wicked (1:1) may suggest a pattern of progression, from "walk," with its implied impermanence; to "stand," with a more

The righteous are described as fruitful trees planted by streams of water. This painting from the Tomb of Nebamun (fourteenth century BC) shows a beautiful garden where date palms, sycamore figs, and mandrake plants ring the pool that provided a constant water supply.

contemplative posture; to "sit," which suggests a more permanent arrangement. On the other hand, the one whose "delight is in the law of the LORD" (1:2) is characterized by permanence also ("like a tree planted by streams of water," 1:3), but a permanence that, like a deeply rooted and well-nourished tree, yields its fruit in the proper season (1:3). This is in stark contrast to the wicked, whom "the wind blows away" (1:4). In this world of rapid change one's spiritual constancy can be a remedy that results in emotional wholeness.

Illustrating the Text

Delight in the Law of the Lord.

Quote: Jonathan Edwards. Edwards, an eighteenth-century American theologian and preacher, said, "God created man for nothing else but happiness."[1] It is not the sensual pleasures of life that he speaks about but the spiritual delight of having one's life rooted in God. In our secular world, many will not understand the delights of God's Word, but it is accompanied by the assurance of God's watchful care that is underwritten by God's love, and who would not want to be surrounded with love!

Meditate on the law day and night.

Theological Book: *The Case for the Psalms*, **by N. T. Wright.** We can illustrate this constant meditation on the law (*torah*) by remembering how the Psalms themselves have been used through the centuries as a source of meditation on God and life. Wright encourages Christians to view the Psalms as representing a biblical "worldview," which is "what you look *through*, not what you look *at*." Praying and living the Psalms will mean for Christians "to weave the Psalms into the very heart of their devotional life and to expect to find as they do this that the way they look out at the world will change bit by bit."[2] This is the kind of saturation of the "law" that Psalm 1 prescribes for those who would choose the "way of the righteous"; and according to this worldview, it is the only legitimate way, for the "way of the wicked leads to destruction" (1:6).

The blessing of commitment to the law of the Lord

Props: Display two potted trees (or plants). One tree should be very healthy, as it has received water and sunlight and has been planted in rich soil. The other tree should be in the final stages of dying from lack of water, sunlight, or nutrients from the soil. Use these two trees as an image for the congregation to understand the blessings of delighting and meditating upon the law of the Lord. In an arid, dry climate, such as existed in much of ancient Israel, trees desperately needed water in order to survive. A tree planted by a stream of water can access that water through its root system, and in Israel's climate those roots have to be very deep. The result is a healthy tree that bears fruit. In the same way, when we choose to meditate on God's law, we are choosing to receive the spiritual and life nutrients that come through his Word. The result of receiving those spiritual nutrients is that we will bear fruit for the kingdom of God. That is, we will become more like Jesus in our character and will be used by God to help transform the world.

"You Are My Son; Today I Have Become Your Father"

Big Idea *God's sovereign control of the universe establishes a touchstone for understanding God's relationship to us and ours to him.*

Understanding the Text

The content and form of Psalm 2 is generally identified as a royal psalm, composed for and used on the occasion of some Israelite king's elevation to the throne. We do not know which king, but given the David collection that it prefaces, it could have been composed as a literary introduction to Book 1 (Pss. 3–41). Hilber has made a case for a prophetic origin based on seventh-century Assyrian royal prophecy.[1] His monarchic dating certainly fits the content and form of the psalm, whether or not it was actually used as a coronation piece.

The Text in Context

We have already observed the relation of Psalm 2 to Psalm 1 (see the sidebar in the unit on Ps. 1) and noted that in the macrocontext of Books 1–3 (Pss. 2–89), Psalms 2 and 89, both psalms of the earthly king, or royal psalms, stood as bookends to this early edition of the Psalter, stamping a royal seal on the collection.[2] Psalm 2 puts kingship, one of the central offices of ancient Israel, in the context of divine sovereignty and casts it in the light of the world of nations, which also falls under the aegis of God's sovereign rule over the world, or the kingdom of God.

Outline/Structure

This psalm centers on the divine decree of kingship (2:6–9):

1. The universal decree of rebellion against the Lord and his anointed (2:1–3)
2. The Lord's response to the universal rebellion (2:4–5)
3. The Lord's royal decree of investiture (2:6–9)
4. Admonition to the kings of the earth (2:10–12)

Historical and Cultural Background

In Israel's world it was anticipated that when a new king came to the throne, the vassal states would take advantage of his political vulnerability and plot rebellion to free themselves of the overlord. In view of this, many scholars consider this psalm to be a coronation psalm, and they see it as a celebration of the crowning of an Israelite king. While that is a possibility, Israel's largest vassal domain developed under David and would not have been in place at his coronation. The prospect of the "anointed" king (2:2) being Solomon is even more remote, since no evidence of such a vassal uprising exists, and added to that, Solomon was hardly the ideal king that the Lord should call him his "anointed," unless, of course, the psalm intends to describe the ideal king, as does Psalm 72, that is, a psalm about Solomon. Another possibility is to view the psalm as a celebration of God's sovereignty over the nations in the most general sense of the word (as Ps. 18), with the "nations," "peoples," and "kings" (2:1–2) being general references to David's enemies, or Israel's, for that matter, who are frequently the subject of Book 1.

Interpretive Insights

2:1 *the nations conspire and the peoples plot.* The idea behind the verb "conspire" is "roar," or "be restless." The revolutionaries form a conspiracy described by four verbs: "conspire," "plot," "rise up," and "band together." The Hebrew word for "plot" also appears in 1:2, where the sense is "meditate" rather than "plot." But the activity of this verb is vocal, not silent, and the reader ought to hear the low-voiced but threatening talk going back and forth in the distance as the nations make their sinister plans.[3] The first two verbs have a different tense. The first question (Hebrew perfect)

Key Themes of Psalm 2

- God is sovereign over the world.
- God's sovereignty is represented in the world by his Anointed One.
- Human rebellion against God and his Anointed One is futile.

In ancient Israel the chosen king was anointed with oil. This ivory flask, from fifteenth-century BC Megiddo, was carved from an animal tusk and held perfumed oils used to anoint the body.

asks the reason for their attempt (already past), and the second (Hebrew imperfect) asks why they imagine that they will succeed (in the future).

2:2 *anointed.* In ancient Israel the king was anointed with oil (2 Sam. 5:3). The term "anointed" came to refer to the messianic king in Judaism and thus in the view of the Gospel writers. In the Hebrew Bible, "Messiah" (*mashiah*, "anointed") does not always refer to a superhuman/divine figure. It stems from the idea of the "anointed" king and eventually comes to designate a future king who will accomplish the ideals of kingship that went so woefully uncomplished by the Israelite monarchy. In this connection Yahweh will intervene and miraculously, through his future "anointed one," bring those ideals to pass.[4]

2:3 *chains . . . shackles.* The metaphor is that of stubborn cattle that break and throw off their restraints.

2:4 *scoffs.* This is an in-your-face attitude. Isaiah uses the verb to describe Assyria's threat against Jerusalem under Sennacherib in 701 BC (Isa. 37:22).

Psalm 2

2:6 *Zion.* David bought the threshing floor of Araunah for the purpose of building the temple there. It was the highest peak of Jerusalem, not the present-day Mount Zion on the elevation south of the city wall. Actually, the kings were not anointed there, but the psalm speaks of Zion as the effective place from which the Lord's decrees go out, in the same sense as the law goes forth from Zion. "My holy mountain" suggests the presence of the sanctuary, although David only moved the ark to Jerusalem, and his son Solomon built the temple on Mount Zion. See sidebar "(Mount) Zion" in unit on Psalm 48.

2:7 *the Lord's decree.* The verbal root of the word "decree" means "to inscribe," thus committing it to permanent status as a legal instrument. Royal protocol in Egypt involved writing down the investiture of legitimate rulers, which became a future validation of their reigns.[5] The father/son language of verse 7b carries the same sense of 2 Samuel 7:14, suggesting that it is a historical reference to the founding of the Davidic dynasty.

become your father. The NIV rendering of this phrase obscures the verb "to beget" used here. While this verb (causative stem) is used of a man's role in the conception of children (a woman "bears," a man "begets," using the same verb in different Hebrew stems), the idea does not seem to be literal here since the "today" of begetting and the proclamation of the king's reign are synonymous.[6] The Old Testament is careful to distinguish Yahweh from the gods of its world, who reproduce like humans.

2:9 *you will break them with a rod of iron ... pottery.*[7] The verb

"break" assumes one Hebrew root (*r'*), while the alternate reading "rule" (see NIV footnote) assumes another (*r'h*, "to shepherd"). The LXX supports "rule" while the Targum the verb "break." In light of the parallel metaphor in the second half of the verse, the translation "break" is preferable, although "to rule" is not out of metaphorical range, since the shepherd "ruled" with his staff by sorting out the sheep (Lev. 27:32; Ezek. 20:37) and fighting off intruders of the flock (Ps. 23:4). Shattering a clay vessel ("pottery") to pieces was a common symbol of destruction (Isa. 30:14; Jer. 19:11). In the Egyptian Execration texts, names and messages were written on pottery sherds or vessels before they were shattered.

2:10 *be wise.* This verb suggests both political shrewdness and spiritual insight.

2:11 *Serve the Lord with fear and celebrate ... with trembling.* The first command, "serve," is the verb often used in the

Describing destroying one's enemies as "dash[ing] them to pieces like pottery" (2:9) is similar to the Egyptian practice of using Execration figurines or texts. Names and curses were written on pottery or clay figurines, like the ones shown here, and then smashed in a symbolic act of destruction (eighteenth century BC).

Old Testament for "worship." The monarchs of the world are called not only to submission but to worship, here implied by making the Lord the object of the verb (also Ps. 100:2). The subsequent command to "celebrate [lit., "rejoice"] . . . with trembling" is a parallel idea and a most appropriate way to combine the notion of awe and joy that must characterize the worship of God. They are complementary, not exclusive.

2:12 *Kiss his son.* This command is problematic in that it unaccountably uses the Aramaic word for "son" (*bar*). However, attempts to amend the text (RSV, NRSV: "kiss his feet") are unnecessary, seeing that it obviously is a call to submission, illustrated by Samuel's kissing Saul on the occasion of his anointing him king (1 Sam. 10:1), thus paying him homage.

Theological Insights

Arguably, no theme in the Old Testament is more important than the sovereignty of God. Psalm 2 teaches this theme in the context of the international arena. While the nations of Israel's world, and ours too, may view their sovereign rights apart from the universal rule of the God of Scripture, it is a false premise, one at which the sovereign Lord laughs (see the sidebar).

Teaching the Text

The key theme of Psalm 2 is God's sovereignty, or we might phrase the theme more colloquially as an answer to the question, "Who is in charge here?" The writer of Psalm 2 asks the same question that echoed through the garden of Eden

The Laughter of God

Three times in the Psalms (2:4; 37:13; 59:8) and once in Proverbs (1:26), God laughs, and all the instances have to do with evil nations or evil people who think they have one up on God. In each case God's laughter is derisive. That is, it is a mocking kind of laughter, the kind that says, "You thought you got the best of me, but I will show you in the end who's in charge." Would it be disrespectful to say that God has the last laugh?

when the serpent boomed out his defiant words, "Did God really say . . . ?" and raised the comparable question of God's sovereignty, or "Who really is in charge here?" It is appropriate to observe that humanity has asked this question all through the centuries, and God in Scripture, and God in the events of our world, answers the question in a myriad of ways: when kingdoms topple, when evil empires crumble, when our selfish designs take a Humpty-Dumpty fall.

Historically, Psalm 2 puts kingship in the light of God's sovereignty and issues the verdict that God is above kings—and, we would add, presidents and prime ministers. While Psalm 1 gives the perspective of God's sovereign rule in the individual's life through the power of his Word, the law, Psalm 2 gives the perspective of God's sovereign rule over rulers and nations.

To be sure that the preacher/teacher does not stand too far from the text, the point can be observed that Psalm 2 celebrates the Lord as King, and Psalm 89, the last psalm in this macrocollection (Books 1–3), also celebrates the Lord's kingship, even when the Davidic dynasty has been exiled to Babylonia.

Textually it is of importance that the psalm begins with the word "why." Why do rulers of the world think they can

Psalm 2

Paul at Antioch of Pisidia applied Psalm 2:7 to God's raising Jesus from the dead, the ultimate proclamation that God is sovereign (Acts 13:33). It was proof positive that God would prevail in history. Who is in charge here? God is! And he has proved that by the resurrection of his Son, Jesus Christ!

The sermon or lesson may include some word about God's laughter (Ps. 2:4; see the sidebar). Human beings may feel their power not merely on the level of kings and presidents but even on the personal level, but God "laughs" at them. In terms of God's saving acts in history, that's what God did in Jesus Christ when he defied the demons of hatred and the idolatry of the human spirit by raising his Son, Jesus Christ, from the dead.

One other aspect of Psalm 2 is important and might be considered as a second sermon on this psalm, which closes with four words of admonition for its ancient audience and for us who live in the twenty-first century. This is the spiritual antidote to the rebellion of the human spirit: (1) "be wise"—take note of the spirit and history of spiritual rebellion (2:10a); (2) "be warned"—God's judgment is certain (2:10b); (3) "serve the Lord"/"celebrate . . . with trembling"—the fear of the Lord is the proper spiritual posture (2:11); (4) "kiss his son"—fall down in humble submission to the sovereign God (2:12; cf. James 4:10). This is the gospel in miniature.

overpower God? And the answer is essentially that God exercises his sovereignty through his "anointed one" (*mashiah*), whom the kings of the earth rebel against. But who is this "anointed one"? In the ancient setting of the psalm, it was the king of Israel, perhaps David; some even believe it was Solomon.

But the New Testament writers look at this psalm and interpret this rebellion in terms of the rebellion of humanity against Jesus Christ. The early church remembered this psalm and equated the nations and peoples with the gentiles, who put Christ to death (Acts 4:25–28). That was the archetypal rebellion of humanity, which simply means we all are involved in that rebellion against the Lord and his Anointed One.

Illustrating the Text

History and parable

History: Psalm 2 represents the raw rebellion of the "kings of the earth" against God and his anointed. It is both history and parable. What happened in David's time is *history*, and as *parable* it presents the stark opposition to God that characterizes all humanity (Acts 4:23–31). Robert Rosenblatt wrote an article in *Time* ("What Really Matters?") that characterizes the twentieth century as a time when American culture decided there should be no moral restraints at all, and any such limits were intrinsically evil (sadly, the twenty-first century is its spiritual offspring). Rosenblatt draws the conclusion about "our age of self-confident autonomy" that "when people are unfettered they are *freed*, but not yet *free*."[8]

Who is in charge here?

Literature: *God Is My Co-Pilot*, by Robert Lee Scott Jr. Colonel Scott's autobiography (1943) covers his role as commander of the Flying Tigers, a collection of some of the best fighter pilots of World War II.[9] The story is compelling, but in light of Psalm 2, the book's title is unfortunate. The idea that God is our "copilot" conveys the thought that we are at least in partial control of the plane (the circumstances of our lives), while God simply sits in the seat next to us and serves as our assistant. In Psalm 2 we are reminded that God is in control of *all* things, and our role is to submit and obey. As we read in verse 11 ("Serve the LORD with fear"), we are to fully surrender to him and allow him to lead and guide our lives as we follow his direction.

The Lord reigns!

Music: Christ's resurrection is proof of God's sovereign reign. While the historical sense of Psalm 2:7 seems to reference the founding of the Davidic dynasty, in Acts 13:33 Paul understands it to extend ultimately to the resurrection of Christ, proof positive of God's sovereignty. J. S. Bach wrote a cantata titled *Heaven Laughs, and Earth Rejoices*. The laughter of heaven concentrated its countless decibels in the empty tomb, echoed up and down the valleys of the cosmos, and resounded through the billions of galaxies. If we could have heard the "laughter" of heaven as Jesus slipped out of the brawny arms of death, it would have deafened us forever. Christ had conquered! Death was vanquished! Christ was alive! The tomb was empty!

"I Will Not Fear Though Tens of Thousands Assail Me"

Big Idea *Sadly, life's conflicts become the baseline of our existence, when it ought to be our trust in the Lord.*

Understanding the Text

The essential elements of lament, according to our definition, are the lament itself and the reason for lamenting. Further, the lament of the individual will generally include one or a combination of three complaints: against one's enemies, against God, or against oneself. In Psalm 3, which is an individual lament, the complaint is against David's enemies (3:1–2). Moreover, psalms of lament will sometimes have, as does Psalm 3, a "confession of trust" (3:3–6).[1] In addition to the lament and the confession of trust, this psalm also has a petition (3:7–8a) and a blessing on God's people (3:8b).

The Text in Context

Psalm 3 is the first of the psalms to be attributed to David (Acts 4:25 later attributes Psalm 2 to David), thus beginning a large collection of Davidic psalms:

Book 1: Psalms 3–41

Book 2: Psalms 51–65; 68–70

Book 3: Psalm 86

Book 4: Psalms 101; 103

Book 5: Psalms 108–10; 122; 124; 131; 138–45

The title, "A psalm of David. When he fled from his son Absalom," belongs to a group of thirteen psalms that have titles linking them to David's life (3; 7; 18; 34; 51; 52; 54; 56; 57; 59; 60; 63; 142). While the connection is easier to identify in some cases than others, Psalm 3 sustains the connection very well (2 Sam. 15:1–19:43). The "many" enemies of Psalm 3:1–2 (cf. 3:6) are thus in keeping with the historical information. The king even sought verification of the notion, shared by the masses, that the Lord had abandoned him (2 Sam. 15:26; see Ps. 3:2). Moreover, Zion, called the Lord's "holy mountain," is the source of God's thunderous answer to David's enemies (2:6) and the place from which the Lord answers his lamenting servant when he cries out to him (3:4).

Psalm 3 faces forward to Psalm 4, where we find similar language of prayer. The psalmist is still surrounded by "many" detractors (4:6), recalling the "many" foes of 3:1–2. The language of sleep also occurs (4:8), as it does in 3:5. By comparison, it is obvious why Psalm 3 has been used as a morning psalm ("I wake again," 3:5) and Psalm 4 as an evening psalm ("in peace I will lie down and sleep," 4:8).

Outline/Structure

The triple invocation ("LORD") provides an easy outline of the psalm, as well as a hint of the "long and intimate communion" the psalmist has with Yahweh.[2]

1. "LORD"—lament (3:1–2)
2. "LORD"—confession of trust (3:3–6)
3. "LORD"—petition (3:7–8a)
4. Concluding blessing (3:8b)

Historical and Cultural Background

Since there is good reason, as shown above, to take the title seriously, the historical background of the psalm is Absalom's rebellion against his father, David, found in 2 Samuel 15:1–19:43. We might wonder, of course, why the psalm does not use Absalom's name. Delitzsch attributes this absence precisely to David's lamentive mood[3] (2 Sam. 19:1). In David's deep anguish, the mention of the name would perhaps have increased the anguish all the more.

As the title denotes, the backdrop of the psalm is war, confirmed by the military terminology (3:2, 3, 7, 8), and laments over war and its consequences were part of ancient Israel's culture. Any decent person deserved to be lamented, and any self-respecting father would certainly

Key Themes of Psalm 3

- David laments over his enemies.
- David acknowledges the Lord's special protection.
- David acknowledges that deliverance is from the Lord.

Psalm 3 is described as "a psalm of David when he fled from his son Absalom." This illustration from the Morgan Picture Bible (ca. AD 1250) shows the battle between the armies of David and Absalom, the death of Absalom, and then David receiving the news of the death of his son.

engage in such an exercise of grief over his deceased child. The activity was more formalized than it is in modern Western culture. Sometimes professional mourners were even hired to aid the process.

Interpretive Insights

Title *psalm.* The Hebrew word *mizmor* was rendered by the Septuagint with the Greek word *psalmos,* from which we get

David asks God to deliver him from his enemies by striking them on the jaw and breaking their teeth. This probably refers to hand-to-hand combat, a scene that this close-up from an Assyrian relief depicts (Nimrud, 865–860 BC).

our English word "psalm." The consensus is that it is a poem to be sung to the accompaniment of music.

3:2 *God.* Note that elsewhere in the psalm, except 3:7, the divine name is "Lord" (*YHWH*). Here David's enemies use the generic title God (*'elohim*), perhaps because Yahweh on the lips of non-believers would be inappropriate. However, the question of the use of the divine name is a complex one (see the sidebar "The Divine Names" in the unit on Ps. 4).

Selah. This word appears at the end of verse 2 (see NIV footnote). It occurs also in verses 4 and 8 (see the sidebar "*Selah*").

3:3 *lifts my head high.* This idea occurs in Genesis 40:13, expressed by a different verb, to indicate favor, and in 40:19 to suggest impaling. Here it is obviously God's favor.

3:6 *tens of thousands.* This term, a derivative of the same root as "many" (3:1, 2), likely alludes to the army Absalom had amassed against his father.

3:7 *Strike all my enemies on the jaw.* Striking one on the jaw was a gross insult (see Matt. 5:39), but here, surrounded by military language, this was probably hand-to-hand combat, as further suggested by the results, "break the teeth of the wicked." God as warrior is a common metaphor in the Old Testament, and here the psalmist engages the bold metaphor of his involvement in hand-to-hand combat, but, as Schaefer comments, to see God "knocking out the teeth of the enemy is an original touch."[4]

Theological Insights

Psalm 3 illustrates the fact that theology and life are congenially related. David's life was filled with conflict, yet he could lie down and sleep at night and awake to a life of trust "because the Lord sustains me" (3:5). Faith shapes practice. The effect is broader than his lying-down-and-rising-up routine, for it takes away the fear of his enemies who assail him by the tens of thousands (3:6). This absence of fear stems not from an unsophisticated view of a reckless world but from the knowledge and experience that the Lord is his shield and the one who lifts up his head (3:3).

Teaching the Text

One of the emphases of this commentary is that the sermon or lesson should arise from the text. While it is not always best to follow the outline of the text, being aware of the structure will help keep the exposition on track. In that mode, we should recognize that Psalm 3 is composed of three addresses.

The first address (3:1–2) gives the baseline of David's lament: his enemies have risen up against him (see "Historical and Cultural Background"). The rebellion of his own son Absalom is the backdrop, and he laments the opposition organized and perpetrated by this uprising. Admittedly, his foes are many, and they have penetrated the media of their time with the claim that God will not deliver David. Here the sermon/lesson may point out the principle that in honest prayer we may and should lay out the circumstances of our lives, as we understand them. This pattern repeats itself in many places in the Psalter.

With the second address (3:3–6), David counters the claim of 3:2b and acknowledges that the Lord is his shield and the one who shows him favor ("who lifts my head high," 3:3), the very opposite of his opponents' claim. The contentment brought by the Lord's answer "from his holy mountain" (3:4) has became an antidote for anxiety.

Salvation

The NIV translates the word for "salvation" (y^eshu'ah, from ysh', "to save") consistently as "deliver" (e.g., 3:2; cf. ESV), and rightly so, since the context is one of war. It is the same word, however, that is translated "salvation" in other contexts. Its range of meaning is rather wide, spanning the width from this basic nuance ("deliver" from battle), to the spiritual notion of "salvation" from evil thoughts and deeds (Ps. 51:12; cf. 51:14), to the idea of "salvation" as a relationship between God and worshiper.

He can sleep at night, and that is a single piece with his rising the next morning to face the day, supported by the knowledge that the Lord sustains him (3:6). This suggests that David's daily routine and trust in God are interwoven, which indeed is the nature of genuine faith.

Life's crises call for a renewal of our faith in the God who answers from his holy mountain. There are obviously good reasons for insomnia and fear, but when our sleep is constantly interrupted by worry, it may be an indicator that we have not yet learned how to rest ourselves in the arms of the one who says: "My yoke is easy and my burden is light" (Matt. 11:30). And further, Jesus instructs his disciples not to be anxious about tomorrow, because tomorrow has enough worries of its own. Our faith in Christ is supposed to be a life-changing, behavior-correcting, emotion-soothing power that flows through our spiritual veins and nourishes every part of the soul.

When we are depleted of spiritual vim and vigor, and weary of the routine of life, we might well use a set of spiritual exercises that could put us back in shape, like those of St. Ignatius of Loyola, or some other spiritual exercise program, or simply find a spiritual mentor. There are no "effortless" exercises, physical or spiritual, regardless of

David could sleep without fear because he recognized the Lord as his shield, providing protection. This Assyrian relief from the king's palace at Nineveh (704–689 BC) features shield bearers.

what advertisers may say. A healthy spiritual lifestyle involves persistent prayer, conscientious study of Scripture, and concentration on the spiritual disciplines of love and mercy. A spiritual "weight watchers" club is not a bad idea, by which we can keep each other accountable and "weigh in" at each meeting on Christ's Sermon-on-the-Mount scale, using the Beatitudes as our guide. There we can discuss our frustrations and failures, and the joy of our achievements through the power of Christ.

In the third address (3:7–8a), David borrows his language, in part, from Numbers 10:35, an old liturgical phrase that Moses used when the ark was taken into battle: "Arise, LORD!" (3:7a). While we will postpone this thought until we deal with Psalms 9 and 10 (see "Teaching the Text" in the unit on Pss. 9–10), the concluding verse of the psalm is a combination of trust and blessing, and a good place to emphasize our need, even in the midst of our own personal crisis, to pray for others in need. David, out of sorts with the popular political winds and under suspicion of divine abandonment, prays for Israel nevertheless: "May your blessing be on your people" (3:8a).

Illustrating the Text

A sacred sorrow

Worship: Plan a service of sacred sorrow, when your congregation has the opportunity to lament about their sins, about the cross where Christ became sin for us, about our lost world, and so on, and closing with our sorrow turned to joy. Use the Psalms,[5] and write your own prayerful laments. It might look something like the following:

A Sacred Sorrow with Jesus (*Psalter Hymnal*, no. 34 [Psalm 22])

A Sacred Sorrow for Our Sins (*Psalms for All Seasons*, no. 34D; *Psalter Hymnal*, no. 96 [Psalm 51])

A Sacred Sorrow for our Savior's Death ("Were You There When They Crucified My Lord?")

A Sacred Sorrow for Christ's Church (*Psalter Hymnal*, no. 80 [Psalm 44])

A Sacred Sorrow for Our Lost World (*Psalter Hymnal*, no. 19 [Psalm 14])

A Sacred Sorrow Turned to Joy (*Psalter Hymnal*, no. 52 [Psalm 30])

Look to the Lord.

Statistics: A Harvard Health Blog post written by Peter Wehrwein reports that the rate of antidepressant use in America among teens and adults (people ages 12 and older) increased by almost 400 percent between 1988–94 and 2005–8. The group (gender and age) that has the highest percentage increase is women in their forties and fifties, with 23 percent taking antidepressants.[6] That is almost one in every four women in that age category. There are legitimate reasons for such a surge, of course, and there are great blessings that have come with these medical advances. But do we as quickly turn to the Lord as David did?

Trust in the Lord.

Story: A woman received a phone call that would change her life forever: "Your husband had a heart attack and has passed away." He had been on a business trip to Europe; now forty-five largely wonderful years of marriage were over. Although she was devastated by the news, the first words out of her mouth after talking to the hospital were, "I wonder what God has in store for me now." The loss was excruciating. The pain was real. But this woman's response was based on a lifetime of trusting a faithful God. She knew she was in the Lord's hands, and ultimately that's all that mattered. Like David, she could lie down and sleep at night, because the Lord sustained her.

Circumstances press us into prayer.

Quote: *The Soul of Prayer*, by P. T. Forsyth. The laments, some less, some more, detail the circumstances that produce them. Forsyth, a renowned Scottish theologian, describes the conditions that press us into prayer:

The joiner, when he glues together two boards, keeps them tightly clamped till the cement sets and the outward pressure is no more needed; then he unscrews. So with the calamities, depressions, and disappointments that crush us into close contact with God. Instant relief would not establish the habit of prayer. If we got all we asked for, we should soon come to treat God as a convenience or the request as magic. The reason of much bewilderment about prayer is that we are less occupied about faith in God than about faith in prayer.[7]

"In Peace I Will Lie Down and Sleep"

Big Idea *God does not do business without a contract (covenant), and its terms, sometimes severe, translate into mercy and blessing when we trust him.*

Understanding the Text

The Text in Context

We have already discussed the relationship of Psalms 3 and 4 (see "The Text in Context" in the unit on Ps. 3), which is not coincidental. In fact, readers of the Psalms have noted the appropriateness of Psalm 3 as a morning prayer (3:5) and Psalm 4 as an evening prayer (4:8), whether the editor of the collection intended that purpose or not.

As noted in our discussion of Psalm 3, the present collection is a Davidic assemblage of psalms. Beginning with Psalm 2, the editor of the collection brings together psalms that set the tone for Book 1, which is David's conflict with his enemies and his trust in the Lord to deliver him. Psalm 4, a psalm of trust (see sidebar "Psalms of Trust" in the unit on Ps. 16), follows on the heels of a psalm that deals with Absalom's rebellion, and the tone of this poem shifts from the crisis mode to reconciliation. Prompted by Joab, his commander in chief, David initiated a policy of reconciliation (2 Sam. 19:1–23), to salvage any vestiges of goodwill that remained after Absalom's death. Rather than the angry words of David's accusers (Ps. 3:2), we hear the query of the former rebels who seek to reposition themselves behind David: "Who will bring us prosperity?" (4:6a). This is followed by David's prayer for divine favor (4:6b) and the joyful outcome of events (4:7).

Outline/Structure

The placement of *selah* (at the end of 4:2 and 4; see NIV footnote) probably reflects the musical performance of the psalm,[1] rather than a logical outline (see the sidebar "*Selah*" in the unit on Ps. 3). The content of the psalm yields a different configuration:

1. The Lord who answers in distress (4:1–3)
2. The psalmist's trust in the Lord and advice to the rebels (4:4–5)
3. Words and prayer of reconciliation (4:6–8)

Historical and Cultural Background

David's opposition includes distress (4:1b), humiliation (4:2a), and by implication, danger (4:8), all pointing to a set of circumstances that would qualify for Absalom's rebellion, as the title of Psalm 3 situates that psalm; but, of course, there were many circumstances in David's life that would qualify.

Psalm 4 gives the reader another window into David's world, the time of harvest. The combination of "grain" and "new wine" (4:7) would suggest that he is summing up the joy of the grain and grape harvests (Deut. 14:22–26; Ruth 3:7). The barley harvest was celebrated at Passover, the wheat harvest at Weeks (Pentecost), and the grape harvest at Tabernacles.

Key Themes of Psalm 4

By trusting in the Lord, the psalmist

- resists the temptation to brood over past wrongs,
- confesses his inner peace,
- confesses his inner joy, and
- holds out hope for his oppressors.

Interpretive Insights

Title *For the director of music. With stringed instruments.* The translation "director of music," or "choir director" (e.g., NASB, NLT), is based on the term's root (*ntsh*), which means "to lead" (Ezra 3:8 [NIV: "supervise"]; 1 Chron. 23:4 [NIV: "be in charge of"]). The suggestion that this is the precentor who led the musicians is plausible. It appears in the title of fifty-five psalms and Habakkuk 3:19.[2] The phrase "with stringed instruments" (*bineginot*) appears in the titles of Psalms 4; 6; 54; 55; 67; and 76, with a variant form in Psalm 61. The noun derives from the verb *ngn*, which means to play a stringed instrument (1 Sam. 16:16). Quite certainly this term means that the psalm was to be recited or sung to the accompaniment of stringed instruments.[3]

4:1 *my righteous God. Give me relief.* The phrase "my righteous God" means that God is the standard of righteousness, the supporter of the righteous, and their defender. (On the name "God," see the sidebar "The Divine Names.") The Hebrew word behind "give relief" means "to

The distress mentioned in Psalm 4 may be the events connected to the rebellion of Absalom. This illustration from the Morgan Picture Bible (ca. AD 1250) shows David being told of Absalom's schemes, Absalom with David's concubines, and David fleeing Jerusalem.

Psalm 4

The Divine Names

The use of the divine names Lord (YHWH) and God ('elohim) in the Psalms is a complex issue. In Book 1 YHWH occurs 278 times, and 'elohim 15. At the same time, Books 4 and 5 use YHWH 339 times and 'elohim 9.[a] Some scholars have spoken of an Elohistic Psalter, which showed a preference for the generic name Elohim. Theoretically, that psalter existed independently and was composed of Book 2 and part of Book 3 (Pss. 42–83), excluding the second Korah collection (Pss. 84–88, except Ps. 86).[b]

The Elohistic Psalter, it was supposed, originated in the northern kingdom and was influenced by Jeroboam's more Canaanite interests.[c] It is dominated by the first Korah collection (Pss. 42–49) and an Asaph collection (Pss. 50; 73–83). In the first collection of Korah psalms, 'elohim occurs 51 times, as compared to 9 for YHWH, while the numbers for the Asaph collection are 55 for 'elohim and 14 for YHWH, with 4 occurrences of the word 'adonay, a substitute for YHWH. In comparison, the second Korah collection (Pss. 84–85; 87–88), which we assume did not come under northern kingdom influences, turns the numbers around, with 17 occurrences of YHWH and 10 of 'elohim.

The idea is that the psalms were most likely composed in the Judean Kingdom and then adapted for use in a northern provenance, where 'elohim would have been more often used in worship. Psalms 14 and 53 provide an illustration of such an adaptation (e.g., "The Lord looks down," 14:2; "God looks down," 53:2). (See the unit on Pss. 42–43 for more on the Elohistic Psalter.)

[a] For these figures, see Goulder, Sons of Korah, 4–5.
[b] See Bullock, Encountering, 74, for an explanation of the "Davidic" nature of Psalm 86.
[c] Goulder, following the work of Peters (Psalms as Liturgies), proposes a northern provenance for the Elohistic Psalter.

---

make wide," and the noun derivative means "plaza" (Ezra 10:9, "plaza of [NIV: "square before"] the house of God"). Spatially, the idea is that the psalmist has been in a narrow place, but now the Lord has given him a wide space.

4:2 *How long will you people . . . seek false gods?* The expression "you people" is literally "children of man" (b^ene 'ish), which is used in conjunction with "children of man" (bene 'adam [i.e., "humankind"]) in Psalm 49:2 ("low and high") and 62:9 (NRSV and ESV: "those ["men"] of low estate" [bene 'adam] and "those ["men"] of high estate" [b^ene 'ish]). The distinction is in the two modifying words, 'ish (an individual man), for persons of distinction, and 'adam (humanity), for persons of common origin. Our term here may allude to the noble class that joined Absalom's rebellion.

The Hebrew word for "false gods" means literally "lies" (see NIV footnote). If, as we have suggested, this psalm is a meditation on the aftermath of Absalom's rebellion, "false gods" does not fit the context. The "lies" are weapons against the king, whose royal and personal "glory" his detractors have turned into "shame." Verse 2 is a description of David's opponents.

4:4 *Tremble.* The word is an imperative verb, just as the Septuagint translates it and as Paul understands it (Eph. 4:26; ESV: "Be angry"). Evidently David refers to a disappointed anger that has developed among the supporters of Absalom and threatens further detriment to their cause if they do not heed David's overture for reconciliation.

4:5 *sacrifices of the righteous.* These are sacrifices that are accompanied by true repentance, reflected by the second line, "trust in the Lord" (see the blessing of Moses in Deut. 33:19).

4:6 *Let the light of your face shine on us.* David knew the priestly benediction (Num. 6:24–26) and the blessing of Moses (Deut. 33), and here he prays with the words of these men of God. Other psalms pray to "see" God's face (Pss. 17:15; 27:8; etc.). We may view here two stages. *Seeing* God's face would be admittance into his presence for an audience, and having God's face to *shine*

The time when grain and new wine abound is during the harvest. Harvesting wheat is still done by hand in parts of Israel today.

4:7 *grain and new wine.* "Grain" and "new wine" are references to the harvest (see "Historical and Cultural Background"). See Deuteronomy 33:28 for this phrase.

4:8 *in safety.* The adverbial term "in safety," or "safely," comes from the verb "to trust." In this phrase we can see in David's life the results of the activity to which he admonished his opponents in 4:5b. See also Deuteronomy 33:28 for this term.

upon one would suggest that God receives one's petition favorably. David modestly requests that he may see a mere reflection.[4] His use of the term "on us" (Num. 6:24–26 is singular) means that he widens the scope of faithful service and worship, just as God has widened David's personal situation (Ps. 4:1) to give him security and peace (4:8).[5] Note the comparisons between the priestly benediction and the Psalms in table 1.

Table 1. Comparison of Numbers 6:24–26 and Psalms

Numbers 6:24–26	Psalms
"The LORD bless you and keep you" (v. 24; also v. 25)	"May God be gracious to us and *bless us* and make his face shine on us" (67:1)
"The LORD make his face shine on you and be gracious to you" (v. 25)	"*Let the light of your face shine on us*" (4:6) "May God be gracious *to us* and bless us and make his face shine on us" (67:1) "*Make your face shine on us*" (80:7, 19) "*Make your face shine on your servant*" (119:135)
"The LORD turn his face toward you and give you peace" (v. 26)	"The LORD blesses his people with *peace*" (29:11)

Theological Insights

Psalm 4 introduces the potent idea of covenant relationship in verse 3: "the LORD has set apart his faithful servant [*hasid*; lit., "godly"] for himself." The NIV renders the noun "servant" because that seems to be the idea behind the statement. However, the term "the godly" gives a perspective that "servant" alone does not imply. The word *hasid* is derived from the Hebrew noun *hesed*, which connotes God's "loving-kindness" (NIV generally translates it "love"; see the sidebar in the unit on Ps. 36). This is one of the major terms used to describe God's covenant with Israel, and we could even render the verse in this way: "the LORD has set apart his *covenant partner* for himself." The second half of the verse reflects Yahweh's responsiveness to the "covenant partner" he has set apart: the Lord "hears" when the suppliant calls. So the word picture is that of the covenant relationship between God and the psalmist, in which God is responsive (4:3b) and the suppliant is obedient (4:4). It is not surprising, then, to hear David pray the best-known benediction upon Israel: "Let the light of your face shine on us" (4:6; cf. Num. 6:24–26).

Teaching the Text

In light of the covenant relationship that stands behind this psalm, we may listen to the *two voices* of the psalm, that of David, which reflects this covenant relationship, and that of his opponents, who, at least in their rebellious state, fall outside covenant obedience.

We will take the voices in reverse order (so that we end on a positive note). In verse 2, David addresses his opponents as "you people." Since the term used here is different from the one that normally designates humanity at large, it may indicate individuals of high standing, thus "nobles" (see the comments on 4:2, above). If these are the nobles who joined Absalom's rebellion, then the king's words in verse 4 are indicting, calling them to search their hearts. Actually, they do not answer the questions of verse 2, as we might expect them to, but we do hear them speak once in verse 6a: "Who will bring us prosperity?" (lit., "Who will show us good?"). This is the voice of the distressed, those who have engaged in rebellion no less, which offers us insight into how God deals with sinners.

In response to their inquiry, we hear the primary voice that dominates the poem, that of David himself. Indeed, his prayer, phrased in the language of the priestly

David encourages his opponents to truly repent and then offer the appropriate sacrifices. This eighth-century BC Aramaean relief portrays a man carrying an animal to be sacrificed.

benediction (Num. 6:24–26), is the answer to their question. Being a covenantal blessing, it both welcomes these rebellious people back into the covenant community and asks Yahweh's blessing upon them. It is David's prayer of reconciliation, a model for our own disposition toward those who do us wrong, quite in keeping with Jesus's own instruction that we pray for our enemies (Matt. 5:44). And historically speaking, it represents the program of reconciliation that David initiated toward those who sided with Absalom and whose cause was lost with Absalom's death (2 Sam. 19).

This suggests that God deals with us, regardless of our circumstances, out of his covenant relationship with us—in Israel's case, the Mosaic covenant, and in ours, the new covenant in Jesus Christ. This indeed is an Old Testament precedent for Jesus's word of instruction. And the change of pronoun in the benediction from "you" (see Num. 6:25) to "us" in verse 6b implies that the psalmist is included among the recipients of grace.

Illustrating the Text

A balanced perspective

Quote: Abraham Lincoln. On April 4, 1864, in a letter to Albert Hodges, Abraham

Lincoln wrote, "If God now wills the removal of a great wrong, and wills also that we of the North as well as you of the South, shall pay fairly for our complicity in that wrong, impartial history will find therein new cause to attest and revere the justice and goodness of God."[6] In the midst of the American Civil War, President Lincoln was willing to acknowledge that the North too was complicit in the "great wrong" of this horrific war that divided the nation. We have a tendency, in conflict, to see the other person as "the unholy enemy" and ourselves as "the righteous victim." The reality is that in almost every conflict, we bear some burden of responsibility, if even limited to what we are thinking about the other person or persons. Even if we are beyond reproach in the conflict, we too are sinners in need of God's mercy. In Psalm 4:1, we see David, the victim of Absalom's revolt, acknowledging that he too is in need of God's mercy. A great challenge for us when we feel wronged is to have a balanced perspective where we recognize not only the other person's sin but our own need for God's grace. As you consider your broken relationships, do you recognize your own need for God's mercy?

Forgive and bless.

Sports: NBA basketball star Chris Paul had just signed to attend Wake Forest University, and the next day he learned that his grandfather had been murdered. Paul's grandfather, Nathaniel Jones, was randomly selected and then robbed and beaten to death by five teenagers. Paul was very close to his grandfather, who was well respected in the community, so you would expect him to be bitter. Rather, in an interview with ESPN's Rick Reilly, Paul says, "These guys were 14 and 15 years old [at the time], with a lot of life ahead of them. I wish I could talk to them and tell them, 'I forgive you. Honestly.' I hate to know that they're going to be in jail for such a long time. I hate it."[7] We see a similar attitude of heart from David in Psalm 4 (vv. 2–5) as he offers his prayer of reconciliation and welcomes these rebels back into the covenant community. Now, follow the example of Chris Paul and King David. Whom do you need to forgive? With whom do you need to experience reconciliation?

"You Are Not a God Who Is Pleased with Wickedness"

Big Idea *God and evil are mutually incompatible, and on the human level, that is effectively demonstrated in the harmful results of evil perpetrated on others.*

Understanding the Text

Psalm 5 is an individual lament (see "The Anatomy of Lament" in the introduction), issuing a complaint that the psalmist's enemies cannot be trusted (not unusual for one's enemies!) and affirming trust in the Lord.

The Text in Context

So far we have seen a lineup of psalms (2–5) that deal with David's enemies. His reign was one of war and conquest, and his enemies were never far from his mind. Evidently in Psalm 5 we have moved outside the context of Absalom's rebellion, although a few interpreters still see hints of it in this psalm.

Like Psalm 3, this is a morning psalm set in the context of the morning service. Unlike Psalm 3, where David is a fugitive, here he is contemplating going to the house of God (5:7).

Outline/Structure

The poet addresses the deity directly as "Lord" (*YHWH*) four times (5:1, 3, 8,

In the opening verse of Psalm 5, David prays for God's help. This illustration by Malnazar and Aghap'ir (AD 1637–38) from an Armenian Bible shows David in prayer (ms. Ludwig I 14, fol. 320v, J. Paul Getty Museum).

12) and as "God" twice (5:2, 10). These addresses do not provide a logical arrangement for the psalm, in contrast to Psalm 3; they do, however, indicate how personal the psalmist's relationship is to God. Kidner has helpfully noted that the psalm falls into five short strophes, "three of which are turned full-face to God," alternating between positive and negative:[1]

1. Listen to my words, Lord (positive; 5:1–3).
2. Evil does not dwell with God (negative; 5:4–6).
3. Lead me, Lord, in your righteousness (positive; 5:7–8).
4. Declare evildoers guilty, O God (negative; 5:9–10).
5. Surely, Lord, you surround them (the righteous) with your favor (positive; 5:11–12).

Historical and Cultural Background

Some interpreters take the references to "house" and "temple" in 5:7 to exclude the psalm from David's authorship. In that case, "of David" would probably mean "for David" in the sense of a dedication. Yet the tabernacle at Shiloh is called a "house" in 1 Samuel 1:7, 9, even though it was a tent. It may be that David's intense desire to build the temple already shapes his vocabulary. There is also the possibility that a later editor upgraded the term.

As in Psalm 3, the psalmist prays "in the morning" (twice in 5:3), which was a time for legal proceedings at the gate (Ruth 4:1–6), as well as the morning sacrifice (Exod. 29:39). If the NIV's reading "I lay my requests" (the Hebrew has no direct object) is the intended sense, then

Key Themes of Psalm 5

- The Lord is King and God.
- God is incompatible with evil.
- Divine mercy is the key to answered prayer.
- God's protection surrounds the righteous.

For Pipes

The Hebrew phrase 'el-hann^{e}hilot in the title of Psalm 5 is often associated with the Hebrew word halil, for "flute." While Braun acknowledges this connection, he objects on the grounds that the Septuagint and the Vulgate render it "heir."[a] In fact, the Midrash on the Psalms also recognizes this connection ("inheritance"), among other suggestions.[b] However, associated with the technical term "director of music," the phrase is more likely to have a musical meaning, although we cannot be certain until further information becomes available.

[a] Braun, Music, 40.
[b] Braude, Midrash, 1:84.

we have a metaphor: the psalmist is laying his requests before the Lord in the morning just as one would lay one's case before the judges at the gate. If it is in the sense of "preparing a sacrifice" (see RSV, ESV), then the morning service is likely in view. I prefer the latter, even though the setting could be that of the law court or the sanctuary.

Interpretive Insights

Title *For the director of music. For pipes.* The title of the psalm suggests a musical connection. While the "director of music" definitely has musical connotations, there are several interpretations of the term "for pipes." Its meaning, however, is best left open (see the sidebar).

5:3 *I lay my requests before you and wait expectantly.* The Hebrew verb for "lay" is used of *laying* wood on the altar (Lev. 1:7), *preparing* a lamp (Ps. 132:17), *setting* a table (Ps. 23:5), *laying out* a legal case (Ps. 50:21), and *setting forth* thoughts (Ps. 40:5; see KJV).[2] The NIV translates the verb in the last sense, supplying the missing object "my requests." The ESV chooses the first meaning, "prepare a sacrifice." Coupled with the imagery of the morning (sacrifice), this meaning seems preferable, although the ambiguity here is quite impressive (see "Historical and Cultural Background"). The verb "wait" has the same meaning in Habakkuk 2:1, where the prophet stations himself in the tower to "watch" (NIV: "look") for the oncoming messenger.

5:4 *with you, evil people are not welcome.* The noun "evil people" can refer to persons or abstract evil. The NRSV translates "evil will not sojourn with you" and the NEB, "evil can be no guest of thine." Either is possible, but the fact that verse 5a says, "The arrogant cannot stand in your presence," seems to picture a journey to the temple where worshipers stand in God's presence. And further, the verb "are not welcome" (*gur*) is used of going to the sanctuary in Psalms 15:1 and 61:4.

5:5–6 *You hate all who do wrong.* The language of "hate" (5:5) and "detest" (5:6) is strong. In Israel's world people thought in terms of opposites, so Malachi records the Lord's words, "Yet I have loved Jacob, but Esau I have hated" (1:3). In this instance it is another way for the Lord to say, "I chose Jacob, but I did not choose Esau." However, our present text is not exactly the same, for it pits God against evil, and the verbs "hate" and "detest" suggest God's absolute rejection of evil because it is the opposite of his nature. Another psalmist views his life in harmony with God's nature when he says, "Do I not hate those who hate you, Lord?" (139:21). The ancients did not distinguish between the "sin" and the "sinner" as we are prone to do.

5:8 *make your way straight before me.* A circuitous path was much more difficult to navigate than a straight one, especially since the enemies hid around the bends and curves to harm the travelers (cf. Prov. 3:5–6).

5:9 *Their throat is an open grave.* The evil words that come out of their throat stink like an "open grave."

5:10 *Declare them guilty . . . Banish them for their many sins.* Using the language of the legal court, the psalmist now prays for the hoped verdict of the Judge, that God will let their own machinations bring them down. That is, the fate of the wicked lies not in God's hatred of them but in the nature of their own rebellious acts (see "Theological Insights").

5:11 *love your name.* The name of God and his person are synonymous, as Exodus

God's protection of the righteous is like a large shield. In this relief, a group of soldiers advance together so that their long, rectangular shields offer maximum coverage and defense (victory stele of Eannatum, ca. 2450 BC).

20:7 suggests. To love God's name is to be loyal to him by obeying his commandments (Deut. 6:4–6).

5:12 *you surround them . . . as with a shield.* The verb may mean "surround" (NIV), "cover" (RSV, ESV), or "crown." With "shield" as its referent, the word "cover" seems best. The reference here is to the large shield (*tsinnah*), compared with the small one (*magen*; e.g., Pss. 3:3; 7:10).[3]

Theological Insights

The path to righteousness is often engineered in the crucible of suffering—in this case, unjust suffering. While the psalmist does not concentrate on the justice of God, he is quite aware that God has an ear and a heart for justice. That is the reason he can pray that the Lord will declare the evil persons guilty and leave them to fall by their own devices (5:10). Western thinkers are able to separate one's person and one's deeds—modern psychology has offered much assistance in this respect. But in ancient Israel a person who did evil was an evil person. Thus God's hatred of evil and his hatred of the person are sometimes synonymous (139:20–22). While this may fall well beneath the New Testament ethic of loving even our enemies, the Old Testament has ample evidence of the love ethic (e.g., Deut. 6:5; 7:7–13; Lev. 19:18), even loving the foreigner (*ger*) as oneself (Lev. 19:34).

The Old Testament does not deal with the problem of evil in abstraction,[4] but rather it addresses the social and ethical issues that evil creates in the real world. Verse 4 may be an exception, and if it is, the psalmist does not dwell long on the abstract but moves naturally to the incarnation of evil in individuals (5:5, 6). And while evil is an abstraction in our minds, it never assumes a passive state but always incarnates itself in human persons, in behaviors, and in circumstances (e.g., natural disasters, illness). Yet, the psalmist insists that God and evil are incompatible, and that is as much of a theological statement on evil as we have anywhere in the Psalms. In verse 5b this is expressed in terms of God's hatred for those who do wrong.

If there is any place in the theology of the Psalms where God's relationship to evil is resolved, it is God's sovereignty, for in that concept and in that reality, evil is overruled. One of the most powerful images of the Psalter occurs in this psalm with the negative assertion that, as the NEB translates it, "evil can be no guest of thine" (5:4b; see the comments on 5:4). The metaphor is that of dwelling or sojourning, to remind us that evil and God are entirely incompatible, at the opposite ends of the ethical and ontological spectrum. No amount of this world's antirejection drugs can achieve compatibility or eliminate the incalculable distance between God and evil. Putting this in human terms, "the arrogant cannot stand" in the Lord's presence (5:5). Yet the psalmist will enter the Lord's house and worship in his holy temple (5:7), and this by no achievements of his own but by God's "great love."

Teaching the Text

Psalm 5 is a personal lament weighted with the psalmist's overwhelming confidence in God, and this weight outbalances the power of evil; formidable as it is, evil is still no match for the God of grace. We may point to three perspectives that open this psalm up.

The first perspective is the psalmist's perspective on God. It is doubtful that the Psalter provides a better description of God's opposition to evil and evildoers than here (5:4). Here is the holy God modeling his holiness, setting himself apart from the evil world. It reminds us of Yahweh's command to Israel: "Be holy, because I am holy" (Lev. 11:44, 45).

The second perspective is on the psalmist himself. He is intimate with God and diametrically opposed to the evil of the world that has done him great harm. He addresses the Lord four times directly by the covenant name "Lord" (*YHWH*; 5:1, 3, 8, 12), twice by the generic name "God" (5:2, 10), and once as "my King" (5:2). He typifies the worshiper who comes into God's presence ("your holy temple," 5:7) through an abundance of God's love (cf. 1 John 3:1).

The third perspective is the picture of evil and evildoers. The six terms of 5:4–6 that crescendo into the shedding of blood and character assassination ("bloodthirsty," "deceitful") utilize the primary colors on the literary artist's palette and describe evil mainly in terms of harmful human relationships. When Paul sets forth his claim that all human beings, gentile and Jew alike, are under the power of sin, he quotes Psalm 5:9, among other passages, to demonstrate his point (Rom. 3:13). The five positive imperative verbs of verses 8 and 11 outline a defensive program against evil and metaphorically straighten out the circuitous path the evildoers have engineered for the psalmist (5:8), leading home all those who find refuge in the Lord, as they sing joyfully and find themselves surrounded by the Lord's protection (5:11). This program countermands the enemies' plan, against which the psalmist prays that the Lord will "declare them guilty," "let their intrigues be their downfall," and "banish them for their many sins" (5:10). Here we may stress the truth that the most effective plan of opposition against evil is a program of doing good, which in psalmic terms is essentially the same as being good.

Illustrating the Text

Follow God's way.

Hymn: "Thy Way, Not Mine, O Lord," **by Horatius Bonar.** In the nineteenth century Bonar published the great hymn "Thy Way, Not Mine, O Lord," which provides a powerful picture of what we see in Psalm 5, David's desire to come before God in reverence and obedience. In fact, we see in this psalm a connection in David's heart between authentic worship and following the righteous path of God. Bonar shares David's heart for righteous obedience, as we see in this hymn:

> The kingdom that I seek
> Is thine; so let the way
> That leads to it be thine
> Else I must surely stray.[5]

This would provide a great opportunity to challenge your listeners to make a similar request of the Lord from their hearts: "Lead me, Lord, in your righteousness . . . make your way straight before me" (5:8).

God takes no pleasure in evil.

Quote: Edmund Burke. Irish orator, philosopher, and politician Edmund Burke is commonly thought to have said, "All that is necessary for the triumph of evil is that good men do nothing."[6] This statement has pricked the conscience of men and women who have made bold and courageous stands against evil and injustice in the world. But evil and injustice can still win the day, because men and women are not sovereign over the world. Psalm 5 provides a great comfort to us that evil and injustice will not ultimately win the day, "For you are not a God who is pleased with wickedness; with you, evil people are not welcome" (v. 4). The sovereign Lord detests sin and takes no pleasure in evil. We are to stand boldly with God against evil and injustice in the world. And as we do, we can take heart even when it seems that evil wins in the moment, for we know that the holy God is still in charge, and he will ultimately be victorious!

The way to begin each day

Church History: Both Psalms 3 and 5 have been considered psalms for morning prayer. The Rule of Benedict (sixth century) prescribes them for morning prayer. The sixteenth-century Reformer John Calvin, following the daily discipline of prayer, began each day with prayer and insisted that prayer must become a routine to be most effective. So Calvin's regimen of prayer looked like this: morning prayer before beginning daily work, prayer before and after meals, and prayer before bedtime.[7]

"Their throat is an open grave" (5:9) is the psalmist's description of the foul, lying, and deceitful words that come out of the mouths of evildoers. Tombs were places of death with the stink of decay. Shown here are the remains of the seventh- to sixth-century tombs at Ketef Hinnom in Jerusalem.

"Have Mercy on Me, LORD, for I Am Faint"

Big Idea *Either an illness or the psalmist's enemies, or both, have driven him to pray for God's mercy, out of which a robust faith bursts forth.*

Understanding the Text

Generally Psalm 6 is considered an *individual lament*, and it is the first of the penitential psalms of the ancient Christian church (6; 32; 38; 51; 102; 130; 143). While the element of penitence seems elusive, this psalm certainly is a prayer for divine mercy one place removed from confession of sin. The suppliant laments either (1) the condition that was caused by sin, or (2) illness that was commonly thought to be the result of sin, or (my preference) (3) the innocent suffering caused by the opposition of his enemies (6:7, 10).

The Text in Context

This psalm follows three psalms (3–5) that have all the earmarks of Davidic psalms and are historically positioned in Absalom's rebellion, with Psalm 5 the least confident of this setting. For the first time, David's enemies, in a general sense, come into view. Psalm 2 deals with his international enemies, while Psalms 3–5 domesticize his enemies, and Psalm 6 introduces us to the nondescript, common company of foes that has caused David so much concern and scholars so much quandary. For the most part, then, with this psalm we have met the three categories of enemies that are the object of so many of the psalms: international, domestic, and common.

Some interpreters have pointed to the psalm's verbal similarities to Jeremiah (Ps. 6:1 with Jer. 10:24 is the most impressive), but these are for the most part echoes, not quotations. Still, the terms shared with other psalms are significant.[1]

Outline/Structure

On the basis of content we can divide the psalm into three parts:

1. The psalmist cries out to God from his anguish (6:1–3).
2. The psalmist cries out to God for deliverance (6:4–7).
3. The psalmist expresses his confidence that God invalidates his enemies' machinations in answered prayer (6:8–10).[2]

Interpretive Insights

Title *sheminith.* This term means "eighth" and seems to direct the singing or playing, perhaps both, in a higher or lower octave.

of David. The term *l'dawid* designates the author (by David), or collection (for David), or dedication (in honor of David). See "The Nature of the Book" in the introduction.

6:2–4 A double-tracking of three verbal similarities ties the first part of the psalm and the final prayer together, and a fourth capitalizes on the answer to prayer with a wordplay. (1) The verb "have mercy" (6:2a) occurs again in nominal form as the psalmist declares that the Lord has heard "my cry for mercy" (6:9). (2) The imagery of "turn" in 6:4 is that of the Lord turning *toward* the contrite worshiper from an opposite direction, while the imagery of "turning back" in 6:10 is that of the enemies who turn *away from* the psalmist to go in the opposite direction, all in answer to his prayer. (3) The use of the verb "dismay" in 6:2 describes the psalmist's physical agony (NIV: "my bones are *in agony*"), while its effect in 6:10 is to describe his enemies who are "dismayed" (NIV: "anguish"), again a reversal, or a transfer of the emotional/physical effect from the psalmist to his enemies. (4) The Hebrew verb used for the entreaty "turn" in 6:4 (*shub*) occurs again

Key Themes of Psalm 6

- The psalmist had suffered innocently.
- Grace is unmerited favor.
- Divine chastisement is love.

in 6:10 ("turn back"), where it forms a word pattern with a similar-sounding verb, "be put to shame" (*bush*). The letters of the two verbs are switched for sound effect: "All my enemies will be overwhelmed *with shame* (y-b-sh) and anguish; they will *turn back* (y-sh-b) and suddenly *be put to shame* (y-b-sh)." Note that the term for "shame" occurs on either side of "turn back," hinting that this return is a shameful defeat and constitutes the answer to the psalmist's prayer.

6:2 *Have mercy on me, Lord, for I am faint . . . my bones are in agony.* The phrase "I am faint" translates a Hebrew verb that is often rendered "languish," used in the Psalms and Job to describe wicked individuals who are doomed to wither away (Ps. 37:2; Job 18:16; 24:24). The verb "have mercy" implies God's favor.[3] The reference to "my bones" is synecdoche for the entire body.

The psalmist calls God to have mercy as his "bones are in agony," which may mean that the psalmist is suffering some sort of illness. This simple prayer contrasts with the complex rituals that would have been enacted as the pagan world sought relief from suffering. Amulets like the one shown here from Mesopotamia were created to ward off sickness, especially illnesses thought to be demon induced. The middle register shows special healers wearing fish-skin robes performing the prescribed ritual over the sick person so that health might be restored (ninth century BC, neo-Assyrian).

Sheol

The Hebrew term *she'ol* is both a place and a state of being. All human beings go to Sheol after death—rich and poor, master and slave. Although *she'ol* is translated by the Septuagint as *hadēs*, a term used also in the New Testament, it is not the same as the New Testament concept of "hell." Rather, in the scope of revelation, Sheol represents an earlier stage of understanding. Sometimes it is used of the extremity of the cosmos (e.g., Deut. 32:22; Isa. 7:11), intended to describe the place or state of being that is the opposite of God, although God can pursue his creatures all the way to Sheol if they try to escape his scrutiny (Ps. 139:8). As the abode of the dead, its clear usage occurs in 1 Samuel 2:6; Isaiah 57:9; Job 17:13; and while it is a place for the wicked (Isa. 5:14; Ezek. 32:27), it is also a place where the righteous go (e.g., Job, Hezekiah, and the psalmist [Ps. 88:3]), although there is some evidence that the righteous hope to escape it (Jon. 2:2; Ps. 16:10). In some instances *she'ol* is merely a synonym of "death" or "the grave" (Pss. 30:3; 49:14),[a] as it appears to be here in Psalm 6:6.

This state of being was one of semi-life, devoid of joy, because those in Sheol did not have the fullness of life that ensured a vital relationship with God in such an intermediate state of existence.[b] God in his wisdom did not choose to reveal the full state of the afterlife until he had revealed himself in the fullness of his glory in Jesus Christ. We might say that God wanted us to long first for a fullness of relationship with him, one that we could understand only in the face of Jesus Christ. Who among us finds the joy of place, however lovely, more appealing than the joy of relationship?[c]

 [a] See Prévost, *Dictionary*, 62–64; Johnston, "Psalm 16."
 [b] Craigie, *Psalms 1–50*, 93.
 [c] See Johnston, *Sheol*.

6:3 *My soul . . . how long?* The word often translated by the English versions as "soul," has a range of meanings. It can denote "life" (107:5) or occur in the place of the personal pronoun (78:50; 120:2). Sometimes it comes close to our concept of personality.[4] The interrogative "How long?" occurs in several psalms (e.g., 74:10; 80:4; 82:2) and usually carries the meaning of "how distressingly long?" (The NIV's second "how long?" is not in the Hebrew text.)

6:4 *unfailing love.* This phrase translates a single Hebrew word, *hesed*, which is close in meaning to "love" and is based on the Lord's covenant faithfulness. See the sidebar in the unit on Psalm 36.

6:5 *from the grave.* The Hebrew is literally "in Sheol" (see the sidebar).

6:6 *I flood my bed . . . my couch.* The Hebrew verb for "flood" means "swim," thus giving the exaggerated metaphor, "All night I caused my bed to swim,"[5] parallel with "drench my couch with tears." The psalmist may position himself socially with the term "couch" ("bed"), because only the wealthy would have a proper bed. The poor would sleep on a straw mat and often cover themselves with their outer garment (Exod. 22:26–27).

6:7 *foes.* The etymology of this word is disputed. Craigie examines the various proposals ("heart," "recess," etc.) and concludes that the sense of "enemies" or "foes," derived from the Hebrew root *tsrr* ("to show hostility"), is the best,[6] with which I concur.

6:8 *you who do evil.* This term (lit., "doers of evil") references those who oppose the psalmist. Their evil is constituted by their unjust opposition to the suppliant, or simply their common practice of evil deeds.

6:9 *The Lord has heard . . . the Lord accepts my prayer.* While the first verb is the Hebrew perfect ("has heard") and the second an imperfect ("will accept"), both types of verbs in Hebrew poetry are quite flexible. Here the second verb carries the present reality, "accepts."

Theological Insights

The early church included Psalm 6 among the seven penitential psalms that were recited on Ash Wednesday (see the

Describing his agony, the psalmist laments, "I flood my bed with weeping" (6:6). Most people slept on mats on the floor, but the wealthy could own an actual bed, perhaps like the terracotta model shown here (Ur, 3000–1750 BC).

comments at the beginning of the "Understanding the Text" section), even though it is not strictly a psalm of penitence. If this choice of the church fathers seems a mystery to us, perhaps it is because we sometimes fail to recognize that anytime we plead for God's grace, we acknowledge our great need and the depravity of our human condition, and this is at the core of confession.

Whatever the cause of the psalmist's suffering, whether it be physical or emotional, it was a time of intense agony that caused him to cry out, "How [distressingly] long, LORD?" (6:3). This cry of anguish issues forth from his deep pain. In the Psalms the cry of fresh anguish is "Why?" The cry of extended anguish is "How long?" Kidner reminds us that "all God's delays are maturings, either of the time (as in Ps. 37), or of the person (as in 119:67)."[7] David's anguish has arisen from the opposition of his enemies (6:7, 10), otherwise undefined in the psalm. Yet, he does not confess guilt, even though the verb "discipline" in verse 1 may imply it. If anything, he dismisses their

opposition as the shaping force in his life (6:1, 8–10) and relies upon God's "unfailing love" (*hesed*; 6:4b) as the shaping power. David has encountered the "no" of God's love in these extended circumstances, whatever form they have taken, which would be unbearable were it not for the knowledge that God's loving-kindness (*hesed*) is the "yes" of God's favor in the broader frame of reference. The verb "discipline" of 6:1 begets the noun "discipline" (*musar*) that is the divine chastisement of love in the direction of righteousness (Prov. 3:11–12). It is the "electric wire that shocks the cattle away from the precipice."[8]

The sudden turn away from the psalmist's overwhelming troubles that occurs in 6:8 is a turn in faith, based on God's "unfailing love" (*hesed*). Thus verses 8–10 are a cry of victory. The psalmist could have succumbed to the character distortion of his enemies and accepted their view of him and his circumstances, but he found the reshaping power of love to be truly transforming. God's reshaping love is painful, but it produces a new perspective on our lives and reshapes the distorted self-image that our "enemies" sometimes try to foist on us.

Teaching the Text

We may begin a message on Psalm 6 by addressing those who are in distress at the hands of those who do them wrong for no reason. While there is a possibility that the suppliant's distress is caused by illness (6:2, 6, 7), which his enemies could interpret as God's disfavor, the poem points in the direction of circumstances, left undefined, that were created by enemy opposition (6:7, 8, 10).

At the same time, Psalm 6 presents us with a very different tone toward David's enemies, which we may also find instructive, in that David here, unlike his imprecatory utterances against them in other psalms (35; 55; 69; 109), simply dismisses their opposition because God has heard his tearful prayer and has acted on his behalf (6:8–9). Paul speaks persuasively on the matter of facing opposition and persecution in 2 Corinthians 4:7–18, declaring that God uses all of this "for your benefit, so that the grace that is reaching more and more people may cause thanksgiving to overflow to the glory of God" (4:15).

The seven imperatives that punctuate the first four verses ("do not rebuke," "[do not] discipline," "have mercy," "heal," "turn," "deliver," and "save") are naturally commanding in force, but emotionally they are pleading petitions. The intensity of the first-person pronouns, "I," "me," and "my," immediately signals the personal desperation of the worshiper and his deeply felt anguish. In fact, that feature is sustained throughout the psalm, even in the prayer of confidence of verses 8–10. Those who are infirm, whether physically or emotionally, may enter that anguish unapologetically and without guilt through this psalm. As Kidner says, "The psalm gives words to those who scarcely have the heart to pray, and brings them within sight of victory."[9]

Jesus uses the language of the psalmist's imperative (6:8) when he speaks of those evildoers who thought their pretense of doing good would get them into the kingdom of God (Matt. 7:23). But their actions spoke louder than their words.

Illustrating the Text

The dark night

Human Experience: When your congregants can relate to the struggle of David, they are more likely to consider David's response in Psalm 6. In the first seven verses we see that David is at a very low point in his life. He has a sense of God's displeasure that has brought emotional and physical fatigue as well as an inability to sleep. As Peter C. Craigie writes, "For most sufferers, it was in the long watches of the night, when silence and loneliness increase and the warmth of human companionship is absent, that . . . pain and grief reached their darkest point."[10] Ask your listeners, "Can you think of a time when fear, grief, or guilt kept you from being able to sleep? Can you think of a time when the troubles of life sapped your emotional, spiritual, and physical strength? How did you respond?" Psalm 6 provides both a connection to our pain (common to the human condition) and the confidence that the Lord hears our prayers.

The power of suffering

Literature: *The Agony and the Ecstasy*, **by Irving Stone.** In this novel, Bertoldo, Michaelangelo's teacher, explains the thorough shaping of a piece of sculpture to his young student: "And so it must be perfect, not only from the front but from every angle. . . . Which means that every piece has to be sculptured not once but three hundred and sixty times, because at each change of degree it becomes a different piece."[11] God is in the process of molding, shaping, and transforming us into the image of Christ (2 Cor. 3:18), and he often uses suffering in this process (James 1:2–4). God can and wants to use every life circumstance to accomplish his purposes (Rom. 8:28).

God's "unfailing love"

Quote: *The Confessions*, by Saint Augustine. God's "unfailing love" (6:4) is the point of appeal for the psalmist. Augustine offers a memorable description of God, which is at the same time a description of his "unfailing love":

> You love, but with no storm of passion; you are jealous, but with no anxious fear; you repent, but do not grieve; in your anger calm; you change your works, but never change your plan; you take back what you find and yet have never lost; never in need, you are yet glad of gain; never greedy, yet still demanding profit on your loans; to be paid in excess, so that you may be the debtor, and yet who has anything which is not yours? You pay back debts which you never owed and cancel debts without losing anything.[12]

David, in anguish of soul, pleads with God for mercy. Several of his psalms were gathered as psalms of confession. Psalm 6, shown here from the English nuns of Saint Brigitta Breviary, is the first of seven penitential psalms that were included in the prayer books used by monks and nuns during their daily services (1490).

Psalm 6

"Their Violence Comes Down on Their Own Heads"

Big Idea *While God's justice is ultimately the solution to the problem of evil, evil also carries in itself the gene of self-destruction.*

Understanding the Text

Psalm 7 is an individual lament, as are Psalms 3–6. The two ingredients that constitute this type of psalm are the lament and the reasons for lament.[1] The lament is against David's enemies, expressed in 7:1, 6, 14, 15, and 16. Whereas the innocence of Psalm 6 was more implied than explicit, here the psalmist is so convinced of his innocence that he establishes it by a threefold oath (7:3–5).

The Text in Context

While we have made a case for Psalms 3–5 as "Absalom" psalms, the Absalom background is less demonstrable in Psalm 6, and this seems true also of Psalm 7. Twice in this psalm we have reference to an enemy's pursuit of the psalmist (7:1-2, 5), and the story related in 1 Samuel 24–26 fits the terms of this psalm quite well. See "Historical and Cultural Background."

Outline/Structure

The position of *selah*[2] after 7:5 (see NIV footnote) appears to divide the psalm into two major parts with two and three

David uses the image of an enemy pursuing when he says, "Then let my enemy pursue and overtake me; let him trample my life to the ground and make me sleep in the dust" (7:5). Assyrian cavalry trample an enemy in this palace wall relief from Nimrud (865–860 BC).

strophes, respectively. Also in Psalm 24 *selah* functions as a strophe divider, although its main function was evidently liturgical.

> Part 1: Innocence established (7:1–5)
>> a. Strophe 1: Prayer for deliverance (7:1–2)
>> b. Strophe 2: Psalmist's innocence established by oath (7:3–5)
> Part 2: Divine justice observed (7:6–16)
>> a. Strophe 3: Prayer for justice (7:6–8)
>> b. Strophe 4: God's justice affirmed (7:9–13)
>> c. Strophe 5: Evil's inherent ruin (7:14–16)
> Final praise/vow (7:17)

Historical and Cultural Background

The title of Psalm 7 gives an enigmatic reference to "Cush, a Benjamite." The word "Benjamite" is key to understanding this reference. While the proper noun "Cush" could refer to the ancient kingdom of Ethiopia or Nubia, connected with "Benjamite" it seems to be an unidentified person, either related to Absalom's death (see 2 Sam. 18:31–32), or more likely to one of Saul's servants (compare David's innocence in 7:3 to 1 Sam. 24:12 and 26:18). The monarchy began with Saul of the tribe of Benjamin, and when David acceded to the throne, his origin in the tribe of Judah was a sore spot in the kingdom for many years. It represented, in fact, a turn from the Rachel side of Jacob's family to the Leah side, an issue that is the concern of Psalm 78:67–72. The Greek translator (LXX) takes the name Cush as a personal name, Chusi: "A Psalm of David, which he sang to the Lord because

of the words of Chusi the Benjamite." The Targum, on the other hand, takes "Cush" to mean Saul.

Six metaphors in the psalm open up windows into the psalmist's cultural world. Four of them are applied to the Lord as warrior, giving us some insight into weapons of war in David's time. The Lord, says David, (1) "will sharpen his sword" and (2) "will bend and string his bow" (7:12; see comments on Psalm 11:2). The sword and bow were major weapons of war, and the Lord makes necessary preparations for battle, although this text does not describe him using the weapons. Just to note Yahweh's careful preparation was enough to put the enemy on notice that defeat was near. (3) David also declares, "My shield is God Most High" (7:10). This defensive weapon (*magen*) was the small shield that protected certain parts of the warrior's body, while the larger shield (5:12) provided full-body protection. (4) David says that the Lord "makes ready his flaming arrows" (7:13), suggesting arrows dipped in pitch or oil and then lit before shooting.[3]

The final two metaphors in Psalm 7 draw from other areas of life. (5) The metaphors of 7:15 are those of hunting, with the subject now changed from the Lord to the evil person. The hunter would dig a pit and camouflage it with brush, and the animals would fall into the trap. In this instance, the

Psalm 7

Oaths

The standard form of an oath begins with the conjunction "if" and concludes with the curse (normally introduced by the Hebrew *ki*) that should befall the individual if the terms of the oath are not kept. Sometimes the oath is not followed by an imprecation, so the translation must be in the negative: "If we had forgotten the name of our God or spread out our hands to a foreign god" (Ps. 44:20) could also be translated, "I swear that we have not forgotten the name of our God." In the same manner, if the oath is negative, it must be translated as a positive. "So I declared on oath in my anger, 'They shall never enter my rest'" (Ps. 95:11), is literally, "So I declared on oath in my anger, *if they shall enter my rest*, . . . [missing imprecation]."

In Psalm 7, however, the threefold oath has the imprecation appended—that is, a threefold imprecation:

> If I have done this and there is guilt on my hands—
> If I have repaid my ally with evil
> [if] without cause [I] have robbed my foe—
> then
> let my enemy pursue and overtake me;
> let him trample my life to the ground
> and make me sleep in the dust. (7:3–5)

hunter (enemy) would fall into it himself. (6) The last metaphor (7:16) is that of a boomerang that recoils upon the thrower. That is, the evildoers will eventually destroy themselves by their own devices.

Interpretive Insights

Title *A shiggaion of David . . . Cush, a Benjamite. Shiggaion* is an enigmatic term that occurs only here in the Psalter, and once in Habakkuk 3:1 (in the plural). It may suggest the singing of the psalm in an agitated manner.[4] On Cush, see "Historical and Cultural Background."

7:1 Lord *my God, I take refuge in you.* The idea of taking refuge in God occurs also in Psalms 11:1; 16:1; 57:1; 71:1. Calvin renders it "in thee do I trust."[5] The form critics suggest that the psalmist speaks of taking refuge in the temple.

7:3–5 David uses a threefold oath to lay out the truth of his personal character and moral standard (see the sidebar "Oaths"). It is to live a life free of another person's blood ("guilt on my hands," 7:3), to treat the peacemaker ("my ally," 7:4) with the same gracious consideration, and to take no advantage of his enemies ("robbed my foe," 7:4).

7:3 *if I have done this.* The demonstrative pronoun "this" refers either to the allegations brought against David or to the hypothetical deeds mentioned in the curses of 7:4 and 5, which spell out the content of "this." Either is possible, but I prefer the former.

7:5 *make me sleep in the dust.* The ESV reading is more literal to the Hebrew: "lay my glory [*kabod*] in the dust." Calvin understands "glory" as a reference to "his memory, or his good name."[6] This term also refers to character in Psalm 4:2 and Job 19:9.

7:6 *Arise, Lord . . . rise up.* The first imperative ("Arise") is reminiscent of Numbers 10:35, associated with the moving of the ark (cf. Pss. 3:7; 9:19; 17:13; 44:26; 102:13; Isa. 33:10; see also "Teaching the Text" in the unit on Pss. 9–10). The second imperative ("rise up") is the Hebrew Niphal stem, which can have a passive or reflexive meaning. Perowne takes it as reflexive and gives the sense as "manifest Thyself in all Thy glory as the true and righteous Judge" (see also Ps. 94:2; Isa. 33:10).[7]

7:7 *the assembled peoples.* Craigie, based on an Ugaritic analogy, prefers "warriors," which would fit well in the context of David's military struggles with Saul and Absalom. It can also be a reference to the "nations," as in Psalm 2:1. In that case, this context would suggest the Lord's universal judgment.[8] In light of verse 8a, this seems the best interpretation.

7:8 *according to my righteousness, according to my integrity, O Most High.* The term "integrity" (*tom*; lit., "innocence") is a parallel term to "righteousness." God is the standard of righteousnss in the world (7:11). The NIV emends the Hebrew preposition at the end of the verse ('*alay*, "upon me") to the name for God, '*elyon* (also 7:10; cf. 7:17), without textual support. However, this preposition is sometimes used to intensify the link between the speaker and the related subject, as it is here, giving the sense of "according to *my own* integrity" (see, e.g., ESV: "the integrity that is in me"). David has put forth the Lord's righteousness as the standard by which men and women must live and by which the righteous Judge adjudicates, and that same divine attribute calls forth his final vow of praise to the "name of the LORD Most High" (7:17).

7:9 *minds and hearts.* Literally, "hearts and kidneys." The word "heart" (*leb*; here it is plural)

approximates our notion of mind (cf. Ps. 17:3), while "kidneys" (*kᵉlayot*) are the seat of emotions. God judges according to the inner motives.

7:10 *shield.* This is the smaller, more portable shield (*magen*). See Psalm 5:12, where the larger shield (*tsinnah*) is in view.

7:12 *If he does not relent, . . . he will bend and string his bow.* The verb "relent" is literally "to return," or "to change one's mind," and the subject is generally understood to be the wicked persons of 7:9. It is quite significant that God stands ready to honor repentance, thus falling in line with the theology of the prophets. The verb "bend" (*drk*; lit., "to tread"; compare our English expression "treading the bow") gives the picture of the archer putting his foot on the bow and pulling back in order to string it.[9]

7:14 *Whoever . . . disillusionment.* Verses 14 and 15 sound like the psalmist is quoting two proverbs (cf. Prov. 26:27a). The NIV's "disillusionment" for the Hebrew word "lie" (*sheqer*) is too weak. "Lie(s)" is stronger and in keeping with the malicious practice described here (see ESV).

The psalmist uses military imagery, such as bending and stringing a bow, to describe God's preparation for action against the wicked. In this Assyrian relief, servants are stringing and testing the king's bows (from the palace at Nineveh, 645–635 BC).

Yahweh and Other Gods in the Psalter

There are at least three possible positions regarding the problem of other deities in the Psalter. (1) The psalmists lived in a *polytheistic* world and accepted the existence of other gods without question. While only occasionally do the Psalms engage in a polemic against idolatry as do the prophets (e.g., Pss. 96:5; 115:4–8), the theme of Yahweh's sovereignty over other gods and wordly powers (e.g., Pss. 2; 93:1–2; 95:3–5), theoretically assuming they exist, rules out this option. (2) The psalmists were actually *henotheists* who believed in one God but did not deny that other gods existed. In reality the prophets make it quite clear that Israel often belonged in this category (e.g., Hos. 8:2; Jer. 2:23). While there was definitely a monotheistic faith in ancient Israel, it was probably not the popular belief—that is, the belief held by the populace—until the exile, when Israel definitely became monotheistic. (3) The psalmists were pure *monotheists* and did not believe other deities existed, but they merely used language that accommodated the people who worshiped them. A pure monotheism prior to the exile was likely exclusive to the writing prophets, a priestly orthodoxy, and a remnant of the common people. The truth of the matter probably rests somewhere between options 2 and 3.

7:15 *falls into the pit they have made.* The Hebrew verbs for "falls" and "made" have similar sounds, creating a wordplay (*wayyippol . . . yip'al*—a play on the *y*, *p*, and *l* sounds).

7:16 *The trouble . . . recoils on them.* For other images of sin that recoils on the sinner, or becomes its own undoing, see Psalms 9:16; 28:4; 35:7–8; 37:14–15; 57:6; 141:10; and Proverbs 26:27.

7:17 *because of his righteousness; . . . of the LORD Most High.* Calvin says God's righteousness "is to be understood of his faithfulness, which he makes good to his servants in defending and preserving their lives."[10] See the comments on 7:8 above regarding the "Most High."

Theological Insights

The title designates the poem as a psalm that David "sang to the LORD." It is a prayer song about the divine name, as Terrien has suggested,[11] a song about God's majesty to save and judge. David's theological vocabulary is rich, using the major names of the deity, and he concludes the poem with the identification that rises to the patriarchal summit of confession, that Yahweh is sovereign over all local deities. David confesses "the LORD Most High" (7:17), a claim from which the generic "god" (*'el*) is removed (see below). All hypothetical deities have yielded their claims and identity to the sovereignty of the one and only God, Yahweh (see the sidebar "Yahweh and Other Gods in the Psalter").

The use of the divine names in this psalm is quite interesting and may hold an interpretive key. The tetragrammaton (*YHWH*) occurs eight times, twice linked to "my God" (*'elohim*, 7:1, 3), and six times alone (title, 7:6, 8 [2x], 17 [2x]). The generic term "God" (*'elohim*) occurs seven times, either as "my God" (7:1, 3, 6), or with another modifier (7:9, 11), or with a complement (7:11, "God is a righteous judge"). Once the shortened

God stands ready to act against the wicked with his sword sharpened and bow and arrows prepared. Gods were often depicted as warriors in the ancient world. This bronze figurine from Megiddo depicts a storm god holding a sword and shield (fifteenth to thirteenth century BC).

form of God (*'el*) occurs (7:11). The climactic divine name is the "LORD Most High" of 7:17, a departure from "God Most High" of the patriarchal narratives (*'el 'elyon*). This combination of the tetragrammaton and *'elyon* ("Most High") is peculiar to the Psalter (Pss. 7:17; 47:2).[12] We are reminded of the story of Abraham and Melchizedek in Genesis 14, in which Melchizedek, "priest of *God Most High*" (*'el 'elyon*) blessed Abraham, and Abraham equated *YHWH* with *'el 'elyon* (Gen. 14:22). In the Psalms the generic term *'el* is removed, and the name is simply *YHWH 'elyon*. One can hardly fail to notice that this term is quite significant, probably implying that Yahweh, Israel's covenant God, is the High God of the world and rules over it in justice. This is also suggested by the use of the universal term *'elohim* in 7:11. In effect, that makes the ethics of this psalm universal, because David's God is universal.

Teaching the Text

While God's attributes may seem at times to be abstract, all who live in this world of evil and believe in justice, justice for others as well as for themselves, can celebrate the *righteousness* of God, which is no abstraction in this psalm. This standard that marks God's own nature is one that he wills to impart to human society. When that standard is violated in the personal dimensions of life, as well as the international, the Lord is the Judge of the situation and can be depended on to intervene when the victims appeal to his name and reputation. "Arise," "rise up," "awake," and "decree justice" (7:6)

are imperatives that engage the divine will in prayer, and God stands ready like a warrior whose sword is sharpened, his bow bent, and his arrows kindled, to accomplish his purposes against evil. While this may sound like a radical program to some, radical evil may require radical solutions, and David is not timid about prescribing them. The preacher/teacher may engage this thought to emphasize the need, indeed the divine mandate, to live a righteous life in this world as a reflection of God's righteousness and God's program for humanity. It is one thing to speak of it abstractly but quite another—and the only option for the psalmist—to live it out in the real world.

Nowhere in the Old Testament do we have a systematic discussion of the nature of evil (see the discussion of evil in "Theological Insights" for the unit on Psalm 5). There are many hints in the Wisdom books, especially Job. But here in 7:14–15 we have a microscopic look at the inherent nature of evil. Using the metaphor of pregnancy and birth, David makes a general statement,[13] then breaks it down into its two stages: "they go into labor with evil [*'awen*]; [that is,] they are pregnant with trouble and give birth to a lie" (author's translation). The fact that the "wicked" of 7:9 are masculine presents no problem for the poet's metaphor. The theological meaning is that the wicked reproduce in their own kind. This is a good opportunity for the preacher/teacher to stress evil's progressive path. James also sketches out its path: "Then, after desire has conceived, it gives birth to sin; and sin, when it is full-grown, gives birth to death" (James 1:15).

Illustrating the Text

A complete surrender

History: On December 17, 1944, approximately 120 Americans surrendered to the Nazi tank force at Baugnez. The American prisoners were taken to a field, and the German SS troops suddenly fired on their prisoners with machine guns. Of the 120 men, only 43 Americans survived, by running from the field and finding refuge. As word of the massacre spread to the Americans, it led to American retaliation against German prisoners.[14] One of the amazing truths of the Bible is that the Lord receives, with joy, the rebellious sinner who surrenders to him. Even though we were at war with God, rebelling against his righteous decrees, he still loved us and received us without punishment (although, as we see in the NT, Jesus paid the price for our rebellion). This is a powerful picture, to view God's *hesed* in comparison to the way we too often respond to our enemies. How grateful we should be for God's loving-kindness! This should also remind us that we should leave retaliation in God's hands, since it is God who is the Judge.

Trust the God of justice.

Statistics: Much of Psalm 7 deals with the issue of God's justice. David asks that God's justice be applied to him (7:3–5) and to his enemies (7:6). Being made in the image of God, we long for justice as well. Sadly, many of us have lost faith in the judicial system's ability to mete out effective and fair justice. For example, in a 2009 government survey of sex abuse survivors across Canada, two-thirds of sexual assault victims indicate that they have little to no confidence in the police, courts, or the criminal justice system.[15] Although these victims cannot put their absolute faith and trust in the government for justice, they can fully trust the Lord. As David writes in Psalm 7:9, "Bring to an end the violence of the wicked and make the righteous secure—you, the righteous God who probes minds and hearts." What a great prayer for us to offer to the Lord on behalf of ourselves and the victims of injustice.

When we surrender to him, God's response is one of loving-kindness, not retaliation. Shown here is the aftermath of the Malmedy massacre, near the towns of Baugnez and Malmedy, Belgium. Corpses lie in the snow after U.S. prisoners of war, primarily from the 285th Field Artillery Observation Battalion, were executed by a German combat force during World War II (1944).

Choices have consequences.

Film: *Iron Man.* We see in Psalm 7:14–16 that choices matter, as David talks about people reaping what they sow (see also Gal. 6:7–8, with regard to eternal consequences). In the movie *Iron Man* (2008), industrialist Tony Stark (played by Robert Downey Jr.) realizes the impact of the weapons that he invented and that have been manufactured by his company. Understanding that choices have consequences, Stark says, "I saw young Americans killed by the very weapons I created to defend them and protect them. . . . I had my eyes opened. I came to realize that I had more to offer this world than just making things that blow up. And that is why, effective immediately, I am shutting down the weapons manufacturing division of Stark Industries."[16] Stark had seen first-hand that the weapons he intended for good (protection of Americans) were being used for evil, and this realization changed the direction of his life. In the same way, we must ensure not only that our choices are righteous but also that the consequences produce God's best.

"LORD, Our Lord, How Majestic Is Your Name in All the Earth!"

Big Idea *God wrote his character into the world of nature, but as awesome as that is, it is no match for the mindful care of his human creation.*

Understanding the Text

The Text in Context

Psalm 8 immediately follows the pledge of Psalm 7:17 to sing praise to "the name of the LORD Most High" (7:17). Now the psalmist does that in majestic words that honor the majesty of the Name.

As in the creation narrative of Genesis 1, the psalmist employs an economy of words that stylistically reveals the Creator's orderly manner and design. In content, the majesty of the Name is manifested in the works of the Lord's creative hands and the delegation of their care to humankind, whose regal crown is studded with the jewels of creation. Verbally this crown is woven from the poetic and prosaic language of the Pentateuch, which Delitzsch says contains all the vocabulary of the psalm, except the noun "children" and the verb "to crown."[1]

Outline/Structure

The content of the poem falls easily into strophes, with the refrain of 8:1a and 9 forming an *inclusio*, suggesting that the thrust of the psalm is the praise of God's majestic name. The swing verse is the ontological question of 8:4.

On the topside of the psalm, David is overcome by the wonder of the created world (8:3), which leads him naturally to ask, "What is mankind " that God lavishes so much care upon them, especially since God has such an awesome world to admire? The following outline is intended to show the *inclusio* of 8:1a and 9 and to call attention to the question of 8:4 as the literary center:

> *Inclusio*/refrain: "LORD, our Lord, how majestic is your name in all the earth!" (8:1a)
> Strophe 1: The Lord's creation of the heavens for his glory with the response of infants chanting his praise (8:1b–2)
> Strophe 2: The psalmist's contemplation of the heavens and his perspective on humanity: "What is mankind that you are mindful

of them, human beings that you
care for them?" (8:3–4)

Strophe 3: God's perspective on
humanity: "You have made them
a little lower than the angels and
crowned them with glory and
honor" (8:5–8)

Inclusio/refrain: "LORD, our Lord,
how majestic is your name in all
the earth!" (8:9)

Historical and Cultural Background

The title attributes the psalm to David,
or it may mean that it is dedicated to him
(see "The Nature of the Book" in the introduction). Yet there is really nothing in
this gem of a psalm to exclude it from
David's writing repertoire, if we are willing to allow that he was a poet of vast
powers, which he had the reputation for
being (2 Sam. 22; 23:1–7). Some would
date it late because of the doctrine of
creation, which some scholars consider
to be a latecomer on Israel's theological

Key Themes of Psalm 8

- The Lord's name is worthy of the highest praise.
- The Creator God has manifested his love to humanity.
- Humans are vice-regents of the universe.

landscape; but this ignores the fact that
Israel's neighbors had very early creation
stories, so why not Israel? Distinctively,
this poem stands out among the cultures
of the ancient Near East in that it does
not deify creation, as do those of Egypt,
Phoenicia, and Mesopotamia.[2] Instead,
animals and the planets are, just as Genesis 1 acclaims, the work of the Creator's
hand.

Interpretive Insights

Title *According to* gittith. Psalms 81 and
84 also have "According to *gittith*" in their
title. The Targum understands this to be a
musical instrument that originated in Gath.
But "Gath" also means "winepress," and
the Septuagint renders it "according to the
winepress," suggesting a vintage song.[3]

The psalmist
does not deify
creation when he
speaks of creation
as the work of
God's fingers. This
contrasts with
the Egyptian view
of the cosmos,
shown here, where
heaven, earth, the
sky, and the sun
are represented
by the deities Nut,
Shu, Geb, and Ra,
respectively.

"What Is Mankind?"

The question "What is mankind?" appears three times in the Hebrew Scriptures. In Psalm 8, David's contemplation of the universe forms the question in his mind: In view of the wonder of creation, why should the Lord be concerned with humans, so small in his vast universe? As David ponders the beauty of the creation (8:3), he asks: "What is mankind that you are mindful of them, human beings that you care for them?" (8:4). He answers in terms of humanity's special status ("a little lower than the angels," 8:5). The sense is that humans, in the psalmist's view, are so insignificant, *yet* the Creator made them almost gods. David marvels at the extraordinary creature God has made, even though the world in which God has placed him was also the object of much deserved admiration.

A second occurrence (Ps. 144:3–4) puts forth the question with two different verbs but the same effect: "What are human beings that you care for them, mere mortals that you think of them?" The question is also a plea, appealing for God to aid the psalmist against his enemies. Is that too much to ask, in view of the shortness of life? The answer is in terms of God's salvation of those who trust him, and that elicits praise (144:15b).

A third occurrence of the question is Job 7:17–18: "What is mankind that you make so much of them, that you give them so much attention, that you examine them every morning and test them every moment?" Its gist is a little different. Job asks the question in the context of his insistence that it is not God's love that is dispensed on him but harassment. Why should God bother if humans are such measly creatures!

The perspective of Psalm 8:4 is informed by Genesis 1, humankind's glory and honor. Psalm 144:3–4 is informed by sin's limitation on life (Gen. 4:6). Comparatively, Job 7 reveals the vast gulf between the Creator and the creature, which was at first the psalmist's perspective (Ps. 8:4). If Job had raised the question after his epiphany (Job 38:1–42:6), he might have espoused the perspective of Psalm 8:5–8, that humankind is a creature of inestimable worth.

8:1 Lord, *our Lord, how majestic is your name in all the earth . . . in the heavens.* Note that the tetragrammaton (*YHWH*, "Lord") appears only twice in the psalm (8:1, 9), and the language of the psalm is descriptive praise. The second part of this address is the common noun for "lord" (*'adonai*) that sometimes is used as a substitute for the covenant name, or in conjunction with the tetragrammaton (the former is lower case, and the tetragrammaton is in small capitals). Also, note the universal character of "all the earth" and its appropriateness in a hymn that adores the Creator of the universe. The idea of "majestic" is "excellent" (KJV) or "glorious" (NEB). No explanation can open up the content of God's majesty. Spurgeon suggests this is the reason "it is left as a note of exclamation."[4] The reference to God's "name" suggests his character and nature. The mention of "the heavens" perhaps suggests that God's glory is too great to fit into the heavens and the created order.[5]

8:2 *Through the praise of children and infants . . . established a stronghold.* The first group includes those who are probably young enough to speak but with no special eloquence. The second term includes babies who are still nursing and can do no more than babble (1 Sam. 22:19). The Hebrew noun standing behind the idea of "praise" has the meaning of "strength," sometimes interpreted as a "bulwark" against the psalmist's enemies. That is, the praise of God rising from the lips of children and infants is more powerful than the assaults mustered by enemy forces.

8:3 *your heavens.* The language of this verse calls to mind Genesis 1 and 2 and is a reminder that this world ultimately belongs to its Creator.

8:4 *what is mankind . . . human beings . . . ?* The noun for "mankind" (Heb. *'enosh*) sometimes connotes frail humanity, as it seems to do in Genesis 4:26 to announce the new era that Seth's birth inaugurated for mankind, corrupted by the fall and marred by Cain's sin (also Pss. 9:19; 90:3; 103:15).[6] This ontological question employs "mankind" ('*enosh*) here and in Job 7:17. On the other hand, Psalm 144:3 has "man" ('*adam*; NIV: "human beings"), but also "son of man," as does this psalm (NIV: "mere mortals"; Heb. *ben-'enosh*). See the sidebar "What Is Mankind?"

In early Judaism, "son of man" (8:4; NIV: "human beings") became a messianic title, but here it is probably a synonym of "mankind." The writer to the Hebrews likely heard the messianic overtone in this phrase, amplified through the megaphone of Jewish interpretation (Heb. 2:6–8). So we may again appeal to Calvin's hermeneutical principle above (see "Additional Insights: Messianic Psalms," which follows this unit).

8:5 *angels*. The Hebrew is "God" or "gods" ('*elohim*), rendered by the Septuagint as "angels." The sense is likely an approximation of divinity, "not quite divine." The Septuagint's "angels" (*angeloi*; Heb. '*elohim*) is used in Hebrews 2:7; perhaps this rendering avoids the appearance of polytheism.[7]

8:6 *You made them rulers*. God's appointment of humans to rule the world is in view here (Gen. 1:28).

8:7–8 *all flocks and herds . . . the birds in the sky, and the fish in the sea*. "Flocks and herds" refers to domesticated animals, while the other two categories, "birds" and "fish," coincide with those of Genesis 1 and are undomesticated.

8:9 LORD, *our Lord, how majestic is your name*. The refrain closes the poem and weaves it into a wreath of praise to God.[8]

Theological Insights

The Bible begins with a statement of the Creator's transcendence and immanence. The opening account of creation presents the picture of the omnipotent God speaking the world into being (Gen. 1), and the following account gives the picture of the immanent God forming humans from the dust of the ground and breathing into them the breath of life (Gen. 2:7). Psalm 8, which draws upon Genesis 1, gives us another such picture of God, who is above the world but in it. As Creator of the world, he has installed his glory inherently in the universe (transcendence), but that same glory is babbled by the lips of children and infants (immanence). David is aware of this as he contemplates the heavens (transcendence) that God formed as a sculptor with his own fingers (immanence;

God has placed human beings as rulers over all domesticated animals like the sheep and goats shown here.

"When I consider your heavens . . . the stars which you have set in place" (8:3). The photo shows the Milky Way as seen from the mountains of San Diego County, California.

cf. Gen. 2:7) and God's care for the human creatures he made (immanence; Ps. 8:4). Divine transcendence and immanence are delicately balanced in the Old Testament, and in the New Testament they are brought together in the two distinct natures of Jesus Christ, embodied in one person, Jesus of Nazareth. He was both God in the absolute sense (transcendence: "truly God") and man in the absolute sense (immanence: "truly man"). Psalm 8 is an Old Testament blueprint of that theological model. Even God's creation of the heavens (8:3), says Kidner, is meant to convey "not His remoteness but His eye for detail."[9]

One cannot read Psalm 8 without recalling the language and categories of creation in Genesis 1: the heavens and the earth (Ps. 8:1, 9), the moon and the stars (8:3), the beasts, fish, and birds (8:7–8), and finally, humanity as the culmination of the works of creation (8:4–6). In Genesis these are concluded with God's deputizing humanity to subdue and rule over creation (Gen. 1:28), something the psalmist is keenly aware of (Ps. 8:6). Even though he does not use the term "image" of God, he is conscious of the general concept and seems to allude to it with the words, "You have made him a little lower than God" (8:5 NASB). Humanity was made *in* God's image, which falls short of Paul's statement that Christ "*is* the image of the invisible God" (Col. 1:15). To be "*in* God's image," however, carries implications for all of life. First, we are a reflection of God, but not divine. Second, we are three-dimensionally relational: to God, because we are in his image; to other humans, because we are "male" and "female" and should "increase in number" and "fill the earth" (Gen. 1:27–28); and to the rest of the created order, because we are to "rule" over it. In ancient Near Eastern thought the gods made human beings to be their slave laborers, but in Psalm 8 they are

God's vice-regents to rule the earth. Even God's crowning humankind with "glory and honor" (8:5) evidently alludes to his work of ruling over creation.

Teaching the Text

Sometimes a psalm contains key terms that open up vistas into its meaning. This method gives the preacher/teacher an opportunity to share the way literary features of a psalm open up the marvels of God's Word. Two terms can provide that opportunity here.

The first term is "what" (*mah*), which is translated "how" in the refrain (8:1, 9) and "what" in verse 4. In the refrain it is used in an exclamatory sense, "How!" (We also use it like this; e.g., "What a beautiful day!" By that we express our surprise or excitement or wonder.) David uses it to express wonder at who God is: "How majestic!" Human language is often inadequate to express our human thoughts, so we resort to exclamations as a summary way of expressing our wonder at God's character and creation. This way of praising God is called *declarative* praise. In the refrain David does not break down God's character and work into their component parts and describe them, but in the psalm he does (8:2–3), and that is called *descriptive* praise.

The "what/how" of the refrain, therefore, calls our attention to the nature of God, and the "what" of verse 4 calls our attention to the nature of humans, giving the psalm a beautiful balance. But still the psalm's focus is God, not humans, for when the psalmist asks the question of verse 4, it is to shine the light even more directly on the Creator, who made such an awesome world and still entrusted so much responsibility to his human creatures (8:5–8). One of the tasks of proclamation/instruction is to explain our human relationship to God, and this psalm does it so well. The Creator of the universe is "mindful of" human creatures (8:4). That is the wonder contained in the "how majestic" of the refrain, a wonder that ought to characterize our faith.

The second term is "all" (*kol*), which occurs four times in the psalm (8:1, 6, 7, 9). The enclosing "all" of the refrain has a universal tone, "all the earth," and, much like Genesis 1, claims the whole earth for God's glory—God's glory is portrayed everywhere. Even the *inclusio* hints that, just as the whole psalm is contained between the duplicate verses, so God's name is majestic in the whole universe. The rest of the psalm is to be viewed in that inclusive frame (also Ps. 19:1). It would be appropriate to observe that God created this world with an inherent orientation toward the Creator. That has many implications for life and suggests that our hearts are restless till they rest in God.[10] Even though we tend to distinguish between special and general revelation, and quite validly so, in Scripture the two are so closely linked that the biblical writers would probably have flinched at such a distinction. God wrote his character into the created world (this is particularly evident in wisdom thought).

The psalmist uses the word "all" two times again in the description of God's deputation of humankind to rule over creation:

> You made them rulers over the works
> of your hands;
> you put everything [*all*] under their
> feet:

all flocks and herds,
 and the animals of the wild,
the birds in the sky,
 and the fish of the sea,
 all [not in the Hebrew, but implied]
 that swim the paths of the
 seas. (8:6–8)

David wants us to see that God's name is majestic "in *all* the earth" (the totality of it, 8:1, 9), and that humankind's rule is over *all* the earth (the totality of it, 8:6b, 7a, 8c). God deputized us to keep this absolutely beautiful and incredibly complex and mysterious universe. The praise of God is one of the most practical dispositions the believer can assume. As the Westminster Shorter Catechism so wisely states, humankind's chief end is "*to glorify God and enjoy him* forever."[11] It is in glorifying God that we come to enjoy him.

God gives dominion over his creation to humankind. This idea of exerting control over the animal world is illustrated in scenes known as the master or mistress of animals. This vessel from the mid-third millennium BC shows a female figure standing on the back of two large felines while grasping a large serpent in each hand. Whether this represents a deity, a hero, or a priest is disputed, but it is clear the depicted figure is exerting dominion and power.

Illustrating the Text

Faith and the universe

Quote: *Why I Believe in a Personal God*, by George Carey. In Psalm 8:3, the psalmist considers the wonder of the heavens, "the work of your fingers, the moon and the stars, which you have set in place." In a similar way, many people look at the universe and its inestimable vastness, complexity, and beauty and contend that there simply has to be a Designer behind it. Former Archbishop of Canterbury George Carey has taken his own look at the universe and observed with wonderment:

> Consider the psychological effect of this piece of information. We are told that the light from the cluster of galaxies in Hydra that reaches us has traveled through space for two thousand million light years. That cluster is only one of the innumerable galaxies, each made up of millions of stars, separated from each other by immeasurable stretches of inter-galactic space.[12]

In comparison to such a vast and ancient universe, one human life seems so insignificant, and yet the Creator of the universe has given humans a special place in creation.

Humans as vice-regents

Quote: C. S. Lewis. In this letter, Lewis was evidently responding to a question by his American lady correspondent (only Lewis's letters are published), inquiring whether he attended the coronation of Elizabeth II. He replied that he had not attended, but his further response suggests that he had obviously seen it on television. Lewis reflected on the ceremony:

The pressing of that huge, heavy crown on that small, young head becomes a sort of symbol of the situation of *humanity* itself: humanity called by God to be His vice-regent and high priest on earth, yet feeling so inadequate. As if He said "In my inexorable love I shall lay upon the dust that you are glories and dangers and responsibilities beyond your understanding." Do you see what I mean? One has missed the whole point unless one feels that we have all been crowned and that coronation is somehow, if splendid, a tragic splendor.[13]

Praise the Lord!

Biography: Joachim Neander. Born in Germany in 1650, Neander was very rebellious in his early years, but then he was converted to Christ through a church service he attended. Still a young man, he was influenced by Philipp Jakob Spener, a pietist who sought to return vitality to the Lutheran church. Neander became director of the Latin School of Düsseldorf, where he served for several years. He experienced considerable opposition there because of his pietism and was eventually dismissed from that position. He then suffered declining health and died at the age of thirty. But even in the face of such difficulty, Neander was filled with joy. He wrote sixty hymns, most of which are hymns of joyful praise, such as the great hymn "Praise to the Lord, the Almighty." Joy and authentic praise are functions not of an easy life but of a life lived in the Lord.[14]

Messianic Psalms

The messianic reading of the Psalms is both a Jewish and a Christian phenomenon, and its roots are deeply fixed in prophetic thought. There are many contributors to messianism; we will mention two. First are the towering personalities of Hebrew history, like David, whose exceptional abilities and accomplishments exceeded those of all other monarchs of biblical repute, and reminded Jewish and later Christian believers of the surpassing potential of human personality, especially when divinely equipped. A second is located at the other extreme of human experience, where hopes are shattered and the human spirit is repressed by tyranny and disillusionment but the spark of faith still smolders.

In Christianity, three hermeneutical approaches have come to some prominence in the messianic interpretation of the Psalms, all revolving around the place of Christ in the Psalms. The first we may call the *All of Christ* approach, classically represented by Augustine (AD 354–430), who typically saw Christ or the church in every psalm.[1] Yet, this method tends to de-emphasize the historical fabric of the Psalms.

The second approach is the *None of Christ* approach, which basically disqualifies the notion of a personal Messiah as being endemic to the Psalms and insists that the generic coming of God to establish his rule, as the prophets proclaimed (e.g., Isa. 43:15; 44:6), is the most we can expect of the Psalms. Sabourin speaks of

"messianism without a Messiah," although he recognizes the messianic interpretation of the Psalms as it developed in the history of interpretation.[2] For example, this critical view recognizes that at some point the prophets connected God's rule to a new Davidic king (e.g., Isa. 9:6–7; Hos. 3:4–5), and many of its proponents insist this occurred only after the Davidic monarchy ended in 586 BC. This is essentially the position of Craigie, who espouses the form critical method and insists that the messianic nuance is not incorporated into the original psalms but came subsequently to be associated with them somewhere in the history of interpretation.[3] While that is certainly a valid way to view the messianism of the Psalms, it seems to me that the strong prophetic hope, also reflected in the Psalter, took shape in those years when the people began to idealize David, perhaps as early as the eighth century prophetic movement (see Isa. 9:6–7; Amos 9:11–12) and long before the exile. Thus some of the psalms may have been written with a messianic baseline. So I believe the position lies somewhere between the *All of Christ* and the *None of Christ* approaches, which we could call the *Some of Christ* approach. Judging from the fact that the book of Psalms is the most quoted Old Testament book in the New Testament, it is quite clear that the New Testament writers believed their messianic hope was written in the lines of the Psalms, not merely projected on to them at a later time.[4]

The messianic hope in the Psalms falls into at least three paradigms. One is the royal paradigm, which takes the shape of kingship and is closely allied with the royal psalms (2; 18; 20; 21; 45; 72; 89; 101; 110; 132; and 144),[5] painting the messiah's portrait with the colors of David's life and reign.

The second paradigm is the priestly, which presents the figure of the "suffering servant," along the lines of Isaiah's Suffering Servant (Isa. 52:13–53:12). Kirkpatrick list Psalms 22; 35; 41; 55; 69; and 109 in this category.[6] Notably, the imprecatory psalms fall in this category and speak of the suppliant's suffering as unjust (e.g., 35:7; 109:3) and for God's sake (69:7; 109:21).

The third paradigm is that of common humanity and rises out of the pitiable lot of humanity in general, attesting how that can be transformed into a life of grace and fellowship with God. These include Psalms 8; 16; 22; 35; 40; 41; 55; 69; 102; and 109, and all of them, except Psalm 55, are applied to Christ in the New Testament.[7] The writer of the Epistle to the Hebrews understood the "son of man" of Psalm 8:4–6 messianically (Heb. 2:5–9), and the use of this phrase in the Gospels is certainly a testimony to Jesus's own understanding of his person and mission.

"The LORD . . . Rules the World in Righteousness"

Big Idea *Acknowledging our humanity is prerequisite to a faith that allows and even expects God to act on our behalf as he has acted for the saints of history.*

Understanding the Text

The Text in Context

Psalm 7 closes with a vow of thanksgiving (7:17), and Psalm 8 is in effect the fulfillment of that vow. Then follows Psalm 9 with a continuation of thanksgiving, followed by the lament of Psalm 10. This order is a reversal of the usual order of lament and thanksgiving. There are certainly psalms that contain mixed types,[1] but the order here may suggest that the editor deemed it more appropriate to follow the thanksgiving of Psalm 8 with another thanksgiving psalm.[2]

Psalms 9 and 10 are generally considered a single psalm, as they are in fact in the Septuagint and Vulgate. The evidence that they were originally one psalm instead of two is rather compelling. First, while Psalms 3–9 all have titles, Psalm 10 does not, indicating that it may be the continuation of Psalm 9. Second, the partial acrostic of Psalm 9 seems to continue in Psalm 10, containing perhaps seven letters of the Hebrew alphabet, while Psalm 9 contains the first nine.[3] Third, the occurrence of *selah* at the end of a psalm rather than internally, as in the case of Psalm 9 (v. 16; see NIV footnote), is unique in the Psalter, suggesting that the psalm continues.[4] Fourth, the two psalms share vocabulary: "seek" (9:10, 12 [NIV: "avenges"]; 10:4, 13 [NIV:

The psalmist uses hunting imagery to describe how the cunning schemes of the enemy nations have backfired. They have fallen into their own pit, been caught in their own net, and become ensnared (9:15–16). This Assyrian relief shows deer being trapped with a net. On the right hand side by the Assyrian hunter, one deer has become entangled in the mesh (from the palace at Nineveh, 645–635 BC).

"call to account"], 15 [NIV: "call to account"]); "forget" (9:12 [NIV: "ignore"], 17, 18; 10:11 [NIV: "never notice"], 12); "times of trouble" (9:9; 10:1); "mortal(s)" (9:19, 20; 10:18); "Arise, LORD" (9:19; 10:12); "for ever and ever" (9:5; 10:16).

On a practical matter, the combination of Psalms 9 and 10 in the Septuagint and Vulgate causes the numbers in those versions to lag one behind the Hebrew and English numbers, beginning with Psalm 10 in the Septuagint and Vulgate (which is Ps. 11 in the Hebrew and the Protestant and Jewish translations; see the sidebar "Varying Numbering of the Psalms").

Outline/Structure

Psalms 9 and 10 form a partial alphabetic acrostic, which does not support a logical progression of thought (see the sidebar "The Alphabetic Acrostic Psalms" in the unit on Ps. 25). Rather than a logical outline, we should probably follow the sequence of the alphabetic letters.[5] However, the following outline approximates a more logical approach:

1. Giving thanks to God (9:1–2)
2. God's righteous judgment of the nations (9:3–6)
3. God's righteous rule of the world and refuge of the oppressed (9:7–10)
4. Singing the praises of God enthroned in Zion (9:11–14)
5. The self-entrapment of the nations and God's care of the needy (9:15–20)
6. The arrogance of the wicked (10:1–11)
7. Prayer for God's intervention on behalf of the afflicted (10:12–18)

Key Themes of Psalms 9–10

- The Lord is the champion of the poor and oppressed.
- God does not forget his people, and he looks unfavorably on those who forget him.
- Those who seek the Lord will find his favor.
- The King of the world is also the protector of the oppressed.

Psalms of Thanksgiving

This category of psalms has two essential elements: (1) the report of a crisis, and (2) the assurance that the crisis has passed (thus the thanksgiving) and deliverance has come. These are typical component parts, but the two essential elements do not necessarily follow in logical order:

- Introduction (e.g., "I will exalt you, LORD," 30:1)
- Report of crisis
- Deliverance as an accomplished fact
- Conclusion

Psalms of thanksgiving: Psalms 9; 13; 30; 31; 32; 40; 66; 92; 116; 118; 120.[a]

[a] Bullock, *Encountering*, 152–59.

Historical and Cultural Background

Psalm 9 is attributed to David or to a Davidic collection. Judging from the theme of the nations and divine justice, the psalm could very well have come from David's pen. It is addressed to the "director of music,"[6] which is followed by an enigmatic phrase translated as a tune name in the NIV, "The Death of the Son." Perhaps such a tune had come into existence as a lamentive tune for the death of Absalom and became associated with Psalms 9 and 10.

The background is one of international strife, which the Lord himself turns in David's favor (9:3–6, 13–20), matching perfectly the general background of Book 1. The

Varying Numbering of the Psalms

In the Greek Septuagint (LXX) Psalms 9 and 10 are combined, and numbered as Psalm 9, which means that the numbers in the LXX lag one behind the Hebrew (and English) text for much of the Psalter. Psalms 114 and 115 in Hebrew are combined into one psalm in the LXX, and numbered as Psalm 113. Two subsequent psalms in the LXX are each divided into two poems: Psalm 116 in the Hebrew appears as Psalms 114 and 115 in the LXX, and Psalm 147 in the Hebrew appears as Psalms 146 and 147 in the LXX, and then the numbers in the Hebrew and Greek Bibles coincide for Psalms 148–150. The LXX has an additional psalm that is not in the Hebrew Bible, giving a total of 151.

Numbering of Psalms in Hebrew and Protestant Translations	Numbering of Psalms in Greek and Roman Catholic Translations
1–8	1–8
9, 10	9
11–113	10–112
114, 115	113
116	114, 115
117–46	116–45
147	146, 147
148–50	148–50
	151

images of Psalms 9 and 10 arise naturally out of their world, with the nations falling into a pit they themselves have dug and caught in the net they themselves have hidden (Ps. 9:15, 16; see also 7:15, 16), reminding one of the inherently reversible nature of evil: it hits its target, but then, by God's design, boomerangs upon its perpetrators.

Interpretive Insights

9:1–2 *I will tell of all your wonderful deeds. I will be glad . . . in you.* Verses 1 and 2 echo the final verse of Psalm 7, particularizing the grounds of praise, which are God's actions ("your wonderful deeds [*nipla'ot*]") and his person ("in you," "your

name").[7] The use of "I will tell" suggests that the psalmist may intend to rehearse these matters in public worship.

9:4 *sitting enthroned.* See 9:7; 93:2.

9:5 *you have blotted out their name for ever and ever.* Naming was a legitimation of one's existence, and the blotting out of the name was the delegitimation. The expression "for ever and ever," composed of two Hebrew words (*'olam* and *'ad*), carries the nuance of a distant future of unthinkable limits.[8]

9:6 *memory of them.* In Israel's world the "blotting out" (9:5) of a person in one's memory meant that he or she virtually ceased to exist.

9:9 *times of trouble.* This Hebrew phrase occurs also in 10:1, but nowhere else.

9:11 *Sing the praises of the LORD, enthroned in Zion.* The injunction to sing praise occurs a number of times in the Psalter (e.g., 30:4; 47:7; 147:7). The Psalms depict the Lord as dwelling, or enthroned, both in Zion and in heaven. Psalm 11:4 sets the two ideas side by side ("The LORD is in his holy temple; the LORD is on his heavenly throne"). God's earthly dwelling replicates a design that he showed Moses on Sinai (Exod. 25:9; 26:30).

9:12 *the afflicted.* Probably refers to the poor and afflicted in general.[9]

9:13–14 *from the gates of death . . . in the gates of Daughter Zion.* The psalmist prays that the Lord may deliver him from the "gates of death" so that he may recount God's praises in the "gates of Daughter Zion." Normally the ancients of the biblical world thought of the netherworld as a city with gates.

9:16 *the wicked are ensnared.* Divine justice was the real reason for the snare, not the wicked's carelessness, a truth that

9:16 lays out. The Hebrew word *higgayon* at the end of the verse (see NIV footnote) may relate to the manner of singing "meditatively."

9:19 *Arise, LORD.* See Numbers 10:35; see also Psalm 10:12, and "Teaching the Text."

9:20 *let the nations know they are only mortal.* As a result of their fall, the nations will know that they are but mortal, not gods.[10]

10:1 *times of trouble.* See the comments on 9:9.

10:4 *In his pride . . . no room for God.* It is the attitude of 14:1 and 53:1, even though it may be more practical than theoretical. The wicked's defenseless victims are the innocent (10:8), and his bravado is nothing more than cowardice emboldened by his superior strength and station.

10:12 *Arise, LORD! Lift up your hand, O God.* While the metaphor of lifting up one's hand is sometimes a gesture of taking an oath (Exod. 6:8; Num. 14:30), here

it suggests divine vengeance (2 Sam. 20:21, Sheba "lifted up his hand against the king").

10:13 *He won't call me to account.* This attitude implies either that the wicked do not think they have done wrong, or that they do not think that God will take issue with them. The latter is likely the case (10:4, 11).

10:14 *the helper of the fatherless.* The "fatherless" is a representative term for all those innocents who are abused by the wicked, or those who are vulnerable without a protector, to whose cries God is especially sensitive (Exod. 22:21–22).

10:15 *Break the arm of the wicked.* God's actions in the Psalms are phrased in terms of physical violence, but God himself is gracious and just. In fact, this is a metaphor that graphically depicts God's dispensing of justice. The principle is that the worse the crime, the more serious the form justice must take.

10:16 *The LORD is King.* This attribution is frequent in the Psalms, both as a noun (the Lord is *King*, 24:8, 10; 29:10; 47:2; 95:3) and as a verb (the Lord *reigns*, 93:1; 96:10; 97:1; 99:1; 146:10). The force of this description is that the Lord, who is King over the nations (10:16), listens to the cry of the oppressed and defends the "fatherless" (10:14), to obviate the repressive power of earth's rulers. Being a just God, he will act for the cause of justice.

10:18 *mere earthly mortals.* Merely human as compared to divine (see "Theological Insights").

Psalms 9 and 10, belonging to the neighborhood of Psalm 8, give their own version of an answer to the question of Psalm 8:4: "What is mankind that you are mindful of them?" While the emphasis there falls on our elevated position in God's sight ("a little lower than the angels," 8:5) and the divine mandate to subdue the earth, David prays in 9:20, "Let the nations know *they are only mortal*" (and not gods). Psalm 10 declares the power of Yahweh as the King who stoops to hear the helpless when they call and comes to their defense "so that mere earthly mortals will never again strike terror" (10:18b).

Theological Insights

In one respect, the ontological question raised in Psalm 8:4 is answered in Psalm 9 in the universal sense (see the sidebar "'What Is Mankind?': The Answer Continued"). The psalmist prays that the nations (universal) may realize that "they are only mortal" (9:20) and asserts that the wicked (individuals) are "mere earthly mortals" (10:18). Thus we have the universal perspective of Psalm 9 balanced by the individual perspective of Psalm 10. Even the Hebrew term "humanity" (*'enosh*) is shared by all three psalms (8:4; 9:19, 20; 10:18). The sobering truth is that human beings are no match for God, who is the just Arbiter of all human disputes and situations. In contrast to human frailty and arrogance, the God who seeks and never forgets his own is the One who will right the world made topsy-turvy by evil (9:7–10).

Teaching the Text

God has given some of his saints the language and spirit of prayer that seem to resound most effectively at the throne of grace. Moses was such a saint, and the psalmists took advantage of that. The prayer he prayed when the ark set out for another location was a powerful entreaty (Num. 10:35) and carried a weight of glory that announced Yahweh's rule and reign in history. This prayer bore repeating, and such a repetition in effect called for an encore of God's extraordinary action: "Do it again, Lord!" Sometimes the saints of one age issue their prayers in the words of the saints of a past era, and thus use their "password" to the throne of grace. Moses's language in Numbers 10:35 becomes a baseline of prayer, applied to the psalmist's new situation.[11] Israel's national enemies are clearly the object of the petition in 3:7; 7:6; 9:19; and 82:8. In Psalms 10:12; 17:13; and 74:22 the object seems to have shifted to the psalmists' enemies in general, not necessarily the nations. The capstone of this prayer usage occurs in 132:7–9, where the psalmist celebrates God's oath to David and the subsequent building of the temple by his son Solomon. To reinforce the point, the Chronicler employs the language of 132:8–9 in Solomon's prayer of dedication for the temple (2 Chron. 6:41), showing how one saint of history (Solomon) prayed the prayer of a previous saint (Moses), thus applying an effective prayer appeal to a new situation. In effect, Solomon was praying, "Do it again, Lord!"

Illustrating the Text

God has a heart for the poor.

Statistics: In Luke's recording of the Sermon on the Plain, we read, "Looking at his disciples, he [Jesus] said: 'Blessed are you who are poor, for yours is the kingdom of God'" (Luke 6:20). How shocking those words must have been for the Jews at the time of Jesus! Many in that day believed that to be rich was a sign of God's pleasure, while poverty was the plight of those who displeased God (views still held by some in our day). And yet, here was Jesus speaking about the blessings of God for the poor. God has a heart for the poor and the oppressed, and we are to share that passion. Consider these truths with regard to just one issue, world hunger:

- Nearly 870 million people, or one in eight people in the world, were suffering from chronic undernourishment in 2010–12.
- Poor nutrition plays a role in at least half of the 10.9 million child deaths each year.
- The world produces enough food to feed everyone.[12]

These truths reveal the seriousness of poverty and oppression in the world. If God is just and never forgets the needy, how can we get involved in these issues and reflect the heart of God? This would be a good opportunity to suggest how your listeners can realistically make a difference.

Our great purpose is to praise God.

Church History: The Westminster Shorter Catechism was completed in 1647 and is used as a creed by many Christian churches and denominations. Perhaps the most famous question of the Shorter Catechism asks, What is the chief end of human beings? Answer: It is "to glorify God, and to enjoy him forever."[13]

The catechism is in accord with Psalm 9:13–14 on this point. In these verses David asks for mercy and to be lifted from the gates of death, in order to declare the praises of God. So often our concerns are limited to our physical, emotional, spiritual, and social needs. But here we see that at a time of need David cries for mercy in order to praise God. If our great purpose is to glorify God, and to enjoy him forever, what should this mean for us as we live our lives? Certainly it means we are to engage in meaningful worship and to have time alone with the Lord as an overriding priority of our lives.

What's in a name?

Applying the Text: As noted in the comments on Psalm 9:5, one's name was connected to one's very existence. This makes the names, titles, and descriptions assigned to God in the Bible very significant. For example, in Psalms 9–10 alone we read that "the LORD is a refuge for the oppressed, a stronghold in times of trouble" (9:9), and "the LORD is King for ever and ever" (10:16). Encourage your listeners to keep a list of the names, titles, and descriptions they discover as they read the Psalms. Also, challenge them to reflect on which of these aspects of God's nature and character they need to experience more fully in their lives.

The Lord is described as a "stronghold in times of trouble" (9:9). A stronghold was a high, inaccessible place where one could flee for safety. Masada, shown here in an aerial view, is a good example of a stronghold.

"In the Lord I Take Refuge"

Big Idea *When our theological foundations are threatened, our fears are disabled by remembering God's just and majestic character.*

Understanding the Text

Psalm 11 is an individual lament. The lament is quite brief (11:1b) and obviously grows out of the immediate threat of danger that David faced (11:2), which itself grows out of the nature of the wicked "who love violence" (11:5). It is that bigger problem that shakes the foundations of faith and life (11:3), until Yahweh's vision from his heavenly throne becomes the vision of the earthlings: "the upright will see his face" (11:7b). To see God's face is to see him in all his glory, and to see him in all his glory is to see ourselves and our world from his perspective. Evidently David had already gotten a glimpse that inspired him to say: "In the Lord I take refuge" (11:1a).

The name of the covenant God (*YHWH*) occurs five times in this psalm (11:1, 4 [2x], 5, 7), and its frequency perhaps stresses Yahweh's constant presence in times of danger (11:1). He is present for the desperate David when his enemies threaten him, and when his well-wishers urge him to choose the fearful alternative ("Flee like a bird to your mountain," 11:1). The Lord is present for the righteous when the ethical foundations are tottering (11:3), and he is

present in his heavenly temple, from which he sees his human patrons (11:4). The Lord is present in judgment (11:5–6), and, most of all, he is present to validate the righteous life that reflects his own righteous nature (11:7).

The Text in Context

If one lays this psalm down on the template of David's many conflicts, especially with Saul, the simple trust that exudes from it reminds one of Samuel's description of David as "a man after his [God's] own heart" (1 Sam. 13:14). From the time of David's coronation (1 Sam. 16) to the occasion of Saul's death (1 Sam. 31), the book of 1 Samuel depicts David's life as virtual conflict. Indeed, his reputation was that of a man of war (1 Sam. 16:18; see ESV). So this psalm could be written against the background of David's reputation rather than a specific incident or phase of hostilities.

Outline/Structure

Psalm 11 is built around the counsel of David's devotees to "flee like a bird to your mountain" (11:1b), followed by the description of the situation that triggers their advice ("For look, the wicked bend their bows," 11:2) and an exclamation of their desperation ("When the foundations are being destroyed, what can the righteous do?" 11:3), set in the frame of David's trust in the Lord (11:1a, 4–7).

1. David's declaration of trust, elicited by the well-meaning advice of his counselors (11:1a)
2. The advice and explanation of the counselors (11:1b–3)
3. David's explanation for his rejection of their counsel (11:4–7)

Historical and Cultural Background

While we cannot be absolutely sure that the psalm was written in direct response to those who advised David to flee from Saul (see above), we are otherwise informed that David on occasion fled to the mountains as he sought refuge from his crazed rival (1 Sam. 23:25–28; 26:20).

Two cultural pictures depict aspects of the world of the psalm. First is the virtual video of stringing and shooting a bow in 11:2 (cf. 7:12). The second is "to shoot in the dark at the upright in heart" (RSV, ESV). This is a metaphor of hunting or war when the enemies hide in the dark or conceal themselves in the shadows (NIV) and ambush their victims. Whether their victims were animals or humans, stealth was their strategy. While I prefer the literal interpretation of the psalm, this is most likely a metaphor (a literal interpretation does not disqualify metaphors), taken from the reality of David's world, and here

Key Themes of Psalm 11

- Trust in the Lord is an antidote for life's threatening dangers.
- The Lord's heavenly enthronement means not that he is isolated from the world but that he is directly involved in human affairs.
- The Lord rewards the righteous and punishes the wicked.

When the psalmist describes God's actions toward the wicked, he says that God "will rain fiery coals and burning sulfur" (11:6). This imagery would have brought to mind the destruction of Sodom and Gomorrah, which is depicted in this AD 1852 painting by John Martin.

applied to political and spiritual assaults by his adversaries.

The Psalms were developed in a world of the spoken word, and hearing was an oral art of the ancient world. A word or a phrase could tell a whole story or bring a graphic scene to mind—as it still can—and that is the case of 11:6, which conjures up the picture of the destruction of Sodom and Gomorrah, even without mentioning the names: "On the wicked he will rain fiery coals and burning sulfur." This word picture creates a message of sure and severe judgment on evildoers.

Interpretive Insights

11:1 *In the* LORD *I take refuge . . . "Flee like a bird."* The adverbial phrase "in the LORD" comes first in the sentence and emphasizes the idea of safety, here in the Lord rather than in a place. The Hebrew verb for "flee" carries the sense of "flit," making it harder for the hunter to aim his sling or arrow and hit his target. David's flight to the mountains in time of danger is affirmed in 1 Samuel 23:25–28; 26:20.

11:2 *the wicked bend their bows; they set their arrows . . . to shoot from the shadows.* The imagery ("bend") is that of stepping on (*drk*) the bow to relieve the tension so the bow can be strung (see the comments on Ps. 7:12). The Hebrew verb "to set" (*kun*) suggests the idea of nocking the arrows in preparation for shooting (also Ps. 7:12),[1] which takes place in the dark, not in the "shadows" (NIV; see "Historical and Cultural Background").

11:3 *foundations.* The Masoretes mark the word *shatot* as a hapax legomenon (a term that occurs only once). It probably comes from the verb "to set" (*shyt*) and likely alludes to established social laws. But ancient Israel made little distinction between social norms and ethical norms, just as they made little distinction between the sacred and the secular. Thus these foundations are more than social customs and imply religious underpinnings.

11:4 *The* LORD *is in his holy temple . . . his eyes examine them.* The reference to the temple could be to the Jerusalem temple, but the second part ("on his heavenly throne") seems to suggest God's heavenly temple, unless "holy temple" is the earthly one, which reflects God's "heavenly throne," a symbol of his universal authority (see

also 22:3; 99:2; 123:1). Reference to God's "eyelids" or "eyes" also appears in Jeremiah 9:18. The verb "examine" (*bhn*) implies testing the quality of an object, as one tests metals (Ps. 66:10; Job 23:10). Here and in 11:5 it means "to subject to close scrutiny."[2]

11:5 *he hates.* The Hebrews thought in terms of opposites, as in Malachi 1:2–3. When the Old Testament speaks of God in this manner, it suggests divine revulsion to evil and evildoers, not hate in the sense of absolute rejection. The God of the Old Testament is the God of the New Testament, and he is love (1 John 4:8). See comments on 5:5–6.

11:6 *he will rain fiery coals and burning sulfur.* The terms recall those of the destruction of Sodom and Gomorrah (Gen. 19:24). The imperfect tense of the verb ("will rain") bears the sense of continuity ("he regularly rains"),[3] thus suggesting that this is God's way in general toward the wicked.

11:7 *he loves justice; the upright will see his face.* The first clause draws a contrast between the Lord—indeed, his character—who "loves justice," and the wicked, who "love violence" (11:5). In the Old Testament human beings are forbidden to see Yahweh's face (Gen. 32:30; Exod. 33:11, 20), which is a metaphor for admission into God's presence and an Old Testament precursor of the final state of redemption in Jesus Christ (Rev. 22:4). See statement at the beginning of the "Understanding the Text" section.

Theological Insights

Trust in the Lord is a spiritual disposition that gives life stability. We might describe it as a frame of mind that shapes our personality and behavior, enabling us to resist the irrational alternatives others would foist upon us. Trust in God will not shield us from the dangers that lurk around us, but it will equip us with the means for dealing with them. And it is more than a human disposition, for it reflects the divine temperament toward the righteous, which results in God's favor toward them (11:7). The question that arises out of the dangerous world of the psalmist is, "When the foundations are being destroyed, what can the righteous do?" (11:3). The psalmist provides the answer in the picture of the Lord enthroned in his holy temple (11:4a). The fact that it is "heavenly" suggests God's sovereign reign over the psalmist's troubled world. Moreover, as a lover of justice, God rewards the righteous with acceptance into his presence (11:7) and, by that same standard, rejects the wicked.

Teaching the Text

In the history of interpretation, Psalm 11 has been viewed in two basic ways. First, a literal interpretation (which is my preference) means that the danger is real and historical and constitutes the background of the psalm. By that hermeneutic we would understand that David's well-meaning advisors urged him to flee to the mountain like a bird to escape the impending danger. Second, a metaphorical interpretation suggests that wicked people are urging the psalmist to forsake his faith in God (11:1; lit., "to wander your mountain like a bird"), an option that David rejects. The mountain would be the Temple Mount, and the arrows that are shot in the dark (see the comments on Ps. 1:2) are unorthodox ideas that the psalmist's detractors have put forth, while the "foundations" (1:3) are the principles of the faith.[4] Yet, while the psalms are replete with metaphors, this one is more allegorical and a bit contrived.

Following the literal hermeneutic, there are four observations the interpreter might make to cover the scope of the psalm.

There were times when David did choose to flee to the rugged terrain of En Gedi to escape King Saul. Shown here are the cliffs at En Gedi, where caves for hiding can be seen.

1. First, we can detect David's perspective, articulated at the very beginning of the psalm, suggesting that it is a settled position: the way out of his troubles is to take refuge in the Lord. While faith in God does not eliminate human problems, it provides a mechanism by which the problems can be faced and dealt with (see "Theological Insights").

2. The second perspective is that of his "friends" who strongly advise him to "flee like a bird to your mountain" (11:1b). There is no reason to doubt that they were well meaning, based on the information that his enemies were arming themselves against him (11:2), while the social/ethical foundations of society were crumbling (11:3). The crumbling of the social/ethical foundations of our world, like Israel's, has everything to do with trust in God, or its absence, for trust becomes the antidote for a society that is falling apart. Changes in our world are inevitable, and there is nothing wrong with many of them, but when they threaten our fundamental trust in the Lord, they can be detrimental, and we should examine them very carefully before embracing them.

3. David, however, judging from his opening affirmation, has already rejected his friends' alternative. Running from one's troubles is a strategy to be rejected when it means abandoning one's trust in God, which is the dilemma here. Sometimes, however, it is therapeutic to take a recess from one's problems so as to reflect and recoup one's thoughts. And certainly, as a general rule, our decision to change course or to abandon a true and trusted direction ought not be made in the midst of our despair. The opening statement (1:1a) suggests that the psalmist's trust in God was a position he had settled outside the counsel of those who recommended he escape. The suppliant's trusting faith is supported by the observations of 11:4–7, which illustrate the third perspective: (a) God has the full perspective on David's world, for he is in his "holy temple" in heaven observing what is going on in the earth (11:4), which buoys David's faith in his refuge; and (b) the Lord is righteous and loves justice (11:6–7), all the more reason to find him to be a great refuge. Here is the spiritual perspective that has stabilized untold millions of saints and drawn myriads of sinners into faith in God and has still not lost its transformative power.

4. The fourth observation is the turnabout in perspective. Just as God is on his throne *seeing* the righteous and the wicked in this world, so the "upright will see his face" (11:7). Indeed, the reward of taking refuge in God is seeing God's face. It is, in a phrase, the story of redemption, God's acceptance of us (to "see his face"), which not only clarifies our vision of his face, but also clarifies our self-perception. Paul views God's acceptance of us in Jesus Christ as the ultimate invitation into his presence (Eph. 1:3–6), and the final metaphor of redemption is to see God (Rev. 22:4).

Illustrating the Text

Trust in the Lord.

Hymn: "Jesus, I Am Resting," by Jean Sophia Pigott. The reason the psalmist did not "flee like a bird" was that his trust was in the Lord, who, he declares, "is in his holy temple, . . . on his heavenly throne." That makes a lot of difference when this world's evils threaten our quietude and it seems that our "foundations are being destroyed."

It is God's sovereign reign that generates the suppliant's trust. Pigott (1845–80), an Irish composer, wrote about resting in the joy of discovering the greatness of Christ's loving heart. There is a story about Hudson Taylor, missionary to China, who, during the Boxer Rebellion at the end of the nineteenth century, sat at his desk, knowing that other mission stations had been destroyed, singing these words:

> Jesus, I am resting, resting,
>   in the joy of what Thou art;
> I am finding out the greatness
>   of Thy loving heart.
>
> Thou hast bid me gaze upon Thee,
>   and Thy beauty fills my soul,
> for by Thy transforming power
>   Thou hast made me whole.[5]

Bible: David and Goliath. We see in this psalm of David, as well as many of the psalms, the call to put our trust and faith in the Lord. In fact, putting our faith and trust completely in the Lord is the antidote to fear and worry. David had a lifetime of experiences with God that enabled him to trust the Lord. For example, as David volunteers to stand against the giant Goliath, he recounts to Saul his successful battles against lions and bears. And, David says, "The LORD who rescued me from the paw of the lion and the paw of the bear will rescue me from the hand of this Philistine" (1 Sam. 17:37). David could trust God as he faced Goliath, because he had found the Lord trustworthy in the past.

How do we deal with fear and anxiety in our lives? Like David the shepherd, we must build a lifestyle of fully trusting God in the daily circumstances, filling our lives more and more with trust, and leaving less and less place for fear.

The King wants to be known.

Children's Book: *Children of the King,* by Max Lucado. Christian author and pastor Max Lucado wrote a children's story called *Children of the King*.[6] In this story the king comes to visit the townspeople, but they do not know or recognize him, and they do not have time to spend with him, because they are too busy preparing the gifts they want to give to the king. But there is one little girl in the village who, not knowing it is the king, serves him with an act of kindness. All she has to offer the king is her heart, and that is all he really wants. This story is a powerful reminder that the Lord has come to us and longs to be intimately involved in our lives. But do we have the time and attention to give to him?

> David could confidently say, "In the LORD I take refuge" (11:1) because when he put his faith and trust in God, he had experienced God's protection. Those times included when he encountered wild animals as a shepherd boy and when he defeated the Philistine warrior Goliath. Shown here is the Valley of Elah, where the battle between David and Goliath took place.

"The Words of the LORD Are Flawless, Like Silver Purified in a Crucible"

Big Idea *In a society where lies and falsehood constitute the "ethical norm," God's flawless words reset the standard and are of a seamless piece with God's character.*

Understanding the Text

Psalm 12 has features of an individual lament (12:1–2), the cause of the lament clearly being the depletion of the righteous and the occupation of society by liars and deceivers.

The Text in Context

Psalm 12 fills out the picture of the scenario outlined in Psalm 11: "When the foundations are being destroyed, what can the righteous do?" (11:3). Those social/ethical foundations, badly crumbling in Psalm 11, have been obliterated in the religious world of Psalm 12: "for no one is faithful anymore; those who are loyal have vanished from the human race" (12:1).

Outline/Structure

The psalm divides into two halves, the first half describing the lies and falsehood of the wicked (12:1–4), and the second, divine intervention (12:5–8), based on and motivated by God's "flawless" word, "like silver purified in a crucible" (12:6). Hakham has pointed out how the two halves correspond to each other, with the first part opening with a description of the morally depleted time and the second part closing with a summary of the times:[1]

First Half	Second Half
"Those who are loyal have vanished from the human race" (12:1)	
"Help, LORD" (12:1)	"I [the Lord] will protect them" (12:5)
"Everyone lies to their neighbor" (12:2)	"The words of the LORD are flawless" (12:6)
"May the LORD silence all flattering lips" (12:3)	"You, LORD, . . . will protect us" (12:7)
"By our tongues we will prevail" (12:4)	[By the NIV's translation there is no contrasting clause in 12:8 but rather a summary of the immoral age]
"[The wicked] freely strut about when what is vile is honored by the human race" (12:8)	

The term "sons of adam" (NIV: "human race") frames the psalm (12:1 and 8), indicating that this psalm is about the human community. The psalm is a conversation between David and God. First, David addresses the Lord with a plea for help (12:1), and his prayer is all the more emphatic because the imperative verb occurs first in the sentence, followed by the direct address: "Help, LORD . . ." After the prayer of 12:1–2, the psalmist hopes, in the third person, that the Lord will cut off all those who flatter and deceive (12:3–4). Then comes the Lord's answer in 12:5, which is the theological center of the psalm, followed by a momentary reflection on the Lord's "flawless" words (12:6). Another prayer in 12:7 pleads divine protection for David and his community ("keep" and "protect us") and is followed by what seems to be another moment of reflection on the problem (12:8). So the pattern is

1. Prayer (12:1–2)
2. Reflection (12:3–4)
3. The Lord's answer (12:5)
4. Reflection (12:6)
5. Prayer (12:7)
6. Reflection (12:8)

Because of the conversational pattern, some scholars suggest that, like Habakkuk 1, this is a prophetic psalm,[2] perhaps used in the temple in some way.

Historical and Cultural Background

Psalm 12 could have a specific historical era as its background, but the oppression

The words of the Lord are compared to flawless silver. Silver was used as currency and in jewelry. Before the advent of coins, payments of silver were made by cutting off appropriate-sized pieces from coils such as the one shown here.

of the poor (12:5) and the faithless conditions expressed by the psalm are rather general points of critique in the Prophets, as well as the Psalms. That means many eras, depleted of the godly and repeopled with liars and deceivers, could qualify as the backdrop. Absalom's rebellion, however, the likely background of Psalms 3–5, could also qualify, based on this rebel son's use of deceptive words to steal the hearts of the people of Israel for his insurgent aspirations (2 Sam. 15:1–6). Nevertheless, we cannot be as confident about the historical setting as we can about the fate of truth (12:2) and the bloated self-assurance of truth's clients, however unjustified. Judging from Psalm 14 and other texts from the Prophets and the historical books, we may say that in Israel's long history there were other times that qualified for this dubious distinction. At the same time, there are no good reasons why the psalm could not be Davidic.

Silver was known in very early biblical times (e.g., Gen. 23:15), both as currency and as jewelry. Psalm 12:6 describes the Lord's words as "flawless, like silver purified in a crucible, like gold refined seven times." The metallurgical process included smelting the ore, then refining it by heating it in a crucible with a baser metal, like lead. The impure properties of the silver combined with the lead, resulting in a purer metal.[3] Repeating this process "seven times"[4] would greatly purify the silver, a most appropriate metaphor for the "flawless" word of God, and the number seven itself being a symbol of perfection. The metaphor, however, should not be taken to imply that the Lord's words were impure and had to be refined; it is the product, not the process, that constitutes the analogy.

Interpretive Insights

Title sheminith. See the comments on the title for Psalm 6.

12:1 *Help,* Lord *... faithful ... those who are loyal.* Psalm 69 also begins with this imperative, "Help" (NIV: "Save me"). The "faithful" (*hasid*) are those who keep God's covenant and fulfill their religious duty (Deut. 33:8–9; Ps. 50:5 [NIV: "consecrated"]). The term for "those who are loyal" parallels "faithful" and comes from the Hebrew verb that gives us the word "Amen," implying affirmation.

12:2 *Everyone lies to their neighbor ... harbor deception.* The NIV verb "lies" is a noun in the Hebrew text (*shaw'*), the same

word used to prohibit taking the Lord's name "in vain," or "falsely" (Exod. 20:7/ Deut. 5:11; NIV: "misuse"). To give "*false testimony*" is a violation of the ninth commandment (Deut. 5:20 [*shaw'*]; cf. Exod. 20:16 [*sheqer*]). The phrase "harbor deception in their hearts" is literally "with a heart and a heart," which means "double-minded." The Septuagint translates the expression quite literally ("with heart and with heart"). The Greek *dipsychos* ("double-minded") of James 1:8 and 4:8 (it does not occur in the LXX or elsewhere in the NT)[5] renders the sense of this expression quite well. However, for James it is most likely a loyalty that is divided between faith and the world, whereas here it is saying one thing and doing another, since the godly have been obliterated from society, and a purely deceitful way of dealing with others has become the norm. Goldingay says that in their minds they think one thing but intend something else.[6]

12:3 *May the* Lord *silence.* The *Midrash on the Psalms* understands this in the legal sense of being "cut off" from the community[7] (lit., "may the Lord cut off all the lips of division").

12:4 *By our tongues we will prevail ... who is lord over us?* Clearly the power of speech is in view here—they were right on that score—but power built on lies and deceit will ultimately lead to ruin, if not in this world, definitely in the world to come. "Lord" is the Hebrew word *'adon* ("lord," "master"), sometimes used as a substitute word for the divine name *YHWH*. Hakham suggests that there is "a hint of blasphemy" in the use of this term. In effect these deceivers are claiming they have no master, not even Yahweh (which the Jews later pronounced as *'adonay*, a form of this noun).[8]

12:5 *are plundered . . . groan.* The word for "plundered" refers to the exploitation of the oppressed, which elicits the groaning of the needy. The word for "groan" references moaning and weeping, like that of Malachi 2:13, where the suppliants cover the altar with weeping and tears (NIV: "wail") because the Lord no longer accepts their sacrifice. This sounds much like the oppressed servant who cries against the oppressor to the Lord (Deut. 24:15; Prov. 21:13). The Septuagint translation (*stenagmos*) is used by Paul in Romans 8:26 to refer to those "groans" or "sighs" in prayer that are too deep for words. When God hears the groans of the oppressed, he is moved to compassion and action, and Paul's words suggest the same response as the Spirit intercedes for us with "wordless groans."

I will now arise . . . I will protect them. The Lord has controlled the situation all along and now at last takes action against this distorted and godless world. This is a veiled statement of God's sovereignty over the world—he never loses control, whatever the circumstances may suggest. The Hebrew behind God's promise "I will protect" means, "I will fight" (*'ashit*). God is

> The words of the Lord are "like silver purified in a crucible" (12:6). This crucible from Tel Akko is dated to the Late Canaanite (Bronze) period (1500–1300 BC).

not merely a defensive God ("protect them"), but he is constantly on the offense on behalf of his people ("I will now arise"). In Psalm 3:6 the same verb (*shyt*, "assail") conveys the notion of war.

those who malign them. The Hebrew word for "malign" means "breathe," which occurs in Song of Songs 4:16 to mean "blow," and in Psalm 10:5 as "sneers" (NIV) or "puffs" (RSV, ESV). In keeping with the psalm, it has to do with malignant speech.

12:6 *the words of the LORD are flawless, like silver purified . . . seven times.* Now the Lord's words are placed in contrast to those of the wicked. "Flawless" is the Hebrew "pure" (*t*e*horot*), which is here a synonym of "true." The Lord's words, like refined silver, are words that have no impurities. Proverbs describes the Torah in terms of the precious value of silver (Prov. 2:4; 3:14). The word "purified" (Hebrew *tsarup*, passive participle) further defines "flawless." Malachi uses the verb to say that the Lord will purify his people as the "refiner" purifies silver (Mal. 3:3). "Seven times" is really the dual form of the number seven and should be understood as "twice seven times," meaning numerous times.[9]

12:7 *You, LORD, will keep the needy safe and will protect us.* The Hebrew has "them" as the direct object of the verbs,

The Lord acts on behalf of the poor who are plundered and the needy who groan like the Judean families being led into exile in the lower register of this Assyrian relief from Nineveh. The upper section pictures Assyrian soldiers carrying spoils from the captured city of Lachish (700–692 BC).

referring to the poor and needy of 12:5. In the second half of the verse, the psalmist switches to the first common plural pronoun ("us").

12:8 *what is vile.* Goldingay renders the hapax legomenon (a word that occurs only once) *zullut* as "triviality" or "worthlessness" and captures what may be the true sense of the sentence in these words: "They turn things upside down, treating the insubstantial as if it counted, the worthless as if it were valuable, and the despicable as if it were honorable. . . . And as they do so they are able to walk about, head held high, because their inversion of standards is accepted within the community as a whole."[10]

Theological Insights

Psalm 12:6 is a testimony to the purity of God's words. They are expressions of his character, as sterling as refined silver, and verses 7 and 8 attest that his character and actions are of a single piece. While some construe this statement as an Old Testament expression of a doctrine of Scripture, it is hardly equivalent to 2 Timothy 3:16. Even when speaking of the divine word(s), the Old Testament is basically concerned with the character of God behind the word, as Isaiah 55:11 indicates. God's word is his envoy sent out to do his bidding, and because God is sovereign, this mission will not fail (Isa. 40:8; 45:23).

Teaching the Text

Those in David's world who are loyal and reliable have been replaced by liars and flatterers (12:2). The sense of verse 2 is that the psalmist's generation is so wicked that not a single pious person can be found.[11] Obviously this is hyperbole, that is, an overstatement of the case, because David himself was considered to be a righteous person. But the theological depravity of the time demanded a hyperbolic description, like Charles Dickens's words that begin *The Tale of Two Cities*: "It was the best of times, it was the worst of times."[12]

This psalm is about Israel, to be sure ("A psalm of David")—all the Psalms are—but its extension is beyond Israel to the world community (note the universal frame "sons of man/adam," 12:1, 8), where words so often get turned inside out and their meanings upside down. Psalm 12 informs this community of how human beings use words to get their own way (not God's), underscoring Martin Buber's appraisal of David's time as "the generation of the lie."[13] It is about both Israel and the world where lies and deceit displace truth, a time that qualifies for the adage, "Superstition, idolatry, and hypocrisy have ample wages, but truth goes a-begging." The rhetorical powers of individuals sometimes inflate their egos and make them feel that they are the master of their own souls ("By our tongues we will prevail; our own lips will defend us—who is lord over us?" 12:4). In fact, the word "lord" is the same word often used in place of the divine name (in our English translations rendered "Lord"), as opposed to the tetragrammaton, "Lord," which is rendered in small caps. Perhaps it is a subtle defiance against the Lord, who rises to protect his people "from those who malign them" (12:5). From the time of Abel, slain by his brother Cain (Gen. 4), the Lord has taken up the cause of the victim. He hears the groans and cries of the oppressed, just as he said he would, when they cry out to him against the oppressor (Deut. 24:15; Prov. 21:13). This picture of a world where lies and flattering words have become the standard by which social institutions operate, where the wicked "freely strut about" (12:8), is frightful indeed, and the outcome is the oppression of the weak (12:5). We might observe that this development described by the psalmist often happens subtly and, at first, almost undetected, and its effect is the eventual reversal of social norms, where "what is vile is honored by the human race" (12:8).

Lies, flattering lips, and a boastful tongue form a contrast with the Lord's flawless words, "like silver purified in a crucible, like gold refined seven times" (12:6). This assuring picture bolsters confidence in the divine oracle of 12:5, which is the opposite of the kind of speech that has become the abysmal norm of human society. As suggested in the "Big Idea," the sterling silver tongue of God is of one piece with his actions in human society, and he renews hope in a world where the godly have vanished and human speech has become a lie. In the vacuum of truth, the Lord arises to protect his people. Interestingly, it is not to defend his word, or justify its truthfulness—even though this would be appropriate—but it is to protect the oppressed from "those who malign them" (12:5).

A point that grows homiletically out of the psalm is the question, "What happens to a society when truth is merely an anomaly, and no longer the standard by which institutions and individuals operate?" Psalm 12 is the picture of a society whose foundations have crumbled (11:3), where "everyone lies to their neighbor" and they "harbor deception in their hearts" (12:2). But the picture of God, who hears the groans of the poor and swings into action (12:5, 7–8), is as sharp and greatly reassuring. To that picture believers must cling.

Illustrating the Text

The struggle for truth

Scenario: As a general rule, many of your listeners probably consider themselves to be honest. In order to help them connect with Psalm 12, ask them to consider how they might respond to the following scenarios:

- Your best friend is making a poor choice, and you know that he is very defensive about his decision and not open to criticism. He asks you what you think, and you know the truth will put your friendship on the line. Would you tell him the truth?

- You are invited to a party but just need a night at home to rest and relax. Will you make up an excuse or tell the truth?

- Your mother gives you a shirt for your birthday that you really don't like. She asks you what

you think about the gift. How would you respond?

- It's World War II, and you are living in Poland. You are hiding Jews in your basement, and the Nazis come to your door and ask, "Are there Jews in your home?" How would you respond? (This is based on an actual event that led to the arrest of everyone in the home.)

The propensity to lie

Statistics: Based on a 2002 study, University of Massachusetts psychologist Robert S. Feldman concludes, "People tell a considerable number of lies in everyday conversation. It was a very surprising result. We didn't expect lying to be such a common part of daily life."[14] The study was based on ten-minute conversations and found that 60 percent of people lied at least once during the conversation with an average of two to three lies per conversation. That's in just ten minutes! Surveys find that 31 percent of people admit to lying on their resumes, and 30 percent of people

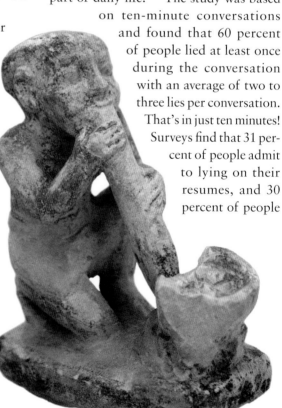

Unlike sinful humankind, where "everyone lies to their neighbor" (12:2), God's words are pure. Here an Egyptian craftsman is probably involved in metallurgy or glassmaking as he uses a blowpipe to increase the flame under the crucible (2477 BC).

admit to lying about their diet and exercise regimens.[15]

Sadly, lying has become a part of our culture and, depending on the circumstances, has become an acceptable sin in the church. We must recognize the contrast between the impurity of our words and the purity of God's word (12:6).

Turning false words into true

True Story: The false and boastful words of David's opponents were destructive, and as he talks to God about it, the Lord says he will arise to "protect them from those who malign them" (12:5). God's counter-force against lies and slander directed at his people is illustrated by a story from the former Soviet Union of how malignant words were turned into God's word:

Some time ago a story was circulated that Christians in the former Soviet Union were without proper printing equipment to produce copies of the Bible. Resourcefully, they collected as much printed Communist literature as they could obtain. Taking those printed texts, they cut out each word and pasted them back together to produce a printed Bible. Originally, these same words, when configured within the Communist documents, had depicted the world of the Communist literature they printed. Once reconfigured as the Bible, these words had quite a different textual meaning.[16]

"I Will Sing the Lord's Praise, for He Has Been Good to Me"

Big Idea *Faith has its personae, from skepticism to personal conflict, but trust, its true persona, sings its way into the joy of God's goodness.*

Understanding the Text

Psalm 13 is an individual lament that leaves the cause of lament uncertain (see below) but calls attention to the joy of buoyant faith (13:5). The biblical laments always hover near words of trust and assurance, and such a question as we have in verses 1 and 2 should send us on a search for words of faith in the lament psalms.

Also, it hardly needs to be said that lament is about some troublesome circumstance, which is often explicit in the poem but other times only a hint. In this psalm it is the latter. Some believe David's problem that gave rise to his lament was conflict with his enemies, while others are inclined to think it was some type of sickness ("or I will sleep in death," 13:3b).

The Text in Context

Psalm 12 dealt with the question of falsity's claim to triumph over truth (12:2–4), while Psalm 13 modulates to the enemies' claim of triumph over this man of faith (13:4).

While we should not overplay the Absalom theme, the trauma of a lost son or daughter, as only parents can know, forms a lamentive tone to whose mournful strains we sometimes grow unconscious. Yet its effect on our actions and words is nevertheless identifiable to the tuneful ear. Kidner implies that behind this probing lament may lie the pain of the Absalom tragedy and that the psalm itself reflects the magnanimity of David's personality, his sense of royal responsibility, and his subservient trust in Yahweh.[1]

Outline/Structure

Delitzsch describes this psalm as a hymn that "advances in waves that are constantly decreasing in length, until at last it is only agitated with joy, and becomes calm as the sea when smooth as a mirror."[2] The first mighty wave is the *lament*; the second breaker, the *petition*, less powerful and foreboding; and the third, after the storm has been stilled, is *trust*.

Looking at the text, Psalm 13 exhibits a lexical outline.

1. The lament (13:1–2) frames the "house of mourning" by *four columns of the agonizing question "how long"* (*'ad-'anah*). The fourfold repetition gives the impression of the protracted suffering David endured[3]—it was painfully drawn out—and covers a wide span of the psalmist's relationships, the first two regarding the Lord ("How long will you forget me?" "How long will you hide your face from me?"), the third, the psalmist himself with his inner struggle ("How long must I wrestle with my thoughts?"), and the fourth, his enemies, who were never very far from David's mind ("How long will my enemy triumph over me?").

2. The suppliant, as it were, enters into his petitionary prayer (13:3–4) within the "house of mourning" framed by his four-column lament and lays *three petitions before the God of grace*: "Look on me," "answer," and "Give light to my eyes" (13:3). Three times David tethers his hope to answered prayer with the little word "lest" (Heb. *pen*, implied in 13:3d), not found in the NIV: "*lest* I sleep the sleep of death" (13:3); "*lest* my enemy say, 'I have triumphed over him'"; "[*lest*, implied] my foes rejoice when I fall" (13:4, author's trans.). It is at the point of "lest" that divine grace will save him or let him go. This word of contingency reminds us of the Hebrew word for

Key Themes of Psalm 13

- God sometimes delays in answering the believer's prayer.
- Faith may have an inner struggle with God.
- Faith has victory in God.

"perhaps" (*'ulay*) on which the prophetic hopes were sometimes suspended (Amos 5:15; Jer. 21:2).[4] Depending on divine grace, the rope will hold or unravel.

3. The conjunction "but" (adversative *waw* in Hebrew) introduces part three of the psalm (13:5–6) and gives us the results of the psalmist's inspection of the tether—it indeed will hold. Here is where David turns the corner and leaves behind the "how long" of part one and puts his full weight of faith on the tether ("lest") of part two. We meet this "but," says Westermann, "somewhere or somehow in every psalm of lament," and he observes: "Only with this 'but' is it possible to understand what trust really means; only in this movement, this clinging to God's goodness, which the facts seem to contradict, can it be seen for what it truly is."[5]

Historical and Cultural Background

The general background for this psalm, as for most of the Davidic psalms, is David's

The psalmist laments, "How long?" four times in the opening verses of Psalm 13. This sundial from Egypt marked time by measuring the length of the sun's shadow cast by the small upright piece when the sundial was aimed at the sun (1540–1075 BC).

encounter with his enemies, foreign and domestic. Kidner astutely observes that the two poles of David's psalms are God and David's enemies.[6] Twice in Psalm 13:4 David mentions his enemy and his foes. Yet, while David's love for his children was a mark of his character, his indulgent attitude toward them sometimes had ill results. One could say that the sorrow of Absalom's rebellion always lurked in David's soul and was never far below the surface.

Psalm 13 does not exhibit the weaponry and brutality of warfare, but those marks of David's world lie just beneath the epidermis of the language of this psalm. "Enemy" and "foes" (13:4) are the most obvious, but the triumphal cry of the enemy, "I have overcome him," comes also from the language of military conflict, as does also the word "salvation" (13:5), which, in theological thought, has long broken loose from its moorings and soared far above the battlefield.

The lament was not only part of the biblical psalms but part of the literary legacy of the ancient Near East,[7] and not surprisingly, since sorrow is a universal sentiment.

Interpretive Insights

13:1 *How long, Lord? Will you forget me forever? . . . will you hide your face from me?* Most of the English translations, quite reasonably, break the single question of 13:1a into two (so pointed in the MT). The single question is found also in Psalms 79:5 and 89:46 (89:47 MT). The question "how long?" (*'ad-'anah*) occurs four times in 13:1–2, suggesting the urgency and emotional intensity of the psalmist's situation. The word "forever" (*netsah*) probably means "utterly,"[8] and the expression "hide your face" (the opposite of Num. 6:26) here denotes God's

"How long will you hide your face from me?" (13:1) asks the psalmist. Mesopotamian wisdom literature echoes this feeling of God's displeasure in the "Poem of the Righteous Sufferer," also known as Ludul bel Nemeqi. In this poem the worshiper laments, "I called to my god, he did not show his face." One of the tablets of the epic poem is shown here.

displeasure. This expression occurs in the ancient Near Eastern literature also in that sense. Hilber cites the Mesopotamian Poem of the Righteous Sufferer, in which the worshiper cries: "I called to my god, he did not show his face."[9]

13:2 *How long must I wrestle with my thoughts . . . ?* Literally, "How long must I set my counsel ['*etsot*] against myself?" Some translations, without textual warrant, emend this word to '*atsawot* ("pains"; cf. RSV, NRSV). The NIV is an accurate rendering of the sense.

13:3 *or I will sleep.* The Hebrew word for "or" (*pen*) is better translated "lest" (see "Outline/Structure").

13:4 *I have overcome him.* The Hebrew verb for "overcome" means "to be able" and here carries the sense of "prevail," the same sense as Genesis 32:28 (32:29 MT), "you have struggled with God and with humans and *have overcome*." See "Outline/Structure" for the occurrence of "lest" (*pen*), which the NIV has translated "and."

13:5 *But I trust . . . in your salvation.* The conjunction "but" (Heb. adversative *waw*) is the fulcrum on which David's faith turns: "*But* I trust . . . ." The "I" is emphatic and is a *casus pendens*: "but *as for me, I* trust in your unfailing love." The backdrop of this verse is most likely political conflict, and thus "salvation" is deliverance from the political danger. This word in time and changing circumstances takes on a spiritual meaning and here very well may have such a nuance, that is, deliverance from the oppressive sense of God's having forgotten the psalmist.

13:6 *for he has been good to me.* The verb expresses the idea of "completeness," or "to deal bountifully."

Theological Insights

"Psalm prayer," says Westermann, "also has always a communal or social aspect: a man is never alone with God."[10] While it is a three-pronged complex (the psalmist, God, and the enemies), it is really a one-way "conversation" between David and God—God never speaks. Nor need he, because it is so clear that he has heard and answered the psalmist's prayer (13:5–6).

But the answer, whether future or already realized, has been long in coming. The "how long" is not so much probing as pleading, and it had been mapped out along a painful path. The tone is incredulity. Perowne expresses it well in his paraphrase: "How long wilt Thou *make as if* Thou wouldst forget me for ever?"[11] It stands apart from the question of Psalm 22:1: "My God, my God, why have you forsaken me?" This latter question probes the mind of God and articulates the sense of incredulity that God could do such a thing, while 13:1 asks the question upon the template of time, "how distressingly long?"[12]

The question the psalmist had, as do we all, is how one is to interpret such a long delay. Is it the maturing of the time or the person that is in play here, as Kidner suggests? Or is there some ineffable attribute in the divine nature that becomes part of the formula? In one sense of the word, since there is no time with God, and God's eternal decrees are *already* accomplished in the eternal realm of realities but sometimes *not yet* realized in the human, the answer is most likely found in the maturing of either the time or the person, or both. Even though David's perspective is truncated by his time and person, he nevertheless trusts in the God of grace (Heb. *hesed*; "unfailing love," 13:5). As Delitzsch eloquently says: "Faith, however, holds fast the love that is behind the wrath, sees in the display of wrath only a self-disguising of the loving countenance of the God of love, and earnestly desires that this loving countenance may once more be unveiled to it."[13] Of course, this face of God can be observed only by the eye of faith.

Sometimes our piety obstructs rather than clarifies our view of God. That is not a censure of piety but an acknowledgment that, though it is the believer's Godward motion, it is still earthbound. In its latter quality it tends to censure us when we ask the hard questions of God ("How can one be so audacious!") or when our pain tends to deprecate God with cries that are inarticulate ("How can you, God, be so indifferent!"). But in the Old Testament, God shows great respect to those people who ask the hard questions, pose the difficult options, and probe the recesses of understanding—Moses, Joshua, Job, and Habakkuk. Perhaps the problem is that our faith is hesitant to stretch the length of piety's full reach. This psalm can help us to lengthen faith's tendons. Calvin, in his deeper grasp of faith's potential, remarks that David "teaches us, therefore, by his example, to stretch our view as far as possible into the future, that our present grief may not entirely deprive us of hope."[14]

However we respond personally to this spiritual challenge, Terrien is right in his observation that the "spirituality of the Psalms and their power of longevity and ecumenicity are partly due to the boldness, close to blasphemy, with which a man of faith challenges his God."[15] For the boldest of us, this psalm can be an instrument of faith, and for the more spiritually timid of us, it can be an amazement that faith could be so bold. Regardless of our spiritual temperament, we will need to walk through the Psalter with a respect for both dispositions, or we will never feel at home in the psalmic world, which is, we must admit, the world of human reality.

The psalmist's triple petition is answered by the faith he expresses in the final confession of trust and his all-too-brief aria of God's grace (13:5–6). We do not know the substantive ways in which the Lord took action in response to his audacious "look on me," "answer me," and "give light to my eyes" (13:3); but somewhere behind "I trust in your unfailing love; my heart rejoices in your salvation" (13:5), there is an answer that comes from the God to whom the psalmist pledges to dedicate his song of divine benevolence.

Teaching the Text

We might employ the "Big Idea" above and talk about the *four faces* of faith's persona that pretty much cover the gamut of the psalmist's world, and ours too. The first is the doubt that troubles the suppliant—doubt too is a natural part of faith. When it drives us to ask the question "How long?" it gives us, as it does the psalmist, a window into our relationship with God (13:1). As the closing lines of the poem attest (13:5–6), he deals with his doubt in the context of God's "unfailing love" (*hesed*). When viewed in that setting, it becomes a supplement to faith rather than an erosion.

The second face is depicted in the suppliant's relationship to himself (13:2a). His

INFINEM
Sque quo one
oblunscerif me in
finem. quo usque auertif
faciem tuam ame
Quam diu ponam consilii
manima mea dolorem
incorde meo perdiem
Siquequo exaltabitur ini
micuf meuf supme refpice

PSALMUS
Rexaudime dne dmf
In lumina oculof meof
neumquam obdormia
in morte
Nequando dicat inimicuf
meuf preualui aduerfuf
cum
Quiteribulant me exulta
bunt fimo cuf fuero ago

DAVID · XII ·
autem intua misericor
dia sperabo
Exultabit cormeum in
falutari tuo. cantabo dno
quibona tribuit mihi
& psallam nomini dni
altissimi

The psalm does not give us the response to the psalmist's request that the Lord "give light to [his] eyes" (13:3), but the illustrations used for Psalm 13, shown here from the Harley Psalter, picture God directing light from a torch toward a man huddled under a tree. Meanwhile, his enemies also wait for God's response as described in 13:4 (Harley 603 f. 7, eleventh century AD).

"thoughts" (see the comments on 13:2, above) are self-deprecating (lit., "counsels against myself"), and evidently constant, "day after day" (lit., "daily"; LXX adds "at night"). One of the marks of a well-adjusted person is a wholesome attitude toward oneself. This is in fact an Old Testament idea (Lev. 19:18) that Jesus taught as part of the second great commandment (Matt. 22:39). Moreover, we might observe that the love of oneself is a reflection of God's own personality, for after the commandment against taking vengeance and bearing grudges in Leviticus 19, he says: "but you shall love your neighbor as yourself: I am the LORD" (ESV). We are never whole in God or complete in Christ until we have a proper attitude toward ourselves, which should be confused with neither an inferiority nor a superiority complex. When we look at the "theology" of the Bible, we can truthfully say that God has, to use our modern phrase, a healthy "self-image." Though he occasionally remorsefully contemplates his actions (e.g., Gen. 6:5–6), even that is done in the context of his unfailing love.

The third face is the psalmist's relationship with his enemies (13:2b). It is spelled out in verse 4 as he contemplates impending death, whether by illness or military conflict, and the thought that his enemies might "rejoice when I fall." How we conduct ourselves amid conflict with others is one of the most revealing facets of faith. Our poet neither curses nor blesses them. This is the countenance of faith where the grimaces of our sins and our hatred toward those who mistreat us can disfigure our face. We ought to review Jesus's instruction to love our enemies and pray for them (Matt. 5:44; Luke 6:27–28), for only the unfailing love of God can change the disfigurement our sins have caused. (See the first illustration in the unit on Ps. 7.)

The fourth face of faith's persona is trust in God (13:5–6). The suppliant's trust in the Lord is most likely both the cause and the result of his triumph. The teacher/preacher might observe that out of the depths of this distress, when one's world (relationships with God, self, others) is falling apart, comes a deep expression of trust in God (13:5). The psalm provides virtually no evidence that the situation has changed, unless verse 6a ("for he has been good to me") represents a new phase in the suppliant's life rather than a general assessment. Even so, verses 3–4 are definitely prayed in the midst of his suffering, reverberating hope in that prayer. Indeed, these three petitions ("look on me," "answer," and "give light") are positioned right in the middle of the poem.

The preacher/teacher could even make these faces four consecutive sermons or lessons and range more broadly on these topics in the Psalms as well as in the larger scope of Scripture.

Illustrating the Text

Lament helps us express before God the pain in life.

News Story: On July 17, 1996, TWA Flight 800 exploded and crashed into the Atlantic Ocean near East Moriches, New York, just twelve minutes after take-off. All 230 people on board were killed, making it the third-deadliest aviation accident to occur in United States territory. Included among the dead were sixteen members of the French club and their five chaperones from Montoursville High School in Pennsylvania. At a memorial service for the students and chaperones, the pastor began the service by reading from Psalm 13, "How long must I wrestle with my thoughts and day after day have sorrow in my heart?" (13:2).[16] It is hard to imagine the depth of pain that the friends and family members of the victims were experiencing. Psalm 13 not only helps the

The psalmist affirms his trust in God despite his circumstances by stating that he will "sing the LORD's praise" (13:6). This brightly painted Egyptian stela depicts a harpist singing a hymn to the falcon-headed god Ra-Horakhty (stela of the harpist Djedkhonsuiuefankh, Twenty-Second Dynasty, 945–715 BC).

reader identify with the sorrow and pain of David but also brings hope as it provides direction.

In the midst of distress, speak honestly with God.

Literature: *Stories for the Journey*, by William R. White. In this book, White shares the story of a seminary professor, Hans, who was devastated by the loss of his wife. The grief was so profound that Hans could not eat and would not leave his home.

Concerned for their colleague, the seminary president and three professors visited Hans at his home. Hans confessed to them, "I am no longer able to pray to God. In fact, I am not certain I believe in God any more." Undeterred, his friends responded, "Then we will believe for you. We will pray for you." The four men continued to meet daily to pray for their friend. Some months later, the four colleagues gathered with Hans to pray. Hans was a different man, and he said, "It's no longer necessary for you to pray for me. Today I would like you to pray with me."[17] A mistake that many people make when they feel disappointed with God is that they turn their backs on him completely. What we see in Psalm 13 is encouragement to continue to look to God, and permission to speak honestly with the Lord. It was this process that brought David to a point of joy and praise even in the midst of sorrow.

Our own story of faith

Testimony: Ask a person from your church who has had a challenging life experience to share his or her story with the congregation. The story should parallel Psalm 13—that is, someone who experienced a great sorrow, continued to turn to the Lord, and has come to a place of trust, joy, and praise. The testimony can be shared live or by video. Having a testimony from someone the listeners know will help the principles of Psalm 13 deepen in the hearts of the congregants and will emphasize the relevance of the Psalms.

"The LORD Looks Down . . . to See If There Are Any Who Understand"

Big Idea *The world's God-deniers will find, maybe to their surprise, that the God they deny is found "in the company of the righteous."*

Understanding the Text

The form of Psalm 14 is sometimes considered to be an individual lament, and in tone, it is, because the psalmist grieves over the vacuum of faith that he perceives in his world. But it does not follow the form of the lament. Others have suggested it is a wisdom psalm, in view of its use of wisdom language. In wisdom terms, the word "fool" stands opposite the "wise," which is here expressed by the two clauses, "any who understand" and "any who seek God" (14:2). Yet that is as much wisdom as we see in the psalm. The truth of the matter is that this is one of those psalms that does not fall into any of the categories form criticism has formulated.

The actions of fools "are corrupt," and "their deeds are vile" (14:1). Perhaps that is why the artist of the illuminations for the Ingeborg Psalter depicted the fool as a man with demons on either side (ms. 66, fol. 56, France, thirteenth century AD, J. Paul Getty Museum).

The Text in Context

In this psalmic neighborhood, there are two competing voices. The first is the sinister sound of those who claim to triumph over the truth (12:4a), adding their voices to

corde suo non est deus;
Corrupta sunt et abhominabiles fach s[
in iniquitatib; non est q faciat bonu[
Deus de celo prospexit super filios ho[

the psalmist's enemies who claim triumph over David himself (13:4). The second, of a nobler character, is the sound of rejoicing from the psalmist, whose defeat was extremely exaggerated (13:3b), added to the multitudinous voice of God's people, rejoicing because the Lord had reversed their ill fortunes (14:7b).

As the Lord "restores his people," Psalm 14 anticipates the gathering at Zion's sanctuary in 15:1, with an ethical examination of those worthy to enter it (15:2–5). This is much like the examination administered to the priests returning from Babylonian captivity, intended to test their knowledge of ritual law and clear them for service in the restored temple (Hag. 2:10–19).

Psalm 14 is virtually duplicated in Psalm 53, with some minor differences, and the major addition of 53:5b–d (in the table below, the addition is in italics; for a fuller comparison of the two psalms, see the table "A Comparison of Psalms 14 and 53" in the unit on Ps. 53):

Psalm 14:5	Psalm 53:5
"There they are, overwhelmed with dread, for God is present in the company of the righteous."	"There they are, overwhelmed with dread, *where there was nothing to dread. God scattered the bones of those who attacked you; you put them to shame, for God despised them.*"

The addition of 53:5 is evidently intended to pronounce judgment on that generation of the godless in whose time the so-called Elohistic Psalter (Pss. 42–83) was collected. The exclusive use of the generic name of the deity, *'elohim* ("God"), rather than the tetragrammaton, *YHWH* ("Lord"), char-

Key Themes of Psalm 14

- The psalmist perceives a vacuum of faith.
- God is found in the "company of the righteous."

Duplicate Psalms

Duplicate psalms or duplicate portions of psalms give some indication of the fluidity of the psalmic literature and offer insight into the process of the compilation of the Psalter (see "The Structure and Composition of the Psalter" in the introduction). There are, of course, many minor duplications, but the major psalm duplicates are the following:

- Psalm 14 = Psalm 53
- Psalm 18 = 2 Samuel 22
- Psalm 31:1–3 = Psalm 71:1–3
- Psalm 40:13–17 = Psalm 70
- Psalm 57:7–11 = Psalm 108:1–5
- Psalm 60:5–12 = Psalm 108:6–13[a]

[a] Adapted from Sarna's list as given by Gruber, *Rashi's Commentary*, 223.

acterizes Psalm 53 (see the sidebar "The Divine Names" in the unit on Ps. 4).

Outline/Structure

Psalm 14 falls into four parts:

1. The fool's perspective (14:1)
2. God's perspective (14:2–4)
3. God's presence among the righteous (14:5–6)
4. Hope for Israel's salvation (14:7)

Historical and Cultural Background

In view of the adaptation of Psalm 14 to fit the context of Psalm 53, the impression is that Psalm 14 is probably the original form. It belongs to the first Davidic collection (Pss. 2–41) and could, in my opinion, have been written by David. Some commentators take the clause "When the LORD restores his people" (14:7) to be a hint of the exile (so A. A. Anderson),[1] since Psalm 126:1 uses an almost exact phrase as a reference to the return ("restored the fortunes"; KJV: "turned again the captivity"). But Perowne calls attention to the metaphorical use of the phrase "to turn the captivity" (Job 42:10; Ezek. 16:53; NIV: "restore the fortunes") and insists that this phrase is not sure proof of an exilic date.[2] Yet it is possible that 14:7 was added as a celebratory colophon, perhaps to celebrate spiritual renewal or temple renovation, which occurred several times in history.[3]

When we look for a time for this psalm's composition, the challenge, given the polytheistic nature of Israel's world, is to discover a time when the widespread sentiment of Psalm 14 ("All have turned away," 14:3) would prevail. Jeremiah searches Jerusalem to find "but one person who deals honestly and seeks the truth" (Jer. 5:1). His time, however, is one not of the absence of faith in God's existence but rather of its perversion: "Although they say, 'As surely as the LORD lives,' still they are swearing falsely" (5:2).

The psalmist describes those who act as if there is no God and whose deeds are corrupt as fools. Isaiah, depicted here, also describes these types of individuals when he says in Isaiah 32:6, "For fools speak folly, their hearts are bent on evil: They practice ungodliness and spread error concerning the LORD." This fourteenth-century painting of Isaiah by Duccio di Buoninsegna was once part of the high altar of the Siena Cathedral in Italy.

The question is whether a philosophical atheism existed in the ancient world. Given the pantheistic beliefs of Israel's neighbors, and sometimes of Israel herself, where is there room for an absolute denial of God's existence? Indeed, the common argument that the psalm cites a time of *practical atheism*, that is, when people acted *as if* there were no God, fits the genre of Israel's world better. Indeed, the fool's claim of 14:1, "There is no God," may be irony of attribution (e.g., the statement that Amos *attributed* to the oppressors of the poor in an attempt to represent their thinking, in Amos 8:4–6). Based on the fool's actions, the psalmist has attributed the statement to him: "The fool says in his heart, 'There is no God.'" It is indeed the actions of his generation that the psalmist indicts in 14:3–4. There is little difference between the fool's spoken theology and his acted theology.

Interpretive Insights

Title *director of music.* See the comments on the title for Psalm 4.

14:1 *The fool says in his heart, "There is no God."* The "fool" (*nabal*) is the equivalent of "scoffer" or "mocker" (see Ps. 1:1; Prov. 21:24). Kidner says that "fool" is "a word which implies an aggressive perversity, epitomized in the Nabal of 1 Samuel 25:25."[4] First Samuel 25 provides a personalized picture of the fool in the person of David's enemy Nabal, who even carried that Hebrew name, or was so designated by the writer of Samuel. Elmslie says this type of person is one whose "whole judgment of life has become perverted."[5] The fool's negativism and its effects are described in four ways: (1) his/her claim: "There is no God" (14:1a); (2) his/her immoral behavior: "they are corrupt, their deeds are vile" (14:1b); (3) the general social decay: "there is no one who does good" (this becomes the refrain of the lament: 14:1b, 3b [note the augmentation, "not even one"]); (4) their lack of prayer: "they never call on the LORD" (14:4c). The expression "says in his heart" corresponds to the Hebrew expression for "to think," or "say to oneself." (Other God-denying thoughts are found in Pss. 10:11; 73:11; Jer. 5:12; Rom. 1:28.)

14:2 *The LORD looks down from heaven on all mankind.* Genesis 11:5 describes the Lord as coming down from heaven to investigate the earthly situation. The verb translated as "looks down" means "look intently," or "to look out" (the window) (see 2 Kings 9:30, 32; Ps. 102:19; Lam. 3:50). It suggests a careful surveying of the human situation (NIV: "mankind"; lit., "sons of adam," b^ene 'adam).

14:3 *All have turned away, all have become corrupt; there is no one who does good, not even one.* The psalmist laments the depravity of the human condition with the terms "all," "together" (ESV; NIV: "all"), "there is no one," and "not even one." With the understanding that "all

have become corrupt," our writer begins the description of what he means by "all have turned away," as he cites their wicked deeds to describe this turning aside. Similar to Jeremiah 5:1, the reference to "no one," "not even one," is obviously hyperbole, a common literary feature.

14:4 *They devour my people as though eating bread.* In the first person ("*my* people") we hear the Lord's voice, perhaps an oracle, or simply the psalmist speaking prophetically on God's behalf. Their evil deeds reach their pathetic climax in the ease and routine with which they destroy God's people, like sitting down to eat their meal and enjoying it (cf. Mic. 3:3).

14:5 *there.* This adverb (*sham*) applies both to the place ("company of the righteous") and time of fear ("overwhelmed with dread") that overwhelm these God-deniers and to the place where they will find God. Verses 5–6 correspond to 53:5 (see above).

God is present in the company of the righteous. This is the same idea as Isaiah 7:14, "God with us," and, while less formulaic than the covenant formula ("that I may dwell in their midst," Exod. 25:8 RSV, ESV), it has the same sense.

14:6 *the plans of the poor.* The "poor" is parallel to the "righteous" (14:5), and they are probably synonymous. The "plans" are likely the intentions of the poor/righteous to keep the covenant, given the covenant nuances of the psalm ("my people," "the LORD," "salvation for Israel," "his people," 14:4, 7). They are the opposite of those who "never call on the LORD" (14:4c).

14:7 *When the LORD restores his people.* This phrase describes the return from Babylonian exile in Psalm 126:1 (with a minor

spelling variant) but is used of other eras also (Job 42:10; Ezek. 16:53; see "Historical and Cultural Background"). While 14:7 may adapt the psalm for Judah's homecoming, it is also included at the end of Psalm 53, which belongs to a different collection, compiled for a particular purpose, and perhaps is used here more as a metaphor than a historical indicator.

Schaefer, with good literary reason, proposes that the seven direct references to God (or Lord) in Psalm 14 (and Ps. 53) create "a sense of the fullness of the divine presence."[6] So the psalm begins with a vacuous absence ("There is no God") and ends with the comprehensive fullness of God's presence. This is one of those numerous instances in the Psalms where the literary structure and nature of the psalm carry a theological message.

Theological Insights

If human depravity is the spiritual malady that marks every generation of human history—and we have good reason to believe it is—the denial of God is common to every age, even though it assumes different forms. It goes without saying that this vacuum of faith is more keenly discerned by men and women of faith. When the psalmist looked at the behavior of the naysayers, he recognized that their disavowal of God's existence had a direct correlation to the moral decline of his day. The deniers were, so to speak, not holding their placards of protest in the public squares, but their evil deeds (14:4) gave loudspeaker clarity to their denial of God.

The evildoers "devour my people as though eating bread" (14:4b)—this is God's analysis report. Their ravenous appetite is so wanton that they no more hesitate when God's people are the entrée than when their daily bread is set before them. They are devoid of human compassion, the default mode of their atheistic living. The correlation between the denial of God and moral decline is written between the lines.

The tragic victims of this ravenous craving for more are the poor (14:6a), in parallel with "the righteous," suggesting they are synonymous. But the tragedy turns into triumph for the righteous, because "the Lord is their refuge" (14:6b); and, further, it is from this tragedy that "salvation for Israel" comes out of Zion (14:7). This is the story of Israel, and the story of humanity in general, as Paul declares in Romans 3:9: "Jews and Gentiles alike are all under the power of sin." The apostle quotes part of Psalm 14:1–3 (13:1–3 LXX), plus a catena of other Old Testament texts,[7] and understands well the principle that sin calls forth God's grace (Rom. 3:5–20), and that is precisely the reaction we see in Psalm 14 (and Gen. 3:15). The God who has been denied his rightful place in the universe by those people who think and act like there is no God—this same God peers out of heaven's window to search through the human race, looking to find "any who understand, any who seek God" (14:2; cf. John 1:10–11). It is a pitiable state of affairs for the world he made.

Teaching the Text

We may draw upon the "Key Themes" to develop a sermon or lesson on this psalm. First, the psalmist draws out the vacuum of faith ("There is no God") that exists in his world, with its practical manifestation of moral decline (see "Theological Insights"). While it may be more a practical denial of God than a philosophical one, the two are interrelated. In fact, this psalm and Old Testament theology in general, to say nothing of New Testament theology, draw a negative correlation between declining belief in the God of Scripture and the shaping of an immoral world (see Rom. 1). This negative correlation is a design of every historical era—in varying degrees, of course—and is the other side of Paul's statement that "where sin increased, grace increased all the more" (Rom. 5:20).

Second, the vacuum of faith turns out to be the proverbial vacuum that seeks to be filled. Faith's vacuum is not a dead spot but a potentially powerful force that, once pricked by the grace of God, will inflate to the full capacity of faith. It is the vacuum in the human heart, reminding us of Augustine's definition of evil as the absence of good. Admittedly, with the negativism of Psalm 14 it is tempting to focus our lesson/sermon on the "atheistic" motif of this psalm, but the focus of the poem is as much on God, if not more so, as on the theologically vacuous world of the psalmist. He insists that there is a place, or an experience, or perhaps a mental state, where God breaks through: "*there* they are, overwhelmed with dread" (14:5). That is, somehow God breaks through with a moment of clarity and certainty, and that moment is God's lightning flash that lights up the landscape before all goes black again. Unbelief is laid down on the palette of a world that God looks down upon from heaven, and he meets its doubters in the venue of his revelation, in the "company of the righteous" (14:5).

But human denial of God is not enough to make God keep his distance. Rather, he will make himself known to the God protestors "in the company of the righteous." God encounters them in the events of life and in the company of his people. Running from God, they meet him on their escape route with his penetrating question *Quo vadis?*[8] "Where are you going?"—that is the surprise. But if they could bring themselves to give the people of God a chance, they would find him there, find him especially there—no surprise at all.

A correlative idea here is that finding God in the "company of the righteous" puts a heavy responsibility on the righteous to live by God's law and be a constant manifestation of his grace. In both the Old and New Testaments God shines forth in the midst of his people, in the Old, Israel, and in the New, the church. While the goodness of the world outside of Israel and the church is not to be demeaned (Calvin speaks of "common grace"), the impact of God's revelation is in and through Israel and his church. If the unredeemed world finds God—and find him it must—it will be *there*, in the "company of the righteous."

We may draw attention also to Psalm 139:7–12, where the psalmist contemplates every possible direction to run from God, only to acknowledge that when he runs from God, he only runs to him, because God is everywhere. God will make himself known in his world because it is his nature to do so, and his special revelation is found only in and among his people. It is certainly appropriate to make an application of the "company of the righteous" to the New Testament church and stress the continuity of the Hebrew people of God and God's manifestation of himself to and among them.

Illustrating the Text

Denying God does not improve human morals.

Science: In our world there is a movement called the "new atheism," championed by such writers as Richard Dawkins and Christopher Hitchens. It is different from the "old" atheism that was largely based on philosophical grounds. Rather, it is based on the growing body of new discoveries, particularly about the universe and its origins. Interestingly, the uniqueness of Psalm 14 (and 53) is that it gives us an inside look into God's mind—by way of the psalmist, of course—a look at how God views those people who deny that he exists. Although the God-deniers of this psalm are most likely not "fools" in the intellectual sense, they look at the universe and cannot see God in the incalculable wonders of nature or hear his voice in the beauty of love. Lamentably our increased understanding of the universe has done little or nothing to change the way we human beings treat one another. While the Holocaust and modern terrorism cannot be blamed on modern science (except the technological means to facilitate such hatred), they are defiant examples of the evil of humankind despite our burgeoning scientific understanding of our world.

Contrasting perspectives

Contrasting Concept: When *GQ* magazine honored actor Matthew McConaughey as one of the 2013 "Men of the Year," he explained in his interview why he chose to "go in the shadows" for a portion of his career: "I got much more selfish. I'm a fan of the word *selfish*. Self. Ish. When I say I have gotten a lot more self-*ish*, I mean I am less concerned with what people think of me. I'm not worried about how I'm perceived. *Selfish* has always gotten a bad rap. You *should* do for you. I wanted new experiences."[9]

Interestingly, in the same magazine, author George Saunders was also honored as the "Life Coach of the Year 2013." In response to the question, "How to Be Decent?" Saunders responded, "The big kahuna of all moral questions, as far as I'm concerned, is ego. How do you correct the fundamental misperception that we are all born with, i.e.: I am permanent, I am enduring, I am central. All of the nasty stuff in this life comes out of that misunderstanding."[10]

God's Word has the power to transform.

Church History: Philip Yancey relates how he went to Sweden after reading the historical accounts of the Vikings. According to Yancey, for 250 years prayers in Europe ended with the words, "Lord, save us from the Vikings." The Vikings were known as a brutal people, guilty of rape, pillaging, and barbarism. And yet, today Sweden is known for charity, cleanliness, honesty, and hospitality. What brought about this change in culture? Yancey explains, "Christianity happened. It took several centuries, but gradually the moral principles of the Christian gospel percolated up to affect all of society."[11] In every culture there are people who are evildoers, corrupt and vile. And yet the Word of God has the power to transform individuals who then transform the culture. No matter how vile a culture, there is always hope (14:7).

The pagan Viking culture was gradually transformed by the power of the gospel. Gamla Uppsala, Sweden, is the location of several large burial mounds dating to the fifth and sixth centuries AD. They adjoin the area of a major ancient cultic center that was replaced by a Christian church in the twelfth century AD.

"LORD, Who May Dwell in Your Sacred Tent?"

Big Idea *Our worship and life in God are grounded more in ethical behavior than in liturgical correctness, though this does not suggest that the latter is unimportant.*

Understanding the Text

Form critics often identify this psalm as an *entrance liturgy* (also Ps. 24), spoken perhaps to the temple gatekeepers (2 Chron. 23:19) before the worshiper entered the sanctuary.[1] Mays moves the discussion in another direction by pointing out that both Psalms 15 and 24, as well as Isaiah 33:14–17 (which is a similar text), seem to be teaching texts for instructing the congregation or community, with no mention of ritual requirements.[2] Based on the ethical content of the psalm, and the question/answer format, others believe it is a wisdom psalm[3] that spells out the conditions of the righteous life.[4] Terrien suggests that the psalm may be a request by a suppliant for temporary asylum in one of the side chambers of the temple (1 Kings 6:5).[5] While each of these opinions carries relative weight, perhaps we ought to let Psalms 15 and 24, as the only ones of their type in the Psalter (Ps. 101 has similarities), stand alone as instructional texts.

The Text in Context

We have already noted in the discussion of Psalm 14 that David hoped for Israel's salvation to come from Zion, which would be accompanied by great rejoicing when the Lord restored Israel's fortunes (see Ps. 126). Psalm 15 is a follow-up psalm that describes those who are ethically prepared to enter Zion's sanctuary (15:1). Delitzsch, quite astutely, comments that Psalm 15 answers the question of who is the "company of the righteous" (14:5) for whom future salvation is intended.[6] In a similar relationship, Psalm 24 supplies the description of those who "will dwell in the house of the LORD forever" (23:6), the final notice of Psalm 23. It is noteworthy that both descriptions are given in ethical, rather than ritual, terms. This falls in line with prophetic religion that shifted the focus from ritual performance to ethical behavior (see Isa. 1:10–20; Amos 8:4–6). Indeed, it would not be an overstatement to say that the Psalter, for the most part, reflects that prophetic shift.

Outline/Structure

Psalm 15 falls into three parts:

1. The question (15:1)
2. The answer (15:2–5b)
3. Concluding word of assurance (15:5c)

Historical and Cultural Background

This poem gives us a window through which we can peer into the social world of ancient Israel. The person whose portrait the psalmist paints is the righteous person (15:2), who constitutes, along with his and her compatriots, the "company of the righteous" (14:5). When this description is turned inside out, we have another portrait of others on the social and ethical spectrum, describing, of course, those who were not prepared to enter the sanctuary on the Lord's holy mountain. The portrait as a whole is a positive one compared with the negative

picture of that person portrayed in Psalm 10:2–11 (see "Theological Insights" below).

The traditional view is that Psalm 15 was composed for the occasion of David's transfer of the ark to Jerusalem (2 Sam. 6:12–19; 1 Chron. 15:16), like Psalm 24. Yet references to the "sacred tent" and "holy mountain" (Mt. Zion) have led commentators in opposite directions. Delitzsch takes these terms to point toward Absalom's time when David was cut off from the sanctuary in Jerusalem and Absalom's devotees were in control.[7] Others see these words as nostalgic and poetic terms for the temple and allow the psalm much more flexibility in dating.[8] Either of these positions is possible, but there are no overwhelming terms that would dictate against Davidic dating.

Interpretive Insights

15:1 *who may dwell . . . Who may live.* The verb "dwell" (*gur*) means "to sojourn," applied to a resident alien (*ger*), and implies impermanence more than does the verb "live" (*shakan*), which relates to a permanent abode (Pss. 37:29 [NIV: "dwell"]; 78:55 [NIV: "settled"]) and is used of God's dwelling in sacred places (Exod. 24:16; NIV: "settled"), although

In Psalm 15, God's holy mountain is Mount Zion, which today is where the Temple Mount and the modern Islamic shrine, the Dome of the Rock, stand. This aerial view shows it in relationship to the ancient city of David (middle of photograph), which lies to the south of the Temple Mount complex.

the two terms are used quite synonymously here (see "Theological Insights").

15:2 *The one whose walk is blameless.* Both the noun and the verb "walk" are used as a metaphor for life. Thus, as an ethical term, "blameless" (*tamim*) describes a life lived in accord with the ethical law, particularly the ethical law described in this psalm. Personal examples of this moral posture were Noah and Abraham (Gen. 6:9; 17:1).

15:3 *whose tongue utters no slander.* The verb translated as "utter slander" is denominative, meaning it comes from a noun, in this case "foot," and expresses the idea of "to go about" or "stumble." The usual meaning is "to go about spying" (Gen. 42:9, the Piel noun; NIV: "spies"), but here and in 2 Samuel 19:27, it means "to gossip or slander."[9]

15:4 *who despises a vile person.* Note the contrast between "despises a vile person" and "honors those who fear the LORD." "Vile person" is a passive participle, from the verb "to reject" (*m's*; see 36:4; 78:67; cf. Isa. 54:6; Jer. 6:30). He is "rejected" because of his immoral condition, which explains the NIV's "vile person."

who keeps an oath even when it hurts. Literally, "he swears to his own hurt."[10] He keeps his oath *even though* it may be inconvenient for him (see Prov. 6:1–5). The thought expressed by "and does not change their mind" literally means, "and does not change" (thus ASV, NASB, and ESV).

15:5 *who lends money . . . without interest; who does not accept a bribe.* The pentateuchal law allows Israelites to charge interest of foreigners but not fellow Israelites (Deut. 23:20; Lev. 25:35–38), lest it impose an additional financial burden on them. In ancient times people did not

A blameless person "lends money to the poor without interest" (15:5). Coinage was not used in Israel until the postexilic period. Instead, payments would typically be made by weighing out bits of silver, although other precious metals and jewelry could be used. Shekel weights, like the ones shown here, were the standard measure. One shekel weighed out 11.4 grams of silver. Shown here are a series of weights. The weight at the top left is a shekel, and then multiples continue to the right. The lower weights are fractions of a shekel.

normally borrow money unless they were in desperate circumstances, so charging interest would only exacerbate their condition.[11]

will never be shaken. The Hebrew word for "shaken" means "to totter," or "be moved or shaken," and with its negatives, it carries the thought of stability or firmness, in this case the stability of the psalmist's relationship with God.

Theological Insights

It is difficult for Christians to understand the world of the psalmist, a world where one must be ritually and ethically qualified to enter the Lord's sanctuary. In ancient Israel this kind of self-examination, or examination by a priest, was standard.

The verb "dwell" implies a journey, or impermanence, while "live" connotes a permanent abode (see the comments on 15:1 above). The ASV captures the different nuances of the synonyms: "Jehovah, who shall *sojourn* in thy tabernacle? Who shall *dwell* in thy holy hill?" (emphasis added). While these nuances ought not be pressed too far, it is nevertheless appropriate to recognize that *sojourning* brings one to *permanent* residence in the Lord's presence.

The answer to the question "Who may dwell . . . ?" comes in the form of a character portrait of the one who can seek and find permanent residence in God's house. It is balanced by four sets of alternating positive and negative statements: three positive, three negative, three positive, and two negative (see table 1).

Table 1. Positive and Negative Statements in Psalm 15

Positive	Negative
• "Whose walk is blameless" • "Who does what is righteous" • "Who speaks the truth from their heart" (15:2) • "Who despises a vile person" • "Honors those who fear the LORD" • "Keeps an oath even when it hurts" (15:4)	• "Whose tongue utters no slander" • "Does no wrong to a neighbor" • "Casts no slur on others" (15:3) • "Who lends money . . . without interest" (lit., "who does not lend his money with interest") • "Does not accept a bribe against the innocent" (15:5)

Schaefer has called attention to the feature that "every imperative stated in Psalm 15 is concerned with the law toward the neighbor."[12] We have already observed the prophetic shift in emphasis from the ritual, which had become a manipulative tool to get Yahweh's attention and favor, to the moral, which is really what God requires in the first place (Mic. 6:8). The eleven qualities are expressed by three categories, though the verbal descriptors of each category may vary: "walks," "does," and "speaks."[13]

The first set of qualities, stated positively, consists of three general statements, probably intended to cover the whole ethical spectrum: "whose walk is blameless," "who does what is righteous," and "who speaks the truth from their heart" (15:2). These life functions are illustrated by the following descriptors, but not arranged as orderly as we might like.

The second set of qualities (15:3), expressed negatively, includes *speaking* ("whose tongue utters no slander" and "casts no slur on others") and *doing* ("does no wrong to a neighbor").

The third set of qualities (15:4), expressed positively, includes *doing* ("despises a vile person," and perhaps also "honors those who fear the LORD" and "keeps an oath"). The first quality in this set may trouble us, especially since Jesus commanded us to love our enemies (Matt. 5:44). Yet there is a strain of theological thought in the Old Testament that expresses obligation to hate Yahweh's haters and to love his lovers (e.g., Ps. 139:21–22). We should, therefore, recognize that with the Psalms, we have not yet come that far in the ethical progress of Scripture, even though there are road signs here and there that we are on our way to the highest ethical plateau of loving and praying for our enemies (e.g., Lev. 19:18).

The fourth set of qualities (15:5), expressed negatively, consists of two, giving us the sum total of eleven character traits. They, again, belong to the category of *doing* ("lends money . . . without interest" and "does not accept a bribe against the innocent").

Thus the portrait is complete, and the question of 15:1 has been answered. Summarily, the result of this righteous life is the degree of security that it ensures, both personally and socially: "Whoever does these things will never be shaken" (15:5c).

Teaching the Text

Following our insistence that the biblical text must shape the message, we can follow the three "Key Themes" to build our sermon/lesson. Early in our discourse, however, we should observe that Psalm 15 begins with a question—and it is not a rhetorical question—which means that an answer is expected. The answer may be a prophetic oracle, or God's words, or a priestly response, or merely the psalmist's answer to his own question (most likely the last option). Yet it still could have been an instrument of priestly or prophetic instruction. This instructional text lends itself to teaching the people of God in any age. We might also make the homiletical observation that there is a great need for the church to recover its role as instructor in the holy life.

We can open our sermon/lesson with the first of the "Key Themes": Who can be guests in the Lord's house? This is an excellent opportunity to demonstrate the ethics of this psalm (see "Theological Insights") and emphasize the moral nature of the biblical faith. Ritual was important, but when it was not accompanied by a holy life, it was an offense to God. The goal of a holy life is to "live" in God's house, which in ancient Israel (and, we should insist, in our own world) involved both a *path* and a *place*. That is, it involves our relationship with God.

The second of the "Key Themes" is the portrait of the guests in the Lord's house. Here we can go into the specifics of the

> The biblical text does not give much information regarding God's dwelling place during the kingship of David. After the ark is brought to Jerusalem, it says in 2 Samuel 6:17, "they brought the ark of the LORD and set it in its place inside the tent that David had pitched for it." Perhaps it was similar to the tent of meeting that was part of the tabernacle. Shown here is the tent of meeting in the tabernacle model at Timna, Israel.

description in verses 2–5b. Like the Ten Commandments, they belong to the ethical underpinnings of the Hebrew Bible, and the biblical faith in general, and still apply to our own lives. The exception is lending money to the poor at interest, but the moral principle that stands behind this prohibition should still be observed.[14] We should not miss this chance to speak about compassionate business practices. In summary, this rubric will instruct us that entrance into God's presence (or our personal relationship to God) demands an ethical life both for entering and for living in relation to him.

The third of the "Key Themes" is the security this lifestyle will bring. Perhaps in the larger sense of the word, our world is no less a changing one than that of ancient Israel, but with modern technology the changes seem so rapid. And with the changing climates—social, political, economic, and so on—we desperately need a sense of stability. We have to acknowledge that family stability in our modern world, for example, is quite a different social spectrum than Israel's tight sense of family loyalty. But even that changing social reality can find remedies in our relationship with God.

Illustrating the Text

The way to God

Bible: Psalm 15 invites us to consider the profound questions, "LORD, who may dwell in your sacred tent? Who may live on your holy mountain?" (15:1). People will respond to these questions in different ways. Some might say the answer depends on church membership or attendance. Others might say the answer depends on how much money a person donates to the Lord's work. Although there are many possible answers to these questions, Jesus has made it clear that there is only one appropriate response: "I am the way and the truth and the life. No one comes to the Father except through me" (John 14:6). And Jesus said that many will be surprised on the day of judgment. He instructs, "Enter through the narrow gate. For wide is the gate and broad is the road that leads to destruction, and many enter through it. But small is the gate and narrow the road that leads to life, and only a few find it" (Matt. 7:13–14). There is only one way to the Father, and that is through belief in Jesus (John 3:16). And we should be aware that believing in Jesus is underwritten by an ethical style of life that authenticates our faith.

Get a spiritual checkup.

Health: According to the Centers for Disease Control and Prevention, regular checkups are important: "Regular health exams and tests can help find problems before they start. They also can help find problems early, when your chances for treatment and cure are better. By getting the right health services, screenings, and treatments, you are taking steps that help your chances for living a longer, healthier life."[15] Regular checkups are important not only for our physical health but also for our spiritual health. Psalm 15 provides a great list of the attributes of one who may dwell in the Lord's sacred tent. Read out each item mentioned in 15:2–5, giving your listeners time to pause and silently reflect on their lives in light of the ethical challenges. After reading the verses, challenge your listeners to make changes in their lives in light of these moral imperatives.

Worship in Spirit and in truth.

Bible: The biblical prophets have a strong aversion to worship that exists for its own sake, or for the sake of the ritual itself. Adrian Nocent comments: "There must be no acts of worship to which nothing corresponds in a man's heart. God is fed up with rote prayers."[16] This advocates an unseverable link between morality and worship and sums up the prophetic urgency. Isaiah censures those who frequent the temple and offer their sacrifices but do not execute justice (Isa. 1:10–17). The antidotal prescription follows: "'Come now, let us settle the matter,' says the LORD. 'Though your sins are like scarlet, they shall be as white as snow; though they are red as crimson, they shall be like wool'" (Isa. 1:18). Amos shares that sentiment and rebukes Israel because they have treated Sabbath worship as nothing but an annoying interruption of their oppressive behavior toward the poor (Amos 8:5–6). Jesus sums up this theology of worship in his declaration that the Father seeks those who will worship him in Spirit and in truth (John 4:23). Thus, a time of self-examination before worship is always appropriate.

"You Will Fill Me with Joy in Your Presence"

Big Idea *The unity of our life in God involves both the journey and the destination.*

Understanding the Text

In literary form, Psalm 16 is an individual psalm of trust.[1] Nowhere in the psalm does God speak, nor do we hear other voices in the psalm—no enemies, no oppressed cries, no accusers. The psalmist is alone with God, and the intimacy of his relationship permeates the poem.

The Text in Context

Psalm 16 represents a plateau in progression from the dismissive fool of Psalm 14, who says there is no God, to the searching suppliant of Psalm 15, who asks about requirements for entry into the Lord's house, to the joyful worshiper of Psalm 16, who knows there is no life apart from God.

The historical allusions in this psalm, discussed below, are of notable value. David was aware of Israel's past, as a king should be, and echoed Israel's sacred writings. His references to Yahweh as his "portion," "lot," and "cup" (16:5) call to mind the Levites, whose portion was the Lord rather than a landed inheritance (Num. 18:20; Deut. 10:9; 18:1).

In Peter's Pentecost sermon he quotes Psalm 16:8–11 from the Septuagint (Acts 2:22–33; Ps. 15:8–11 LXX), saying that David prophesied Christ's resurrection. The fact that Paul also quotes from Psalm 16 (Acts 13:35–37) would suggest that this was a key apostolic Old Testament witness to the resurrection of Jesus.[2] Some commentators believe that the apostles,

Both Peter and Paul quote from Psalm 16 when speaking about the resurrection of Jesus. The empty tomb proclaimed that his body had not seen decay. Shown here is a first-century AD rolling stone tomb in lower Galilee.

having experienced the glorious resurrection of Christ, placed their template of the resurrection of Christ on the psalm, and thus the New Testament application. The apostles, however, and Jesus himself, looked at the Old Testament as the source of the prophetic word. They believed the template was the Old Testament, not the New Testament events, and in the presence of the events, the prophetic voice of the psalm could finally be clearly heard.

Outline/Structure

For the most part Psalm 16 is a prayer from beginning to end, with reflective moments woven into the direct words of the prayer:

1. Prayer (16:1)
2. Report of prayer (16:2)
3. Reflection (16:3–4)
4. Prayer (16:5)
5. Reflection (16:6)
6. Intent to praise (implied prayer) (16:7)
7. Reflection (16:8)
8. Concluding prayer of faith (16:9–11)

Historical and Cultural Background

Perowne proposes that David wrote this psalm when Saul had driven him out into the Wilderness of Ziph, where David said to Saul: "They have driven me today from my share in the LORD's inheritance and have said, 'Go, serve other gods'" (1 Sam. 26:19).[3] David draws upon the language of the conquest and settlement of Canaan to affirm his strong trust in the

Key Themes of Psalm 16

- Cast your lot with God alone.
- There is joy in God's presence.

Psalms of Trust

Trust is a relationship that is built by experience. This is evident in the psalms of trust, in which either an event or circumstance that has taught the suppliant to trust the Lord is described; or the event or circumstance that lies behind trust is alluded to or merely implied. The essential elements that compose these psalms are *a declaration of trust*, sometimes the first statement of the psalm, and often but not always, a use of the language of trust (especially *bth*). Inclusive of these two essential elements, the six that may be found in these psalms, of which we have both *individual* and *community* examples, are (1) a declaration of trust in the Lord, (2) an invitation to the community to trust, (3) the basis for trust (not the crisis itself but Yahweh's character, for example), (4) a petition, (5) a vow to praise the Lord or offer a sacrifice of thanksgiving, and (6) an interior lament (which specifies or alludes to the occasion that has taught the psalmist to trust). Individual psalms of trust are Psalms 4; 16; 23; 27; 62; and 73. Community psalms of trust include Psalms 90; 115; 123; 124; 125; and 126.[a]

[a] Bullock, *Encountering*, 166–76.

Lord: "portion," "lot," "boundary lines," and "inheritance" (Ps. 16:5–6).

Interpretive Insights

Title *A miktam.* Occurring here for the first time in the Psalter, this term also occurs in the headings of Psalms 56–60. Here and in Psalm 60 it is literally "a *miktam* for/to David," while in Psalms 56–59 the order is "for/to David a *miktam*." Rashi leans toward the idea of a literary style,[4] and Delitzsch moves in a similar direction, noting that the *miktam* has two literary features: (1) memorable expressions are sometimes introduced by the verbs "he spoke," "and he said," and "I said"; (2) and sometimes these expressions are used as a refrain (Pss. 56:4, 11; 57:5, 11; 59:9b–10a, 17).[5]

16:1 *in you I take refuge.* The metaphor of refuge seems to suggest the tradition of finding asylum in the sanctuary,[6] but it may also suggest a spiritual disposition.

16:2 *I say to the* LORD, *"You are my Lord."* Sometimes, as here and many other places, the generic term "lord, master" (*'adonay* = Lord, lowercase in English translations) occurs in place of the tetragrammaton (*YHWH* = LORD, small caps in English translations). Here it is parallel to the shortened generic *'el* ("God," 16:1; rather than *'elohim*). Both designate the all-powerful God of the Old Testament.

apart from you I have no good thing. The Hebrew preposition behind "apart from" is "over" or "upon" (*'al*). While the NIV emends the text to read "apart from you . . . no" (*bal bil'adeyka*), A. A. Anderson suggests "my welfare surely (rests) upon you (alone)."[7] "Good" occurs in contrast to the sorrows of verse 4 and is equivalent to "my portion and my cup" (16:5) and "delightful inheritance" (16:6).[8] A similar sentiment occurs in Psalm 73:25: "Whom have I in heaven but you?" The whole of the psalmist's "good" includes the experience of walking in the path of life until David is satiated with the joys of being in God's presence.

16:3 *of the holy people who are in the land . . . "They are the noble ones."* These very difficult verses are generally viewed in one of two ways. The first approach views verse 3 as an affirmation of the loyal devotion of the psalmist expressed in verses 1 and 2. The NIV adopts this approach, adding "I say" in verse 3, assuming that the "I

say" that begins verse 2 still applies to verse 3. That means that the "holy ones" of verse 3 (NIV: "holy people," *q^edoshim*) would be the faithful Israelite believers ("saints"), thus reaffirming the suppliant's devotion. The translation of verse 3 then, looking back to verses 1 and 2 (the conjunctive approach), would be as follows: "Concerning the saints who are in the land, that is [Hebrew conjunction *waw*], the noble ones in whom is all my delight" (author's trans.). The NIV, ESV, and ASV, for example, espouse this hermeneutic.

Other interpreters look at verse 3 as a reference to idolatry. This approach is based largely on two considerations. First, verse 4 clearly deals with idolatrous practices, since "libations of blood" are not practiced in Israelite worship. Second, in Ugaritic literature the word *q^edoshim* (NIV: "holy people") often means "gods" and is used as a synonym of the word for gods (*'elim*). Therefore, these interpreters disjoin verse 3 from verses 1 and 2 (disjunctive approach) and insist that verse 3 is facing on toward verse 4 and the idolatrous practices alluded to there. The "holy ones" (NIV: "holy people") would then be idols, and "the noble ones" (or "mighty ones") would be their devotees. This understanding would require a translation similar to the JPS: "As to the holy and the mighty ones that are in the land, my whole desire concerning them is that those who espouse another [god] may have many sorrows!" Thus verses 3 and 4 distance the worshiper from idolatry, which is affirmed in v. 4b–c. Then in verse 5 the psalmist appeals again to the exclusive worship of Yahweh that he has espoused in verse 2, acknowledging that the Lord alone is his "portion" and "cup." Based on the language of the text, either interpretation is possible, but an overdependence on the Ugaritic language makes this interpreter a bit uncomfortable, and therefore I would prefer the former hermeneutic.[9]

16:4 *Those who run after other gods will suffer more and more.* The suffering here likely refers to the sorrows of human existence, perhaps a metaphorical allusion to the "sorrows" or "pains" of childbirth pronounced as a curse upon Eve (Gen. 3:16, from the same Hebrew root; also Ps. 147:3 [NIV: "wounds"] and Job 9:28 [NIV: "sufferings"]). These became the symbol of creation's "pains" that anticipate and herald the coming of redemption (Rom. 8:22–23). A literal translation would be, "Their sorrows will increase; they run after another ["god" is implied]."

libations of blood . . . their names. The major sacrifices were sometimes accompanied by libations, but never blood libations. These are either libations associated with bloody sacrifices (the blood was "poured out") or libations made by individuals who had blood on their hands.[10] In view of my preference for the first interpretation above (see the comments on 16:3),

I would then choose the first option. Also, "their names" refers to the names of the gods.

16:5 *you alone are my portion and my cup . . . my lot.* "Portion" reflects the appointment of the Levites for service in the tabernacle, which also denied them landed property, because the Lord was their "portion" (Num. 18:20; Deut. 10:9; 18:1). The word "cup" is metonymy for the food and drink that sustain individuals, and the word "lot" perhaps is an allusion to the practice of casting lots that determined the tribal claims (Josh. 14:2).

16:6 *The boundary lines . . . in pleasant places; . . . a delightful inheritance.* The "boundary lines" refer to the survey of the land to mark off tribal inheritances (Josh. 17:5; NIV: "tracts") and is used metaphorically to describe the fellowship with God that the psalmist enjoys (see also Mic. 2:5). The term for "pleasant places" is parallel to "a delightful inheritance" in the second half of the verse. The Hebrew word for

Suffering is one of the penalties of running after other gods. One of the gods that the Israelites worshiped was Baal. This stele found at Ras Shamra depicts Baal (fifteenth to thirteenth century BC).

Psalm 16

"pleasant places" is from the same root as the "pleasures" David enjoys in the Lord's presence (16:11). The overtones of 1 Samuel 26:19 may be heard in the phrase "delightful inheritance," where David complains that Saul has driven him away from his rightful "inheritance" (see "Historical and Cultural Background"). Here the word is metaphorical for the covenant relationship that David and Israel enjoy. The word translated as "delightful" has the basic sense of "rub" in order to make smooth, and thereby shiny and beautiful.[11]

16:8 *I will not be shaken.* This verb is a connecting link for Psalms 15 (15:5), 16 (16:8), and 17 (17:5; NIV: "stumbled"). Its root meaning is "to move, stumble, totter," and by negation suggests stability and security (see the comments on Ps. 15:5).[12]

16:9 *my tongue.* The Hebrew has "my glory," and the Septuagint has "my tongue." Calvin accepts the Septuagint reading in deference to the use of the same word, "my glory" (*kᵉbodi*), in Genesis 49:6 (NIV: "me"), which seems to carry the sense of speech (in the assembly).[13]

16:10 *not abandon me to the realm of the dead, nor will you let your faithful one see decay.* "Realm of the dead" is *shᵉ'ol* in Hebrew, the state of death.[14] Whatever circumstances David has faced, they threatened death, and he is now assured that he will not die, or if he does, the Lord will not abandon him. "Your faithful one" is translated as "Holy One" (capitalized) in the KJV and NASB, suggesting a prophetic reference to Jesus Christ, as Peter (Acts 2:25–28) and Paul (Acts 13:35–37) understood it (see "The Text in Context"). The historical meaning, however, is David himself.

The Hebrew word for "decay" is "corruption" (*shahat*).[15] This suggests the decay of the body and probably means that God will not allow the psalmist to experience premature death. In comparison, the Septuagint has "decay" (*diaphthora*) and in that sense means the decomposition of the body. As a reference to the resurrection of Jesus, the Septuagint is an easier reference, which only "made it marginally easier to interpret the psalm as referring to the actual destruction of the human body in the grave."[16]

16:11 *path of life . . . joy in your presence.* The phrase "path of life" belongs also to the language of wisdom (Prov. 2:19 [pl.]; 5:6; cf. 10:17; see also Matt. 7:14). It is life from God, with God, and in God (Deut. 30:15), who is life itself,[17] and it climaxes in the presence of God. "Your presence" is literally, "your face." In the Old Testament seeing God's face was so awesome that it carried the penalty of death (Exod. 33:20). Yet that continued to be the spiritual aspiration of the great worthies of faith, to see God's face and live. Historically speaking, this is a reference to worship in the temple (Ps. 11:7), and in the history of redemption it is symbolic of the ultimate state when believers will see God's face (Rev. 22:4).

eternal pleasures at your right hand. The term "right hand" is a metaphor of privilege and authority (see Gen. 48:12–20; Pss. 109:31; 110:5; 121:5). Perowne, among others, understands this text to reveal a hope, even promise, of eternal life.[18]

Theological Insights

If the progression of Psalms 14–16 in the canonical order reflects the mind of the editor of Book 1—and I think it does—the worshiper of Psalm 16 is already in God's presence in the temple or tabernacle, having passed through the gate of the Lord's house in Psalm 15. Leaving behind the worries and cares of the world that have troubled him, he comes to this plateau of faith and prays, "You satisfy [pres. ptc.] me with joy in your presence" (16:11b, author's trans.).

Whatever the psalmist's circumstances, he implies that some danger is lurking in his world: "Keep me safe, my God" (16:1); and in the concluding prayer he testifies to an answer to his supplication, since he is assured that God will not abandon him to the grave (16:10–11). Hardly has he offered his petition before he lays out the major premise of his faith, "You are my Lord; apart from you I have no good thing" (16:2). Metaphorically, Yahweh is the psalmist's

"good," his "portion," "cup," and "lot" (16:5), meaning that what worldly possessions are to some, Yahweh is that and more to him. The journey from the world's foolishness (Ps. 14) along the road of righteousness (Ps. 15) into the presence of God (Ps. 16) has left the world's attractions farther and farther behind, until David can say, "Apart from you I have no good thing."

David acknowledges that the Lord is his "delightful inheritance" (16:6). Contained in the word "inheritance" (*nahalah*) is a sense of the past, a sense of belonging, of a permanent home. David has found that in the Lord, and it corresponds to the "pleasant places." It is in the light of the "pleasant places" and "delightful inheritance" that we are to understand the psalmist's joy of being in the Lord's presence (16:9, 11).

The "path of life" (16:11) that the Lord has made known to David is so real that he cannot imagine being abandoned to death. This phrase occurs in wisdom literature (Prov. 5:6; 6:23; 10:17; 15:24) and has the sense of a full life of joy that only those who have achieved wisdom can experience.[19] We should note that it is the "path of life" that leads to joy in the Lord's presence and "eternal pleasures" at his right hand (16:11). While we look toward the "eternal pleasures," we cannot afford to miss the joy of the journey. In fact, the "pleasant places" that the psalmist has experienced in this world (16:6) and the "pleasures" at God's right hand come from the same Hebrew root (see the comments on 16:6). It may not be an overstatement to say that the "pleasant places"—those the psalmist experiences along the way—are an adumbration of the "eternal pleasures" in God's presence. So we dare not miss them as we travel. One is reminded of the concept of eternal life in John's Gospel. It is a present reality that comes to eternal maturity in the afterlife.

Teaching the Text

To build our sermon/lesson, we may speak about David's spiritual modus operandi: "I have set the LORD always before me; because he is at my right hand, I shall not be shaken" (16:8 ESV). David's spiritual journey was characterized by joy: "Therefore my heart is glad and my tongue rejoices" (16:9a). And the destination was to celebrate the Lord as his "delightful inheritance" (see "Theological Insights"). Thus the outcome was a life about which he could say: "LORD, you alone are my portion and my cup" (16:5a). It is another way to say: "Love the LORD your God with all your heart and with all your soul and with all your strength" (Deut. 6:5). Calvin draws the conclusion that "none are taught aright in true godliness but those who reckon God alone sufficient for their happiness."[20] David rose above his world of sexual sin, personal guilt, war, and family strife to a journey of faith that drew him irresistibly toward God. In fact,

1 Samuel tells us that what God was looking for in a king, he found in David, "a man after his own heart" (1 Sam. 13:14).

This psalm draws a contrast between those who "run after other gods" (16:4a) and those who have chosen the Lord as their portion and cup (16:5). We can draw an illustration from Israel's history, especially seen through the eyes of the prophets. Hosea puts the story in the form of marriage and divorce, and ultimately God's reconciliation with unfaithful Israel. The outline of that history lies behind the theology of this psalm. Our temptation is to move from monotheistic belief to polytheistic practice, and we must constantly examine how our faith conforms to our practice.

A logical step in our discourse is to draw attention to the joy that the psalmist finds in God's presence (16:11). The suppliant draws out the correlation between one's fidelity to God and the joy that one finds in that relationship: the greater one's faithfulness, the greater one's joy. Even the "path of life," that is only speckled with joy, merges into the joy of God's presence and leads

Even as David prayed for the Lord to keep him safe (16:1), he recognized that with the Lord at his right hand he need not be afraid. This is a military picture. A bodyguard would stand to the right of the king, his shield in his left hand to protect the king and his sword in his right to defend the king. In Assyrian battle reliefs, like the one shown here, warriors are often shown fighting in pairs. One is actively using his weapon, while the other is offering protection with a shield (Nimrud, 865–860 BC).

all the way into eternal pleasures at God's right hand (16:11).

Illustrating the Text

The journey matters as much as the destination.

Personal Testimony: A pastor was leading a group of high school students on a backpacking trip. Being a prudent planner, he had two scoutmasters and an Eagle Scout on the trip to ensure the safety of the students. Wanting to show his value to the team, the pastor went out front to blaze the trail, to show the scouts that he could read the map and stay on the trail. Hiking at a rapid pace, he arrived at the day's destination long before the scouts. Puffing up with pride, the pastor asked the scouts as they arrived, "What took you so long?" The scouts merely smiled and complimented him. A little later one of the scouts asked the pastor what he thought about the American bald eagles that had been flying overhead. Another scout asked him what he thought about the beautiful redwood trees. Still another asked if he had stopped to see the trout that the fishermen along the river had caught. The pastor had to admit he had not seen any of this. Why? Because he was so focused on the destination that he missed the value of the journey! So often we become so enamored with our goals and destination that we do not pay attention to the journey. As we see in the book of Exodus, the journey matters as much to God as does the destination.

Be fully devoted to the Lord.

Hymn: "Forth in Thy Name," by Charles Wesley. This hymn is largely based on Psalm 16:2, 8, and 11. Through this hymn Wesley expresses his dedication to Christian discipleship and service. The central theme of the hymn is devotion to God alone in all our work. The first stanza expresses this well:

> Forth in thy name, O Lord, I go,
>   My daily labour to pursue;
>   Thee, only thee, resolved to know,
>   In all I think, or speak, or do.

Charles's brother John shared this commitment to complete dedication; he wrote, "I determined, through His grace, to be all devoted to God, to give Him all my soul, my body, and my substance."[21] The hymn "Forth in Thy Name" also captures the spirit of Psalm 16 in its final stanza:

> For thee delightfully employ
>   Whate'er thy bounteous grace hath
>   given,
> And run my course with even joy,
>   And closely walk with Thee to
>   heaven.[22]

This hymn provides an opportunity to challenge listeners to consider what idols (see 16:4) might keep them from being fully devoted to the Lord.

"When I Awake, I Will Be Satisfied with Seeing Your Likeness"

Big Idea *When we encounter false accusations, through faith we hope to awake in the wonder of God's likeness, which is true reality.*

Understanding the Text

Some scholars identify Psalm 17 as a prayer of innocence, based particularly on 17:3–5.[1] Others, in view of 17:1–2 and 6–9, consider it an individual lament. While the categories of form criticism are helpful, the psalmists were not working with those categories as such, and they were sometimes inclined to mix genres. Obviously the psalmist is lamenting false accusations by his enemies (17:10–12), and although he does not receive the answer he asks for, he is confident he will (17:15).

The Text in Context

We have already observed that Psalms 15, 16, and 17 are tied together with the thread of the verb "to totter, be shaken, stumble," expressing the psalmist's confident faith in God (15:5; 16:8; 17:5; see the comments on 16:8). In our discussion of Psalm 16, we noted a progression from the atheistic claim of the fool in Psalm 14, to the searching spirit of Psalm 15, to the confident claim that there is no life apart from

God in Psalm 16. Psalm 17 seems to lead the reader down the other side of a bell-shaped collection to consider the wicked again, as in Psalm 14. But this time in the light of the ecstatic reality of seeing God's face, this poem sustains the theological momentum attained in Psalm 16:11. It has the effect of showing how truly foolish evildoers are, that they would exchange the joy and peace of God's presence for the transitory pleasure and power of evil.

The shared ideas of Psalms 16 and 17 are worth noting:

Psalm 16	Psalm 17
"For in you I take refuge" (16:1)	"Those who take refuge in you" (17:7)
"Even at night my heart [*kelayot*; lit., "kidneys"] instructs me" (16:7)	"Though you probe my heart [*leb*], though you examine me at night" (17:3)
"With him at my right hand, I will not be shaken [*mut*]" (16:8)	"My steps have held to your paths; my feet have not stumbled [*mut*]" (17:5)

Metaphorically, Psalm 17 is a good illustration of how the Psalms draw on other portions of Scripture, citing terms from Deuteronomy 32:10–11 (Song of Moses; Ps. 17:8) and Numbers 10:35 (Ps. 17:13).

Outline/Structure

The psalm is a single prayer, divided into its distinctive parts:

A prayer . . .
1. For God's vindication (17:1–5)
2. For God's intervention (17:6–9)
3. For God's deliverance from enemies (17:10–14)
4. Of assurance (17:15)

Historical and Cultural Background

In those legal cases that were too difficult for the courts, individuals could go to the temple and appear before the priest or

Key Themes of Psalm 17

- Speech can be an instrument of righteousness.
- Moral uprightness, while not obligatory, matters at the throne of grace.
- Wake up to God's likeness.

the judge and receive his decision (Deut. 17:8–13). Some scholars propose that Psalm 17 reflects such an instance, and the defendant stayed overnight to receive the decision the next morning (17:3, 15).[2]

The form critics are inclined to date this psalm in the late preexilic or early postexilic era, assuming that the psalmist is in the temple (17:3) awaiting his answer.[3] However, the psalmist's location is not clear, and it is hard to find substantive reasons for denying the psalm to David. Delitzsch suggests that David wrote the psalm out of his experience in the Desert of Maon when he barely escaped Saul's pursuit (1 Sam. 23:24–28).[4] On that occasion Saul's troops surrounded David, paralleling the psalmist's description of his enemies (17:9).

The imagery of the eagle protecting her young (17:8b) is a frequent metaphor in the Psalms.[5] Some would link it to the cherubim in the tabernacle/temple,[6] but the plausibility that it is an echo of Deuteronomy 32:11 supports nature as its source, as is definitely the case in the Song of Moses. The presence of lions (17:12) in the ancient Near East is well attested, and the Psalms often compare the psalmist's enemies to lions (e.g., Ps. 7:2).[7]

"Hear me, LORD. . . . Hear my prayer" (17:1). This fifteenth-century AD illumination by Willem Vrelant from the Arenberg Hours shows David in prayer (ms. Ludwig IX 8, fol. 163, J. Paul Getty Museum).

Psalm 17

Interpretive Insights

Title *A prayer of David.* "Prayer" is the Hebrew word *t^epillah*, which occurs in Psalm 72:20 to designate the first two Davidic collections (Books 1 and 2, Pss. 1–72). "Psalm" is the traditional translation. As the designation of a single psalm, it occurs in the titles of Psalms 17; 86; 90; 102; and 142, and once as "A prayer of Habakkuk" (Hab. 3:1), suggesting perhaps that this word designates a particular type of psalm. However, the word occurs in various contexts as a general designation of prayer (as Ps. 72:20 implies), and we should probably understand it in that sense.

17:1 *my plea is just . . . my cry.* The word "just" or "righteousness" (*tsedeq*) forms an *inclusio* (17:1 and 15), suggesting that the entire thought of the psalm is framed by the psalmist's righteousness. The supplicant begins by asking God to hear his righteous plea (lit., "hear, O Lord, righteousness"). In the psalm he profiles his innocence: his prayer "does not rise from deceitful lips" (17:1); "my mouth has not transgressed" (17:3); "I have kept myself from the ways of the violent" (17:4). Predominantly, then, he defines his righteousness in terms of speech. That is also the way David describes the person who is permitted to enter the sanctuary, again a description of the righteous person (15:2c–3a). The Hebrew word for "cry" (*rinnah*) most likely denotes a sung prayer, sometimes lamentive and sometimes joyful.[8]

17:2 *Let my vindication come from you.* This is the language of the law court used in the Psalms and the Prophets to speak of God as the dispenser of justice.

17:3 *Though you probe my heart . . . examine me at night.* The verbs "probe" (*bhn*; lit., "test") and "examine" (*pqd*) are parallel, describing God's scrutiny of the psalmist's moral profile (also 17:1b).

though you . . . test me, you will find that I have planned no evil. Just as silver or gold is refined by repeating the process, so God has applied his moral purifying process until all the impurities are eliminated (see Zech. 13:9 and "Historical and Cultural Background" in the unit on Ps. 12). The Hebrew verb for "planned" means "to muzzle" and denotes "I have silenced myself."[9] The ESV translates, "you have tested me and found nothing; I have purposed that my mouth will not transgress."

17:4 *Though people tried to bribe me.* The NIV has translated the initial words (ESV: "With regard to the works of man") as "Though people tried to bribe me," in an attempt to remove an ostensible contradiction (lit., "Concerning the works of man, by the word[s] of your lips I have indeed kept the paths of the violent"). Obviously it contradicts the claim to innocence in verse 3, and the parallel line in verse 5 says just the opposite, which is precisely what we would expect an innocent person to say. Delitzsch's solution is quite satisfactory. Taking the prefixed preposition "though" (or "for", Heb. letter *bet*) as introducing a difficulty, he then understands "by the word of your lips" as an allusion to God's word, which has been the strength by which he has guarded (*shmr*, "to guard" or "be careful"; NIV: "kept") his steps against the influences of the wicked: "Notwithstanding the doings of men, by the word of Thy lips I have guarded myself against the way of the violent."[10] That makes the parallel thought of 17:5 an affirmation of 17:4b–c.

17:5 *My steps have held to your paths.* The word "steps" comes from a verb "to step." The noun occurs in Psalm 40:2 (NIV: "place to stand") and the verb in Proverbs 4:14 (NIV: "walk"). The Hebrew verb for "held" (*tmk*) is an infinitive absolute used in place of the first common singular ("I have held fast").[11] Calvin understands "your paths" to be a metaphor for the law,[12] which is quite possible, especially since the ninth commandment ("you shall not give false testimony against your neighbor," Exod. 20:16) seems to stand behind the psalm.

17:6 *my God.* As in Psalm 16:1, the divine name is *'el*, the abbreviated form of *'elohim*. See Moses's prayer in Numbers 12:13.

17:7 *Show me the wonders of your great love.* This verse is packed with the vocabulary of the psalmist's faith. First, the verb "show the wonders" (Hiphil of *pl'*) means to perform wonders or mighty acts. Its noun means "wonders" or "miraculous acts." Here David prays for God to act in the same miraculous power that he displayed before the patriarchs, matriarchs, and Israelites in Egyptian slavery (Gen. 18:14, "Is anything too hard [too wonderful] for the LORD?"). Second, God's "great love" (lit., "your loves") is in the Hebrew a plural of intensity (thus "great") and is the foundational term of Yahweh's covenant with Israel (*hesed*). The extension of this idea in the New Testament is God's love (*agapē*). Third, the participle of the verb "to save" is here a noun, "Savior" (the NIV translates it verbally, "you who save"). The ESV renders it as a direct address: "Wondrously show your steadfast love, O Savior of those who seek refuge from their adversaries at your right hand." In the Psalms

As the psalmist reflects on God's actions on behalf of his people, he asks God to once again show his wondrous power. One such marvelous work was the provision of a son to Abraham and Sarah in their old age. This mosaic shows Abraham's hospitality to the three visitors who reveal that Sarah would give birth to a son (Basilica of Santa Maria Maggiore, Rome, Italy, fifth century AD).

it primarily connotes the one who saves from evil circumstances and persons, but, as Kidner observes, this concept "can pass readily into the spiritual realm, as in 51:12, 14."[13] Fourth, the participle "those who take refuge" is a verb that is characteristic of the psalms of trust, and other contexts as well, describing Yahweh's role as protector and closely allied with his role as Savior. Fifth, the final term of the verse in Hebrew, "your right hand" (NIV has rearranged the verse), is equivalent to "your power," the right hand being God's strong hand.

17:8 *the apple of your eye . . . the shadow of your wings.* The metaphor "apple of your eye" (lit., "apple of the daughter of [your] eye") clearly refers to something very precious to the Lord—here to the psalmist himself, but in Deuteronomy 32:10 to Israel, and in Proverbs 7:2 to the Torah. Generally this is understood as the "pupil," and the Hebrew word may mean "little man" (*'ishon*), as is reflected in the pupil of one's eye when looking at another person.[14] This metaphor and "the shadow of your wings" are found together in the Song of Moses (Deut. 32:10–11), with which the psalmist is probably familiar (see also Pss. 36:7; 57:1; 63:7; 91:4).

17:10 *They close up their callous hearts.* Literally, "They close up their own fat." In ancient times fat was considered a symbol of stupidity, arrogance, and rebellion (Ps. 119:70; Isa. 6:10; Job 15:27).[15]

17:12 *They are like a lion hungry for prey.* The verb translated as "hungry" means "to be eager,"[16] and, metaphorically, it describes the ravenous assault of the enemies (Pss. 7:2; 10:9; 22:13).

17:13 *Rise up, LORD.* See Numbers 10:35 (see also "Teaching the Text" in the unit on Pss. 9–10).

17:14 *By your hand save me . . . from those of this world whose reward is in this life.* This verse is difficult. Judging from the request of verse 13, it seems to be a continuation of that thought, that God would deliver the psalmist from the wicked people who have set their sights on his downfall. "World" (*heled*) is used poetically of this world (Ps. 49:1), but the term is sometimes translated "life" or "lifespan" (Pss. 39:5 [NIV: "span of my years"]; 89:47; Job 11:17). Perowne calls attention to the contrast between the people of this world "whose reward is in this life" and those who have raised their sights above the purely fleshly pursuits of this life.[17]

17:15 *when I awake . . . seeing your likeness.* Either the psalmist is speaking of waking up in the temple to hear the judicial decision that awaits him, or he is speaking of waking from death. If this is a reference to life after death, then the difficulties of 17:14 are partly resolved—he is contrasting the life of the wicked in this world with that of the righteous who have hope in the world to come (Job 19:25–27).

The enemies of the psalmist are described as lions hungry for prey. This register from the Black Obelisk of Shalmaneser III (858–824 BC) shows a lion pursuing a stag.

The Scriptures instruct us that Moses saw "the form [t*emunah*] of the LORD" (Num. 12:8), the same word used for "likeness" in 17:15. David may very well have Moses's experience in mind to describe his own communion with God.

Theological Insights

Drawing upon the "Key Themes," we may observe that the psalmist considers right speech as an instrument of righteousness. As the book of Proverbs attests, the power of speech can build up or tear down (e.g., Prov. 6:12–15; 18:6–7, 21). The power of the ninth commandment (Exod. 20:16) lies behind this psalm.

God's "great love" (17:7; lit., "your loves") is code language for the covenant between Yahweh and Israel. When David prays, "Show me the wonders of your great love [*hesed*]" (17:7a), this is covenant language, which draws upon the wonderful and mighty acts of God in history. These words summon the Old Testament story of redemption, from the patriarchs to deliverance from Egyptian bondage and beyond. This language is born out of an intimacy between God and Israel and, in the case before us, between God and the psalmist. Only one who enjoyed this intimacy could make such a bold request of God (there is no defiance here).

The concluding idea of satisfaction upon awaking in God's likeness (17:15) can have a historical and an eschatological explanation. While this may not be the doctrine of the resurrection or the afterlife, as we have in Daniel 12:2 and Job 19:26–27, in the progress of revelation it merges into that doctrine. Kidner states this theological truth eloquently: "This superb verse soars straight up from the prosperous lowlands of verse 14, where all was earthbound."[18]

Teaching the Text

We can prepare a lesson/sermon on the idea of whether our moral condition matters when we pray. Admittedly if moral perfection were the requirement for God to hear our prayers, we would all be at a great loss at the throne of grace, some more than others. However, in light of Psalm 17 our moral condition is not an entirely negligible factor when we pray. James certainly affirms that principle: "The prayer of a righteous person is powerful and effective" (James 5:16).

First, we should look at the psalmist's relationship to God, which is characterized by two conditions: obedience and love. The psalmist goes to God in prayer with a clear conscience. He even calls his prayer "righteousness" (see the comments on 17:1), which means it grows out of a right relationship with God and with his fellow human beings. His prayer does not rise out of "deceitful lips," since he has been careful about how he has represented his neighbor (17:1b), and his speech has not been sinful (17:3). Moreover, he has treated his neighbor with respect and has not engaged in violent actions (17:4). Thus, the psalmist believes that this right character gives him an advantage in prayer. In fact, should the Lord want to conduct his own thorough examination, he would find nothing against the suppliant (17:3).

Yet we should stress that the psalmist is not totaling up his merits, demanding that God honor his prayer on that basis. Rather he speaks about the good life that God respects because it is what God commands.

We would do well to take this kind of inventory of ourselves from time to time, especially during a time of self-examination, like the Lenten season.

Second, the psalmist's requests that the Lord keep him as "the apple of your eye" and hide him under "the shadow of your wings" (17:8) are requests that grow out of the intimate relationship God has with him, the imagery being based in God's relationship with Moses (Deut. 32:10–11). In these petitions the psalmist draws upon God's covenant grace, reminding us that divine grace is written in God's saving acts in history. And just as Israel drew upon the Sinai covenant and Yahweh's saving acts on their behalf, Christians draw upon the saving grace of Calvary and the resurrection, recognizing that they are an extension of Old Testament grace. Thus the psalmist's bold petitions arise much more out of the boldness of grace (*hesed*) than out of the suppliant's own righteous actions (Heb. 4:16). Yet, so confident is he in the grace of moral innocence that he also copies the words of Moses (Num. 10:35) to his own profile,

The psalmist asks for refuge from his enemies when he prays, "Hide me in the shadow of your wings" (17:8). The Egyptians captured an image of protective wings in this statue of Horus as a falcon standing above King Nectanebo II (360–343 BC).

requesting God's intervention (Ps. 17:13). It is a bold move, but God issues his facsimiles of grace in every age, based on his self-revelation in the wonderful deeds of salvation history. Based on this and many other psalms, it falls within the bounds of permissibility to review one's moral demeanor before God, so long as one acknowledges oneself, in the final analysis, to be ultimately the product of God's covenant grace.

Illustrating the Text

When wrongly accused, look to the Lord for vindication.

News Story: Just after 1 a.m. on July 27, 1996, a bomb exploded in Atlanta's Centennial Olympic Park. Richard Jewell was working as a private security guard at the park and helped lead many of the spectators to safety. He was called a hero. Then everything changed. A story was leaked to the papers that Jewell was not a hero but was actually the man who had planted the bomb. He was ridiculed by the media and followed by the FBI. It took many weeks of investigation before the FBI finally acknowledged that Jewell was not a suspect in the bombing. But Jewell's life changed forever. His attorney, Lin Wood, said, "It's a war! Why in this bevy of stories does not anyone point out the fact that Richard was a hero one day and a demon the next? They have destroyed this man's life!" When interviewed a decade later, Jewell confessed that he was still angry about the false accusation and the devastating impact it had on his life.[19] David was also falsely accused and suffered for many years. But David wisely looked to the Lord for vindication, as we see in Psalm 17.

God's love is powerful.

True Story: A high school student, Lori, was invited to church summer camp. Lori made it clear to the pastor that she was not a Christian and had no intention of becoming a follower of Jesus, and that she was not even going to bring a Bible to camp. Her goal was simply to spend time with her friends. Each morning at camp the students were sent off to spend an hour alone with the Lord. They were instructed to bring only their Bible with them. The first two days Lori took the time to lie down on her bunk and rest. But on the third day she borrowed a Bible and spent the entire quiet time reading it. That same day Lori sought out the pastor to tell him that she had given her life to Jesus. Surprised, the pastor asked her what happened. She said that during the quiet time she opened the Bible and read Psalm 17, and she felt that the Lord was speaking directly to her heart as she read the prayer of David in verses 7–8. Lori had come from a very difficult home and had longed to be loved by a father. As she read this psalm, she sensed the powerful love of the Father draw her to himself. There will be many in your congregation who, like Lori, are longing to be "the apple of God's eye" and who deeply desire to experience the wonders of his great love. Challenge your listeners to make this prayer of David their own prayer.

"I Love You, Lord, My Strength"

Big Idea *In David's life, as in ours, God shows himself to be powerful in deliverance and intimate in grace.*

Understanding the Text

Psalm 18 is generally classified as a royal psalm because it is attributed to King David and deals with his political and military victories. It has the features of an individual psalm of thanksgiving, including the report of the crisis, which has passed (18:4–19), and the vow to give thanks to the Lord (18:49).[1] Perhaps in the history of Psalms usage it functiond as an instrument of other kings to celebrate their victories as well.[2] The response in 18:46–50 indicates that it was used in the tabernacle and temple in a service of thanksgiving, with the congregation affirming the psalmist's thanksgiving.

The Text in Context

Psalm 18 and 2 Samuel 22 are virtual duplicates, with only minor variations.[3] Both texts may be taken from a common source, or one of them may be the original, but that is difficult to determine. The fact that the psalm is quoted in Proverbs 30:5 (18:30) and Habakkuk 3:19 (18:33) indicates that it is earlier than either of these. In addition, verse 31 contains echoes of the Song of Moses (Deut. 32:4, 31), holding the Lord up as Israel's Rock and declaring that there is no one else like him. Such stock phrases had become imbedded in the liturgical memory of Israel, and they contribute to the possibility that it is a genuine composition of David.

Set in the context of David's victories over Saul, as well as other enemies, 2 Samuel 5–20 is a special account of this period of conflict. It is possible that an early editor of Book 1, as the collection was beginning to form, installed Psalm 18 as a conclusion to an early "Davidic" collection, consisting of Psalms 3–17.

The apostle Paul quotes 18:49, along with other Old Testament texts,[4] as a prophecy

When David says, "I love you, Lord" (18:1), he is using a word for love that conveys a child's love for its mother. This figurine from Ur shows a mother holding her child (2000–1750 BC).

of the inclusion of the gentiles ("nations") into the gospel (Rom. 15:9–12).

Outline/Structure

Part 1 is framed by the verb "take refuge" (18:2 and 30), registering its total effect in the question that follows: "For who is God besides the Lord? And who is the Rock except our God?" (18:31). Part 2 (18:31–45) is the implicit answer to that question, articulating the response, "There is no god besides Yahweh."

Part 1 (18:1–30)
    a. Introductory hymn of praise (18:1–3)
    b. Account of the crisis (18:4–6)
    c. The theophany and rescue (18:7–19)
    d. The psalmist's righteousness (18:20–24)
    e. The Lord's response (18:25–30)
Part 2 (18:31–45)
    a. Confession of praise (18:31–36)
    b. David's rehearsal of his exploits (18:37–42)
    c. David's rehearsal of God's deliverance (18:43–45)
Doxology (18:46–50)

Historical and Cultural Background

David's conflict with Saul and his family was long and deep, and what had been a political and family feud in the first generations of the monarchy eventually became a mystery in the theological memory of Israel, especially the shift of the monarchy from the tribe of Benjamin (Rachel tribes) to the tribe of Judah (Leah tribes), a phenomenon dealt with in Psalm 78:67–72.

Key Themes of Psalm 18

- The Lord is mighty in power but personal in love.
- Righteousness is the standard of God's action.
- Obedience has rewards.
- The Lord lives.

Loving God and Keeping His Commandments

The commandment to love God, first made to Israel in Deuteronomy 6:5, is a huge order. But it comes out of the context of God's love for Israel (Deut. 7:7–11), which makes the order realistic—it is much easier to love a God who loves us. While Deuteronomy uses the verb "love" (*'hb*), David here takes a word from the vocabulary of motherly love (*rhm*). The echo we hear from this verb is that of the mother's love for her child, or the child's love for his or her mother. This relationship, unique in the human family, is one of the most intimate terms of covenant language. *Targum Onqelos* uses a verb from the same root (*rhm*) to translate the verb "love" (*'hb*) in Deuteronomy 6:5, suggesting that the Aramaic translator considered these verbs synonymous. The fact that this term is taken from covenant vocabulary, involving the covenant stipulations and promises, affirms the thought that the moral commandments of the Torah are summed up and fulfilled in the piety of the psalmist. The union of Torah precepts and spiritual devotion to God is attested also in the Ten Commandments (Exod. 20:5–6; Deut. 5:9–10): "for I, the Lord your God, am a jealous God, punishing the children for the sin of the parents to the third and fourth generation of those who hate me, but *showing love [hesed]* to a thousand generations *of those who love ['hb] me and keep my commandments*." Loving God and keeping his commandments are complementary. One cannot exist without the other (see 1 John 2:3–5).

Military language characterizes the psalm, especially 18:31–36, and in that respect confirms the information in the title.

Interpretive Insights

Title *the servant of the Lord.* The designation "servant of the Lord" is used of only three persons in the Old Testament—Moses, Joshua, and David—while others are called God's servants (e.g., "my servant Abraham," Gen. 26:24). It is applied to David here and at the beginning of Psalm 36.

when. The phrase "on the day" (e.g., RSV, ESV) should be taken not literally but as an adverb, "when," just like the same expression in Genesis 2:4. The psalm was written sometime after the crisis with Saul had passed.

18:1 *I love you.* The phrase "I love you" is not found in 2 Samuel 22:2. See the sidebar for a discussion of this verb.

18:3 *who is worthy of praise.* This passive participle ("praised," masc. sg. Pual) begins the verse, literally, "*Worthy to be praised*, I call upon the LORD."

18:4–5 *The cords of death . . . the cords of the grave.* The Hebrew word for "grave" is *sheʾol* (see the sidebar "Sheol" in the unit

on Ps. 6). The imagery is that of a hunter who lays his traps to snare his prey.

18:6 *I called to the* LORD; *I cried to my God for help. From his temple he heard.* While the word for "called" is the normal Hebrew verb for "cry out" (*qrʾ*), the word for "cried for help" means "to cry out in prayer" (*shwʾ*).[5] The Hebrew concept was that God dwelled in his heavenly temple.[6]

18:7 *The earth trembled and quaked.* This is the beginning of God's epiphany, described in terms of the revelation on Mount Sinai (Exod. 19:18–19), suggesting that "*all* his acts of salvation form a

> God's appearance in response to the psalmist's call for help is described similarly to God's coming before the Israelites at Mount Sinai. Thunder, lightning, thick clouds, fire, smoke, and earthquakes accompany God's presence. Jebel Musa, shown here, is the traditional Mount Sinai.

single, never-ending whole,"[7] extending from Moses to David, and beyond.

18:9 *He parted the heavens and came down.* The picture is of Yahweh bending the canopy of the sky toward the earth and descending on a platform of dark clouds.

18:10 *He mounted the cherubim and flew; he soared on the wings of the wind.* In Genesis 3:24 the "cherubim" were the guardians at the entrance of the garden. Here they are the drivers of God's chariot throne, as they are in Ezekiel 10. The invisible Lord mounted his chariot and flew with a strong tailwind at his back (see Ps. 99:1).

18:12 *Out of the brightness of his presence . . . bolts of lightning.* Even though darkness surrounds the invisible deity, his presence is represented by bright light. Out of his presence shoot forth streaks of light that remind the psalmist of streaks of lightning.

18:13 *The LORD thundered from heaven; the voice of the Most High resounded.* One of God's names is God Most High (*'el 'elyon*, or *YHWH 'elyon*; Pss. 7:17; 9:2; see "Theological Insights" in the unit on Ps. 7). God speaks in the thunder of nature.

18:16 *he drew me out.* The verb "drew" (*msh*) is used of taking Moses out of the Nile (Exod. 2:10), probably echoing God's mercy and power to save David like he saved Moses.

18:19 *he delighted in me.* Delitzsch calls this the "principal thought of the hymn."[8] This is an Old Testament version of "For God so loved . . ." (John 3:16).

18:20 *according to my righteousness.* See also 5:4–6; 17:1–5. Note the virtual duplicate of this statement in 18:24, the thought being that the psalmist has kept the Torah,

and this is the basis of his righteousness (see "Teaching the Text" in the unit on Ps. 17). This is a more general statement on Torah keeping than Psalm 15, and the psalmist draws out the meaning of the legal terms of 18:21–22 ("ways," "laws," "decrees") in the ethical blueprint of 18:25–29, spelling out the practical benefit of keeping the law in 18:29.

18:22 *laws . . . decrees.* "Laws" (*mishpatim*) and "decrees" (*huqqot*) are the terms of the written law (e.g., Deut. 26:17), suggesting that David knew the law, and also anticipating the description of the law in 19:7–11, where the ethical and personal dimensions of keeping the Torah are spelled out in inimitable language.

18:23 *I have been blameless before him.* See Deuteronomy 18:13; Psalm 15:2.

18:25–27 *To the faithful you show yourself faithful.* See "Theological Insights."

18:28 *my lamp.* God, through his law, is both the Enlightener and Enabler (18:29).

18:29 *With your help I can advance against a troop.* The benefit of keeping the Torah is not merely spiritual and ethical but includes the practical dimension of David's military valor.

18:30 *As for God, his way is perfect.* In 18:30, 32, and 47 the expression "the God," or "this God" (*ha'el*), stands at the beginning of the verse, drawing attention to God's awesome power, and functions as a *casus pendens* (that is, a pending case), "as for God." The fact that God's "way is perfect" (*tamim*) means that God is totally capable and unrelentingly reliable in his dealings with the psalmist. Proverbs 30:5 uses the language of this verse.

18:31 *For who is God besides the LORD?* This is not a rhetorical question, because

David answers it in military language with a description of what God does (18:32–36).

18:33 *He makes my feet like the feet of a deer.* The deer is known for its swiftness and sure-footedness.

18:35 *your help has made me great.* The Babylonian Talmud (*Megillah* 31a) draws attention to the contrast between God's sovereign might and his condescension.

18:37–42 *I pursued my enemies . . . in the streets.* Here the psalmist recounts his exploits in battle, enabled by the Lord himself, and observes that his enemies, whose prayer, says Delitzsch, "was wrung from them by their need,"[9] cried for help just like the psalmist did (18:41, same verb as in 18:6, *shw'*, meaning "to cry out in prayer"), but the Lord did not answer them.

18:46 *The Lord lives!* The Hebrew phrase "the Lord lives" (*hay-YHWH*; lit., "the life of Yahweh") usually is used as an oath ("as the Lord lives"), but here it is an exclamation. This is the climax of the psalm,[10] and the present reality of God's life extends its effects to David his servant in a very personal way. It is because God lives that David has been saved from Saul and his enemies (see title), and that the Lord mounted the cherubim's chariot, lit up the heavens with his fireworks of liberating power, and drew the psalmist out of deep waters. This truth is not confined to the halls of history. The participles and Hebrew imperfects of 18:46–50 affirm God's ongoing activity.

"He makes my feet like the feet of a deer" (18:33), swift, nimble, and sure footed. Fallow deer similar to these were common in the Middle East during the time of David.

18:47 *He is the God who avenges me.* Vengeance belongs to the Lord (Deut. 32:35) and is governed by justice, not vindictiveness.

18:50 *he shows unfailing love to his anointed.* This is a formulaic way to say that God is faithful to his covenant with Israel, and specifically with David, his anointed king (2 Sam. 7). Paul quotes this verse in Romans 15:9–11, along with Deuteronomy 32:43 and Psalm 117:1, as psalmic proof that salvation belongs to the gentiles as well as the Jews.

Theological Insights

The sentiment that positions the psalm theologically is David's opening words, "I love you, Lord, my strength." The psalmist's "righteousness"—in this case legal terminology ("the cleanness of my hands"), understood in the light of his personal love of the Lord (18:1)—is the reason for the Lord's favorable treatment of David (see the duplicate declaration of 18:20 and 24).

It is the precise mixture of law and piety to which we are introduced in Psalm 1. If this is the concluding psalm in an early Davidic collection, it is the editor's witness that David is truly the pious person described in Psalm 1 (see "The Structure and Composition of the Psalter" in the introduction).

David attributes his personal relationship to his "righteousness" (18:20, 24), which he defines in terms of keeping the law (Torah): "the ways of the LORD" (18:21), "all his laws," "his decrees" (18:22). And then he inserts the beautiful theological principle of 18:25–29. Yet it does not mean that we, by our own behavior, determine God's attitude toward us, but rather God responds to our behavior in appropriate ways: "To the faithful you show yourself faithful," and so on (18:25–29). That is, God rewards us in kind. In fact, keeping his commandments is our duty as God's servants, and God does not owe us anything for doing our duty. The image behind verses 25–27 is that of servant and master, but it does not define the totality of divine grace. In fact, the "faithful," "blameless," and "pure" are equipped by God's flawless word (vv. 30–36). While the language of this psalm is not strictly the New Testament notion of unmerited favor (which is not foreign to OT theology), the underlying grace of God meets individuals in their strength (vv. 25–29) as well as in their weakness (v. 36). Not included in this dimension is God's gift that is matched by no human obedience, which Paul expresses in his memorable words: "But God demonstrates his own love for us in this: While we were still sinners, Christ died for us" (Rom. 5:8).

Teaching the Text

We may begin a sermon/lesson by making two preliminary observations: (1) The entire poem is in the psalmist's voice, beginning with his explicit words, "I love you, LORD, my strength" (18:1). This affirmation is important because it sets the tone for the whole psalm. (2) We may also observe that this relationship of love is the highest level of devotion in Scripture, the goal of the spiritual life, both in the Old Testament and the New Testament (Deut. 6:5; 1 John 4:19). It is the characteristic that sets Christianity and Judaism off from all other religions.

Then, drawing upon the "Key Themes," the leader may present the main thrust of the psalm that is found in its two portraits of God, for the most part following the natural division of the psalm: *God who is mighty in power* and *God who is intimate in love*. We can stress the historical fact that David lived in a world of conflict like ours, but the portrait of the psalmist is that of a man who has fallen in love with God. Although the psalm is a celebration of victory in David's long struggle with domestic enemies, like Saul and Absalom, foreign enemies, like the Philistines, and personal enemies like himself, this affirmation of faith says much about the way he approached his problems and the way he trusted God to bring him through them. Putting our conflicts in the light of our love for God and his love for us should provide the context for confronting and dealing with life's issues.

To develop the point further, "God who is mighty in power" draws attention to the "conflict" mode in which the poem originates. We may stress the fact that terms for God were cut out of the fabric of his world (in military language: "my strength," "my rock," "my fortress," "my deliverer," "my shield," "the horn of my salvation" [18:1–2], and "Rock" [18:31]), not that he was pouring God into earthly vessels, but God had chosen to shape his revelation to those realities. The God of Scripture speaks also to us in the routine conflicts of our lives and teaches us that we can triumph through them and over them.

For some people, however, describing God in military terms may be a bit repulsive, since it raises so many questions about the ethical dimensions of war and nature. Yet God's accommodating of himself to the harsh realities of our world is not so much an endorsement of them as it is the reassurance of his presence with us in their midst. This is the place when the contextualizing thought of the psalm can be reintroduced: "I love you, LORD." We may conclude the lesson/sermon on the topic of grace (see the sidebar), emphasizing David's affirmation in the larger context of God's love for Israel corporately (Deut. 7) and for him personally (18:19; 91:14). Broadly speaking, we do not learn to love as much by loving as we do by being loved (1 John 4:19). It is mandatory, indeed, that we read the whole of Scripture in the context of God's love. When the Lord told Israel that he chose them only because he loved them, he intended for them to understand the covenant in light of his love. In a similar way, John puts the Christian gospel in the light of God's love (John 3:16), and Paul insists in his Letter to the Roman church that Israel's history, especially as represented by the gift of God's law, should be viewed in the context of God's love (Rom. 13:10).

Illustrating the Text

God is mighty in power.

Testimony: The intimacy of the Psalms provides a great opportunity to share stories of God's activity in the lives of people today. The God of the Psalms is the same God we worship today. He is the same yesterday, today, and forever. In order to communicate this reality it will be helpful to share personal stories from your life or the lives of people in your congregation who have experienced the God who is powerful in deliverance. Look for people who have stories to tell about how God delivered them from spiritual bondage, bitterness, brokenness, emotional struggle, relational turmoil, physical danger, financial stress, and so on.

Love is the frame of Scripture.

Bible: We have to read the whole of Scripture in the context of God's love. The standard "creed" of Israel's faith, the Shema (Deut. 6:5–8), commanded them to "love the LORD" with all their hearts. To show the reciprocity of that love, Deuteronomy informs us that the Lord chose Israel not because they were more numerous than other peoples but because he loved them (Deut. 7:7–8). John wrote that immortal text in chapter 3 of his Gospel to say that we have to view the life and death and resurrection of Christ in light of God's love (John 3:16). Jesus himself, when asked what is the greatest commandment, answers that it is to love God with all our heart (Matt. 22:37–40). Paul's rhapsody of love in 1 Corinthians 13 makes love the sine qua non of the Christian faith and comes close to John's declaration that "God is love" (1 John 4:8). And the doxology of the Revelation of John in 1:5, virtually forming the title page of the book, sets human history in the framework of God's love in Jesus Christ (Rev. 1:4–6). The whole of human history and the kingdom of God are framed in light of God's love. Love is reciprocal—God loves Israel and the world, and calls us to love God—setting Israel's faith apart from all others. In Psalm 18:1 David joins that innumerable chorus as he sings, "I love you, LORD."

Church History: Bernard of Clairvaux. Bernard (twelfth century) spoke of a four-step ladder of love, with a progression ranging from self-absorption (step 1), to God-absorption (step 3), to the ultimate state of human absorption in God (step 4):

1. We love ourselves for our own sake; then,
2. We love God for our own sake; then,
3. We love God for God's sake; then,
4. We love ourselves for God's sake only.[11]

In this fourth step we have fully devoted ourselves to God, choosing to deny ourselves, take up our cross, and follow him (Luke 9:23). Challenge your listeners to consider which rung of the ladder they are currently on and how they might go to the next step.

David uses military terms to describe God's power and might. Looking at the remains of the walled fortress city of Arad, shown here, gives visual meaning to David's declaration, "The LORD is . . . my fortress" (18:2).

"The Heavens Declare the Glory of God"

Big Idea *We see God's ubiquitous revelation in the world he created and his unique revelation in the Torah.*

Understanding the Text

The Text in Context

Mays has made a convincing case for the pairing of the Torah psalms (Pss. 1 and 2; 18 and 19; 118 and 119)[1] in order to present the eschatological kingdom of God, which will come in the context and through the instrumentality of Torah piety.[2] In the case of Psalm 18, David's deliverance from Saul is a foreshadowing of future salvation. Psalms 18 and 19 both give a picture of God's appearance, Psalm 18 in terms of the exodus and Sinai (18:7–15), and Psalm 19 in terms of the heavens' declaration of God's glory (19:1–6) and the Torah's enlightenment (19:7–11).[3]

When one should have expected the Lord to speak from his heavenly temple in 18:6b, David gave witness to the silent, yet powerful, voice of God that articulated God's mighty acts in David's time, akin to the mighty acts of God in the time of the exodus and Sinai (18:7–15). Again, in 19:1–4, rather than human speech, we hear God's voice in the wonders of nature.

Verbal links between Psalms 18 and 19 are the following:

Psalm 18	Psalm 19
"Servant of the LORD" (title)	"Your servant" (19:11, 13)
"[My] Rock" (18:2, 31, 46)	"My Rock" (19:14)
"Blameless"/"perfect" (*tamim*) (18:23, 25, 30, 32 [NIV: "secure"])	"Perfect" (*tamim*) (19:7)

At the same time there are verbal links between the two parts of Psalm 19:

The heavens speak a word (*'omer*, 19:2, 3)	Suppliant's *words* (*'emer*, same root, 19:14)
Nothing *hidden* (*nistar*) from the heat (19:6; NIV: "nothing is deprived of its warmth")	Asks forgiveness from *hidden faults* (*nistarot*, 19:12)

While we may suppose that these verbal links are mere coincidences that stem from the nature of the language, the frequently recurring pattern of verbal links in the Psalms is often part of the artistry of the psalmist, as it is here.

In Romans 10:18 Paul quotes Psalm 19:4 to answer his question "Did they [Israel] not hear?" and ratifies the divine message spoken universally by the heavens. In fact, this message, if not the word of Christ himself (see Rom. 10:17), is the penultimate word of God, spoken in the silent voice of the heavens, on the way to Christ.

Outline/Structure

Psalm 19 falls clearly into two strophes, with a concluding meditation:

Strophe 1: Creation's silent proclamation of God's voice (Word) (19:1–6)
Strophe 2: Torah's oral proclamation of God's Word (19:7–11)
Conclusion: The psalmist's reflection and prayer (19:12–14)

Historical and Cultural Background

Unlike Psalm 18 (18:50), David is mentioned only in the title of Psalm 19, but the similar phrases "servant of the LORD" and "your servant" may further link these poems together as Davidic psalms (see "The Text in Context").

Key Themes of Psalm 19

- The heavens are a silent witness to God's glory.
- The Torah is a vocal witness to God's glory.
- The Torah life is sweet.

Torah Psalms

The three psalms devoted to the Torah are Psalms 1; 19; and 119. Many other psalms express Torah theology: Psalms 18; 25; 33; 78; 89; 93; 94; 99; 103; 105; 111; 112; 147; and 148.[a]

[a] See Wenham, *Psalms as Torah*, and Bullock, *Encountering*, 214–26.

Interpretive Insights

19:1 *The heavens declare the glory of God*. Psalm 148:1 and 4 also picture the heavens praising God. They report in scribal fashion (*meṣapperim*), as if reading from the book of divine creation, because God has written his word there and they cannot refrain from proclaiming it. Note that the "heavens" (*shamayim*) and the "firmament" (*raqiʿa*; NIV: "skies") are parallel, as they are in Genesis (see esp.

David could have been remembering a similar view to the west when he composed the opening of Psalm 19, "The heavens declare the glory of God; the skies proclaim the work of his hands" (v.1). Here the photographer is looking west from the Mount of Olives over the Old City of Jerusalem.

Wedding/Marriage Ceremony in the Old Testament

We do not know a lot about the wedding ceremony in ancient Israel, even though marriage was the basic social institution. From the first allusion to marriage in Genesis (2:18, 23–24), the institution is associated with the payment of a *marriage gift* (*mohar*, Gen. 34:12; Exod. 22:17; 1 Sam. 18:25), paid by the groom to the bride's father, and the payment of a *dowry* by the bride's father to the groom's father (Gen. 16:1 implies that Hagar was part of Sarah's dowry), creating a reciprocal relationship between the two families. Feasting was attendant to the marriage ceremony, in some cases lasting one week (Gen. 29:22, 27–28; Judg. 14). Songs and music were also typical (Ps. 78:63; 1 Macc. 9:39; Song 4). *Betrothal* was as serious a commitment as the marriage itself (Deut. 22:23–24). The marriage consisted of two ceremonial acts: moving the bride into the husband's family's house, and the consummation of the marriage. The bridal *chamber* (*huppah*) was the place where the consummation took place. It is mentioned twice in the Old Testament, here in Psalm 19:5 and in Joel 2:15–16, where the bride must vacate her bridal "chamber" during a fast.[a]

[a] See Mary E. Shields, "Marriage, OT," *NIDB* 1:818–21.

Gen. 1:8, "God called the vault [*raqiʿa*] 'sky' [*shamayim*]"). The sense is similar to Ezekiel 43:2, where the "glory" of God alludes to the splendor and light of God's presence. Hakham observes that this verse "intimates that the light from the heavenly bodies is but a flicker of the wondrous light of God's glory."[4]

19:2 *pour forth.* The metaphor is the bubbling of a spring, which is the basic meaning of the verb translated as "pour forth" (see also Prov. 18:4, "rushing").[5]

19:4 *Yet their voice goes out into all the earth . . . In the heavens God has pitched a tent for the sun.* The word translated by the NIV as "their voice" (*qavvam*) is "measuring line" in Hebrew (thus KJV: "their line"). The NIV and other translations follow the LXX, which has "their voice" (*phthoggos*), which fits the context better. Some commentators see an underlying hymn to the sun in this poem (e.g., Weiser),[6] but the more likely background of the metaphor is the wedding festival, and the nuptial tent where the bride and groom consummated their marriage, or the bridal house from which the bridegroom departs (as the rising sun) to claim his bride.

19:5 *like a bridegroom coming out of his chamber . . . rejoicing.* Depending on how we understand the metaphor, the "chamber" (*huppah*, "tent"; see the sidebar "Wedding/Marriage Ceremony in the Old Testament") is either the nuptial tent or the home prepared for the bride. The word "rejoicing" (*yasis*) also carries the nuance "to move energetically."[7]

19:7 *The law of the LORD is perfect, refreshing the soul. The statutes . . . making wise the simple.* The "law" (*torah*) is a general term for God's self-revelation. It comes from a verb (*yrh*) that means "to point out" or "teach," thus giving us "instruction," a meaning the Prophets and Wisdom literature often give to the term (e.g., Ezek. 7:26; Prov. 13:14). This law is "perfect" (*temimah*, "whole" or "complete"; see comments on Ps. 15:2), "refreshing the soul" (Ps. 23:3 uses the same Hebrew terms). The Greek idea of "soul" is not intended here, but in Hebrew parlance, "soul" (*nepesh*) was the self or the essence of the person. The word translated "statutes" is really a singular noun (*ʿedut*), bearing the meaning of attested truth. In Exodus 25:16 it refers to the "testimony" (NIV: "tablets of the covenant law") placed in the ark. The Lord's statutes make the uninstructed ("the simple") wise.

19:8 *The precepts of the LORD are right, giving joy to the heart. The commands . . . light to the eyes.* The word "precepts" (*piqqudim*) carries the meaning of "regulations" (see, e.g., Ps. 103:18). These precepts are morally right and bring joy to the heart. The Lord's "commands" (sg. "commandment," *mitswah*) illuminate one's understanding ("eyes") just as the sun illuminates the world.

19:9 *The fear of the LORD is pure . . . The decrees of the LORD are firm . . . righteous.* Now David turns to the human response to God's law and describes it as "pure," with the same word that is used of something ceremonially "clean" (e.g., Lev. 10:10), used in a moral sense rather than ceremonial. Thus the fear of the Lord renders one acceptable to God. While the noun "decrees" (*mishpatim*) can mean judicial decisions, here it may be quite general, seeing that it concludes the six statements, which would correspond to the general nature of Torah in 19:7. The word "firm" (*'emet*) means "true" and signifies the reliability of the divine ordinances, which are both "true" and "righteous" (see Deut. 4:8). That is, they measure up to the standard of truth and righteousness.[8]

19:10 *more precious than gold, than much pure gold; they are sweeter than honey.* The worth of the Torah is communicated through universal metaphors: "more precious than gold" and "sweeter than honey." The Hebrew word for "precious" corresponds to the expression "pleasing to the eye" in Genesis (3:6; NIV: "desirable"). Gold was the most desirable real commodity of the ancient world. The second term for gold, "pure gold" (*paz*), is likely refined gold. Each phrase takes the thought further toward refinement, not just gold, but "much pure gold," not just honey, but "honey from the honeycomb."[9] There is some discussion about what kind of honey is in mind here, whether it was the product of bees or a fruit nectar. However, the story of Saul's son Jonathan eating honey attests to bees' honey in the time and place of this

The psalmist describes God's commands as "sweeter than honey, than honey from the honeycomb" (19:10). This replica shows what a beehive from the first century BC would have looked like.

psalm (1 Sam. 14:27; Judg. 14). Moreover, the problem seems to have been solved by the discovery of beehives at Tel Rehov in the Jordan Valley that date from the tenth to ninth centuries BC.[10]

19:12 *who can discern their own errors? Forgive my hidden faults.* English versions generally add the personal pronoun "his" or "their" before "errors," which is understood in Hebrew. Judging from the entreaty "Forgive my hidden faults" (lit., "Cleanse me from hidden [faults]"), David is alluding to his own sin.

19:13 *Keep your servant also from willful sins; may they not rule over me.* Note the title of Psalm 18, "servant of the LORD." "Willful" sins may be equivalent to the sins "with a high hand" (e.g., Num. 15:30 ESV; NIV: "defiantly") that were done out of willful disobedience. Sin seeks to "rule over" the individual, which may be an allusion to the Lord's instruction to Cain that he "must rule over it" (Gen. 4:7).

19:14 *LORD, my Rock and my Redeemer.* Above we observed that "Rock" as an epithet

The law, statutes, precepts, and commands of the Lord that are refreshing and trustworthy and bring wisdom, joy, and light were given by God as he revealed himself to Israel through Moses at Sinai. This section from the sarcophagus of Agape and Crescenziano (AD 330–360) shows Moses receiving the law. The law was so precious because, unlike the gods of the ancient world, the God of Israel told his people how to live to please him.

for God occurs in Psalm 18 (vv. 2, 31, 46; see "The Text in Context" in the unit on Ps. 18) and denotes the stability and solidity of God's care. The "redeemer" (*go'el*) was the next of kin who took measures to help a relative in trouble (see Job 19:25). As the psalmist prays that his words may be acceptable to God, he also affirms his faith in God's securing and redeeming power. Goldingay observes that this latter term, by its basic meaning, puts us in God's family and recognizes God's commitment to us.[11]

Theological Insights

Drawing upon the "Key Themes," we observe that the heavens silently declare God's glory in the everyday cadences of the cosmos (19:1). Verses 1–6 portray the Creator God of Genesis 1, who stands over and apart from his world. The only possible departure from this portrait is the personification of the sun that rises like a bridegroom from his tent and streaks across the sky in a parade of strength and joy to the other extremity of the firmament. Parallel to that universal witness is the Torah (19:7–11), which presents God's personal involvement with the world, as does Genesis 2–3, but with the Lord using the instrument of Torah to create human society. The Genesis narrative is so embedded in the psalmist's mind that his language echoes its vocabulary: "soul" (19:7; Gen. 2:7 [NIV: "being"]), "eyes" (19:8; Gen. 3:5–7), "precious" (19:10; Gen. 3:6 [NIV: "desirable"]), "gold" (19:10; Gen. 2:11).

The psalmist's reflections in 19:12–13, interestingly, focus

Table 1. The Torah Life in Psalm 19

Noun	Adjective	Participle	Genitive/Adverb	Verse
Torah/law (of the Lord)	Perfect	Refreshing	The soul	7a
Statutes (of the Lord)	Trustworthy	Making wise	The simple	7b
Precepts (of the Lord)	Right	Giving joy to	The heart	8a
Commands (of the Lord)	Radiant	Giving light to	The eyes	8b
Fear (of the Lord)	Pure	Enduring	Forever	9a
Decrees (of the Lord)	Firm		All of them are righteous	9b

on the power of sin, which is the center-piece of Genesis 2–3. As he contemplates his own sin, he even employs the verb that came to describe sin's overpowering force in the early history of the human family ("rule," 19:13; Gen. 4:7). The "hidden faults" (19:12; a synonym is used for "hid" in Gen. 3:8), the willful sins, and the great transgression (the latter two not specifically mentioned in Genesis) are echoes of the primordial fall. Now David faces the situation again on a personal scale.

For the most part, the nouns in verses 7–9, while they have their fine nuances, are synonyms of the Torah, with the exception of "the fear of the Lord" (which is the human response to God's instruction; 19:9). The adjectives are the pigments on the palette of the life of Torah, and the participles are the brush that paints the lovely portrait of the Torah life on the canvas described by the genitives and adverbs (see table 1). Kidner concludes: "Together, these terms show the practical purpose of revelation, to bring God's will to bear on the hearer and evoke intelligent reverence, well-founded trust, detailed obedience."[12] David estimates its value in terms of the world's most precious commodity (gold) to enrich life materially, and the sweetest delicacy (honey) to increase life's pleasure (19:10). This is the perfect life enabled by the perfect law.

The shift from the cosmos to humanity in 19:7 is no coincidence, for the psalmist highlights the power of the Torah to transform human life, and to ensure that the Torah rather than sin rules over life. This may be seen as an implicit application of the Torah (the spoken and written word of God) to the story of Genesis 2–3, which would have produced a totally different outcome. The Genesis story itself was a challenge to God's word ("Did God really say . . . ," Gen. 3:1). If the message of this psalm had been the answer that the woman gave the serpent, the history of humanity would have been radically different.

Teaching the Text

An obvious but easily overlooked feature of the text is the use of the divine names. "God" (*'el*, shortened form of *'elohim*) in 19:1 refers to the Creator of the world, reminding the reader of Genesis 1 (the longer form *'elohim* occurs there). Then, when the poem shifts to the meditation on the Torah, "Lord" (*YHWH*), the name of the covenant God, occurs seven times in verses 7–14. We can speak of the *transcendent* God of Genesis 1, who is distinct from creation, and the *immanent* God of Genesis 2–3, who enters into a personal relationship with creation through the covenant.

This can lead us into a brief discussion of the literary beauty and theological balance of the psalm. Lewis has called it "the greatest poem in the Psalter and one of the greatest lyrics in the world."[13] The theological balance brings the two concepts of the *creative word* (19:1–6) and *the redeeming word* (19:7–14) into perfect equilibrium.

The heart of the sermon/lesson may be articulated in the following two points, which are the central thrust of the psalm. First, David hears the voice of the *creative word*, or the voice of nature, God's creation. It is, in fact, a whole choir, singing the oratorio of creation (19:1–4), even though its audience is like the deaf Beethoven hearing the spiritual rather than the audible symphony. Paul confirms that in creation we can see that there is a God—his eternal power and deity (Rom. 1:20). The message of the planetarium choir, the multiple billions of celestial bodies, is this: the God of Scripture made the universe (Ps. 100:3).

We may point to the ageless human effort to equate the God of creation with the creation itself. Sinful human nature leans in the direction of pantheism. It is invoked in the temptation narrative: "The woman saw that the fruit of the tree was good for food and pleasing to the eye, and also desirable for gaining wisdom" (Gen. 3:6)—the fruit was virtually a substitute for God.

Second, we hear the voice of Scripture (19:7–11) informing us about what kind of God is the God who speaks in nature. John Calvin is attributed with the saying, "From nature we know only the hands and feet of God, but from Scripture we know His heart." The heavens cannot tell us that "God so loved the world, that he gave His only begotten Son" (John 3:16 KJV).

We can effectively emphasize here the transforming power of God's word and its value for life, illustrated by the two metaphors of gold and honey (see the comments on 19:10). As a further illustration, the leader may point to Ezekiel's consumption of the scroll, which left him with the same taste sensation (Ezek. 3:3). In that vein, John reminds us that God's "commands are not burdensome" (1 John 5:3). On the contrary, it is our sins that are burdensome (19:12–13), from which the divine word releases us. The catalogue of qualities in verses 7–9 reminds us that God, through the instrument of his word, remakes, reconstitutes, and re-creates us into the persons he intends us to be.

Illustrating the Text

All creation declares the glory of God.

Props: In Psalm 19:1–2 we read, "The heavens declare the glory of God; the skies proclaim the work of his hands. Day after day they pour forth speech; night after night they reveal knowledge." Consider placing beautiful pictures or paintings of creation in the church lobby as people arrive. These images can include pictures of the ocean, the mountains, individual trees, animals, the sky, people, and so forth. As you preach, reference these pictures and talk about how all of creation reveals and declares the glory of God. Share specifically what these images reveal to you about the nature and character of God. At the end, hold up a Bible and explain that God's glory is revealed not just in nature but in his Word as well. Share specifically how God has used the Bible to reveal his character and nature to you and what difference that has made in your life.

Psalms and hymns grow out of life experience with God.

Hymn: "How Great Thou Art," by Stuart K. Hine. Hine was an English missionary to Poland in the 1920s. During his time there, he heard a Russian version of a Swedish poem put to a Swedish melody. Later, Hine made his own arrangement of the Swedish melody and added English words, creating the hymn we sing today. The first three verses were written based on experiences Hine had in the Carpathian Mountains. After climbing to a village in the mountains, he heard the thunder echoing through the mountains and wrote the first verse. Pushing on, he crossed the mountain frontier into Romania and then into Bukovina. As he wandered through the woods and forest glades, listening to the birds singing in the trees, he was inspired to write the second verse. Throughout his journey, Hine preached the gospel. The third verse was inspired through the conversion of many of the people who lived in the Carpathian Mountains. Like the Psalms, the hymns and worship songs we sing have a context, coming out of people's lives and experiences with God. Hine, overwhelmed by the glory of God, was moved to write this great hymn of praise.[14]

The value of God's Word

Global Christianity: There are countries throughout the world where possessing or distributing Bibles is illegal or dangerous.[15] Pakistan is one country that has religious freedom guaranteed by its constitution but where Christians often face prosecution under blasphemy laws or persecution from neighbors. One pastor, "Edward John," held sewing classes at a sewing center in Karachi. A student, Abia, was curious about the daily Bible readings and asked repeatedly to have a copy of her own. So one day Pastor Edward gave her a Bible, and he never saw her again. Instead, five men (one, Abia's brother) came and shot up the center and brutally beat Pastor Edward.[16] Despite dangers like these, there are Christians all over the world who treasure their Bibles and who seek to put God's Word into people's hands, even at great personal risk.

Nature silently declares God's glory to the whole earth, announcing that he is the Creator. Like the psalmist, we still gaze in awe at the heavens as we see things in even greater detail with the aid of space telescopes. This picture of the Seagull Nebula, described by astronomers as a site for star formation in the Milky Way, was captured by NASA's Wide-Field Infrared Survey Explorer.

"Some Trust in Chariots . . . , but We Trust in the Name of the LORD Our God"

Big Idea *While reliance on our own resources is a mark of achievement, it can also become an obstacle to trusting in the Lord.*

Understanding the Text

Psalm 20 is a royal psalm because it concerns the king ("anointed," 20:6; "the king," 20:9)[1] and his success in battle. Indeed, the psalm is concerned with the king's obedience to the law of God (Deut. 17:16). Craigie calls the psalm a royal liturgy for use in the sanctuary,[2] and Goldingay considers it a dialogue between the people and the king,[3] assuming that verse 6 records the king's words rather than those of a prophet or priest. However, the prospect that a Levite (or priest) is speaking the word of assurance in 20:6 seems stronger, based on the pattern laid out in 2 Chronicles 20: Jehoshaphat's prayer (20:5–12), a Levite's word (20:15–17), the Levitical chorus of praise (20:18–19), Jehoshaphat's prebattle words (20:20), the chorus of praise that initiates the battle (20:21–22). In Psalm 20, the congregation's prayer (vv. 1–5) replaces Jehoshaphat's, and with that adaptation, we might allow for the king's word in verse 6

rather than a priest's or Levite's, but obviously there is no certainty.

The Text in Context

At first glance Psalm 20 may seem to interrupt the theme of Torah that was begun in the second strophe of Psalm 19, but at second glance Psalm 20:7 applies a divinely ordained national policy from the Torah (Deut. 17:16; 20:2–4), that kings should not amass great numbers of horses for military purposes. David seemed to have observed this policy, seeing that he hamstrung the captured horses of Hadadezer, King of Zobah, and saved only enough of them for a hundred chariots (2 Sam. 8:3–4), implying David's limited use of horses and chariots. Psalm 20:7 would thus be an affirmation of David's obedience of the Torah, at least that particular provision, thus connecting Psalm 20 to Psalm 19.

Goldingay has pointed out the verbal links of Psalm 20 to Psalm 18 (see table 1),

Key Themes of Psalm 20

- The people bless their king.
- God gives heavenly sanction of their endorsement.
- Trust in the Lord.

Torah, with Psalm 20 pointing to David's obedience to the military policy that the Torah imposed upon Israel's kings. Compositionally, if Psalm 19, celebrating the Torah, is the crown of an early collection of psalms, then Psalm 20 may be viewed as the compiler's bridge to connect that collection to his own larger edition of Book 1.

the latter being David's psalm of lament and victory (18:43–50).[4] Psalm 19, as the middle psalm in this triad, may be considered a hymn of praise to the Lord of the

Table 1. Verbal Links between Psalms 18 and 20

Psalm 18	Psalm 20
The king speaks of Yahweh's "help" that makes him great (18:35; from same root, 'nh, as "answer")	The people promise that Yahweh will "answer" ('nh) the king (20:1)
The king speaks of being in "distress" (tsar, 18:6)	The people refer to the day of "distress" (tsarah, 20:1)
The king describes Yahweh as "my stronghold" (misgabbi, 18:2, from the verb sgb)	The people promise that Yahweh will place the king in a "stronghold" (here a verb, sgb, 20:1; NIV: "protect you")
The king testifies to the way Yahweh "sustains" him (s'd, 18:35)	The people promise that Yahweh will "sustain" the king (s'd, 20:2; NIV: "support")
The king sings praises to Yahweh's "name" (shem, 18:49)	The people promise that the "name" (shem) of the God of Jacob will protect him (20:1)
The king's enemies "fell" (npl) and "could not rise" (qum, 18:38)	The enemies "fall" (npl), and the people "rise up" (qum, 20:8)

Outline/Structure

A simple outline of Psalm 20 is the following:

1. The people bless the king (20:1–5).
2. The psalmist (or prophet or priest) affirms God's answer (20:6).
3. The congregation affirms God's faithful response to obedient faith (20:7–8).
4. The congregation prays for the king (20:9).

Historical and Cultural Background

It was customary in ancient times to pray for the king and for the king to pray before going into battle (2 Chron. 20:5–12). It was also common practice for the king, along with the people, to offer sacrifices in those circumstances (1 Sam. 7:9–10; 13:9–23; Ps. 20:3).[5] The general opinion is that Psalm 20, besides its use in David's day, was used on other occasions prior to battle. Here we are speaking of the original purpose of this psalm, rather than its editorial purpose. They are two different functions (see "The Text in Context").

The words of the psalm paint mental scenes that we see only in outline form. Here the king is offering sacrifices before he goes into battle (20:3), and the people who bless him in 20:1–5 anticipate victory that will be accompanied by singing and celebration (20:5). Banners were used by the troops (Num. 2:2; Song 6:4), and by celebrants too, as suggested by 20:5, cheering the troops returning from battle.

The motto that enunciates the thrust of the psalm (20:7) is a reminder that chariots and horses were popular weapons of warfare in the ancient Near East. The Canaanites, in fact, were well known for their chariots and horses, which made them militarily superior to the Israelites (Judg. 4:7, 13; 5:22, 28), until Deborah and Barak defeated them in the Valley of Jezreel (Judg. 4–5). Solomon, not surprisingly, was the first Israelite king to use chariots and horses extensively in warfare (1 Kings 4:26; 9:17–19), marking a military advance, albeit a violation of the Torah.

Craigie points out that preparation for war included two phases, one spiritual, involving prayers and sacrifices, and the other military.[6] Psalm 20 reflects them both.

Interpretive Insights

20:1 *May the* Lord *answer.* The verbs of 20:1–4 are all Hebrew imperfects, normally translated as future ("The Lord *will answer*"), which the NIV translates as optatives (expressing a wish): "*May the* Lord *answer*," and so on. This is the case, for example, with the priestly benediction in Numbers 6:24–26 (e.g., see NLT).

20:3 *your sacrifices . . . your burnt offerings.* The basic meaning of the word translated as "sacrifices" is "meal offerings," which were flour mixed with oil and frankincense (Lev. 2:1–2). Here, however, the term seems to be a general designation for sacrifices (as in 1 Sam. 26:19, etc.).

20:5 *and lift up our banners.* Banners were used by troops in battle and by those who celebrated victory after battle.

20:6 *Now this I know . . . from his heavenly sanctuary.* Some believe that a priest or prophet speaks here ("I know"), affirming that God has accepted the king's sacrifices. Goldingay thinks it is more natural to view the "I" as the psalmist himself.[7]

20:7–8 *Some trust in chariots . . . but we trust in the name of the* Lord *our God.* This verse is the theological center of the psalm. Although the verb "trust" is implied, it is certainly the intended meaning of the sentence (lit., "These in chariots, and those in horses"; see below). The reference to "some" refers to Israel's enemies, but it may also refer to Israel, especially those kings who relied heavily on horses and chariots, as did David's son Solomon (1 Kings 10:26–29) and his successors (cf. Deut. 17:16 and 20:2–4). Psalm 33:16–19 expresses a similar sentiment. For the use of the Lord's name in battle, see David's words to Goliath (1 Sam. 17:45).

Here is a literal translation of verse 7:

These in chariots, and those in horses, but, as for us, we the name of the Lord remember / call to mind.

This literal translation notes that the verb "trust" stems from a nuance of the verb

"call to mind" (*nazkir*). The contrast is drawn in 20:8 as the people point to the outcome of their relationship to God, compared to those who rely on their martial forces:

> They [i.e., those who trust in chariots
>   and horses] bow down and fall,
> but, as for us, we rise and stand firm.
>   (author's trans.)

The contrast is highlighted in the words "some" (lit., "these"), "they," and "we": "*Some* trust . . . , but *we* trust . . . *They* bow down and fall . . . , but *we* rise."

20:9 *the king.* This is the only reference to the king, except for the synonym "anointed [one]" in 20:6, but it is enough to place the psalm in a royal setting.

Theological Insights

The blessing of 20:1–5, though not called a blessing, is a string of Hebrew imperfects used in a modal sense ("May the LORD answer you"), expressing what the people hoped the Lord would do, perhaps even expressing the substance of their prayer. A blessing is the transfer of God's favor from one person to another. In the Old Testament people can bless one another (Ruth 2:4), bless the king (Ps. 72:15; 1 Kings 1:47; 8:66), and bless the Lord (Ps. 103:1). God also blesses his people, and priests bless them too (Num. 6:24–26; Deut. 10:8; Ps. 118:26).[8]

The program of "blessing" outlined here is the formula for the king's success in battle, spelling out the exclamation of 20:9: "LORD, give victory to the king!" In Israel's world the welfare of the king and that of the people were inextricably tied together.

The people's response to the Lord's answer "from his heavenly sanctuary" (20:6) was to phrase their trust in overtones of the Torah's instruction to the king: "Some trust in chariots and some in horses, but we trust in the name of the LORD our God" (20:7).

Teaching the Text

To begin our lesson/sermon, we could use this analogy: reading the Psalms is like listening to the radio—we have to imagine what actions are taking place behind the voices. The literary images and metaphors become the sound effects that form our mental picture. The words of Psalm 20:3, for example, paint a scene on our mental TV screen: "May he remember all your sacrifices and accept your burnt offerings." The image is that of altar, fire, and sacrifice, of priests and worshipers watching, working, and singing. Similarly, verse 5 provides the mental picture and sounds of a victorious celebration, banners and all, to commemorate a great victory. Here in the psalm we hear the words but do not see the actions. Those are left to our imagination. The king offers sacrifices before he goes into battle (20:3), and the people bless him in verses 1–5, anticipating his departure (20:5) (see "Historical and Cultural Background").

For success in battle, the pagan kings of the ancient Near East depended on their horses and chariots, but Israel was to trust the Lord. Here four Assyrian soldiers go charging into battle in their horse-drawn chariot (Nineveh, 645–635 BC).

Now we are ready for the substance of the message. First, the psalm is a warning against trusting our own resources. Behind the pronouncement of verse 7 lies the law of Deuteronomy 17:16 (see also Deut. 20:2–4; Ps. 33:16–19). We should insist that this is not a formula for defeat but a formula for trust. Human resources are needful, but they can become a substitute for God's help. Thus the rationale behind the Deuteronomic law is our natural tendency to trust in ourselves and our resources rather than God's. Self-reliance is our sinful predisposition, and it will ultimately work against us and rob us of God's favor and of experiencing the marvel of what God can do. We might even give the example of Solomon, who was the first Israelite king to use horses extensively, and draw attention to his general self-reliance, including his numerous diplomatic marriages to win the good will of his political neighbors (1 Kings 10:26–11:4).

Second, the psalm provides the alternative mode of faith over against self-reliance. It is not overstating the case to say that this is, or ought to be, Israel's motto, and ours too: "Some trust in chariots and some in horses [self-reliance], but we trust in the name of the Lord our God [God-reliance]" (20:7). The verb that governs both clauses, coming at the end of the Hebrew verse, is "remember / call to mind / mention" (Hiphil imperfect). Certainly "trust" is the sense of the verb, but it goes beyond that. Behind "trust" is remembering, or recalling past experience—in short, remembering God. Few of us trust in something we know nothing about. Thus to "trust" in the name of the Lord is to recall and rely on his character and his past actions (note the historical implications of "God of Jacob" in 20:1).

While the application should be obvious throughout the lesson or sermon, we might conclude by putting the question more pointedly: "How would our lives change if verse 7 were intentionally our motto?"

Illustrating the Text

In ourselves we trust?

News Story: On September 11, 2001, the United States changed forever. On that day four passenger airliners were hijacked by terrorists with the goal of flying them into buildings in suicide attacks. When the day was over, almost three thousand people were dead. Many changes occurred in the United States that day and in the days that followed, not the least of which was the realization that even with the greatest military might in history, America could not protect its own land and people. We now live with the constant awareness that such an event can occur again at any moment. What was America's response? The Transportation Security Administration (TSA) implemented procedures that included stricter guidelines on passenger and luggage screening. The government created the Department of Homeland Security, which has created or combined over two hundred agencies. We engaged in two wars in the Middle East.[9] But are we really any safer today? Listen to David's perspective in Psalm 20:7, "Some trust in chariots and some in horses, but we trust in the name of the LORD our God." Where does our faith ultimately rest, in our boast of military might or our trust in the Lord?

In God we trust.

Prop: Hold up a coin and read to your listeners the words "In God we trust." These words were first placed on coins in the nineteenth century as a result of appeals from Christians during the Civil War. One such request was from Rev. M. R. Watkinson to Secretary Chase, whose letter read, in part: "One fact touching our currency has hitherto been seriously overlooked. I mean the recognition of the Almighty God in some form on our coins. . . . This would place us openly under the Divine protection we have personally claimed." Then, on July 30, 1956, the president approved a joint resolution of Congress declaring "In God We Trust" as the national motto of the United States.[10] But is this motto, in fact, indicative of the heart of the United States today? Does the nation put its faith and trust in God? Do we, as Christians, put our faith and trust in God? Or is our trust in our bank account, jobs, family, friends, doctors, technology, or possessions?

Pray for our leaders.

Applying the Text: It was a common practice in ancient times to pray for the king. We see in the New Testament that we are called to pray for all who are in authority over us (1 Tim. 2:1–2). Prior to teaching from this passage, make contact with various local, state, and national leaders, asking them how you can specifically pray for them as they carry out their work. Challenge the congregation to pray for all who are in authority over us, specifically that they will lead us in ways that uphold justice and righteousness and acknowledge that God is sovereign ruler of the universe.

"The King Rejoices in Your Strength, LORD"

Big Idea *God's overpowering strength plus his overpowering love not only saves us but provides a life of joy.*

Understanding the Text

This psalm belongs to the broad genre of royal psalms. Like Psalm 20, Craigie calls it a *royal liturgy*,[1] which suggests that it was used in worship. It is as if we are standing outside the temple and hearing the voices of worship, and we have a vague idea of what is going on inside the building as we try to picture the action in our mind's eye. The question that the form critics put forward, and quite validly, is, What was taking place behind the words of the psalm, a scene for which the words of the psalm are either a description or an illusion? Since one liturgy, to continue the analogy, has just ended (Psalm 20), the strains of that service are still in our memories when we begin to hear similarities as we listen to Psalm 21. The Lord is directly addressed at the beginning and end of Psalm 21, continuing the direct address of Psalm 20:9 (the only direct address in Psalm 20), and thus implying a continuation of the prayer of Psalm 20. The speaker is not named, although it could be a priest or the congregation, or even, but less likely, the king (since "the king" is referred to in the third person).[2]

Kidner has pointed out the relationship of these two psalms, although his proposal that they are paired as "petition and answer"[3] may not be entirely convincing, since

God bestows rich blessings and welcomes the victorious king's return by placing a crown on his head. In this relief from the Ramesseum in Thebes, Egypt, Pharaoh is being crowned by the gods (thirteenth century BC).

Psalm 20 is not precisely petition. In the first part, at least, it is blessing. It is more likely that we ought to view Psalm 21:1–6 as the congregation's confession (note the first plural of 21:13, "we") that the Lord has made their blessing of the king (20:1–5) a reality. While the blessing of Psalm 20 was spoken by the congregation to the king, here we have a direct prayer to God by the congregation, a prayer of thanksgiving, in fact, phrased in the second-person singular ("you"). Psalm 21:7 is essentially the swing verse, as well as the theological center of the poem, where the congregation or a priest or prophet acknowledges the faith of the king. Then in 21:8 the subject changes to the second-person singular again ("you"), and the congregation or a priestly or prophetic voice now assures the king of victory and blessing. After the assurance of 21:7–12, Craigie again hears the congregation's voice (heard first in 21:1–6) speaking the final word of praise in 21:13.[4]

The Text in Context

Taking our cue from Psalm 20:5 ("May we shout for joy over your victory"), Psalm 21 is the congregation's promised response to the realization of their blessing of the king. Psalm 20 was the prayer before his departure for battle, and Psalm 21 is the thanksgiving upon his return.[5] It is an acclamation of the Lord's strength (21:1 and 13), which issues in victorious conquest, extending the king's life (21:4) and bestowing on him splendor and joy (21:5–6). The psalm of thanksgiving (21:1–6), so fresh in the wake of recent conflict, is phrased with past and future verbs, but they seem to reference the recent past. This prayer of thanksgiving is complemented by a prayer

of trust (21:7–12), in which the congregation affirms its confidence in God's "unfailing love" (21:7).

Outline/Structure

Viewing 21:7 as the theological center, and the psalm to be bounded on either end by the notion of God's strength, the following outline reflects that structure:

1. The Lord's strength as context (21:1–6)
2. Covenant love as center (21:7)
3. Confidence as mainstay (21:8–12)
4. Concluding word of exaltation in the Lord's strength (21:13)

Historical and Cultural Background

Our discussion of this psalm assumes the backdrop of the king's departure for battle, much like the Chronicler describes (2 Chron. 20), accompanied by the congregation's blessing. Psalm 21 is the response to his victorious return home. Thus Psalms 20 and 21 are properly viewed as a dramatic pair of poems that depict the success of the king who remembers the name of the Lord and does not put his trust in horses and chariots. While neither he nor the congregation explicitly asks for his life in Psalm 20, the prayerful exclamation of 20:9, "LORD, give victory to the king!" is essentially such a request. Psalm 21 attests to the gift of "life" and "length of days"

(21:4), which, says the psalmist, the king asked for, but this may simply be a reference to the congregation's prayer on his behalf.

Interpretive Insights

21:1–8 The multiple use of vocabulary terms is a hermeneutical key to understanding a psalm, in that it cues the reader to themes and emphases that are on the psalmist's mind: (1) "rejoices," "make glad" (*smh*, 21:1, 6); (2) "victories" (*yᵉshu'ah* [sg.], 21:1, 5); (3) "granted," "gave" (*ntn*, 21:2, 4); (4) "placed," "granted," "make," "make" (*shyt*, 21:3, 6, 9 [see ESV, "you will *make* them as a blazing oven"], 12); (5) "not" (a poetic negative, *bal*; 21:2, "have *not* withheld"; 21:7, "he will *not* be shaken"; 21:11, "they *cannot* succeed"); (6) "blessings" (*bᵉrakot*, 21:3, 6); (7) "lay hold," "seize" (*mts'*, "to find," 21:8 [twice]).

21:1 *The king rejoices in your strength,* Lord . . . *in the victories.* The speaker is not stated, but it is perhaps a priest or prophet. Some even insist that the king is speaking of himself in the third person. The word "victory," or "salvation" (Hebrew root *ysh'*), links the psalm to 20:5, 6, and 9, where the same root word occurs.

21:3 *rich blessings . . . and placed a crown of pure gold on his head.* Some have suggested that this is an allusion to the crown of the king of Rabbah that was placed on David's head (2 Sam. 12:30). However, it is likely a general reference to the king's coronation. The phrase "rich blessings" is literally "blessings of good," which are most likely the abundant living resources associated with royalty.

21:4 *length of days, for ever and ever.* Because this description exceeds what normal human beings expect of life, the Targum and other commentaries have interpreted this psalm messianically. While there is hermeneutical warrant for that, it could also reference "the absolute fullness of the length of human life, as opposed to being cut off in one's prime."[6] I would prefer the latter understanding but not rule out the former.

21:5 *you have bestowed on him splendor and majesty.* The verb "bestow" occurs in another royal psalm (89:19), with the meaning to bestow royal investiture.

21:6 *you have . . . made him glad with the joy of your presence.* The verb "make glad" and the adverbial phrase ("with the joy") emanate the joy of God's presence, which is the source. Calvin comments: "It would not be enough for God to take care of us, and to provide for our necessities, unless, on the other hand, he irradiated us with the light of his gracious and reconciled countenance, and made us to taste of his goodness, as we have seen in the fourth Psalm."[7]

21:7 *For the king trusts in the* Lord; *through the unfailing love of the Most High.* Note the covenant terms in the psalm, illuminating this theological center: Yahweh ("Lord"), God's covenant name, which occurs four times (21:1, 7, 9, 13); "Most High," the patriarchal name for God (21:7; see below); and God's "unfailing love" (21:7).

Note that the king is mentioned in 21:1 and 7. Except for this verse in the third person, the psalm is spoken in the second-person singular because it is a prayer to Yahweh. This third-person comment, referring to the king and Yahweh in the third person, sounds like the psalmist's commentary. Melchizedek refers to his God by the title "Most High" (*'elyon*; Gen. 14:19–20), and Abraham equates *'elyon* with Yahweh: "LORD, God Most High, Creator of heaven and earth" (Gen. 14:22). It occurs also in Psalms 7:17; 9:2; and 18:13.

21:8 *Your hand will lay hold . . . will seize.* The meaning of the future tenses is a point of contention. Craigie thinks they should be future "and were, perhaps, addressed to the king by a prophet or priest participating in the liturgy."[8] While 21:1–6 constitutes the recognition of God's blessings on the king (a fulfillment of 20:1–5), 21:8–13 turns to the malevolent outcome of the king's engagement of his enemies, but all brought about by Yahweh's own power, indicated by the second person ("you").

21:9 *When you appear for battle.* Hakham insists that the word "appear" (noun *paneka*; lit., "your face") bears the same meaning ("your anger") as it does in the story of Hannah.[9]

blazing furnace. The Lord's victory against the king's enemies is described as "a blazing furnace." The Hebrew word refers to a household oven (Exod. 8:3; Lev. 2:4; 7:9). Constructed of earth, brick, and potsherds, it was bell shaped, with an open top that served as a chimney. When the oven was fired, the sides served as heat reflectors, directing the heat onto the objects to be baked.[10] It is a metaphor of divine punishment (Hos. 7:7; Mal. 4:1).

21:11 *Though they . . . devise wicked schemes, they cannot succeed.* The Hebrew word for "wicked schemes" means an evil plot (Ps. 10:2–4).[11] The word "not" (*bal*, in "cannot") is a strong negative used in poetry and occurs three times in this psalm (21:2, 7, 11).

21:12 *You will make them turn their backs.* In other words, they will turn around and flee from the Lord (Exod. 23:27).

21:13 *Be exalted in your strength,* LORD. Literally, "Arise, O LORD, in your strength." Ezekiel 38:18–23 declares that when the Lord takes vengeance on his enemies, his name is exalted. This may be a congregational response to the prayer.[12] Note that "your strength" occurs in verses 1 and 13, forming an *inclusio*. In verse 1 the king rejoices in "your [Yahweh's] strength," and in this verse the congregation joins in a song of praise for "your [Yahweh's] strength."

The image for the fate of the king's enemies is that they will be burned up "as in a blazing furnace" (21:9). This furnace is a *tannur*, or oven, and may have looked like this replica from the first century BC.

The psalmist begins and ends this psalm praising God for his strength. This all-powerful nature of God was given the term *pantokrator* in Greek. As images of Christ were created in the early Christian church, the depiction of Christ that is shown here became known as Christ Pantocrator, portraying Christ as the all-powerful Judge. This beautiful mosaic piece is part of a larger fourteenth-century AD mosaic located in the southern dome of the inner narthex of the Chora Church Museum in Istanbul.

Theological Insights

When one reads through the Old Testament, one is struck by the frequency and the assumed normality of war. And, of course, those who accept the teachings of Jesus find this feature of history extremely troubling. How do we explain, not to mention defend, the endorsement of war? One explanation is to say that Israel lived in a warmongering world, and they merely reacted to threat and conflict in the same way their neighbors did. In fact, if they had not, they would have been extinguished by their enemies. The problem becomes more formidable when Yahweh is depicted as a warrior (e.g., Ps. 24:8). Is it merely accommodation to their world and the warrior gods of their world? That complicates the problem even more, limiting the range of Old Testament revelation. While there is no totally satisfying answer, one may say that the God of justice must sometimes engage in warfare against the enemies of justice, so the warrior God is a needful image to preserve this fundamental plank of Old Testament religion. To exacerbate the issue even further, the endorsement of holy war in Deuteronomy 20:16–18 puts the question to the ultimate ethical test. While our discussion here cannot be as nuanced as it deserves, the Deuteronomist believed the *herem* (total destruction) was necessary or the Canaanite nations would corrupt the Israelites. While that still may not satisfy the ethical urgency of most readers, it is nevertheless his underlying rationale. Perhaps we have to leave the issue somewhat unresolved, but as we do, we must examine our own ethical persuasions and determine what shape our respect for life ought to assume.[13]

Teaching the Text

We can use the "Key Themes" to put our lesson/sermon together. As we develop the first idea, that God's strength surrounds the king, we may point out that this message is illustrated by the structure of the psalm, as well as its content. As already observed, the phrase "in your strength" forms an *inclusio*, a literary term suggesting a framework, or bookends, for the thought of the psalm. Then at the center of the psalm (21:7) is the "unfailing love [*hesed*] of the Most High." David is bringing together these two divine attributes, power and love, and indicating by the structure of the psalm that the Lord's exercise of power occurs within the covenant framework of his love (*hesed*). It should not surprise us that David believes he serves a powerful God. The theologians call God omnipotent or all-powerful. When one enters an Orthodox Christian church, one will generally see a figure of *Christ Pantokrator* ("Pantokrator" is the Greek term for "Almighty") painted in the dome of the church to symbolize the fact that God Almighty in Christ rules over our world and watches over us. Schaefer counts fourteen divine actions in the psalm, eight in the first part and six in the second,[14] a feature that provides a perspective that exposes the power of God that exudes from the psalm, a power that derives from the king's trust in the Lord (21:7). Although the psalmist never uses the term "covenant" itself, he nevertheless employs terms from covenant vocabulary (see the comments on 21:7).

Second, the saving message of Scripture is that our all-powerful God, who is love, can and does save us. We can make the application that he is there in the midst of our battles, fighting them for us, and putting our enemies (human, emotional, social, spiritual, etc.) to flight. John 3:16 affirms the central message of God's love, and God is powerful enough to save us from perishing, both in the pursuits of this life and in the hope of eternity.

The leader might also bring in Paul's words about this relationship of power and love. Paul knew that the power of God was exercised in love, and nothing could separate us from that (Rom. 8:35, 37). Moreover, it was so strong that Paul knew that the power of God and the love of God are forever united in the theological truth that God did not even spare his own Son (Rom. 8:32).

Third, we may make another observation that rises out of this psalm. We can write this formula: our all-powerful God + God's unfailing love = a life of joy. That is, the explanation of the king's joy is that he serves an all-powerful God who loves him unfailingly and who has made a commitment to him (covenant) that cannot be broken. Though circumstantially different, it is not unrelated to the "joy of your salvation" that David prayed that God would restore (Ps. 51:12a). In Israel's world—and ours is hardly different—rampant suffering and political unrest made joy a precious commodity, and an elusive one. But the gospel of Psalm 21, and the Christian gospel, is that divine power and love exude a joy that surpasses human understanding (Phil. 4:7). Our all-powerful God has not changed, nor has his unfailing love diminished, nor has the ultimate covenant sealed on the cross been canceled. That's enough to keep us singing (21:13).

Illustrating the Text

Give thanks to the Lord.

Bible: Luke 17:11–19. Luke 17 records the story of ten men with leprosy who were healed by Jesus. But only one, when he saw he was healed, came back to give thanks.

How often are we like the nine who failed to come back to thank the Lord for what he had done? Caught up in the busyness of our lives and focused on the next life challenge, we forget to take the opportunity to thank God. Psalm 21 was written as a psalm of thanksgiving upon the return of the king. Take a few moments of silence to give the listeners time to reflect and give thanks to the Lord for the great things he has done. Or you might want to take a moment for a few testimonies of how God has graciously provided.

Joy is God's partially concealed attribute.

Quote: *Orthodoxy*, **by G. K. Chesterton.** Chesterton ruminates about God's public exhibition of his nature and advocates that his joy has often been concealed:

> Joy, which was the small publicity of the pagan, is the gigantic secret of the Christian. . . . The tremendous figure which fills the Gospels towers in this respect, as in every other, above all the thinkers who ever thought themselves tall. His pathos was natural, almost casual. The Stoics, ancient and modern, were proud of concealing their tears. He never concealed His tears; He showed them plainly on His open face at any daily sight, such as the far sight of His native city. Yet He concealed something. . . . There was something that He hid from all men when He went up a mountain to pray. There was something that He covered constantly by abrupt silence or impetuous isolation. There was some one thing that was too great for God to show us when He walked upon our earth; and I have sometimes fancied that it was His mirth.[15]

Psalm 21 is a psalm of thanksgiving giving credit to God for the victory and safe homecoming of the king. In the New Testament account of the ten lepers who ask Jesus for help, only one returns to give thanks to Jesus after all are miraculously healed. This event is portrayed in this early twentieth-century lithograph by William Brassey Hole.

Trust in the Lord and his unfailing love.

Hymn: "How Can I Keep from Singing?," by Robert Lowry. Lowry's hymn (also known as "My Life Flows On in Endless Song") captures what most of us would consider an inconsistency, the joy of singing and the earth's lamentation. But Lowry's theme is essentially the same as the psalm: "we will sing" even though this world is filled with war and its evil effects. The reason is the king trusts in the Lord in such a conflicted world because of "the unfailing love [*hesed*] of the Most High" (21:7). Generally the joy that constitutes a major theme in the

Psalter is the song that resounds over the noise of this world's evil, a distant echo, as Lowry put it, "that hails a new creation." The psalmist registers a similar thought. The congregation or a soloist might sing this beautiful hymn as a response.

My life flows on in endless song,
    above earth's lamentation.
I hear the clear, though far-off hymn
    that hails a new creation.

Refrain:
No storm can shake my inmost calm
    while to that Rock I'm clinging.
Since Christ is Lord of heaven and
      earth,
    how can I keep from singing?

Through all the tumult and the strife,
    I hear that music ringing.
It finds an echo in my soul.
    How can I keep from singing?

What though my joys and comforts
      die?
    I know my Savior liveth.
What though the darkness gather
      round?
    Songs in the night he giveth.

The peace of Christ makes fresh my
      heart,
    a fountain ever springing!
All things are mine since I am his!
    How can I keep from singing?[16]

"My God, My God, Why Have You Forsaken Me?"

Big Idea *Even when God seems to have forsaken us, he is still present in the praises of his people, so our worship should continue.*

Understanding the Text

Psalm 22 is an individual lament that covers the spectrum of complaint: against God (22:1–2, 15c), against the psalmist himself (22:6–8), and against his enemies (22:7–8, 12–13).[1]

The title of this poem contains what is most likely a tune name, "The Doe of the Morning."[2] Sadly, none of the ancient tunes has survived. It is also called "a psalm of David," as are all the psalms in the Psalter so far except Psalms 1, 2, and 10. As already explained, this phrase may attribute the authorship of the psalm to David, or it may comprise a dedication of the psalm to David.[3] As for other psalms in Book 1 (1–41), it is not easy to identify historical circumstances in which a particular psalm was written. However, the dreadful vacuum that the psalmist feels in his soul would make sense in the setting of Absalom's tragic death. But there is no certainty.

The Text in Context

While some soul-distressing questions have already resounded among the psalms

As the inspired Gospel writers reflected on Christ's crucifixion, they saw parallels with David's suffering recorded in Psalm 22. Christ is mocked and insulted, lots are cast for his clothing, and he utters the words from Psalm 22:1 as he hangs in agony. This painting by Lucas Cranach the Elder (1538) depicts the crucifixion. Men rolling dice for his clothing can be seen at the lower right.

we have looked at so far,[4] this is by far the most antagonizing interrogation of God that we have heard or will hear in the totality of the Psalter. In fact, the entire Old Testament will not be able to articulate a more painful question than this one, because it represents the lowest rung of human despair. In the New Testament, the death of the Son of God was the occasion for this distressing question to be asked again. If the background is Absalom's death, the question was formed on the father's lips. On the occasion of Christ's death, it was formed on the Son's. For Christians it has a special significance because Christ uttered these words from the cross (Matt. 27:46/ Mark 15:34—quoted in Aramaic rather than Hebrew), turning human despair into divine despair, if such a term has any validity.

This psalm, not surprisingly, has stamped its impression on the Gospel writers. The dividing of his garments and casting lots for them (22:18) is alluded to by all the Gospel writers (Matt. 27:35/Mark 15:24/Luke 23:34/John 19:24). The hurling of insults (22:7) is alluded to by Matthew and Mark (Matt. 27:39/Mark 15:29), and the psalmist's trust in God (22:8) is remembered by Matthew (27:43). These quotations and allusions are enough to support the conclusion that Psalm 22 was seared in the messianic consciousness of the early disciples.

Further, the writer to the Hebrews, after he has asserted that Christ is not ashamed to call his followers "brothers and sisters" (Heb. 2:11), quotes verse 22 to affirm that Christ and his followers are all of the same family (Heb. 2:12), and to attest Christ's perfect identification with them.

It is also noteworthy that, while Psalm 21 is about Israel's earthly king (21:1, 7), Psalm 22 is about Israel's heavenly King, who dwells in Israel's praises (22:3) and whose "dominion" (or "kingdom") extends over the nations (22:28). In this sense these two psalms complement each other.

Outline/Structure

Some scholars divide Psalm 22 into two parts, and others into three. I have followed the latter practice, because verse 22 seems to introduce a new movement in the psalmist's experience, to which he will now turn his attention, and he will invite the congregation ("You who fear the LORD," 22:23) to join him in praising God for the 180-degree turn God has made in his relationship to the psalmist: he "has listened to his cry for help" (22:24b).

A common feature of this psalm is the use of multiple terms to magnify the complaint and praise of the psalm,[5] if not in succession (as "My God, my God," 22:1), then in a distributive pattern. For example, the idea of God's remoteness occurs at the beginning of the psalm (22:1c, "so far from my cries of anguish") and sets the tone for both complaints of the first and second sections (22:1–11: "Do not be far from me" [v. 11]; 22:12–21: "do not be far from me" [v. 19]).[6]

Another literary feature is the distribution of the subject pronouns in the psalm.

There are three pericopes that are dominated by the first-person singular pronouns (I/me: 22:1–2, 6–8, 12–18), and three dominated by the second-person singular (you: 22:3–5, 9–11, 19–21), which produces an alternating pattern. Then from 22:26 to the end the pronouns are third person. The significance of this is pretty obvious, seeing that the personal poles of the psalm are God (you) and the psalmist (I/me), until he turns his attention to the generations yet unborn (22:31), who will enjoy the fruits of divine blessing.

The poem consists of three parts, the first two (vv. 1–11 and 12–21) focused on the complaint, and the third a celebration of victory (vv. 22–31). Part 1 presents two grievances of the psalmist (vv. 1–2, 6–8), as does also part 2 (vv. 12–15 and 16–18), with part 3 celebrating victory (vv. 22–31).

1. The complaints (vv. 1–11)
   a. Complaint: against God (vv. 1–2)
   b. Reasons for trusting God (vv. 3–5)
   c. Complaint: against himself and his compatriots (vv. 6–8)
   d. Reasons for trusting God (vv. 9–10)
   e. Petition (v. 11)
2. The complaints (vv. 12–21)
   a. Complaint: against distant enemies (vv. 12–15)
   b. Complaint: against domestic enemies (vv. 16–18)
   c. Petition (vv. 19–21)
3. The celebration (vv. 22–31)
   a. First vow to praise (v. 22)
   b. Call to praise (v. 23)
   c. Reason for praise (v. 24)
   d. Second vow to praise (v. 25)
   e. Praise by the Lord's adherents (v. 26)
   f. First declaration of worship: all nations (v. 27–28)
   g. Second declaration of worship: the rich and the poor (v. 29)
   h. Third declaration of worship: future generations (vv. 30–31)

Historical and Cultural Background

David's familiarity with the ferocious animals of his world—bulls, lions, and dogs—is not a surprising insight. He had a reputation for killing a lion and a bear (1 Sam. 17:34–37), and to add bulls and dogs to the list is only to enlarge it. While dogs, mainly scavengers (Ps. 59:6, 14; Jer. 15:3), were not domesticated in ancient Israel until a much later date,[7] it does appear that they were used for shepherding (Job 30:1). Eventually lions and bears were eliminated from Israel's forests (which themselves were deforested) and became only a metaphor for ferocious enemies.

Interpretive Insights

22:1 *Why . . . ?* Psalms 10 and 13 both begin with a question. See also 42:9; 43:2; 88:14, all of which raise an ultimate question, but none quite so absolute as 22:1. Many psalms express the opposite sentiment (9:10; 27:9–10; 37:25; etc.).

22:3 *enthroned as the Holy One; you are the one Israel praises.* The reading in the NIV text disregards the disjunctive accent after "Holy One" and joins this word to the following participle, "enthroned" or "inhabiting" (on the punctuation of the text by the Masoretes, see "Hebrew Poetry" in the introduction). The reading in the NIV footnote is preferable: "Yet you are holy, enthroned on the praises of Israel" (see also ESV, NRSV). "The praises of Israel" is in effect the object of the participle "inhabiting," thus giving the sense "inhabiting the praises of Israel." Other instances of the participle in construct relationship to a following noun are 80:1, *"the shepherding one* of Israel" (who shepherds Israel), and 135:21, *"the inhabiting one* of Jerusalem" (who inhabits Jerusalem). The idea of Yahweh's enthronement occurs elsewhere in the Psalter (2:4; 55:19; 99:1; 123:1). Perhaps on the basis of Deuteronomy 10:21 ("He [Yahweh] is the one you praise"), and Jeremiah 17:14 ("you are the one I praise"), the NIV has joined the pronoun "you" that begins the sentence to the final phrase, "praises of Israel," and given the sentence a different sense. A more natural rendering is: "And you are holy, inhabiting the praises of Israel."

22:6 *I am a worm and not a man.* The terms of 22:6b–7 explain why the psalmist thinks of himself in such degrading terms. See also Isaiah 41:14 and Job 25:6.

22:7 *All who see me mock me; they hurl insults, shaking their heads.* See Matthew 27:39/Mark 15:29. Shaking one's head was an offensive gesture.

22:8 *He trusts in the LORD.* The verb (*gll*) is not the same word used to describe the suppliant's faith in 22:9 (*bth*). The

connotation of this verb is found in Psalm 37:5 and Proverbs 16:3 ("commit"). See also Matthew 27:43.

22:9 *you brought me out of the womb.* While Yahweh is the actor, the actions are those of a midwife.

22:10 *from my mother's womb you have been my God.* Jeremiah 1:5 also traces Yahweh's relationship back to the prenatal state.

22:11 *Do not be far from me.* See also 22:19a. This is a prayer for the reversal of the condition expressed in 22:1.

22:12 *strong bulls of Bashan.* Amos was aware of the popularity of cattle grown in Bashan, on the eastern side of the Sea of Galilee (Amos 4:1). The word for "strong bulls" occurs in this sense in Isaiah 34:7 ("great bulls"). Note the order of animals, metaphors for David's enemies (22:12–16: bulls, lions, dogs), and its reversal in 22:20–21 for literary effect (dogs, lions, bulls).

22:14 *poured out like water . . . my bones are out of joint . . . My heart has turned to wax.* Craigie offers the colloquial phrase "completely washed out" as the sense of the clause "poured out like water."[8] For the image of the bones being out of joint, Goldingay suggests the colloquialism "I am falling apart."[9] Finally, the metaphor of the heart turning into wax combines with "poured out like water," "all my bones are out of joint," and "my mouth is dried up like a potsherd" (22:15) to convey the psalmist's failing physical condition or declining emotional well-being in light of the terrible persecution he has endured.

22:15 *you lay me in the dust of death.* He believes himself close to death, and God has a hand in it. The description of his ailments sounds like he is physically ill, but other statements sound equally descriptive of an emotional state (22:14b, 24). Both may be the case.

22:16 *they pierce my hands and my feet.* This traditional reading, dependent on the Septuagint, is not quoted in Matthew's Passion Narrative. The Hebrew text literally reads: "like a lion, my hands and my feet," with the verb missing (see NIV footnote). Some scholars, with little manuscript evidence, take "like a lion" (*ka'ari*) to be a corrupted verb, "pierced" (*krh*). Hakham insists that the preceding verb also governs these two nouns, reading: "they have encircled me, my hands and my feet, like a lion." The imagery would be that of a lion caught in the hunter's net.[10]

22:17 *All my bones are on display.* This is not a metaphor but a word picture of the psalmist's emaciated condition. Both emotional and physical disorders have taken effect.

22:18 *They divide my clothes among them and cast lots for my garment.* This was one of the final things an enemy would do to dispose of the effects of the deceased. See Matthew 27:35/Mark 15:24/Luke 23:34/John 19:23.

David cries out to the Lord saying, "Rescue me from the mouth of the lions" (22:21). David's enemies, described as dogs, lions, and bulls or oxen, are endangering his life. This ivory plaque found at Nimrud (800–750 BC) shows a lioness killing a man.

22:19 *do not be far from me. . . . come quickly.* This is the third time the psalm speaks of God's remoteness (also 22:1 and 11). Verses 19–21 climax the "you" sections of the psalm and are the point where the psalm turns from lament to thanksgiving. This is the hinge on which the psalm turns from abandonment by God to a celebration of deliverance. The urgency of the situation is pointed out by the plea "come quickly" (lit., "hasten," *hushah*; see also 38:22; 70:5; etc.).

22:20 *Deliver me from the sword, my precious life.* While this psalm does not contain many military terms, "sword" gives a certain ambience to David's situation, suggesting there was a military component. The phrase "my precious life" literally translates "my darling one [y*ehi-dah*]." While some take this as a reference to the soul, it is parallel to "life" (*nepesh*) in the first half of the verse and should be understood in that sense. The NIV has understood the feminine form to carry a diminutive nuance, thus "precious" (y*ehi-dah* rather than *yahid*).

22:22 *I will declare your name to my people.* Now the psalmist states his intention to join the congregation (called the "great assembly" in 22:25; see also 40:9, 10), most likely in a service of thanksgiving. He further addresses them directly: "you who fear the LORD" (see also 22:25), "all you descendants of Jacob," and "all you descendants of Israel" (22:23). The temple was the national sanctuary, where such inclusive terms of address would be appropriate.

22:23 *praise him.* This verse picks up the language of praise, and it summons Israel to join in ("praise him," "honor him," "revere him"). Note also 22:3, 25, and 26.

22:24 *he has not hidden his face.* We are not aware of the moment when this change of direction and attitude occurred, but we have hints of it in the psalmist's review of Israel's past (22:3–5) and his contemplation of the Lord's care at his birth (22:9–10).

22:25 *From you comes the theme of my praise in the great assembly . . . I will fulfill my vows.* Literally, "From you comes my praise," and that makes the point clear: his praise comes from God, and, not surprisingly, it is because the Lord inhabits Israel's praise (22:3). This praise takes place in the congregation and is preceded by the offerings that the psalmist has vowed. The intention to fulfill vows denotes two things: the payment of a debt, for making a vow

establishes a debt that the person has to pay; and bringing a peace offering, part of which was burned on the altar, but the bulk of which was shared by the worshipers (Lev. 3:1–17; 7:11–16; 22:21; 1 Sam. 11:15).[11] See the sidebar "Vows" in the unit on Psalm 76.

22:28 *for dominion belongs to the LORD and he rules over the nations.* The word translated as "dominion" is literally "the kingdom" (*hammelukah*). The scope of the psalmist's world broadens from his very personal interrogation of 22:1 to this recognition that, while he may have felt abandoned, the world of nations was the much wider range of God's sovereign concern. This was not to diminish his state of dereliction but to put it in perspective, much like the Lord reminds Job that he, the Creator of the universe (Job 38:4–24), is concerned about the whole world, much of which humankind has never even set foot on (Job 38:25–27). In effect, the psalmist's personal question modulates from the minor key of 22:1 to the rhapsody of God's sovereign rule over the world (22:27–31), where the psalmist's voice blends with the congregation's (22:25), unites with the voices of the poor (22:26), and merges into the universal song of God's sovereign rule (22:27–31).

22:29–30 Finally, the psalmist's eyes turn to the future when the "rich of the earth" (22:29) shall bow before God's majesty, and future generations shall proclaim what he has done.

22:31 *He has done it!* Kidner sees a prefigurement of Calvary, which ranges from the cry of dereliction (22:1) to this closing word of finality, which, says Kidner, is "an announcement not far removed from our Lord's great cry, 'It is finished.'"[12]

Theological Insights

Drawing upon one of the "Key Themes," we are acutely aware that the opening question of Psalm 22 reverberates through the soul of every believer who has fled to God for refuge. The very idea that God may abandon his own is both shocking and perplexing. How could he! Why would he! The mystery of God is wrapped up in the psalmist's destiny. It was not enough for the suppliant to ask this probing question, but he reinforced the vacuous nature of his life in several ways in the psalm (see "Teaching the Text").

While our remotest thoughts may leave some place for the idea that God can, and even would, forsake his servants, the recesses of our rational beings, by the very contradiction of terms, shut off the notion that God can, and even would, forsake his own Son (Matt. 27:46/Mark 15:34). Some say Christ was merely speaking like a human, but that violates his incarnate and inseparable God/man nature. Others say that, even though Christ could not be held by the power of death (Acts 2:24), he nevertheless was not altogether exempted from its harm. Calvin reminds us that Christ, as our representative, appeared before the judgment seat of God as a sinner (2 Cor. 5:21).[13] What better way for the Son of God to express to our human ears the mystery of that transaction of grace than to take upon his lips the words of Psalm 22:1!

Calvin further comments on the fact that the address to God comes before the question, suggesting that the psalmist "has given the first place to faith."[14] This is confirmed by the content of the psalm. Our writer takes confidence from the fact that the ancestors of the faith trusted in the Lord, and they too, as did the psalmist (22:2, 5—two different but synonymous verbs for "cry/cried"), cried out of their deep faith ("trust[ed]" occurs three times in 22:4–5) and were not ashamed that they had trusted in God. This sense of community with the ancestors of the faith buoys the psalmist in his hour of despair. Moreover, his and their praise is the Lord's habitation (22:3; lit., "You are holy, dweller of Israel's praises"), an Old Testament concept that is only a step away from the doctrine of the incarnation. The God who took up residence in Israel's praises also took upon himself our human flesh.

Some will raise the question why God commands us to praise him. Does he "need" our praises, or is he so egotistical that

"From my mother's womb you have been my God" (22:10) expresses the psalmist's faith in God. Shown here is a figurine of a pregnant woman (sixth to fourth century BC).

he "wants" our praises? Lewis says that pleasure in being praised is not pride.[15] If we know ourselves and our work to be worthy of praise, then we should receive it truthfully—no denial—and gratefully. J. S. Bach is worthy of our praise. In his case he signed his works with the letters *S.D.G.*, the Latin attribution *Soli Deo Gloria* ("to God alone be the glory"). He passed the praise on to God the Giver. But there is no one to whom God owes allegiance or gratitude, and he himself receives our praise, for the Creator and Redeemer of the world is worthy. That is what the twenty-four elders before God's throne recognize when they cast their crowns before God and declare him worthy (Rev. 4:11).

Of the metaphors describing God's relationship to Israel, one of the most tender is found here in 22:9 and 10. Like a midwife, the Lord has assisted in the psalmist's birth and laid him on his mother's breast, and he has made him trust in the Lord. Indeed his faith, like Jeremiah's (Jer. 1:5), began in his mother's womb. This puts the question of verse 1 in the light of faith, which at the same time intensifies the emotion of forsakenness, seeing that his whole life has been one of trust in Yahweh.

Teaching the Text

Our first phase of preparation might involve considering the nature of the psalm: it consists of *lament* and *praise*. If the literary sense of these terms does not get our audience's attention, the emotional sense should: these are the two poles of our lives. There are a lot of degrees in between, of course, but so often we measure the incremental degrees by the opposite poles. Then we can look briefly at the lament of all laments: "My God, my God, why have you forsaken me?" To reinforce David's sense of abandonment, draw attention to the way David paints a vacuous picture of his God-forsaken world: no answer (22:2); no one to help (22:11); no water (22:14–15); and no strength (22:15). He further expands on that picture in the description of his inferiority feelings (22:6–7), the "bullying" he has endured (22:12), and his sense of impending death (22:15). At this point, there can be no doubt why he started off with his question about divine desertion.

The second phase of our preparation is to recognize that lament is counterbalanced with praise, one of the really beautiful things about this psalm. The psalmist plants ideas here and there that tell us he knows that God is somewhere in the shadows, somewhere in the margins of life, and the most striking of these statements is found in verse 3: "Yet you are holy, enthroned on the praises of Israel" (ESV; see the comments on 22:3).

We may take another angle on Israel's—and our—praises. All of us would admit that our praises are not absolutely pure—sometimes they are tinged with ulterior motives. The praises of the best of the saints are probably at times tinted with shades of insincerity. They rise from human lips, and from human motives, and we can never be absolutely sure they are 100 percent pure. Even if they are totally sincere, they still are marred by our deficient understanding of the One we praise. But look at what God does: he inhabits our praises. Does that not hint at one of the greatest truths of Scripture, the incarnation, that the Word became flesh and dwelled among us, tabernacled among us (John 1:14)? Israel's praises were *words*, and David was articulating, in a different mode, of course, and in a different time, the incipient doctrine of the *incarnation*, in this case, in Israel's praises.[16] It is quite noteworthy that, despite the importance and centrality of lament in the Psalms, God took up residence not in lament but in Israel's praises.[17]

That's not far from Psalm 22:3. When God became flesh in Jesus of Nazareth and tabernacled among us, he did not re-create human flesh in its prefall innocence and tabernacle in that, but he took up residence "in the likeness of sinful flesh" (Rom. 8:3). God's "inhabiting the praises of Israel" was a work of both identification and redemption. Thus, in the praise of God we will find his redeeming presence, and that can restore our spiritual equilibrium. Praise the Lord!

Illustrating the Text

Our suffering and the suffering of Christ

Quote: Dietrich Bonhoeffer. From his incarceration during the Nazi regime—he would eventually be hanged as a traitor—Bonhoeffer wrote this response to Psalm 22:1:

> But not only is Jesus Christ the goal of our prayer; he himself also accompanies us in our prayer. He, who has suffered every want and has brought it before God, has prayed for our sake in God's name: "Not my will, but thine be done." For our sake he cried on the cross: "My God, my God, why hast thou forsaken me?" Now we know that there is no longer any suffering on earth in which Christ will not

Referring to Christ's words from 22:1 and work on the cross, Elizabeth Barrett Browning (1806–61) writes, "It went up from the Holy's lips amid his lost creation, / That, of the lost, no son should use those words of desolation!" (from "Cowper's Grave")

be with us, suffering with us and praying with us—Christ the only helper.[18]

As the author of Hebrews writes, we have a high priest who is able to empathize with our weaknesses (4:15). You are not alone, and God understands your pain and suffering!

Worship God in the midst of suffering.

True Story: John Ortberg shares an amazing story about a woman named Mabel who lived in a state-run convalescent hospital for more than twenty-five years. Blind and partially deaf, Mabel lived much of her life strapped to a wheelchair or to her bed. One side of Mabel's face had been eaten away by cancer so that her face was completely distorted. A seminary student regularly visited Mabel because of her evident joy in the midst of such hardship. One day the student asked Mabel what she thought about, day after day, since she was not even able to know if it was day or night. And Mabel simply responded, "I think about Jesus. I think about how good he's been to me. He's been awfully good to me in my life, you know. . . . I'd rather have Jesus. He's all the world to me." And then Mabel began to sing an old hymn worshiping God for his amazing love and care.[19] Do you have that kind of joy? Are you able to worship God with authenticity and integrity, even when life is hard?

The death of Jesus and Psalm 22

Poetry: "Cowper's Grave," by Elizabeth Barrett Browning. This poem captures one aspect of the meaning of our Lord's cry of dereliction from the cross. The words reflecting the abandonment of Jesus were echoless, says Browning, so that no human being would ever have to utter that cry again:

> Deserted! God could separate from His
>   own essence rather;
> And Adam's sins have swept between
>   the righteous Son and Father;
> Yea, once, Immanuel's orphaned cry
>   His universe hath shaken—
> It went up single, echoless, "My God, I
>   am forsaken!"
>
> It went up from the Holy's lips amid
>   His lost creation,
> That, of the lost, no son should use
>   those words of desolation!
> That earth's worst phrensies, mar-
>   ring hope, should mar not hope's
>   fruition,
> And I, on Cowper's grave, should see
>   his rapture in a vision.[20]

"The Lord Is My Shepherd, I Lack Nothing"

Big Idea *The Lord as David's shepherd watches over him and, with his gentle agents of goodness and mercy, pursues him into the Lord's house.*

Understanding the Text

Psalm 23 is an individual psalm of trust (see the sidebar "Psalms of Trust" in the unit on Ps. 16).[1] Psalms of trust arise out of some trouble that the psalmist has experienced, although we cannot always determine specifically what it was. Yet through this experience the psalmist has learned to trust in the Lord. Sometimes these psalms include a petition (e.g., 4:1, 6) and a vow to praise God (e.g., 16:7), but Psalm 23 contains neither. As Goldingay says, it is "radically a psalm of trust."[2]

The Text in Context

While we do not want to contrive canonical associations among the psalms, we do want to recognize, even insist, that the psalmists and the editors of the book worked with word and phrase associations, and sometimes a word or phrase was enough to place two psalms next to each other and proclaim a message that the compiler of the book wanted to get across. This is illustrated in the relationship of Psalms 22 and 23. That is, Psalm 22 closes with the vision of a great feast in the kingdom of God (22:29) with a view to proclaiming the Lord's righteousness (22:31). As a follow-up, Psalm 23 relates that, indeed, the Lord leads in "paths of righteousness" (23:3a ESV; NIV: "right paths"). The festival imagery is picked up in 23:5, both images affirming the present and ongoing reality of the kingdom of God, which in Psalm 22 was still future.

Outline/Structure

This incredibly beautiful poem that has captured the hearts and imaginations of Jews and Christians alike over the centuries has traditionally been divided into two strophes, each controlled by a metaphor. The first likens the Lord to a shepherd and the psalmist to a lamb (23:1–4), and the second describes the Lord as the host and the psalmist as a guest or king (23:5–6).[3] I would prefer to see the first strophe under the metaphor of the divine Shepherd and the lamb, with the second strophe as a reflection on the divine Shepherd and the king, giving us the following simple outline:

1. The divine Shepherd and the lamb (23:1–4)
2. The divine Shepherd and the king (23:5–6)

Historical and Cultural Background

Proposed dates for this psalm have ranged from David's time to the exile. Delitzsch locates it in the period of Absalom's rebellion.[4] Understandably, the thought of David's trust in God being so personal and confident in so troubled a time is certainly attractive. However, the connections are tenuous at best. Perhaps the end of David's life is more probable. It makes a lot of sense to think of David writing this psalm at the end of his life, when his children's disloyalty was a distant memory, when the kingdom had been firmly established against the unfriendly nations, when his own personal sins had long been forgiven and almost forgotten, and when he was ready to hand over a peaceful kingdom to his successor, Solomon. Out of that rich legacy of life and faith, he looked back and reflected on the Lord's goodness.

This king played a significant role in making Jerusalem the worship capital (2 Sam. 24), as he had made it his political capital (2 Sam. 5). Although the tabernacle had likely

been destroyed, David transferred the ark of the covenant to Jerusalem and established a temporary tent for it. Psalm 23 calls the place of meeting "the house of the LORD" (23:6), which some suggest dates the psalm during the temple period. However, "the house of the LORD" and the "temple of the LORD" are sometimes used interchangeably,[5] but in the story of Samuel, when the worship center was definitely a tent (tabernacle), it is called "house of the LORD" (1 Sam. 3:3).

The application of the metaphor of shepherd to ancient kings and gods was common practice in the ancient Near East. Even Isaiah calls the Persian king Cyrus the Lord's "shepherd" (Isa. 44:28). The metaphor carried the dual notion of authority and compassion.[6] This psalm not only contains the metaphor but also references the functions and equipment of a shepherd. "Green pastures," "quiet waters,"

The metaphor of king as shepherd is visualized when Egyptian pharaohs are depicted holding the crook and the flail. The crook, a shepherd's tool, is symbolic of his shepherding role. The flail is thought to be an agricultural tool (funerary figurine from King Tutankhamun's tomb, fourteenth century BC).

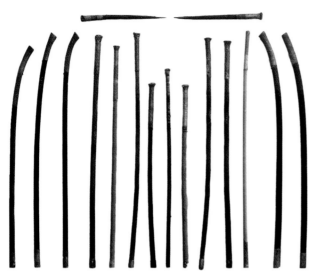

"Your rod and your staff, they comfort me" (23:4). The staff served as a walking stick, a weapon, and a prod to guide the sheep. This array of staves from ancient Egypt is on display at the Egyptian Museum, Cairo.

reflections on David's kingship, perhaps in the peaceful time when the Lord had given him rest from his enemies (2 Sam. 7:1).

Interpretive Insights

23:1 *The* LORD *is my shepherd.* Yahweh as Shepherd of Israel occurs in Psalms 77:20; 78:52; and 95:7, but here he is *David's* Shepherd. (On "I lack nothing," see "Theological Insights.")

23:2–3 *he leads me . . . he refreshes my soul. He guides me along the right paths.* The verb "leads" (*nhl*) is used to describe Yahweh's guiding Israel through the wilderness to the promised land, as is also the verb "guides" (*nhh*; Exod. 15:13; also Ps. 77:20; see "Theological Insights"). The verb "refreshes" may also be rendered "restores" (ESV), which may allude to the shepherd's retrieval of a stray or endangered lamb. The word (Hebrew causative stem, Polel) occurs also in Isaiah 49:5 to speak of the Lord's bringing Jacob back to him. While the phrase "right paths" (or "paths of righteousness," ESV) may have an ethical nuance, its literal meaning is "paths along which one does not lose one's way."[7]

23:4 *the darkest valley.* The literal meaning of the valley imagery (*ge' tsalmawet*, "valley of the shadow of death," KJV; see NIV footnote) is a valley where the danger of death lurked because of robbers and wild animals. Hakham identifies it geographically as "a path that runs between two cliff embankments."[8] Job uses the term *tsalmawet* for death (Job 10:21–22; NIV: "utter darkness"), and the prophet Jeremiah employs it metaphorically for the wilderness that God brought Israel through after the exodus (Jer. 2:6).

"the darkest valley"—these are pictures of security and protection that the shepherd provides for the sheep. The standard picture of the shepherd would also include a rod, attached to a belt, to fight off animals of prey, and a staff in the shepherd's hand, to provide support and to shake olives from tall trees for the sheep.

The metaphors of "shepherd" and "king" are mixed in the second strophe (23:5–6). The divine Shepherd anoints David as king and blesses his reign: the imagery of a feast following victory over David's enemies (23:5a, "you prepare a table before me in the presence of my enemies"), his coronation as king (23:5b, "you anoint my head with oil"), the success of his reign (23:5c, "my cup overflows"), the Lord's trailing pursuit of David despite his failures (23:6a, "surely your goodness and love will follow [lit., "pursue"] me"), and his passion for the temple (23:6b, "and I will dwell in the house of the LORD forever")—these are all *for you are with me; your rod and your staff, they comfort me.* The conjunction and pronoun "for you" begins the sentence to emphasize the Lord's presence. The rod was used as a weapon, and the staff for support. Here they stand at the beginning of the clause as a *casus pendens* (a pending case): "as for your rod and staff, they comfort me."

23:5 *You prepare a table . . . You anoint my head with oil.* Form critics understand the word "table" to suggest a liturgical feast at which some victory was celebrated. While Psalm 23 was likely used on more than one occasion, this term, in view of "enemies" and "anoint" (words that were familiar to David as warrior-king), likely alludes to the victory celebration after battle. In Psalm 78:19 it is a metaphor for God's provision for Israel in the wilderness. "To lay a table for someone" is the act of a gracious host (Prov. 9:1–2).[9] The anointing with oil, while included in times of pleasure and joy (Eccles. 9:8; Ps. 92:10), is here more likely an allusion to David's elevation to the throne.

23:6 *Surely your goodness and love will follow me.* The word normally translated "surely" (*'ak*) carries here the nuance of exclusivity: "Only goodness and love," excluding the psalmist's enemies.[10] The word picture is that of "goodness and love," rather than his enemies, benevolently pursuing (*rdp*) the psalmist for his whole life. The result is the psalmist's dwelling in the Lord's house continually. (On "follow," see "Teaching the Text.")

Theological Insights

As one looks at Psalm 23 in the context of the Hebrew Scriptures, the words of this

---

"For His Name's Sake"

God's leading of his people "for his name's sake" (23:3) indicates that (1) God has acted in his own self-interests, or on behalf of his own reputation (see Ezek. 20:9, 14, 22), and in accord with his own nature, and (2) Israel was totally dependent upon Yahweh. Theologically speaking, when God acts in his own best interest, it is simultaneously an act in Israel's (and our own) best interest.

In the Lord's Prayer we pray that God will perform his will on earth just as he does in heaven, and this will be the "kingdom of God," the best state of life that could possibly happen: *thy kingdom come, thy will be done on earth as it is in heaven.* The goal of redeeming grace is to bring humanity into perfect agreement with and practice of the will of God. Thus God's action "for his name's sake" is the best thing he could do for David and for us.

---

magnificent poem begin to connect to other portions and stories of Israel's history, the main story being the exodus from Egypt. Just as David's experience as shepherd (1 Sam. 16:11; 17:20) and king engraved its language on this psalm, the archetypal story of the exodus is also echoed in its language. Psalm 23 is an example of the archetypal story, that is, a large segment of history or biography is represented under symbols and metaphors, while other psalms recount the story in historical language (e.g., Ps. 106:7–8). Verses 2 and 3 share two verbs for "guide" (*nhl* and *nhh*) with the strains of the Song of the Sea, and the same word for "pastures":[11]

> In your unfailing love you will lead
>   [*nhh*]
>   the people you have redeemed.
> In your strength you will guide [*nhl*]
>   them
>   to your holy dwelling [lit., "your
>   holy pasture"].[12] (Exod. 15:13)

The "quiet waters" (lit., "waters of rest") of 23:2 may recall the "place of rest" to which the ark of the covenant guided Israel (Num. 10:33); and "I lack nothing" in 23:1 is the same verb (*hsr*) that recounts Israel's lack of nothing during the forty years in the wilderness (Deut. 2:7). The table that God spread for David in the presence of his enemies is reminiscent of the Lord's provision for Israel in the wilderness, which they at first doubted (Ps. 78:18–19). Finally, the purpose of God's guidance of the psalmist, "for his name's sake" (23:3), is synonymous with God's saving Israel from Egypt "for his name's sake" (Ps. 106:8). The language of the Torah functioned for the psalmists as a dialect of faith, from which they drew their vocabulary and imagery.[13] Ezekiel too drew on this same thought as he reflected on Israel's deliverance from Egypt (Ezek. 20:9).

We should remember that the exodus was the time of God's great presence and guidance in Israel's history. The very suggestion that Yahweh as David's Shepherd would lead him personally, as he had led Israel out of Egypt and through the wilderness, supports the position that ancient Israel, even as early as David's day, had a sense of individual personality, not merely corporate. God looked on Israel as a corporate people, and on individuals as persons, and his concern encompassed both. There is a Jewish saying that all Jews should celebrate the Passover as if the Lord took each Jew by the hand and led him or her out of Egypt. Christians have inherited this marvelous view of personhood from Judaism—that it was both corporate and individual—and to celebrate our personal redemption at Calvary, we can sing, "Were you there when they crucified my Lord?"[14]

David's hope to dwell in the house of the Lord "forever" (lit., "for length of days"; 23:6b) is parallel to "all the days of my life" in the first half of the verse (23:6a) and should be understood in that sense. The fact that Christians have given this phrase an eschatological meaning calls not so much

Jesus adopts the image of God as Shepherd when he says in John 10:11, "I am the good shepherd." Figurines of a man carrying a sheep on his shoulders, such as this one from the fourth century AD, became portrayals of Jesus as "the good shepherd" in early Christian art.

for a reprimand of our exegesis as it does a commendation of our hope. If, then, we take seriously the allusions to the exodus from Egypt, David's dwelling in the "house of the LORD" is nothing short of the imagery of the promised land when that hope became a reality, a reality for a permanent house and a permanent dwelling, in distinction from the mobile tabernacle that moved from place to place. Thus, when Psalm 23 is held up to the light of Israel's history, the picture of the journey from Egypt to the promised land is stamped on it like a watermark.

The theology of this psalm arises out of the practice of life, the practice of the lowliest of occupations, shepherding sheep. In the broad outline of biblical theology, it is not an exaggeration to say that this imagery is a hint of the incarnation of God in human flesh. That God would condescend to the level of a shepherd is remarkably assuring, and a clue that he would humble himself and take the form of a servant (Phil. 2:5–11). Isaiah too saw the shepherding aspect of Yahweh's nature and reassured Israel that "he will feed his flock like a shepherd, he will gather the lambs in his arms, he will carry them in his bosom, and gently lead those that are with young" (Isa. 40:11 RSV). In the context of the Old Testament, the imagery of the Lord as Shepherd generally carries the corporate notion that he is *Israel's* Shepherd (Pss. 77:20; 78:52; 95:7), but in Psalm 23 the Lord is David's *personal* Shepherd.

The New Testament picks up the imagery of God as Shepherd, and Jesus applies this image to himself in John 10:11: "I am the good shepherd." While this application may be more closely connected to Ezekiel 34 than Psalm 23, the significance is that the image belongs to the language of the incarnation and the loving care of God in Jesus Christ. The writer to the Hebrews remembers Christ as "that great Shepherd of the sheep" (Heb. 13:20), and Peter calls him "the Chief Shepherd" (1 Pet. 5:4).

Teaching the Text

As we look at this psalm we see two pictures of the way God guides our lives. The first is found in that memorable clause, "he leads me beside quiet waters" (23:2b). In that picture, metaphorically speaking, the shepherd is in front, and the sheep are following him to the quiet waters. That is a common picture of the shepherd leading the sheep, the shepherd in front and the sheep following.

But we have to admit that sometimes we do not follow very well. As sheep are wont to do, we get distracted by things on the right and on the left, rather than looking at the Shepherd. That is where the second picture is so important, and so graphic. "Surely your goodness and love will follow me all the days of my life" (23:6). The verb "follow" translates the Hebrew root *rdp* ("pursue"). The KJV translates it "shall follow me," but it means "follow me" *in pursuit*. And that puts a different hue on the landscape. We may stress the shift in the metaphor. Something has distracted the sheep, and the Shepherd, personified by "goodness and love," has dropped behind them, and they pursue us "all the days" of our life. A Scottish preacher said, "The Lord is my Shepherd, aye, and he has two fine collie dogs, goodness and mercy. They will see us safely home."[15]

Isaiah uses this kind of imagery too. He speaks of Israel on her way home from Babylonian exile. They arrived in Babylonia in the first place by meandering from side to side along the moral path, and not keeping their eyes on the Shepherd. When the Lord brought them back home (about 536 BC), they could hear him behind them saying, "This is the way; walk in it" (Isa. 30:21)— more *pursued* than *led*. Isaiah combines the two metaphors in 52:12 to describe that awesome and treacherous journey of the exiles on their way home, and he promises that the Lord will go "before you" and will also be "your rear guard." In this case the Lord was their Vanguard and Rear Guard.

We may emphasize the fact that life's circumstances sometimes force us to follow God where we would not normally have gone, and those circumstances turn out to be the voice of the Lord as he drops behind us, to use the metaphor, and "goodness and love" gently drive us home, saying, "This is the way; walk in it."

Illustrating the Text

Overcome by the shadow of death

Biography: **Donald Grey Barnhouse.** Billy Graham shares a story about the great American preacher Dr. Donald Grey Barnhouse, whose first wife died of cancer, leaving him with three children under the age of twelve. On the day of the funeral, Barnhouse and his family were driving to the service when a truck passed them, casting a large shadow across their car as it went by. Turning to his oldest daughter, who was deeply grieving the loss of her mother, Barnhouse asked, "Tell me, sweetheart, would you rather be run over by that truck or its shadow?" Looking at her father, she replied, "By the shadow, I guess. It can't hurt you." Speaking to all his children, he said, "Your mother has not been overridden by death, but by the shadow of death. That is nothing to fear."[16] This response of Dr. Barnhouse is a great reminder to all of us that as Christians we have nothing to fear in death. Jesus has overcome the grave; he has conquered death and sin. His victory is our victory!

God's goodness and mercy pursue us.

Poetry: **"The Hound of Heaven," by Francis Thompson.** Thompson's poem, published in 1893, tells the tale of a person who has wandered away from God's path, and like a hound, the Lord graciously and lovingly follows until the person turns back to God. The poem begins with the words "I fled Him, down the nights and down the days; I fled him, down the arches of the years." And then Thompson completes his poem with these words: "I am He Whom thou seekest! Thou dravest love from thee, who dravest Me."[17] If possible, you might want to share how you have experienced God as "the hound of heaven." That is, how has God pursued you? You might also want to project one or more of the twenty-three paintings by the American painter R. H. Ives Gammell, who painted a pictorial sequence based on Thompson's poem.

The leading of the Shepherd

Church History: Calvin tells his own story in the preface to his *Commentary on the Psalms* and informs us of how God led him to Geneva against his will. At age twenty-six he had already published the first edition of his *Institutes of the Christian Religion,* one of the greatest theological works of the Christian church, and he was on his way to Germany, where he intended to isolate himself in study and writing. En route, however, he stopped to spend the night in Geneva. When William Farel, a leader of the fledgling Reformation church in Geneva, heard that Calvin was in town, he went to see him and asked that he remain in Geneva to help the fledgling Reformation church. Calvin resisted, and he tells the story like this:

> And after having learned that my heart was set upon devoting myself to private studies for which I wished to keep myself free from other pursuits, and finding that he [Farel] gained nothing by entreaties, he proceeded to utter an imprecation that God would curse my retirement and the tranquillity of the studies which I sought if I should withdraw and refuse to give assistance when the necessity was so urgent.[18]

Thankfully Calvin did stay in Geneva, pursued by God's "goodness and love," and changed the history of the church and the history of Western civilization.

John Calvin (1509–64) talks about God's guidance in his life in the preface to his commentary on the Psalms. He says, "God so led me about through different turnings and changes, that he never permitted me to rest in any place, until, in spite of my natural disposition, he brought me forth to public notice."

Psalm 23

"The Earth Is the Lord's, and Everything in It"

Big Idea *Entering the King's presence is an awesome privilege, and in worship we join the psalmist in preparation for that tremendous experience.*

Understanding the Text

Psalm 24 is titled "Of David. A psalm [*mizmor*]." First occurring in Psalm 3, the term *mizmor* is generally understood to mean a poem that is sung to musical accompaniment (see comments on the title for Ps. 3). While the order of the words is reversed here (not "A psalm of David," as it usually is), the order does not seem to have much significance.

The Text in Context

In Psalm 23:6 David affirms that when "goodness and love" have pursued him into the Lord's house, he will dwell there forever. As a natural follow-up psalm, Psalm 24 is directly concerned with who will or may ascend the mountain of the Lord (24:3).

Psalm 24 is a companion to Psalm 15, with Psalm 24:3–6 corresponding to Psalm 15:2–5b (see table 1). Both psalms pose the question of who may enter the Lord's sanctuary and then give an answer in ethical terms. Note that both instructional texts begin with a general and positive description of the person who may enter the

The mountain of the Lord in Jerusalem was Mount Zion, where Solomon's temple and all of Israel's future temples were built. Today, the Temple Mount marks the location of the Roman-era temple complex and also the probable site of Solomon's temple. This view from the Kidron Valley looks up at the southeast corner of the Temple Mount with its Ottoman-era walls and provides a perspective of the climb necessary to get there.

Lord's sanctuary, and then Psalm 24 turns entirely negative in its particulars, while Psalm 15 is more balanced between positive and negative particulars. Both texts conclude, as they begin, with a positive affirmation, 15:5c basing this affirmation on the suppliant's behavior, and 24:5 upon God's.

In 1 Corinthians 10:26 Paul quotes the first verse of Psalm 24 to establish the principle that no food should be considered "forbidden," because the earth, and everything in it, belongs to the Lord.

Outline/Structure

The following outline is based on the assumption that the question/answer format is one between the Levites and priests.

Key Themes of Psalm 24

- The world belongs to God.
- Religion is an ethical matter.
- Metaphorically speaking, God is too big to enter the gates of his own temple.
- God condescends to meet his people.

1. Celebration of creation (24:1–2)
2. The liturgical procession to the temple (24:3–10)
   a. The liturgical question asked by the Levites (24:3)
   b. The answer of the priests (24:4–6)
   c. The priests order the temple gates to enlarge so the King of glory may enter (24:7)

Table 1. Correspondences between Psalms 15 and 24

Psalm 15	Psalm 24
"The one whose walk is blameless, who does what is righteous, who speaks the truth from their heart" (15:2)	*"The one who has clean hands and a pure heart"* (24:4a)
[general description of the moral life, including external behavior and internal purity]	[general description of the moral life, including external behavior and internal purity]
[no reference to idolatry]	"Who does not trust in an idol" (24:4b)
"Whose tongue utters no slander" (15:3a), "who does no wrong to a neighbor" (15:3b), "and casts no slur on others" (15:3c)	"Or swear by a false god" (24:4c)
[deals with evil speech and the harm it can do to one's neighbor, corresponding in a certain degree to 24:4c]	[deals with evil speech and the harm it can do to one's neighbor, oaths often relating to interpersonal relationships]
"Who despises a vile person but honors those who fear the Lord; *who keeps an oath even when it hurts*, and does not change their mind; *who lends money to the poor without interest*; who does not accept a bribe against the innocent" (15:4–5)	[See 24:4c for oaths, evidently regulating oaths sworn in the name of false gods]
"Whoever does these things will never be shaken" (15:5c) [this word of affirmation depends upon the suppliant's activity]	*"They will receive blessing from the Lord and vindication from God their Savior"* (24:5) [this word of affirmation depends upon God's activity]

Note: Positive particulars are marked in italics; negative ones are indicated with underlining.

d. Levites ask the Deity's identity (24:8a)

e. Priests answer (24:8b–c)

f. The priests, a second time, order the temple gates to enlarge so the King of glory may enter (24:9)

g. Levites ask the Deity's identity a second time (24:10a)

h. Priests answer a second and definitive time (24:10b–c)

Historical and Cultural Background

Psalm 24 was likely used many times, perhaps even routinely, as a ritual psalm in ancient Israel on the approach of the Levites and priests to the temple. The form critics have called it an *entrance liturgy*. Some believe it was written for the occasion of the ark's relocation from Kiriath Jearim to Jerusalem (1 Sam. 7/1 Chron. 13), accompanied by songs and musical instruments (1 Chron. 13:8). Psalm 132 certainly celebrates this event, and perhaps Psalm 68:24–27 does also.[1] Still others—including this writer—would assign the psalm to the time when Solomon brought the ark into the holy of holies (1 Kings 8). The description of the gates in 24:7 and 9 suggests this, since the tabernacle had doors but not gates. In that case, "Of David" in the title is a dedication rather than an ascription of authorship. In Israel's early history, the ark of the covenant accompanied the Levites as they made their processional way to the temple. When the ark was no longer a part of the ritual and was permanently housed in the temple, the Levites or priests, on their way to serve their

appointed time in the temple, would ask the entrance question ("Who may ascend the mountain of the LORD?"), and an unnamed voice posed the identity question ("Who is this King of glory?"). The identity of the speakers is not clear, but I have suggested it is an interchange between the Levites and priests.

The Mishnah informs us that in the Second Temple period the Levites recited

When the psalmist talks about the Lord founding the earth on the seas, he is referring to the view common in the ancient Near East that pictured the earth as a flat disk surrounded by water. In this tablet from the seventh century BC, the earth is drawn as a circle with Babylon in the center. The circle is surrounded by another circle that marks the boundaries of the ancient ocean.

Psalm 24 in the temple on the first day of the week (Sunday),[2] and in some Jewish traditions it is still recited on that day. The reason for the first day of the week is that God began to create the world on that day, which Psalm 24 celebrates.

It is quite obvious that the orientation of the psalm is the temple, and even though the speakers are not identified and the ark is not mentioned, based on other information from Scripture (e.g., 2 Sam. 6), we assume that the ark accompanies the procession to "the mountain of the LORD."

The question-and-answer format of 24:3–10 suggests the antiphonal nature of the religious liturgy being enacted. Certain terms fill out the word picture of this scene: the procession *ascends* Mount Zion ("*ascend* the mountain of the LORD," 24:3) and *stands* in the court ("*stand* in his holy place" [sitting in the court was forbidden], 24:3b;[3] also 135:2 [ESV], the priests "stand" in the house of the Lord); with the procession now positioned at the massive gates, a voice commands the gates to enlarge, so the King of glory, the Creator of the world, too big, metaphorically speaking, to pass through the massive temple gates, may enter ("Lift up your heads, you gates,"[4] 24:7, 9).

Interpretive Insights

Title *A psalm.* For the designation "a psalm" (*mizmor*), see the comments above and on the title for Psalm 3.

24:1 *The earth is the LORD's, and everything in it . . . and all who live in it.* The theological truth behind the statement "the earth is the LORD's" is based on the Pentateuch, found especially in Exodus 9:29 and Deuteronomy 10:14, and, of course,

generally attested by the creation narrative of Genesis 1–2.

24:2 *for he founded it . . . established it.* The personal pronoun "he" comes before the verb to emphasize that it is God who did this ("for it is he who founded it"). The root word for "establish" (*kun*) means to "build" a house.[5] Psalm 8:3 uses the same verb in the sense of "create" (NIV: "set in place").

24:3 *Who may ascend the mountain of the LORD? Who may stand in his holy place?* David bought the threshing floor of Araunah, on which Solomon ultimately built the temple (1 Chron. 21:18–22:1). The question/answer format occurs here and in 24:8 and 10.

24:4 *clean hands and a pure heart, who does not trust in an idol.* "Clean hands" were a symbol of a "pure heart." One's "hands" were a metaphor of one's exterior life (toward neighbors), and the "heart" a metaphor of one's interior life (toward God; Ps. 73:1). The verb "trust" literally means "to lift up" and is technical language for taking an oath ("to lift up the hands" in swearing an oath). The ESV translates: "who does not lift up his soul." The word "his soul" (the Septuagint reading) is actually "my soul" in the Masoretic Text and has a long-established textual authenticity. We have here an instance of direct and indirect speech together. When the worshiper swore, he would say, "I swear by my life." Here the term "my life" (direct speech) is retained, while the "I swear" (direct speech) has been changed to indirect, "who does not swear to an idol by 'my life.'" Here also two negative commandments of the Torah are in view, idolatry and false testimony (Exod. 20:3, 16).

24:6 *Such is the generation . . . who seek your face, God of Jacob.* The Hebrew reads literally, "This is the generation" (see KJV). If the psalm celebrates the new temple of Solomon, the psalmist is acknowledging the Godward orientation of this generation that succeeded in building the long-awaited temple. Exodus 33:7 uses the phrase "to seek the Lord" (NIV: "inquiring of the Lord") to describe those who go to worship in the tabernacle. To "see" God's face (Pss. 11:7; 17:15) and to "seek" his face are synonymous, except in degree (Ps. 27:8). "Jacob" is a poetic designation for Israel (Ps. 14:7). It is probable that the Hebrew clause "who seek your face, O Jacob" (see KJV) should be read, "who seek your face, O God of Jacob" (Ps. 20:1; Isa. 2:3, and so LXX).

This verse ends with *selah*, a liturgical term, here marking the end of a strophe and indicating where the Levites made a liturgical response (see NIV footnote; see also sidebar "*Selah*" in the unit on Ps. 3).[6]

24:7 *Lift up your heads, you gates; be lifted up, you ancient doors.* "Heads" is a metaphor for the lintels of the temple gates. Yahweh was so marvelously great that the temple could not contain his presence. Therefore, the gates must, figuratively speaking, enlarge themselves high and wide to let the King of glory pass through. On the occasion of the dedication of the temple, Solomon prays, "But will God really dwell on earth? The heavens, even the highest heaven, cannot contain you. How much less this temple I have built!" (1 Kings 8:27). In that mode of thought, the voice in Psalm 24 commands the lintels of the gates to lift themselves up to allow the King of glory, the Creator of the universe (24:1–2), to come in.

24:8 *Who is this King of glory? The Lord strong and mighty.* The question here is a liturgical response, not a formal request for information. The word translated as "strong" is found in only one other place in the Old Testament (Isa. 43:17; NIV: "reinforcements"), where it describes a powerful army. The word "mighty" (*gibbor*) is quite common and is repeated in the following phrase, identifying Yahweh as a God who is powerful in military conflict (Exod. 15:3).

24:9 *Lift up your heads . . . that the King of glory may come in.* As if the gates did not hear or respond to the first command, a second is issued. This name for God ("King of glory") is found nowhere else in the Hebrew Bible, although Psalm 29:3 has "the God of glory." It is used five times in this psalm.

24:10 *Who is he, this King of glory?* Part of the beauty of the liturgy is repetition. A second time, in response to the liturgical question, another voice asks for further clarification, and the pronoun presses for precision: "Who is *he*, this King of glory?"[7]

The Lord Almighty. "Lord Almighty" translates the phrase "Lord of Hosts [*ts^eba'ot*]." The term "hosts" references the angels and the stars (Pss. 103:21; 148:2; NIV: "heavenly hosts"),[8] a veiled allusion to Yahweh's creation. In 1 Samuel 4:4 and 2 Samuel 6:2 the phrase "Lord of Hosts" designates Yahweh, who sits on the cherubim of the ark. Thus the psalm closes as it began: the God of creation, the One to whom everything belongs, the Creator of the heavenly hosts, is the God who seeks entry into his temple. Syntactically the responders pick up the pronoun "he" of the preceding question to press their answer:

"The LORD of hosts—*he* is the King of glory," and no one else.

Theological Insights

This psalm begins where Scripture begins, with creation, and declares that the world, with everything in it and all its inhabitants, is the Lord's because he created it. Like Genesis 1, it begins on a universal note and writes God's name on the world and all its creatures. The reader should recognize that the description of creation in 24:2 is a visual account, the earth appearing to rest upon the vast waters of the sea (see Gen. 1:9–10).

That Hebrew religion was an ethical faith is unmistakable in the Torah, despite the volume of legal and liturgical detail found there. The legal and liturgical elements of the Old Testament faith were the crucible in which the ethical content of the faith was contained. This balance can also be seen in Psalm 24. It is, as Goldingay labels it, a processional liturgy,[9] and the liturgy sets forth an ethical faith and an awesome and holy God. The concern of the liturgical convoy is "Who may stand in his holy place?" The undefined "who" of 24:3 is given clarity in the answer of 24:4: "The one who has clean hands and a pure heart," and is further defined by the exclusion of idolatry ("who does not trust in an idol," 24:4b; cf. the second commandment, Exod. 20:3) and the prohibition of false witness, presumably against one's neighbor (the ninth commandment, Exod. 20:16). This reinforces our observation that the ethical nature of the Hebrew faith (and the Christian faith follows suit) was the heart of that faith, and the liturgical/legal elements were secondary ("secondary" does not mean unimportant; see Mic. 6:8).

Teaching the Text

Rather than developing one of the "Key Themes" as our sermon/lesson, we might take all of them seriatim and thus give the message of the psalm the broad exposure it deserves. First, we may observe that the basic principle of this psalm is that the world belongs to God (24:1). Verse 2 explains

Whether it is the gates of the city or the gates of the temple referred to here, the "King of Glory" is invited to enter. We find a visual picture of a god entering his sanctuary at the ruins of a temple at Ain Dara, Syria. Here we see giant footprints as if the god himself were walking in.

this claim: the Lord "founded it." Then there is an interesting shift from the world to the temple in verse 3. The question has cosmic implications for who is worthy to appear in the presence of such a God.[10]

Second, as the psalmist turns our attention to the temple, he seeks to establish the identity of those who are worthy to enter it, or to enter God's presence, and he does so in ethical terms (24:4–6). This question calls for an examination of the heart and perhaps applies not only to priests but to all worshipers who would enter the temple. The metaphor of "clean hands" is an allusion to the exterior life of the worshiper, maybe even to his or her relationship to others, while a "pure heart" is a metaphor that suggests the worshiper's relationship to God (see 1 John 4:20). We might mention Jesus's teaching on the two great commandments (e.g., Mark 12:29–31). Micah 6:8 raises a similar question and gives a similar answer in terms of the relationship to one's neighbor ("to act justly and love mercy") and one's relationship to God ("to walk humbly with your God"). The profile is expanded in verse 4b with the requirement of the second commandment ("who does not trust in an idol or swear by a false god"; see Exod. 20:4–6). We may emphasize the conjugal nature of ethics and liturgy, the latter an offense without the former. Our liturgy must always reflect our commitment to a holy life.

The third attention center is the address to the gates of the temple in preparation for God's entrance. He is too great to get through the restrictive gates of Mount Zion's temple without some spacious adjustments, so the gates are commanded to raise their "heads" (lintels) so that the King of glory might come in (24:7–9). Here is an opportunity to stress the greatness of our God. The world he made cannot contain him, nor can our little personal world. This should be a spiritual incentive to faith.

Fourth, the psalm closes as it begins, by turning the floodlight on the person of God, this time, the "King of glory" (24:10). This is the God who "founded" the earth and who is, figuratively speaking, too great to walk through these gates. Yet the Creator of the world condescends to enter the earthly sanctuary to meet his people, just as he condescends to dwell in Israel's praises (Ps. 22:3). The concept of divine condescension and self-humiliation is written indelibly into the Christian gospel, and it is not a New Testament novelty but has its beginnings in the Hebrew Scriptures.

Illustrating the Text

The earth belongs to the Lord.

Quote: *God and the Astronomers*, by Robert Jastrow. The acknowledgment that God is the Creator of the universe is a basic premise of the biblical faith. The fact that the Bible begins with the story of creation is no coincidence but quite intentional, and creation is a frequent theme in the Psalms. Recognizing the need for faith, Jastrow concludes his book with these words: "For the scientist who has lived by his faith in the power of reason, the story ends like a bad dream. He has scaled the mountains of ignorance; he is about to conquer the highest peak; as he pulls himself over the final rock, he is greeted by a band of theologians who have been sitting there for centuries."[11]

God has a registered patent on the universe.

Science: One of the great intellectual violations of our time is the denial of the Creator of the world. With advancing knowledge of the universe, especially our own Milky Way galaxy, we know that the universe is infinitely huge and interminably complex. As of February 2014, scientists working on NASA's Kepler planet-hunting telescope have confirmed a count of "more than 3,600 planet candidates, of which 961 have been verified as bona-fide worlds,"[12] and from this kind of information, scientists have extrapolated that there may be a whopping 100 billion planets in our galaxy alone.[13] If that does not give you a sense of awe, just think of this: the observable universe—that is, the region that we can observe with our best exploration instruments—has a radius of about 46 billion light years. Compare that to our galaxy, whose diameter is about 100,000 light years[14] (a light year is about 6 trillion miles). That is the universe God made, and the universe that belongs to him. David did not have those statistics in his mind, of course, but he knew that God was the Creator of the world, and that fundamental premise underwrites the theology of Psalm 24.

Lift up your heads, that the King of glory may come in.

Hymn: "Lift Up Your Heads, Ye Mighty Gates," by Georg Weissel. This hymn was written during the Thirty Years' War

Although our view of the earth, shown here, is very different from that of the ancient Near East, we can still affirm God as Creator and say with the psalmist, "The earth is the Lord's, and everything in it" (24:1). This image is a montage of photographs from the Suomi NPP satellite.

(1618–48), a devastating time of suffering in Europe that also has given Christianity some of its greatest hymns.[15] With a clear connection to Psalm 24, the hymn begins with these words, "Lift up your heads, ye mighty gates: behold, the King of glory waits!" The second stanza then brings this incredible challenge, "Fling wide the portals of your heart: make it a temple, set apart from earthly use for heaven's employ, adorned with prayer and love and joy."[16] You may want to sing it as a congregation or simply read the words of the hymn.

Psalm 24

"Show Me Your Ways, LORD"

Big Idea *As students in the school of faith, we have the Lord as our Teacher, and his ways (and will) are our curriculum.*

Understanding the Text

This psalm is another example of reflective prayer (see Ps. 16), in which the suppliant talks to God and then reflects on the subject of the prayer (see "Outline/ Structure" below), either alone or in company with others. Goldingay proposes that it has an instructional purpose, to teach people to pray.[1] Generically, Psalm 25 is generally typed as an individual lament, while Craigie insists that the language is more descriptive of a psalm of confidence (psalm of trust).[2] Its connections with wisdom poetry have also been noted, especially the use of the terms "way(s)" (25:4, 8, 9, 10, and 12; the noun is turned into a verb, "guide," in 25:5 and 9), "fear" (25:12, 14), and "good" (25:8, 13 [NIV: "prosperity"]), as well as the acrostic form of the psalm (see the sidebar).

The Text in Context

The psalmist puts his trust in God (25:1), in contrast to those who put their trust in that which is false (24:4). Put in reference to the question of Psalm 24:3, Psalm 25 translates the content of that question into spiritual relationship (25:12)

and answers it in covenantal, rather than liturgical, terms (25:14).

Outline/Structure

1. Prayer (25:1–7)
2. Reflection (25:8–10)
3. Prayer (25:11)
4. Reflection (25:12–15)
5. Prayer (25:16–22)

Historical and Cultural Background

The title "to/for David," for the most part, fits the psalm into a Davidic frame. David's enemies preoccupy his thoughts in many psalms. The enemies of Psalm 25 (25:2, 19) have not yet gotten the upper hand in the psalmist's life, and David prays that their increased numbers and augmented hatred would not triumph, nor give any semblance that he has been rejected.

Interpretive Insights

25:1 *I put my trust.* This expression (lit., "I lift up my soul") suggests hope or desire (Pss. 86:4; 143:8).[3] The physical gesture of lifting up the hands or lifting up the evening sacrifice may be the liturgical derivative.[4] In light of Deuteronomy 24:15 (NIV: "counting on it") and Jeremiah 22:27 (NIV: "long to"), where lifting up the "soul" occurs also, the idea here as there is that of hope and desire, which is in harmony with the stress on hope (25:3, 21) and trust (25:2).

25:2 *do not let me be put to shame.* This verb occurs here and in 25:3 and 20, framing the psalm. For one to be "put to shame" involved a sense of rejection socially or the experience of being forgotten by God.[5] In view of this, the trifold prayer that God would remember him (25:6, 7) makes all the more sense.

25:3 *No one who hopes in you will ever be put to shame.* Literally, "Let all who hope in you not be ashamed." The verb "hope" carries the basic idea of "wait," suggesting the nature of hope, which has its eye on the future (see "Theological Insights"). In fact, hope has been called "faith on tiptoe," a metaphor that beautifully

This cuneiform tablet contains a portion of Ashurbanipal's Hymn to Marduk, an acrostic prayer where the first letter of each section (sections are separated by the horizontal lines) arranged sequentially form the sentence, "I am Ashurbanipal who calls on you. Give me life, Marduk, I will glorify you."

Key Themes of Psalm 25

- The psalmist seeks God's guidance.
- The psalmist desires God's remembrance of his mercy but not the psalmist's sin.
- Goodness is part of God's character.
- God's covenant grace spares one from personal shame.
- The psalmist expresses both community and personal identity.

The Alphabetic Acrostic Psalms

The Psalter has eight alphabetic acrostic poems (9–10; 25; 34; 37; 111; 112; 119; 145). These poems follow the order of the letters in the Hebrew alphabet (with some variations). The literary purpose of an alphabetic psalm is mnemonic, to assist in memorization and recall, which could also have been a way to assist students in learning the alphabet. Or it may code a message, such as Ashurbanipal's Hymn to Marduk and Zarpanitu, in which the Akkadian first letters of each line spell out a message.[a] The alphabetic pattern allows the composer freedom to range through various subjects rather than follow a sequence of ideas, even though ideas may be grouped together under a particular rubric (e.g., Ps. 119, on the Torah; see the discussion of Ps. 34).

The theological purpose of the acrostic is more elusive, but likely it represents symbolically that the poet has scanned the entire alphabet (compare the expression "from a to z") and thus figuratively utilized the entire language to articulate the subject; or it suggests "that the meaning of the whole is greater than the sum of the parts."[b] This purpose is most obvious in Psalm 119, which scans the alphabet to cover the meaning of Torah.

Outside the Psalter, Lamentations is the best example of this pattern. Poems (chapters) 1, 2, and 4 begin the first line of each strophe with a new letter of the alphabet, but the following lines of the strophe do not maintain that pattern. However, Poem 3 does follow the pattern of Psalm 119, where each line of the strophe begins with the same letter of the alphabet. Poem 5 consists of the number of letters in the alphabet (22 letters) but is not an acrostic.[c]

[a] Hilber, "Psalms," 420; see also Goldingay, *Psalms*, 1:377; Wilson, *Psalms*, 566.
[b] Hilber, "Psalms," 420.
[c] Bullock, *Encountering*, 41–42; Craigie, *Psalms 1–50*, 128–31.

expresses the relationship of faith and hope.[6]

25:4 *Show me your ways . . . your paths.* "Ways" and "paths" are synonymous terms for God's will. "Show me your ways" uses the causative inflection (Hiphil) of that verb, "*make* me *know* your ways," as does verse 14: "he *makes* his covenant *known*" (infinitive construct Hiphil). The fact that the poem is an alphabetic acrostic (see the sidebar) may suggest that the poet ran the scope of the whole alphabet to explore the subject of his need for divine guidance and God's gracious answer to that prayer.

25:5 *Guide me.* The verb "guide" is a denominative verb (derives from the noun "way," *derek*) that suggests the mapping out of a path, a prayer for guidance in the way forward. It occurs again in verse 9.

25:6 *Remember.* The psalmist prays that God will recall his covenant "mercy [*raham*] and love [*hesed*; both nouns are plural here, possibly to imply their abundance] from of old," most likely a reference to the Mosaic covenant.

25:7 *Do not remember the sins of my youth . . . for you,* LORD, *are good.* The psalmist's "youth" is in contrast to

the antiquity of Yahweh's mercy and love.[7] Delitzsch equates God's goodness with his love, suggesting that it is an equivalent of "God is love" (1 John 4:8).[8]

25:8 *therefore he instructs sinners in his ways.* The verb "instruct" (Hiphil of *yrh*, from which the word *torah* also derives) gives the picture of Yahweh as Teacher, and Israel as students (also Ps. 32:8; Prov. 4:11). See verse 12 for a similar statement ("He will instruct them in the ways").

25:10 *loving and faithful . . . toward those who keep the demands of his covenant.* The covenant context is critical for understanding this psalm. The Lord's ways are a reflection of his "loving" (*hesed*) and "faithful" (*'emet*) nature, and this divine character shapes the covenant he has made with Israel and the relationship he has with the keepers of the covenant. The same two terms are also found in the second revelation to Moses on Mount Sinai, describing God's "abounding in *love* and *faithfulness*" (Exod. 34:6). This echo of the Mosaic covenant implies that the psalmist was familiar with this important text.

25:11 *For the sake of your name,* LORD, *forgive my iniquity.* Regarding the phrase "for the sake of your name," see "Theological Insights" and the sidebar "For His Name's

God's covenant was made with Israel through Moses on Mount Sinai. This sculpture depicts Moses holding the tablets of the law (ca. 1170, Cathedral of Noyon, France).

Sake" in the unit on Psalm 23. The character description of Yahweh noted in 25:10 is also associated with forgiveness in the second Sinai revelation (Exod. 34:7), where the more common verb for "forgive" (*ns'*) occurs; it occurs for the first time with this meaning in the Psalter in 25:18. The word in this verse (*slh*) is, according to Goldingay, the closest word the Hebrew language has for a technical term for forgiveness, since it is only used with Yahweh as subject.[9] Rashi comments: "It is appropriate for the Great [God] to pardon Great Iniquity."[10] This verse may be considered the core verse of the psalm.[11]

25:12 *Who, then, are those who fear the* Lord? This question is another version of the question of 24:3, stated in terms of spiritual piety. The Hebrew is literally, "Who is this man who fears the Lord?" obviously pointing to "David" as the immediate answer.

25:14 *The* Lord *confides in those who fear him.* The Hebrew word for "confides" is a noun (*sod*), meaning "secret" (KJV) or perhaps "counsel" (see HCSB). The Septuagint's "strength" and the ESV's "friendship" both show the difficulty it poses for translators. In any case, this verse is a restatement of the thought of 25:12, the fear of the Lord being the link. Perhaps Abraham is a good illustration of this thought (Gen. 18:17–19; cf. Amos 3:7).

25:15 *My eyes.* Note the resumption of the first person, which is also the grammatical person of 25:1–7, suggesting the personal nature of the psalm.

25:18 *my affliction and my distress.* The terms "affliction" (*'oni*) and "distress" or "suffering" (*'amal*) were used in the response the Israelites made when they brought the firstfruits to the sanctuary (Deut. 26:7): "and the Lord . . . saw our *affliction* and our *suffering*, and our oppression" (author's trans.). Here David personalizes the "affliction" and "distress," as the psalmists often do of national experiences. The reference is more likely to emotional problems associated with the psalmist's unforgiven sins, rather than to physical illness.

25:19 *how numerous are my enemies.* This verse, along with 25:2, highlights the problem the suppliant's enemies have caused him. Their hatred, as hatred directed toward any person's life, has contributed to David's sense of alienation and elevated his consciousness of sin, which only God can alleviate.

25:21 *May integrity and uprightness protect me.* The psalmist's faultless and upright character is the source, even the instrument, of his well-being. These character attributes, in a personified way, have become the sentinels of the psalmist's life (see also the personification of attributes in Pss. 23:6; 43:3).

25:22 *Deliver Israel, O God, from all their troubles!* Note that here a personal psalm turns toward Israel's corporate well-being. It is possible that this grows out of the suppliant's love for his nation, which ought certainly to be part of a king's passion for his people. If so, it contributes an excellent balance to the psalm's personal orientation. It is also possible, as suggested by Delitzsch[12] and others, that it is a virtual gloss in the form of a congregational response, used in worship by later generations. That is, a later generation applied this psalm to their own situation, much like David applied the ancient words of the

Mosaic covenant to his personal life. Other psalms that add the communal aspect at the end of the psalm are Psalms 3:8; 31:23, 24; 130:7, 8; and 131:3.

The initial letter of verse 22 (*pe*) falls outside the alphabetic acrostic. Goldingay sees a code word formed by the initial letters of the first, middle, and final verses (25:1, 11, 22), forming a Hebrew word that means "to learn" or "teach" ('*lp*, used in Prov. 22:25; Job 15:5, etc.), suggesting that this psalm was designed to "teach" one to pray.[13]

Theological Insights

With reference to our "Key Themes," Psalm 25 outlines two modes of prayer as the psalmist seeks God's guidance. The first employs four different verbs to convey the idea of seeking God's instruction and guidance: "show" / "make known," "teach," "guide," and "instruct" (see table 1). While these are not strict synonyms, their common thread is God's instruction in his ways, which sums up his will, and this he has imparted to Israel in his covenant. Instruction and guidance are intertwined, a good principle for us to keep in mind.

The second mode of prayer employs the verb "remember," used twice to make a positive request and once to implore God negatively (see table 1). In light of the psalmist's earnest desire to know God's ways, that is, his will, it is not surprising to hear him plead that the Lord will remember his "mercy" and "love" (25:6, 7b), two covenant terms flowing out of God's character of goodness (25:7, 8). The negative side of that coin is to ask the Lord *not* to remember the sins of his youth (25:7a), a plea that he

Table 1. Instruction, Guidance, and Remembrance in Psalm 25

"Show"/"make known" (Hiphil of *yd'*)	"*Show me* your ways" (25:4a) "He *makes* his covenant *known* to them" (who fear the Lord; 25:14b)
"Teach" (*lmd*)	"*Teach* me your paths" (25:4b) "*Teach* me" (25:4b) "*Teaches* them his way" (25:4b)
"Guide" (Hiphil of *drk*)	"*Guide* me in your truth" (25:4b) "He *guides* the humble in what is right" (25:9a)
"Instruct" (*yrh*)	"He *instructs* sinners in his ways" (25:8b) "He *will instruct* them" (those who fear the Lord; 25:12)
"Remember" (*zkr*)	"*Remember*, Lord, your great mercy" (25:6) "Do not *remember* the sins of my youth" (25:7a) "According to your love *remember* me" (25:7b)

will forgive the suppliant as he forgave the ancient recipients of his covenant grace.

David's "enemies," who are never far from his mind, are connected with the prayer that Yahweh not allow him to be put to shame (25:2, 19–20). The covenantal language of the psalm would imply that the suppliant is putting his relationship with his enemies in the covenant context. Twice the noun "covenant" occurs (25:10, 14), and once "testimonies" (25:10; NIV: "demands"), along with what is perhaps the innermost covenantal term, "love," or "loving-kindness" (*hesed*, 25:6, 7, 10; see the sidebar in the unit on Ps. 36). The central thrust of the psalm is covenant faithfulness, conveyed by Yahweh's faithfulness to his own name (25:11), and the suppliant's

A PSALMVS
ote ofſe Leuaui
animam meam df
meaſ ime confido. noneru
beſcam
Neque irrideanc me inimi
ci mei. &enim uniuerſi
quire exſpecſtaſ dñie nonſ
funденcur
Conſfundancur iniqui faci
ſ

DAVID
nui coraidie
Reminiſcere miſeracionuim
cuarum dñe. &miſericor
diae cuae que aſeculo
ſunt
Delicſta iuuencucſ meſ
&ignorancicaſ meaſ ne
memineriſ dñie. ſecdm
magnam miſericordiaſ

XXIIII·
bre manſuecoſ inaſ ſuaſ.
Vniuerſſe uiſſ dñi miſerſ
corſha &uericaſ requiroli
buſ ceſtamenicaſ eiuſ &
ceſtimonia eiuſ
Propter nomen tuu
propicianperiſ pec
copioſum eſt er
Quiſeſt homo

authentic hope in God (25:3, 5, 21). This hope, virtually acting as bookends for the psalm (25:3 and 21), is the Hebrew word for "wait," conveying the essence of hope, for it anticipates its reality in the future. It is not inert, however, for hoping is an active waiting. Isaiah affirmed that waiting on the Lord would bring renewal of strength (Isa. 40:31). David affirms his faith in the covenant God by waiting for him, and God reveals his covenant love by sparing him from shame (25:14). The question raised in 24:3 has been answered in terms of who: David is the man who may ascend the mountain of the Lord and stand in his holy place.[14]

Teaching the Text

Based on the fact that this is a teaching psalm, we may build an effective sermon/lesson on the ideas of Yahweh as Teacher, his ways as the curriculum, and the psalmist and all who fear the Lord as his students. As we have pointed out (see "Theological Insights"), there are four verbs that deliver

the message of this relationship: "show," "teach," "guide," and "instruct." All four occur two or more times in the poem, and this accumulation of virtual synonyms is a literary device to indicate how intense David's search for guidance and understanding is and, by application, how powerful ours ought to be.

First, the Teacher is obviously Yahweh, and the psalm gives us a "bio" that informs us of his character: he is good (25:7, 8) and loving (25:6). So we should expect his instruction to reflect his character (25:10), and with this exemplary character, there should be no reluctance to listen to and follow his instruction. This imagery of the good Teacher who designs his curriculum by his gracious and merciful character provides the kind of "classroom" experience every student needs.

Second, the Teacher's curriculum is to "instruct sinners in his ways" (25:8; see also 25:9). His "ways" (25:4, 8, 9, 10, 12), most likely a designation of his laws in the specific sense, and his covenant in the more general sense (25:10, 14), suggest a journey, and the Lord's instructions are designed to "instruct them in the ways they should choose" (25:12; lit., "instruct him [David] in the way he should choose"). The idea of the journey is further suggested by the promise that his offspring would inherit the land, recalling the land of Canaan (25:13), and the sojourner is well aware of his untutored life, alluded to as "the sins of my youth and my rebellious ways" (25:7; see also 25:18).

Third, there is no evidence in the psalm of a sophomoric mentality, for the psalmist recognizes his sins. This is a state of mind to which we must come as students in the school of faith. The psalmist was, as we must be, open to instruction. His circumstances, described as "affliction" and "distress" (25:18), have driven him into the classroom of faith as he has prayed for God's forgiveness, as sometimes our life circumstances drive us. But the learning experience, with the Master Teacher and his well-crafted curriculum of truth and love (25:5, 7) and his character-reflecting pedagogy, generates a life of hope (25:3, 5, 21). And the psalmist can say—and we can join his affirmation—"my hope, LORD, is in you" (25:21).

Illustrating the Text

Learning for a lifetime

Cultural Institution: In the United States, one function of government is education, which is administered through the public school system by the Department of Education. Although the federal government has an interest in education, the states have primary responsibility for the maintenance and operation of public schools through the twelfth grade. There is such great value placed on education in the United States that the Equal Education Opportunities Act of 1974 provides that no state shall deny equal educational opportunity to an individual on the basis of race, color, sex, or national origin.[15] However, once a student has satisfied the requirements of a twelfth-grade education, the government tends to stop emphasizing the importance of education. Sadly, many Christians carry this notion into their Christian experience. Instead of realizing their need for spiritual continuing education until the day they die, many Christians wrongly believe that all they need to know can be gained through a half-hour sermon once a week. Psalm 25 shows David's realization of his need to continue to learn and grow as he repeatedly asks the Lord to teach him.

In Psalm 25, the writer confesses his sin, asks for forgiveness, and looks for guidance from the Lord. Our pride should not keep us from seeking God. We should not be like lost travelers who refuse to ask for directions because of insecurity or pride.

Pride can prevent us from trusting in the Lord.

Psychology: Dr. Mark Goulston wrote a self-analysis on why men stereotypically prefer to be lost rather than ask for directions. His list of eight explanations boils down to insecurity and pride. For example, his first two points are "to ask for directions is to admit I am lost" and "to admit I am lost is to feel both anxious and incompetent."[16] Many of us deal with issues of pride and insecurity that keep us from admitting our inadequacies and human need. What a contrast to Psalm 25, where David openly acknowledges his need for direction and confesses his sin (25:11).

Shame and guilt

Psychology: Shame and guilt are related but different experiences. Donald R. Hands says shame hits people at the core of their being and is a constant reminder of their failure, whereas guilt is an item-by-item experience and can be expunged from their psychological portfolio more readily than shame. Shame is less therapeutic than guilt.[17] The Psalms frequently speak of shame as a condition of moral breakdown, as in 25:2–3, where it is the near opposite of trust. Indeed, "no one who hopes" in God will ever be the victim of shame. If guilt is more therapeutic than shame, it may be a spiritual malady that has resulted from our blasé attitude toward sin. Our politically correct society insists that we should not be condemnatory toward human behavior that transgresses God's moral commandments, so we have developed an immunity to shame. And the more impervious we are to shame, which is a consequence of our sin, the less we feel our need of grace.

"Lord, I Love the House Where You Live"

Big Idea *The love of God's house is evidenced in the psalmist's personal conduct—the two cannot be separated, for David's life is an illustration of how worship shapes one's life.*

Understanding the Text

Craigie, following Vogt,[1] classifies Psalm 26 as an *entrance liturgy*, or pilgrim prayer, related in both form and content to Psalms 15 and 24. In form, however, the prayer that God will vindicate the psalmist and examine his heart has replaced the liturgical question of Psalms 15:1 and 24:3, and even the explicit answer of Psalms 15:2–5 and 24:4 is missing, blending into the suppliant's defense of his innocence. Since the poet largely lays out the case for his innocence, a *psalm of innocence*, as Gunkel has labeled it, seems a much better choice.[2] The editor(s) of Book 1, or this particular subcollection, makes a case for the righteous person who is morally worthy to enter the temple of the Lord, so the psalm may be a more general consideration of his moral character, that he is worthy to enter the Lord's house, than a specific liturgy in the sense of Psalms 15 and 24.

The Text in Context

Psalms 25 and 26 share verbal links. The psalmist trusts in the Lord (25:2; 26:1) and prays for redemption (25:22; 26:11) and mercy (25:16; 26:11). Wilson observes that the psalm has a broader context in

One large laver, or water basin, was required in the tabernacle so that the priests could wash their hands and feet before performing sacrifices or entering the tent of meeting. The laver and altar in the tabernacle model at Timna, Israel, are shown here.

the sequence of Psalms 23–30, all of which have their focus on the "house" or "dwelling" of Yahweh.[3] Further, as we have seen in our study of the Psalms, sometimes the editors have arranged the individual poems in a fashion so that one psalm provides an explicit or implicit identification of the righteous person, that person, in a rhetorical sense, being David (see unit on Psalm 25, n. 14). From Psalm 15 the editorial line of this section of the Psalter runs along the theme of ceremonial/personal righteousness and entrance into the Lord's house, which in effect is the goal of the faith of the Psalms, sometimes expressed as joy in God's presence (16:11; 21:6; 23:6) and seeing God's face (17:15). The general question of who can enter the temple is answered in terms of those who conduct their lives in a godly way and who fear the Lord, two ways of saying the same thing, or, to phrase it another way, two complementary ways of describing the righteous individual. The psalmist (and the editors also by their arrangement of the psalms) puts David forth as the exemplar of righteousness and the one who is worthy, by his personal conduct and God-fearing demeanor, to ascend the mountain of the Lord and enter the sanctuary. In this psalm the ceremonial and the ethical are brought together in one scene, as the supplicant rejects the company of evildoers by washing his hands in the sanctuary (26:5–6) and going about the altar praising God (26:7). Here we have a brief but crisp picture of worship in the temple, which involved washing, going to the altar of burnt offering, and rehearsing the mighty acts of God in Israel's history (26:6–8; see also 68:24–27).

Key Themes of Psalm 26

- Associate with sinners but disassociate with their lifestyle.
- God's unfailing love is the center of life and the biblical gospel.

Outline/Structure

The psalm is framed by "I walk in my integrity" (NIV translates "walk" as "led," 26:1, and "lead," 26:11), and within that frame the supplicant requests the Lord's attention to his innocence with four positive imperatives and two negative affirmations.

1. First positive imperative: "*Vindicate* me" (26:1)
   Psalmist's righteousness presented in positive terms:
   - "I have led a blameless life"
   - "I have trusted in the LORD and have not faltered"
2. Second and third positive imperatives: "*Test* me, LORD, and *try* me" (26:2a)
3. Fourth positive imperative: "*Examine* my heart and my mind" (26:2b–3)
   Psalmist's defense in positive terms:
   - "For I have always been mindful of your unfailing love" (26:3a)
   - "And have lived in reliance on your faithfulness" (26:3b)
4. First and second negative affirmations (26:4–5)
   a. "*I do not sit* with the deceitful, nor do I *associate* with hypocrites" (26:4)

b. "*I abhor* the assembly of evil-doers and *refuse to sit* with the wicked" (26:5)
5. The psalmist in worship (26:6–8)
   a. The psalmist's worship activity (26:6–7)
   b. The psalmist's worship attitude (26:8)
6. The psalmist's disassociation with evildoers (26:9–10)
7. Conclusion/restatement of theme and vow (26:11–12)[4]

Historical and Cultural Background

The practice of washing one's hands to symbolize innocence (26:6) was observed by Israel's elders (Deut. 21:6–7). The priests washed their hands in the great laver that sat in the tabernacle/temple court in preparation for service at the altar of burnt offering (Exod. 40:30–32).[5] Here we have a camera view of the court in front of the sanctuary where both the altar of burnt offering and laver were located. In 26:6–7 we have the service in minuscule: the washing of the hands, attendance at the altar (either as priest or worshiper), and proclaiming the wonderful deeds of Yahweh in Israel's history.

Interpretive Insights

Title *Of David.* Psalms 25–28 are titled "Of David," and there are no solid reasons why these psalms could not have been written by him. Certainly David's desire to build a permanent house for the Lord (2 Sam. 7) provides the historical and emotional positioning for 26:8.

26:1 *Vindicate me,* LORD. Form critics see a judicial proceeding behind the verb "vindicate" (also in Pss. 7:8; 35:24; 43:1), and some scholars suggest that the suppliant has taken refuge in the temple, as sometimes offenders used the sanctuary as a place of asylum (Exod. 21:13–14; 1 Kings 1:50–53; 2:28–30). However, it is more likely that the psalmist is simply dealing with his moral innocence before God.

I have led a blameless life . . . have not faltered. In Hebrew the phrase "I have led a blameless life" is literally, "I walk in my integrity [*tom*]," suggesting that he is free from sin (also Prov. 10:9). "Walk" (26:1, 3, 11; NIV: "lead a life," or "live") and "stand" (26:12) form a merism that describes the whole of life's activity.[6] The imagery behind "have not faltered" (see also Ps. 37:31; NIV: "do not slip") is that of a sure-footed traveler walking along a narrow mountain path.[7]

26:2 *Test me,* LORD, *and try me, examine my heart and my mind.* The words for "test" (*bhn*) and "examine" (*tsrp*) also occur in Psalm 17:3 ("probe" and "test," respectively; see the comments on that verse). The verb for "examine" is from the vocabulary of metallurgy, describing the melting down of the metal by fire to remove the dross (Pss. 12:6; 66:10, etc.). (See "Historical and Cultural Background" in unit on Psalm 12.) "Test" (*bhn*) and "try" (*nsh*) occur as synonyms in Psalm 95:9 ("tested," *nsh*; "tried," *bhn*). The Hebrew equivalent of "my heart and my mind" is "my reins and my heart." My "reins" (*kᵉlayot*) are the kidneys, which register one's emotions, while "heart" (*leb*) is the mind (see the comments on Ps. 7:9).

26:3 *your unfailing love . . . your faithfulness.* "Love" (*hesed*) and "truth" or "faithfulness" (*'emet*) are covenant terms, which form the grounds of the suppliant's prayer of faith. See Psalm 25:10 (*hesed* and *'emet*).

26:4 *the deceitful . . . hypocrites.* Delitzsch describes "the deceitful" as "the very opposite of being filled with the fullness of God and with that which is good, which is the morally real" (see Job 11:11).[8] The word for "hypocrites" is the Niphal participle from the verb "to hide," suggesting those who try to hide their real character.

26:5 *assembly of evildoers.* David has rejected this assembly in preference of the "great assembly" (26:12; NIV: "great congregation").

26:6 *wash my hands in innocence, and go about your altar.* For washing hands in innocence, see Exodus 40:30–32 and Deuteronomy 21:6–7 (see also "Historical and Cultural Background"). "[I] have washed my hands in innocence" occurs in Psalm 73:13 and connotes a pure heart.[9] The *Midrash on the Psalms* associates this activity with the circling of the altar each day of the festival of Sukkot, when Psalm 118:25 ("Lord, save us!") was recited.[10] The same ritual procession seems to be in view in 118:27: "With boughs in hand, join in the festal procession up to the horns of the altar."

26:7 *proclaiming aloud your praise and telling of all your wonderful deeds.* The first phrase is literally "proclaiming with the voice of thanksgiving." God's "wonderful deeds" (*nipla'ot*) are his saving deeds. In Exodus 3:20, this term refers to the exodus event and its attendant wonders, as it does also in Micah 7:15.[11]

26:8 Lord, *I love the house where you live, the place where your glory dwells.* The center of the psalmist's life was the sanctuary. "The house where you live" is literally "the habitation of your house" (see KJV). The noun "habitation" (rendered verbally in NIV) originally meant a hiding place or retreat, and in Old Testament poetry it has the sense of God's dwelling place, both in heaven and on

During their service in the temple, the priests purified themselves before performing sacrifices or entering the holy place. Temple furnishings for purification included a large basin, known as The Sea, for the priests, and ten movable bronze cart-stands, which held basins of water for washing utensils used in sacrifices. This wheeled cart, which many scholars believe is a laver stand, was designed to hold a vessel or basin and may have served a similar ritual function in Cyprus (1250–1100 BC).

earth (Deut. 26:15; 2 Chron. 36:15; cf. 2 Chron. 7:1–3; Ezek. 43:4–5; 44:4).[12] God's glory was the evanescent presence of God dwelling in the holy of holies and streaming from the temple (Ps. 63:2; see also Ezek. 11:23; 43:1–5). While Yahweh was invisible, from time to time he manifested himself visibly or in a vision.

26:9 *Do not take away my soul along with sinners.* "Soul" (*nepesh*) sometimes is used in place of the personal pronoun ("me"). The supplicant prays that God will not add him as "collateral damage" to the lot of sinners, which option he has already rejected (26:5). It is a negative plea that parallels the positive plea of 26:1–2.

26:10 *wicked schemes . . . right hands are full of bribes.* Their hands, which should delicately hold the welfare of their neighbors, hold instead the cunning schemes of evildoers. The word "schemes" (*zimmah*) normally means sexual sins,[13] but here in parallelism with "bribes" it implies dishonest actions that would undermine their neighbors' legitimate rights. Hakham, however, suggests that the three violations mentioned here reference the three serious transgressions of the Ten Commandments: "men of blood" (NIV: "bloodthirsty")—murder; "mischief" (NIV: "wicked schemes")—adultery; and "bribes"—theft (see Exod. 20:13–15).[14]

26:12 *on level ground.* Metaphorically, we may understand "level ground" to mean that the psalmist has reached a state of moral equilibrium in his struggle with sin and sinners. He fights on level ground, where his moral innocence provides him great advantage, as would level ground for warriors, as opposed to a rocky landscape.

Theological Insights

Except for the title and final verse, this psalm is exclusively a prayer to God. While David does not underscore the judgment of God that accrues to doing evil, his plea for divine scrutiny of his character, and his prayer that God not "take away" his soul with sinners (26:9), implies a consciousness of divine judgment. In fact, despite his innocence, he obviously is a close associate with the ways and schemes of evildoers—otherwise he could not have rejected them—and he feels himself on the cusp of experiencing God's judgment (26:9–10). His plea for redemption and divine mercy (26:11b) is probably an appeal that he not, by mere proximity, be the object of God's displeasure with wicked people.

There is no way the righteous can live in a separate world from evildoers—that is contrary to reality. The protestation of the psalmist's innocence is necessarily in terms of the evil behavior he has avoided, and that not by distance but by choice. But even rejection of evil, a response that implies its closeness, carries the risk of being entrapped by its implications. The innocent, like the prophets Jeremiah and Ezekiel of the sixth century BC, did not escape the consequences of divine judgment. Jerusalem fell, and Ezekiel was exiled to Babylonia and Jeremiah taken to Egypt against his will; the suffering they saw and endured was beyond human description (see Lamentations). The psalmist prays for redemption from such "collateral" judgment.

Yet the love for the Lord's house is the centerpiece of the psalm (26:8). David is on his way morally and ritually to the house where God's glory dwells. It is love of the Lord's house that leads him along the path of character formation to the place of God's glory. Any stress or discipline is easier when the goal is tempered by love. David's world is incredibly evil, and the cost he pays as Israel's monarch is substantial, both politically and personally, but he has been steadied on his feet (26:12) by the love of God's house. Another patron of the Lord's house speaks of the ways to the temple as being in the hearts of the pilgrims ("in whose heart are the ways of them," Ps. 84:5 KJV). It was more than planning the pilgrimage; it was making the pilgrimage the essence of their life.

Teaching the Text

It is virtually axiomatic to prescribe how one should write a good essay: *state one's theme*, then *explain one's theme*, and then in summary *state one's theme again*. That is precisely what David does in the psalm. He states his theme in verse 1: "I have led a blameless life"; then he develops that theme in verses 2–10; and last, he states his theme again in verse 11: "I lead a blameless life." This can be a helpful outline for a sermon/lesson. We should explain to our audience that "blameless life" (lit., "I have walked in my integrity") is not one of those terms we ought to define before we discuss the rest of the psalm, but we should allow the psalm to define it for us. So we should bring our students or congregation along with us as we explore verses 2–10—and this is the "essay" proper.

Here we may speak of two ways that David defines and describes the theme of the psalm. First, he talks about his personal conduct in both positive and negative terms, praying that God will conduct his own "laboratory" tests (26:1–5; see "Outline/Structure"). The center of his faith and conduct has been his consciousness of God's "unfailing love" (26:3). That truth is not only the substance of the Old Testament covenant but is also the constituent truth of the New Testament gospel, which is an opportunity to make a connection between the

The psalmist proclaims, "Lord, I love the house where you live, the place where your glory dwells" (26:8). The place of God's presence was the holy of holies, first in the tabernacle, then in the temple. It is not clear, however, how the Israelites thought about God's presence during this time. Archaeological excavations at the city of Arad uncovered a tenth-century BC temple where YHWH was worshiped. It includes an altar and an area that has been named the holy of holies (shown here) because of the two incense altars that flank the doorway and the two standing stones that designate it as sacred space (though archaeologists are uncertain whether all four of these pieces would have been in use at the same time).

Testaments and stress God's bonds of love that the Testaments have in common. This is indeed the center around which his whole life revolves: "LORD, I love the house where you live, the place where your glory dwells" (26:8). Here he does what a good writing teacher would tell her or his students to do: when you develop your theme, develop it in two or three ways, each slightly different but appealing. It is a given fact that every aspect of our lives revolves around something, someone, or some activity. If we look at these "centers," there is, generally speaking, a deeper motive that determines what that center is. It can be egocentric (self), humanitarian (others), or theological (God), to name the basic concentrations (one does not have to be exclusive of the others, of course). David's was theological, for the centerpiece of his life was the Lord's house, as stated in verse 8, developing the theme of verses 1 and 11.

Second, David focuses on two "assemblies," the "assembly of evildoers," which he has rejected (26:5), and the "great assembly/congregation" (26:12), or the worshiping community, which he has embraced and where he feels safe from the lurking evils of his world. At the same time, this is not inconsonant with God's "unfailing love." While it implies an "associate" relationship with sinners, it also demands a "disassociate" relationship with their lifestyle.

To stress God's power over that of evil, the psalmist uses six synonyms for sinners

Psalm 26 begins and ends with the psalmist declaring, I have led, v. 1, or I lead, v. 11, a blameless life. He tells the Lord to test him, to examine his heart and his mind (26:2). This brings to mind the weighing of the heart ritual (shown here as a drawing on papyrus) that Egyptians believed occurred as the deceased passed through the netherworld. The heart was weighed to determine if it was pure (fourth to first century BC).

and by them forms a picture of the world he faces: the deceitful and hypocrites (26:4), evildoers and the wicked (26:5), sinners and the bloodthirsty (26:9). At times he has felt as if he was about to be swept away with this evil influence, and he has prayed: "Do not take away my soul along with sinners" (26:9a; see "Theological Insights").

Yet over against that malicious world, the psalm has a way of showing us that there is a power beyond the power of sin, that where "sin abounded, grace abounded much more" (Rom. 5:20 NKJV). Over against the *six* synonyms for sinners, the Lord's name occurs *six* times, with one instance of the epithet "your glory" (26:8)—seven occurrences—which offset the power of evildoers. We might call this code language, but that is one of the literary riches of the Psalms. Evil is powerful—six is close to seven, only one less—but seven, the perfect number, represents the Lord's overpowering grace.

In conclusion we should call attention to the fact that verse 12 is our conclusion, and as such, it *restates* the theme of the psalm introduced in verse 1 and developed in verses 2–10: "My feet stand on level ground; in the great congregation will I praise the LORD." David's whole life has been "on the way" to the Lord's house, a concept that has tempered his life and shaped his character. The path is not just a way for one's feet but a path engraved in one's heart (Ps. 84:5).

Illustrating the Text

Writing our autobiography

Personal Testimony: When we look at Psalm 26:8, we see the principle that motivates David's life. It is the centerpiece of the psalm: "LORD, I love the house where you live, the place where your glory dwells." David is developing his theme of verses 1 and 11 as he tells us what influence has caused him to lead a "blameless life." This is really the theme of his autobiography.

All of us are writing our autobiography. We may never put it down on paper, and it may never be published; however, we are writing it, and somebody is reading it. A few years ago, an elderly woman came through our offices at Wheaton College selling copies of her autobiography. So far as I know, she was not famous, nor had she written anything else that would make one want to read this volume. She was just a lady who wanted others to know about her life. This was her maiden composition. I have no idea how many copies she sold in the department, but I was so touched by her effort and motive that I bought a copy.

Quote: Albert Schweitzer. Schweitzer was a German theologian, missionary doctor, and musician. He wrote about leaving home to go to school and how homesick he got. He said he longed much for the church at Guensbach, where his father was pastor: "I missed my father's sermons, and the services I had been familiar with all my life." So many years later he was still reading his father's autobiography.[15]

"The LORD Is My Light and My Salvation—Whom Shall I Fear?"

Big Idea *Our lives, guided by a single purpose, find their security in our relationship to God.*

Understanding the Text

This psalm has two distinct parts, which leads some interpreters to suggest that it was originally two separate poems.[1] Part 1 (27:1–6) has the qualities of an individual psalm of trust (see the sidebar "Psalms of Trust" in the unit on Ps. 16),[2] while part 2 (27:7–13) takes the form of a complaint[3] or lament. The difference in genre cannot, of course, be the definitive word, since the psalms sometimes mix them.[4] If they are two distinct poems, the evidence seems to point in the direction that part 2 was composed with part 1 in view, rather than the psalm being the combination of two independent poems.[5] It seems, however, that the poet was describing his deep trust in God alongside his plaintive lament, two frames of mind that, in the complexities of life, do sometimes exist together.[6] Even though the duplicate use of key terms in the two parts does not solve the problem (see table 1), it certainly does point to the compositional relationship and at least leaves the single-author option open, much like the two-part composition of Psalm 19.

Table 1. Corresponding Terms between Parts 1 and 2 of Psalm 27

	Part 1 (27:1–6)	Part 2 (27:7–13)
"My salvation"/"Savior"	27:1	27:9
"My enemies"/"foes"	27:2	27:12
"My heart"	27:3	27:8 (cf. 27:14)
"Break out"/"rise up"	27:3	27:12
"Seek"	27:4	27:8
"Life"/"living"	27:4	27:13

Note: The list of terms is adapted from Craigie, *Psalms 1–50*, 230–31.

Craigie has proposed that the psalm is a *royal liturgy*, used by a king to celebrate the occasion or anniversary of his coronation in the tradition of the Davidic covenant. After part 1, the king declares his faith and trust in God before the congregation and then offers sacrifices of thanksgiving. After part 2, a priest or temple prophet delivers an oracle (27:14) that provides an answer to the king's prayer in part 2.[7]

The Text in Context

David's love of God's house, declared in Psalm 26:8 ("LORD, I love the house

198

where you live"), appears again in 27:4: "One thing I ask from the LORD, . . . that I may dwell in the house of the LORD all the days of my life." This links the two psalms together. Moreover, at the sanctuary the psalmist stands on "level ground" (26:12, *mishor*), the same kind of level-footed place where he meets his oppressors (27:11; NIV: "*straight* path").

Outline/Structure

Part 1: The psalmist's trust in the Lord and desire to dwell in God's house (27:1–6)

Part 2: The psalmist's prayer for God's mercy (27:7–13)

Final counsel: Wait for the Lord (27:14)

Historical and Cultural Background

In Book 1 of the Psalter, Absalom's rebellion is never far out of mind.[8] "In the day of trouble" (27:5) sounds like a specific situation may be in mind, but that does not have to be the case, since David's life was filled with wars and rumors of wars.

Key Themes of Psalm 27

- The Lord is our light and salvation.
- The psalmist longs to dwell in the Lord's house.
- God's goodness is in "the land of the living."
- Wait for the Lord.

The military language ("stronghold," 27:1; "my enemies and my foes," 27:2; "army" [lit., "camp"], "war," 27:3; etc.) is part of Craigie's reason for typing this psalm as a *royal liturgy*. David was a man of war (2 Sam. 17:8), and his life was filled with conflict—military, political, family. It is therefore not surprising that his speech reflected that. In this case, the idea of a royal liturgy may be more a product of form criticism than David's historical situation. Even Craigie himself admits that the liturgical elements are implied.

Interpretive Insights

27:1 *The LORD is my light and my salvation . . . the stronghold of my life.* Not only is Yahweh "light," but he is also called a "lamp" (2 Sam. 22:29) and is the one who kindles and trims the lamp (Ps. 18:28). The word "stronghold" (*ma'oz*) refers to a place of refuge, especially from one's enemy (Nah. 3:11; NIV: "refuge"). All

The psalmist will not fear a besieging army because he trusts in God as his stronghold. Shown here is the Assyrian army attacking the fortified Judean city of Lachish, which they subsequently conquered. This siege began in 701 BC as Sennacherib invaded, punishing many Judean towns for not paying the required tribute. Like David, King Hezekiah trusted in the Lord, and God defended the city of Jerusalem. It did not fall.

three nouns position this psalm in a military context: "light," which was absolutely necessary for successful battle; "salvation," or victory, in battle; and "stronghold," the place of safety from one's enemies.

27:2 *When the wicked advance against me . . . it is my enemies who will stumble and fall.* "Advance" means "come near" to fight (Deut. 20:2; NIV: "about to go"). The double verb of defeat ("stumble and fall") is very close to Psalm 20:8: "They are brought to their knees and fall." The final clause gives the sense of the enemies' failed purpose.

27:3 *Though an army besiege me . . . even then I will be confident.* The Septuagint renders the prospect of "besiege me" as past, whereas the Hebrew is tentative. Also, in the last clause, the NIV does not render the demonstrative pronoun literally ("in *this*"), shifting the reference from the psalmist's faith in Yahweh to the circumstances ("even then"). The demonstrative pronoun, in fact, reflects back on the nature of God described in 27:1, the fact that the Lord is his light, salvation, and stronghold, the basis of the suppliant's confidence.

27:4–6 Verses 4–6 constitute the heart of the poem, the suppliant's desire to be in God's house, which is another way of expressing his desire to be with and to know his God.

27:4 *to gaze on the beauty of the Lord.* Perowne suggests that the best translation of the Hebrew word for "beauty" (*no'am*) is "favor" (Ps. 90:17), combining the ideas of beauty, personality, and kindness (cf. Prov. 31:30).[9] In Psalm 90:17 Moses uses the same word to pray that the beauty of the Lord would be upon Israel, and that he would establish their work.

to seek him in his temple. Four different words, all synonyms, are used for the sanctuary (see below): "house" (*bayit*) and "temple" (*hekal*, 27:4), "tabernacle" (*sukkah*, 27:5; NIV: "dwelling"), and "tent" (*'ohel*, 27:6). If the psalm is of Davidic vintage, "temple" (*hekal*) occurs here as a reference to the tabernacle, as it does also in 1 Samuel 3:3 (but see 27:5 below).

27:5 *he will keep me safe in his dwelling . . . the shelter of his sacred tent . . . high upon a rock.* According to 2 Chronicles 1:3–4, Moses's "tent" (tabernacle) was still located at Gibeon at the beginning of Solomon's reign, to be distinguished from the tent that David prepared in Jerusalem to receive the ark of the covenant. "Dwelling" (*sukkah*) is the term for the sanctuary (Ps. 76:2; NIV: "tent"). The thought of "hiding" is in deference to the danger the psalmist faces. The place "high upon a rock," a place of safety and security, is parallel to the sanctuary as a place of safety (Ps. 18:2), "where the surge of earthly perils cannot reach him."[10] The sanctuary was a place where one could flee from one's enemies and find safety.

27:6 *my head will be exalted above the enemies who surround me; at his sacred tent I will sacrifice.* Still in the sanctuary, David now reflects on the battlefield. The long form of the imperfect verb "sacrifice" implies that this is a vow to make a sacrifice of thanksgiving.[11] Craigie understands this to suggest that the king is about to offer sacrifices, perhaps as a renewal celebration of the Davidic covenant.[12]

27:7 *Hear my voice . . . be merciful to me.* With this verse we hear a dramatic shift in the tone of the psalm (27:7–12). The tone of confidence that dominated verses

The psalmist asks the Lord to hear his voice and answer (27:7). This stele shows an Egyptian praying to his god. Notice the ears along the top left side. These were included in the painting to assist the god in hearing the prayers (Thebes, 1200 BC).

God's faithfulness, which becomes an affirmation of faith to precede his petition for divine mercy and help. This frame of mind is affirmed by the reaffirmation of confidence in 27:13.

27:8 *My heart says of you, "Seek his face!"* Obviously the psalmist is speaking ("My heart says"), which calls attention to the grammatical problem: the grammatical persons of "my heart [psalmist]" and "seek [masc. pl.] my [God] face" do not match up. The Septuagint and the Targum, however, do not try to "correct" the reading. We would expect: "My heart says of you, 'Seek his face!' Your face, LORD, I will seek." And that is precisely how the NIV has rendered it, unfortunately without textual warrant. It is quite likely that this is an ellipsis, the psalmist reporting what his heart heard of Yahweh: "My heart says of you [ellipsis: "what I had heard you say to me"], 'Seek my face!' Your face, LORD, I will seek." The fact that the imperative "seek" is plural should pose no problem—it was in the congregation that he heard the voice. The suppliant's intention is to go to the sanctuary, the very thing that is the passion of his life (27:4). In any case, this is both a command and a promise, as Weiser observes,[15] for the Lord has said, "But if from there [exile] you seek the LORD your God, you will find him if you seek him with all your heart and with all your soul" (Deut. 4:29).

1–6 now becomes a passionate prayer for mercy, assuming a lamentive frame of mind. Why the sudden change? Some assume that the first part of the psalm was a review of God's faithfulness in the past, as a preliminary statement to the psalmist's petition for mercy.[13] Others believe that in part 1 he laid out his vision for the future, and in part 2 he awakes from his dream to the reality of present dangers.[14] I prefer the first option, in the sense that he lays out his trust in

Psalm 27

David Cast in the Profile of Joshua

The Psalms often employ the interpretive principle that the psalmist, and especially David, could relive, or at least reenact, the life of the heroes of the faith, like Moses and Joshua. Psalm 27 clearly illustrates this principle as David echoes the words of Moses to Joshua:

David (Ps. 27)	Moses (Deut. 31)
"Be strong and take heart" (27:14)	"Be strong and courageous" (Deut. 31:7; cf. Josh. 1:6, 7, 9)
"Whom shall I fear?" (27:1) "My heart will not fear" (27:3)	"Do not be afraid" (Deut. 31:8)
"Do not . . . forsake me" (27:9)	"He will never . . . forsake you" (Deut. 31:8; cf. Josh. 1:5)

27:9 *Do not reject me or forsake me, God my Savior.* Sometimes there is a psychological benefit in asking God not to do what we know he would never do. We need recurring affirmation. Weiser captures the tension here between faith and uncertainty: "It is precisely the blending of divine judgment and divine grace which constitutes the peculiar tension so characteristic of the experience of faith."[16]

27:10 *Though my father and mother forsake me, the LORD will receive me.* Most likely, this is not a reference to anything in David's life but a hypothetical thought, "even though." The apodosis expresses the reality of God's taking the psalmist into his house (cf. Deut. 22:2).[17]

27:11 *straight path.* The metaphor stems from the terrain of Palestine, where a straight path is more direct and less risky as one moves toward one's destination. Here it refers to good and righteous behavior.[18]

27:12 *spouting malicious accusations.* Literally, "he breathes out violence."

27:13 *in the land of the living.* The psalmist, having in part 2 (27:7–13) thrust himself into the reality of the present situation, affirms that he fully expects to live through the danger and survive it well. Some believe that he is expressing a view toward the afterlife. If not, his soul is reaching forward toward a reality that the salvation from his enemies portends in a better day.[19]

27:14 *Wait for the LORD; be strong and take heart and wait for the LORD.* This urgent admonition to "be strong and take heart," sandwiched between the double "wait for the LORD," recalls the words of Moses to Joshua (see the sidebar). Compare with Isaiah 40:31 (see ESV). See "Theological Insights" in the unit on Psalm 25.

Theological Insights

The association of God with light (27:1) is a theme that begins with creation. As Creator of light, who established its line of separation from darkness (Gen. 1:3–5), God identified himself forever with light and by implication established his rule over darkness. When the psalmist on another occasion thinks darkness can hide him from God, he feels God's hand taking hold of him as he crouches under its elusive cover (Ps. 139:11–12). The prophet Micah also assures the Israelites that when they sit in the darkness of defeat, "the LORD will be my light" (Mic. 7:8). Normally we think of light and darkness as different spheres of the real world, as they are in the creation narrative, but it is imperative that God be understood as Lord *over* darkness, as well as the God of light. The eschatological description of the church, redeemed in glory, declares that there will be no need for sun and moon, for the glory of God lights the city of God, and the Lamb is its lamp (Rev. 21:23).

God's power to turn the circumstances in his favor is a recurring theme of the Psalms. Here it takes the form of a battle raging against the psalmist, and contrary to all opposing expectations, the battle turns in the psalmist's favor (27:2–3). The position of the personal pronoun standing at the front of the half line gives this sense: "It is they [not I] who will stumble and fall" (27:2). The same reversal of events has taken place in the psalmist's heart as that unfolding on the battlefield.

The miraculous reversal of events, that is, God's bestowal of light and salvation, awakens in David and intensifies the "one thing" his heart longs for: "that I may dwell in the house of the LORD all the days of my life, to gaze on the beauty of the LORD and to seek him in his temple" (27:4). This passion preoccupies 27:4–6, using several synonyms for the tabernacle or temple (see the comments on 27:4). Dwelling in the temple "all the days" of his life does not suggest that the psalmist was a priest or Levite but indicates that he desired frequent, likely even daily, access to the sanctuary for the rest of his life. There he would "gaze on the beauty of the LORD," meditating on the gracious deeds of the Lord in Israel's and his personal experience.

The heartthrob of the suppliant's life, which war and opposition could not stop, issues in an oath—so sure is he—that he will see the Lord's goodness while he is still alive (27:13). Thus he can cast himself in the character of Joshua, drawing on Moses's words to his successor, in order to commend to his own soul or some other fellow traveler the way forward, the way to the promised land: "Wait for the LORD; *be strong and take heart* and wait for the LORD" (27:14, italicized words echo Moses's words; see the sidebar).

Teaching the Text

We might well begin the lesson or sermon by referring back to Psalm 26, where we made the observation that David was always *on the way* to the Lord's house. It was his passion, a way of life for him. Psalms 23–30 all have their focus on the Lord's house, but Psalm 27 brings clarity to this theme. It is not merely the *house* that attracts David but the LORD *of the house*,

Walking along a straight path meant that one's behavior was righteous and upright. Because of Israel's terrain, straight, level paths, like the one shown here for a short way in the Ein Avdat National Park, are not the most common.

who illuminates his way and removes the fear that otherwise stalks his path.

To understand the depth and solidity of David's trust, we need to look for hints of his story. As we know, one's story is not always related in short-story form but often comes in phrases and metaphors (see "Theological Insights" in the unit on Ps. 23). When he measures his faith in God, he finds the measuring rod on the field of conflict (27:2–3). The NIV translates the last half of verse 3 as "even then I will be confident" (that is, even in the face of battle), but the Hebrew says: "In this I am trusting" (KJV: "In this will I be confident"). The demonstrative pronoun "this" bundles up David's confidence that has grown out of those times when the battle seemed lost and then the enemies stumbled and fell (see "Theological Insights" regarding the personal pronoun in 27:2).

It certainly is within the bounds of good homiletical theory to apply this to the hostile forces of our own lives that configure to send us into retreat. And when the "battle" seems lost, the circumstances may miraculously turn, and the hostilities may be defused by a rush of the adrenaline of grace, taking away the fear and restoring confidence.

Illustrating the Text

"The Lord is my light."

Bible: The centrality of light in the Scriptures is attested in many places. Here David's statement "The Lord is my light" summons to our minds the primordial light of the universe (Gen. 1:3–5) and one of Jesus's "I am" sayings in John's Gospel, "I am the light of the world" (John 8:12). Psalm 139:12 teaches that even when we try to escape from God's watchful eye into the darkness of this world, we only discover that "the night will shine like the day, for darkness is as light to you," strongly implying God's sovereign control over darkness. John's proclamation is all the more understandable when we perceive God's nature as light: "The light shines in the darkness, and the darkness has not overcome it" (John 1:5). So this announcement points toward the creation and the new creation. Perhaps John's word picture of ultimate salvation is the capstone of this biblical theme, "The city does not need the sun or the moon to shine on it, for the glory of God gives it light, and the Lamb is its lamp" (Rev. 21:23).

Be anchored to the Lord.

Metaphor: An anchor is a heavy object attached to a rope or chain

God was David's anchor during the storms of life. These ancient anchors are on display at Caesarea, Israel.

and is used to moor a vessel to the sea bottom. The power of an anchor is that it can hold a boat in one place regardless of the sea conditions. The wind may blow, and the waves may pound the boat, but the properly anchored vessel will withstand the storm. Psalm 27 provides a powerful picture of David being anchored to the nature and character of God. How did David withstand the dangerous and fearful storms of life? He chose to anchor himself to the Lord, who was the stronghold of his life (27:1). David knew that God was his light, protector, and savior. David knew the love and power of God firsthand. It is this intimate knowledge of God that brings hope in the midst of the fears, insecurities, and dangers of life.

God is for us!

Bible: Romans 8. In Romans 8:31, Paul captures the essence of Psalm 27 in his declaration, "If God is for us, who can be against us?" God's help is more than sponsorship but is a total giving of himself to save us, proved by the great sacrifice of his Son: "He who did not spare his own Son, but gave him up for us all—how will he not also, along with him, graciously give us all things?" (Rom. 8:32). That is proof of God's great love. There are times, during life's storms that all of us face, when we doubt God's love and provision. When these thoughts come, we must stop and remind ourselves what God has already done for us in Christ. The circumstances do not shape God, but God shapes the circumstances.

"Do Not Drag Me Away with the Wicked"

Big Idea *The menaces of leadership are myriad, sometimes posed by cordial faces with malicious intentions, and we pray that God will be the real Shepherd.*

Understanding the Text

Gunkel lists Psalm 28 among the individual complaint songs, the genre that, in his view, forms the basic material of the Psalter.[1] Gerstenberger, based on the elements of petition, thanksgiving, and intercession, agrees and considers this psalm a model representative of the individual complaint psalm,[2] commonly referred to as the individual lament. Based on the individual nature of these psalms, Gunkel objects to the inclination of some scholars to interpret the "I" of the Psalms as corporate Israel.[3] The suppliant's concern for his personal situation could not, however, be isolated from his concern for corporate Israel, evidenced in 28:9 by the shift from his private anxiety to his public concern for Israel. Both the individual and corporate perspectives are vital to an understanding of the Psalms, especially to the powerful appeal they have for individuals in Israel's and the church's history.

The psalms of lament are composed of the lament itself and the reasons for it, the latter sometimes only hinted at.[4] Kidner suggests that the reason for this lament is likely illness or despair,[5] but Craigie's proposal, based on 28:5, is more appealing: the reason for the lament was the psalmist's enemies and their ill treatment of him and others.[6]

The Text in Context

The verbal links between Psalms 27 and 28 are not impressive (both call Yahweh a "stronghold" [ma'oz, 27:1 and 28:8 (NIV: "fortress")]), even though the similar concern with the psalmist's enemies makes for compatible content, as does also the presence of the temple (27:4–6 and 28:2). In fact, the internal links within Psalm 28 are more impressive than the inter-psalmic ones:

First Occurrence	Second Occurrence
"My cry for mercy" (28:2)	"My cry for mercy" (28:6)
"Lift up my hands" (28:2)	The shepherd's "lifting up" (or "carrying") of his sheep (28:9)
"Those who do [p'l] evil" (28:3–4)	"Deeds [root p'l] of the LORD" (28:5)
"Their hands" (28:4)	"His hands" (28:5)
"Blessed" (NIV: "praise") (28:6)	"Bless" (28:9)

These parallel terms likely suggest a unity of authorship, and most certainly a unity of thought, which means part 2 was most likely composed in light of part 1.

Several commentators have observed that the theme of the Lord's house forms a bond for Psalms 26–28. In Psalm 26 the worshiper, much like the supplant of Psalms 15 and 24, is concerned about the ethical requirement for entrance into the temple (26:2–8), finally arriving there for worship (26:12), where the security and joy of the temple make him want to stay forever (27:4). In Psalm 28 he engages in worship there, lifting up his hands toward the holy of holies (28:2).

Outline/Structure

Part 1: The king's prayer and the Lord's answer (28:1–5)
  a. The king's prayer (28:1–4)
  b. The answer in the third person (28:5)
Part 2: A song of praise and the "shepherd's prayer" (28:6–9)
  a. The king's song of praise (28:6–8)
  b. The "shepherd's prayer" for his people (28:9)

Historical and Cultural Background

The traditional dating of Psalm 28 is the period of Absalom's rebellion,[7] suggested by the longing for the temple, which, it was thought,

Key Themes of Psalm 28

- Collateral punishment can result in the suffering of the righteous along with the wicked.
- Hypocrisy is evil.
- The Lord is the Shepherd of Israel.

reflects David's absence from Jerusalem and the sanctuary (2 Sam. 15:13–20:3). As we have seen earlier in Book 1, Absalom's rebellion forms the historical background and the emotional setting for several of the psalms in Book 1. While this date is possible, David's more general concern for the sanctuary is well attested outside that historical context (2 Sam. 6–7). With Craigie we might prefer a more general date reflecting the violation of a political covenant between Israel and another nation.[8]

As Psalms 26 and 27 include allusions to worship activities in the temple (26:6; 27:6), so Psalm 28 alludes to the lifting up of one's hands toward the holy of holies (the sanctuary; 28:2), a practice that is attested both in Israel (e.g., Exod. 9:29; 1 Kings 8:38) and in other ancient Near Eastern cultures.[9]

Interpretive Insights

28:1 *To you, Lord, I call . . . my Rock.* The Hebrew verb for "call" (*qr'*) carries the idea of prayer that is accompanied by a great cry (e.g., Ps. 18:6; see comments on that

The psalmist lifts up his hands as he prays for help. This pose for prayer and worship was common in the ancient Near East as illustrated by this seventh-century BC Egyptian figurine discovered in Ashkelon, Israel.

Psalm 28

verse).[10] Yahweh is called "rock" in other Hebrew poetry (Gen. 49:24; Deut. 32:4), as he is in other places of the Psalter (e.g., Ps. 18:2). It may have been an allusion to Mount Sinai, or even to the temple that was built upon a rock, symbolizing security and strength.[11]

do not turn a deaf ear to me. For if you remain silent . . . pit. The clause "do not turn a deaf ear to me" is literally "do not be silent to me," which implies that the Lord has ignored the psalmist.[12] The negative phrasing of a request is sometimes a more effective expression than a positive one, because it implies the alternative: what a sad outcome if God does not hear the psalmist's plea! The Hebrew verb for "remain silent" occurs in Isaiah 62:1 in parallel with the verb "to be quiet." The line here begins with the Hebrew word *pen* ("lest"; NIV: "For if"), a word that introduces a situation the psalmist wishes to avoid.[13] The word "pit" refers to the netherworld, or Sheol (also Pss. 30:3; 40:2).

28:2 *Hear my cry for mercy . . . as I lift up my hands toward your Most Holy Place.* "Cry for mercy" occurs also in verse 6. It is a cry for divine favor, sometimes accompanied by tears (cf. Jer. 31:9). "Most Holy Place" translates the Hebrew word *dᵉbir*, a term for the holy of holies that is used in the books of Kings and Chronicles, and which occurs only here in the Psalter. In Solomon's prayer of dedication of the temple, he refers to the practice of praying with outstretched hands toward the temple (1 Kings 8:38).

28:3 *Do not drag me . . . with those who do evil.* The verb "drag" describes Joseph's brothers dragging him out of the pit to sell him to the passing Midianites (Gen. 37:28;

also Ezek. 32:20; Job 24:22). An identical expression to "those who do evil" occurs in Psalm 5:5 ("who do wrong").

speak cordially with their neighbors but harbor malice. Jeremiah describes those who speak peaceably with their neighbors but set a trap for them in their hearts (Jer. 9:8). The Hebrew has a wordplay on the terms "their neighbors" (*reᵉhem*) and "harbor malice" (*raᵉah*, from a similar root with a different meaning).

28:4 *Repay them for their deeds.* The assumption is that God punishes his enemies; Psalm 9:16 turns the truth to a different angle, saying that the wicked are snared by their own works (Prov. 11:5 is similar). The Hebrew word for "deeds" (*poᵉal*) usually means evil deeds (Jer. 25:14), although the term is used of the Lord's "deeds" in 28:5.[14]

28:5 *Because they have no regard for the deeds of the LORD.* Here the grammatical person changes from the second—*you*, Lord (see 28:1)—to the third person, where God is spoken of rather than addressed. The change of person may suggest that this is the answer to the king's prayer, spoken by a priest or Levite or prophet. If these are Israel's national enemies who have not seen God's works on Israel's behalf, they are culpable still, even though they do not stand within the covenant.

he will tear them down and never build them up. The verb "tear down" is used in reference to an enemy in Exodus 15:7 (NIV: "threw down"), as these people have indeed become. These two verbs describe Jeremiah's role as prophet (Jer. 1:10), the first, "to tear down" (NIV: "overthrow"), in parallel with "to destroy," and the second, "to build," in parallel with "to plant." Here, in contrast to Jeremiah's prophetic instructions, the tearing down is to be permanent. Wilson suggests that the picture is that of a conquering king who "tears down" and does not build up again.[15]

28:6 *Praise be to the LORD.* This word of praise (*baruk*, "blessed") begins part 2 of the psalm. Since the sacrifice of thanksgiving was often accompanied by the congregation's recitation of a psalm of thanksgiving, 28:6–7, or maybe even 28:6–8, may well be such a psalm, or the remnant of one.[16]

28:7 *my strength and my shield . . . My heart leaps for joy . . . with my song I praise him.* The terms "strength" and "shield," both from the vocabulary of battle, suggest safety and refuge (Pss. 3:3; 18:2).[17] Here, joy is the outcome of the psalmist's trust in God. If the "song" or its representative is preserved here, 28:8 may be a continuation of the song.[18] The longer form of the verb "to praise" ("to give thanks") occurs here (*'ahodennu* rather than *'odennu*), giving more force to the verb (also Ps. 45:17).

28:8 *The LORD is the strength of his people . . . for his anointed.* The Hebrew reads *"their* strength," but a consonant change (addition of an *ayin*) could make it "the strength of *his people,*" and was so read by the Septuagint and the Syriac, which the NIV has followed. The king is called

"anointed" (*mashiah*), which gives us our English "Messiah" (e.g., Pss. 2:2; 18:50). In other ancient Near Eastern societies also the king was anointed. Oil was even used in marriage contracts, perhaps underscoring the covenant relationship.[19]

28:9 *Save your people and bless your inheritance; be their shepherd and carry them forever.* This brief and beautiful prayer closes the psalm, just as a prayer (28:1–4) opens it. Both "people" and "inheritance" occur in the Song of Moses (Deut. 32:9). One's inheritance (*nahalah*) was property passed down through the family line and held in perpetuity by the family. No one can lay claim to Israel, God's inheritance.[20] The NIV's "be their shepherd" is literally "shepherd them" in Hebrew. The shepherd carried (*ns'*) his lambs on his shoulders or against his chest (Isa. 40:11) to protect them and cuddle them. It is also used to describe a man carrying his child. In fact, it may reflect the statement of Deuteronomy 1:31, where Moses says the Lord has carried Israel through the wilderness like a man carries his son.

The expression behind the word "forever" (*'ad-ha'olam*) refers to a long period

Military terminology is again used to describe the Lord's protection and help. "The Lord is . . . my shield" (28:7) and "a fortress of salvation" (28:8). In this close-up of the Assyrian relief depicting the assault on the Judean city of Lachish, Israelite soldiers protect themselves behind shields as they defend the city from the heights of its fortified walls and towers (700–692 BC).

of time, whether in the past or the future. Hakham observes that 'ad may not be a preposition here but may intimate the idea of "eternity."[21] While we should be careful not to read our New Testament concepts into the Psalms, we should also exercise care that we do not restrict the Psalms to such earthbound thoughts that can rise no higher than the time and place limitations of their world. That aptitude is best illustrated by the prophetic spirit that could not accept the limitations of the world's kingdoms as the last word but superseded them and projected a life far beyond their boundaries. The "forever" of the Psalms falls in this category and awaits the New Testament expansion.

Theological Insights

One of the topics that often arises in the Psalms, or is always just beneath the surface, is that of moral integrity. The Hebrew faith required a consistency of thought and action. The tenth commandment moves us from the sphere of action to the world of thought and commands a consistency between what we do and what we think. After prohibiting the *deed* of adultery in Exodus 20:14, three verses later the Ten Commandments prohibit committing the same sin in *thought* (20:17). Indeed, one of the great sins of the biblical faith—of humanity in general, for that matter—is hypocrisy, precisely the sin of these evildoers "who speak cordially with their neighbors but harbor malice in their hearts" (28:3). The reason that consistency of *deed* and *thought* is so important is that truth stands at the heart of the universe—truth about nature, truth about human society, truth about personal motives and behavior, truth about God. We

The psalmist asks the Lord, "Save your people . . . be their shepherd and carry them forever" (28:9). This plaque shows a king carrying a goat kid in his arms (second millennium BC, Mesopotamia).

are reminded of the depressing assessment of society that the psalmist gives in Psalm 14:1: "There is no one who does good." Selderhuis describes Calvin's view of the human heart as being "so riddled with sin that even what appeared to be good was really cloaked in hypocrisy and deceit."[22] This certainly would fit the view of Psalm 14, even though Psalm 28 has a more positive view of humankind as a whole. Yet the evildoers of the human family, for whatever reasons, whether purely sinister or politically beneficial, often resort to a division of mind and heart. One is reminded of the double-minded individual whom James indicts, marked by instability and deprived of divine blessings (James 1:8). In this case, however, we are likely dealing with an international situation involving unreliable diplomacy, rather than a personal one, but the matter of integrity is the same. Hypocrisy on any level shatters relationships and violates truth, the bond that holds the universe together.

Teaching the Text

Psalm 28 raises an ethical issue that is as contemporary as our humanity. David introduces the issue in verse 3: "Do not drag me away with the wicked, with those who do evil." That is, he prays that he not become collateral damage, so to speak, along with evildoers. Calvin expresses the "collateral damage" idea: "God should not mingle the righteous with the wicked in the same indiscriminate destruction."[23] We all know stories where innocent bystanders have suffered at the hands of those who sought to do harm to others. They were not the target but were dragged away with the wicked.

Sadly, the nature of punishment, as well as the nature of evil, is such that it is not self-contained. Some suffer either directly or indirectly when evil acts are performed or when evil is punished. We might point out that, when Jerusalem was sacked by the Babylonians in the sixth century BC, there were some covenant-abiding people there, a remnant, who suffered collaterally from the disaster that came upon Jerusalem.

Jeremiah, for instance, was taken to Egypt against his will by the conspirators who plotted the murder of Judah's governor, Gedaliah (Jer. 41–44). It may seem unjust—and it is—but it is the nature of human society. When divine judgment falls on the human community, it is directed but not laser focused.

However, that does not answer the question of fairness or justice. We should observe that, while David raises the issue, he does not instruct us on how to handle this problem—except that he prays. Of course, we could get angry with God, or angry at the perpetrators, or at some other innocent bystander in the situation. But that inner anger will not accomplish anything. In fact, it will harm us all the more. If we use Joseph as an example ("You meant evil against me, but God meant it for good," Gen. 50:20 ESV), we must point out that this is not David's explanation but quite another way of dealing with the issue. As we use other Scriptures to develop our lesson or sermon, we must be faithful to the text we are exposing.

David's way of dealing with the problem, however, was to lay the issue out before God in prayer. Sometimes the answer to prayer is an ability to cope with the problem. In fact, there is no evidence that David's problem was solved or the issue laid to rest, but in prayer, affirming his trust, he found strength in the Lord and even exuberant joy (28:7). We should also note that this spiritual disposition was expansive, turning David's attention outward to the Lord's people (28:8). Verse 9 of the psalm is one of the most beautiful and moving prayers in the entire Psalter, a prayer for the wounded lamb that has lost its way, for the sheep that

An embassy provides a diplomatic presence for one country in another and may be a place of refuge for its own citizens while they are on foreign soil. Shown here is an entrance to the Embassy of the United States in Ottawa, Ontario, Canada.

have been the victims of the preying lions of this world. As David looks on his beloved Israel, he prays that God will "carry them" like a shepherd. Thus we see that David begins with a focus on his own problems, and through the power of prayer, he turns toward the Israel he loves and commits them to the Great Shepherd of the sheep.

Illustrating the Text

Sometimes the innocent become collateral damage of this world's evildoers.

Church Missions: Nancy Shuman Davis had been a missionary in Mexico for forty years, working in orphanages and planting churches, with her husband, Sam. On January 26, 2011, while she and her husband were driving through northern Mexico, she was murdered, allegedly by a drug cartel that wanted the late-model pickup they were driving. While Mrs. Davis was serving her Lord in Mexico, she became collateral damage of the drug cartel. Mary Gardener was a missionary with Wycliffe Bible Translators in Togo, Africa. Her lifelong passion was, in her own words, to "share the Word of God that has given me such joy and peace."[24] She lived to see the completion of the New Testament in the Ifè language in 2009. Then, on March 23, 2011, while studying translation technique in

Jerusalem, she took a bus into the city on her day off to meet some friends. And at the central bus station, Mary was standing closest to a concealed bomb, which exploded and took her life. A life of devotion to God's Word was lost, for no reason of her own. She was collateral damage to the power of evil that works in this world. There are many lunatics in our world who do not think anything about turning a gun on innocent people, often to take revenge on somebody else, or on the society, for some imagined wrong they have been done. We do not know whether these missionaries had ever prayed such a prayer as David's in Psalm 28:3, and if they did, why the Lord did not answer their prayer. But we can join David in his prayer of commitment: "Be their shepherd and carry them forever" (28:9b).

A place of sanctuary

International Law: There is an international law that sets aside diplomatic missions in host countries, such as embassies and consulates, as native territory of the sponsoring country. They may not be entered by the host country without permission, and these provide effective refuge from a host country's national authorities.[25] In Psalm 28:8 we see that David refers to the Lord as "a fortress of salvation." The temple itself was often seen as a place of safe refuge, and the psalmist describes himself as dwelling safely in the temple (Ps. 27:5). However, ultimately the Lord himself is the refuge, and our suppliant calls him "my Rock" (28:1), a place of security and protection from harm.

The "shepherd's prayer"

Imagery: The prayer found in 28:9 is particularly potent since David, himself a shepherd, takes the title place in the psalm.

First, he understood that sometimes circumstances necessitated that the shepherd pick up the sheep and carry them in his arms. Second, he had also confessed the Lord as his Shepherd, and this had become an article of faith. And third, knowing his people, he was painfully aware that they were often wounded and even more often strayed, so the Shepherd might need to carry them "forever," or at least carry them farther than they could walk on their own strength.

"Ascribe to the LORD the Glory Due His Name"

Big Idea *God has many voices, sometimes proclaiming his majesty and power through nature, while his people acclaim the message in worship.*

Understanding the Text

In this beautiful psalm of praise, the "voice of the LORD," the central thrust of Psalm 29, heard in the frightful storm, announces in nature's accent the lordship of Yahweh, ending in the peaceful lull of the storm. In Psalm 96 (v. 10a) the announcement of the Lord's reign sends the heavens and the earth and all creation into passionate jubilation.[1] See the sidebar "Psalms of Praise" in the introduction.

The Text in Context

In both a literary and theological sense, Psalm 29 is beautifully balanced. The call to worship of 29:1–2 is balanced by 29:10–11, the final announcement of God's enthronement as "King forever," and from that truth issues forth the blessing of strength and peace for God's people. The middle part of the psalm (29:3–9) develops the reasons why the Lord should be praised and why he as "King forever" can, by virtue of his enthronement, give strength to his people and bless them with peace. In this central section

"the voice of the LORD" occurs seven times, in much the same sense that the covenant name "LORD" appears seven times in the second half of Psalm 19 (19:7–14) to mark his perfection and his perfect manifestation in the law. The repetition in the poem, far from being tedious, builds with the intensity of an incredible storm, which starts in the sea (29:3), sweeps in waves of awesome power from Lebanon in the north to Kadesh in the south, centering its calm and peaceful eye on the temple, where everything and everybody in unison utter the climactic praise of God as they shout, "Glory!" (29:9).[2] Perowne observes that the meteorological cues are the structural girders of the psalm. Each strophe "begins with a burst, and closes with a lull in the tempest."[3]

Commentators have rightly called attention to the psalm's similarity to Psalm 96:7–13 (verbal differences are italicized):[4]

Psalm 29	Psalm 96
"Ascribe to the LORD, you heavenly beings, ascribe to the LORD glory and strength" (29:1)	"Ascribe to the LORD, *all you families of nations*, ascribe to the LORD glory and strength" (96:7)

Psalm 29	Psalm 96
"Ascribe to the LORD the glory due his name" (29:2a)	"Ascribe to the LORD the glory due his name; *bring an offering and come into his courts*" (96:8)
"Worship the LORD in the splendor of his holiness" (29:2b)	"Worship the LORD in the splendor of his holiness" (96:9a)

Outline/Structure

1. The ascription (29:1–2)
2. The voice of the Lord (29:3–9a)
   a. Description of the voice of the Lord over the waters (29:3–4)
   b. Effect of the voice of the Lord on the cedars of Lebanon (29:5–7)
   c. Effect of the voice of the Lord on the Desert of Kadesh (29:8–9a)
3. Response of the people to their King (29:9b–11)

Historical and Cultural Background

The Septuagint augments the title of Psalm 29, "A psalm of David," with "For the following day of Sukkot" (*exodiou skēnēs*; cf. Num. 29:35). It is recited on the first day after Sukkot.[5]

Key Themes of Psalm 29

- The voice of the Lord is heard in nature and in special revelation.
- The Lord's kingship over the world issues in blessing.

Judging from the geographical terms, the storm described in 29:3–9a apparently begins in the Mediterranean Sea ("over the waters"), sweeps inland over the majestic forests of Lebanon in the north, and leaves a wide trail of devastation from Mount Hermon (Sirion) to Kadesh in the south.[6] While there is no hint of Baal, the god of the storm, a counterstatement to that myth may be implied, since he figures so prominently in the religious psyche of Israel, both as a henotheistic option and as a rival of Yahweh, who overpowers and outmatches this god of nature. That was the object of

The strength and majesty of the voice of the Lord is illustrated by a powerful storm that devastates the forests of Lebanon, home of the renowned cedars. These evergreen trees, like the ones shown here, can reach a height of one hundred feet and have trunks six or more feet in diameter.

Elijah's ministry, and interestingly, when the writer of 1 Kings wants to draw the contrast between Yahweh and Baal, he traces the line through a powerful storm, a shattering earthquake, and a subsequent fire, to the "still small voice" of Yahweh, distinguishing the real Deity from the mythical one (1 Kings 19:11–12; see RSV). David, compared to 1 Kings 19, uses only the imagery of the storm to demonstrate God's power, and his description decrescendos into God's gift of "peace," perhaps comparable to the "still small voice" (KJV) of Elijah's experience. If Psalm 29 is Davidic and thus prior to the Kings story, the comparison is more parabolic than imitative, which means there is no textual dependency.

Interpretive Insights

29:1 *Ascribe to the* LORD, *you heavenly beings, ascribe to the* LORD. Note this same kind of repetition in other poetry: Genesis 49:22; Judges 5:12. The exhortation appears elsewhere in the Psalter only in 96:7–8 (1 Chron. 16:28–29 quotes this text), and its object there as here is "honor and strength" (see comparison above).

The Hebrew equivalent of "heavenly beings" is literally "sons of *'elim*,"[7] the latter term being the plural of *'el* ("God"). The phrase likely means "heavenly beings" or "angels." Calvin, however, understands *'elim* to mean "mighty" (cf. Job 41:25 NIV) and translates it "mighty rulers," thus identifying the scene as the earthly court rather than the heavenly. The majority opinion, however, favors the "heavenly" (but not divine) meaning of the term and the heavenly court[8] (see Job 1:6; 2:1).

29:2 *worship the* LORD *in the splendor of his holiness.* The primary meaning of the verb for "worship" is to bow down (thus, to worship). The phrase "splendor of his holiness," found also in 96:9 (also the parallel in 1 Chron. 16:29; 2 Chron. 20:21), alludes to the "splendid attire" of the priests (KJV "beauty of holiness").

29:3 *The voice of the* LORD *is over the waters; the God of glory thunders.* Here begins the main section of the psalm (29:3–9), which is a description of the Lord's "glory and strength" alluded to in 29:1.[9] Psalm 104:7 describes the Lord's voice in creation (Gen. 1:9–10) as "the voice of Your thunder" (NKJV).

Perowne insists that each of the three "voice" strophes "begins with a burst, and closes with a lull in the tempest."[10] The first strophe begins with thunder (29:3) and ends in the quieter tone of divine majesty (29:4). The second strophe renews the fury of the storm (29:5) and falls to a lower key in the flashing lightning of verse 7. The third strophe begins with one long peal of thunder after another (29:8) and then is lost in "the music and songs of the heavenly host" (29:9b),[11] concluding with the Lord's blessing of peace (29:11b).

The "waters" may be the Mediterranean Sea, or the waters "above the firmament,"[12] or the waters of the storm clouds.[13] In view of the other geographical locations in the psalm, the Mediterranean Sea fits well.

29:4 *majestic.* The term suggests kingly power and adornment (see 29:10).

29:5 *The voice of the* LORD *breaks . . . the cedars of Lebanon.* The cedars of Lebanon had a reputation for their stately beauty and size, like the sequoias of California. Yet at the thunderous voice of God in the storm, they splinter into toothpicks. The word "breaks" is a Qal participle, while the second line ("breaks in pieces") has the Piel imperfect of the same verb plus the *waw* consecutive, implying a repeated breaking. Ancient Middle Eastern kings, including David and Solomon (2 Sam. 5:11; 1 Kings 5:6–9),[14] boasted that they had secured lumber for their buildings from Lebanon.

29:6 *He makes Lebanon leap like a calf, Sirion like a young wild ox.* The beautiful imagery of the mountains leaping like a calf and an ox (Ps. 114:4) implies a happy frolic as a response to the Lord's voice. Located in northern Israel, Sirion is the poetic name for Mount Hermon, whose height is 9,232 feet.

29:7 *flashes of lightning.* The phrase is literally "flames of fire," usually translated "lightning."

29:8 *shakes the desert . . . the Desert of Kadesh.* The NIV renders the Hebrew word *midbar* ("wilderness") as "desert," but there is no desert as such in Israel. The exodus may be in view here. This is the

only occurrence of "Desert of Kadesh" in the Old Testament, and here it refers to the Wilderness of Zin (Num. 20:1; 33:36; Deut. 1:19, 46) in the region of Kadesh Barnea. The scope of the storm, then, is from the sea, inland to the Lebanese mountains, and southward to the Wilderness of Zin. Similar imagery of shaking occurs in Psalms 68:8–9 and 114:7.

29:9 *twists the oaks . . . in his temple all cry, "Glory!"* The meaning of the phrase *yᵉholel 'ayyalot* (NIV: "twists the oaks"), with the Polel form of the verb, is to "make the deer go into labor." However, the NIV translates the noun "deer" (*'ayyalot*) as "oaks" (probably because of the parallelism with the following half line, "and strips the forests bare"), even though the trauma of the storm could certainly cause the deer to go into labor

> Sirion and Hermon were both names for the portion of the Anti-Lebanon range that marked the northern border of Israel. The peaks, shown here, are so high that they remain snow covered most of the year.

(thus KJV and NJPS, which is preferable; see the NIV footnote). These "all" who cry "Glory!" are those worshiping in the temple, perhaps even joined by the heavenly worshipers. The temple is where the climax of God's glory occurs. The word "glory" forms an *inclusio* with 29:1 and 2, especially completing the idea of "the glory due his name." Now it is finally offered by the worshipers in the temple.

29:10 *enthroned over the flood*. This word for "flood" occurs only in Genesis, in relation to the flood narrative (Gen. 6–11), suggesting by its exclusivity that God's manifestation in nature, both in Noah's time and in David's, was the "supreme example of natural forces,"[15] and that he in both times exercised his dominion over the natural world. This psalm declares in its own lovely way what the psalms of the heavenly King proclaim in their distinctive declaration: "The LORD reigns!"[16] Thus the poem ends where it began, in the heavenly court with Yahweh seated on his throne. See the sidebar in the unit on Psalm 93.

29:11 *The LORD blesses his people with peace*. God's sovereign peace follows the horrible storm that has now passed. Delitzsch

writes: "*Gloria in excelsis* ["Glory (to God) in the highest"] is its beginning, and *pax in terris* ["peace on earth"] its conclusion."[17]

Theological Insights

As we have seen in Psalm 19, God speaks in both nature and the law. Psalm 19 attests the divine word in the routine of nature and in the words of the law in a complementary way. Psalm 29 offers a similar comparison, first the divine word in the tumultuous storm of 29:3–9a, and then the brief but climactic shout of "Glory!" by all in the temple in 29:9b. The two expressions of God's word are complementary, as they are also in Psalm 19. But in effect, the content of God's voice in the powerful storm is divulged in the descriptive language of the psalm. God is powerful—he breaks cedars, makes

The Lord is portrayed as "enthroned over the flood" to describe his power over nature. In this stone plaque, the Babylonians pictured their sun god, Shamash, sitting on a throne atop waters carved as wavy lines (early ninth century BC, Sippar, Babylonia).

Lebanon leap like a calf, and strikes with flashes of lightning (29:5, 6, 7). God has many voices, but they speak to us differently. This, in fact, is what the psalmist wants us to recognize, and he issues a call to the angels (NIV: "heavenly beings"; see the comments on 29:1) to recognize the Lord's "glory and strength" and to worship him in the sacred regalia of the heavenly temple ("the splendor of his holiness," 29:2). It may very well be that the call is not only for recognition but to yield all "glory and strength" to God, who is their rightful Possessor.[18] Of the three voices in the psalm, we do not hear the voice of God, except in the powerful work of nature (29:3–9a). Even the voice of the heavenly beings, unlike Isaiah's seraphim (Isa. 6), is only implied. Yet they may join the cry of "Glory" (29:9b), giving us a combination of the "heavenly beings" in the heavenly temple and the celebrants in the earthly sanctuary.

This manifestation of power attests to God's kingship over the primordial flood (see the comments on 29:10) and thus his rule over the work of nature. As he spoke to the world through Noah's flood, and thereby established his lordship (or kingship) over the world, so he has again spoken in waters and winds of nature's force to tell the world once more that he is "King forever" (29:10b). Out of his strength the Lord "gives strength to his people" and "blesses his people with peace," a welcome peace after the storm (29:11).

Teaching the Text

In a literary sense, Psalm 29 is one of the most beautiful psalms in the entire Psalter.

Here is an excellent opportunity to build a lesson or sermon on the voice of God, structuring the sermon on the three voices we hear in the psalm: the psalmist's voice (29:1–2, 10–11), the Lord's voice in nature (29:3–9a), and the congregation's voice (29:9b).

First, we can draw attention to the fact that the psalmist's voice begins and concludes the psalm (29:1–2 and 10–11), thus giving a balance to the structure of the psalm. It starts out with praise and ends with praise, first addressing the angels, and then concluding the middle section (29:3–9a) by letting us listen in on the acclamation of God's people in the temple as they join the chorus (29:9b). It would be appropriate to stress worship as inclusive praise of God. That is, worship is in part confession and petition, but all within the frame of and to the end of the praise of God. The range of praise in this psalm begins in heaven, proceeds in the works of God in nature, and concludes with the earthly chorus rising from the temple, much like we have in Revelation 5.

Second, we will listen to the featured voice of the psalm, the Lord's voice (29:3–9a), not in spoken words but in actions of nature, similar to Psalm 19:1–6, except the tone of his voice is different from that of Psalm 19 (see "Theological Insights"). Quite significantly the phrase "voice of the LORD" occurs seven times in verses 3–9, the number seven authenticating the voice as the Lord's voice. In this setting God speaks in a tumultuous storm, revealing himself as the majestic (29:4b) and omnipotent God ("strength," 29:1b; "powerful," 29:4a). Then the psalm centers God in the Jerusalem temple, where we hear the congregation's response as they join the heavenly chorus: "And in his temple all cry, 'Glory!'" (29:9b), a response to the command of verse 2a: "Ascribe to the LORD the *glory* due his name." In Psalm 29 we hear one of God's many voices as he says to Israel through his work in nature: "I am powerful, majestic, sovereign."

While Psalm 29 does not itself communicate this message, some teachers and preachers will feel that concluding on the note of God's power may leave us with an unfinished gospel. That is, we need to stress that God is "love." And the Psalms, as we have observed, are filled with that message, a message we want and need to hear, even though the psalmist evidently thought the message of the hour was God's power and sovereignty. But not to detract from that word, we may augment the message of this psalm with the fuller message of love that the psalms teach so clearly and the New Testament relates so graphically in the cross. In this regard we might say that if God is not powerful ("omnipotent" is our theological term), then how can we trust his love? God's power is conditioned by his love.

Third, we may return to the voice of the congregation (29:9b) and make the point that the final two and a half verses of the psalm leave us emboldened to live in this difficult and evil world as they emphasize the fact that the sovereign God gives *strength* to his people and blesses them with *peace* (29:11). The word "peace" (*shalom*) is a product of God's "love" (*hesed*), even though the latter term does not occur in this psalm. And he is King forever!

Illustrating the Text

God is majestic and powerful.

Film: *Twister*. Much of Psalm 29 focuses on the power and majesty of God expressed

Nature reveals God's power. A tornado is a terrifying example of the power of a violent storm.

through nature. Imagery from Psalm 29:3–9 might be visualized by thinking about the devastation wrought by tornadoes, such as is seen in the 1996 movie *Twister*. This movie is a fictionalized account of storm chasers who are seeking to understand tornadoes. The destruction of the wind is incredible as it levels buildings, uproots trees, and destroys everything in its path. At one point in the film, the characters discuss the Fujita scale for measuring tornadoes. The most powerful type of tornado, the F5, is in hushed tones referred to as "the finger of God." The movie shows the power of nature and, when connected with Psalm 29, provides a great visual of the power and sovereignty of God.

God is the sovereign King.

Cultural Institution: Americans will have a much harder time understanding and appreciating the institution of kingship than will the British or people of other nations that have a monarchy. The attribution of kingship to God is common in the Bible, and the Greek notion of democracy never influenced the Scriptures. But God's kingdom implies his kingship. A King who does "not judge by what he sees with his eyes, or decide by what he hears with his ears," but judges the world in righteousness (Isa. 11:3–5) is the perfect King. Moreover, a King who is love and who can dispense his love because he is all-powerful is King of kings. The kingdom of God is thus a theocracy, and we have nothing to fear as subjects in that realm. So the psalmist declares: "The Lord is enthroned as King forever" (29:10b). On the other hand, a human-centered government brings with it the sinful inclinations of its citizens. Calvin's experiment in Geneva sought to move this human community in the direction of a theocracy, although Calvin himself was well aware that such an earthly city could never rise to the level of the new Jerusalem. But it could be a station on the way. Calvin's motto was "improve the world, begin with Geneva."[19] We would do well to post this motto across the lintel of our church doors and on the foreheads of our own personal lives—with only the names changed.

"His Anger Lasts Only a Moment, but His Favor Lasts a Lifetime"

Big Idea *Life's pendulum swings from sorrow to joy, and faith's lintel is inscribed with "weeping may stay for the night, but rejoicing comes in the morning" (30:5).*

Understanding the Text

Like other psalms that straddle two or more genres, Psalm 30 is sometimes classified as an individual psalm of thanksgiving, or, as Kraus advocates, a prayer song of the sick (30:1–3, 8–9).[1] The more traditional form-critical classification is an individual psalm of lament (it contains complaints against God [30:5a, 7] and against enemies [30:1c]),[2] which also borders on an individual psalm of trust, since the element of trust is so pervasive.[3] The psalmist laments the divine anger he has experienced (30:5, 7), perhaps looking back over a lifetime, and celebrates God's deliverance (30:11–12).[4]

Craigie proposes a cultic setting for the psalm, taking the form of a ceremony of thanksgiving, apparently held in the temple.[5] While the contents of the psalm do not mention sacrifice and the payment of vows, the reference to "saints" (30:4; NIV: "you his faithful people") suggests a tabernacle/temple setting where the congregation participates.

The Text in Context

Wilson calls this psalm "a fitting summation of the group of psalms extending from Psalms 23 through 29,"[6] especially in view of the group's featured theme of the temple. Here we have one illustration of how the book of Psalms came into being. Sometimes a group of psalms came to be associated by a common theme, as well as authorship (e.g., the Korah psalms [42–49] that begin Book 2), and the editor kept the group together and incorporated it into the collection.

Outline/Structure

1. Introduction: Reason for praise (30:1–3)
2. Call to "saints" to join the psalmist's praise (30:4–5)
3. Narrative of the psalmist's circumstances (30:6–10)
   a. The psalmist's sense of security (30:6–7a)
   b. The fall into disfavor (30:7b)

c. Prayer for God's mercy
(30:8–10)
i. Report of prayer for mercy
(30:8)
ii. Content of prayer for mercy
(30:9–10)
4. God's response recounted
(30:11–12)

Historical and Cultural Background

The title "for the dedication of the *house*" (NIV: "temple") could imply the dedication of David's royal palace (2 Sam. 5:11), which was a point at which David realized that the Lord had established his kingdom, certainly a reason to reflect and celebrate. At the same time, it could also reference the dedication of the tent that David erected for the ark in Jerusalem (2 Sam. 6:17), which would connect well with the psalmist's dancing (Ps. 30:11/2 Sam. 6:16), if we are to take that literally. It is possible, of course, to view it metaphorically, the "wailing" and "dancing" describing the extremes of David's life, while the parallel terms, "sackcloth" and "joy," constitute a metaphor of transition to the joyful occasion. In that case, the sickness that brought the psalmist to the brink of death (30:2–3, 9) would be a fitting metaphor for David's biography.

Of course, in view of David's preparations for the temple project (1 Chron. 22), there is the possibility that the psalm was written for the dedication of Solomon's temple, perhaps even written by David in anticipation of that occasion, or later

The Talmud reveals that Psalm 30 was used during the rededication of the temple after it was desecrated by Antiochus IV Epiphanes, whose face is shown on this coin. He offered pagan sacrifices to Zeus in the temple in 167 BC.

applied to that occasion, and noted by the title. Moreover, the Talmud gives witness to the psalm's use in the rededication of the temple (ca. 164 BC) after Antiochus Epiphanes had desecrated it in 167 BC.[7] If the phrase "dedication of the house" belongs to a time later than David, the psalm still could be composed by David, since psalms were reused for liturgical purposes on various occasions.[8]

Interpretive Insights

Title *A psalm.* For the designation "A psalm" (*mizmor*), see the comments on the title for Psalm 3.

30:1 *I will exalt you, Lord, for you lifted me out . . . my enemies gloat over me.* The verb "exalt" comes from the Hebrew verb *rum*, "to be high." While human beings cannot raise God any higher than he already is, they can indeed acknowledge his unsurpassable greatness. The verb "lifted out" describes drawing water from a well (Exod. 2:16, 19; Prov. 20:5), and the imagery is that of pulling a drowning person out of the water.[9] The verb "gloat" is the Hebrew verb "rejoice" (*smh*) and refers to the rejoicing of his enemies had they triumphed over him (also 35:19, 24, 27; 38:16; the same root is used for "joy" in 30:11).

223   Psalm 30

30:2 *you healed me.* The verb implies that some illness was involved. Rashi says this is a metaphor for forgiveness[10] (see "Historical and Cultural Background" for the view that this is a metaphor for the psalmist's life, rather than for a specific experience).

30:3 *You, LORD, brought me up from the realm of the dead.* The "realm of the dead" is the word *sheʾol* in Hebrew and is parallel to "pit" at the end of the verse (see the sidebar "Sheol" in the unit on Ps. 6).

30:4 *Sing the praises of the LORD, you his faithful people; praise his holy name.* The imperative verbs are plural, addressing the congregation. "Make music" and "give thanks" are better translations of these two verbs (respectively), and they occur again at the end of the psalm (30:12). In Hebrew "his faithful people" is literally "his saints." Coming from the same Hebrew root as *hesed* ("loving-kindness"), a covenant term, the word *hasidim* ("saints") designates members of the worshiping community who have experienced God's loving-kindness as a result of their incorporation into God's covenant family. "His holy name" is literally "memorial of his holiness." Calvin holds open the possibility that this may refer to the tabernacle, since the ark of the covenant was the memorial of God's presence. However, he prefers to consider "memorial" as a synonym for "name,"[11] as does the NIV.

30:5 *For his anger . . . in the morning.* The first half of the verse represents the general principle of the psalm (God's anger and favor), illustrated by the second half of the verse (weeping and rejoicing). Both 30:5 and Exodus 20:5–6 make a character statement about Yahweh, whose "anger" against sin is short-lived compared to his favor. The NIV has "lifetime" for "life" (*hayyim*). The contrast works well in the English translation ("a moment," "a lifetime"), but unfortunately *hayyim* does not elsewhere mean "a lifetime."[12] In view of the parallelism, however, it seems to demand that sense here.[13]

The Hebrew verb for "stay for the night" implies "spend the night." The noun "rejoicing" (*rinnah*) comes from the Hebrew verb "to rejoice" (*rnn*), and means a "shout of joy,"[14] like the exuberant "shout of joy" (NIV: "songs of joy") coming from the exiles returning from Babylonian captivity (Ps. 126:2). The Hebrew phrase is striking in its simplicity: "at dawn, a shout of joy."[15] Note the parallelism between the contrasting pairs.

30:6 *When I felt secure, I said, "I will never be shaken."* This begins the psalmist's account of his experience, logged from the time he enjoyed the Lord's secure favor, through divine abandonment, and finally to joyful restoration. Note that his confidence ostensibly has assured him against any trauma. The negative framing of the verb "be shaken" occurs in other psalms to indicate a spiritual and ethical steadfastness (15:5; 16:8; 17:5).

30:7 *when you favored me, you made my royal mountain stand firm.* Now the suppliant explains why he felt so secure—the Lord "favored" him (lit., "in your favor"). The clause "you made my royal mountain stand firm" is difficult. While the exact translation may be elusive, the sense of the statement, in contrast to the feeling of dismay that the psalmist experienced, is clear. The JB gives the attractive rendering: "Your favour, Yahweh, stood me on a peak impregnable." It may be a metaphor for the security and expansiveness of David's kingdom established in time.[16]

but when you hid your face, I was dismayed. The hiding of God's face means a loss of divine favor on which the psalmist had leaned so heavily (see Ps. 27:9). The Niphal of the verb "was dismayed" suggests "terrified out of one's senses."[17] The absence of the conjunction "and" in Hebrew makes the sequence of the verbs more emphatic:[18] "you made my mountain stand strong; you hid your face; I was dismayed" (ESV).

30:9 *What is gained if I am silenced . . . ? Will the dust praise you?* In the mood of Psalms 6:5 and 88:10–12, the suppliant poses these rhetorical questions to ask what profit his death would be to God, especially since there would be one fewer of his faithful to praise him (see also Job 7:21).

30:10 *Hear, Lord*. In a petition similar to Psalm 27:7, the psalmist prays for God's help.

30:11 *you removed my sackcloth and clothed me with joy*. Sackcloth was worn as a sign of mourning and deep sorrow. God replaces the suppliant's mourning clothes with a festal garment.[19]

30:12 *that my heart may sing*. The syntax is difficult. The NIV renders the Hebrew noun for "glory" (*kabod*), the obvious subject of the verb, as "my heart." Wilson makes the very attractive proposal to take "glory" as an exclamation, just as it is in 29:9. Thus the psalmist ends by shouting, "Glory!" just as the temple worshipers were doing in Psalm 29.[20] This would require, however, amending the verb from the third masculine singular to the first singular (perhaps following the Syriac): "that I may sing, 'Glory!' and not keep silent."

Theological Insights

Psalm 30 is a reflection on David's personal recovery from a crisis, and the heading of the psalm links the poem to the "dedication of the house" (NIV: "temple"; see "Historical and Cultural Background"). How do we draw the trajectory from one to the other? Certainly the presentation of life as opposites is a feature of the psalm. Despite its general nature, Wilson observes: "It is not often that we find such a clear and linear description of the circumstances behind lament and thanksgiving."[21] Kidner understands this trajectory to suggest the life-and-death struggle that marked David's long reign as king.[22] On a national scale, Israel's history could be charted along a path between extremes. The "dedication of the house," whether it be the temple or the palace, would be the positive pole of history's wide vacillations. In fact, the writer of Samuel remarks that David's building of his palace marked that point when he "knew that the Lord had established him as king over Israel and had exalted his kingdom for the sake of his people Israel" (2 Sam. 5:11–12).

A metaphorical interpretation of the psalm makes a lot of sense, since it can be viewed as charting the broad swings of David's life. In fact, sometimes we record our autobiography best when we observe the extremities of life's pendulum (here mainly 30:6–7), filled in with the bare details that authenticate the story.

God has removed the psalmist's sackcloth, the conventional clothing of mourning in the ancient Near East, and replaced it with joy. This end panel from the sarcophagus of King Ahiram shows grieving women wearing sackcloth (tenth century BC).

We may also observe that the mood of this poem is basically joy, summarized in the aphoristic statement of 30:5, which is so beautifully expressed in the KJV: "weeping may endure for a night, but joy cometh in the morning." The psalm is framed by and centered on the idea of joy (30:2b, 5, 11). Moreover, the psalmist calls for a musical celebration of life's extremities (30:4, 12).

Teaching the Text

We can begin our lesson or sermon by observing that in Psalm 30 we hear David's story in terms of the extremes of his life, which match up quite well to our own lives, noting that they move from the negative pole to the positive: from sickness to healing (30:2), from death to life (30:3), from God's anger to God's favor (30:5, 7), from weeping to joy (30:5), from sackcloth to gladness (30:11), from silence to praise (30:12). Taking verse 5 as the theme of the psalm, we need to stress that the framework of the psalm is joy (30:1 and 11; for the vocabulary, see the comments on these verses, above):

> At the beginning (30:1): "For you lifted me out of the depths
> and did not let my enemies gloat [lit., "rejoice"] over me."
> At the middle (30:5): "Weeping may stay for the night,
> but rejoicing comes in the morning."
> At the end (30:11): "You turned my wailing into dancing;
> you removed my sackcloth and clothed me with joy."

The natural instrument of joy is music, and David twice calls for a celebration of life's extremities in song (30:4, 12). Sometimes the only human language that can tune itself to the farthest boundaries of joy and sorrow is music.

To expand on this, we may point out that if we opened up the chapter of David's life titled "From Weeping to Joy," we would likely read the story of his adultery with Bathsheba and his confidence in God's forgiveness (Ps. 51:17), the account of his innocent son's life weighed in the balances of uncertainty (2 Sam. 12:22), and the narrative of the loss of his adult son Absalom (2 Sam. 18:33). We may also point out David's boldness in reminding God of the obvious, that he would get more praise from the living than from the dead (Ps. 30:9). It is here also that we can insert our own personal autobiography, most of which reveals the same pattern, and this psalm can be a word of admonition for those who are somewhere on the spectrum of "weeping to joy."

Our autobiography cannot be written without emphasizing the extremities—that is the nature of life—but neither can we forget that there is an energizing power that spans the difference. Note the verbs that describe God's effective power: "you lifted," "you healed," "you brought up," "you spared" (30:1–3). God is the subject of the supplicant's autobiography, as he should be the subject of ours. Life is about us in a secondary sense of the word; it is about God in the primary. God went beyond the process of deliverance and shaped an outcome of joy: "You turned my wailing into dancing; you removed my sackcloth and clothed me with joy" (30:11). Yet in the Psalms the praise of God is not merely an outcome of deliverance but a goal of life, and that goal, when reached, is a life of joy.

There were many events in David's life that caused him to weep and mourn. In the account of his sin with Bathsheba (2 Samuel 11 and 12), David confesses his sin and receives forgiveness yet loses the child born out of that sin. With fasting and sackcloth, he pleads for the child's life, and after the child dies, David's response is to worship the Lord. This bronze relief showing David and Bathsheba responding in grief to Nathan's words from the Lord and the death of their son illustrates the eighth commandment on the door of the Madeleine Church in Paris. It was carved by Baron Henri de Triqueti around 1837.

The writer to the Hebrews even describes the Savior's journey to the cross as underwritten by joy ("For the joy set before him he endured the cross," Heb. 12:2).

Illustrating the Text

From lament to praise

History: Natan Sharansky, a noted Jewish dissident who became a member of the Israeli parliament, tells the story of his imprisonment by the KGB in the Soviet Union. During those years his one constant companion was a book of Psalms that his wife had given him. Not a particularly religious man himself, he nevertheless found that the laments in the Psalms and their hope of deliverance became an encouragement to him. When his nine years in prison were over, he was taken to an airport outside Moscow to be flown to East Germany and then to freedom. The Soviets had made sure that photographers were on hand to capture this act of "humanitarianism" as the authorities led him out of the car to the waiting airplane. As this exchange took place, Sharansky asked, "Where's my Psalm book?" A KGB officer responded that he had received everything that was permitted, and he ordered that the prisoner be put on the plane. But Sharansky boldly proclaimed, "I won't move until you give me back my Psalm book." When nothing happened, he fell down in the snow and started shouting, "Give me back my Psalm book!" The photographers were aghast and pointed their cameras toward the sky. After a brief consultation, he was given his Psalm book. On the plane Sharansky opened his book to fulfill a promise that he had made to himself while in prison: his first act of freedom would be to read Psalm 30.[23]

The pendulum of life

Personal Stories: When facing times of difficulty, many people quickly grow discouraged, largely because their expectation is that life should be void of hardship. Why, if God really loves me and is in control, am I going through this life challenge? The reality is that all of us struggle in our lives. Using a pendulum to illustrate (e.g., you could use a timepiece on a string), talk about some of the highs and lows from your own life. Describe times you have struggled and how God has taught and encouraged you through those times. Also, talk about times of great joy and peace in your life. It is important to emphasize that everyone goes through hard times and good times. The truth is that we will get through most of the challenges and periods of suffering we will face in life. Also, after times of struggling there typically do come periods of peace. This can be a great encouragement for people who are presently going through a life challenge.

Psalm 30

"Into Your Hands I Commit My Spirit"

Big Idea *Life's opposition forces are formidable, but God holds powerful sway over the evil forces that assail us.*

Understanding the Text

Psalm 31 is an individual lament.[1] The lament proper is found in 31:10–13, where the psalmist complains about his crisis, which, judging from the anatomical language of 31:9–10, was an illness, interpreted by his enemies as God's ill favor. In view of the declaration of trust in the Lord (31:6, 14), the attestation of his deliverance (31:7–8, 21–22), and the affirmation of God's goodness as the basis of his trust (31:19), it could be considered an individual psalm of trust.[2] Yet, it is not unusual that trust is an integral part of lament.

The unity of the psalm has been disputed because of the repetitious nature of the content and the awkward transition between 31:18 and 19. Craigie's division of the psalm into parallel sections, however, makes a good case for its unity (see "Outline/Structure").[3]

The Text in Context

The similarity of the suppliant's backward glance at his life in Psalm 30:6 and 31:22 has created some commentary on the matter, but actually the two statements are quite different. Psalm 30:6 is a remembrance of his sense of security in the past, while 31:22 declares that he has been removed from God's watchful care, two quite different themes. However, in terms of liturgical participation, the "faithful people" (30:4; 31:23), members of the covenant (note the similarity of covenant language, *hesed*, "covenant love," and *hasidim*, "love covenanters"; see the comments on Ps. 30:4), are participants in the worship experience of both psalmic occasions.

From this psalm Jesus, in his dying hours, uttered the words of Psalm 31:5a, "Father, into your hands I commit my spirit" (Luke 23:46). For the Lord Jesus, it was a gesture of trust in the "God of truth," who could save him not from death but out of death through the resurrection. His address of "Father," not found in Psalm 31, is not a coincidental addition but captures the spirit of trust that exudes from this psalm. Mays calls Psalms 22; 31; and 69 "a kind of commentary on the passion of Jesus."[4] They indeed bring the Christian believer close to the cross and reveal the heart of the God whom Jesus trusted and who also holds our times in his hands.

Outline/Structure

The lament, according to Craigie's outline, stands at the center of the psalm (C), being supported on either side by corresponding materials:

1. Prayer (31:1–18)
   A Prayer (31:1–4)
     B Trust (31:5–8)
       C Lament (31:9–13)
     B′ Trust (31:14)
   A′ Prayer (31:15–18)
2. Thanksgiving and praise (31:19–24)[5]

Historical and Cultural Background

The psalm is attributed to David, and older commentators looked for some incident in David's life that fits the circumstances, which Delitzsch has found in the conflict between David and Saul.[6] More recent commentators, especially form critics, look for the occasion of the psalm in cultural or liturgical rather than historical

circumstances. In this case, Psalm 31 seems to have arisen out of some personal setback, most obviously illness, that led the psalmist's friends and enemies to attribute his trouble to moral failure (although this is more assumed than explicit; see 31:11–13). It is quite likely that his eventual recovery led him to the temple, where he celebrated with fellow worshipers (31:23). The form-critical approach intercalates a prophetic or priestly answer between 31:18 and 19, though it is not heard, and this leads David to a final section of thanksgiving and praise (31:19–24), which results in public witness to God's mercy in worship. On that occasion he calls upon the "saints" (NIV: "faithful people"), his fellow worshipers, to "love the LORD" (31:23).

Verse 11 gives us a snapshot of the ancient city in the Hebrew word for "street," which carries the sense of "marketplace."

The psalmist is ostracized when he goes out in public. Because city streets were narrow, people tended to gather in the larger public spaces such as the marketplace or the temple court. The ancient city of Dan was designed with a large plaza and marketplace just outside the city wall. This view shows the partially excavated marketplace in the foreground, which borders the plaza in front of the city gate.

The cities were small and the streets narrow, so the marketplace, probably at the city gate, and the temple court were the two places spacious enough for a large crowd to gather.

The military language of the psalm is what we have come to expect of David—that was his world. The images are similar to those of Psalm 18. Even when David was dealing with some personal crisis other than a military one, he was inclined to use military metaphors to describe it. In addition to the military language, the hunter's language also enters the psalm in 31:4.

The world of the psalmists would be incomplete if we did not recognize the widespread idolatry that was practiced in Israel and neighboring countries. A frequent issue for the prophets, it was less so for the psalmists, but from time to time it became the focus of their religious indictments (e.g., Pss. 24:4; 97:7). Generally speaking, the psalmists went right to the primary concern and dealt with the "gods" that stood behind the idols.

Interpretive Insights

Title *A psalm.* For the designation "A psalm" (*mizmor*) see the comments on the title for Psalm 3.

31:1 *In you, Lord, . . . let me never be put to shame; deliver me in your righteousness.* The object "you" begins the verse to place emphasis on the Lord, the object of the psalmist's trust. The Hebrew verb translated as "be put to shame" is the lengthened form, "which reinforces the request": May I never be disappointed in my trust in you (similarly 25:2, 20).[7] "Your

righteousness" is a reference to God's character, out of which his covenant faithfulness proceeds.

31:2 *come quickly.* The adverb "quickly" precedes the Hebrew verb to emphasize the speed of God's deliverance, "quickly come."

31:3 *for the sake of your name lead and guide me.* These two verbs, "lead" (*nhh*) and "guide" (*nhl*), appear together in Psalm 23:2–3, connected also with the phrase "for the sake of your name." In the Song of the Sea (Exod. 15:13), the same pair of verbs describes Yahweh's guidance of Israel in the wilderness (see "Theological Insights" in the unit on Ps. 23). For a discussion of "for the sake of your name," see the sidebar "For His Name's Sake" in the unit on Psalm 23.

31:4 *Keep me free from the trap.* The imagery is that of animals escaping the hunter's net.

31:5 *Into your hands I commit my spirit; deliver me, Lord, my faithful God.* The psalmist's "spirit" (*ruah*) was his "life," but more than what was represented by the Hebrew noun *nepesh*, also commonly used for "life." It included his conscious experience as a human being (Eccles. 3:21), not merely his physical life. The imperative "deliver" (a perfect verb used imperatively; also Ps. 3:7, "*break* the teeth of the wicked") is a petition that God will deliver him from the crisis described by the psalm, whether illness or political danger. The "faithful God" is the One who can be relied on "because he is true to himself" and continues to be true to his covenant.[8]

31:6 *I hate those who cling to worthless idols; . . . I trust in the Lord.* Some manuscripts have "you hate," but either pronoun is a bit shocking, whether from

The psalmist asks God to protect him from being ensnared in any traps that are set. This is hunting imagery as nets were used to capture wildlife such as deer, fish, and, in this painting from the tomb of Nebamun, birds (fourteenth century BC).

the standpoint of God's character or that of our character, which should imitate God's. However, the idea of the psalmist hating those who hate God is found also in 139:21–22. The idea seems to be that he "rejects" the idolaters. The Hebrew syntax heightens the contrast between the idolaters and the suppliant: "But as for me—in the LORD I trust." The verb "trust" (*bth*) normally takes an object preceded by the preposition *b* ("in"), suggesting "adhering to," but here it takes the preposition *'el* ("to"), which means "hanging on."[9] The "worthless idols" (*hable-shaw'*) are literally "idols without substance."[10] See also Jonah 2:8, and comments on 39:8.

31:7 *I will be glad and rejoice in your love, for you . . . knew the anguish of my soul.* The double verb of joy emphasizes the psalmist's present state of mind,[11] even though the NIV makes it future. Note the vocabulary of joy shared with Psalm 30 (vv. 5, 11).

31:8 *in a spacious place.* The Hebrew word for "spacious place" (also Ps. 18:19) contrasts with the narrow path, perhaps on a cliffside, where one's footing is not so sure, especially when the enemy is pursuing. From a narrow place to a broad place is the path of relief (Ps. 118:5).

31:9 *my eyes grow weak with sorrow . . . my soul and body.* This phrase is Psalm 6:7a verbatim (except for the preposition), another example of formulaic language. Note the body language, "my eyes" and "body," which suggests that the NIV's "soul" (*nepesh*) should be rendered by the literal meaning of *nepesh*, "throat."

31:10 *my years by groaning.* The word rendered "groaning" means "sighs."[12]

31:11 *I am the utter contempt of my neighbors . . . on the street.* The conjunction (*waw*) before "of my neighbors" can mean "even" or "especially" (as in 2 Sam. 1:23): "I have become an utter contempt *even* to my neighbors."[13] See Job 19:13–19; 30:9–18, for a similar lament.

31:12 *like broken pottery.* "Broken pottery" is useless (cf. Hosea 8:8 ESV).

31:13 *"Terror on every side!" They conspire . . . and plot.* The content of the whisper, "Terror on every side," is the slanderous word being disbursed so as to generate fear (see Jer. 6:25; 20:10; 46:5; 49:29). A similar expression to the verb "conspire," from the same root, is used in Psalm 2:2 (NIV: "band") to describe the foreign rebellion forming against Israel's king. "Plot" implies evil intent.

31:14 *I say, "You are my God."* This is a personal confession of the covenant formula (Lev. 26:12), which otherwise was a salvation formula for the nation.[14]

31:15 *My times are in your hands.* This is not merely a general acknowledgment that the psalmist's life is in God's hands but refers to the special events and circumstances of life (1 Chron. 29:30).[15] It is closely parallel to the trust represented by 31:5: "Into your hands I commit my spirit."

31:16 *Let your face shine on your servant.* This is an allusion to the priestly benediction (Num. 6:25; see table 1 in the unit on Ps. 4). See also Psalms 4:6; 27:9. David prays this blessing on himself to suppress the feeling of uncertainty that plagues him.[16]

31:17 *Let me not be put to shame, LORD, . . . let the wicked be put to shame.* An answer to this prayer against his enemies (31:17–18) would confirm his trust in God and bring his problem to resolution. Verses 21–22 suggest that the answer indeed has come.

31:19 *How abundant are the good things . . . on those who take refuge in you.* Verses 31:19–24 form a parallel track to the prayer of 31:1–18.[17] The NIV's translation "good things" in place of "your goodness" obscures the fact that this is an exclamatory word of praise for the "goodness" of God's character ("Oh, how abundant is your goodness," ESV), in the same sense as Exodus 33:19, where the Lord denies Moses's request to see his glory but causes his "goodness" (cf. Ps. 25:7 ESV) to pass before him.

31:20 *In the shelter of your presence you hide them.* See Psalm 27:5.

31:22 *"I am cut off from your sight!" Yet you heard my cry for mercy.* Twice in the psalm we hear the suppliant reminding the Lord of his former words and thoughts (31:14, 22). This is truly a perilous moment in his life, but the Lord holds even those moments in his hands (31:15). The word "yet" (*'aken*) means "nevertheless."[18]

31:23 *Love the LORD, all his faithful people!* The psalmist turns to his comrades and exhorts them to "love the LORD" (see Deut. 6:5). On "faithful people," see "The Text in Context."

31:24 *Be strong and take heart, all you who hope in the LORD.* Based on his own experience of answered prayer, in language reminiscent of Joshua's call to Israel (see the sidebar "David Cast in the Profile of Joshua" in the unit on Ps. 27), the psalmist can confidently call upon his fellow worshipers to "be strong and take heart" (Ps. 27:14). The two verbs reissue Moses's admonition to Israel (Deut. 31:6, 7, 23) and the Lord's to Joshua in the face of the daunting challenge of the conquest (Josh. 1:6, 7, 9, 18; 10:25). On hoping in the Lord, see Psalm 130:7.

Theological Insights

The contrast between God's hands and the enemies' is striking. Twice the suppliant refers to his enemies' hands (31:8a, 15b), once praising God that he has not delivered him into them and once petitioning the Lord that he would not do so. In his tendency to dual-track his ideas, he commits his spirit into God's hands (31:5a) and confesses that the significant moments of his life are in God's hands (31:15a). A metaphor for God's power, God's hands are a symbol not of brute power but of God's compassionate control over the lives of the faithful who, because of God's abundant goodness, fear God and take refuge in him (31:19).

The personalization of the covenant faith is further evidenced in David's call to the congregation to "love the LORD" (31:23). It is a rearticulation of the opening command of Israel's platform of faith found in the Shema (Deut. 6:5). While there are many other examples of this kind of total commitment, which can be translated into the commandment of love, there must be no better one than Psalm 31.

This psalm is a model of the artful weaving of words and phrases into a poem as a delivery system of theology. First of all, the covenant name for God ("LORD") appears ten times, a good biblical number to indicate completeness. Second, the poet knows how to turn nouns into realities of his personal world: he uses *covenant love* (*hesed*) three times (31:7, 16, 21), and from that covenant context he calls the *covenant people* (*hasidim*) to *covenant faithfulness* ("Love the LORD, all his faithful people!" 31:23). Third, he plays on the Hebrew word *ki* ("that," "because"/"for," "indeed"), and seven times this conjunction bears the weight of his lament or trust:

1. "*For* you are *indeed* my rock" [NIV: "since"] (31:3)
2. "*For* you are my refuge" (31:4)
3. "*For* I am in distress" (31:9)
4. "*For* my life is consumed" [NIV does not translate this one] (31:10)
5. "*For* I hear many whispering" (31:13)
6. "*For* I have cried out to you" (31:17)
7. "*For* he showed me the wonders of his love" (31:21)[19]

Fourth, his tapestry of words is replete with dual verbs: "to take refuge" (31:1, 19), "to be ashamed / put to shame" (31:1, 17), "to deliver/rescue" (31:2, 15), "to save" (31:2, 16), and "to trust" (3:6, 14). Moreover, his war experience has left him sufficient vocabulary to describe his opponents: "enemies" (*'oyeb*, 31:8, 15) and "adversaries/distress" (root *tsrr*, 31:9, 11). The poetic artistry of the psalm is quite

In Psalm 31, the image of God's hands providing protection and deliverance is contrasted with the hands of the enemy. We also find the arms and hands of deity portrayed on Egyptian reliefs. Here the sun disk, Aten, reaches out toward the pharaoh Akhenaten and his family with the ankh symbol of life and hands of blessing (eighteenth dynasty, ca. 1350 BC).

compelling and may be attested by the formulaic use of phrases in other psalms and nonpsalmic materials, as well as the aphoristic sayings that have stuck in the memories of faithful Jews and Christians.

The Insanity ride at the top of the Stratosphere Tower in Las Vegas, Nevada.

Teaching the Text

Drawing upon one of our "Key Themes," we can build a sermon/lesson on the idea of trust in the Lord. The lament is surrounded by statements of trust (see "Outline/Structure"), and structurally this is part of the message—one's personal suffering and social alienation have to be surrounded by trust—in this case, trust in the God who is absolutely trustworthy. This fact is reinforced by the psalmist's commitment of his life into God's hands (31:5), and as a consequence he is confident that God holds the events of his life in his gracious hands (31:15).

In a world where lying has often replaced truthfulness as the norm, how do we restore our world and our life to a spirit of reliance and responsibility? First, we must rediscover the *source* of our trust. The psalmist finds it in God, who is his rock and fortress, one he can depend on to "lead and guide" him (31:3)—that implies trust. Second, we have to understand the nature of our *source*, and our suppliant knows that the God he trusts is strong and reliable (31:1–3). Third, we need a mutually trusting relationship with the *source* of trust. The psalmist's confession of trust and confession of God ("You are my God," 31:14) are made in the same breath, as he

also confesses his confident entrustment of the events of his life to God. The quest is worth whatever effort we must expend to restore this world of trust, so with Moses's admonition to Joshua, the psalm closes: "Be strong and take heart" (31:24). As it was for Joshua, this is a new world and a formidable challenge, and, most important, God's promise of the new land "flowing with milk and honey."

Illustrating the Text

Know the God we trust.

Popular Culture: The Stratosphere Hotel in Las Vegas boasts an extreme ride called "Insanity." The ride extends 68 feet over the edge of the 1,149-foot Stratosphere Tower, not only providing a great view of the city but also challenging the faint of heart. The maximum speed is 40 miles per hour, with a 70-degree seat angle, and includes a spin up to three Gs.[20] There are many people who would look at this ride and say, "No way would I ride Insanity!" But there are others who would gladly pay the fee and enjoy every moment of the ride. What's the difference? Unless there is a related health issue, it may have to do with confidence in the designer and those who ensure that the ride is safe (government agencies and the hotel). If we trust the design and maintenance of the ride, then we know there is nothing to fear. When it comes to life in this world, there will be times when we will feel like we are on Insanity, times when life is frightening and we do not feel as if we are in control. It is in these times that we must remember we can trust the One who designed us and maintains our lives. Our ability to live with joy in these moments is a function of how well we know and trust God.

Belonging to God

Church History: Soon after the introduction of Protestantism into the Palatinate in southern Germany in 1546, the controversy between Lutherans and Calvinists broke out. In order to put an end to religious disputes in his nation, Frederick III determined to put forth a catechism, or formal confession of faith. From this decision came the Heidelberg Catechism, written principally by Zacharias Ursinus.[21] The catechism begins with the question "What is your only comfort in life and in death?" The response to this question begins with these words: "That I am not my own, but belong—body and soul, to my faithful Savior Jesus Christ."[22] This answer to the first question of the Heidelberg Catechism reflects the heart of David with regard to his understanding that he belonged to the Lord.

Famous last words

History: There are examples of famous last words that provide an interesting insight into the hearts and minds of people. For example, P. T. Barnum, the great circus entrepreneur, reportedly said as his last words, "How were the receipts today at Madison Square Garden?" Barnum obviously did not take any money with him as he left this world. In fact, he did not take anything with him. American actor John Barrymore's last words were reportedly, "Die, I should say not, dear fellow. No Barrymore would allow such a conventional thing to happen to him." As successful as Barrymore was in this world, he left it like anyone else would. Contrast these statements with the last words of English prelate Robert Abbott: "Come Lord Jesus, come quickly, finish in me the work that Thou has begun; into Thy hands, O Lord, I commend my spirit, for Thou has redeemed me. O God of truth, save me Thy servant, who hopes and confides in Thee alone."[23] Although Abbott left this world in the same manner as Barnum and Barrymore, he was focused on his eternal destination, the arms of God! On the cross Jesus used the words of Psalm 31:5 as his ultimate surrender to the Father, in whose will and care surrender became the ultimate victory (Luke 23:46).

"Blessed Is the One Whose Transgressions Are Forgiven"

Big Idea *The story of saving grace begins with the confession of a repentant heart and climaxes with joyful witness in the congregation of God's people.*

Understanding the Text

Psalm 32 is generally classified as an individual psalm of thanksgiving, a genre that incorporates the report of a crisis and the account of deliverance as an accomplished fact.[1] The crisis (32:3–4) is nondescript and could stem from a physical, psychological, political, or spiritual trauma, or all of the above. In this psalm the brief account of deliverance follows immediately and partially comprises a key to the crisis (32:5), which stemmed from the suppliant's sin, unacknowledged and unconfessed (see "Theological Insights").

This psalm is also sometimes classified as a wisdom psalm, based on the wisdom-like admonition and similes of 32:9, the use of "blessed" (32:1, 2; cf. 1:1), typical wisdom vocabulary,[2] and a typical wisdom explanation of retribution (32:10). However, the unambiguous characteristics of the thanksgiving psalm weigh heavier on that side of the scales.

The Text in Context

Psalm 33 has no title (it is called an "orphan psalm"), although the Greek text (Ps. 32 in LXX), as it is wont to do, gives it a title, "Of David." Some commentators take this to mean that Psalms 32 and 33 were linked, much like Psalms 9 and 10. However, we do not have the same literary

In Israel horses were used primarily for pulling war chariots. Mules were ridden by royalty or used to transport heavy loads. Bits and bridles had been developed to better control these animals. The horse on this relief from the palace of Sargon at Khorsabad wears an elaborate bridle (ca. 700 BC).

link as we do with Psalms 9 and 10, which exhibit the features of a partial alphabet acrostic.[3] Nor are the contents of these two psalms so closely allied that they would appear to be a single psalm, as are Psalms 42 and 43. Yet Psalm 32 ends with a call to sing songs, "Sing, all you who are upright in heart!" (32:11), and, with no title, Psalm 33 flows naturally from it, beginning with such a call to "sing joyfully to the LORD, you righteous" (33:1). Looking back at Psalm 31, the linguistic link is minimal: "hiding place" (*seter*, 32:7; 31:20 [NIV: "shelter"]).

Paul quotes Genesis 15:6 to remind the Roman church that Abraham's faith "was credited to him as righteousness" and then follows that up with a quotation of Psalm 32:1–2 (Rom. 4:1–8), where the same verb, "to credit" (*hshb*), occurs (NIV: "whose sin the LORD does not *count* ["credit"] against them").

Outline/Structure

The following outline reflects the two components of the individual psalm of thanksgiving (report of a crisis and deliverance as an accomplished fact). The psalm is composed of two movements (vv. 3–5 and 6–19), with an introduction and conclusion:[4]

1. Introduction (32:1–2)
2. The first movement: the crisis caused by sin (32:3–5)
   a. Suffering (32:3–4)
   b. Confession (32:5)
3. The second movement: salvation as an accomplished fact (32:6–9)
4. Conclusion: Lessons learned and call to rejoice (32:10–11)

Key Themes of Psalm 32

- We should acknowledge our sin and confess it.
- There is a connection between sin and sickness.
- The psalmist seeks a time when God can be found.

Historical and Cultural Background

Psalm 32, like most of the psalms in Book 1, is attributed to David, and the imagery of "hiding place" (32:7) and the metaphors for forgiveness (32:1–2), which David personally knew so much about, are certainly suitable for such an author. Moreover, the metaphorical use of "bit and bridle" would not have been out of context for David, a man of war, who also used horses in warfare, at least in a limited way (see "Historical and Cultural Background" in the unit on Ps. 20). So the aphorism of 32:9 ("Do not be like the horse or the mule, which have no understanding but must be controlled by bit and bridle") belongs naturally to the general context of the psalm. Consequently we may not be compelled to assign the psalm to wisdom thinking. Rather, this is just the way a man like David would have thought. Delitzsch has proposed that David wrote Psalm 51 in the midst of his moral crisis with Bathsheba and Psalm 32 after he had "recovered his inward peace."[5] Whether or not Delitzsch's sequence is correct, his idea is good, in that Psalm 32 reveals a matured view of divine forgiveness.

Interpretive Insights

Title *Of David. A maskil.* The heading of the psalm, in addition to "Of David," brings to our attention for the first time in the Psalter the word *maskil* (a noun with the form of the Hiphil participle, from *skl*, "to instruct," or "to be skilled"). Hakham

The Language of Forgiveness

Psalm 32 contains three verbs and three nouns that describe the divine transaction of forgiveness. The first verb, "to forgive" (*ns'*, Qal passive participle; 32:1), is literally "to be lifted up, carried away"; it is used of both human and divine forgiveness (e.g., Gen. 50:17; Exod. 10:17) and suggests a metaphorical "carrying away" of one's sins. The second verb, "to cover" (*ksh*, also Qal passive participle; 32:1), means "to conceal" from sight, in the sense that God does not see one's sin. The third verb, "to count, impute" (*hshb*, 32:2), is the same verb as used of Abraham's faith in Genesis 15:6: "Abram believed the LORD, and he *credited* it to him as righteousness." Here in the psalm, of course, we have the negative sense, "whose sin the LORD *does not count* against them." That is, God does not record it against the sinner.

The nouns are also instructive. The first, "transgression" (*pesha'*, 32:1), is from the verb "to rebel," a root that has political implications; Isaiah uses the verb in the sense of moral rebellion against God (Isa. 1:2). The second noun, "sin" (*hata'ah*, 32:1), has the root meaning of "to miss the mark." The third, "iniquity" (*'awon*, 32:2; NIV: "sin"), comes from a Hebrew root that means "to bend, twist" (Ps. 38:6; NIV: "bowed down") and is used of moral perversion; in Psalm 32:2, however, as in Exodus 34:7 and Leviticus 16:21, it seems to be a summary term for sins.

represents the view of some scholars that a *maskil* teaches a moral lesson (thus a didactic psalm), suggested by 32:8, where the participle occurs (same form as the noun), "*I will instruct* you and teach you in the way you should go."[6] Besides Psalm 32, however, other psalms that have *maskil* in their titles (thirteen in all: 42; 44; 45; 52–55; 74; 78; 88; 89; and 142; also occurs in the text of 47:7 [NIV: "psalm of praise"]) are not didactic in nature, except for Psalm 78. Kraus draws attention to 2 Chronicles 30:22, where this participle describes skilled Levitical service in worship ("And Hezekiah spoke encouragingly to all the Levites who *showed* good *skill* in the service of the LORD," ESV), and suggests that the word has something to do with skillful

and artistic style.[7] Perhaps this is the best our understanding can do.

32:1 *Blessed is the one.* The word "blessed" (*'ashre*) begins the whole Psalter (see the comments on Ps. 1:1). This is the person who is favored by God's forgiveness, which is preceded by repentance (32:5). Verses 1 and 2 are a general benediction on the repentant and forgiven life. The crisis that led to this "blessed" life is described in 32:3–4.

32:2 *whose sin the LORD does not count.* The three terms for sin in 32:1–2 occur in Exodus 34:7 and the confession of the Day of Atonement in Leviticus 16:21, suggesting a summary catalogue of sins (see the sidebar).

32:3 *my bones wasted away through my groaning all day long.* David describes a similar physical debility in 31:9–10.

32:4 *your hand was heavy on me; my strength was sapped.* The psalmist considers his deteriorating condition a consequence of God's actions. The Hebrew word translated as "strength" literally means "marrow" and occurs only here in that sense.[8] In Numbers 11:8 it means "cake" (NIV: "something"). The suppliant has experienced the broiling heat of Israel's summers, which saps him of his strength, and that becomes an appropriate metaphor for the waning of his physical strength.

32:5 *Then I acknowledged my sin . . . I said, "I will confess . . ." And you forgave the guilt of my sin.* The verb "acknowledged" (Hiphil of *yd'*, "to admit, reveal") means disclosing something that was hidden or unknown. This acknowledgment was a turning point in the suppliant's experience. Healing begins with confession ("I will confess"). The word "guilt" (*'awon*) is in construct with "my sin," and Hakham cites this as a case where the construct stands in the place of the conjunction *waw*, meaning "my iniquity and my sin."[9]

32:6 *Therefore let all the faithful pray to you while you may be found.* "Therefore" is the expression "for this," referring to what he said in the last part of 32:5. The subject "all the faithful" (*hasid*) references those who are within the covenant, since *hasid* is a derivative of the covenant noun *hesed* ("love"). The subject "you" (i.e., Yahweh) is assumed by most of the English translations, even though it is missing from the Hebrew. It is literally "at a time of finding." Immediately after the infinitive "find" the Hebrew word "only" occurs, but it carries the force of "surely," as it does in Deuteronomy 4:6—thus, the NIV's translation of 32:6b, "*surely* the rising of the mighty waters will not reach them."

32:7 *You are my hiding place . . . songs of deliverance.* "Hiding place" (*seter*) occurs also in 31:20 (see "The Text in Context"). Since "hiding place" is a military term, the "songs of deliverance" are songs of victory sung by the troops or the waiting people when the army returns from victorious battle.

32:8 *I will instruct you . . . I will counsel you with my loving eye on you.* "Instruct" is the Hiphil imperfect verb of the participial noun (*maskil*) found in the heading (see comments on the title above). One can easily see why some commentators consider the noun in the title to mean a "didactic psalm." In view of the clause "I will counsel you with my loving eye on you," the "I" is most likely the Lord himself. All these activities—"instruct," "teach," "counsel," and the idea of watching over—describe God's relationship to his people and so confirm the view that the "I" is God.

32:9 *Do not be like the horse or the mule, which have no understanding.* "Understanding" designates the difference between humans and animals.

32:10 *but the LORD's unfailing love surrounds.* In 32:7 the verb "surround" describes the "songs of deliverance" that celebrate the psalmist's victory over the crisis he encountered, while here the same verb describes the Lord's covenantal "unfailing love" (*hesed*) that

The psalmist experiences that unconfessed sin has physical consequences, and he describes it as "my strength was sapped as in the heat of summer" (32:4). Israel experiences periodic heat waves with temperatures climbing close to 120 degrees Fahrenheit in the south. An acacia tree provides the only shade to get relief from the sun.

surrounds those who trust in the victor, "the one who trusts in him." In the Hebrew text, "the one who trusts in the LORD" is a *casus pendens* (a pending case), "But as for the one who trusts in the LORD," making the contrast stronger by putting the person of contrast out front in the clause.

32:11 *Rejoice in the* LORD *and be glad, you righteous; sing, all you who are upright in heart!* Three verbs of joy, "rejoice," "be glad," and "sing," change the person to the plural. Moses uses the same concluding verb, "sing," to call Israel to break into singing (Deut. 32:43; NIV: "Rejoice").

Theological Insights

The modernity of the notion of sin and forgiveness in Psalm 32 is striking. The psychosomatic relationship between sin and suffering belongs to the timeless category of humanity, even though modern psychology has been more inclined to understand it. At the same time, it is a timeless phenomenon that the psalmists verbalized so well. Yet the Old Testament does not lack the disavowal of this connection, with Job posing the major objection. In the story of the paralytic, Jesus begins with forgiveness and subsequently pronounces the man physically healed (Mark 2:1–12). Once his sins are forgiven, if his paralysis has been caused by sin, should not the spiritual healing correct it? One wonders if, in addition to proving himself capable of forgiving sin and performing physical healing, Jesus is implying that the two, at least in this case, are not connected. Clearly, he denies the link in the case of the man born blind (John 9:3), but that does not mean an absolute denial; Paul acknowledges a link in 1 Corinthians 11:29–30.

Teaching the Text

Let us call attention to the fact that the introduction of this psalm is about *forgiveness* (32:1–2), but that implies the underlying problem of *sin*. Only one who is forgiven, like the psalmist, can make such a pronouncement about that new condition with the term of life's renewed perspective, "blessed" (see comments on 32:1). The first movement of the psalm (32:3–5) concludes with a resolution of the crisis—the forgiveness of sin is an *accomplished fact*: "You forgave the guilt of my sin" (32:5b). But as is often the case with those who are forgiven, the psalmist feels the urgency to rehearse the crisis

(32:3–5a). The prayer proper is contained in verses 4–7, as he implores the Lord, based on his own experience of God's forgiveness (32:6, "therefore"; lit., "for this"), to replicate that transaction in the lives of all the godly (*hasid*) who call on God while he may be found. At this point the teacher or preacher might speak about the use of the term "sin" in the public square (see Karl Menninger's story in "Illustrating the Text"). The Westminster Shorter Catechism gives an axiomatic definition of sin: "Sin is any want of conformity unto or transgression of the law of God."[10] That is, sin is both omission and commission. The psalmist suggests that his sin is an offense against God, implied by the fact that, though he does not, the Lord ought to count it against him (32:2a; see also 51:4).

The second movement in the psalm represents a new voice of instruction (32:6–9), obviously the Lord's, who counsels the godly not to be stubborn and disobedient like a horse or mule. The plural number of the verb in 32:9 alerts us to a wider audience than the psalmist alone, likely his fellow worshipers—he is sharing the good news. This, of course, is a textual hint that we may take advantage of and urge one another to share the reality of sins forgiven.

As subpoints, the lesson may include observations about the psalmist's silence with its psychosomatic effect (32:3–4). The powerful truth of Psalm 32 is, in part, that unconfessed sin has serious consequences. Perhaps only one who has experienced those burning, hot summers in the land of Israel will comprehend the full measure of his metaphor in verse 4a.

We have to wonder if our society is not getting morally worse because we refuse to acknowledge our sin. But the new life that broke into David's world is contained in the word "blessed." In this connection, we may call attention to Paul's quotation of Genesis 15:6 and then his follow-up quotation of Psalm 32:1–2 in Romans 4:1–8 (see "The Text in Context"). The key to connecting Abraham and David to the doctrine of righteousness by faith is the verb "to credit" (*hshb*, Ps. 32:2; Gen. 15:6). Even though David falls within the covenant and thus is a recipient of God's promises to Abraham's descendants, Paul's point is to draw a line from Abraham, justified by faith *before he was circumcised*, to gentiles who belong to the spiritual family of Abraham because they too are justified by faith. So before Abraham could be called the "father of the race," he could already be called the "father of the faith" (Rom. 4:9–12).

In this second movement we have the sober warning of verse 6: "Therefore let all the faithful pray to you while you may be found." The Scriptures teach that God is available to those who call on him; yet on occasion—here in verse 6 and in Isaiah 55:6—there seems to be some restriction on God's availability. Sometimes it is just our imagination, or our state of mind, that prohibits us from finding God, but Amos speaks of a time when Israel will "stagger from sea to sea and wander from north to east, searching for the word of the LORD, but they will not find it" (Amos 8:12). On the other hand, Isaiah recognizes that he prophesies at a time when the Lord "may be found" (Isa. 55:6), perhaps a reference to the temple or the availability of the prophetic

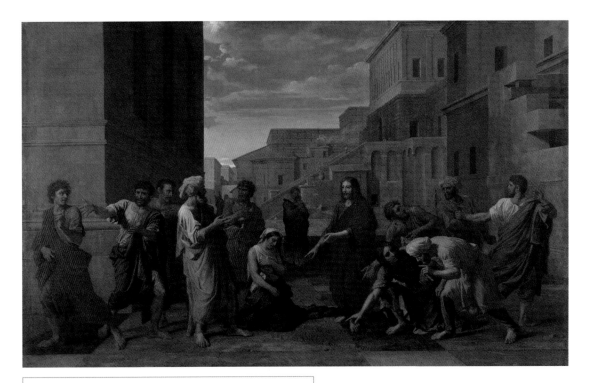

"Blessed is the one whose transgressions are forgiven" (Ps. 32:1). The woman caught in adultery experienced that forgiveness when Jesus said, "Neither do I condemn you" (John 8:11). This painting by Nicolas Poussin shows Jesus with the adulterous woman as her other accusers begin to leave the scene, thwarted in their plan to trap Jesus.

word. In any case, the phrase "while you may be found" should not be taken lightly. Whether it is a matter of God's availability or our perceptiveness, the biblical faith warns us that spurning God's grace is a serious matter (Ps. 95:7c–9). Nevertheless, the psalmist paints the door of grace as wide open and admonishes us to take advantage of it.

Illustrating the Text

Connecting guilt with depression

Psychology: A study conducted by clinical neuroscientist Roland Zahn of the University of Manchester has identified how the brain links knowledge about social behavior with moral sentiment. Of particular interest to Zahn was the connection between guilt and depression. He explains, "The most distinctive feature of depressive disorders is an exaggerated negative attitude to oneself, which is typically accompanied by feelings of guilt."[11] In Psalm 32:3–4, David expresses the emotional pain associated with guilt. For those who have struggled with depression, David's description will sound familiar. But there is good news. God has dealt with our deep need of forgiveness through the atoning death of Jesus on the cross!

Forgiven!

Bible: In John 8 we read an amazing encounter between Jesus and a woman who was caught in the act of adultery. A crowd has dragged her before Jesus. The teachers of the law and the Pharisees are using this moment to try to trick Jesus. It is in this encounter that Jesus speaks the words, "Let any one of you who is without sin be the first to throw a stone at her" (8:7). But the most remarkable part of the encounter is what occurs next.

> At this, those who heard began to go away one at a time, the older ones first, until only Jesus was left, with the woman still standing there. Jesus straightened up and asked her, "Woman, where are they? Has no one condemned you?"
> "No one, sir," she said.
> "Then neither do I condemn you," Jesus declared. "Go now and leave your life of sin." (John 8:9–11)

Imagine the power of these words for this woman caught in a life of sin. Imagine the healing in her heart to hear, from the lips of the God-man, that she is forgiven.[12]

Whatever happened to sin?

Popular Culture: In 1972, on a sunny day in the Chicago Loop, a stern-faced man stood on the street corner, and as a person would pass along the street, he would lift his right arm and, pointing straight at that person, call out, "Guilty." He elicited some eerie looks from pedestrians, even one remark from an "accused" man who said, "But how did *he* know?" Karl Menninger, the famous psychiatrist of the last century, tells this story in his book, *Whatever Became of Sin?*[13] In that book Menninger points out how the word "sin" has disappeared from the public vocabulary and many private vocabularies. He remarks that if we use the term at all, it is often with some kind of sneering tone, "That's a sin!" when we are referring only to some minor departure from etiquette. How seriously do we take the word "sin"?

"May Your Unfailing Love Be with Us, LORD"

Big Idea *The story of humanity, from creation to redemption, is tied together with the golden thread of God's unfailing love.*

Understanding the Text

Psalm 33 is atypical of the psalms in Book 1 in that it has no title, sharing this feature only with Psalm 10 (assuming, of course, that Psalms 1 and 2 are introductory). It is a good example of the *hymn*, which represents the "purest form" of praise to God, expressing who he is and what he does.[1]

The absence of a title has led to the speculation that this psalm was a continuation of Psalm 32, much like Psalms 9 and 10. In fact, Wilson cites at least ten Hebrew manuscripts that treat these two psalms as a single unit.[2] However, both the Masoretic Text and the Septuagint treat Psalm 33 as a separate psalm, and the Septuagint gives the psalm a title, "of/to David."

Though not attributed to David in the Hebrew Psalter, Psalm 33 does contain ideas that belong to the Davidic psalms, like the "victory cry" of 33:3 (NIV: "shout for joy"), the foiled plans of the nations (33:10), the blessing on the nation whose God is the Lord (33:12), and the folly of the king's trust in his military resources (33:16–17; cf. 20:7).

The Text in Context

The penultimate verse of Psalm 32 contains the promise that the Lord's "unfailing love [*hesed*] surrounds the one who trusts in him" (32:10), and the declaration of Psalm 33:5 is a universal expansion of that truth, "the earth is full of his unfailing love [*hesed*]." The psalmist reiterates this theme in 33:18 to affirm God's watchful care of those "whose hope is in his unfailing

Table 1. Shared Vocabulary between Psalms 32 and 33

Psalm 32	Psalm 33
"Blessed" (*'ashre*; 32:1, 2)	"Blessed" (*'ashre*; 33:12)
"My [Lord's] eye" (32:8)	"Eyes of the LORD" (33:12)
"Trust" (*bth*; 32:10)	"Trust" (*bth*; 33:21)
"Unfailing love" (*hesed*; 32:10)	"Unfailing love" (*hesed*; 33:5, 18, 22)
"Rejoice" (*smh*; 32:11)	"Rejoice" (*smh*; 33:21)
"Sing" (*rnn*; 32:11)	"Sing joyfully" (*rnn*; 33:1)
"Righteous" (*tsadiqim*; 32:11)	"Righteous" (*tsadiqim*; 33:1)
"Upright in heart" (32:11)	"Upright" (33:1)

love," with a concluding prayer that unites God's "unfailing love" with the hope of God's people, which has now become the medium of love's expression (33:22). Thus the two psalms are an expression of God's covenantal love. Additionally, they share an abundance of other vocabulary (as indicated in table 1). This linguistic interweaving is much like that of Psalms 1 and 2,[3] suggesting that Psalm 33 was written with Psalm 32 in view.

Outline/Structure

Among the standard elements of the hymn are the call to praise and the reasons for praising, both represented here in duplicate.

1. Call to praise (33:1–3)
2. Reasons for praise (33:4–7)
3. Intermediate call to praise (33:8)
4. Further reasons for praise (33:9–19)
5. Concluding prayer (33:20–22)

Historical and Cultural Background

Unmistakably this is a musical psalm. There are two verbs for "sing" (*rnn*, 33:1; *shir*, 33:3), used synonymously. The product of this call is a "new song" (33:3). The third musical verb is to "play" a musical instrument (*zmr*, 33:2), in this case the "harp" and the "ten-stringed lyre" (33:2; also 144:9; see the sidebar "Musical Instruments in Psalm 33").

Musical Instruments in Psalm 33

The "harp" (*kinnor*, 33:2) was a widely used instrument of the biblical world. The general opinion is that it was the lyre, possibly made out of almugwood, imported from Lebanon in Solomonic times (Braun suggests this otherwise unknown wood was sandalwood) and used for making the *kinnor* and *nebel* (1 Kings 10:11–12; 2 Chron. 9:11). Ancient sources differ in their opinion of the number of strings, varying from ten (Josephus, *Jewish Antiquities* vii.12.3) to seven (*b. Arakhin*) to six (Jerome). It was played with the fingers or a pick.[a]

The "ten-stringed lyre" (*nebel 'asor*, 33:2) was most likely an instrument similar to the *kinnor*, made from the same almugwood (1 Kings 10:12) and used for similar purposes of worship and entertainment. This instrument (*nebel*, not necessarily ten-stringed) may have been specifically used by the Levitical guilds (1 Chron. 15:16, 20; 25:1, 6) and at victory celebrations. The term *nebel* sometimes occurs without the "ten-stringed" modifier (*'asor*), so these instruments probably varied in the number of strings. Rabbinic sources relate that the strings of the *nebel* were made of a sheep's large intestine, and those of the *kinnor* of small intestines.[b]

[a] Braun, *Music*, 16–19.
[b] Braun, *Music*, 22–24.

The harp (*kinnor*) and lyre (*nebel*) were the stringed musical instruments commonly played in the biblical world. The harp may have looked like the one painted on this pottery jug from Megiddo, eleventh century BC.

The Musicality of the Psalms

Psalm 33 is an excellent illustration of the musicality of the Psalms. Teachers of the Psalms must insist that if we do not give attention to the musical nature of the Psalms, we have not done justice to the book. Unfortunately, we cannot recover the tunes or be certain about the musical notations, but we still can be confident that most of the Psalms were composed for singing or chanting, often to the accompaniment of musical instruments. In the genealogy of Cain (of all places!), we have a paragraph that mentions the beginnings of three basic institutions of human civilization: shepherding, music, and metallurgy (Gen. 4:19–22). It is no accident that music is included, directing the reader's attention to the central role of music in Hebrew society. In this connection we should note that the last verse of Psalm 32 calls the "upright in heart" to sing, and Psalm 33 is the response to that call. Psalm 33, in fact, contains two verbs for "sing" (33:1, 3), the names of two instruments, and one verb for playing musical instruments (33:2; see "Historical and Cultural Background"). The worthy product of this musical effort is a "new song" (33:3), which is probably the content of verses 4–19.[a] It is new in that it is a "new" composition, but the ideas of the song are old, celebrating the creation of the world (33:6) and Israel's redemption from Egypt (33:7; see the comments on that verse). We should note the shift from the singular "you" to the plural imperative in 32:9, thus setting the stage for the communal performance of the psalm. Since Psalm 33 is the response to the call in 32:11, we may point out that the second plural imperative of 33:1–3 ("[you] sing joyfully") continues the call to corporate worship, only to turn into the congregation's response in 33:20–22 ("we").

[a] The temple services were filled with music. In 1 Chronicles 24 we have a list of David's temple musicians, and it is quite extensive.

Interpretive Insights

33:1 *Sing joyfully to the* Lord. Psalm 32 ended with the same root verb, "sing [joyfully]" (*rnn*, 32:11b). Note the second-person plural imperatives in 33:1–3, continuing the same verbal forms that began with the aphoristic injunction of 32:9, implying a corporate setting for the psalm in the tabernacle or temple.

33:2 *harp . . . ten-stringed lyre.* See the sidebar "Musical Instruments in Psalm 33."[4]

33:3 *Sing to him a new song; play skillfully.* The suppliant offers a freshly composed poem. "New song" occurs also in 40:3; 96:1; 98:1; 149:1 (see also Rev. 5:9; 14:3). The idea of a "new song" marking "new" works of Yahweh seems to be the meaning of this phrase. God's "new" work of forgiveness, celebrated in Psalm 32, could be the reason for the song, just as God's great work of redemption is the reason for the "new song" of Revelation 5 and 14. Isaiah 42:10 uses the phrase also to celebrate Yahweh's "new" acts of deliverance. The verb "play" (*ngn*) means to "touch" or "pluck" (see the comments on the title for Ps. 4).

33:4 *For the word of the* Lord *is right and true.* Craigie says the word "imparted to the created order the divine characteristics of the Creator—truth, righteousness, justice, and lovingkindness (33:4–5)."[5]

33:6 *By the word of the* Lord *the heavens were made, their starry host by the breath of his mouth.* This verse implies a familiarity with Genesis 1. The "word of the Lord" is an allusion to God's speaking the world into existence, "And God said." The psalmist mentions only the "heavens," because he wants to call attention to their "starry host." But immediately 33:7 turns our attention to the earth by reference to "the waters of the sea," using the plural form of the word for "deep" (*t^ehomot*), which along with the phrase "breath [*ruah*] of his mouth" (33:6) brings to mind Genesis 1:2: "Darkness was over the surface of the *deep* [*tehom*], and the *Spirit of God* [*ruah 'elohim*, "Spirit of God" or "breath of God"] was hovering over the waters." The implication of "breath of his mouth" seems to be the creative Spirit, which we may assume operates in and through the spoken word, "And God said." "Spirit of God" and "breath of his mouth" are equivalent terms, virtually synonymous with the "word of the LORD."

33:7 *into jars; he puts the deep into storehouses.* The Septuagint has "bottle" for "jars," evidently reading the Hebrew *ned*, "heap," as *no'd*, "bottle." The NIV follows this reading, but in effect it obscures the allusion to the miracle at the Red Sea and the Jordan River (Exod. 15:8; Josh. 3:13, 16; Ps. 78:13), which seems to be intended. The psalmist conflates the creation story and redemption at the Red Sea and Jordan River, joining them with the psalmist's present history. See Job 38:22 for a similar use of "storehouses."[6]

33:9 *For he spoke, and it came to be; he commanded.* This is precisely the description of creation in Genesis 1. In fact, it is the verbal equivalent of "And [God] said, 'Let there be . . .'" (e.g., Gen. 1:3). The verb "commanded" is not used in the creation narrative of Genesis 1, but the jussive form of the verbs ("Let there be," "let gather," etc.) are in effect commands.

33:12 *Blessed is the nation . . . the people he chose for his inheritance.* In the midst of this essay on God's control of the world (33:10–15), the congregation affirms Israel's special significance in history. God chose them as his "special inheritance" (*nahalah*), a term that signifies a family inheritance held in perpetuity.

33:13–15 *the LORD looks down and sees all mankind.* In 33:13–15 we have four verbs

Israel is not alone in its view that God spoke and "it came to be" (33:9). The Egyptians also have a creation account where Ptah creates as he speaks. Known as the Memphite Theology, it is inscribed on this surface known as the Shabako Stone. Here it says, "It is Ptah, the very great, who has given [life] to all the gods and their kas through this heart and through this tongue" (translation from M. Lichtheim, *Ancient Egyptian Literature: A Book of Readings*, vol. 1 [Berkeley: University of California Press, 1975], 54).

that describe God's omniscience: "looks down," "sees," "watches," and "considers." The trifold "all" in these three verses ("all," "all," "everything"; cf. "hearts of all") reinforces the idea of divine omniscience, extending it to all humanity (see "Teaching the Text").

his dwelling place. The expression "dwelling place" is the same expression found in Exodus 15:17 ("the place . . . you made for your dwelling").[7]

hearts of all. The idiomatic sense of the Hebrew word "all" (*yahad*, "together") is "one and all."[8]

33:16 *by the size of his army . . . by his great strength.* Note the repetition of the Hebrew word *rob* ("size of," "great"). Combine the thought of verses 16 and 21 and we have the idea of Psalm 20:7.

33:17 *A horse is a vain hope for deliverance.* Like 32:9, this saying sounds a bit aphoristic.

33:18 *unfailing love.* This term (*hesed*) occurs three times (33:5, 18, 22), to put the psalm in a covenantal framework.

33:20 *We wait in hope for the LORD.* Alter translates the initial "we" (lit., "our soul") as "we urgently" to recognize the position (first word) and emphasis of the noun.[9] The verb translated as "wait [in hope]" occurs once more in the Psalter (106:13).

33:22 *May your unfailing love be with us, LORD.* For the most part, this psalm is not a direct prayer, even though it is sung in praise of God. This is the first time, in fact, that God is addressed, and it is a prayer that God's "unfailing love" may be upon Israel as they hope in him.

Theological Insights

The Old Testament does not systematize its theology in any formal sense, but this psalm is as good a treatise on the providence of God as we have in the Psalter. Citing the primordial events of providence, the "new song" that the congregation sings begins with creation, drawing on Genesis 1 and Moses's Song of the Sea (Exod. 15; Ps. 33:6–7). The vocabulary of Genesis 1 forms a template for this description of creation: heavens, breath (spirit) of his mouth (Gen. 1:2, "spirit/breath of God"), the deep, "God said . . . And it was so." Yet, the imagery is a bit more poetic, perhaps dependent upon the Song of the Sea (Exod. 15:8), where, "by the breath [NIV: "blast"] of your nostrils" (cf. 33:6, "by the breath of his mouth") the waters stood up in a "heap" (see ESV). In comparison, our poem describes the Lord

as bringing the "starry host" into being "by the breath of his mouth" (33:6b). In any event, the miracle at the Red Sea elicited from Israel the fear of the Lord (Exod. 14:31), the response to which the psalmist calls "all the earth" (33:8).

In addition to making the story of creation and redemption a single narrative, our psalmist breaks this subject out to include the particulars of history (33:10–19). In broadest outline, the Lord is sovereign over the plans and purposes of the nations, foiling their designs but making his firm and secure (33:10–11), a normal outgrowth of his authority over the creation (33:9, "He spoke, and it came to be; he commanded, and it stood firm").

God is not only omnipotent but omniscient, observing all humankind and their actions (33:13–15). If there is any doubt about these attributes, one need only look at Israel, whose history illustrates the fact that salvation is attained not by great strength but by his "unfailing love" that delivers from death and saves in time of famine (33:16–19), constituting the basis of Israel's present and future (33:10–22).

Teaching the Text

The psalmist does a beautiful thing in this poem by connecting the creation of the world (33:6) to Israel's redemption from Egyptian bondage at the Red Sea: "He gathers the waters of the sea as into a heap" (33:7 NIV footnote; see the comments on this verse above). That is the description of the Red Sea *and* the Jordan River when the Lord rolled them back so that the Israelites could pass over. The exodus and the Red Sea are Old Testament symbols of redemption, and Psalm 33 brings them together—it connects the God of creation and the God of redemption. God is Redeemer precisely because he is Creator. God did not find an alien world that had gone bad and impose himself on it as Redeemer. Rather, he himself created this world, and he had every right to redeem it. Luther in his typical candor once said, "If I were as our Lord God, and had committed the government to my son, as he to his Son, and these vile people were as disobedient as they now be, I would knock the world in pieces."[10] But God did not do that, and, of course, Luther celebrated that grace. God's strategy is one of love, and the psalm says this in at least three ways.

First, the Lord surrounds those who trust him with "unfailing love" (33:18). That means he has a special relationship to those who trust him. Rather than kicking this contrary world to pieces, he said, "I love you," and set up a special relationship with Israel (33:12).

Second, he fills the earth—the earth he made—full of his "unfailing love" (33:5b), and he not only fills it but is constantly looking down from heaven on "all mankind,"

watching over them, forming their hearts, aware of all their activities (33:13–15), not in an accusatory way but in the love with which he has filled the world.

Third, in that same spirit of love, God defeats the plans of the nations and puts his own plans into effect (33:10–11). The plans of the nations cause us human beings a lot of anxiety, but they do not cause the Lord one anxious moment. He has plans for the world he created and the world he redeemed, the world he loves, and he puts these plans into place. We can take confidence from that and renew our hope through that assurance. Psalm 2:4 tells us that the Lord just "laughs" at the cocky plans of those people who have no regard for his sovereign rule. In a similar vein the psalmist deflates the foolish notion that kings and military might can save (33:16–17). If we could view history through God's

Psalm 33 is a hymn of praise, speaking of God's creative power and his deliverance to illustrate God's unfailing love. One miraculous act of redemption was the rescue of Israel from slavery in Egypt. The carving on this fourth-century AD sarcophagus shows Pharaoh and his army being engulfed by the waters while Moses and the Israelites are safe on dry land.

eyes, it would take away the anxiety we feel in a world that is extremely troubled and combative. While it would not remove the threat or reality of war, it would give us the peace that God is in control, and moreover that the God who controls this world is a loving God (20:7). All our human resources are fickle and unreliable compared with God's "unfailing love" (33:18–19).

The concluding prayer of the psalm (33:20–22) could be the constant prayer of the church:

> May your unfailing love be with us,
> LORD,
>   even as we put our hope in you.
>   (33:22)

The hope of Israel and the church is found in the presence of God's "unfailing love," the tie that binds the Testaments together and gives us a sense of God's redeeming purpose in the world.

Illustrating the Text

God's unfailing love

Quote: *A Room Called Remember*, by Frederick Buechner. Buechner writes about an experience when someone he loved was near death, and though God did not seem close by, he desperately needed God and sensed his love:

> Though God was nowhere to be clearly seen, nowhere to be clearly heard, I had to be near him—even in the elevator riding up to her floor, even walking down the corridor to the one door among all those doors that had her name taped on it. I loved him because there was nothing else left. I loved him because he seemed

to have made himself as helpless in his might as I was in my helplessness. I loved him not so much in spite of there being nothing in it for me but almost because there was nothing in it for me. For the first time in my life, there in that wilderness, I caught a glimpse of what it must be like to love God truly, for his own sake, to love him no matter what.[11]

"But the eyes of the LORD are on those who fear him, on those whose hope is in his unfailing love" (v. 18).

God reaches out to us in grace.

True Story: Anne Graham Lotz (daughter of Billy and Ruth Graham) has shared a story about learning of God's grace from her father. One day as she was speeding down a mountain road, Anne hit her neighbor's car. It was her fault, and she did not know how to tell her father. Finally, her dad was waiting for her in the kitchen, and she ran into his arms, confessing what she had done. Billy said four things in response to his daughter. First, he told her that he already knew what she had done. Second, he reminded her that he loved her. Third, he assured her that the car could be fixed. Finally, he told her that she would be a better driver because of the accident.[12] What an incredible lesson of grace a father taught his daughter that day! God is a God of grace who reaches out to us, already knowing the depth of our failure and sin (vv. 13–15). But here it is not so much through eyes of judgment that he sees us, but through eyes of love (v. 18). This love (*hesed*) peaks in God's sacrificial gift of his Son, after which God always sees us through the lens of Calvary.

When fearful events occur, like the terrorist attacks on September 11, 2001, we can put our hope in the Lord, who is in control of all things and "stand firm forever" (33:11). In this photo, smoke billows from the World Trade Center Towers after terrorists crashed commercial airliners into each of them.

Hope in hopeless times

News Story: At almost any time in history there are reasons to fear the future. For example, consider the condition of the United States in the year 2013. The official unemployment rate averaged 7.35 percent.[13] The federal deficit continued to climb with no remedy in sight.[14] The city of Detroit filed for bankruptcy. Nations such as Iran and North Korea continued to develop nuclear weapons and threaten their neighbors and the United States with nuclear annihilation. In April 2013, two terrorists set off bombs during the Boston Marathon. At any given moment there is much to fear in the world. But Psalm 33 provides hope during seemingly hopeless times. We read in verse 11, "But the plans of the LORD stand firm forever, the purposes of his heart through all generations." The Lord rules over the universe, and his plans will stand firm, ruling and overruling our human plans and plots. We do not need to fear, because God is ultimately in control!

"Taste and See That the LORD Is Good"

Big Idea *Having experienced God's goodness, we invite others to "taste and see that the LORD is good" and thus experience the assuagement of their fears.*

Understanding the Text

In addition to being an alphabetic acrostic,[1] Psalm 34 shares at least three other features with Psalm 25, another acrostic: (1) the *waw* (the sixth letter of the Hebrew alphabet) is missing from both poems; (2) each closes with a supernumerary verse beginning with the Hebrew letter *pe*; and (3) the same verb begins each of these closing verses, *pedeh* (imperative, "redeem," NIV: "deliver") in 25:22 (also in 26:11) and *podeh* (participle, "redeems," NIV: "rescues") in 34:17. This verb, as both petition (Ps. 25) and affirmation (Ps. 34), is at the heart of Israel's life and faith, and these acrostic poems that, at least by their formal engagement of the complete alphabet, have covered the gamut of the poem's topic, have still not said everything necessary until they have petitioned or affirmed Yahweh's redemption of Israel. Regarding the consonant *waw*, it is quite possible at this stage of the development of the Hebrew language that it had not yet taken its place as a legitimate consonant of the alphabet and is thus absent. On the other hand, the addition of the *pe* verse at the end, also attested in a medieval Hebrew version of Ben Sira 51 (second century BC), linguistically brings the number of verses, excluding the title

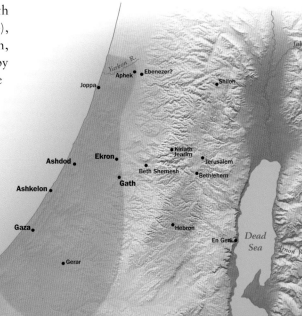

The title of Psalm 34 refers to the time when David acted like a madman in the presence of King Achish of Gath. Gath was one of the five major Philistine cities and the hometown of Goliath. This map shows the location of the major Philistine cities and the territory controlled by the Philistines during the early monarchy period.

verse, to twenty-two, the standard number of consonants when the alphabet had completed its development, and theologically prays the ultimate prayer for redemption. The shift also means that the poem, now with twenty-three verses, including the title (which is v. 1 in the Hebrew), has a middle verse (v. 12 Heb.; v. 11 Eng.), and taking the first letter of the first, middle, and final verses, the balanced structure now produces a wisdom code word *'lp*, meaning "to learn, to teach" (Prov. 22:25; see the comments on Ps. 25:22). There is, of course, the possibility that the final verse was a congregational response.[2]

The first part of the psalm (34:1–7) has the features of an individual psalm of thanksgiving, containing both the report of a crisis (only alluded to in 34:4 and 6) and the suppliant's deliverance as an accomplished fact (34:4, 6).[3] Yet the second part (34:8–22) has the characteristics of a wisdom poem, which is, for the most part, a collection of aphorisms.[4]

The Text in Context

The title of Psalm 56 places that poem also during David's experience in Gath ("When the Philistines had seized him in Gath"), and it is an individual psalm of thanksgiving, as is Psalm 34, in which David also implores God's help in time of trouble.

In relation to its next-door neighbor (Ps. 33), our present psalm has twenty-two verses because it is an acrostic (see above), while Psalm 33 also has twenty-two verses (with no title). Whether the acrostic structure of Psalm 34 has influenced the number of verses in Psalm 33 is not clear, but it is possible.

Key Themes of Psalm 34

- David is the righteous man.
- The fear of the Lord is a dual theme.
- God is not safe, but he is good.

As we have seen with neighboring psalms, they often share verbal links. In this case, Psalm 33:18 affirms that "the eyes of the LORD are on those who fear him," and 34:15 virtually duplicates this affirmation: "The eyes of the LORD are on the righteous."

This psalm has long been considered to have messianic implications. John quotes 34:20 in his account of the crucifixion to portray Jesus's unbroken bones as fulfilling this prophecy (John 19:36). Peter draws on the Greek version of this psalm (33:13–17a LXX; 34:12–16a Eng.) in support of his admonition that one should not "repay evil with evil or insult with insult" but "repay evil with blessing" (1 Pet. 3:9–12). It is likely that he sees in the admonition of 34:14 this principle of repaying evil with blessing. Sadly, in our Christian effort to understand the power of saving faith, we sometimes neglect the nexus of *faith* and *practice*. Peter's words can gratefully serve as a corrective.

Outline/Structure

Title
1. Thanksgiving for God's deliverance (34:1–7)
   a. Praise and call to praise (34:1–3)
   b. Personal history and the Lord's protection (34:4–7)
2. Affirmation of God's goodness (34:8–22)

a. A call to experience the Lord, with the assurance of God's goodness (34:8–10)

b. Invitation to learn the "fear of the LORD" and the Lord's attentive care of the righteous (34:11–20)

   i. Learning the fear of the Lord (34:11–14)

   ii. The Lord's attentive care of the righteous (34:15–18)

   iii. The Lord's protection of the righteous (34:19–20)

c. Final contrast between evil's power to slay the wicked and God's will to deliver the righteous (34:21–22)

Historical and Cultural Background

The title alludes to an event recorded in 1 Samuel 21:10–15, when David feigned madness before Achish, king of Gath. The name Abimelek ("my father is king"), rather than Achish (evidently a personal name), is generally explained as a title for the Philistine king, like Pharaoh in Egypt. The name Abimelek is also used to designate the Philistine ruler in the narrative relating Abraham's visit to Gerar (Gen. 20 and 21) and later Isaac's visit to the same Philistine region (Gen. 26).

In Saul's pursuit of David, the newly anointed King David fled to the Philistine city of Gath, a place where Saul could not follow, but when David realized that he faced danger from the Philistine king, he pretended to be mad so that they would let him go. Perhaps this event also led the Philistines to believe that a mad king would be no threat to them.[5]

Interpretive Insights

Title *When he pretended to be insane before Abimelek.* While it is more difficult to see the connection of the title to the second part of the psalm (34:8–22) than the first (34:1–7), the whole psalm celebrates those who fear the Lord (34:7, 9, 11) and "take refuge" in him (34:8, 22) and those who seek the Lord (34:10). On the account with Abimelek, see "Historical and Cultural Background." "Pretended to be insane" is literally "he changed his 'good sense'" (cf. Ps. 119:66).

34:2 *I will glory in the LORD.* The verb translated as "glory" means "to boast," as in 1 Kings 20:11, or "to glory in" or "to rejoice," as it does in Isaiah 41:16.

34:3 *Glorify the LORD with me; let us exalt his name together.* The plural verbs imply an audience, as do also the plural imperatives of verses 8, 9, and 11, probably the worshiping congregation.

34:4 *he delivered me from all my fears.* These "fears" are not the fear of verses 7 and 9 but fears generated by threatening circumstances, mortal fears (34:6). In fact, "fears" has a different verbal root (*gur*) from the verb "to fear" (*yr'*) the Lord that dominates this psalm (34:7, 9, 11; see "Teaching the Text").

34:5 *Those who look to him are radiant.* The word picture of Isaiah 60:5 helps us understand the radiance of these faces—metaphorically, Jerusalem's face "lights up" as she sees the exiles returning.

34:6 *This poor man called.* The prepositive (occurs before the word it modifies) "this" (normally it is postpositive, occurs after the word it modifies) brings emphasis to the subject "poor man," very likely a reference to the psalmist.

34:7 *The angel of the* L<small>ORD</small> *encamps around those who fear him.* Sometimes "angel of the L<small>ORD</small>" is a synonym for the Lord (e.g., Gen. 16:7). When it is not the Lord himself, it is the divine messenger.[6] Although there are many occurrences of this phrase in the Old Testament, surprisingly it occurs only three times in the Psalter, the other two times in Psalm 35 (vv. 5, 6).

Interestingly, the psalmist's "enemies" are referenced by secondary terms, "all my fears" (34:4), "all his troubles" (34:6), and "the afflictions" (34:19 ESV; NIV: "troubles"). In fact, "this poor man" of verse 6 is likely a reference to David himself, who has been delivered from all his mortal fears (34:4b) and enjoys the company of "those who fear" the Lord and experience the encircling protection of the "angel of the L<small>ORD</small>" (34:7).

34:8 *Taste and see that the* L<small>ORD</small> *is good; blessed is the one who takes refuge in him.* "Try him" is the sense of the imperative "taste." The suppliant's challenge grows out of his experience of deliverance in verses 6–7. The verb "to take refuge" (34:8, 22) forms an *inclusio*, linking this second part together. For the term "blessed" (*'ashre*), see the comments on Psalm 1:1.

34:9 *for those who fear him lack nothing.* With this term "lack" (*hsr*, 34:9, 10), Moses reminds the Israelites that in the wilderness they "have not lacked anything" (*hsr*, Deut. 2:7); the same verb occurs also in Psalm 23:1 (see "Theological Insights" on

Psalm 34 and the Lord's Supper

In early church history Psalm 34 became part of the liturgy of the Eucharist, largely because of 34:8, "Taste and see that the L<small>ORD</small> is good." Reciting the Psalms during the celebration of the Lord's Supper was attested during Augustine's day, and a wordplay in the Greek version of this particular psalm augmented the connection. The Greek word for "good" (*chrēstos*) is close to the Greek word for "Christ" (*Christos*), so the invitation "Taste and see that the L<small>ORD</small> is good [*chrēstos*]" in the Septuagint is easily heard as "Taste and see that *Christ* [*Christos*] is the Lord."[a] Even in our modern Protestant liturgies of the Lord's Supper, the use of 34:8 has persisted.[b] When our Lord said to his disciples, "Take and eat; this is my body" (Matt. 26:26), it was more than a mystical matter. It was the reality of living in, and living out, the presence of Christ.

[a] Holladay, *Psalms*, 180, citing Dimitri E. Conomos, *Communion*, 12.
[b] E.g., *Book of Common Worship*, 125.

The phrase "taste and see that the L<small>ORD</small> is good" (34:8) became a part of the liturgy of the Eucharist early in church history. Shown here is a restored silver chalice originally from AD 500–600. Similar chalices were used to serve the wine during the celebration of the Lord's Supper.

Ps. 23). The meaning of "lack nothing" is clarified in verse 10, "lack no good thing."

34:10 *The lions may grow weak and hungry.* The "lions," or "young lions" (ESV), are generally strong enough to get the prey they want, but even if they cannot, by analogy, the Lord is strong enough and willing to supply the needs of "those who seek the L<small>ORD</small>."

34:11 *Come, my children, listen to me.* The teacher, in wisdom style, addresses his students as "my children" (lit., "sons"; cf. Prov. 5:7; 7:24).

34:12 *Whoever of you loves life.* The Hebrew begins with an interrogative pronoun:

In contrast to the wicked, "the eyes of the LORD are on the righteous" (34:15). In the ancient world, when the god watched someone, it usually meant that the person was offered protection. In Egypt, the eye of Horus became a symbol of protection used for amulets, like the one shown here.

"Who is the one who desires life, [and] loves long life [lit., "days"] in order that he may see good?" (author's trans.). It is the equivalent of the liturgical questions of Psalms 15:1 and 24:3, which are followed by an ethical description of the one who may enter the Lord's house (15:2–5; 24:4). Here also the question is followed by an ethical description of the one who fears the Lord (34:13–14). Unfortunately, the NIV's "Whoever of you" (translating "who" [*mi*] as a relative pronoun) obscures the question and, therefore, the connection to the liturgical inquiry.

34:14 *Turn from evil and do good; seek peace and pursue it.* "Peace" and "good" are parallel terms, as in Psalm 122:8–9 (see ESV). Note the positive use of "pursue" (*rdp*) in Psalm 23:6 ("follow") and Proverbs 21:21.

34:15 *The eyes of the LORD . . . his ears.* The Lord's "eyes" and "ears" are terms that suggest the Lord's attentiveness. Note that verse 15 begins a series of affirmations intended to show that the Lord is good (34:15, 16, 18, 19, 20, 22).

34:16 *but the face of the LORD is against those who do evil.* When the Lord sets his face against someone, it presages ill (Lev. 20:5–6), whereas setting his eyes on someone carries a favorable connotation (Gen. 44:21; Deut. 11:12).

34:18 *The LORD is close to the brokenhearted.* The "brokenhearted" are those who have suffered affliction and who humble themselves before the Lord (Ps. 51:17). The terms "heart" and "spirit" are parallel and denote the human will and mind. To such persons God is very near (Deut. 4:7).

34:20 *all his bones, not one of them will be broken.* "Bones" is a synecdoche that means the whole body. There is a wordplay on "brokenhearted" of verse 18 and "broken" of this verse. The brokenhearted have no broken bones, the latter a metaphor of divine protection.

34:21 *Evil will slay the wicked.* The verb "slay" (Polel of *mut*, "to die") means "bring death nearer."[7] With "evil" as the subject of this verb, the violent picture is that of evil finishing off the wicked, who were already wounded and dying (see 1 Sam. 14:13).

34:22 *The LORD will rescue his servants.* For comments on the concluding verse of the acrostic, see the introduction to "Understanding the Text." The verb "rescue" (*pdh*) means "to redeem" or "to deliver." See the prayer in Psalm 25:22: "*Deliver*

Israel, O God, from all their troubles" (see also 130:8). What better verb ("redeem") to form a prayer and a statement of trust on Israel's behalf!

Theological Insights

The editor(s) of Book 1 sought to establish David as the truly "righteous" man, as we have maintained elsewhere,[8] perhaps not so much in the personal but in the rhetorical sense,[9] and Psalm 34 constitutes a fundamental statement to that effect.[10] The "righteous" portrait picks up where the "fear of the LORD" portrait leaves off. Obviously the singular, which we would expect if David is the referent, is not consistently the case in the psalm, and in fact it is never the case with "fear" (see 34:7, 9, 11). The lesson David seeks to teach his "children" is "the fear of the LORD," thus the plural form. He even pluralizes the "righteous" in verse 15 to reflect his teaching audience.

The heart of the poem is evident in the ethical imperative that comes to full expression in verse 8: "Taste and see that the LORD is good." While this may seem a little abstract for Old Testament thought (also 34:21), typically the abstract yields to the practical as the psalmist breaks down the "fear of the LORD" into ethical terms of obedience ("listen to [obey] me," 34:11a) and then translates the fear of the Lord into guarding against deceitful speech (34:13). The fear of the Lord is not abstract but changes one's spiritual perspective and personal behavior.

The narrative voice of the psalmist is heard throughout, but twice he steps forth and speaks in the first person. In the first instance he states: "I sought the LORD, and he answered me; he delivered me from all my fears" (34:4). Then in the following verses (34:7–11) the supplicant directs the audience's attention to the "fear of the LORD" that counterbalances mortal fear (34:7, 9, 11), concluding with his second first-person statement: "I will teach you the fear of the LORD." Whereas David has rhetorically appeared in Book 1 as the "righteous" man, Psalm 34 also depicts him as the "teacher" of the "fear of the LORD," which suggests a proactive righteousness.

Teaching the Text

We can structure a lesson/sermon on Psalm 34 by using John Newton's hymn "Amazing Grace," drawing on the words, "'Twas grace that taught my heart to fear [saving fear], and grace my fears relieved [mortal fear]." The psalmist recognizes, as did Newton, that grace has two functions: it teaches us to fear (the fear of the Lord—saving fear), and it relieves our fears (fear of what others can do to us—mortal fear). If that sounds like grace working against grace, we should observe that this is precisely the dilemma of the psalmist, but in the opposite order: "he delivered me from all my fears" (34:4), which carries the sense of "dread" or "terror," especially dread or terror in the presence of one's enemies (Num. 22:3; 1 Sam. 18:15).[11] Thus the "fears" of verse 4 were the "fears" that arise from the threatening circumstances of life, corresponding to Newton's "and grace my fears relieved."

The heart of the psalm, however, is the spiritual disposition that Newton expresses in his line "'Twas grace that taught my heart to fear," and that is the fear of the Lord. Verses 7, 9, and 11 focus on this kind of fear and employ a different word for fear, *yr'*, which signifies awe and reverence for God, even love. Indeed, that was David's lesson plan: "Come, my children, listen to me; I will teach you the fear of the LORD" (34:11). This is the "fear of the LORD" that, in the direst of circumstances, even summons the help of heaven: "The angel of the LORD encamps around those who fear him, and he delivers them" (34:7). The fear of the Lord issues in the condition that "those who fear him lack nothing" (34:9), a sufficiency that is found more in the sufficiency of God than the sufficiency of things, even though the latter is not excluded (Matt. 6:28–34).

We should point out also that as the "fear of the LORD" grows, it does so in reverse relationship to the negative fear that would harm us. The more we fear the Lord, the more the dread and terror of circumstances lose their hold on us. The answer to the question posed by the middle verse, "Who is the person who desires life and would love to see many good days?" (34:12, author's trans.), is answered by the larger psalm—it is the one who fears the Lord. The moral code of verses 13–14 is an ethical description of that person, and the implications of this lesson are life transforming.

Illustrating the Text

The Lord helps in times of trouble.

Testimony: In Psalm 34, David talks about the provision of the Lord in times of trouble. David specifically talks about the Lord hearing his plea (34:6), answering him (34:4), and delivering him (34:4, 6). Ask one of your congregants to share a personal testimony of how he or she turned to the Lord in a fearful time of life, saw the Lord respond (hearing, answering, and delivering), and observed how his or her mortal fears turned to the fear of the Lord. Verses from Psalm 34 could be woven through the testimony.

Spiritual awakening

Biography: John Newton. The story of the conversion of Newton, author of the hymn "Amazing Grace," is a great illustration of the "fear of the Lord" that leads to salvation (34:7, 9, 11). Newton lived the first twenty-two years of his life far from the Lord. At age eleven he became a sailor and later engaged in slave trade. But at age twenty-three, while he was on a voyage to

The grave of John Newton is located in the churchyard of the Parish Church of St. Peter and St. Paul, Olney, England, where he served as curate between 1764 and 1780. The epitaph, which he composed, speaks of his transformation from sinner to servant by God's mercy. It reads, "John Newton, Clerk, once an infidel and libertine, a servant of slaves in Africa, was, by the rich mercy of our Lord and Saviour Jesus Christ, preserved, restored, pardoned, and appointed to preach the faith he had long labored to destroy."

England, Newton's ship was overcome by a fierce storm, and for weeks the disabled vessel was tossed and drifted about by the waves and winds. This gave Newton opportunity to think deeply about his life. At first he concluded that his sins were too many and too great to be forgiven, a reality that nearly brought him to despair. But as he read a New Testament on board that wandering vessel, Newton reflected on the death of Jesus. As great as was his sin, the blood of Christ was even greater. By the time the ship arrived in Ireland, Newton was a new creation in Jesus Christ, saved by the grace and mercy of God.[12] As we read in Psalm 34:9, "Fear the LORD, you his holy people, for those who fear him lack nothing."

The fear of the Lord

Children's Book: *The Lion, the Witch and the Wardrobe*, by C. S. Lewis. This book contains a powerful quote that is a good reminder of the nature of God and how we relate to him. In the story, Aslan, the great lion, portrays Jesus. In a conversation between Susan (one of the four children in the story) and Mr. Beaver, we are reminded of the "fear of the Lord." Mr. Beaver says, "Aslan is a lion—the Lion, the great Lion." "Ooh," says Susan, "I'd thought he was a man. Is he quite safe? I shall feel rather nervous about meeting a lion." "Safe?" says Mr. Beaver. "Who said anything about safe? 'Course he isn't safe. But he's good. He's the King, I tell you."[13]

The Lord of Scripture is not "safe," but he is good (v. 8a). "Safe" means that God is custodian of our security, and nothing more. But that he is "good" means our security is in the Custodian, not in the place of refuge. Indeed, we take refuge in him (v. 8b), but it is more abiding in his love than relaxing in our security.

Imprecatory Psalms

The *imprecatory psalms* ("curses") are prayers that God will requite the evil deeds of the psalmists' enemies. They include Psalms 35; 55; 59; 69; 79; 83; 109; and 137. The three that most honestly earn this title are Psalms 35; 69; and 109. Yet "imprecatory" is not the best label for this subgenre because, as we see, Psalm 35 contains no curses in the strict sense of the word. Perhaps "psalms of anger" or "psalms of wrath" would be better, but "imprecatory psalms" has been the standard label, so we will retain it for our discussion.

The problem of these psalms for Christians and Jews alike is how to square their vengeful nature against the commandment to love God and to love one's neighbor as oneself (Deut. 6:5; Lev. 19:18). Christians face a challenge beyond that, which is how to obey Jesus's instruction to "Love your enemies and pray for those who persecute you" (Matt. 5:44). How can that command be lived out if the spirit of these psalms is allowed to stand as an authentic piece of biblical ethics?

Many "solutions" have been put forward, even though there is probably not a solution in the best sense of the word. First, since they are poetic, some believe they tend to overstate the situation they describe and exaggerate the resolution of the problem. Eric Zenger acknowledges that this may be part of the "solution," though certainly not the whole.[1] Second, Sigmund Mowinckel saw the explanation in the practice of black magic in the psalmists' world. As they uttered their words of revenge against their enemies, they also engaged, it is supposed, in a ritual that acted out their vengeful wishes.[2] The Old Testament, however, is highly negative toward this type of "spiritual" manipulation of people and circumstances. Third, still other interpreters have written off these "psalms of anger" as an inferior ethic to the ethic of Jesus and insisted that they are not to be taken

The desire for the deity to act in justice that is expressed in the imprecatory psalms is also recorded in this sixth-century BC prayer to Marduk by a son of Nebuchadnezzar who has been wrongly imprisoned. He says, "O Marduk, slay the worker of artful deeds against me. . . . Surround the malefactors with the same cruel web with which he artfully surrounded me" (translation from B. Foster, "The Lament of Nabu-shuma-ukin," in *Before the Muses*, 3rd ed. [Bethesda, MD: CDL, 2005], p. 854, ll. 41, 49).

seriously. Admittedly, Old Testament ethics range all the way from the law of retaliation ("an eye for an eye," Deut. 19:21) to the law of love (Deut. 6:5; Lev. 19:18), and this range ought not be ignored. These psalms theoretically could fall somewhere in that range. Fourth, some interpreters prefer to view these "imprecations" as predictions rather than pronouncements, but their circumstances are too real to ignore, and their words of vengeance too fresh to pass off as mere predictions. Fifth, the messianic interpretation is that they are prophetic references to the Messiah, and that is attractive, especially since Jesus himself quoted Psalm 35:19/69:4 to explain why the world hated him (John 15:25). The "curses" then would be against the enemies of Christ rather than those of the psalmists. Yet even this can be only a partial explanation, especially since the speakers in the psalms are so personally involved.[3] Sixth, a few scholars insist that these psalms are about national rather than personal enemies, but that is to neglect the very personal nature of most of these psalms (Pss. 79 and 83 do speak of national enemies). Seventh, the psalmists are quoting their enemies' words of imprecation spoken against the psalmists themselves, not vice versa. While this interpretation has been applied frequently to Psalm 109 (see the "Additional Insights" following the unit on Ps. 109), it does not apply as well to other imprecatory psalms.

In our opinion there is no solution to the problem of the imprecatory psalms as such, even though several of the foregoing explanations might be helpfully employed. The best we can do is to put them in theological perspective and provide several angles from which to view them. First, the psalmists perceive that they have suffered ill-treatment from their persecutors, since the psalmists have, at least sometimes, been repaid evil for the good they have done to their enemies (e.g., 35:12). And on some occasions the evildoers were their friends, which compounded the wrongs done to the psalmists (109:4–5). Second, on other occasions the psalmists make the point that they have been done ill for no cause of their own (35:7, 19; 59:3–5; 69:4; 109:2–3). Third, the suffering they lament is for the Lord's sake (69:7–9), giving the suppliants strength of character to endure. Fourth, the psalmists' faith in God's goodness is still intact (e.g., 109:21), even though their faith in human beings has taken a downward plunge. Fifth, at times the suppliants were very confident in the support of their community that hoped for their vindication (35:27). Sixth, the psalmists, whether stated or unstated, do not take vengeance into their own hands but leave it to God (e.g., 109:26–29; see Deut. 32:35; Rom. 12:19). Thus this theological context gives us a perspective, even though it still cannot countermand such harsh rhetoric as we find in Psalm 137:9, "Happy is the one who seizes your infants and dashes them against the rocks."[4]

While trying to understand these perplexing poems and their caustic prayers for vengeance on the psalmists' enemies, we should not at the same time forget that divine judgment is a reality that both the Old and New Testaments take seriously. C. S. Lewis also points out that these psalms can remind us that there is still a place in Christian piety for a sense of righteous indignation.[5]

"May the Net They Hid Entangle Them"

Big Idea *Rather than taking vengeance for injustice into our own hands, we can pray that its perpetrators will become victims of their own contrivances.*

Understanding the Text

Psalm 35, the first of the imprecatory psalms, deals with the issue of divine justice in a bare-bones way. In one sense, it is an individual lament (Craigie), but in its total effect, it is more a prayer for deliverance (Wilson). The form critics, seeking the cultural context for such prayers, are inclined to view the psalm as a royal or national lament,[1] and based on verses 20 and 27, the speaker is assumed to be the king.

This psalm belongs among the imprecations ("curses") of the Psalter, and is one of the three psalms designated as the imprecatory psalms (Pss. 35; 69; 109),[2] although they do not hold exclusive rights to imprecations (see the "Additional Insights" that precedes this

The psalmist asks God to act to bring justice on his behalf because of enemies who have acted against him "without cause" (35:7, 19). Deities were considered the administrators of justice in the ancient Near East. This statue of an old Babylonian god may represent Shamash, who was known as a god of justice.

unit). In fact, there are really no statements in this poem that can be designated "curses" in a strict sense—35:4–8 provides the closest examples—certainly not in the clear sense of Psalm 109.[3] Psalm 35 is a prayer that God will deal out justice to those who, without cause (35:7), have dealt injustice to the psalmist.

The Text in Context

In the immediate neighborhood, Psalm 35 appears to be a companion to Psalm 34, the two sharing the only references to the "angel of the Lord" in the Psalter (34:7; 35:5, 6). The gentle admonition of Psalm 34 is that the saints "turn from evil and do good; seek peace and pursue it" (34:14). In contrast, the king's enemies in Psalm 35 "do not speak peaceably" (v. 20; lit., "they do not speak peace"). The psalm is an enlargement of the portrait of those who reject the admonition of 34:13–14 and a theological treatment of how God should deal with the unjust portrait that their rejection has cultivated.

Among the prophets Jeremiah sometimes assumes a vengeful spirit toward his many and violent enemies, but, like the psalmists, he does not take vengeance into his own hands but leaves it to God. Jeremiah 18:18–23 is such a caustic prayer in which he petitions God to bring personal tragedy on his persecutors (the spirit of Jer. 21–22 especially runs in that vein). Jeremiah's prayer is introduced with information about how the people have been plotting against him, much like the plot that spawned his earlier prayer (Jer. 11:18–23). His critics have claimed that Jeremiah's words are certainly no replacement for the words of the priest, the wise, and the prophet (perhaps these three groups were the major source of the charges). Yet Jeremiah's disposition is not one of total denunciation, for he reminds God of how he has pleaded for their welfare (18:20b), putting a compassionate face on Jeremiah's preaching. He, like Jonah (Jon. 4:2), knows God's gracious nature and wants to direct God's response into the channel of punitive action.

Jesus knows this psalm and quotes 35:19 in one of his discourses in John's Gospel, in which he speaks to the disciples about his and their undeserved persecution: "But this is to fulfill what is written in their Law: 'They hated me without reason'" (John 15:25). It is of interest that Jesus refers to this statement as "written in their *Law*," not the Torah as such, but in the Psalms, which was, in a sense, a compendium of the Torah (see the discussion of Ps. 1). In its totality, Psalm 35 may not be messianic, but it certainly has messianic overtones, as do the imprecatory psalms generally (see quotes from Pss. 69 and

109 in Acts 1:20; Rom. 11:10). Some consider these words not so much curses against David's enemies as prophecies against Christ's.[4]

Outline/Structure

The psalm is composed of three parts, each ending in praise. The following outline highlights the various elements of the psalm.

1. Part 1 (35:1–10)
   a. The scheming (35:1–8)
      i. Prayer of petition (35:1–3)
      ii. Prayer against enemies (35:4–6)
      iii. Explanation of enemies' behavior (35:7)
      iv. Prayer against enemies (35:8)
   b. Praise (35:9–10)
2. Part 2 (35:11–18)
   a. The mobbing (35:11–17)
      i. Explanation of enemies' behavior (35:11–12)
      ii. Psalmist's behavior compared to theirs (35:13–14)
      iii. Enemies' behavior compared to psalmist's (35:15–16)
      iv. Psalmist's prayer for mercy (35:17)
   b. Praise (35:18)
3. Part 3 (35:19–28)
   a. The gloating (35:19–27)
      i. Psalmist's prayer for mercy against evil intent of enemies (35:19–21)

ii. Psalmist's prayer for God's
actions (35:22–27)
b. Praise (35:28)[5]

Historical and Cultural Background

Delitzsch hints that the "curses" of the imprecatory psalms are reserved largely for Saul and, by prophetic extension, for Jesus's enemies.[6] This is certainly possible, but unfortunately, in this case, we cannot be so sure that Saul's persecution of David was the historical context for the "curses." David had many enemies besides Saul, both inside and outside Israel.

While the "curses" of Psalm 35 hardly come up to the standard of those in Psalms 69 and 109, entreating God to bring curses on one's enemies was a common practice in ancient Israel, as it was also among Israel's neighbors.

Interpretive Insights

35:1 *Contend,* Lord, *with those who contend with me.* The verb "contend" and the object, "those who contend," come from the language of the law court. Some form critics insist that this reflects a liturgical/legal use of the psalm, which may also be a hint of its provenance—the law court. That Yahweh should "contend" with "those who contend," and "fight with those who fight," is reflective of the same principle in Psalm 18:25–26, where human actions seem to shape divine actions (see "Theological Insights").

35:2 *Take up shield and armor.* Two types of shields are in view, the first (*magen*) being the small shield that could be wielded in the left hand with the sword in the right, and the second (*tsinnah*, "armor"

or "buckler") referring to the large shield that virtually covered the warrior's whole body and was probably carried by an infantry aide (see the comments on Ps. 5:12).

35:3 *Brandish spear and javelin.* The battle gear of the ancient warrior is listed here in terms of the defensive (shield and armor) and offensive (spear and javelin) weapons. The Hebrew word for "javelin" is contested (e.g., the KJV translates the Hebrew *sᵉgor* as a verb, but it probably should be pointed as *sᵉger* and rendered as the NIV does, "javelin"; see also the NIV footnote).[7]

35:5 *chaff.* See Psalm 1:4 for a picture of winnowing. The wheat was placed on the threshing floor, where the grain was beaten out of its husk, then tossed into the air, allowing the wind to blow away the lighter chaff, with the heavier grain falling to the threshing floor.

35:7 *without cause.* The Hebrew word *hinnam* ("without cause") occurs twice in 35:7, with 35:8 stipulating the punishment.

35:8 *may the net they hid entangle them, may they fall into the pit, to their ruin.* This principle of Old Testament ethics, that one's evil deeds should "entangle" the evildoer, picks up on the same thought as 34:21 and is basic to Old Testament jurisprudence.

35:9 *Then my soul will rejoice in the* Lord. The Hebrew word for "soul" (*nepesh*) is not the Greek concept of "soul," the disembodied spirit, but rather the idea of the human person. The phrase "living being" (*nepesh hayyah*, Gen. 1:20; NIV: "living creature") is very close to the Hebrew notion. In view of this, it could be translated as the personal pronoun "I" (the parallel noun in 35:10 is "my whole being"; lit., "all my bones").

35:10 *Who is like you,* Lord? This is an allusion to Moses's words in the Song of the Sea (Exod. 15:11; variations occur in Pss. 71:19; 89:8; Isa. 44:7; Jer. 49:19; 50:44; see the sidebar).[8]

35:11 *Ruthless witnesses.* The phrase is literally "witnesses of violence," the noun "violence" (*ḥamas*) connoting violence that involves bloodshed. Wilson sees here "damaging false testimony in a case involving the death penalty."[9] The legal setting that gives rise to the language of the psalm is again evident in the word "witnesses,"[10] with the nature of the legal conflict dominating 35:11–16.[11]

35:12 *They repay me evil for good.* This sets the problem in perspective. David has done them no wrong but, in fact, has done them good.

35:15 *when I stumbled, they gathered in glee.* The evil intent of David's persecutors is clearly in evidence here. They are not moved to pity when he stumbles but are prompted all the more to rejoice over his fall.

35:17 *my precious life.* The imagery of the Hebrew word *yᵉḥidah*, which is feminine (see also 22:20), suggests a dearly beloved only daughter, whereas the masculine noun elsewhere describes Isaac as "your only son [*yaḥid*], whom you love" (Gen. 22:2). Here it refers to the psalmist's life.[12]

35:19 *those who hate me without reason . . . wink the eye.* Jesus applies this verse to the hostility of his and his followers' enemies (John 15:25; see "The Text in Context"). Again the psalmist insists on his innocence. To "wink the eye" is a metaphor that suggests insidious intentions (Prov. 6:13; 10:10; 16:30).

35:21–22 *With our own eyes we have seen it.* Here we have a wordplay on the idea of seeing. The enemies claim they have

seen with their own eyes (*ra'ᵃtah*) the false deeds that they have accused David of, and then the psalmist turns immediately to exclaim that it is the Lord who has seen (v. 22, *ra'itah*) the falsity of their vision (implied).

35:26–27 *exalt . . . be exalted.* The contrast is between those "who exalt themselves" and those who proclaim, "The Lord be exalted" (35:27).

Theological Insights

The notion that God's attitudes and actions are motivated by, or react to, human attitudes and actions is reflected in 35:1 ("Contend, Lord, with those who contend with me; fight against those who fight against me"). This relationship between divine and human actions is also the topic of Psalm 18:25–26:

> To the faithful you show yourself
>   faithful,
>   to the blameless you show yourself
>   blameless,
> to the pure you show yourself pure,
>   but to the devious you show yourself
>   shrewd.

How does one explain this connection? Are God's attitudes and actions determined by our human ones? Or are they *reactions* and not *actions* at all? The mystery of divine/

human relationships is written all over the Psalms, and here we have an insight into that mystery, however dense it may at first appear. Even to suggest that God is unaffected by our deeds and attitudes is to obscure a huge part of the theology of the Psalms and, for that matter, the Old Testament as a whole. God is moved to compassion by our repentance (Ps. 51:17) and provoked by our sin (18:26b). Psalm 35:1 describes the second part of this mystery, "Contend with those who contend," and "fight against those who fight." Human actions and God's response have a direct connection. On the other hand, Psalm 18:25–26 depicts both sides of the formula, exhibiting "the device of repeated reciprocity to encourage the faithful to adopt a fruitful relation to Yahweh."[13] It is in effect an expression of the covenant relationship stated in Psalm 18:24: "The LORD has rewarded me according to my righteousness, according to the cleanness of my hands in his sight." God's righteousness is the standard by which men's and women's righteousness is judged, and in that sense all other good attributes of human character are reflections of God's character: "Be perfect, therefore, as your heavenly Father is perfect" (Matt. 5:48). God is favorably responsive to those who reflect his nature and adversely responsive to those who do not.

Another issue that Psalm 35 raises concerns the treatment of our enemies. See the "Additonal Insights" section following this unit for further discussion.

Teaching the Text

Psalm 35 is among the psalms that have long portions omitted in the Liturgy of the Hours (35:3a, 4–8, 20–21, 24–26; also Pss. 59 and 69, while Pss. 58; 83; and 109 are omitted altogether).[14] Even though this psalm, along with the other imprecatory psalms, is included in the standard Psalters for worship, just how often they are used in public worship is anyone's guess. My personal practice is to use these psalms as teaching instruments, but not for preaching, except as they may yield their messianic dividends (but see "Teaching the Text" in the unit on Ps. 109). The issues require a complex discussion and theological nuancing that do not fit the time frame and the audience-speaker dynamic of the sermon, but they can be useful as instruments of instruction, especially the justice of God and our reaction to it (see "Theological Insights" and the "Additional Insights" that precede and follow this unit).

Illustrating the Text

Spiritual perception sees the world as God intends.

Science: The image perceived by the human eye is thrown upon the retina in an inverted position. The brain knows what to do with that image so that it is perceived right-side up. But what if the brain did not know what it should do with the inverted image? What if the brain read it just as it appears on the retina? In the Gospels, Jesus gives us a picture of the world turned right-side up and instructs us that this is the panorama of the kingdom of God. For example, Jesus says, "Whoever wants to become great among you must be your servant, and whoever wants to be first must be your slave" (Matt. 20:26–27). That's the right-side-up version. But what if our spiritual brain did not have the capacity to turn the inverted image right-side up? It might read: "Whoever would be great among you must be rich and powerful, and whoever would be first among you must not allow anyone to get ahead of him." One of the tragedies of the secularization of the church is that our spiritual brain has sometimes lost its capacity to handle the inverted image that is cast by a sinful world upon the retina of our spiritual eye. The psalmist's ocular capabilities were quite excellent, and he insists that the world, turned upside down (35:12), is one that he has envisioned turned right-side up (35:13), and one that the Lord himself intends to turn right-side up (35:27).

Evil for good and good for evil

Applying the Text: One strong idea that emerges from Psalm 35 is the psalmist's innocence, asserted in the phrase "without cause" (vv. 7, 19). His sterling character is further affirmed by his treatment of his enemies, "They repay me evil for good" (v. 12a). He defines the good he did to them when they were in trouble, "I put on sackcloth and humbled myself with fasting. When my prayers returned to me unanswered, I went about mourning" (vv. 13–14a). But something transformed the suppliant's good thoughts about his enemies somewhere along this journey, for now he is wishing them woe (v. 8). Perhaps it was their reaction to his misfortune, "But when I stumbled, they gathered in glee. . . . They slandered me without ceasing" (vv. 15–16). When our assailants

reject our kindness, and even our compassion for them in trouble, that is one thing, but when they then turn on us and mock us when we stumble, that is quite another matter. But that is not to imply that it is morally acceptable at that point to turn on them and pronounce our "curses" against them. Rather it is to point out that when our opponents return evil for good, that is a test of our character. One might conclude that David's subsequent attitude that led to his prayer for their harm was a character failure. Could he not, should he not, have continued to nurture the "good for evil" principle that he practiced in the first phase of this troubled relationship? If he had achieved the ethical principle of loving one's neighbor as oneself, the answer is definitely "yes." But one wonders if the ethical currency of the day was that high a norm, especially when the "good for evil" principle had been rebuffed by its beneficiaries. I suspect that what is missing here is the clear teaching of that Son of David who taught us, "Love your enemies and pray for those who persecute you. . . . If you love those who love you, what reward will you get?" (Matt. 5:44, 46). While the psalmist had not achieved that status of ethical behavior, he had nevertheless reached a high plateau, and his enemies could not say, "We have swallowed him up."

Cursing or Loving Our Enemies

Curses against the psalmist's enemies do and ought to arouse a spirit of resistance inside us, mainly because Jesus has said that we should pray for our enemies, even love them (Matt. 5:43–48).[1] If cursing our enemies provokes a reaction in our minds, loving our enemies elicits a certain kind of resistance as well, since that is so contrary to our sinful nature. How can we possibly love our enemies! While Jesus interprets the curses of the psalms (Pss. 35:19; 69:4) to have been fulfilled in his own suffering (John 15:25; see also Rom. 15:3 [Ps. 69:9]), nowhere in the Gospels does he use an imprecation against his enemies. He both prescribes and practices a new standard of behavior toward one's enemies, best expressed by his words from the cross, "Father, forgive them, for they do not know what they are doing" (Mark 23:34).

At the same time we may ask the question whether we should make a distinction between interpersonal relationships, on the one hand (in which we are to love our enemies and turn the other cheek, etc.), and the behavior of those responsible for carrying out justice in society, on the other. It is generally recognized that Jesus in the Sermon on the Mount is talking about how we should live as kingdom people, not about how society should function or how governing officials should deal with crime. Surely they are not to turn the other cheek and let crime go unchecked. With this caveat in place we can recognize that God's actions are those of the one who is responsible to carry out justice. When God is carrying out justice, his interpersonal relationships are not at issue.[2]

The bold metaphors of the Psalms are sometimes shocking, such as that of 35:2–3. The suppliant prays that God will take up the weapons of battle and use them against his enemies. It is essentially a challenge for Yahweh to equip himself for battle. Yahweh as warrior has been a recurring concern of Old Testament theologians.[3] While this is more a metaphor than a virtual description of Yahweh's battle worthiness, its bold effect is nevertheless notable, and for some readers it is disturbing. It is reminiscent of the audacious metaphor of Yahweh's striking the psalmist's enemies on the jaw and breaking their teeth in Psalm 3:7. While this picture of Yahweh as violent opponent may vibrate negatively to our sensitivities, we should remember that it is a measured reaction against his enemies' violence. The psalmist's complaint is of a serious nature, for the "ruthless witnesses" (35:11; see comments on that verse) are those who accuse the psalmist of blood-violence (*hamas*), a crime deserving death.[4]

The first principle of justice that the psalm presents is that evildoers may be ensnared by their own machinations (35:7–8). That, of course, is not to ignore the fact that in the world of Old Testament jurisprudence, as in the phenomenal world, every ethical action has, or ought to have, an equal and opposite reaction ("the punishment fits the crime"). If this ethical law fails in human affairs, then the second principle of justice presented by the psalm comes into effect, that Yahweh may initiate punitive action. In fact—and this is of great significance—the poets of the imprecatory psalms never take vengeance into their own hands but leave it in God's ("Vengeance is mine . . ."; see Deut. 32:35; Rom. 12:19). God as initiator of punishment is further confirmed when the suppliant entreats the Lord to make his enemies chaff, "with the angel of the LORD pursuing them" (35:5–6). God as the expediter of punishment in order to establish his justice is a significant idea, and while it does not resolve the ethical dilemma that the imprecatory psalms present, it nevertheless provides one perspective that helps us understand why they are contained in the Psalter.[5]

Yet, this principle, despite our own vicious age, troubles some people because they, like Marcion of the second Christian century, have extracted judgment from their god profile, regardless of what the Scriptures may teach. But if God does not deal appropriately with injustice, how can we view him as a just God? Some retributive aspect is necessary for a balanced view of justice. The modern Western world is correct to insist on an appropriate measurement of punitive justice, but a total elimination of that aspect would make the system lopsided and essentially "unjust." By the same analogy, we cannot eliminate the punitive aspect from the biblical profile of God and still maintain the profile of a just God.

The innocence of the suppliant is obvious in his reminder, "They repay me evil for good" (35:12a), while he has done the opposite (35:13–14). This moral code belongs in the upper stratum of Old Testament ethics, in the same category as "love your neighbor as yourself" (Lev. 19:18); and certainly the psalmist exceeds the "eye for an eye" principle by miles and institutes an ethic of love, very close to what Jesus himself has taught. To be sure, it is unnatural for us, because by our sinful nature we tend to return others' behavior in kind. Yet this position only breeds further resentment and violence. The range of the Old Testament ethic extends upward from the ground-zero code of retaliation, to "Love the LORD your God with all your heart" and "your neighbor as yourself" (e.g., Mark 12:29–31). David's demeanor illustrates the upper range. Admittedly, however, one may treat another person with consideration and respect without loving him or her, but at least this behavior puts one in closer range of love.

The psalmist asks the Lord to arm for battle with a spear and a javelin in Psalm 35:3. Shown here are bronze spearheads from several excavation sites in Israel, eleventh to sixth century BC.

"Your Love, LORD, Reaches to the Heavens, Your Faithfulness to the Skies"

Big Idea *The absence of the fear of the Lord that characterizes the wicked is outmatched by the covenant love of the Lord, which encompasses the world, humans and animals alike, and reaches the heavens.*

Understanding the Text

The literary genre of Psalm 36 is a bit elusive. Dahood says it has elements of wisdom in 36:1–4, becomes a hymn in 36:5–10, and then is a lament in 36:11–12. This, of course, is not the only instance when the form-critical method of analyzing the Psalms fails. In Dahood's words: "The coexistence of three literary types within a poem of thirteen verses [in Hebrew] points up the limitations of the form-critical approach to the Psalter."[1] Craigie prefers the classification of a wisdom psalm but recognizes that the form does not give much reason for it.[2] Ultimately, we simply have to admit that Psalm 36 represents a multiple-genre composition and remind ourselves that the psalmists were not working by the form-critical method.[3] The method, with much in its favor, is for our benefit, and we need not be surprised when the biblical writers do not meet our expectations.

The Text in Context

Psalm 36 follows the injunction of praise in 35:27 that celebrates the Lord's delight in the "well-being of *his servant.*" If we allow the title of Psalm 36 to inform us, then "his servant" is likely David, and in a prophetic voice ("an oracle"; see below) he recounts the godless disposition of the wicked, commemorates the covenant love of the Lord, and prays that God will continue his covenant love and prevent any further damage by the "foot of the proud" and the "hand of the wicked" (36:11; cf. 36:1). Like Psalm 14, which laments the godless disposition of David's world, this lamentation comes close to that but stops short of saying that people deny God's existence, with perhaps only a hair's breadth between "there is no God" (14:1) and "there is no fear of God before their eyes" (36:1). Indeed, the disposition of the wicked as expressed in 36:1b is a good summary of the kind of evil represented by the subjects of Psalm 35, who have no regard for the innocent, the social equivalent of their flagrant spiritual mood. Psalm 36 presents a picture of a totally different world where the love (*hesed*) of God reaches the heavens and exceeds the height of the mountains. This is the world known to God's servant David and the "upright in heart" (36:10).

Only here and in Psalm 18 (title) is David called the "servant of the LORD." In fact, the two titles are exact duplicates, except for the historical note appended to the title of Psalm 18. In view of Moses's role as prophet par excellence (Deut. 18:15–22), Craigie proposes that the first word in the body of the psalm (*neʾum*, "an oracle"; NIV: "message") be treated as an introduction to a prophetic message, as it is in the last words of David ("oracle of David, son of Jesse," 2 Sam. 23:1) and the oracle of Balaam ("the oracle of Balaam the son of Beor," Num. 24:3 ESV). In that case we would ignore the *maqqef* (a connecting mark of punctuation) in the Hebrew text that joins the word to the following word ("sinfulness"). Generally, however, *neʾum* is used as a concluding word of a prophecy, especially in Isaiah, Jeremiah, and Ezekiel, and can be translated nominally ("oracle of the LORD") or verbally ("says the LORD"; e.g., Jer. 1:8).

Outline/Structure

Craigie draws attention to two terms in this psalm that give a chiastic structure of thought: "wicked" (36:1) and "love" (36:5), and the reverse order of "love" (36:10) and "wicked" (36:11). The predominant place of these terms in each of these four sections

Key Themes of Psalm 36

- Creation serves as a framework for the love of God.
- Flattery may be a blinder to one's own sin.

sets the theme of the psalm, with the term "wicked" forming an *inclusio*:[4]

A The behavior of the *wicked* (36:1–4)
  B The Lord's *love* (36:5–9)
  B′ Prayer for *love* (36:10)
A′ Prayer for protection from the *wicked* (36:11–12)

Historical and Cultural Background

As we have seen already in our study, the world of the Psalms was a vicious world, where personal and political evil was rampant, and often the innocent suffered and had no reprisal. In Psalm 35 that innocent person was the king, victimized by a host of evildoers who had no sense of justice. With Psalm 36, in that world of injustice and stark evil, something absolutely astonishing has happened: God has revealed his covenant love

David declares that with God "is the fountain of life" (36:9). Similar images of life-giving water coming from the gods are found in the ancient Near East. This eighth-century BC statue of a Mesopotamian deity stood at the entrance of the Nabu temple in Khorsabad. Streams of water flow from the vessel he holds.

to Israel and offered them a "fountain of life" to slake their intense thirst and a light to guide them through that dark world (36:9).

Interpretive Insights

Title *the servant of the Lord.* See "The Text in Context." Wilson suggests that, since most of the references to "servant of the Lord" are to Moses, this occurrence "may well suggest that a messianic interpretation of David . . . is already in operation here rather than a straightforward historical one."[5]

36:1 *I have a message . . . concerning the sinfulness of the wicked.* Taking the phrase "concerning the sinfulness of the wicked" as part of the oracle, and wickedness ("sinfulness," *pesha'*) as a personification, the sentence would read: "An oracle. Wickedness [speaks] concerning the evil one, that there is no fear of God before his eyes." (On *ne'um*, "message," as "oracle," see "The Text in Context.")

no fear of God. Whether the last part of the verse is intended to be a direct quotation of the wicked's words or merely a summary of that person's words,[6] it provides the reader with the essence of the wicked person's attitude. The word "fear" (*pahad*) is used in a double sense, "fear [*pahad*] of God" because he is Judge, and the "fear [*yir'ah*] of God" because he is Savior (e.g., 34:11). Along with several Old Testament texts to support the argument, Paul quotes Psalm 36:1b in Romans 3:18 to declare that both Jews and gentiles are under the power of sin. Paul very likely hears this universal note in the phrase "sons of man" (36:7; NIV: "people").

36:2–4 *In their own eyes they flatter themselves too much to detect or hate their sin.* Verse 2 is difficult to translate (especially the last phrase) and may mean, as the NIV renders it, they "flatter themselves" to the extent that they cannot recognize *their own sin* so as to hate it. As verse 3 explains, "the words of their mouths are wicked and deceitful." The process begins in their self-deception, is expressed in their words, and perverts their actions ("they fail to act wisely or do good," 36:3), culminating in a life totally bent to their wicked way of thinking ("on their beds" and "a sinful course [or "way"]," 36:4a, b).[7] The final disposition, parallel to their failure to "do good," is that they "do not reject what is wrong" (36:4c). The progression then, like that of Psalm 1, is laid out in sinister clarity. See Psalm 12:3 for the notion of "flattery."

The words of their mouths are wicked and deceitful. The words "wicked" (*'awen*) and "deceit" (*sheqer*) occur together also in Psalm 7:14, where "deceit" is parallel to "falsehood" (*sheqer*; NIV: "disillusionment"). The latter part of the verse shows that moral decline has spiraled down from thought to actions.

Even on their beds they plot evil . . . and do not reject what is wrong. The verbs here are Hebrew imperfects, implying continuous action—it has become a practice of life for them. The reality that they "do not reject what is wrong" is a summary of the final stage of the downward spiral. The verb "reject" (*m's*) is used in Psalm 78:67 to speak of Yahweh's rejection of the Leah side of Jacob's family (Saul) in favor of the Rachel side (David). It is a clear rejection of one alternative over another.

36:5 *Your love, Lord, reaches to the heavens, your faithfulness to the skies.* Here begins the stanza (36:5–9) that is dominated by the four nouns of 36:5 and 6: "love" (*hesed*), "faithfulness" (*'emunah*), "righteousness" (*ts*ᵉ*daqah*), and "justice" (*mishpat*). The psalmist means to say that as the mountains are established on the "great deep," the entire world is founded upon love, faithfulness, righteousness, and justice.[8] See also Psalms 57:10; 89:14.

The extent of God's "love" is measured by the altitude of the heavens.[9] The created world, of course, is in view, and one cannot avoid the idea of the Creator who sustains the world with his love. The phrase "your faithfulness to the skies" is parallel to "your love, Lord, reaches to the heavens." In Deuteronomy 32:4 "a God of truth/faithfulness" (*'emunah*; NIV: "faithful God") means that God conducts the world in a just manner.[10] The word translated as "skies" means "curtains" and refers evidently to thin, lacelike clouds.

36:6 *like the highest mountains.* Literally, "like the mountains of God [*'el*]." Jonah 3:3 uses the divine name *'elohim* ("God") in a similar way to suggest greatness: "Nineveh was a very large city" (lit., "a great city *to* God"). The fact that the

mountains are not as high as the heavens should not be taken to suggest that God's righteousness is less significant than his love and faithfulness. They are metaphors of greatness.

your justice like the great deep. God's "judgments" (NIV: "justice") are the principles by which God sustains the world, principles based on justice and righteousness.[11]

The "great deep" (*t*ᵉ*hom rabbah*; see Gen. 7:11; Amos 7:4; cf. Ps. 78:15) in ancient cosmology was the waters, or the seas, on which the foundations of the earth rested. God's judgments, therefore, are firm and enduring like the waters of the seas (see Jon. 2:6–7). For the notion of God preserving "people and animals," see Genesis 8:1 and 9:15. Three words in this verse appear both in the Genesis narrative of creation (Gen. 1) and the Noah story: "the deep," "man" (*'adam*; NIV: "people"), and "cattle." Israel's God is the same God who created the world and then delivered evil humankind from the flood.

36:7 *How priceless is your unfailing love . . . take refuge in the shadow of your*

Hesed—God's Love

This noun occurs 245 times in the Old Testament, 127 of those in the Psalms. This term is typically translated by the KJV as "mercy" or "lovingkindness," sometimes by the ESV as "steadfast love," and generally by the NIV as "love" or "unfailing love." *Hesed* ("love") is an attribute of God that defines his character and further defines his relationship to Israel and the world. The Decalogue put God's *hesed* up against evil, revealing that, while the sins of the fathers may fall on the third and fourth generation, the Lord shows *hesed* to thousands (of generations) of those "who love me and keep my commandments" (Exod. 20:6; cf. 34:7). The backdrop of God's *love* in Psalm 36:5–9 is the Creator God of Genesis 1, who brings the world into existence and, according to our psalm, sustains it by his *love*.[a]

[a] See H. Stoebe, "Hesed," *TLOT* 2:449–64.

wings. "How" (*mah*) implies astonishment (cf. Ps. 31:19, "How great is Your goodness" [NASB]). The mother bird's fledglings take refuge under her wings (Deut. 32:11; Ruth 2:12; Pss. 17:8; 57:1; 91:4; Matt. 23:37). Some commentators see an allusion to the wings of the cherubim in Solomon's temple or on the ark of the covenant, but since there seems to be no indication of this psalm's use in worship (which, of course, does not rule it out), the metaphor can stand on its own.

36:8 *the abundance of your house . . . your river of delights.* The word for "abundance" is literally "oil" or "fat," which represents the abundance (Pss. 23:5; 63:5). Perhaps the idea of drinking from God's river is an allusion

to Genesis 2:10: "A river watering the garden flowed from Eden." The word translated as "delights" is a derivative from the Hebrew word for "Eden," alluding perhaps to the pleasures of the garden of Eden.

36:9 *For with you is the fountain of life; in your light we see light.* The word for "fountain" is the "spring" or "source" of water (Prov. 25:26 [NIV: "well"]; Zech. 13:1). Note Jeremiah's statement, "They have forsaken me, the spring of living water" (Jer. 2:13). Perhaps the reference to "light" is also an allusion to Genesis 1:3–5, the primordial light by which the whole world is lighted. Note also that "light" and "life" are parallel terms, light being a symbol of life.

36:10 *Continue your love to those who know you . . . to the upright in heart.* The two groups, "those who know you" and "the upright in heart," are synonymous (Pss. 7:10; 11:2; 32:11; Deut. 9:5).

36:11 *the foot of the proud.* The anatomy of the wicked is completed here with

"People take refuge in the shadow of your wings" (36:7) communicates God's protection. The wings of two divine creatures envelope the god Horus at his birth on this ivory carving from Arslan Tash (eighth century BC).

"foot" and "hand"; these body parts, used for movement and actions, complement the members of sight and speech in 36:2 and 3. These four members form a merism to suggest the entire person. Now the suppliant prays that the "foot of the proud" and the "hand of the wicked" would not do him the harm that they have the potential for doing. The physiognomy of the wicked (eyes, mouth, foot, and hand; 36:1–3, 11)[12] implies their total dedication to sinister purposes.

36:12 *See how the evildoers lie fallen— thrown down, not able to rise!* This implies that the psalmist's request has been granted. It represents the opposite of what is promised to the righteous in Proverbs 24:16: "though the righteous fall seven times, they rise again."

Theological Insights

In addition to outlining the progression of evil (see the comments on 36:2–4), verse 2 gives us another discerning insight into the profile of evil: "In their own eyes they flatter themselves too much to detect or hate their sin." How one perceives oneself is critical to one's spiritual well-being. An inflated or a deflated view of oneself has spiritual implications. The matter here is that the evildoers who flatter themselves cannot recognize their own sin and hate it—their flattery covers it up. It is an expression of pride, sometimes defined as an over-inflated view of oneself, and reflective of the original sin of Genesis 3. When confronted, Adam blamed Eve, and Eve blamed the serpent. In his lineup of the seven deadly sins, Gregory the Great insists that pride is the head sin from which all others have their origins.[13] Whether the problem of the prideful person is an inability to detect his or her sin or an inability to acknowledge it—two different stages of spiritual consciousness—it nevertheless represents evil's power to deceive and set its patrons on a fixated course against God's world and God's love.

Teaching the Text

The Psalms basically speak of evil in terms of those who perpetrate it rather than in abstract terms, and Psalm 36 is a good example of that. Verses 1–4 describe the general attitude of the wicked ("There is no fear of God before their eyes") and how they live out that disposition in self-flattery, deceitful talk, and relentless plotting. Then verses 5–10 draw a sharp contrast between this portrait and God's love (*hesed*), and the vocabulary of the psalm puts God's love in the context of the creation story: heavens, deep (*tᵉhom*), mountains, man (*'adam*), and beast. One of the beautiful features of this psalm is that it declares the love of God to be ubiquitous in this world that God made—it "reaches to the heavens" (36:5a). The presence of evildoers is a formidable problem in every age of history, but the love of God is simply "priceless" (36:7a).

If we are not careful, verse 2 will become a red herring to lead us on the wrong trail in our quest for the substance of the psalm—it is not the world's wickedness but God's love that takes center stage. The psalmist paints his own picture of the multiplex of divine virtues: God's love, faithfulness, righteousness, and justice (36:5–6). And it is important to remind ourselves that these are communicable attributes—God shares them with us, and God commands that we imitate them. While this mandate is not the subject of Psalm 36, it certainly is a major theme of the Psalter. God's love, indeed, is the way to overcome in this evil world.

The final verse of the psalm gives us a snapshot of the battlefield strewn with evil's fallen comrades, a picture of the triumph of good. We may remind ourselves of John's equivalent message of the triumph of good over evil: "the one who is in you is greater than the one who is in the world" (1 John 4:4). It is the victory of God's love.

Illustrating the Text

Compared to what?

Popular Culture: In the United States today, the majority of people claim to be Christian. The reality is that Christians often compare their lives to the norms of our culture rather than to the standard of biblical truth. An example of this is the divorce rate in America. We often hear the claim that Christians divorce at roughly the same rate as non-Christians. Actually, this is misleading. According to Bradley Wright, a sociologist at the University of Connecticut, people who identify themselves as "Christian" but rarely attend church have a divorce rate of about 60 percent. However, the divorce rate of those who attend church regularly is only 38 percent, far below the national average.[14] In Psalm 36 we see that there is a marked difference in perspective, and morality, of those who walk with God and those who do not (the "wicked"). When we evaluate our lives, we must do so in light of God's Word and not in light of what is normative in the culture. There should be a significant difference between the way God's people live and the lives of nonbelievers.

Photo taken of General George Armstrong Custer (1839–76) in 1865. His pride may have played a role in the military decisions that led to the death of everyone under his command.

The danger of pride

History: For many people, the name General George Custer is synonymous with pride. Custer was known as a daring, impetuous leader with high ambitions. Some historians believe his foolish attack at Little Big Horn was motivated, in part, by his desire to be president. What is clear from that day is that Custer, seeking personal glory, made military decisions that would ensure that the credit for the victory would go to him and his Seventh Cavalry. His pride led to his demise. Had Custer followed orders that day, he would have probably been reinforced by General George Crook's two thousand men and survived the day.[15] Pride is always a danger, and we are reminded of its impact in Psalm 36. Here we see that pride can keep us from looking honestly at our own lives so that we do not even see our own sin. Pride can lead to disaster when it keeps us from seeing the danger of our faults and weaknesses.

Come clean before God.

Bible: Even we who believe can have times where we flatter ourselves to the point where we do not see our own sinful nature. We feel smug because we compare ourselves to "the people of the world" rather than examine ourselves in the light of God's Word. Read Matthew 22:36–40, and ask your listeners to reflect on these questions:

- Is the Lord the first love of your life?
- Are you giving obediently and sacrificially to the work of God?
- Do you love and serve your enemies?
- Have you forgiven those who have hurt you?
- Are you sacrificing for others?

These questions reflect God's standards. The reality is that not one of us is innocent. But as we read in Psalm 36, not only is God righteous and just, but his love is unfailing and faithful (see 1 John 1:9).

"Trust in the LORD and Do Good"

Big Idea *Whatever disconsolation the prosperity of the wicked may create for the righteous, they can find consolation in trusting the Lord and doing good.*

Understanding the Text

Psalm 37 is a wisdom psalm replete with wisdom terms (see the sidebar "Wisdom Psalms").[1] The subject of the prosperity of the wicked is a typical topic of wisdom, here expressed particularly in proverbial truths (37:16, 17, 21–22, 37). The literary form is the alphabetic acrostic, using all twenty-two letters of the Hebrew alphabet, each new strophe beginning with the new letter, except *waw* (37:10, 11), *heth* (37:14, 15), and *kaph* (37:20), which are duplicated in their stanzas.[2] Topically speaking, the acrostic gives the composer the liberty to range broadly.

The speaker of this psalm steps forward in two instances (both times employing the verb "see": "I have never seen," 37:25; "I have seen," 37:35), to share his personal experience with his audience. In the first instance (37:25–26), he identifies himself as an old man, patterned after the wisdom teacher, and shares his long experience of God's faithfulness with his students. In the second instance, he offers a word about the "wicked," asserting that the wicked, "like a luxuriant native tree," will soon pass away (37:35–36).

The Text in Context

Here David takes up the theme that preoccupies Psalm 73 as well, the prosperity of the wicked, although Psalm 73 finds the

There are five references to "inheriting the land" in Psalm 37. Israel initially inherited the promised land as a result of the conquests of Joshua. The inheritance that each of the individual tribes received is recorded in Joshua 13–19 and shown on this map.

resolution in worship (73:17). Yet there may be little difference between David's conclusion in 37:13 that "their day is coming" and 73:17, "I understood their final destiny."

Also, Jesus turns the teaching of 37:11 into the third beatitude: "Blessed are the meek, for they will inherit the earth" (Matt. 5:5). As we observe below, "inheriting" the land is a major motif of this psalm, suggesting the importance of obedience and trust for security in the promised land (see Jer. 7:5). Jesus expands this historical reality into the meek's possession of the earth. In fact, the "meek" (or "poor"; see comments on 37:11) are synonymous with those who trust in Yahweh, already implying a spiritual interpretation.

Outline/Structure

The acrostic psalms are not easily broken down into a subject outline, because the acrostic allows a lot of freedom in choice of subject as the poem moves from one letter to the next. Generally, however, the following outline sums up the content of this poem:

1. Admonition to trust in the Lord (37:1–9)
   - Note the three occurrences of "do not fret" in 37:1, 7b, 8b, which capture the anxious spirit of those to whom the psalm is addressed.
   - Instead, one should "trust in the LORD and do good" (37:3).
2. Contrast between the wicked and the righteous (37:10–22)
   - The wicked plot against the righteous and gnash their teeth at them (37:12).

- The Lord laughs at the wicked, for he sees that their day is coming (37:13).
3. Solution contemplated (37:23–40)
   - The Lord establishes the steps of the righteous (37:23), and the psalmist is a personal witness to this care (37:25–26).
   - The wrongdoers will be destroyed (37:28b), and the psalmist is a personal witness to this truth (37:35–36).

Psalm 37

Historical and Cultural Background

As is often the case, Psalm 37 must be viewed against the backdrop of the conquest of the land of Canaan ("inheriting" the land). Perhaps in a historical context in which Israel was still threatened with dispossession, the lesson of the psalm is to trust in the Lord, and "he will do this"—give them the "land" (37:5). The climate of threatening war, or at least social violence in the nation, hangs about this psalm with plotting (37:12), violence against the poor (37:14–15), and hunting down the righteous to kill them (37:32). The social injustice of the ancient world was not a pretty scene. Amid swords and bows (37:14–15), the psalmist found images among the flora of his world to describe the fate of the wicked: grass that withers, green plants that fade (37:2), and trees that flourish and die (37:35–36).

Interpretive Insights

37:1 *Do not fret because of those who are evil.* The verb "fret" occurs three times in the early verses (37:1, 7, 8) and sets the tone for the psalm, admonishing the reader not to be angry or anxious about evildoers and their prosperity.

37:2 *for like the grass they will soon wither.* This is the first solution to the problem of evildoers that the psalmist introduces—they will not last long.

37:3 *Trust in the LORD and do good; dwell in the land and enjoy safe pasture.* The first part of this verse is really the alternative program that the psalm puts forward (see Prov. 3:5). The image of dwelling in the land is a metaphor taken from Israel's historical experience of dwelling in

the land of Canaan (see Exod. 20:12). The beautiful rendering of the phrase "enjoy safe pasture" takes the sense of the verb (*r'h*, "to pasture") into account.

37:4 *Take delight in the LORD.* This is another way to commend trust in the Lord—it is no less than delight. When one's desires become totally synonymous with the will of God, that person "can desire nothing but God, with whose will his own is thoroughly blended in love."[3] The desires often alluded to in the Psalms are bounded by the constraints of the moral law.

37:5 *Commit your way to the LORD.* Literally, "Roll your way on the LORD." This is another way to commend trust in the Lord.

37:7 *Be still before the LORD . . . when they carry out their wicked schemes.* The verb "be still" (*dmm*) implies resignation. "Schemes" are plans designed to cause other people trouble.[4]

37:8 *Refrain from anger and turn from wrath.* The avoidance of anger is a common theme in wisdom literature (e.g., Prov. 22:24–25; 29:22).[5]

37:10 *A little while, and the wicked will be no more.* This reiterates the idea of 37:2 that the wicked will soon wither like the grass.

37:11 *But the meek will inherit the land.* The Septuagint renders the Hebrew *'anawim* as *praeis* ("meek"), since the *'anawim* are the poor and helpless who accept their impoverished condition and appeal to the Lord for help.

37:12 *gnash their teeth.* A gesture of anger (Ps. 35:16).

37:13 *the Lord laughs.* The Lord knows that the day of judgment is coming for evildoers, so he laughs at their naïveté, or better still, at their arrogance that God would

The triumph of the wicked over the poor and needy will end as their weapons are turned against them or made useless. This Assyrian relief shows a defeated Elamite officer cutting his bow as he is seized by an Assyrian soldier poised to kill (the palace at Nineveh, 645–635 BC).

37:25 *I was young and now I am old*. Here and in 37:35–36 the psalmist speaks in the first person, sharing his own experience with those whom he addresses (the admonitions are in the second masc. pl.).

37:27 *Turn from evil and do good; then you will dwell in the land forever*. The admonition to "do good" is evidently spoken to the same audience as 37:3, suggesting that they have already begun to engage in evil practices. This is a society on the verge of disaster. (For the concept of dwelling in the land, see "Theological Insights.")

37:30 *The mouths of the righteous utter wisdom*. The verb "utter" (*hgh*) occurs in Psalm 1:2 to describe those who constantly meditate on the Torah, the result being a stability equivalent to what we have here, "their feet do not slip" (37:31).

37:34 *Hope in the* LORD *and keep his way. He will exalt you*. This is a direct address to the psalmist's audience, evidenced by the pronominal suffix on the verb "he will exalt *you*," and also the pronominal suffixes on the nouns in 37:5 and 6 ("*your* way," "*your* righteous reward," "*your* vindication"). Generally the second masculine singular verbs of the psalm are rather impersonal, but here the audience steps forward as does the psalmist in 37:25 and 35.

37:35–36 *I have seen a wicked and ruthless man . . . though I looked for him*. A second time the psalmist offers his personal observation, in 37:25 about the righteous, here about the wicked. Here the solution to

overlook their evil schemes (Pss. 2:4; 59:8; Prov. 1:26).[6]

37:14 *bend the bow*. Literally, "tread" (*drk*) the bow (see the comments on Ps. 7:12).

37:15 *But their swords will pierce their own hearts*. This principle that perpetrators of evil become victims of their own actions is a common principle of justice in the Psalms (see, e.g., Ps. 35:8).

37:21 *The wicked borrow and do not repay, but the righteous give generously*. This prophetic promise is found in Deuteronomy 15:6; 28:12, 44, and here the psalmist affirms that the promises given to the patriarchs are fulfilled in those who are blessed of God.[7]

37:23 *The* LORD *makes firm the steps of the one who delights in him*. The verb "delights" (*hpts*) is not the same as that in 37:4 (Hitpael of *'ng*), but they are synonyms.

The Principle of Retribution

The law of Exodus 21:24 is the classic expression of the principle of retribution: "eye for eye, tooth for tooth, hand for hand, foot for foot." It involves no mercy and prescribes punishment of the offense in equal and like kind. Although the Western world still exercises jurisprudence by this principle (the death penalty, for example), there are many degrees of adaptation. While the Psalms do not abandon this principle (e.g., Ps. 28:4), they nevertheless present an important modulation that diminishes the society's role as dispenser of justice and makes the offender and the offense the delivery system of punishment. That modulation is visible in the hope that the offender's sword "will pierce their own hearts" (37:15). This inflection of the retribution principle is frequent enough in the ethical system of the Psalms to lead us to believe that it was an alternate way to deal with the harsh nature of the *lex talionis* and perhaps to alleviate the society's role in carrying it out. The psalmists declare that the nations will fall into a pit they themselves have dug (9:15, 16; also 7:15, 16); and David's enemies fall into the pit they have dug for him (57:6). More abstractly, the nature of evil forms a parallel track in the ethical system of the Psalms. Evil has an inherent quality that causes it to recoil on itself (54:5), and the evil the psalmist's enemies have plotted against him instead falls on them (27:2; 64:8). While the ethics of the Psalms do not easily allow for systematization, this inflection is a stage on the way (albeit measured in miles) to the ethic of Jesus that when we are struck on one cheek, we should turn the other also (Matt. 5:39).

the problem of the prosperity of the wicked is the same as that of 37:10: they pass away and can no longer be found.

37:37 *a future awaits those who seek peace.* "Future" is literally "hinder part," and here we have a window into the psychology of the Hebrew mind. Their back was to the future—it could not be seen; and their face to the past—it could be seen because it had been experienced.

37:40 *The LORD helps them and delivers them.* Verse 40 summarizes the theology of the poem that is found in verse 34: "Hope in the LORD and keep his way. He will exalt you to inherit the land; when the wicked are destroyed, you will see it" (37:34). The

righteous will see it just like the psalmist himself has seen it (37:35).

Theological Insights

This psalm, much like Psalm 73, puts the problem of evildoers over against the benefits of trust in the Lord. The prosperity of the wicked is the problem that challenges the psalmist (37:1, 7b, 12, 14, 32, 35–36), a problem that was not theoretical but quite a reality ("when people succeed in their ways," 37:7b). The psalmist contemplates two potential reactions to the problem: become envious (37:1b) or become vindictive (37:8). Neither solution suited him. The resolution he came to express was that the wicked will soon wither like the grass (37:2, 20), be destroyed (37:9a), even by their own sword (37:15), and "go up in smoke" (37:20). In fact, the Lord "laughs at the wicked" because he knows their day of reckoning is coming (37:13), a fact they seem to be incognizant of. (See "Additional Insights" following this unit.)

To counterbalance the obvious prosperity of the wicked, our psalmist admonishes his audience to embrace the lifestyle of faith: trust in the Lord (37:3), commit your way to the Lord (37:5, 34), be still and wait patiently (37:7, 9, 14, 34), and depart from evil and do good (37:27). The addressees are likely the righteous (37:16), the poor and needy (the equivalent of the righteous; 37:14), and the saints who are tottering on temptation's edge of turning to evil rather than maintaining the good (37:27–28). In fact, judging from the sustained emphasis on dwelling in the land (37:9, 11, 18, 29, 34), the audience may very well have been individuals, even the nation, that were on the slippery precipice of moral decay, and dwelling in the land was contingent on their moral behavior.

The benefits of the life of faith are the possession of the land—that is, the land inherited from the Canaanites—and security in it (37:3, 9b, 11, 22, 29, 34), the fulfillment of their desires (37:4), God's defense of those who trust him (37:5–6), posterity ("future," 37:37; cf. Jer. 29:11), and abundance in time of famine (37:19, 25). These are all more or less tied to the inheritance of the land (37:18). Those of us who live in a mobile society have a hard time appreciating the concept and reality of "landedness," but those in the ancient biblical world understood it perfectly. Property, which was held by the same family in perpetuity, was a security second only to security in God.[8]

Faith as represented in Psalm 37 is definitely a journey, symbolized by the use of the word "way" (37:5, 7, 34) and signified by their dwelling in the land (37:3, 27, 29). Israel's life in the land was contingent on their obedience to God's laws (Deut. 28:15–24), and the curses and blessings that Moses pronounced against them (Deut. 27–28) governed their life there: "Those the LORD blesses will inherit the land, but those he curses will be destroyed" (37:22).

Teaching the Text

As we begin to shape our lesson/sermon on Psalm 37, we should make the point that this psalm is about the age-old question of *theodicy*: Is God just? The issue of this psalm, however, is not so much how one solves the problem but how one lives with it.

Right away we should observe that one of the beautiful things about Psalm 37 is

The righteous reap the benefits of God's care. For example, "in days of famine they will enjoy plenty" (37:19). Famine was a real concern in the ancient Near East as shown on these Egyptian reliefs from Saqqara, Egypt, 2375–2345 BC. Here people are depicted in a state of starvation with ribs showing and emaciated limbs.

that the psalmist steps up and offers his personal observation in two instances (37:25–26 and 35–36), both personal words about justice. In the broad sense, the first instance is a window on God's care for the oppressed, the poor, the outcasts, and all of those who are the victims of injustice: "I was young and now I am old, yet I have never seen the righteous forsaken or their children begging bread" (37:25). Perhaps in this statement is conceived our own responsibility for making sure the suppliant's vision is fulfilled ("do good," 37:3 and 27).

It is important to note that the psalm lays out a program for dealing with the realities of an unjust world, consisting of a series of injunctions, aphorisms, and personal observations (37:3a, 4, 5, 7a, 11, 16, 17b, 18, 22a, 23, 25, 26b, 27b, 29, 31, 37b). Their gist is that the righteous have a relationship with God, who is just, does justice, and honors the just. While we will never find the answer to the problem of injustice in the sense of "this is why," it is nevertheless in that relationship that we find the *solution*—which, of course, is not an answer as such but a program for dealing with its reality. In fact, twice David says, "Do good" (37:3, 27), and do not take revenge. It is a relationship that causes us to run to God when there is no place to hide and prompts us to "take refuge in him" (37:40).

The second personal observation from this wise man is a word about the wicked, the evildoers in this world: "I have seen a wicked and ruthless man flourishing like a luxuriant native tree, but he soon passed away and was no more" (37:35–36). Here the Lord tells us something about the evil in this world and those who perpetrate

it: it won't last forever; they won't get by with it perpetually. And the psalm is full of these disclaimers (37:2, 9a, 13b, 15a, 17a, 20, 38). Yet the closing verses sum up the *living solution*, that God is always there in times of trouble to deliver us (37:39–40). In fact, one wonders if God does not allow some formidable problems in life so that we might "take refuge in him," and taking refuge in God is the ultimate solution.

Illustrating the Text

Injustice

Testimony: Anyone who has lived in this world for a while knows what it feels like to be the victim of injustice. Most of us have seen the injustice of "the wicked," those who cheat and lie in order to get ahead, often at the expense of the powerless. Ask a person from your congregation to share an experience of injustice. It might be a person who has lost his or her business to a dishonest competitor or who was mistreated by a rich landlord. Whoever shares his or her testimony should emphasize the impact of the injustice in terms of finances, personal stress, relational struggle, and so forth. Encourage them not to use names in their testimony and to ensure that they are being respectful even toward the person who mistreated them. To fully appreciate Psalm 37 we need to help people identify with the struggle of the suffering of the righteous at the hands of the unjust.

The world put right

Bible: The Psalms often describe our twisted world, with its focus on God's enemies and on sin, slander,

The psalmist reflects on God's care when he says, "I have never seen the righteous forsaken or their children begging bread" (37:25). This pottery piece inscribed with the Hebrew word for "your brother" may have been used to collect donations for the poor (Beth Shemesh, eighth century BC).

deception, and an innumerable host of immoralities. On occasion, however, we are privileged to get a glimpse of the world put right, as we do in Psalm 37:11: "But the meek will inherit the land." Obviously that is not the usual way the system works. Indeed, Jesus takes this statement and makes it part of the picture of the world as it should be, the picture of the kingdom of God that he gives us in the Sermon on the Mount (Matt. 5:5). Rather than the world turned upside down—it certainly is not what we are used to seeing—the Sermon on the Mount is a picture of the world turned right side up.

Hope for the unjust

Film: *Braveheart.* This 1995 movie is the story of William Wallace (played by Mel Gibson), a commoner who begins a revolt against the cruel English tyrant who rules Scotland. Wallace was motivated by his passion for a free Scotland, as well as his anger over the injustices carried out by the English, who killed his wife. In the movie the Scottish rebels, led by Wallace, face off against their enemy. In order to avoid a battle, the two sides talk under a white flag of truce. Wallace gives the English this ultimatum: "Lower your flags and march straight back to England, stopping at every home you pass by to beg forgiveness for a hundred years of theft, rape, and murder. Do that, and your men shall live. Do it not, and every one of you will die today." The hope of an unjust world lies in marching straight to God and asking forgiveness, in light of Jesus's death, for acts of injustice.

Wealth and Wickedness in Psalms 37, 49, and 73

These three psalms deal with the problem of the wealthy and the wicked, which are virtually synonymous, in the same way that, at a later time of Old Testament history, the poor and the righteous were practically synonymous. Whatever we think of the synonymity between wealthy and wicked, and poor and righteous, it was the observation of these biblical writers that the two conditions carried the implication of vice and virtue, respectively. Practically speaking, it is easy to understand the connection, and it certainly troubled the psalmists. Judging from other Old Testament considerations of the problem of wealth and power, with its social implications, we are not surprised that it was felt deeply by the citizens of that world. Nor is it surprising that some individuals came to articulate the problem very well and also advanced solutions. There is no uniformity, however, in the solutions offered. But the practicality of these considerations was unquestionably helpful to victims of wealth and power in that world, and in our world as well, since the problem is a persistent one. God as refuge from the oppression created by the powerful who care nothing for justice, and the thought of the brevity of life for oppressors, are certainly comforting to a degree, the former more than the latter, but obviously neither assuages the pain of the oppressed in this life.

From the viewpoint of the victims, the righteous, Psalm 37 contemplates two outcomes: one could become envious (37:1b) or vindictive (37:8). Neither solution, however, is satisfactory to the psalmist, and he stresses the fact that the wicked will soon wither like the grass (37:2, 20) and be cut off (37:9a). This, however, is never the most comforting solution for those who may not live to see it, so there needs to be a more existential answer. That is where the theology of the psalmist makes itself delightfully apparent: trust in the Lord (37:3), let him direct your way (37:5, 34), and be patient (37:7, 9, 14, 34). But theology is not only passive but active, and on this side of the ledger, one's personal conduct

In spite of their wealth and prosperity, the wicked will wither away like this grass during the dry season in the Arabah in Israel or like herbs when their growing season is done.

must reflect one's theology: depart from evil, and do good (37:27). This advice will serve effectively in times of ethical conflict, even if it does not provide the permanent solution the righteous long for.

In a sense, Psalm 73 illustrates this spiritual posture by focusing faith in worship (the sanctuary). When the prosperity of the wicked becomes so troubling as to be spiritually disorienting, this teacher too insists that the wicked will meet their fate in this life (73:18–20), much like Psalm 37; but in the world of human nature—what other world do we know!—patience and justice are not the most congenial traveling companions, or we do not travel with them so amiably. Yet, in the absence of justice accomplished, we must learn to cope, and the singer of Psalm 73 learns this lesson in the sanctuary (73:15–17). Either he "solves" the problem to his satisfaction in the context of worship, the equivalent of trust (Ps. 37), or in the same spiritual environment he learns how to live with the problem. But he cannot leave the issue there, because he realizes, like Job, that he has an advocate in heaven (Ps. 73:25; see Job 16:19; 19:25), and he moves on to reveal that he hopes, like Psalm 49, for a continuing relationship with God, who will "take" him into glory (73:24; see 49:15).

While the "glory" of Psalm 73 may be the elevated spiritual state of being in God's presence in the temple, it certainly creates some space for the New Testament concept of heaven and life after death. I am convinced that the New Testament doctrine is not unattached to the Old Testament hope of an enduring relationship with God, both in this life and after death. The problem we have in the Old Testament is that the concept is elusive, and where it occurs at all, it is vague. But that is not unusual for Old Testament theology, since there are other doctrines we refer to from time to time in this commentary (e.g., the incarnation) that have their theological roots in the Old Testament. Here our ears tingle with an echo of two other Old Testament saints, Enoch and Elijah, whom God "took" out of this earthly sphere (saved from death), even though both stories stop short of ascribing the afterlife to this experience.

Psalm 49, like Psalms 37 and 73, finds a "solution" in a relationship with God. And perhaps this poet feels the problem even more deeply than the other two teachers—at least, he experiences it differently—for to him, the "evil days" encompass him and make life into a prison from which no one but God can ransom him (49:7–8). He has reached a tentative "solution" in the lesson he has learned and taught, that death equalizes the difference between the righteous and the wicked (49:12–14, and refrain), a theme not contained in the other two psalms. While the first half of verse 15 asserts that God will redeem his life from death (Sheol), the second half does not have an adverb of place or state after the verb, simply "he will take me." In parallel with the first half, however, it appears to repeat the idea that God will take the suppliant from death, that is, spare his life. Psalm 49, like Psalm 73, thus rises above the temporal solution offered by Psalm 37 and identifies the ultimate solution as a unique relationship with God. If Psalms 49 and 73 do not teach the doctrine of the life to come, they lay out a grid on which the doctrine can and would be laid.

"I Confess My Iniquity; I Am Troubled by My Sin"

Big Idea *When our sins and their consequences are misconstrued by our adversaries, God will dispense his discipline without malice.*

Understanding the Text

Psalm 38 is an individual lament (esp. 38:2–14) about the psalmist's sickness that, in his view, has been caused by his sin, which he confesses (38:3–4, 18). Generally this genre includes, according to Westermann, complaints against God, against an enemy, and against the psalmist himself.[1] While a lament need not contain all three, Psalm 38 does: against God (38:2–3), against his enemies (38:11, 12, 19–20), and against himself (38:4–5).

Though not an acrostic, the poem conforms to a twenty-two-verse structure (excluding the title). The influence of the acrostic form of Psalm 37 on the length and structure of this poem is a possibility.

The title contains the phrase "to remember" (*le'hazkir*; NIV: "a petition"), which the ESV renders as "for the memorial offering," and the KJV simply as "to bring to remembrance." Since the suppliant recalls his sin, this could be the unstated object of this Hiphil infinitive construct (root *zkr*, "to remember"). In this vein, Weiser translates the phrase tentatively, "For the purpose of making a confession."[2] There is also the possibility, which is my own preference, that the phrase suggests that the psalmist "remembers/recalls" his sin, a very natural connection of this phrase to the contents of the psalm. The early church fathers understandably included it among the seven penitential psalms.[3] The Chronicler informs us that David appointed the Levites "to minister before the ark of the LORD, to extol, thank, and praise the LORD" (1 Chron. 16:4), where the word "to extol" (*le'hazkir*; ESV: "invoke") applies to confession of sin.

The Text in Context

The first line of Psalm 38 is Psalm 6:1 almost verbatim (see comments on 38:1). The content of the two psalms is different, however. While both are laments, and both are occasioned by illness (38:2, 3, 5, 7, 10, 17), the writer of Psalm 6 does not try to connect his sickness to sin, nor does he confess his sin. Rather, he laments his physical plight, prays for healing, and dismisses his enemies, who likely took the occasion as evidence of sin, although that is only implied. On the other hand, Psalm 38 is a lament about both the suppliant's sickness and the sin that brought it about.

Some interpreters have identified an echo of Psalm 38:11 in the Passion Narrative of Luke 23:49, "But all those who knew him, including the women who had followed him from Galilee, stood at a distance, watching these things."[4] The bystanders in Psalm 38:11, however, are antagonists, whereas in Luke they are sympathizers.[5] While, then, the literary expressions are parallel, the motives are not.

Outline/Structure

The main body of the psalm is a description of the psalmist's sickness and the surrounding social and emotional implications, with an invocation on either side. The first invocation bears the weight of the illness, while the closing prayer leaves that aside and prays simply for God's deliverance.

1. Opening invocation, describing the psalmist's sickness (38:1–4)
2. Description of sickness and the enemies' accusations (38:5–20)
   a. The physical aspects of the psalmist's suffering (38:5–10)
   b. The social aspects of the psalmist's suffering (38:11–20)
3. Closing invocation and prayer for deliverance (38:21–22)

Key Themes of Psalm 38

- Is sickness God's discipline?
- Confessing one's sins may lead to God's healing.

Historical and Cultural Background

Psalm 38 keys in to a common theme in the ancient Near East, which explains sin as the cause of suffering. Even though this was not the exclusive explanation for sickness, it was a shared one in that world, Israel included.[6] Job's friends represent the view that an indissoluble link binds the two together, a view that Job strongly refutes. Our writer espouses the view of Job's friends, even though he is not as dogmatic as they are. The writer of Psalm 38 does not even try to explain his illness—he just operates on the assumption that sin is its root cause.

Interpretive Insights

Title *A petition.* See the introduction to "Understanding the Text." The term for "petition" (*lᵉhazkir*), which also appears in the heading of Psalm 70, may be explained by the appearance of the same term in 1 Chronicles 16:4: "to extol [*lᵉhazkir*, or "make petition"], thank, and praise." Wilson relates these to the major

Like the psalmist who believed that his sickness was a punishment for sin, other ancient Near Eastern cultures also believed that illness could have a supernatural origin whether attributed to gods or demons. Apotropaic wands like this one were used in Egypt to ward off evil and provide protection especially for infants and the mother and child during childbirth (Middle Kingdom, Twelfth Dynasty, ca. 1985–1773 BC).

form-critical categories of psalms: lament, thanksgiving, and praise.[7] Delitzsch suggests that psalms such as 38 and 70 accompanied the memorial (*'azkarah*) sacrifice, in which a portion of the offering was burned on the altar, sending smoke into the heavens to *remind* Yahweh of the sufferer's need, even though Psalm 38 gives little evidence of its use in worship.[8]

38:1 Lord, *do not rebuke me in your anger or discipline me in your wrath*. The psalmist does not pray for no divine discipline at all, but he prays that it will not be angry and wrathful. Jeremiah prays: "Discipline me, Lord, but only in due measure—not in your anger, or you will reduce me to nothing" (Jer. 10:24).

This verse is identical with Psalm 6:1, except for two differences: (1) for "anger," 6:1 uses a synonym, *'ap*, rather than the word here (*qetsep*); (2) before the second half of the verse, 6:1 inserts the negative word *'al*, while here it is implied.

38:2 *Your arrows have pierced me*. Arrows may be a military term here, but they are also a metaphor, not necessarily military, to describe the sharp pain the psalmist has endured (see Job 6:4).

38:3 *Because of your wrath there is no health in my body*. Through the use of the repeated words "because of" (38:3a, b, and 5), which imply source, the psalmist is obviously attributing his sickness to his sin. Kidner says it would be as wrong to think there is never a connection between sin and illness as to think there is always one.[9] The word for "health" means a "healthy spot" ("not a *healthy spot* on my body"), as in Isaiah 1:6 ("soundness").[10]

38:4 *My guilt has overwhelmed me like a burden too heavy to bear*. This is a very good rendering of the Hebrew (see Ezra 9:6). Calvin remarks that the suppliant's sin overwhelms him like a heavy weight and certainly deserves God's wrath, but it is too severe for him to bear (compare Cain's complaint in Gen. 4:13).[11]

38:5 *My wounds fester and are loathsome*. "My wounds" are pus-filled with a foul odor.[12]

38:6 *I am bowed down and brought very low*. The verb "bowed down" occurs in Jeremiah 3:21 to describe the "twisted" (NIV: "perverted") motive of evildoers.

38:7 *My back is filled with searing pain; there is no health in my body*. The verse begins with the Hebrew conjunction *ki* for emphasis ("because," "for"; not translated in the NIV). The NIV translates the Hebrew word for "loins" as "back." Outside of Leviticus, this word only occurs here and in Job 15:27. It may mean "sinews" or "tendons."[13] The phrase "there is no health in my body" is a repetition of the clause in 38:3, strengthening the description of the suppliant's ill health.

38:8 *I am feeble . . . I groan in anguish of heart*. Genesis 45:26 uses the same verb,

"Your arrows have pierced me" (38:2). Pointed arrowheads were usually made of flint, bone, or metal, typically bronze or iron. These iron arrowheads are from Lachish, eighth century BC.

translated here as "feeble," to describe Jacob's reaction when his sons, just returned from Egypt, inform him that Joseph is alive: "and his heart *fainted*, for he did not believe them" (RSV). The latter part of the verse is a description of the psalmist's emotional state of being ("anguish"), like Psalm 22:1.

38:9 *All my longings lie open before you, Lord.* The psalmist addresses the Lord, as he did in 38:1, saying that the Lord (*'adonay*) is aware of his longings.

38:10 *My heart pounds.* The Hebrew verb doubles the two root letters (*heth* and *resh*: *seharhar*, root *shr*) to indicate intensity (e.g., *halaqlaqqot*, root *hlq*, "slippery," Ps. 35:6).[14]

38:11 *My friends and companions avoid me because of my wounds.* Three groups of acquaintances are mentioned: "my friends" (lit., "those who love me"), "my companions" (or, "my friends"), and "my neighbors." The last term may also mean "relatives." The Hebrew word behind the idea of avoiding or standing afar means "far away, but within the range of vision, within sight" (see Gen. 21:16; Deut. 32:52).[15]

38:12 *talk of my ruin . . . scheme and lie.* The word "ruin" (*hawwot*) means "utter destruction"—that is what they talk about; and to accomplish this purpose, they "scheme and lie." Calvin observes that the supplicant's friends will do nothing to help him, while his enemies vigorously make their sinister plans.[16]

38:13 *I am like the deaf, who cannot hear.* As the supplicant watches his world disintegrate, the physical torment and social alienation immobilize him so much that he cannot defend himself against his enemies.

38:15 LORD, *I wait for you.* Given his inability to react, the psalmist appeals to the Lord. The verb "wait" (*yhl*) carries the nuance of "hope" (see Ps. 31:24).

38:17 *For I am about to fall.* The word that stands behind "about" means "ready," and together with the noun translated as "to fall," gives the same sense as the expression in 38:16, "when my feet slip."

38:19 *those who hate me without reason are numerous.* They have evidently interpreted the supplicant's sickness as an ill omen, and even though he has confessed his sin, the fact of his illness has led them to intensify their lying schemes against him. The NIV emends the difficult phrase "my *living* [*hayyim*] enemies" (see NIV footnote) to "my enemies *without cause* [*hinnam*]" (cf. Ps. 35:7).

38:20 *though I seek only to do what is good.* This attitude of the psalmist is proof of his moral integrity, which is further attested by his honest confession of sin.

38:22 *my Lord and my Savior.* The term translated "Savior" (lit., "salvation") is the less common of the two words that come from the Hebrew verb "to save" (*ysh'*; the more common word for "salvation" is *yeshu'ah*).

Theological Insights

The psalmist, honest and candid, prays that God will not rebuke him in anger or discipline him in wrath. He confesses that he has sinned (38:3–5, 18), connects his sin to his sickness (38:3, 17–18), and prays that God's discipline will not be motivated by anger (38:1). In all honesty, however, God's heavy-handed reaction to his sin and the guilt the psalmist experiences as a result seem to violate the principle of divine

God's discipline results in the psalmist's friends and companions avoiding him (38:11) and his enemies plotting against him. Like these men from this seventh-century Nineveh palace relief who are carrying nets, stakes, and twine in preparation for the hunt, "those who want to kill me set their traps" (38:12).

the kindness he has paid them.

The psalmist's sickness is not merely a psychosomatic disorder resulting from his sin, but there is a theological link between the two (38:3b). Our understanding of psychosomatic illness has been greatly enhanced by modern medicine and psychology, and we may be less reluctant to assume this theological link than some in earlier generations, but connecting sin and illness was also a common understanding of Old Testament theology. And even if we do not make the connection as readily as the ancients, we have to acknowledge nevertheless that our sins, whether they be substance or sexual abuse, or any myriad of social and physical exploitations, have a causal effect. That is not to impose a modern explanation upon the psalmists—their understanding was less complex than that—but it is to recognize that the link between sin and physical illness is not so implausible, even though the modern explanation cannot be equated to the ancient (see "Theological Insights" for the unit on Ps. 32).

mercy, as Calvin observes: "God has promised that he will chastise his servants, not according to their deserts, but as they are able to bear."[17]

Moreover, the social ostracism by friends, companions, and relatives is the human overlay of God's heavy-handed response. They too have overreacted (38:19), especially since the psalmist's sin does not seem to have been directed toward them, for he has sought "only to do what is good" (38:20). We may assume that the overreaction stems from the intensity of the psalmist's suffering, leaving the impression that his sin is of such gravity that they can ignore

Teaching the Text

We may begin our sermon/lesson by explaining what has brought on the psalmist's remarks about discipline. He has become very sick and believes that his sins have caused his illness. Perhaps we are less inclined to enter this discussion enthusiastically, but it is undeniable that certain forms of behavior precipitate physical issues. Nor is this a modern discovery. Gregory the Great (sixth century AD) made this connection in his book *A History of the Cure of Souls*. While it is not absolutely necessary to delve into this issue, the astute listener is going to be thinking about it and may raise the question in a class session, while the sermon format likely would not present such an opportunity.

The main topic of the psalm, however, is divine discipline. Does God discipline his children? The psalmist believes God does, and his illness is a case in point. His concern is that God not apply his discipline too severely, or that he not dispense his discipline in an angry spirit: "LORD, do not rebuke me in your anger or discipline me in your wrath" (38:1). While the psalmist is not opposed to discipline—he expects it and is not surprised by it—he asks the Lord not to overdo it, a bold prayer indeed. While this is not the point of the psalm, it is a subsidiary idea that can produce profitable dividends when put in the broader setting of bold and honest prayer in the Psalms. It is an approach to prayer that should be more commended than demeaned (see Exod. 32:11–14; Josh. 7:6–9).

Observe that the psalm draws the reader into the intensity of the poet's suffering by the repetition of an adverbial phrase, "very" (38:6) or "utterly" (38:8): "I am bowed down and brought *very* low"; "I am feeble and *utterly* crushed." In addition, to intensify to the audience the extent of his suffering, the poet repeats the clause "there is no health in my body" (38:3, 7).

Depending on the audience, of course, this may be an excellent opportunity to speak about the dynamics of language, how effective writing and speech can draw one's audience into the narrative.

At this point one could speak about the purpose of discipline. If God disciplines his children—and the psalmist believes he does—what is the purpose of God's discipline? It obviously varies from occasion to occasion, and from person to person, and probably no one but the individual involved is able to state God's purpose with a great degree of confidence. Others may suggest and counsel, but they must take care not to orate, as did Job's friends. Our psalmist personally confesses that sin is behind the discipline. The writer to the Hebrews quotes Proverbs 3:11–12 and draws out the purpose of divine discipline, meted out of love, to be spiritual refinement (Heb. 12:5–11). In conclusion one might draw attention to the fact that the psalm is a prayer from beginning to end, and the suppliant is laying out his problem before God in prayer. The urgency of his situation is evident not only from the intensity of his suffering but also from the desperation in his closing lines (38:21–22). The Lord has not yet come, and the psalmist's suffering calls for a rapid response. The psalm ends, not with a period, but with a dash—

Illustrating the Text

The power of God's discipline

Children's Book: *The Voyage of the Dawn Treader*, by C. S. Lewis. In this book, which is part of the Chronicles of Narnia series, Lewis has a character named Eustace who becomes a dragon (reflecting his selfish heart). Eustace does not want to be a dragon, so he keeps trying to peel off his scales, only to find another layer beneath. Then the great lion, Aslan (representing Jesus), comes to Eustace. He recounts:

> Then the lion said—I don't know if it spoke—You have to let me undress you. I was afraid of his claws, I can tell you, but I was pretty nearly desperate now. So I just lay down flat on my back to let him do it. The very first tear he made was so deep that I thought it had gone right into my heart. And when he began pulling the skin off, it hurt worse than anything I've ever felt. The only thing that made me able to bear it was just the pleasure of feeling the stuff peel off.[18]

The discipline of the Lord can be painful, but if only we understood the potential God sees in us, then with joy we would lay ourselves before him and invite him to do his work.

God's discipline works through us.

Scenario: Ask your listeners to imagine that they have a Christian friend who is a coworker. The friend is married, but you notice that he is spending too much time with a female coworker. It seems to you that an attraction is developing between them. Would you say something to your friend? The Bible clearly teaches that we have a responsibility for one another (see Gal. 6:1, for example). In a very real sense we are our "brother's/sister's keeper." We do have a responsibility to speak the truth in love to one another with the goal of restoration. Is there a Christian brother or

The psalmist views his sickness and pain as God's discipline because of his sin. In contrast, Job continually affirmed his righteousness in spite of his afflictions. The sarcophagus of Junius Bassus, AD 359, includes a depiction of the suffering Job with his wife and friend standing nearby. A cast of that relief is shown here.

sister whom God is calling you to gently restore?

A unique approach

Everyday Life: Parents must be able to recognize and adapt to the unique differences that exist between each child. Author and speaker Lisa Whelchel writes,

> Think of yourself as a sculptor shaping and molding the lives of your young ones. With each child, you may be working

with a different medium. You could be endeavoring to form one youngster who appears to be as hard as marble. As an artist, you might use a chisel, hammer, even water, while sculpting your masterpiece. You may have another child who is more pliable, like clay. Even then, as a potter, you might use fire, a knife, and your bare hands.[19]

Whelchel then provides creative discipline ideas for children's issues like lying, tantrums, resisting bedtime, and so on. She presents multiple ideas for each topic because the best response depends on the nature and character of each child. In the same way, God's discipline in the life of each person is unique. God provides discipline that is most effective for that individual. Our responsibility is to be open to God so that we recognize his discipline and learn from it.

"The Span of My Years Is as Nothing before You"

Big Idea *Once the repressed thoughts about our transitory lives are verbalized, valuable lessons about our status as foreigners in this world can be learned.*

Understanding the Text

Psalm 39 is an individual lament, perhaps prompted by sickness, as was Psalm 38, and the supplicant prays that God will remove his "scourge" (39:10) from him so that he not die.

The Text in Context

This psalm shares resemblances to Psalm 38[1] and anticipates shared ideas with Psalms 40 and 41 (see tables 1 and 2). It also has striking similarities to Psalm 62.[2]

First Chronicles 29:15 provides a link with this psalm, for there David likens Israel to "foreigners and strangers" in God's sight, "like all our ancestors," a virtual quote of the Chronicles verse, which adds the observation that our earthly life is "like a shadow, without hope," the same idea as 39:4–5, but in different words. In view of the similarities, the psalm may have been written to spell out the implications of David's sentiments on that special occasion when he gave thanks for the Lord's provisions for building the temple, as recorded in Chronicles.[3]

Outline/Structure

The content falls into two major parts, with the second part constituting the prayer:

1. The psalmist's report about silent waiting (39:1–3)
2. The psalmist's prayer (39:4–13)
   a. Life's brevity (39:4–6)

The muzzle that the psalmist will figuratively use to guard his tongue is the same word used in Deuteronomy 25:4 where it says, "Do not muzzle an ox while it is treading out the grain." This Egyptian tomb painting shows oxen at work on the threshing floor.

b. Confession of sin (39:7–11)

c. Prayer for deliverance (39:12–13)

Historical and Cultural Background

Already in the Psalter we have encountered the restraints for horses (Ps. 32:9), recognizing the use of horses in the ancient world of the Bible, and also noting that Israel's use of horses on a large scale did not happen until Solomon's reign.[4] Here the psalmist uses a different term, "muzzle" (39:1). The muzzle was used to keep the animal from eating the grain as it was working near it.

The mention of another cultural term, "handbreadth," occurs in 39:5, a term of smaller measurements (also found in Exod. 25:25 and 1 Kings 7:26/2 Chron. 4:5). It was the width of the palm, measured across the hand from the thumb to the end of the little finger, approximately 7.5 centimeters (or 3 inches).

Interpretive Insights

Title *For Jeduthun.* "Jeduthun" was one of the three senior temple musicians

Key Themes of Psalm 39

- Like our ancestors, we must see ourselves spiritually as foreigners and strangers.
- Sometimes in the presence of conflict, silence is the best strategy.

Table 1. Shared Topics between Psalms 38 and 39

Topic	Psalm 38	Psalm 39
God's rebuke or discipline	"LORD, do not rebuke [Hiphil of *ykh*] me in your anger or discipline [Piel of *ysr*] me in your wrath" (38:1)	"Remove your scourge from me; I am overcome by the blow of your hand. When you rebuke [pl. noun from *ykh*] and discipline [Piel perfect of *ysr*] anyone for their sin" (39:10–11a)
Tenuous nature of life	"For I am about to fall, and my pain is ever with me" (38:17)	"Show me, LORD, my life's end and the number of my days; let me know how fleeting my life is. . . . Everyone is but a breath" (39:4–5) "Surely everyone is but a breath" (39:11)
Silence	"I am . . . like the mute, who cannot speak" (38:13)	"I said, 'I will watch my ways and keep my tongue from sin; I will put a muzzle on my mouth while in the presence of the wicked.' So I remained utterly silent, not even saying anything good" (39:1–2) "I was silent; I would not open my mouth" (39:9)
Deafness	"I have become like one who does not hear [*shmʿ*]" (38:14)	"Hear [*shmʿ*] my prayer, LORD, listen to my cry" (39:12)
Blows of God's hand	"Your hand has come down on me" (no mention of "blows"; 38:2) "My friends and companions avoid me because of my wounds [*negaʿ*]" (no mention of "hand"; 38:11)	"Remove your scourge [*negaʿ*] from me; I am overcome by the blow of your hand" (39:10)
The Lord's presence	"All my longings lie open before you, Lord" (38:9)	"The span of my years is as nothing before you" (39:5)

Table 2. Shared Topics among Psalms 38–41

Topic	Psalm 38	Psalm 39	Psalm 40	Psalm 41
Sickness	"There is no health in my body" (38:3, 7)	"My heart grew hot within me" (39:3)		"The LORD sustains them on their sickbed and restores them from their bed of illness" (41:3)
Hope	"LORD, I wait [Hiphil of yhl, "to hope/wait"] for you" (38:15)	"But now, Lord, what do I look for [Piel of qwh, "to wait"]? My hope [Hiphil noun from yhl]" (39:7)	"I waited [Piel of qwh] patiently for the LORD" (40:1)	
Personal sin as cause of God's judgment	"There is no soundness in my bones because of my sin [noun from ht']" (38:3) "My guilt ['awon] has overwhelmed me" (38:4) "My wounds fester and are loathsome because of my sinful folly ['iwwelet]" (38:5) "I confess my iniquity ['awov]; I am troubled by my sin [hatta'ah]" (38:18)	"When you rebuke and discipline anyone for their sin ['awon]" (39:11)	"My sins ['awon] have overtaken me, and I cannot see" (40:12)	"I said, 'Have mercy on me, LORD; heal me, for I have sinned [ht'] against you'" (41:4)

in David and Solomon's era, along with Asaph and Heman (1 Chron. 16:41–42; 2 Chron. 5:12).

39:1 *I will watch my ways and keep my tongue from sin; I will put a muzzle on my mouth.* The "ways" he needs to watch are his speech. At first the psalmist expresses his intention to keep silent "while in the presence of the wicked." The reasons for silence are related to his concern that he might sin against God and, likely, that the wicked might provoke him to misspeak. In Job 2:10 "to sin with one's tongue" (NIV: "Job did not sin in what he said") is an allusion to blasphemy. The verbal form of the term for "muzzle" occurs in Deuteronomy 25:4 (see "Historical and Cultural Background").

39:2 *So I remained utterly silent, not even saying anything good.* The Hebrew verb for "I remained silent" (*'lm*) is used to describe the servant's silence in Isaiah 53:7. There is the possibility that the psalmist does not take the witness stand lest he should have to admit his sin in the presence of his detractors. The idea of "not even saying anything good" reminds us of Jeremiah, who thought of being silent, but the fire shut up in his bones reversed his restraint (Jer. 20:9). The psalmist's strategy of silence in the presence of the wicked so as not to say the wrong thing is well intended, but repressing his speech only increases the anxiety, prompting him to speak at last (39:3).

39:3 *my heart grew hot within me . . . then I spoke with my tongue.* This expression implies an inner compulsion to act, in this case, to speak. Some interpret this to suggest that the psalmist suffered from a high fever.[5] As a consequence of his inner compulsion, he renounces his resolve and speaks out.

39:4 *Show me,* LORD, *my life's end.* His concern, interestingly enough, is not about sin but about the brevity of life. He wants to know when he will die, not so much to mark the calendar but to understand better the brevity and frailty of life.

39:5 *a mere handbreadth; the span of my years is as nothing before you.* Small things were measured in handbreadths (see "Historical and Cultural Background"). A comparable saying might be that our life is measured in inches rather than yards. Here he answers the request he made in 39:4. (For his years being "as nothing before you" see Psalm 90:4.) In the previous verse he used the word *hadel* (NIV: "fleeting"), and here he uses the noun *heled* "life" with a similar sound (NIV: "span of years"), creating a play on words.[6]

39:6 *Surely everyone goes around like a mere phantom; in vain they rush about.* In the Hebrew, verses 5b, 6a, and 6b [Heb. 6b, 7a, and 7b] begin with an emphatic word, translated "surely" or "yes" (*'ak*), and it occurs a fourth time in the middle of verse 11 [Heb. 12]. The NIV does not translate the word in 39:5b and 6b, losing the emphatic tone of these clauses. The ESV, however, is consistent: "Surely all mankind stands as a mere breath! Surely a man goes about as a shadow! Surely for nothing they are in turmoil" (39:5b–6b). "Surely all mankind is a mere breath!" (39:11c). The nonsubstantive nature of life is described as "a mere

Because the psalmist mentions keeping his "tongue from sin" (39:1), the opening illumination for this psalm by the Master of the Ingeborg Psalter shows David pointing to his mouth while a demon stands close by tempting him to sin with his speech.

phantom" (*tselem*, "image, likeness"). The term "in vain" (*hebel*) is the word that Ecclesiastes capitalizes on, translated "vanity, breath, vapor." (In Ecclesiastes the NIV renders this word as "meaningless.") Life is described as vaporous, as its patrons heap up wealth without even knowing whose it will be after their death. Ecclesiastes features this same theme (Eccles. 2:18–23; 4:7–8).

39:7 *But now, Lord, what do I look for? My hope is in you.* He asks the question and answers it too. He may use *'adonay,* the substitute term for Yahweh, because

God's Complicity in Suffering

The suppliant's sense of God's complicity in his suffering (39:9b–11) is both troubling and reassuring. It is troubling in that God is implicated in human suffering—its cause, in fact. But that is not a foreign idea in the Old Testament, for God is the cause of everything, both evil and good. Not until the exilic or postexilic era did the common Israelites become monotheistic (the priests and prophets and a remnant of the common people were already monotheists). God's collusion in human suffering was inevitable in that kind of thought system.

In another sense, God's complicity in suffering is comforting: God is personally involved in our lives (e.g., Ps. 41:3), and even divinely initiated sickness means that the deity is not ignoring the human subject, even though, as in Job's case, he or she does not celebrate the gesture. Yet—and this is the beauty of the thought—God enters not only into a causal but also into an empathetic relationship, and this makes suffering more bearable. He enters into our situation and becomes our shepherd ("my shepherd," Ps. 23:1), identifies with us by enthroning himself on the praises of Israel (Ps. 22:3), and even enters our conflicts and battles with us (Ps. 64:7–8).

he describes God's heavy hand that afflicts him, thus avoiding direct reference to the divine name Yahweh in such a context.[7]

39:8 *Save me from all my transgressions.* He believes his sins are the cause of his illness.

39:9 *I was silent; I would not open my mouth.* He returns to the silence of 39:2. Here the explanation, not given in verse 2, is rather perplexing: "you are the one who has done this." What has Yahweh done? Evidently he has caused the psalmist's condition, whether it be emotional or physical, that forced him into silence and then an outburst of anguish (39:1–3). Interestingly, this psalm accuses not the psalmist's enemies but God for the psalmist's trouble.

39:10 *I am overcome by the blow of your hand.* At this point there is no doubt that the psalmist believes his affliction has come by the hand of God.

39:11 *When you rebuke and discipline anyone for their sin, you consume their wealth like a moth.* The word "rebuke" carries the double nuance of punishment and discipline (Prov. 3:11). The Hebrew word for "wealth" describes Esau's "beautiful" clothes in Genesis 27:15 (NIV: "best") and here may describe the healthy and beautiful flesh of the suppliant before God afflicted him (as in Job 20:20).[8] The verb "consume" is the shortened Hiphil of the root *msh*, "to melt." The picture is that of healthy flesh melting away at the slow, persistent work of a moth (see Hosea 5:12).

39:12 *as a foreigner, a stranger.* The sociology of the ancient world comes into view in the nouns "foreigner" (*ger*) and "stranger" (*toshab*) of 39:12. The "foreigner" was the person who took refuge in Israel, driven from his or her homeland by economic or political hardships. Abraham was called a *ger* in Hebron (Gen. 23:4), Moses in Midian (Exod. 2:22), and the Israelites in Egypt (Exod. 22:21), and Elimelek and his family were said to "sojourn" (*gur*) in Moab (Ruth 1:1 KJV).[9] The term "stranger" includes those residents who were probably less assimilated into Israelite society than the "foreigner."[10] Here, however, and in 1 Chronicles 29:15, the two terms are synonymous.

39:13 *Look away from me, that I may enjoy life again before I depart and am no more.* This is similar to Job's request that God not look at him lest God's disfavor be realized (Job 7:19). The phrase "and am no more" is close to the description of Enoch's translation: "and he was not" (Gen. 5:24 ESV). Different from Enoch, however, the psalmist anticipates merely that he will "depart," while God "took" Enoch.

Theological Insights

Here the meanings of "foreigner" (*ger*) and "stranger" (*toshab*) merge into the story of the ancestors (lit., "fathers"; 39:12), an allusion to Abraham and his family, who were foreigners in Canaan. Even though they had permanent domicile there, the land still did not belong to them. The writer to the Hebrews has caught the sense of Abraham's dilemma: "By faith he made his home in the promised land like a stranger in a foreign country; he lived in tents, as did Isaac and Jacob, who were heirs with him of the same promise. For he was looking forward to the city with foundations, whose architect and builder is God" (Heb. 11:9–10). This is a metaphor of the tentative relationship the suppliant has with God, particularly in view of life's brevity and his impending death. Whether we should view this description as provisional or more constant is a difficult decision to make, but most of us have at times felt the "provisional" nature of our life with God. It partly stems from the provisional nature of life itself (39:4–6), an existence the psalmist describes as a "phantom" (39:6), that is, not quite substantive but with a shadowy quality. But perhaps even more significant than that is the "painful barriers sin has erected" between the psalmist and God.[11]

In his prayer, the psalmist tells the Lord that he dwells with him "as a foreigner" (39:12). In Exodus 22:21, the same word, also translated foreigner, is used to describe the Israelites in Egypt. This painting, 1890 BC, from the tomb of Khnum-hotep III at Beni Hasan, shows Semitic people from Syro-Palestine arriving in Egypt. The hieroglyphics above the leader of the group (not shown) identifies him as the "ruler of a foreign land."

Both the temporary nature of life and the sin that weighs us down combine to give us a sense of our status as "foreigner" and "stranger," as all our ancestors were.

With seven imperatives, five positive and two negative (39:8–13), our poet urges himself on God with a keenness of his own condition and circumstances, perhaps much more keen on himself than God. But he is human—who can deny it! And he is painfully aware of his sins and the grief they have caused him (39:8a, 8b, 9a, 12a, 12b, 12c, 13a–b). This painful awareness and the attendant grief are the stuff out of which repentance is made. The path to our awareness of God is plotted through a self-awareness of the distance our sin has generated between us and God.

Teaching the Text

Psalm 39 is a poetic essay on the brevity of life and its implications. All of us at some point should engage in this train of thought, and when we do, hopefully we will find that this thought accrues benefits for a more meaningful life. It is quite possible that these are the thoughts the suppliant has suppressed (39:1–3), because when he emerges from his self-imposed silence, they are the concern of the first prayer he prays: "Show me, LORD, my life's end" (39:4a).

We should point out to our congregation or class that this psalm typically treats its subject in less than a systematic way, although we can discover the dimensions of the topic by a careful reading of the psalm. The central topic, in fact, is marked off by an *inclusio*, "Everyone is but a breath" (39:5c and 11c). Between these duplicate observations is a mini-essay on the real values of life, and we can make this the heart of our message, growing out of the suppliant's recognition of life's brevity.

First, this recognition has led him to examine the value of material wealth, as it should all of us who come to grips with this grim but freeing reality. People rush about amassing their wealth (39:6b), not knowing whose it will be when they are gone—a shortsighted perspective. While the psalm does not attest to this thought, we can still raise the question whether the drive to amass wealth is not, at least sometimes, a way to suppress the thought of life's brevity and a way to escape dealing with it. There are, of course, many other reasons, but this certainly contributes to the rush and hurry of building our portfolios.

A second benefit that the psalmist's recognition has produced, found outside this *inclusio* (thus the lack of systemization), is his consciousness of being a "foreigner" and a "stranger" in this world (39:12). The world that we love so much has a way of holding on to us, or perhaps we should say, we have a way of holding on to it. This admission has freed the psalmist of the power of possession, and he can hold on to the world more loosely because he realizes the impermanent status of his citizenship. An auxiliary benefit, quite beautiful in itself, is attached to this one: that he belongs to a large group of people, his "ancestors" (39:12c), and that abode is more his home than this transient world of foreigners and strangers. While the first expression of this second benefit is freeing, this auxiliary benefit gives him the sense of belonging that he really needs in order to manage his life in a world of conflict and transience.

Let us not, however, make the mistaken assumption that this is a message for the aged, because a life freed from the tyranny of possession and given a new sense of belonging to our fathers and mothers who have prepared the way for us will enrich the young incalculably along their journey.

Illustrating the Text

Foreigners and strangers

Quote: *Jesus Rediscovered*, by Malcolm Muggeridge. One of the paradoxical dilemmas believers face is living in an alien world, ever aware that it is not our home. Abraham is the archetypal "stranger" making his abode in the alien society of Canaan, looking for a city "which has foundations, whose builder and maker is God" (Heb. 11:10 RSV). The effectiveness of our Christian witness depends to a large degree on how well we live out this life. Malcolm Muggeridge, the English satirist and journalist, feared that we might fail to recognize this call: "The only ultimate disaster that can befall us, I have come to realise, is to feel ourselves to be at home here on earth. As long as we are aliens we cannot forget our true homeland, which is that other kingdom You proclaimed."[12] The psalmist affirms that his life with God is as a "foreigner" and a "stranger" (v. 12), and in that respect he identifies with the patriarchs, who were foreigners in Canaan. We must assume the same spiritual posture as individuals and as the church, with our eyes fixed on the horizon of the future kingdom of God (Col. 3:1).

Brevity of human life

Music: Psalm 39:4–7 is the text of a major movement of Johannes Brahms's incredibly beautiful *German Requiem*. The themes are the brevity of life (especially in relation to God's life), life's fleeting nature (a subtheme of brevity), and the vanity of wealth, which one must leave to others. These themes are common to the Psalms and Wisdom literature. Job laments that "man who is born of a woman is few of days and full of trouble" (Job 14:1 ESV), and the psalmist joins the dirge as he prays, "Teach us to number our days, that we may gain a heart of wisdom" (Ps. 90:12). This means that the more keenly we recognize how brief our life is, the more fulfilled our life will be, because we will hopefully "redeem the time." While Psalm 39:4b does not formally constitute a result clause ("*so that* I may know how fleeting life is"), it could be read like that (so KJV), and indeed that seems to be the purpose of the prayer.

Pilgrims and strangers

Literature: *What's Mine's Mine*, **by George MacDonald.** In MacDonald's novel, Ian, one of the main characters, says to his farmer brother Alister:

Johannes Brahms, shown in this photo taken in 1870, used the text from Psalm 39:4–7 in the third movement of his first major composition for chorus and orchestra, the *German Requiem*, written between 1865 and 1869.

But I am sometimes not a little afraid lest your love for the soil get right into your soul. We are here but pilgrims and strangers. God did not make the world to be dwelt in, but to be journeyed through. We must not love it as he did not mean we should. If we do, he may have great trouble and we much hurt ere we are set free from it.[13]

Even though there is a delicate balance between being a "pilgrim and stranger" in this world and a "permanent resident," this "pilgrim and stranger" perspective is one endorsed by Psalm 39, and one that will help us to possess the world rather than being possessed by it (Matt. 5:5).

"I Waited Patiently for the LORD; He Turned to Me and Heard My Cry"

Big Idea *Waiting on the Lord through trouble and opposition opens our hearts to doing God's will.*

Understanding the Text

Psalm 40 is an individual psalm of thanksgiving, which is typically composed of the report of a crisis (40:12) and the celebration of deliverance (40:1–3), and these elements do not necessarily occur in that order.[1] Some commentators insist that this psalm is a combination of two independent psalms, an individual psalm of thanksgiving (40:1–10) and an individual lament (40:11–17). In reality, however, thanksgiving and lament naturally belong to the individual psalm of thanksgiving, since the suppliant as a matter of course rehearses the crisis (lament) from which he has been delivered.[2]

As for the usual order of lament followed by thanksgiving, Psalms 9–10 pose a similar challenge to this order and show that the order is not sacrosanct.[3]

The Text in Context

A thematic editorial principle definitely plays a role in the order of the Psalms. In the present case, the theme of "waiting," or "hoping," occurs in Psalms 37:7, 34; 38:15; 39:7 and was likely a factor in the

The opening verses of this psalm express thanksgiving, probably for a military victory. The slimy pit and mud and mire may express the general mess of David's predicament or the location of the battle in some type of swampy, muddy environment. Shown here is a battle scene from one of Sennacherib's campaigns where fighting occurs in a marshy area (640–620 BC, Nineveh palace relief).

placement of Psalm 40 here in the collection, especially in view of the fact that this is the initial theme of the psalm (40:1).[4]

The last five verses of Psalm 40 (40:13–17) constitute Psalm 70, with a slight change in the title and minor variations in the text itself. As is characteristic of Books 2 and 3 (Pss. 42–72 and 73–89), three times Psalm 70 substitutes the divine name 'elohim for the tetragrammaton (YHWH, "Lord"; 70:1a/40:13a; 70:4b/40:16b;[5] 70:5a/40:17a ['adonay to 'elohim]), and even once, at the very end, replaces 'elohim (40:17b/70:5b) with YHWH.

The Epistle to the Hebrews (10:5–10) quotes Psalm 40:6–8 from the Septuagint and applies it to Christ.[6] The writer hears the voice of Christ speaking in the psalm: Christ came into the world with the attitude of understanding and doing God's will (40:8) and went to the cross with this intention ("Here I am, I have come to do your will," Heb. 10:9).

Outline/Structure

Psalm 40 divides naturally into two parts, the first part being a reflection of the psalmist's experience, crowned with a word of blessing (40:1–4), and the second being the prayer itself (40:5–17), which may constitute the "new song." Some, however, would limit the "new song" to 40:5–10 (e.g., Waltner).[7]

1. The psalmist's reflection on the past, concluding with a benediction (40:1–4)
   a. A reflection on deliverance (40:1–3)
   b. A benediction on the one who trusts in the Lord (40:4)
2. The "new song" and lament (40:5–17)

Key Themes of Psalm 40

- God's preference for the psalmist to do God's will preempts the sacrificial system.
- God's law in one's heart is the goal of those who do God's will.
- Waiting on the Lord involves endurance and expectancy.

The Use of 'Elohim ("God") in Books 2 and 3

The preference for the divine name 'elohim (God) has generally been explained as an editorial or a geographical preference.[a] If Books 2 and 3 of the Psalter had their origin in the northern kingdom, with its focus on the sanctuary of Dan, as John P. Peters advocates,[b] a preference for the generic name 'elohim rather than YHWH would be easy to understand, given the semipagan origins of the northern cult under Jeroboam. But then the question remains as to what interest at all the northern worship tradition would have in the Psalms, which are so replete with Judean traditions of the Jerusalem temple and the Davidic dynasty. It is more likely that the entire book finds its compositional and editorial stimulus in Judah. Therefore, the preference for the divine name 'elohim in Books 2 and 3 is more likely to be found in an editorial/liturgical rather than a geographical motive, particularly the broadening international outlook of Judah, with its sights set on a world where a common name for God ('elohim) carried certain ecumenical implications. Particularly in view of the fact that Book 3 closes with the crisis generated by the fall of the Davidic dynasty, Judah's peripheral vision widened during the Babylonian exile, and their religious language underwent corresponding changes. This may account for the editorial philosophy of Books 2 and 3. Indeed, this view coheres with Craigie's suggestion that Psalm 70 could be a "salvaged psalm" for use during the exile when the monarchy no longer existed.[c] See sidebar "The Divine Names and the Elohistic Psalter" in the unit on Psalms 42–43.

   [a] See Bullock, Encountering, 75–77.
   [b] Peters, Psalms as Liturgies, 9–11.
   [c] Craigie, Psalms 1–50, 314.

   a. The "new song": An individual prayer of thanksgiving (40:5–10)
      i. A declaration of God's "wonders" (40:5)

ii. Gratitude expressed not by sacrifices but by observance of the Torah (40:6–10)

b. An individual lament (40:11–17)

　i. Prayer for mercy (40:11)

　ii. Confession of sins that "have overtaken" the psalmist (40:12)

　iii. Prayer for deliverance (40:13–17)

Historical and Cultural Background

The king's role of offering sacrifices makes Psalm 40, especially 40:6–8, sound like a royal psalm,[8] in which case the deliverance of 40:1–2 would be a military victory, and indeed the imagery of 40:2 suggests that. The king had almost suffered disaster when victory came, and the Lord put a "new song" in his mouth. Delitzsch assigns the psalm to the military conflict between Saul and David,[9] and Calvin also believes it was not illness that David was delivered from but "a multitude of dangers."[10]

Interpretive Insights

40:1 *I waited patiently for the* LORD. The infinitive absolute before the finite verb ("I waited patiently") implies constancy and perseverance.[11] Hakham renders it: "I hoped with all my heart."[12] Compare Psalm 18:6–9.

40:2 *He lifted me out of the slimy pit, out of the mud and mire.* The phrase translated as "slimy pit" refers to "a pit of devastation, of destruction, of ruin." See Genesis 37:20–28; Jeremiah 18:18–20, 22. The words "mud" and "mire" are really a single phrase in the Hebrew, meaning "mire of the marsh."

40:3 *He put a new song in my mouth . . . Many will see and fear the* LORD. The "new song," a "hymn of praise" (*teḥillah*), is in response to God's deliverance (on the content of the song, see "Outline/Structure"). The later part of the verse seems to define the purpose of the new song. Fearing the Lord is expressed positively as "put their trust in him." The one who does this is "blessed" in the following verse (40:4).[13]

40:4 *who does not look to the proud, to those who turn aside to false gods.* In Isaiah 3:5 the root word for "proud" (*rhb*) refers to children who treat their parents insolently ("The young will *rise up* against the old"). The verb for "turn aside" means "stray" in Numbers 5:12, and here it may

One of the purposes of sacrifices for cultures of the ancient Near East was to meet the god's need for food. Since YHWH has no needs, the sacrificial system in Israel played a different role. This Egyptian tomb painting shows an offering table piled high with food for the god Anubis (Temple of Hatshepsut, Karnak, Egypt, sixteenth century BC).

denote those who are idol worshipers (lit., "strayers of a lie," the "lie" being the false god; cf. NIV footnote).

40:5 *Many . . . are the wonders you have done, the things you planned for us.* The "wonders" (*nipla'ot*), according to Delitzsch,[14] are the "thoughts of God realized," while "the things you planned" are those that are being realized (Jer. 51:29; Isa. 55:8). The noun "wonders" often refers to past events in Israel's history. For the phrase "none can compare with you," see Psalm 89:6.

40:6 *Sacrifice and offering you did not desire—but my ears you have opened.* The verb "desire" may be understood in the sense of "to take pleasure in," suggesting that it is not the sacrifice itself that the Lord has taken pleasure in, but, as David implies in Psalm 51:16–17, it is the spirit behind it that he delights in. The word for "opened" (*krh*) means "to dig" (Ps. 7:15), perhaps suggesting the gesture of opening a stopped-up ear (see also "The Text in Context," concerning Heb. 10:5–10, and the endnote there). The message the psalmist hears may be the last part of the verse: "Burnt offerings and sin offerings you did not require." That message would require a divine transaction of opening the psalmist's ears (understanding), since it was such a radical turn away from the plain teaching of the Torah.

The four words for sacrifice have specific meanings but also can be used to comprehend the whole sacrificial system:[15] "sacrifice" (*zebah*, thanksgiving offering); "offering" (*minhah*, meal offering); "burnt offering(s)" (*'olah*, whole burnt offering); "sin offering(s)" (*hata'ah*).[16]

40:7–8 *Then I said, "Here I am, I have come—it is written about me in the scroll."*

The Moral Law and Sacrifice in the Psalms

There is a theological stream in the Psalms that recognizes, despite the Psalter's strong interest in the sanctuary and sacrificial system (e.g., 50:23), the auxiliary role of sacrifice and the primary function of the moral law (see, e.g., 40:6–8). In a voice that portends the voice of Christ, the psalmist declines to endorse the sacrificial system, favoring instead moral obedience to God's law. In the same tone, Psalm 50:7–15 summons Israel to "listen" or "hear," implying obedience and harking back to an earlier covenant renewal (Deut. 5:1; 6:4). Yet, in an effort to balance sacrifice against obedience, Psalm 50, sharing prophetic affinities,[a] seeks to clarify the meaning of sacrifice. God neither disallows sacrifice nor needs it; yet so long as sacrifice is made in thanksgiving and obedience and confirmed in moral conduct, God endorses it, for only then does it become the instrument of covenant relationship between Israel and God, which is the original purpose of sacrifice. Indeed, God does not *need* it, for he already owns all the beasts of the field and the birds of the air (50:10–11). Further, he has no need to be fed (50:12) and certainly does not, unlike the perception of the Mesopotamian deities, gorge himself on flesh and blood (50:13). Rather, the meaning of sacrifice is found in relationship with God (50:14, 15). The following psalm, Psalm 51, finds David, again in a prophetic voice, asserting that God does not "delight in sacrifice" or "take pleasure in burnt offerings" (51:16). On the contrary, he honors the sacrifice of a "broken and contrite heart" (51:17). In a statement akin to Psalm 50, David prays in 141:2 that his prayer "be set before you like incense; may the lifting up of my hands be like the evening sacrifice." In a vein of thought much like the postexilic compensation for the loss of sacrifice, incense and lifting up hands have become a substitute for sacrifice.

[a] Delitzsch, *Psalms*, 3:140–43; Bullock, *Encountering*, 77–79.

This is the servant's obedient response to God's call, like Samuel's "Here I am" (1 Sam. 3). The "scroll" is likely a synonym of "your law," in this context, written on his heart or innermost being (lit., "bowels," the seat of the emotions; 40:8). This is basically a Deuteronomic idea, that the "law" (*torah*) was to be an inner reality (Deut. 6:6), an idea that Jeremiah made the distinguishing feature of the new covenant

(Jer. 31:33; see "Text in Context" for the messianic resonances; see also "Additional Insights: Messianic Psalms" following the unit on Ps. 8). Even Israel in Isaiah's time was known as "the people in whose heart is my law" (Isa. 51:7 ESV). See also Proverbs 7:3; 22:18.

40:9–10 *I proclaim your saving acts in the great assembly.* The "great assembly" is either the worshiping congregation in Jerusalem or the larger body of Israel, most likely the former. In this setting he rehearses the "saving acts" (lit., "righteousness") of God—the great redeeming events in Israel's history. Verse 10 contains a rephrasing of the psalmist's message in the congregation.

40:11 *Do not withhold your mercy from me, LORD.* Delitzsch comments that "in accordance with the true art of prayer, petition develops itself out of thanksgiving."[17]

40:12 *For troubles . . . my sins have overtaken me, and I cannot see.* These "troubles" may be an allusion to those who want to take his life (40:14). This is the first time in the psalm that the suppliant confesses his sins, which are "more than the hairs of my head." The fact that the consequences of his sins have overtaken ("caught up with") him is another Deuteronomic idea (Deut. 28:15). The crisis has produced two outcomes: the psalmist cannot see (perhaps see his life in proper perspective), and he is fearful ("my heart fails within me").

40:14 *May all who want to take my life.* While the suppliant's sins are the main problem, for the first time he alludes to his enemies, who seem always to be present.

40:15 *Aha! Aha!* These words are used to rejoice over another person's misfortune (see Ps. 35:21).

40:16 *But may all who seek you rejoice and be glad in you.* This is the opposite request of 40:14.

Theological Insights

When it comes to the value and meaning of sacrifice, there is a parallel theme of ostensible disparagement that runs between the Prophets and the Psalms, with some expression of sympathy in the Wisdom books. Even though some would insist that this negative attitude toward sacrifice was exilic or postexilic, most likely it belongs to the preexilic period, when Israel often used sacrifice as a manipulative tool, to get something from God without rendering true worship and loyalty (e.g., Amos 8:4–6). It is universally recognized that the prophets proclaimed a strict moral code of religion. They condemned the religiosity of Israel that gave only ritual credence to Yahweh,

David realized that sacrifices and offerings alone were not what God desired. Obedience to God's law was most important. The sacrificial system used altars such as this one found and reconstructed at Beersheba, Israel. As part of the ritual connected with the sin offering, blood was sprinkled on the horns of the altar.

and they demanded moral obedience. In fact, they recognized that the core of the Hebrew faith was the ethical demands of Yahweh, represented in the Torah by Deuteronomy 6:5; Exodus 20; Deuteronomy 5; and Leviticus 19:18, to name only a few such texts.

To reinforce their emphasis, the prophets were sometimes inclined to reduce the faith to its moral essence, in order to put another layer of argument on the ethical nature and the simplicity of Yahweh's demands. That tendency, for example, is represented in the Saul story when he preempts the priestly function of the altar in Samuel's absence and earns Samuel's reproof that "to obey is better than sacrifice" (1 Sam. 15:22). Isaiah takes the matter a step further and asserts that God has "no pleasure [*hpts*] in the blood of bulls and lambs and goats" (Isa. 1:11), but what he really demands is moral obedience (Isa. 1:16–17). Jeremiah is yet more explicit and proclaims that the Lord did not demand sacrifices of Israel when he brought them out of Egypt but instead demanded their obedience (Jer. 7:22–23): "But I gave them this command: Obey me, and I will be your God and you will be my people." Hosea, in a more theological than historical mode, announces, "For I desire mercy, not sacrifice, and acknowledgment [or "knowledge"] of God rather than burnt offerings" (Hosea 6:6; see also Amos 5:10–20). One of the most memorable expressions of this negative view of the sacrificial system occurs in Micah 6:6–8. In a ritual reminiscent of the ethical inquiries of Psalms 15 and 24, the prophet turns the question slightly from "who" can approach the Lord to "how" one must approach him, giving the answer in ethical terms (Mic. 6:8).

This theme has a lower profile in the Wisdom literature, but a visible one nevertheless. The book of Proverbs downgrades the sacrifice of the wicked, which is understandable, and gives commendation to the "prayer of the upright" (Prov. 15:8), as if the "prayer of the upright" is a substitute for sacrifice. Clearest, however, is Proverbs 21:3, where the wise man declares that doing "what is right and just" is a more acceptable alternative than sacrifice.

Teaching the Text

We may begin our lesson/sermon by first calling attention to the opening idea of the psalm, waiting on the Lord. Grammatically the verb "wait" (*qwh*) has an accompanying verbal form (infinitive absolute) to indicate its intensity, rendered by the translations as "patiently." This idea is one of intense expectancy. The companion verb "to wait" (*yhl*) carries the nuance of endurance ("hang in there"), and the two occur in parallel in Psalm 130:5 ("wait" and "hope"), implying both endurance and expectancy.[18] These nuances suggest that waiting on the Lord is not an idle but an active waiting, involving expectant faith, and expectant faith is not dormancy.[19] This spiritual discipline is essential in the lives of all believers, even though it takes various expressions in each individual's faith: patience, endurance, and suffering, to name only the obvious.

Second, Psalm 40 contains a germ of the gospel in that it sets forth God's redemptive design to put his law in human hearts (40:8). Jeremiah's new covenant statement (Jer. 31:33) is the best-known text in that regard. Yet Deuteronomy already points in this direction by predicating that God's words are to be "on" Israel's hearts (Deut. 6:6). Isaiah endorses this idea and may represent a lesser-known parallel to Jeremiah (Isa. 51:7). See Hebrews 8:1–13 and 9:1–18.

Further, a connected idea is that, while God's "law" (*torah*) in the broadest terms involves the full scope of legislation given to Israel on Sinai, here it is expressed in summary form: "to do your will" (40:8). It is the voice of the psalmist articulating the idea that would become Jesus's summary of the kingdom of God in the Lord's Prayer, "Thy will be done on earth as it is in heaven." When that is written in our hearts, everything else is of secondary importance, even sacrifice (see "The Text in Context" for the way the writer to the Hebrews interprets this psalm).

Titled *"My wife and my mother-in-law. They are both in this picture—find them,"* this drawing by the British cartoonist W. E. Hill was published in *Puck*, an American humor magazine, in 1915.

Illustrating the Text

The essential commandment

Judaism: There is a midrash that says the 613 commandments given to Moses (the traditional Jewish number) were reduced by David to eleven (Ps. 15:1–5), by Isaiah to six (Isa. 33:15), by Micah to three (Mic. 6:8), and by Habakkuk to one (Hab. 2:4). Psalm 40:6–8 operates in that vein of thought as it reduces the sacrificial law to the simplified and unadorned statute "to do your will, my God," a law that God has placed in the psalmist's heart. Jesus joined this company of prophets, reducing the Torah to a single commandment, to love God with all one's heart, soul, and mind (Matt. 22:36–40).

An offering of life

Applying the Text: Instead of offering an animal sacrifice, David comes before the Lord to offer his life in obedience to God. Lead the congregation in a time of commitment prayer. For example, using the parts of the body you might pray,

Lord, we offer our mouths to you, that we might speak your truth in the world. God, we offer our minds to you, that we might meditate on your word. Lord, we offer our hands to you, that we might serve your people and those in the world. God, we offer our hearts to you, that our worship would focus solely upon you.

Lord, we offer our feet to you, that we might bring the good news of the gospel to the ends of the earth.

After praying each part, take moments of silence for the congregants to consider how they might use that part of their body to serve the Lord. As you close in prayer, ask your listeners to join with you as together you recite Psalm 40:8, "I desire to do your will, my God; your law is within my heart." The hymn "Take My Life and Let It Be" could be fitting in conjunction with this psalm and prayer.

Turn your heart to God.

Props: Show an optical illusion that contains two different images combined into one, such as the old lady and the young woman or the two faces in profile that form a candlestick. What makes these images fascinating is that some people will immediately see one subject while others will quickly recognize another. This is simply a difference in perspective. In the same way, when people face life challenges, some are energetic and hopeful, while others are discouraged and defeated. What's the difference? Perspective plays a key role. One of the beauties of Psalm 40 and the Psalms in general is that the authors often focus on praise and thanksgiving (e.g., Ps. 40:2, 3, 5), regardless of their circumstances. The more we focus on the nature of God and the great things he has done, the greater will be our hope!

"Blessed Are Those Who Have Regard for the Weak; the LORD Delivers Them"

Big Idea *Irrespective of the cause of our illnesses, the Lord cares for us in our vulnerability.*

Understanding the Text

The literary type of Psalm 41 has been the topic of much discussion, since the poem does not seem to fall easily into any single type. Perhaps Kraus's "prayer song of the sick"[1] is appropriate for this psalm, although we might simply designate it as an individual lament. The psalm, in fact, begins with a benediction on those who "have regard for" the sick (see the comments on 41:1). Craigie identifies the setting of the psalm as the sanctuary where the suppliant prays for healing. While this may be true, in order to arrive at that conclusion, certain parts of the liturgy are assumed.[2] Yet it does make sense that such a momentous event would be celebrated publicly in some way.

The Text in Context

This psalm concludes Book 1 (Pss. 1–41), employing the same term of blessing (*'ashre*) that began Book 1 (Ps. 1:1). Since, however, Psalm 1 was likely installed

as an "introduction" to the entire book, and perhaps later than the composition of Psalm 41, the editor likely picked up the term from Psalm 41 in order to provide a literary balance, not vice versa. Of course, this assumes that the fivefold division was very early.

The selection of Psalms 40 and 41 as a conclusion to Book 1 accomplishes two things. First, they verbally connect the profile of David to the beginning of the book to establish him, rhetorically speaking, as the righteous person par excellence, in much the same way as the book of Job establishes Job as the wise man (Job 28:28).[3] The repeated use of the word *'ashre* ("blessed," 1:1; 40:4; 41:1) is the initial hint. Book 1 has rhetorically developed the profile of David from various angles as the righteous man, and now he is seen to be the one who "has regard for the weak" (or "sick," 41:1). And quite importantly, David has concluded Psalm 40 by acknowledging that he is "poor and needy," and he appropriately opens

Psalm 41 with this benedictory word for "those who have regard [lit., "the one who has regard"] for the weak." The portrait of Psalm 40 corresponds almost perfectly to that of the "righteous one" in Psalm 1 in that the "blessed" person is that one "whose delight [root *hpts*] is in the law of the LORD" (1:2), while the speaker of Psalm 40 declares, "I desire [*hpts*] to do your will, my God; your law is within my heart" (40:8). In fact, it is not sacrifice that God wants but doing his will, which is contained in the Torah, which is in the suppliant's heart (40:6–8), and in which the psalmist delights (1:2).

Second, Psalms 40 and 41 quite appropriately compile a summary of the struggles and sentiments of David represented in Book 1, presenting David as the *prototype* of the righteous man. David indeed is the "blessed" person who "has regard for the weak" (41:1). As already observed, this ideal profile actually begins in Psalm 40:4, where the benedictory term *'ashre* occurs to draw attention to the person who has set his trust in the Lord. Moreover, the rhetorical profile of the righteous person continues as the psalmist freely confesses his sin (41:4) and explains that God upholds him because of his integrity (41:12a). Further, God sets the psalmist in his presence, fulfilling David's desire (often expressed in Book 1) to appear before Yahweh in the sanctuary (41:12b). Yet the capstone assessment is found in 41:11a: "I know that you are pleased [*hpts*] with me." The profile of the righteous person, therefore, has received its final touches in Psalm 41, and David, rhetorically speaking, is that man (see "Theological Insights" in the unit on Psalm 34, and particularly endnote 9 in that unit).

Key Themes of Psalm 41

- God is a "nurse" of the sick.
- God's grace is "upholding" grace.

Jesus quotes Psalm 41:9 during his last meal with his disciples when he tells them that one of them will betray him. Jesus says, "I am not referring to all of you; I know those I have chosen. But this is to fulfill this passage of Scripture: 'He who shared my bread has turned against me'" (John 13:18). Judas Iscariot would later betray Jesus with a kiss in the garden of Gethsemane. This scene is illustrated by Simon Bening in his illumination of the Prayer Book of Cardinal Albrecht of Brandenburg (sixteenth century).

At the same time, the characterization of David's enemies, so prominent in Book 1, corresponds to their general profile as presented in this collection. They have spoken evil against David (41:7), wished for his demise (41:5, 7), interpreted his illness in negative terms (41:8, "a vile disease"), turned from friend to foe (41:9), yet last, and most significant, not triumphed over him (41:2c, 11).

See John 13:18–30, where Jesus applies Psalm 41:9 to Judas's betrayal.

Outline/Structure

Assuming that this psalm is a profile of David as the righteous man in whom the Lord is pleased, the psalm divides into three parts:

1. David, the "blessed one," has regard for the weak/sick (41:1–3).
2. David recalls his own sickness (41:4–9).
    a. He recalls his confession of sin (41:4).
    b. He recalls his enemies' ill treatment (41:5–9).
3. Pleading God's grace, David prays for mercy and acknowledges God's pleasure with him (41:10–12).

Verse 13 is the closing doxology for Book 1 (see the comments on 41:13 below). For more on the doxologies, see "Trends in Psalms Studies" in the introduction.

Historical and Cultural Background

This psalm may arise out of David's conflict with his son Absalom, at least that general period, especially in view of the betrayal of his close friend who ate bread with him (41:9). Perowne suggests that the friend was Ahithophel, whose sympathies in fact turned to Absalom (2 Sam. 15:12).[4]

An interesting word picture occurs in 41:3 with the use of two phrases: the phrase "sickbed" (lit., "bed of illness") in the first line and "his whole bed you turn over when he is ill" (NIV: "and restores them from their bed of illness") in the second line. This parallel expression, using different Hebrew vocabulary, appears to describe turning the bed over after the patient has been lying on it for several days.[5] Rashi, citing a midrash, says this was done on the seventh day, while the *Midrash on Psalms* says it was done on the fourth day when the illness was considered to be more grave.[6] While the rabbinic interpretation may reflect a later healthcare practice, the metaphor is definitely a beautiful picture of Yahweh's tender care of the psalmist.[7]

Interpretive Insights

41:1 *Blessed are those who have regard for the weak.* On "blessed" (*'ashre*), see "The Text in Context" (see also Pss. 112:1; 119:1; 128:1). Kidner asserts that the word "regard" (*maskil*) describes the practical wisdom of the man of affairs[8] (see the use of the participle in Ps. 32:8; see Neh. 8:13 for "giving attention to" the law, using the same verb). Generally the Hebrew word for "weak" (*dal*) occurs in contrast to the wealthy (Ruth 3:10; Prov. 10:15; 19:4, 17; 28:11).[9] It can also mean "poor" (Exod. 30:15), as well as "sick," as in 2 Samuel 13:4 (NIV: "haggard"),[10] and perhaps in this context the rendering "sick" is the most logical.

41:2 *The LORD protects and preserves them—they are counted among the blessed in the land.* The first part of the verse refers to the Lord keeping the psalmist alive. The word that the NIV renders "counted among the blessed" (root *'shr*) is similar to the word that begins the psalm, *'ashre* ("blessed"), and may be translated in this way. Another meaning, however—and my preference—is "to take steps" (Prov. 9:6). It would be translated "he will take steps on the earth," which is a logical sequence to the psalmist's restoration from his sickness (i.e., "he will walk again").

41:3 *The* L<small>ORD</small> *sustains them on their sickbed and restores them from their bed of illness.* See "Historical and Cultural Background." The NIV translates the verb in the second half of the line as if it is third-person singular[11] ("he restores them"), evidently to agree with the third-person singular in the first half of the verse, but the verb is second masculine singular, addressed to God: "You restore him to full health" (ESV). The change is unnecessary, however. While we tend to keep our grammatical persons consistent in English, it is not uncommon in the Psalms for the suppliant to change persons abruptly. The psalmist does the same thing in the second half of 41:2 ("You do not give him up to the will of his enemies," ESV). The verb rendered as "restores" is the Hebrew verb *hpk*, which can mean turn over or upside down. Hakham gives the sense as follows: "You, O Lord, overturned his entire bed, in the manner of someone attending a sick person, who turns over the bed on which the sick person is lying, in order to clean and arrange it."[12]

41:4 *I said, "Have mercy on me,* L<small>ORD</small>; *heal me, for I have sinned against you."* Although the psalm begins in the third person ("those who"; the Hebrew is singular), the poem is really about the psalmist, as the first-person verbs indicate (41:4, 9, 10, 11) and the generous use of the first-person

pronouns "me" and "my" in verses 4–12 also attests. Note the belief that sickness is caused by sin, shared by Psalms 38–40 (see table 2 in the unit on Ps. 39).

41:6 *When one of them comes to see me, he speaks falsely, while his heart gathers slander.* Operating as friends, but in effect enemies, these people visit the suppliant in his illness, and then they go away and slander the patient. Evidently verse 8 is the content of their slanderous talk.[13]

41:7 *All my enemies whisper together against me.* Gaster sees this whispering as "incantations" and hears the Hebrew word for "whisper" (*yitlahashu*) as onomatopoetic, reproducing the hissing sounds of the incantations.[14]

41:8 *A vile disease has afflicted him.* The term for "vile disease" is *dᵉbar-bᵉliyyaʿal*

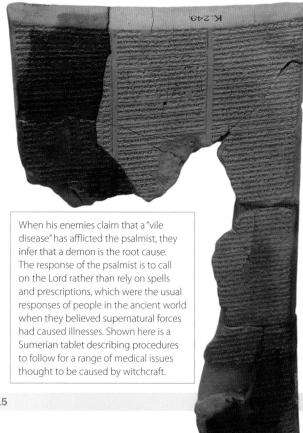

When his enemies claim that a "vile disease" has afflicted the psalmist, they infer that a demon is the root cause. The response of the psalmist is to call on the Lord rather than rely on spells and prescriptions, which were the usual responses of people in the ancient world when they believed supernatural forces had caused illnesses. Shown here is a Sumerian tablet describing procedures to follow for a range of medical issues thought to be caused by witchcraft.

("worthless pestilence"). See the exact expression also in Psalm 101:3 (NIV: "anything that is vile"). The implication here is that the cause of his illness is demonic, but the psalmist believes it is due to a breakdown in his relationship to Yahweh.

41:9 *Even my close friend, someone I trusted, one who shared my bread, has turned against me.* "My close friend" is literally "the man of my peace," that is, someone who is committed to his well-being (see "Historical and Cultural Background"). See Psalm 55:12–14 for the same idea. The verse ends with the statement of betrayal, literally, "he has magnified [his] heel against me" (NIV: "has turned against me"; see NIV footnote). The word 'aqeb ("heel," "deception") is related to the name "Jacob," who was known for his deceptive ways (e.g., Gen. 27), and some translations render the phrase more literally (e.g., RSV: "has lifted his heel against me"). In a metaphorical sense, the lifting of the heel may suggest the turning and walking out on one in time of need or lifting the heel and crushing one's opponent.[15]

41:10 *that I may repay them.* The psalmist's motive to "repay them" for their deeds is a bit surprising. Even in the imprecatory psalms, the psalmist leaves vengeance to God. Kidner, however, puts this in the context of David's kingship, which gave him authority to take actions against his enemies.[16]

41:11 *I know that you are pleased with me.* Literally, "In this I know that you are pleased with me." "In this" (not in the NIV)—by his own prayer that he has offered, he discerns God's favor; or more likely, by what is said in the rest of the verse: his enemies have not triumphed over him.

Like the psalmist who believes his sickness is a punishment for sin, other ancient Near Eastern cultures also believed that illness could have a supernatural origin, whether attributed to gods or demons. Amulets were created to ward off demon-induced sickness. In this section of an amulet from Mesopotamia, special healers wear fish-skin robes as they perform the ritual prescribed to restore the health of the sick person (ninth century BC, Neo-Assyrian).

This is the evidence that God is pleased with him.

41:12 *Because of my integrity you uphold me and set me in your presence forever.* "Integrity" (*tom*) is innocence (Gen. 20:5–6 [NIV: "clear conscience"]; 2 Sam. 15:11; 1 Kings 22:34/2 Chron. 18:33 [NIV: "at random"]) and also a consistency of good character, as well as spiritual fortitude.[17] The verb "uphold" (*tmk*; see also Ps. 63:8) suggests that God is supporting the psalmist in his sickness, and even in the opposition his pretentious friends have raised against him. The suppliant is assured of the fulfillment of this longing, to appear before God's face—that is, to appear in the temple.

41:13 *Praise be to the LORD, the God of Israel, from everlasting to everlasting. Amen and Amen.* This doxology closes Book 1, as all five books are similarly closed (Pss. 72:18–19; 89:52; 106:48; 146–50; see "Trends in Psalms Studies" in the introduction for discussion of the closing doxologies). The Hebrew word for "praise be" is the passive participle *baruk* (often translated as "blessed"). We have called attention above to the use of "blessed" (*'ashre*) that opens the psalm, here applying that general ascription of Psalm 1:1 to David, the ideal righteous man. The word *'ashre* is a recognition that the person is healthy, prosperous, and spiritually well balanced. In comparison, *baruk*, the word that closes the psalm (closes Book 1, in fact) is an ascription that recognizes an inherent worth in God or the person who is "blessed" (the NIV, "praise be," calls for an active offering of praise to God).

While the phrase "from everlasting to everlasting" (*meha'olam w^e'ad ha'olam*) may not mean "forever" in our understanding of the term, it nevertheless edges up to eternity. Hakham speaks of the *'olam* of man and the *'olam* of God and observes that *'olam* is written with the definite article in both instances, suggesting that this is the *'olam* that belongs to God alone.[18] The word "amen" means "to affirm, be so." The repeated "amen" (also Num. 5:22; see ESV) reinforces the affirmation, "Praise be to the Lord, the God of Israel, from everlasting to everlasting." The implication is that this is the affirmation of all affirmations.

Theological Insights

The honest confession of the psalmist is heartening, but we know only the outcome of his inner struggle, not its details. Whatever the nature of it, the result is the confession of sin (41:4), prayer for healing (41:4, 10), and restoration (41:11–12). It is a process of honest confession and reflection that in the end God honors: "Because of my integrity you uphold me" (41:12a). The suppliant's relationship to God, described with the verb "uphold," is not without an ethical commitment on his part, particularly defined by his "regard for the weak" (41:1) and ready confession of sin. In this case, God's "upholding" grace does not take place in a moral vacuum. Rather, it is the kind of grace that works in and through the suppliant's personal life, the moral life to which God has called him.

Teaching the Text

Since we want to get to the heart of the psalm, we can draw attention to the fact that this poem accents the divine attribute we know as "grace." The term *hesed* is not even present here, but the reality is everywhere. Likewise, in the opening psalms of Book 2 (Pss. 42–43), the word does not occur, but its ubiquitous presence is nevertheless there because the God of love is there, and this God meets us in the daily routine of life.

Two word pictures in Psalm 41 open up this truth for us. They remind us that God's grace is a reality every day. They occur in verses 3 and 12, but if we speak of them in reverse order, the most tender of the two will conclude our lesson or sermon, and that aspect of teaching and preaching is very important. The last word should always be grace.

The first word picture is expressed in these words: "In my integrity you uphold me" (41:12a). The picture is that of God holding David up or supporting him. That is what the verb "uphold" (*tmk*) means, "to bear the weight of, to support," which is the effect of daily grace. It can be the burden of our sin, or an illness, or the weight of our everyday worries and cares.

David prays for the Lord's mercy and requests healing, trusting in God's gracious character. In contrast, this papyrus reconstruction of a stele relief shows an Egyptian priest with a deformed leg who is offering sacrifices to the goddess of healing, hoping that his gifts will persuade her to grant his request.

The second word picture is found in verse 3b and is a rather surprising one, but all the more beautiful: the Lord will "restore them from their bed of illness." Literally, the text reads: "you [LORD] turn his whole bed over in his illness." Verse 3 opens the door to the patient's room and shows us Yahweh's bedside manner as he attends the psalmist, who is suffering from a serious illness. Yahweh even turns the bed over to make the patient more comfortable: "Most carefully you make his bed when he is sick" (JB). This is a picture of patient care in the ancient world of Israel, but more tenderly, it is a picture of the Lord's tender care of David, and of us all. This picture tells us that God is a hands-on God who attends to our cares, not as a once-in-a-lifetime event, but on a daily basis. We may also recall Jesus's words about his easy yoke in Matthew 11:28–30 and note that it is in the daily toil of the oxen that the metaphor is meaningful, as it is in the details of life that God manifests his grace.

We are reminded of the hands-on creation narrative in Genesis 2, where the Lord God takes the dust of the earth and forms a man from it. It is all too easy to lose God's immanent care in the grandeur of his transcendent reign over the universe. This word picture of God as the "nurse" of the sick reminds us that God always comes near.

Illustrating the Text

Ministry of comfort

Literature: *The Diary of a Country Priest*, by Georges Bernanos. In Bernanos's novel, a young priest lies dying and asks for absolution, whereupon his friend sends for a priest. When no priest comes, the friend is obliged to express his regret to the dying man that absolution cannot be given. The friend later recounts the young priest's response: "He then uttered these words almost in my ear . . . 'Does it matter? Grace is everywhere.'"[19] This provides a picture of the reality that we do not need a religious person in order to come to God. Rather, God is already there, and we encounter him through faith in Jesus.

Cause and effect

True Story: A young man volunteered one evening to take a nursing home patient to see a movie. Feeling good about his act of service, the young man brought the woman back to the nursing home and then headed home. On the way, a car ran a stoplight and plowed into his car, injuring him. Although the injuries were not serious, he needed to be treated. The experience created a crisis of faith for the young man, who wondered, "Why would God allow this to happen when I was doing a good deed?" Actually, the same question can be asked about David. He is presented in the Psalms as a righteous man whom God has blessed, but he is also a man who suffers much at the hands of enemies and even supposed friends. Many people have a "cause and effect" perspective on faith. That is, they expect bad things to happen when they have been bad, and good things to happen when they have been good. But as we see with David, that is simply not the case. We need to broaden our understanding of biblical faith to recognize that our circumstances do not always yield to a "cause and effect" explanation, but the psalmist reminds us that the Lord delivers us in times of trouble (41:1).

God is ever present.

Personal Stories: *Abba's Child*, **by Brennan Manning.** In his book, Manning shares a story about the daily care of the ever-present God. A woman asked a priest to visit her father, who was dying of cancer. As the priest entered the man's room, he saw an empty chair, which he assumed had been placed there for his visit. But the man explained that it was his "prayer chair." The dying man said that he had found prayer very difficult and had given up on it until a friend made a suggestion. The friend said he might place an empty chair in front of him and, in faith, picture Jesus in the chair and have a conversation with him, which he had been doing ever since. The priest prayed with the man and then a few days later heard from the daughter that her father had died. She said, "But there was something strange, Father. In fact, beyond strange—kinda weird. Apparently just before Daddy died, he leaned over and rested his head on a chair beside his bed."[20] The God of the universe provides daily comfort to his people who look to him! "The LORD sustains them on their sickbed and restores them from their bed of illness" (41:3).

"As the Deer Pants for Streams of Water, So My Soul Pants for You, My God"

Big Idea *Even in adverse circumstances of place, atmosphere, and our own troubled thoughts, we can rally our hearts to joy and hope in God.*

Understanding the Text

Psalms 42 and 43 are distinct psalms in the Hebrew (MT), Greek (LXX), Syriac, and Vulgate, which suggests that they were separate compositions. Yet the seamless relationship of the two poems is indicated by these factors: (1) they share a refrain (42:5, 11; 43:5); (2) Psalm 43 has no title (Ps. 71 is the only other exception in Book 2); (3) both psalms share the lament meter of 3+2; and (4) they share a similar subject.[1]

The psalm is an individual lament, stating the reason for the lament, which is the psalmist's inability to visit the Jerusalem sanctuary (42:1, 4, 6; 43:3–4) and the mockery of his compatriots (42:3, 9; 43:2), evidently because of his religious devotion (43:1). There is no resolution to his dilemma, except in hope that God will in time resolve it.

The supplicant's prayer for vindication against an "unfaithful nation" (43:1; see the comments on this verse) implies that,

given his location in the northern kingdom, he keenly feels Israel's unfaithfulness. One possibility is that the psalmist's absence from Jerusalem was due to exile related to David's flight from Absalom (but David fled in the opposite direction from Mount Hermon). Psalm 43 may very well have been written as a response to Psalm 42 (as Goldingay proposes),[2] leaving the time quite undefined, but certainly before the Babylonian exile, since Book 3 concludes with a theological quandary about the implications of that event (Ps. 89).

The Text in Context

Book 1 ends with the psalmist's confident assertion that the Lord sets him in his presence forever (Ps. 41:12), and Book 2 begins with longing for that same intimacy with God, which did or should characterize every age of Israel's national history. Indeed, this longing characterizes the kingly line (David is its representative) in Psalms 16; 23; 26; 27; and 63. Further, one would expect the sons of Korah, a Levitical family (representing the priestly line), to long for restoration to their temple and profession. The fact that Book 2 begins with this longing, now applied specifically to the Levitical line ("sons of Korah"), partially completes the picture of the appropriateness of this longing as stretched across the lines of ancient Israel, kings, priests, and commoners alike. The geographical provenance of this Psalm in the northern kingdom may be a hint of the origin, or most likely the adaptation, of the Elohistic Psalter. Here the soulful longing of David for the temple and encounter with God has, in an editorial way, been planted firmly in the hearts of the Levites by this powerful liturgy of yearning to see God's face. Behind the king himself (Ps. 41), it was only reasonable that the priestly/Levitical officiants longed too for the temple and the awesome presence of God and that this longing be represented in the Psalter.

Psalm 84, a key psalm in Book 3, helps us to position Book 3 in the same theological frame. In fact, Delitzsch insists that Psalm 84—also a "psalm of the sons of Korah"—and Psalms 42–43, were written

by the same author, and he draws attention to their verbal correlations: [3]

Psalms 42–43	Psalm 84
"Living God" (42:2)	"Living God" (84:2)
"The place where you dwell" (Hebrew is plural; 43:3)	"Your dwelling place" (Hebrew is plural; 84:1)
"Altar of God" (43:4)	"Your altar"/"altar of God" (NIV: "a place near your altar"; 84:3)

As for their general emotional range, both poets acknowledge their absence from the sanctuary, and both deeply yearn to be there.

Two collections of the Korah psalms serve as bookends to the Elohistic collection of psalms (see below), with a cadre of eight Korah psalms beginning Book 2 (Pss. 42–49) and a second collection (Pss. 84–85; 87–88) concluding Book 3. In between, heading up Book 3, is a collection

When the psalmist asks for vindication "against an unfaithful nation" (43:1), he may be referring to the northern kingdom of Israel, where alternative worship centers were set up around golden calves. One of these centers was at Dan, and the remains of the sanctuary with its altar and high place can be seen here.

The Divine Names and the Elohistic Psalter

The use of the divine names "LORD" (*YHWH*) and "God" (*'elohim*) in the Psalms is a complex issue. In Book 1 *YHWH* occurs 278 times, and *'elohim* 15. Books 4 and 5 use *YHWH* 339 times and *'elohim* 9, obviously a predominance of *YHWH*.[a] But Psalms 42–83 (Book 2 and part of Book 3) exhibit a preference *for 'elohim*. Because of that, these forty-two psalms have been called the Elohistic Psalter. They contain *'elohim* 200 times and *YHWH* 44 times, quite a reversal of the pattern in Books 1 (Pss. 1–41) and 4 and 5 (Pss. 90–150).[b] The Elohistic Psalter is dominated by the first Korah collection (Pss. 42–49) and an Asaph collection (Pss. 50; 73–83). In the first collection of Korah psalms, *'elohim* occurs 51 times, as compared to 9 for *YHWH*, while the numbers for the Asaph collection are 55 for *'elohim* and 14 for *YHWH*, with 4 occurrences of the divine name *'adonay*, a substitute for *YHWH*. In comparison, the second Korah collection (Pss. 84–85; 87–88), which may not have come under northern-kingdom influences and do not belong to the Elohistic Psalter, turns the numbers around, with 17 occurrences of *YHWH* and 10 of *'elohim*.

One wonders why, once the shift to *'elohim* in the Elohistic Psalter had occurred, the preference for *YHWH* did not mandate a restoration of the tetragrammaton. We may make two assumptions (this whole area is speculative). First, we assume that the Elohistic Psalter developed sometime before or soon after the fall of the northern kingdom (722 BC), to represent the theological interests of Israel, thus the preference for the generic *'elohim*. Second, the larger Psalter (Books 2 and beyond) developed under Judean influences during the exile and postexile, this expansion coming at a time when the hopes of the reunion of the two kingdoms, Israel and Judah, and the restoration of the Davidic dynasty were still part of the political platform (see Jer. 3:11–20; Ezek. 37:15–28). Even the strategic placement of *YHWH* within these psalms, at least in some instances, may be a feature of that editorial process. This helps to explain not only the use of the generic *'elohim*, which was both political and theological, but also the strong Davidic interest of the Elohistic Psalter (see sidebar "The Editing of Book 2" in the unit on Ps. 70).

[a] For these figures, see Goulder, *Sons of Korah*, 4–5.
[b] See Bullock, *Encountering*, 74, for an explanation of the "Davidic" nature of Psalm 86.

of eleven Asaph psalms (Pss. 73–83), also a Levitical collection (see 1 Chron. 25), giving the Levitical stamp to Book 3 as well. Even with the stamp of the Davidic seal

on Book 2 ("This concludes the prayers of David son of Jesse," Ps. 72:20),[4] the Elohistic collection of psalms in Books 2 and 3 still, with the positioning of the Korah and Asaph psalms,[5] gives the impression of the unmistakable Levitical seal. We might suggest that, by the time Books 2 and 3 were edited, it was quite obvious that the psalmic material belonged to the sanctuary and thus to the Levites who composed its musical staff, and such an editing as we see in Books 2 and 3 was both the Levitical seal of approval and the Levitical contribution. The question of why *'elohim* is overwhelmingly used as the divine name in this section of the Psalter has been much discussed (see the sidebar). Although the substitution of *'adonay* for the divine name *YHWH* was a practice that developed, probably a bit later, in Judaism, we may have here an early development in this direction. The preference for *'elohim* over *YHWH* to protect the sacredness of the covenant name may have an early history in the preexilic age.

Outline/Structure

The refrain, with slight deviations, divides these two psalms into three strophes:

Strophe 1: Lament (42:1–4)
Refrain: Hope (42:5)
Strophe 2: Lament (42:6–10)
Refrain: Hope (42:11)
Strophe 3: Prayer for vindication (43:1–4)
Refrain: Hope (43:5)

Historical and Cultural Background

The attribution of the psalms to the "sons of Korah" follows a long history of this family in the Jerusalem sanctuary. Korah was the grandson of Kohath, one of the three sons of Levi (1 Chron. 6:22). Korah himself was a victim of God's wrath that resulted from his rebellion against Moses and Aaron (Num. 16), but his sons were spared (Num. 26:11). They are an example that the sins of the fathers were not always visited on the next generation, for in David's time the house of Korah was one of the most famous families of the Levitical house of the Kohathites, with some of them, at least, supporting David's claim to the throne (1 Chron. 12:6). In David's revision of the temple service, the Korahites retained their role as gatekeepers of the temple, along with the family of Merari (1 Chron. 26:1–19). According to the Chronicler, they even had a place in the postexilic temple as gatekeepers, among other functions (1 Chron. 9:19, 31–32).

Interpretive Insights

Title A maskil *of the Sons of Korah.* The enigmatic term *maskil* (a Hiphil participle of the verb *skl*) occurs in the headings of thirteen psalms (Pss. 32; 42; 44; 45; 52; 53; 54; 55; 74; 78; 88; 89; 142).[6] It occurs internally in Psalm 14:2/53:2, where it means "to act wisely" (NIV: "understand"). The other internal occurrence is 47:7, where it designates, as in the thirteen headings above, a type of psalm. Kraus proposes that, in view of its use as a type of psalm, and based on 2 Chronicles 30:22, which describes Levitical activity with this word, it may mean "well-crafted songs."[7] This of course raises the question whether they were well-crafted musically or stylistically, or both. I suspect both. For the reference to the "sons of Korah," see "Historical and Cultural Background."

42:1 *As the deer pants for streams of water.* The verb "pants" also occurs in Joel 1:20, where the nuance is to stretch the head in a certain direction.[8] In 42:1 the impulse for relationship with God is found in the psalmist ("so my soul pants for you"), while in 43:3 the imagery changes, and the impulse is with God. There the suppliant prays that God might send forth his light and truth (NIV: "your faithful care") and lead him to the house of God. Both are valid ways of talking about our longing for God, and both have their source in God, whose loving character creates the spiritual thirst.

my God. The occurrence of the divine name Elohim twelve times, in comparison to only one appearance of the covenant name Yahweh, alerts the reader to the change in presentation but not theology that occurs in Books 2 and 3 (see "Historical and Cultural Background"). This is especially noticeable in light of the frequent use of the covenant name in Book 1, and particularly the six occurrences of the covenant name in the neighboring Psalm 41, with only one occurrence of Elohim, a virtual reversal of pattern. As we have suggested above, this is more a liturgical accommodation than a theological change, although it may also have political implications.

42:2 *My soul thirsts . . . when can I go and meet with God?* See Psalm 63:1, where the verb "thirst" is also used metaphorically for the human longing for God. "When can I go and meet with God" is literally, "When can I go and appear before [or "see"] God?" The suppliant is longing for the sanctuary. The expression "appear before God / the LORD" occurs in Exodus 23:17 and 34:23 in the sense of appearing in the sanctuary. It is the Niphal form of the verb "to see," whereas the Syriac and Targum boldly have "see" rather than "appear." Perhaps the Niphal form, a bit more indirect (literally a passive verb), is intended to avoid the direct sense of "seeing" God, which, according to Exodus 33:20, would mean death. Here, however, it is in a spiritual sense, or a liturgical sense, that the psalmist sees God, but it still reflects the ultimate spiritual gravity of seeing God. Amid his hopelessness, the psalmist's faith and confidence produce the hopefulness that this reality will eventually materialize, and he affirms this hope three times (42:5, 11; 43:5). That indeed is the heart of the psalm, highlighted by the refrain.

42:3 *My tears have been my food day and night . . . "Where is your God?"* The terms of the psalmist's longing are "tears" and "day and night," one indicating the emotional depth of his longing and the other the extent of it in time. The concluding question is a summary of the taunting words of the psalmist's enemies who deride him because he cannot go to the temple, obviously in view of their knowledge that he longs so deeply to do so. See also Psalm 115:2.

42:4 *These things I remember . . . how I used to go to the house of God.* The phrase "these things" connected to the verb "remember" implies that he is thinking about the past joys of pilgrimages (so NIV's punctuation).

42:5 *Why, my soul, are you downcast? . . . I will yet praise him, my Savior and my God.* This refrain occurs for the first time here and is repeated almost verbatim in 42:11 and 43:5. The psalmist's inner struggle of faith is intense, and he does not allow it to be recast by his depressed spirit.[9]

42:6 *heights of Hermon—from Mount Mizar.* The noun "Hermon" is plural (lit.,

"Hermonites," hence the NIV rendering "*heights of* Hermon"), which is perhaps a textual error. "Mount Mizar" means "little mountain," which some would take as a gentle jibe, in view of Mount Zion, which was considered to be the high point of the whole land, but in theological importance only, since Mount Hermon was a much higher elevation. Mount Mizar has never been identified. Perhaps it was one of the peaks of Hermon.

42:7 *Deep calls to deep in the roar of your waterfalls.* These "waterfalls" produce wafts of roaring waves that make each wave seem to summon the next. Such falls can be found near the sources of the Jordan River, south of Hermon.

42:8 *By day the* LORD *directs his love.* The Hebrew reads, "Yahweh commands his love [*hesed*]," Yahweh being the Master and "love" being his servant. Note the personification of "light" and "faithfulness" (NIV: "faithful care") in 43:3.

42:10 *My bones suffer mortal agony as my foes taunt me.* It is the taunting question, issued over and over by his "foes," that causes the "crushing" (lit., "killing"; see HCSB; cf. Exod. 20:13, same root) agony in his soul, so similar to the comparable agony in his bones.

43:1 *plead my cause against an unfaithful nation. Rescue me from those who are deceitful and wicked.* The "deceitful" and the "wicked" are evidently the same "foes" of 42:10, and corporately, the "unfaithful nation" of 43:1. The term "unfaithful [*lo'-hasid*] nation" could very well be a reference to Israel, the northern kingdom, in whose territory the psalmist now is confined. Since the adjective *hasid* ("faithful") is a derivative of the key covenant term

The roar of a waterfall can be heard near Banias in northern Israel. Its waters are one of the sources of the Jordan River.

hesed, the description here is reminiscent of Hosea's description of Israel as a land of *'en-hesed* ("no love," Hosea 4:1).

43:3 *Send me your light and your faithful care.* "Light" and "truth" (*'emet*; NIV: "faithful care") are personified, as is also "love" (*hesed*) in 42:8. The NIV's "faithful care" obscures the fact that the psalmist mentions two distinct character traits of God, "light and truth," that become his emissaries of grace. See "Teaching the Text."

43:4 *Then I will go to the altar of God, to God, my joy and delight . . . O God, my God.* This is the goal of his longing, the moment of return to the temple, where he experiences the God of his greatest joy (lit., "God of the joy of my delight"; ESV, "God my exceeding joy"). The psalmist calls the deity "God, my God," in place of "Lord, my God" (*YHWH 'elohay*; e.g., 7:1, 3), which we would expect to find in the non-Elohistic psalms.[10]

43:5 *I will yet praise him.* The psalmist, for the third time, expresses his hope that he will yet worship in the sanctuary in Jerusalem.

Theological Insights

There is a pattern of prayer in Psalms 42 and 43 that is characteristic of the psalms of lament. The psalmist moves from complaint to confidence, a movement powered by faith and guided by hope. His circumstances, foreign to his former way of life (42:4), have been exacerbated by the mockery of his compatriots, enhancing the agony of his soul. Yet he cannot permit the scornful atmosphere of the alien circumstances to triumph over the power of faith that someday, not merely in memory but in reality, he will return to the sanctuary and experience the intimate presence of God (42:5, 11; 43:5). It is so easy for circumstances to tower over faith, a fact that the writer to the Hebrews recognizes (Heb. 11); yet faith by its very nature is stronger than circumstances. And that is a truth the psalmist has to keep reminding himself of in the refrain. Nor does it happen all of a sudden, but, as Delitzsch remarks, in the third stanza (43:1–5) "resignation and hope are rendered complete by the addition of confident prayer."[11] To consider resignation and hope as common links in the same chain as confident prayer may seem bold, but they belong there in the spiritual reality of saints who have struggled with God and their own inner consciences and have found their way through the maze of faith to the open presence of God.

The personification of "light" and "truth" (see comments on 43:3) as the psalmist's guides to the sanctuary in Jerusalem remind us of the same phenomenon in Psalm 23:6, where "goodness" and "mercy" (or "love"; *hesed*) gently pursue David into the sanctuary of God. Here "light" and "truth" are the vanguard; there in Psalm 23 "goodness" and "mercy" are the rearguard (cf. Isa. 52:12; see "Teaching the Text"). Prior to this wonderfully guided pilgrimage as formed in the eyes of faith, we have already seen God "command" his love (*hesed*), like a master his servant (42:8). So God is totally in control of the pilgrim's circumstances, making his hope secure.

The psalmist, presently in the region of Mount Hermon rather than Mount Zion, thinks of that moment when he will again "go to the altar of God" (43:3), and neither the mockery of his enemies nor the surroundings of an "unfaithful nation" (43:1) can repress the joy that begins to swell up in his soul. And its source is the God whom he longs to meet, "God, my joy and my delight" (43:4). This image draws him all the more toward the sanctuary. Over against the lamentation, the anger, and the deep anguish of the psalmists' souls runs a joy that is unspeakable, a joy whose fullness is only experienced in the presence of God (Ps. 16:11).

Teaching the Text

We can begin a lesson or sermon on these two psalms by observing that the idea of faith as a *journey* is basic to understanding these twin psalms. While the supplicant is somewhere in northern Galilee, he is prevented from making his journey to worship in the Jerusalem temple. His yearning to make that journey is as severe as the thirsty deer's panting for streams of water (42:1). To exacerbate the restrictive circumstances, the people he lives with have mocked him for his faith in God (42:3b).

We should also observe that in this difficult and depressive situation, our psalmist prays that God may send his "light" and "truth" (NIV: "faithful care") to conduct him to the house of God (43:3). This is a personification of these divine attributes, unseen but

nevertheless very real (see "Illustrating the Text" for the ideas of vanguard and rearguard). If we want to make a connection to the incarnation of God in Christ, we may point out that Christ is not a personification of light and truth but their incarnation, the perfect Guide (John 8:12; 14:6).

To connect with the tone of the psalm, we should note that the psalmist calls God his "joy" and "delight" (43:4), quite an elevated description for one who is depressed, deprived, and derided. This is a strong point, and one that can further advance our New Testament appeal, particularly if we look at the message of Hebrews 12:1–3, where the saints of the ages are gathered in the grandstands of history to watch us as we take up their torch and begin to run our stage of the race, looking not to the right or left but to Jesus, who is our Guide.

If we would like to extend the lesson and expand on the imagery of the vanguard, we can appeal to Psalm 23:6 to find the imagery of "goodness and mercy" pursuing us all the way to the house of God, not so much as guides, but as one commentator remarked, as "collie dogs,"[12] making sure we get home (see "Teaching the Text" in the unit on Ps. 23). They are again personifications, acting as the rearguard rather than the vanguard. Isaiah puts the two together and describes the Lord as Israel's vanguard and rearguard leading Israel home from exile (Isa. 52:12).

Illustrating the Text

Guarding the flanks

History: The Scriptures speak of divinely appointed guides that lead and pursue believers to the house of God (Ps. 43:3; see "Teaching the Text"). James S. Stewart, chaplain to the queen in Scotland (1952–66), related this story in a sermon called "Vanguard and Rearguard." Before Napoleon began his retreat from Moscow to return to Paris in 1812, he appointed Marshal Ney to serve as his rearguard and protect his decimated flanks from the Russian army at any cost. One day, after Napoleon's army had safely reached Paris, some officers heard a knock at the door while they were playing cards in their quarters. When they opened the door,

> there stood before them the most disheveled figure they had ever seen, old and bent and emaciated, his clothing tattered, his hands trembling and lines of terrible suffering carved deep into his features. "Who are you?" they cried, startled. But suddenly, to one of them, there came a flash of recognition. "Why," he exclaimed, springing to his feet, "it's the Marshal! It's Marshal Ney!" And the others rose and saluted. "Tell us, Marshal," they said, when they had conquered their astonishment, "tell us—for we have been wondering—where is the rearguard?" And the bent, broken figure squared his shoulders a moment, and looked them in the face: "Sirs," he said, "I am the rearguard!" And it was a fact. He alone had seen it through.

Dr. Stewart's application continues:

> Who is this that cometh from Edom, with dyed garments from Bozrah, this that is red in His apparel, His garments stained in blood; this whose visage is marred more than any man, and His form more

than the sons of men; this from whose head and hands and feet sorrow and love flow mingled down? This is the Christ. "*I am* the rearguard," says Jesus.[13]

A hunger for God

Biography: Frank Laubach. There have been many Christians in history who have earnestly sought the Lord, reminiscent of the psalmist in 42:1–2. One example is Frank Laubach (1884–1970), who served for many years as a missionary to the Philippines. It is estimated that through his efforts one-half of the ninety thousand people who lived in the region in which he ministered learned to read and write. Laubach sought not only to educate and plant churches but also to live each moment with a sense of God's presence. He hungered and thirsted for God. In *Letters from a Modern Mystic*, letters written by Laubach while he was in the Philippines, he says, "There has been a succession of marvelous experiences of the friendship of God. I resolved that I would succeed better this year with my experiment of filling every minute full of the thought of God than I succeeded last year."[14]

"As the deer pants for streams of water, so my soul pants for you, my God" (42:1). This ibex finds refreshment at a stream.

"For Your Sake We Face Death . . . as Sheep to Be Slaughtered"

Big Idea *Sometimes when we have been faithful to God and bad things still happen to us, the best and only explanation is that it is for God's sake.*

Understanding the Text

Psalm 44 is a community lament that follows some national defeat of Israel's army (44:9), even though the psalmist, speaking on behalf of the king, cannot understand why this has happened, since Israel has not forgotten God or "been false" to his covenant (44:17).

The Text in Context

Psalms 42–43 celebrate the psalmist's hope that he, isolated and dejected in a foreign land, will someday worship in the Jerusalem sanctuary again. Psalm 44 is an expression of theological—not geographical—isolation. God's past act of giving the land of Canaan to Israel is clear in the psalmist's mind, but his understanding of why God has not kept his covenant promise and secured faithful Israel on their land lags behind his historical knowledge. Theologically he is still isolated from the "land" of understanding God's ways. But he is not angry, and he too, like the previous singer of Israel, trusts the God who

sometimes acts unapologetically for his own sake (44:22) and whose "unfailing love" is the source of and the empowerment for the future (44:26).

In Romans 8:36, Paul quotes Psalm 44:22 and applies it to the suffering of the first-century church, "not with the despair of the 'more than defeated' . . . , but the conviction that 'in all these things we are more than conquerors through him who loved us.'"[1] It is the last word in the psalm, "unfailing love" (*hesed*), that provides the reality check.[2]

The Greek text (LXX) that Paul used even renders the final word of the Hebrew psalm ("your unfailing love") as "for the sake of your name," evidently picking up on the phrase in 44:22 to reinforce the concept. Although the apostle does not include that final verse, one wonders if his mind recalled the final word of the Hebrew psalm alongside the Greek, which moved him to comment: "No, in all these things we are more than conquerors through him *who loved us*" (Rom. 8:37).

Outline/Structure

In terms of subject matter, Psalm 44 falls into two main sections: the review of God's gift of the land of Canaan (44:1–3), and the lament that God has failed to honor the people's faithfulness (44:4–26). Another way to outline the psalm is to listen to its voices:

Part 1 Congregation's voice (choir) reviewing God's gift of Canaan (44:1–3)

Part 2 Lament about God's failure to honor Israel's faithfulness (44:4–26)

  a. Psalmist's voice confessing God's past faithfulness (44:4)

  b. Congregation's voice confessing God's past faithfulness (44:5)

  c. Psalmist's voice disavowing victory through weapons (44:6)

  d. Congregation's voice confessing God's affirming victory through God's power (44:7–8)

  e. Congregation's voice lamenting defeat in battle despite God's past faithfulness (44:9–14)

  f. Psalmist's voice lamenting defeat (44:15–16)

  g. Congregation's voice lamenting humiliating defeat despite their innocence (44:17–22)

  h. Congregation's voice petitioning the Lord to help them (44:23–24)

  i. Congregation's final lament (44:25)

  j. Congregation's final plea for help (44:26)

Historical and Cultural Background

Attempts to date this psalm have run the wide gamut of history, all the way from the time of David (Delitzsch),[3] to the time of Jehoshaphat, to the Maccabean period (Calvin).[4] More cautious proposals put the psalm simply in the preexilic era (Kidner, A. A. Anderson).[5] Notwithstanding Craigie's understandable objections to the historical connection in 2 Chronicles 20,[6] which relates the impending threat by the Moabites and Ammonites during Jehoshaphat's reign (870–848 BC), the psalm

It was God who fought the battles for Israel, keeping his promise to give the land promised to Abraham to his descendants. In Joshua 6:2, the Lord says, "See, I have delivered Jericho into your hands." The first battle as Israel entered Canaan was at Jericho. An aerial view of the remains of that ancient city is shown here.

in 2 Chronicles 20:6–12 nevertheless provides a life setting for Psalm 44, even if it does not provide a historical one. It even includes the picture of a prophetic oracle to instruct King Jehoshaphat, a picture of the praise of God led by the Kohathites and Korahites, and the king's assignment of "men to sing to the LORD and to praise him for the splendor of his holiness as they went out at the head of the army" (2 Chron. 20:21). The latter feature is missing from our psalm, but the activity of the Levitical singers is attested, and the dynamics of the threatening situation are laid out.

Interpretive Insights

Title *Of the Sons of Korah. A maskil.* See the comments on the title for Psalms 42–43.

44:1 *We have heard it . . . O God; our ancestors have told us what you did.* The psalm begins by invoking God (cf. ESV). The NIV unfortunately shifts the direct address to the end of the sentence and thus weakens both a character trait of the Elohistic Psalter and the prayerful appeal to God that is the heart of the psalm. Based on 44:17–22, Israel has not only heard but also been faithful to the covenant. See also Psalm 78:3.

44:2 *With your hand you drove out the nations . . . you crushed the peoples and made our ancestors flourish.* God's promise to Moses uses the same verb "drive out" (Hiphil of *yrsh*) to describe the dispossession of the Canaanites (Exod. 34:24). In place of "the nations," God "planted our ancestors" (Joshua and the Israelites who possessed the land). The imagery is that of planting a tree or vine (Ps. 80:8; Isa. 5:3). The verb "crushed" (*tara'*) is taken by some

to be an imperfect of the verb "to do evil" (*r'*), but Hakham takes it to mean "crush" and cites the Targum, which renders it *tabbarta*, "you broke."[7] The metaphor is that of breaking down trees and planting them (Jer. 11:16; Amos 2:9).

44:3 *It was not by their sword . . . it was your right hand, your arm, and the light of your face.* The NIV omits the Hebrew conjunction *ki* at the beginning of the verse, which means "for/because," explaining the statement in the prior verse.[8] The psalmist is not denying that the Israelites used weapons to defeat the Canaanites but is saying that the Lord, not their weaponry, made them victorious. God's "right hand" and "arm" are used synonymously for his power (Exod. 15:6, 16; Isa. 51:9–10). The mention of God's "face" alludes to his blessing (see the priestly benediction, Num. 6:24–26).

44:4 *You are my King and my God, who decrees victories for Jacob.* The idea of God as King is frequent in the Psalter, especially the psalms of the heavenly King (Pss. 47; 93; 95–99). The Hebrew has "God," whereas the Greek (LXX) and Syriac have "my God," which the NIV follows.

44:5 *Through you we push back our enemies; through your name we trample our foes.* The word translated "push back" occurs in poetic sections of the Bible (e.g., Deut. 33:17 [NIV: "gore"]) in reference to smiting Israel's enemies.[9] The verb "trample" (*bus*) is used of trampling Israel's enemies (e.g., Isa. 63:6). The verbs are Hebrew imperfect, suggesting a review of Israel's past practices: "Through your name we would trample our enemies." The imagery is that of an ox that gores its way forward as it also tramples those in its path.

The psalmist declares that it is the Lord who brings victory, not the swords of the warriors. Shown here are some examples of fifteenth- to fourteenth-century BC bronze swords and daggers from Akko and Tell el-Aijul in Palestine.

44:6 *I put no trust in my bow, my sword.* Literally, "Indeed [*ki*], I do not trust in my bow" (author's trans.). The NIV omits the first word, *ki*, "indeed"; this word brings an emphasis to the fact that the speaker does not trust his bow. The bow was usually made of wood or an animal's horn. The sword was the most common weapon of ancient Israel and made of bronze or iron; most likely this is the short, straight-bladed sword.[10] Compare Psalms 20:7; 33:16.

44:9 *But now you have rejected and humbled us.* Up through 44:8, the poem sounds like a victory celebration, but with verse 9 the present and perplexing reality sets in, "but now"—that is, the present situation defies our understanding of what we know about God from the past. Psalm 44:9

can also be found in Psalm 60:10, with some variations.

44:10 *our adversaries have plundered us.* This detail gives us the picture of defeat, since plundering followed defeat.

44:11 *You gave us up to be devoured like sheep and have scattered us among the nations.* The picture of defenseless sheep is one that ought to elicit compassion (compare with 2 Sam. 12:1–6). The description of scattering among the nations is borrowed from Leviticus 26:33, where the Lord informs Israel of the consequences of disobedience to the covenant.

44:12 *gaining nothing from their sale.* This idea appears in the Song of Moses (Deut. 32:30), describing a situation when Yahweh had switched to Israel's enemies' side as a result of Israel's sin. One of Israel's enemies could not chase a thousand, and two, ten thousand, unless Yahweh had shifted his support to the enemy. Here God is acting like he is on the enemy's side (see Isa. 50:1). Isaiah adapts the expression to speak of redemption: "You were sold for nothing, and without money you will be redeemed" (Isa. 52:3).

44:13 *the scorn and derision of those around us.* The noun translated "derision" occurs in verbal form in the story of the children mocking ("jeering") the prophet Elisha (2 Kings 2:23).

44:15–16 *and my face is covered with shame at the taunts of those who reproach and revile me.* For the first part, see Psalm 69:7. Sennacherib's messengers "reviled" Judah in a loud voice, for which Isaiah rebuked them (Isa. 37:23; NIV: "blasphemed").

44:17 *All this came upon us, though . . . we had not been false to your covenant.*

According to the Torah, a breach of the covenant would result in punishment (Deut. 4:25–31; 6:13–15; 8:19–20), but obviously they were unaware of any such breach. Kidner comments: "In the heart-searching of verses 17–22, the important fact begins to emerge that disaster is one thing, and disgrace quite another. The defeats which seemed to prove God's withdrawal in wrath, now suggest only His refusal to be hurried (23ff.) or to do what everyone has expected of Him. The psalm is exploring the baffling fluctuations that have their counterpart in Christian history: periods of blessing and barrenness, advance and retreat, which may correspond to no apparent changes of men's loyalty or methods."[11]

44:18 *Our hearts had not turned back.* Now the psalmist uncovers another layer of Israel's loyalty, their thoughts. Even there ("our hearts"), they have not been unfaithful. Compare Exodus 20:17, the tenth commandment, which governs the mind.

44:19 *But you crushed us and made us a haunt for jackals; you covered us over with deep darkness.* The sense is that they have not been unfaithful "even though" (*ki*, which the NIV omits), God has crushed them.[12] On "deep darkness" (*tsalmawet*), see the comments on Psalm 23:4.

44:20 *If we had forgotten the name of our God or spread out our hands to a foreign god.* This is the form of an oath: "I swear that we have not forgotten the name of our God." The hands of the worshiper were spread out toward the deity (Exod. 9:29, 33; Pss. 88:9; 143:6; Isa. 1:15), toward the temple (1 Kings 8:38; Ps. 28:2), or toward heaven (1 Kings 8:22, 54).[13]

44:21 *since he knows the secrets of the heart.* Dahood proposes "the dark corners of the heart," deriving the noun "secrets" from the root *'lm*, "to be dark."[14] Compare Job 28:11. See Goldingay's statement on God's "secrets."[15]

44:22 *Yet for your sake we face death all day long.* See "Theological Insights."

44:23 *Awake, Lord!* The psalmist refers to God by the substitute name for Yahweh (*'adonay*). Note that the covenant name Yahweh does not occur in the psalm at all, perhaps because God's absence as Israel's helper is so prevalent in the psalm as not to merit the use of the name of Israel's God. Even so, the presence of Israel's Lord hovers over the prayer and gives boldness to the

"We are brought down to the dust; our bodies cling to the ground" (44:25) is an image of a defeated people face down before the conquering power. In this relief from one of the bronze bands of the Balawat Gates, local officials show their submission to Shalmaneser III during his expedition to the source of the Tigris in 853 BC by kneeling and kissing the ground before his feet.

final petition "because of your unfailing love" (*hesed*). This is an anthropomorphic statement, especially since Psalm 121:4 says the Lord never sleeps. For that reason, the second-century BC high priest John Hyrcanus gave the Levites orders not to use this verse (*b. Sotah* 48a).

44:25 *our bodies cling to the ground.* Literally, "our belly clings to the ground."

44:26 *Rise up and help us.* The long form of the imperative verb translated as "help" may be a poetic form of the verb[16] or may be used to make the verb more emphatic. Numbers 10:35 uses the verb "rise up" in relation to taking up the ark to move it to another place (see "Teaching the Text" in the unit on Pss. 9–10). The psalmist may be alluding to that verse here. The psalm ends with the key word of the covenant relationship, "your unfailing love [*hesed*]." It is in the covenant that they have lost their perspective, and it is in that relationship that it has to be recovered.

Theological Insights

Job, before his theological crisis, could say only, "My ears had heard of you," but after the voice of God out of the whirlwind, he could say, "Now my eyes have seen you" (Job 42:5). In comparison, our psalmist can say only, "We have heard it with our ears" (Ps. 44:1), but his spiritual reserves are deposited in the final word of the psalm, the "unfailing love" of God (44:26).[17] In fact, despite the daunting circumstances that have left much unexplained, the suppliant resorts to the mystery of God, expressed in one simple phrase, "for your sake" (44:22). This phrase takes a slightly different form than the phrase popularized by the prophets, especially Ezekiel,

"for the sake of my name" (Ezek. 20 and 36). This short phrase sums up God's activity on his people's behalf, the actions he will take to rehabilitate his name among a languishing people who have, by their actions and humiliated condition, profaned his name.[18] Our psalmist's faith and that of other psalmists join the prophets in declaring that God acts "for his own sake."[19] This faith has come in our present psalm to the brink of disaster, when the psalmist throws himself on this small phrase with a huge meaning, "for your sake." Kidner aptly comments: "This psalm is perhaps the clearest example of a search for some other cause of national disaster than guilt and punishment. It comes within sight of an answer at the point of its greatest perplexity: 'Nay *for thy sake* we are slain.'"[20] Sometimes this is the only and, if we trust the eyes of faith, the best answer we can give.

Teaching the Text

Building on our statement in "Theological Insights," it is possible to structure a sermon/lesson around one phrase in this psalm, "for your sake" (44:22a), and still be faithful to the meaning of virtually the whole psalm. This phrase, here composed simply of a preposition and its object (God), carries the meaning of "in your own interest." Israel has been defeated in battle, for no moral infractions of their own, and now they face death like innocent "sheep to be slaughtered" (44:22b).

According to Ezekiel, God rehabilitates his profaned name, profaned by the actions and the condition of his people in exile. He does so by acting on behalf of his people, doing what they cannot do. In Ezekiel 20 and 36, God reminds Israel that he has always acted for the sake of his own name, even when the visible circumstances demand another strategy. God's actions in history have always been directed, unapologetically, toward himself, *for his own sake*, and the prophets and psalmists know that in God's self-directed course of action can be found the best that Israel can ever hope for or imagine. The mystery is bundled up, not in the "secrets" of Israel's heart (44:21), which God knows so well, but in God's unfailing love (44:26). Yet even when the phrase "for your sake" is resolved in the chord of "your unfailing love," the mystery still remains, and we trust not in the mystery but in God's "unfailing love," which is God's greatest revelation and his greatest mystery.

But what does this mean in the real world? When God acts for his own sake (not for ours), how does that benefit us, if at all? In this second phase of the sermon/lesson, we can try to resolve the mystery, as a minor chord is resolved in a major. In Psalm 44 God listens to Israel speak, but he himself never speaks at all. He just acts. That is so typical of our own life experience. We see God's actions that often defy reason and resist explanation. Yet Psalm 44 lays out a way of

resolving the mystery: we interpret God's actions in terms of his "unfailing love." We sometimes are acting in our children's best interests when it appears to them that it is for *our own sake*, not theirs. Similarly, when every other picture of God fails, we have to throw ourselves on God's unfailing love, for "God is love" (1 John 4:8). When we cannot understand what is happening in our lives, and why, especially when it does not seem to be related to moral failure, as with Israel (44:17–18), we can see a parallel between Israel's dilemma and ours.

We may conclude with Paul's use of this psalm in Romans, when he asks: "Who shall separate us from the love of Christ?" He answers his question by quoting Psalm 44:22, recognizing that the psalmist has resolved the mystery of why we suffer "as sheep to be slaughtered" when we have done nothing wrong: it is to make us conquerors through "him who loved us" (Rom. 8:35–37). When we do not understand God's actions in our world and cannot figure out God's work in our own lives, we throw ourselves on the "unfailing love" of God "that is in Christ Jesus our Lord," from which nothing in all creation can separate us (Rom. 8:39).

Illustrating the Text

The King and kingdom citizens

Everyday Life: The image of the Lord as King is one of the most common pictures of God in the Psalms. And the psalmist's confession "You are my King" (44:4) is an acknowledgment

The Israelites could not understand why they were oppressed because they had not forgotten the name of their God or spread out their hands to a foreign god (44:20). This bronze figurine shows a man with his hands spread out in worship (Egypt, 1186–664 BC).

that he is one of the citizens of the kingdom. There are, of course, numerous degrees of citizenship, and we may employ some analogies from the American experience. Some citizens new to the kingdom are like new immigrants, still uncomfortable in the new country and speaking the language of the old country. There are others who represent a different stage, feeling more at home in the new country and even speaking its language, but with the accent of the old country. Still another degree is that of the citizens who are conscious of their ethnic origin but are totally acclimated to the new country and the new language—at home, no less. Our psalmist, or the community—both speak—would likely belong in this last group, for they have "not turned back" and have not strayed from the King's path (44:18).[21]

Remember whose daughter or son you are.

Personal Stories: I had a wonderful high school English teacher who was the daughter of a Methodist pastor. She related to our class that when she was young and would go out at night, her mother would say, "Now, Frances, remember whose daughter you are." She was to be on her best behavior for the sake of her father's and mother's reputation. Some young people might resent that and think their parents are just thinking about themselves. But if their parents are thinking about their own moral integrity, to which the children should comply, they are acting in the best interest of their children as well as themselves. If we would remember whose daughter or son we are, and live by that reputation, we would be more like God and be better persons because of it. "Be holy, because I, the LORD your God, am holy" (Lev. 19:2).

A gift greater than fairness

Bible: The sentiments shared by the psalmist in Psalm 44 are similar to those shared by Habakkuk as the prophet wrestles with God's fairness. The matter at issue for Habakkuk is how God can use a godless nation like Babylon to bring discipline on Judah, a more righteous nation. And as the prophet continues to wrestle with his thoughts, something incredible happens. At the end of his book, Habakkuk concludes with these words:

> Though the fig tree does not bud
>   and there are no grapes on the vines,
> though the olive crop fails
>   and the fields produce no food,
> though there are no sheep in the pen
>   and no cattle in the stalls,
> yet I will rejoice in the LORD,
>   I will be joyful in God my Savior.
> The Sovereign LORD is my strength;
>   he makes my feet like the feet of a deer,
>   he enables me to tread on the heights. (Hab. 3:17–19)

Use Habakkuk as a way to encourage those listeners who can relate to the struggle of the prophet and the psalmist.

"Ride Forth Victoriously in the Cause of Truth, Humility and Justice"

Big Idea *Great value is put on leaders who, by their own lives, exemplify the virtues of truth, humility, and justice.*

Understanding the Text

Psalm 45 belongs to the genre of royal psalms, which celebrate the king and his reign, not as a lone-standing king, but as a stand-in for Yahweh as king. It is better to think of these psalms as constituting two subgenres, psalms of the heavenly King, which celebrate Yahweh as king, providing the model for all kingship, and psalms of the earthly king, which shine the spotlight on Yahweh's representative in this world (see the sidebar). The latter, according to the form critics, were performed either in the sanctuary or in the royal palace. Psalm 45 falls into this category and was most likely performed, perhaps even by its author, in the palace on the occasion of the royal wedding (45:1). At the same time, it is reflective of the heavenly King as the model and defender of truth and justice (45:4, 6–7).

The Text in Context

It is tempting to look for information and clues to what brought Psalms 44 and 45 into next-door proximity, but they are difficult to find. Perhaps the best we

Psalm 45 was composed for and perhaps performed in the wedding celebration of the king and his beautiful foreign bride, adorned in "gold of Ophir" (45:9). This eighth-century ostracon, which mentions the "gold of Ophir," was found at Tel Qasile near Tel Aviv. The location of Ophir is debated, but it was known for very high quality gold.

can do is to recognize the general themes of the two psalms. Psalm 44 is a poem spoken by the king, in which he acknowledges that he trusts not in his weaponry but in God (44:6–8), despite the fact that he has suffered defeat and humiliation. This downturn of events falls outside the pale of understanding, because Israel has been faithful to the covenant (44:17–21). With this conundrum unresolved, the king throws himself on the mystery of God's actions in history, which God sometimes does for his own name's sake, leaving his people to trust him in the midst of the mystery.

The mystery has disappeared when we come to Psalm 45, and the scene is an event that grips the heart of a nation, the marriage of its king to a foreign bride, whose beauty complements the handsomeness of the king. Yet there is a kinship between these two psalms that, intentional or not, calls the reader to listen carefully to these two monarchs. The covenant loyalty of the monarch of Psalm 44, that he trusts no weaponry apart from God's power to save, connects to the ideal monarch of Psalm 45, who understands the true meaning of being a king. He exists for the sake of truth and justice (45:4). Thus if we are looking for a portrait of the ideal king, we find it here in the companionship of these two psalms. Perhaps that justifies the scribe's addressing the king as "god" (see comments on 45:6), since he comes close to the character of God.

Kidner calls this psalm a "wedding benediction," taking his cue from the title, "a love song" (NIV: "a wedding song"), and relates it to the Song of Songs,[1] which is a very different genre, but he finds a close comparison to Psalm 45 in the procession of Song of Songs 3:6–11.[2]

Key Themes of Psalm 45

- This psalm is a chapter in the plan book for God's future kingdom.
- Truth, humility, and justice are hallmarks of kingdom leaders.

Psalms of the Earthly King

In the Psalms we have two kingships, that of Yahweh and that of Israel's king, and the psalms that celebrate these kingships are called *royal psalms*; but we can distinguish two subgenres here, the psalms of the heavenly King and the psalms of the earthly king. As is often done, we could treat them together because they share the concept of "kingship," but for practical purposes we will deal only with psalms of the earthly king here, since that is the subgenre of Psalm 45. See the sidebar "The LORD Reigns: Psalms of the Heavenly King" in the unit on Psalm 93.

Psalms of the earthly king (1) refer to the "king"; (2) use the term "anointed" (*mashiah*, messiah); (3) and refer to David by name, although all of these features do not characterize every such psalm. We will consider the following psalms in this category: Psalms 2; 18; 20; 21; 45; 72; 89; 101; 110; 132; and 144.

Of these eleven psalms, seven of them use the term "king" (2; 18; 20; 21; 45; 72; 89); six refer to the "anointed" (2; 18; 20; 89; 132; Ps. 45 uses the verb); eight refer to David by name, four of these in the title or colophon (18; 89; 132; 144; in title or colophon: 20; 21; 101; 110).

Outline/Structure

In effect we hear only one voice in the psalm, the voice of the poet. God never speaks, nor does the king or the queen. But the recipients of this ode are the criteria that sort out the structure for us. They are the scribal poet, the king, and the queen, giving us the following structure:

1. Title / the poet's signature (45:1)
2. Praise of the royal groom/king (45:2–9)
3. Praise of the royal bride/queen (45:10–15)

4. Promise of the king's progeny (45:16)
5. The poet's purpose / the poet's signature (45:17)

Historical and Cultural Background

As we have observed above, this psalm, by its own claim, is recited on the occasion of the king's wedding to a foreign princess. Since Solomon capitalized on the practice of diplomatic marriages, it was only natural to identify him as the unnamed king, and the queen as the princess of Egypt who became his bride (1 Kings 3:1; 9:16). However, since the psalm represents this king as a military figure (45:4), it does not quite match up with Solomon as a "man of peace," as he is called in 1 Chronicles 22:9.³ There is the possibility, of course, that our scribe was giving a full portrait of the king and that the reference to military exploits, real or ideal, was necessary to complete the picture. Other possibilities are that the bride is some unknown princess of Tyre, since this city is mentioned as bringing a gift to the royal couple (45:12), and Jehoram's marriage to Athaliah, the daughter of Ahab.⁴ The poem, whose beauty and power cannot be replicated, could have been the love song for many such occasions.

The palatial setting of royalty, including garments "fragrant with myrrh and aloes and cassia" (45:8), "embroidered garments" (45:14), a gown "interwoven with gold" (45:13)— in fact, the gold of Ophir,

the finest gold that wealth can afford (45:9)—and palaces "adorned with ivory" (45:8), points to a time when international trade was vigorous, like the time of Solomon, although such activity was not confined to that period. Putting the final touch of elegance and festivity on the occasion was the presence of music (45:8).

Interpretive Insights

Title *To the tune of "Lilies."* . . . *A wedding song.* The phrase "to the tune of" is not in the Hebrew, but the phrase "on lilies" (*'al-shoshannim*) may be a tune title. It occurs again in the title of Psalm 69, and its companion form is found in Psalm 60 (*'al-shushan 'edut,* "according to the lily of covenant"; cf. Ps. 80). (See "Interpretive Insights," title, in the units on Pss. 69 and 80.) The phrase for "wedding song" literally reads, "a song of love(s) [*yᵉdidot*]."

H. T. Tur-Sinai suggests that the word *yᵉdidot* is another form of Solomon's alternate name, Jedidiah (*yᵉdidyah,* 2 Sam. 12:25).⁵

45:1 *the pen of a skillful writer.* The "scribe" (NIV: "writer") had one of the most respected professions in the ancient world. In Israel scribes wrote on papyrus

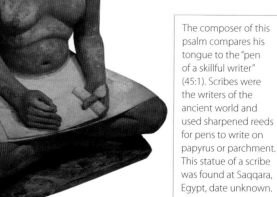

The composer of this psalm compares his tongue to the "pen of a skillful writer" (45:1). Scribes were the writers of the ancient world and used sharpened reeds for pens to write on papyrus or parchment. This statue of a scribe was found at Saqqara, Egypt, date unknown.

or leather (parchment) with a stylus made from a reed.[6] This scribe compares his tongue to the "pen of a skillful writer." What we know about the scribal trade suggests that scribes composed both orally and in written form.

45:2 *You are the most excellent of men.* The clause "you are the most excellent" is a single verb (*yph*) and rare in the Old Testament. It means "you are handsome," just like the groom in the Song of Songs (Song 1:16) and also like David (1 Sam. 17:42). The king is not only handsome but articulate ("your lips have been anointed with grace"). That would fittingly describe Solomon, who had a literary reputation.

45:3 *Gird your sword on your side, you mighty one.* The military function of the king as commander in chief was integral to the idea of kingship. If Solomon is the unnamed king of the psalm, even though he was a "man of peace" (1 Chron. 22:9), the military role was still a part of his job description (see "Historical and Cultural Background").

45:4 *In your majesty ride forth victoriously in the cause of truth, humility and justice.* As Yahweh's proxy in the world, the king rides forth into battle in defense of the virtues of the faith: truth (*'emet*), humility (*'anwah*), and justice (*tsedeq*). While the NIV takes the words "humility" and "justice" as separate terms, the Hebrew text (MT) writes them together: *'anwah-tsedeq.* The Septuagint translates all three terms as distinct virtues, "truth, humility, and justice." "Humility" and "justice" (NIV: "righteousness") also appear together in Zephaniah 2:3.

45:6 *Your throne, O God, will last for ever and ever; a scepter of justice will be the*

scepter of your kingdom. Hilber cites the ancient Near Eastern texts that speak of the king as the god's representative. While in Egypt the king was considered divine, this was not generally true in the ancient Near East. In Israel the king was thought of as God's son (Ps. 2:7), and priests of the temple were sometimes called *'elohim* (Exod. 21:6; 22:8–9).[7] Hakham translates the verse "Your throne, of God, is forever and ever," and he alleviates the tension by expanding the verse as follows: "Your throne is the throne of God, and it will remain forever and ever" (cf. 1 Chron. 29:23).[8] However, the Epistle to the Hebrews resolves the issue simply by recognizing this usage of *'elohim* as a reference to Christ as King (Heb. 1:8–9). That is, the author views the psalmist as speaking beyond his time and outside his historical context, describing Christ as divine. The regal character of the occasion calls forth the psalmist's prophetic powers to speak of the King of kings and Lord of lords, whose scepter will be one of justice. Dispensing justice and ruling the kingdom were virtually synonymous.

45:7 *You love righteousness and hate wickedness.* See Isaiah 61:8.

45:8 *your robes are fragrant with myrrh and aloes and cassia; from palaces adorned with ivory.* "Myrrh" comes from the resin of the *Commiphora* plant, native to Arabia, producing an oil used for perfume, or dried for incense. "Aloes" (*Aquilaria agallocha*) also are extracted from the resin of the aloe tree that grows in India. "Cassia" (*Cinnamomum cassia*) is a perfume manufactured from the bark of the cassia plant. These three terms are used in a connected phrase (a *waw*, "and," occurs between the first two terms but not between

The king's palace is described as being "adorned with ivory" (45:8). Beautiful ivory carvings were used to decorate the furniture in royal residences. These ivory panels were once part of the backrest of a couch from eighth-century BC Nimrud.

the second and third),[9] suggesting perhaps that they are three perfumes used together. The phrase describing the palaces literally reads, "palaces of ivory." Because of the delicate nature of ivory, palaces were certainly not built out of it, but certain rooms were inlaid with ivory (1 Kings 10:18; 22:39; Amos 3:15; 6:4).

45:9 *Daughters of kings . . . at your right hand.* The plural term may refer to other wives of the king or female attendants in the royal court. Among them is the "royal bride," a synonym for the queen.[10] Her place at the king's "right hand" signals her important position.

45:10 *Listen, daughter . . . Forget your people and your father's house.* Now the scribe turns his attention from the king to the queen. The bride is to turn her loyalties from her ethnic home to the king's realm, counsel on which her future as queen hinges.

45:11 *Let the king be enthralled by your beauty.* Now the scribe praises the beauty of the queen as he has praised the king's in 45:2.

45:12 *The city of Tyre will come with a gift, people of wealth will seek your favor.* See "Historical and Cultural Background." Situated on the Phoenician coast, Tyre had a reputation as a wealthy city (Ezek. 27:1–33), whose wealth had come about through international sea trade. This reference may serve merely as a symbol of the wealthy guests present at the wedding. The phrase translated as "seek your favor" is used of those who come seeking help from the generous in Proverbs 19:6.

45:14 *In embroidered garments she is led to the king.* Now the scene turns from description to action as the bride is led away, accompanied by her maidens, to the king's bedroom for the consummation of the marriage. Kidner suggests that this description is behind Paul's picture in 2 Corinthians 11:2, "to present you as a pure bride to her one husband" (RSV).[11]

45:16 *Your sons.* The address has now changed from the bride to the groom (the pronominal suffix, "your," is masculine).

45:17 *I will perpetuate your memory through all generations.* This is precisely the function of a court scribe.

Theological Insights

There is no question that Israel's monarchy served as God's *proxy* in the ancient world. And among the mysteries with which God has endowed human beings to reflect his image and remind us of his true nature is marriage. In fact, marriage is, above all Old Testament metaphors, the most intimate metaphor of relationship between the human and the divine.

The prophets speak in these terms (Hosea 1–3; Isa. 62:1–5; Jer. 2:1–3; Ezek. 16; 23), and the bold audacity of the metaphor is the marriage of God and Israel! It follows naturally, then, that New Testament spokespeople, including Christ himself, should utilize this intimate metaphor for the relationship of Christ and the church (Matt. 9:15; John 3:29; Eph. 5:21–33; Rev. 19:7–9; 21:2; 22:17). This has become the hinge on which many interpreters find Christ in Psalm 45, supported by the direct address of 45:6, "Your throne, O God, will last for ever and ever." Whether by the *fuller sense* (*sensus plenior*) or *typology*, this psalm seems to many interpreters, including this one, to outstrip the realm of human meaning and rise to a level where only God can qualify for the terms of its language. Thus the messianic interpretation that the king is God/Christ and the princess is Israel/church was and may be made unapologetically. The Epistle to the Hebrews, however, quoting 45:6–7, sees the king as God's Son, and the writer finds this to support the claim of Christ's divinity, especially since the psalmist addressed him as God (Heb. 1:8–9).

The superlative of superlatives in the royal vocabulary is "King of kings." It means the best of human monarchs. But our psalm looks higher than earth's kingdoms to a King whose throne "will last for ever and ever"—itself a superlative way to say it—and whose kingdom is ruled by a "scepter of justice" (45:6). Indeed, this King is the same monarch Isaiah sees in the coming kingdom of God (Isa. 9:6–7), for whom the whole world longs, but they do not long as deeply to receive as God longs to give.

Teaching the Text

We might call the Old Testament a "glimpse book," giving us glimpses of the future of God's kingdom and its leaders. Psalm 45 is a chapter in that book, a picture view of the ideal king, snapped by this talented poet on the occasion of the king's wedding, and gaining messianic clarity, like the increasing clarity of a photo,[12] as history moves toward its climax in the appearance of the King of kings.

A sermon/lesson can be built around the definition of the king's role, outlined in verse 4. Since we are speaking about leadership, it is quite appropriate to apply these terms of the king's leadership to all leaders in the body of Christ. First, the king exists for the cause of *truth*. While some interpreters will object to viewing this as abstract truth, Israel was not unaware of the abstract, even though they generally thought more practically. This term overlaps our concept of the abstract truth, suggesting that which is real, accurate, and faithful to the facts. It is the opposite of a "lie" (*kazab*), a word that describes falsehood in the Psalms. We might mention the subtle ways human beings have of cloaking their lies and making them appear like truth, a problem for the psalmists' time and all times. Lies make pretenders out of us and cause us to act in ways that are not true to reality.

The second royal cause is *humility*, a character trait that is adverse to the misrepresentation of truth and reality. It is related to the root that describes those people who are humbled by life's circumstances and by unjust perceptions that other people impose on them. The king was their champion, again representing God, who was their ultimate Defender. The application of this text to all leaders, to all believers, in fact, is quite in keeping with the biblical mandates for leadership (see 1 Tim. 3).

The third royal cause is *justice*, and that, above all other causes, was at the top of the king's job description. So often we come at this cause from its opposite, injustice, because so many people have lived in that category of experience, some only fender benders but others tragic collisions. It has many dimensions, social and political being two that we are most often conscious of. We might entertain the hypothetical idea of a world where justice is always done, where human motives are always transparent, so there is no miscarriage of justice. This is the vision of the psalmist, the portrait of the ideal of the king, and the prophetic portrait as well (Isa. 11:3b–4b).

The ideal king holds the scepter of justice because he loves righteousness and hates wickedness. Shown here are two scepter heads from the tenth to seventh century BC.

character. We try to deceive people by making them believe we are something we really are not. The king of Psalm 45 is challenged to "ride forth victoriously in the cause of truth, humility and justice" (v. 4). These qualities represent God's character, and the king is his representative. Our challenge is to remember, though we are not monarchs, that we are God's representatives in this world, and others will know who he is by our character portrait.

Illustrating the Text

Lies and deception

Film: *The Mask*. The 1994 movie *The Mask* presents a man named Stanley (played by Jim Carrey) who is too nice for his own good. Stanley finds a mask, and when he puts it on he becomes his inner self, a cartoony romantic wild man. The interesting aspect of this movie is that the mask actually brings out Stanley's true character—meaning that the Stanley without the mask was really the deception. We all have a tendency to project something that is not true to our real

Renew your vows of commitment.

Television: *The Office*. Psalm 45 provides an insight into the heart of God with regard to marriage. Here we see an entire chapter of Scripture dedicated to the blessing of the marriage between the king and the queen. God created marriage, and he honors it. In the final season of the television show, *The Office*, Pam and Jim have been struggling in their marriage. In "Paper Airplanes" (season 9, episode 20), Jim is preparing to leave for Philadelphia for a second job, which has been a source of conflict between the two of them. Jim reaches out to hug Pam, but she does not reciprocate. Suddenly there is a flashback to their wedding and the reading of 1 Corinthians 13:7–13. The scene cuts back to Pam and Jim in the parking lot, and Pam, recalling the words from the Bible and her vows, embraces Jim as they say, "I love you," to each other. When we came to faith in Jesus, we entered into a sacred commitment through our vow, "Jesus is my Savior and Lord." The relationship between king and queen in this psalm was one underwritten by love ("Let the king be enthralled by your beauty," [v. 11] is more than infatuation) and commitment ("Forget your people and your father's house," [v. 10b]). See Ruth 1:16.

Marriage as a parable

Classic Sermon: Psalm 45 celebrates a royal marriage, and in a sense every marriage is intended to be "royal," but more than that. Indeed, God has given us the gift of marriage partly to help us to better understand our relationship with him

and what it means that "the church is the bride of Christ." Pastor Timothy Keller of Redeemer Presbyterian Church in New York preached a sermon called "Sex and the End of Loneliness" (February 1996), in which he emphasized this spiritual reality. In this sermon, Keller talks about sex in a committed heterosexual marriage and states:

> The ecstasy and joy of sex is supposed to be a foretaste of the complete ecstasy and joy of total union with Christ. The moment we see Christ face to face . . . we will be naked, yet so delighted in [our nakedness that] we will be unashamed. . . . The Lord God will look at us through Jesus and say, "I love you." . . . Great sex is a parable of the Gospel—to be utterly accepted in spite of your sin, to be loved by the One you admire to the sky.[13]

"God Is Our Refuge and Strength, an Ever-Present Help in Trouble"

Big Idea *Human effort is necessary to build God's kingdom, but the final word is that we should "be still" and recognize that God is the real Builder.*

Understanding the Text

Psalm 46 is a type of poem that challenges form criticism's assumptions. Gunkel has identified it as a subtype of the hymn, which he labels "Zion Songs."[1] Goldingay helpfully lays out the features of this psalm that overlap with other types and concludes that the psalm of trust is the best choice of categories.[2] Indeed, the spirit of trust in God as refuge pervades the poem. More specifically, the plural pronouns and first common plural verbs point to the community psalm of trust, along with Psalms 90; 115; 123; 124; 125; and 126.[3]

The Text in Context

The city of Jerusalem is not mentioned by name in Psalm 46, but its identification as the "city of God" is unmistakable. Other psalms celebrate Jerusalem, or Zion, as Israel's theological center because of God's presence there and his association with Jerusalem (48; 76; 84; 87; 122). In fact, Psalm 46 belongs to a minicollection

Certain words and phrases used by the psalmist in Psalm 46 allude to the song in Exodus 15 that Moses and the Israelites sang to the Lord after their deliverance from the Egyptian army. A haggadah for Passover from the fourteenth century AD contains this illustration of the Israelites successfully crossing the Red Sea while the Egyptians drowned.

of psalms (46–49) that have their general focus on the sanctuary in Jerusalem or its worship.

The psalmists are not inclined to quote from other portions of Scripture. In fact, this is a general observation that can be said of most genres of the Hebrew Bible. Yet, judging from their many allusions to the Torah, Prophets, and Writings, we conclude that the psalmists were steeped in the language of those writings, especially the poetic sections.[4] So students of Scripture can discover verbal remnants of certain eras and institutions reflected in those allusions. Psalm 46 affords us the opportunity to look through those portholes and see the larger theological canvas on which the poet paints his verbal picture of refuge and security in God. It is another layer of meaning that, once perceived, gives fullness to the text.

The writer has a mental and spiritual knowledge of the biblical tradition that forms the presentation of the psalms, and this is of great importance. With that observation, we may take note that Psalm 46 has a universal perspective on God's presence in the world. That is, God's presence in the "city of God" is not an isolated presence but a presence that is to be understood in the context of creation. Five times the term "earth" appears (46:2, 6, 8, 9, 10), implying God's sovereign control over it. The simple picture of creation is perhaps in the writer's mind (and should be in the reader's) as he describes the reverse action of the mountains receding into the "sea," bringing to mind the emergence of the dry land from the waters, which yielded their generic titles, "earth" and "seas" (Ps. 46:2; Gen. 1:9–10). The extension of the

creation picture is reflected in the "river whose streams make glad the city of God" (46:4), reminiscent of the river that flows through Eden to water it (Gen. 2:10), and whose branches complete the system of navigation.

This code language is interwoven with the allusion to the Melchizedek story, where Abraham identifies Yahweh with Melchizedek's God 'elyon (Ps. 46:4; Gen. 14:18–24, esp. 14:22). The tapestry continues by interweaving allusions to Moses's Song of the Sea (Exod. 15): God's "strength" (Ps. 46:1; Exod. 15:2), and God's dwelling place ("the holy place where the Most High dwells," Ps. 46:4, lit., "the holy place of the tabernacles of the Most High"; Exod. 15:17, lit., "place of your dwelling"—synonymous terms). In close textual proximity to the Song of the Sea, the story of the Red Sea relates how Moses stretches out his hand, and the sea goes back into place "at daybreak" (Exod. 14:27), the exact phrase with which the psalm describes God's intervening help "at break of day" (Ps. 46:5). So the pigments of Israel's past are dotted on the psalm's wider canvas, giving a fuller range within which to see the present security that God's presence brings.

Outline/Structure

If one uses the refrain to divide the psalm into its parts, then it likely consists of two parts: 46:1–7 and 46:8–11.[5] Those who take their cue from the liturgical term *selah* that occurs after verses 3, 7, and 11 (see NIV footnote) insist that the refrain of 46:7 and 11 originally stood after 46:3 also, and they generally divide the poem into three parts (46:1–3, 4–7, and 8–11). There is probably no compelling reason to endorse this view, since Hebrew poetry does not exhibit the same kind of symmetry we expect of classical Western poetry,[6] and, further, the meaning of *selah* remains somewhat in doubt.[7] We will follow the two-part division, which seems to align with the content a little better than the three-part division.

1. God as refuge from natural disasters (46:1–7)
   Refrain (46:7)
2. God as refuge from political disasters (46:8–11)
   Refrain (46:11)

Historical and Cultural Background

Traditionally Psalm 46 was understood against the background of some great military victory, such as victory over the Assyrians in the late eighth century (2 Kings 18:13–19:36/Isa. 36:1–37:38). With the rise of form criticism, the discussion generally turned from historical background to cultic or worship settings as a way to understand the Psalms. As a result, some form critics proposed an autumn festival at which Yahweh was "reenthroned," a festival that for the most part has proved to be a modern myth, but with some scholars, myths die slowly.[8] Craigie, whose form-critical method has led him in some helpful directions, proposes, following Eissfeldt, that Psalm 46 can be seen as a celebration of David's successful establishment of the royal cult in Jerusalem.[9] In view of the "sons of Korah" connection to the psalm, some Davidic associations are certainly possible, although it is impossible to describe them with any sense of confidence.

Interpretive Insights

46:1 *God is our refuge and strength, an ever-present help in trouble.* The first clause is verbless (the verb is understood), putting the emphasis on the nouns. The latter clause literally reads, "He is found very much [to be] a help in troubles." Note the phrase "at break of day" in 46:5b, which suggests the prompt availability of God's help (see also "The Text in Context," and Pss. 27:9; 44:26; 63:7).

46:2 *though the earth give way and the mountains fall into the heart of the sea.* The implied imagery is that the earth might slip and fall into the waters by which it is supported. In ancient cosmogony the earth was viewed as supported by the sea. The mountains are a symbol of stability and strength, meaning that their disappearance would deprive the world of its point of reference. Some commentators associate the "sea" with the mythological idea of chaos. Whether or not there is a mythological insinuation here, the sea was nevertheless a symbol of instability, with its tossing and turning, its storm-tossed waves, and the ebbing and flowing of the tides. See "The Text in Context" for associations with Genesis 1.

46:3 Selah. See "Outline/Structure."

46:4 *a river whose streams make glad the city of God . . . where the Most High dwells.* The "river" may be an allusion to the river in the garden of Eden that flowed through the garden to water it (Gen. 2:10), and whose four branches (here "streams";

In contrast to the chaotic ocean with its damaging waves, a river and its streams "make glad the city of God" (46:4). In this relief from the palace of Ashurbanipal at Nimrud (645 BC), streams of water flow from an aqueduct to water a garden that surrounds an altar and shrine for the deity.

Gen. 2:10, "sources" [NIV: "headwaters"]) nurtured the whole of Eden (see "The Text in Context"). Others see another mythological allusion to the springs that were situated in the dwelling place of the Canaanite god El. The purpose of the river, not stated in Genesis, is to "gladden" the city of God ("city of God" occurs elsewhere only in Ps. 87:3, but 48:1 and 8 are similar), or Jerusalem, which is never named in Psalm 46. From there the whole world would become joyful. The last part of the verse further defines the "city of God." It recalls the name of the deity in Melchizedek's Jebusite city of Salem (Jerusalem), 'el 'elyon ("God Most High"; here "God," 'el, is not part of the phrase as it is in Genesis 14). Thus it is an allusion to Abraham's God, Yahweh, whom he equated with 'el 'elyon (Gen. 14:22).

46:5 *God is within her, she will not fall; God will help her at break of day.* The important thing about the city of God is God's presence, not its fortifications. The NIV's translation times God's help at the rising of the sun. But other suggestions have been proposed, like the administration of

justice in the morning (see 2 Sam. 15:2). The phrase "at break of day" (*lipnot boqer*) occurs in the description of the exodus event, when Moses lifts his hand and the waters return to their place "at break of day," and the Egytians are drowned (Exod. 14:27).

46:6 *Nations are in uproar, kingdoms fall; he lifts his voice, the earth melts.* Craigie calls this verse the central section of the psalm.[10] Some commentators hear a mythological allusion to the forces of chaos (46:2–3), but the Psalms are generally concerned with the threatening and rebellious nations (e.g., Ps. 2), a theme that has not played loudly in Book 2 up to this point. The voice of God is incredibly powerful and works uncanny changes on nature, here melting the earth and in Amos 1:2 withering the top of Mount Carmel (see also, e.g., Exod. 15:15; Isa. 14:31). Psalm 29 speaks of the power of God's voice as it thunders over the mighty waters. Kidner comments that God's voice "will be as decisive in dissolving the world as it was in creating it (cf. 33:6, 10)."[11]

46:7 *The LORD Almighty is with us; the God of Jacob.* The refrain, which picks up on the theme that God is in the midst of the city, is equivalent to Isaiah 7:14's "Immanuel" ("God with us"). God's presence with his people is at the heart of Israel's religion. The phrase "God of Jacob" adds another allusion to the Genesis narrative and gives the psalm an additional "covenant" touch.

46:8 *Come and see what the LORD has done.* The verbs are plural and most likely spoken to the nations, since they have just been mentioned in verse 6. Yet it could be a summons to Israel also, since the poem is a meditation on Israel's struggle with the troubles of their world and the power of their God. After reviewing God's mighty acts in nature, performed by the Creator God, Abraham and Jacob's God, Israel invites the nations to "come and see" what the Lord has done in their history.

46:9 *He makes wars cease to the ends of the earth . . . he burns the shields with fire.* The general declaration of causing wars to cease means there are no limits on God's power and realm. Then the psalmist breaks it down into specific images: "he breaks the bow and shatters the spear," and "he burns the shields with fire." This is a description of God that the belligerent nations need to hear. The Hebrew word behind "shields" (*'agalot*) means "wagons," but nowhere is it used of "war chariots." The Septuagint reads the word as "shields," which the NIV follows.

46:10 *Be still, and know that I am God; I will be exalted.* The quotation in 46:8 is Israel's summons to the nations. This is God's. The NIV takes the liberty to prefix "He says" to the verse (absent from the Hebrew), identifying the speaker.

Theological Insights

An important feature of the Psalms is that the present and the future are often framed in terms of the historical events of the past, of which Psalm 46 is an excellent example. In verses 2–3, the psalmist describes a future crisis in terms of the disordering of nature, or the reversal of the creation process described in Genesis 1:9–10 (the waters gather into one place, and the land emerges out of the waters; reverse: the sea roars and foams, and the mountains slip back into the seas and disappear beneath the waters). Verse 4 describes the river that runs through the city of God—a reflection of the river that flowed through Eden to water the garden, dividing into four rivers (Gen. 2:10). So the psalmist takes the picture of Eden and uses the pigments of that portrait to paint the picture of the kingdom of God that is in the making.

The theme of "the city of God" is quite widespread in the Psalms, even though this precise term appears only one other time (87:3; similar forms are "city of our God," 48:1, 8; "city of the LORD of hosts," 48:8 ESV). Jerusalem, or Zion—neither name appears here—is the place where God dwells, and his presence, represented by the sanctuary, or represented simply by the larger city, is its identifying mark. The following two psalms

God Almighty "makes wars cease.... He breaks the bow and shatters the spear" (46:9). The Akkadian king Naram-Sin announced his military victory in this stele found at Susa (2250 BC). The defeated soldier to the right of the tree holds a broken spear.

(Pss. 47 and 48) celebrate that city, especially its God and worship. The prophets join the chorus in various ways, and Ezekiel, representing the melodic theme, gives it the eschatological name of *YHWH Shammah* ("The Lord is there," Ezek. 48:35). Psalm 46 maps out the water sources of the city, which were in geographical reality limited to the spring of Gihon, and makes the city a virtual replica of the garden of Eden (see "The Text in Context"; see also Pss. 65:9; 87:7; Ezek. 17:1–12; Joel 3:18; Zech. 14:8). Some commentators object to an eschatological interpretation of this psalm, but when Jerusalem takes on the features of the Edenic paradise and absorbs the colors of Abraham's Canaanite victory and Moses's triumph over Pharaoh's army, it is not removed from historical circumstances, to be sure, but it rises to new levels as a shelter of strength and security.

Teaching the Text

Now let us use this observation to build our sermon/lesson. As we have observed, Psalm 46 speaks about the disordering of nature, in fact, the reversal of the creation process described in Genesis 1:9–10. The picture is that of the primordial waters gathering into one place and the land, composed of plains and mountains, emerging out of the waters. So we see a picture of this troubled world as the reversal of the creation process: the sea roars and foams, and the mountains slip back into the seas and disappear beneath the waters. And this is the message: the God of creation who separated the waters and caused the plains and mountains to emerge from beneath them can control the situation when the process is going in

reverse, in the disordering of the world and of life. When the landmarks of our world begin to dissolve and our orientation loses its reference points, we still can declare, "The Lord Almighty is with us; the God of Jacob is our fortress" (46:7, 11). God is, in fact, our orientation, not the landmarks of our world.

Now let us see the second word picture from the psalm: "There is a river whose streams make glad the city of God, the holy place where the Most High dwells" (46:4). To understand the picture behind this statement in the psalm, we need to read another part of the Genesis story: "A river flowed out of Eden to water the garden, and there it divided and became four rivers" (Gen. 2:10 ESV). It is a description of the world under the metaphor of Eden, and when the new world God is making is complete, it will be like the "city of God," like Jerusalem in its idyllic form. That is precisely the image John uses when he paints the final picture of the kingdom of God and describes the new Jerusalem as coming down out of heaven from God (Rev. 21). So the psalmist is taking the picture of Eden and using the pigments of that portrait to paint the picture of God's kingdom. Similarly, John takes those same pigments, improved, refined with sharper tones and hues, and paints the picture of heaven for us. God is making a new world. Psalm 46 calls us into it and sets forth our manner of living in it: "Be still, and know that I am God; I will be exalted among the heathen, I will be exalted in the earth" (46:10 KJV). It is not a call to a quiet and serene lifestyle but a summons to stop fighting the Lord's battles for him. Stop trying to be God, and let God be God. It is a summons to

say to his friend Melanchthon, "Let's sing the Forty-Sixth Psalm." This psalm became so important to the Reformation that when Protestants were forced into exile or martyrs went to their death, they would often be heard singing this hymn. It was even referred to as "The Battle Hymn of the Reformation."[13] When you read the words of Psalm 46, it is not hard to understand why it was so inspirational in a time of religious warfare and persecution. Even when it seems all is lost, we may be comforted by the reminder that the Lord is in control. As Luther wrote in his hymn, "And though this world, with devils filled, should threaten to undo us, we will not fear, for God hath willed His truth to triumph through us."

"Be still, and know that I am God."

Quote: Robert E. Lee. Robert E. Lee was an American military officer who is best known for having commanded the Confederate Army of Northern Virginia in the American Civil War. And he was very committed to faith in Jesus Christ. He once said, as a great summary of Psalm 46, as well as an expression of his personal faith and philosophy:

> The truth is this: The march of Providence is so slow and our desires so impatient; the work of progress so immense and our means of aiding it so feeble; the life of humanity is so long, that of the individual so brief, that we often see only

surrender, not to our enemies, but to God, and to let God himself build his kingdom (see 2 Chron. 20:15). While the plural imperative of verse 8 is obviously addressed to the nations, this summons (also plural) may be addressed to them also. Yet, like so many other instances, especially in the Prophets (the oracles against the nations, for example),[12] when God addresses the nations, it often becomes a message of comfort and reassurance to Israel as well.

Illustrating the Text

A mighty fortress is our God.

Hymn: "A Mighty Fortress Is Our God," by Martin Luther. When Luther wrote this great hymn, he based the words on Psalm 46. During times when the Protestant Reformation seemed lost, Luther would often the ebb of the advancing wave and are thus discouraged. It is history that teaches us to hope.[14]

There are times when we get frustrated with God because he is not moving according to our time frame. Lee reminds us that our perspective is limited, and we would be wise to be still before God and to reflect on his pace in history and his mode of building the kingdom.

The God of hope

Testimony: Psalm 46 draws on what God has done to provide encouragement for the present and the future. We must not only remember what God has done through history as revealed in the Bible but also meditate on what he has done in our own lives. By remembering, we are empowered to know who God really is! In a world of shifting sands, God is our point of reference. One possible illustration for remembering who God is and what he has done is through a "cardboard testimony." Ask volunteers to write on one side of a piece of cardboard some crisis or struggle they have experienced and write on the other side how God responded (bringing comfort or relief through an actual change in circumstances). With music playing, ask the volunteers to come before the congregation together. Then have one person at a time step forward, silently hold up one side of the cardboard (indicating the struggle), and then the other side (indicating God's response). Examples of what could be written on the cardboard: Was considering divorce / Have reconciled with my wife; Was far from God / Reading the Bible every day; Was addicted to alcohol / Christ has set me free. Following this, read Psalm 46 as a reminder of the God we worship!

"The LORD Most High Is Awesome, the Great King over All the Earth"

Big Idea *God's covenant of grace with Abraham, far from being exclusive, is an implicit call to the people of the whole world to become members of this covenant.*

Understanding the Text

Psalm 47 is a good example of what Gunkel calls a *hymn*, and he includes it in a subcategory of Zion songs. Mowinckel has followed Gunkel's study by proposing a new classification, the enthronement psalms,[1] postulating that ancient Israel celebrated a fall festival at which they reelevated Yahweh to his throne, or at least celebrated his enthronement.[2] Belonging as it does to the Elohistic collection of psalms, the royal acclamation here is "God reigns" (47:8a), rather than "Yahweh reigns," as the acclamation appears in Psalms 93:1; 96:10; 97:1; and 99:1. It is not a declaration that Elohim has *begun* his reign or that he has *become king*. It is rather a declaration that God *is* king, that he *reigns*, unrestricted by time, and unconstrained by geographical boundaries. Psalm 47 alludes indeed to Israel's acts of

worship ("God has ascended amid shouts of joy," 47:5), but these are celebrations of God's timeless reign.

The Text in Context

Since the other psalms of the heavenly King are contained in Book 4 (Pss. 93; 95–99), Psalm 47, which shares their style and content, is obviously separated from those psalms (see the sidebar "The LORD Reigns: Psalms of the Heavenly King" in the unit on Ps. 93). But the content of Psalm 46 helps us understand why these two psalms

The psalmist tells the people of all the nations to clap their hands for the Lord is King. This relief from the tomb of Kheruef in Luxor, Egypt, shows four women clapping their hands as they celebrate the pharaoh's jubilee festival (fourteenth century BC).

occur together—not, of course, to imply that Psalm 47 ever belonged to the aggregate of the psalms of the heavenly King in Book 4 and has been moved to this place. An analogy is the separation of Psalm 50, an Asaph psalm, from Psalms 73–83, a collection of Asaph psalms.[3] But to address our question, the final admonition of Psalm 46 is an apostrophe,[4] spoken to the nations, much like the prophets spoke to the nations who were out of hearing range (see, e.g., Ezek. 25–32): "Be still, and know that I am God; I will be exalted among the nations, I will be exalted in the earth" (46:10). For that reason, the compiler(s) of Book 2 may have chosen Psalm 47 to follow Psalm 46, which also begins with an apostrophe to the nations and celebrates Yahweh's kingship.

Further, Psalms 46 and 47 share words and phrases. First, the divine name *'elyon* ("Most High") occurs in 46:4 and 47:2, joining them both to the patriarchal story of Abraham and Melchizedek (Gen. 14). Second, both psalms are connected to the patriarchal tradition of Jacob, one using the phrase "God of Jacob" (46:11), and the other the "pride of Jacob" (47:4). These terms place both psalms in a covenant context that leaves the covenant imprint on Yahweh's sovereign reign. Neither psalm alludes to other gods, as some psalms do, but they appeal to the terms and story of the covenant God to establish his supremacy. Third, they share a story of Israel's past, stretching all the way from creation to Moses, in the case of Psalm 46, and from Abraham to the conquest, in the case of Psalm 47 (see "Historical and Cultural Background"). This "code" language of Israel's story was buried in the subconscious mind of the psalmists, and when they spoke and wrote, they addressed

Key Themes of Psalm 47

- God's reign is universal.
- God's covenant is inclusive.

spiritual realities in words, phrases, and descriptive terms that divulged the larger story.

Outline/Structure

Psalm 47 is structured around the trifold use of a single conjunction, "for/because" (*ki*), giving reasons why the nations should praise the Lord and acknowledge his sovereignty.

"Clap your hands, all you nations;
shout to God with cries of joy" (47:1)
> *For/because*
>> "The LORD Most High is awesome, the great King over all the earth" (47:2)
>> "He subdued nations under us" (47:3)
>> "He chose our inheritance for us" (47:4)
>> "God has ascended amid shouts of joy" (47:5)

"Sing praises to God, sing praises" (47:6)
> *For/because*
>> "God is the King of all the earth" (47:7)
>> "God reigns over the nations" (47:8a)
>> "God is seated on his holy throne" (47:8b)

"The nobles of the nations assemble as the people of the God of Abraham" (47:9a)
> *For/because*
>> "The kings of the earth belong to God; he is greatly exalted" (47:9b)

Historical and Cultural Background

Since the text is our point of reference, we need to sensitize and resensitize ourselves to it, and when we do, we often discover that the text tells a story, sometimes by explicit biblical references and sometimes only by allusions. In the case of Psalm 47, we have two explicit historical references, to Abraham (47:9) and to Jacob (47:4). Here as in Genesis 14, Abraham appears in company with 'elyon ("Most High"). The other significant patriarch, Jacob, comes along with the information that Yahweh "loved" "the pride of Jacob."[5] More implicit are the allusions to the conquest under Joshua ("He subdued nations under us," 47:3) and to the promised land ("our inheritance," 47:4). Against this patriarchal backdrop, the psalmist summons the nations to clap their hands and shout to God joyfully (47:1).

Interpretive Insights

47:1 *Clap your hands, all you nations; shout to God.* The clapping of hands accompanied a king's coronation (e.g., Joash's in 2 Kings 11:12). Here it acclaims Yahweh's kingship. The verb translated as "shout" denotes a high, staccato sound of an instrument or a human voice.[6]

47:2 Lord *Most High.* The use of the epithet "Most High" ('elyon) for God, first occurring in the Melchizedek story of Genesis 14, evidently derives from the verb 'lh, which means "to go up," implying that Yahweh is the "high God." Abraham identifies 'elyon as Yahweh (Gen. 14:22).

47:3 *He subdued nations under us, peoples under our feet.* The language suggests the conquest (Pss. 135:8–11; 136:10–22). In the ancient Near East, the theme of placing one's enemies under one's foot was common (Ps. 110:1).[7] This form of the Hebrew verb "subdued" (*yadber*), with this meaning, is found only here and in Psalm 18:47.

47:4 *He chose our inheritance for us, the pride of Jacob, whom he loved.* In the phrase "pride of Jacob," the word "pride" (*ga'on*) literally means "heights." A related word (*ga'awah*) is found in Psalm 46:3, where it has the sense of "rising up" (NIV: "surging"). So here it refers to the "rising up" of Jacob's land—the mountainous spine that extends from Galilee to the Negev.[8] Parallel to the term "our inheritance" in the previous line, this noun is clearly a reference to the land of Israel.

47:5 *God has ascended amid shouts of joy.* When David brought the ark to Jerusalem, it was accompanied by shouts and trumpets, an exact quotation from

"He subdued nations under us, peoples under our feet" (47:3). To actually portray enemies or prisoners under the feet of the conquering king or deity is a common motif in the ancient Near East. This example from the great temple at Abu Simbel shows captives from Nubia carved on the stone slab under the feet of the statue of Pharaoh (thirteenth century BC).

2 Samuel 6:15. The "trumpet" (*shophar*) was made from the ram's horn.

47:6–7 *Sing praises to God . . . sing to him a psalm of praise.* Five times in these two verses the command to "sing praises" occurs (Piel of *zmr*, "make music," either with an instrument or the voice). The word *maskil* ("a psalm of praise") appears in some psalm titles to designate a type of psalm.[9]

46:8 *God reigns over the nations; God is seated on his holy throne.* The verb "reigns" (*mlk*) is the same verb used to describe the earthly king's reign (e.g., 2 Sam. 15:10; 1 Kings 1:11). "His holy throne" is a hapax legomenon and probably is a reference to God's heavenly throne. Other texts speak of God's throne in the heavens (1 Kings 22:19; 2 Chron. 18:18; Ps. 103:19; Isa. 66:1).

47:9 *the nations assemble as the people of the God of Abraham . . . kings of the earth.* (See "Historical and Cultural Background.") This is in keeping with God's promise to Abraham (Gen. 12:3), a fulfillment that has already begun in Genesis 14. "Kings" is literally "shields" and may allude to the Abraham story as well: "Praise be to God Most High, who delivered your enemies into your hand" (Gen. 14:20); "I am your shield [*magen*]" (Gen. 15:1). But here it is a reference to kings.

Theological Insights

With the widespread exclusiveness that we find in the Old Testament, Psalm 47 is a welcome acclamation of God's universal reign, a sovereign reign of saving proportions. Psalm 87 shares this saving perspective, as it reorients Israel's cantankerous neighbors to Zion, the city of God, and issues them a "born-in-Zion"

birth certificate. From the beginning, God's saving plan has had a universal perspective (Gen. 12:1–3). One can appreciate the subtle way the psalm draws the nations under the aegis of the covenant. To begin with, the psalmist calls them to join joyfully the celebration of God's sovereign reign (47:1), and five times he bids them "sing praises" to "*our* King" (47:6–7). The summons itself implies that God has had designs on the gentiles all along, and when the "nobles" (kings) of the nations gather as "the people of the God of Abraham," the designs are transparent. Now the only remaining piece of the picture is an acknowledgment from the covenant side of the aisle that "the kings of the earth belong to God" (47:9).

But what does this covenant context have to do with the gentile nations? And here is one of the remarkable features of this psalm: the bold acclamation of God's sovereign reign over the nations is made under the aegis of his covenant with Israel. This psalm stands on tiptoe and looks directly across history to the salvation of the gentiles and God's universal reign over the world.

Yet it is not the salvation of the gentiles that is the subject of the poem—this is implied—but it is the sovereignty of Yahweh that forms the heart of the psalm. He is "Lord Most High" (47:2a), the "great King over all the earth" (47:2b), "ascended amid shouts of joy" (47:5), "our King" (47:6), "seated on his holy throne" (47:8), and "greatly exalted" (47:9). If verse 5 describes David's transfer of the ark to Jerusalem, or some other ritual of Yahweh's acclamation, the nations have become coheirs of this event. It was not likely part of their memory bank, but the heirs do not have to know their Benefactor's history for the legacy to be valid.

Teaching the Text

The gentile nations normally fall outside the Abrahamic/Mosaic covenant in the Old Testament. In fact, the salvation of the gentiles is often considered a latecomer to Old Testament theology. While a date for this psalm may be late in the preexilic era, the salvation of the gentile nations has thankfully become fixed in psalmic theology. This psalm is more developed in that sense than most of them. The psalm is clearly addressed to the nations (perhaps a link to "nations" [*goyim*] in Ps. 46:6). The *inclusiveness* of the poem is quite striking in its description of the "nobles of the nations" assembling as "the people of the God of Abraham" (47:9). Christians claim that the Old Testament is *their* testament too, and this psalm is a testimony to the validity of that claim. Perhaps this can be used as an occasion to introduce Christians to the Old Testament covenant and make them feel a bit more at home than many are prone to feel.

The theme of the psalm is really God's sovereign reign over the world. Three times the conjunction "for/because" introduces reasons why the nations should bow to

One of the earliest Christian festivals is Ascension Day, when Psalm 47 is read as part of the liturgy. This painting depicting the ascension of Jesus was once part of an altarpiece in the Carthusian monastery in Thuison-les-Abbeville, France, late fifteenth century.

God's sovereign rule (see "Outline/Structure"). The first follows the summons to all nations to "shout to God with cries of joy" (47:1) and gives the reason that God is the awesome and universal King (47:2). We even get a glimpse of God's "coronation" as King of the universe (47:5). The second follows the summons to "sing praises to our King," probably also spoken to the nations (47:6), and states the reason: "For God is the King of all the earth" (47:7). The third follows a description of the kingdom of God as the "nobles of the nations assemble as the people of the God of Abraham" (47:9).

The theological implication of God's sovereignty is that all nations and individuals are his subjects. That is a message written between the lines of the psalm and calls us to obedience and worship.

Illustrating the Text

A contribution of Psalm 47

Christian Year: Psalm 47 is the psalm for Ascension Day in the Christian church year. Ascension Day is the fortieth day of Easter and is a holiday that commemorates Jesus Christ's ascension into heaven. It is one of the earliest Christian festivals, dating back to the first century. It marks the end of the Easter season and occurs ten days before Pentecost. Thus Psalm 47, with its call to the worship and exaltation of the Lord, along with its reminder that the gospel is to go to the very ends of the earth, is a perfect selection for this Christian festival. The connection between the ascension of Jesus and Psalm 47 is rightly expressed by Scott Hoezee: "Jesus has ascended to God's right hand and is, right now, the King of kings and Lord of lords; the President of presidents and Prime Minister of prime ministers. Jesus rules. Jesus is in charge—whether people know it or not, whether they like it or not. Ascension Day is not a day for modest claims!"[10]

Worship is God-focused.

Quote: J. I. Packer. Psalm 47 provides wonderful expressions of God's sovereign reign and is a great reminder that worship flows from that truth. Theologian J. I. Packer once reflected,

> Worship—in the sense of telling God his worth by speech and song and celebrating his worth in his presence by proclamation and meditation—has largely been replaced, at least in the West, by a form of entertainment calculated to give worshipers the equivalent of a sauna or Jacuzzi experience and send them away feeling relaxed and tuned up at the same time. . . . The question is not whether a particular liturgical form is used, but whether a God-centered as distinct from a man-centered perspective is maintained—whether, in other words, the sense that man exists for God rather than God for man is cherished or lost. We need to discover all over again that worship is natural to the Christian heart, as it

was to the godly Israelites who wrote the psalms, and that the habit of celebrating the greatness and graciousness of God yields an endless flow of thankfulness, joy, and zeal.[11]

Authentic worship of an authentic God

Quote: Psalm 47 pulses with a genuine spirit of worship because "the LORD Most High is awesome, the great King over all the earth" (v. 2). That means that the most authentic thing we do is to worship the authentic God. Eugene Peterson looks perceptively at our world and observes: "We live in a pragmatic age and are reluctant to do anything if its practical usefulness cannot be demonstrated. It is inevitable that we ask regarding worship, is it worth it? Can you justify the time and energy and expense involved in gathering Christians together in worship?"[12] Peterson then goes on to quote theologian Helmut Thielicke, who had a clear sense of what worship is:

> Look at the mower in the summer's day, with so much to cut down ere the sun sets. He pauses in his labour—is he a sluggard? He looks for his stone, and begins to draw it up and down his scythe, with rink-atink, rink-atink, rink-atink. Is that idle music—is he wasting precious moments? How much he might have mowed while he has been ringing out those notes on his scythe! But he is sharpening his tool, and he will do far more when once again he gives his strength to those long sweeps which lay the grass prostrate in rows before him.[13]

In worship we are sharpening our tools for future worship in this life and worship with the church triumphant in the world to come.

"Within Your Temple, O God, We Meditate on Your Unfailing Love"

Big Idea *Jerusalem, like Jerusalem's God, generates awe in her worshipers and terror in her enemies.*

Understanding the Text

Like Psalms 46 and 47, Psalm 48 is a hymn that belongs to the subcategory of Zion songs (Pss. 46; 47; 48; 76; 84; 87; 122). It is an appropriate companion to Psalm 47 in that Psalm 47 is addressed to the nations, acclaiming Yahweh as King of the nations and announcing God's kingly acclamation. Psalm 48 idealizes Mount Zion (Jerusalem), but it capitalizes on the fact that Mount Zion is the "city of our God" (48:1) and that God is there ("in her citadels," 48:3). Further, Psalm 48 parades the kings of the nations past Jerusalem, perhaps looking at the city from the Central Highway, and the very sight of its impregnable defenses sent the kings fleeing in terror (48:4–6).

The Text in Context

Psalm 48 belongs to a joyful collection of Zion songs (Pss. 46–48) that one would naturally expect to find in a collection written by or dedicated to the Levitical family of Korah. In these psalms (Pss. 42–49) the temple and its idyllic location in Zion are both a memory and a present reality. Even Psalm 45, while not focused on Jerusalem as such, is set in this city.

Psalm 48 gives us a picture of the beauty of Zion, with its impenetrable fortresses that can repel kings bent on conquest and send them in terrorized retreat (48:4–6). Yet those who look on the city as the place where the Lord dwells see the beauty of "its loftiness, the joy of the whole earth" (48:2), the security of her towers and citadels, and a story to tell their children (48:12–13). When the city was destroyed by the Babylonians in the sixth century BC, the sympathetic passersby wondered if this devastated city could really have been "the joy of the whole earth" (Lam. 2:15).

In this minicollection of Zion songs (Pss. 46–48) the preferred name of the city is Zion, or Mount Zion, since that is the religious name of the city. The name Jerusalem conjured up political thoughts, while the name Zion invoked religious and spiritual impressions. In fact, the name Jerusalem does not appear in any of the Korah psalms, and only here in Psalm 48 does Zion, the religious designation of the city, appear in the Korah collection. In scope, these three psalms exhibit an advancing pattern. Even though they are called Zion songs, Psalm 46 does not use the name Zion at all but speaks of the city with epithets, which were well understood, of course, but more allusive. Most assuredly the place of refuge was "the city of God" and "the holy place where the Most High dwells" (46:4), and that was the point—not the place but God's presence. That psalm was a confession by God's people that God is their refuge, a confession of faith in an informal sense. Psalm 47 picks up the threads of a multilayered history of this city, acclaiming Yahweh to be "the great King over all the earth" (*melek gadol 'al-kol-ha'arets*, 47:2) and summoning the nations to join the acclamation, still with no mention of the name Zion but only an allusion to worship activity there (47:5). With Psalm 48 we reach the summit of our ascent, as the psalmist proclaims the Lord's greatness in "the city of our God, his holy mountain" (48:1), "the city of the Great King" (*qiryat melek rab*, 48:2). And if there be any doubt about its identity, doubt no longer, because the city is Mount Zion (48:2, 11, 12), where the temple stands (48:9) and where God takes his place "in her citadels" (48:3).

Key Themes of Psalm 48

- God will be our guide to the end.
- God's name is who he is.
- Meditate on God's unfailing love.

From that summit we can view Zion with the kings (48:4) and admire her towers and citadels with the pilgrims as they make their circular inspection (48:12–13). In a literary sense we have "ascended amid shouts of joy" and "sounding of trumpets" (47:5), and in a religious sense we have finally seen with our eyes the evidence we have only heard about with our ears (48:8).

Outline/Structure

When we listen to the voices of the psalm, we hear only the psalmist's voice—God never speaks, nor do the kings or Zion's pilgrims. However, the psalmist thinks their

Jerusalem, the city of God, is described as well fortified, causing invading kings to flee in terror. Shown here is the excavated area known as the "stepped-stone structure" located in the ancient city of David. Thought to have originally been part of the Jebusite city and then enlarged by David, it may have supported a large civic structure such as a fortress.

(Mount) Zion

The origin of the name Zion is uncertain, but its historical and religious significance is beyond dispute.[a] The first mention of the word is recorded in 2 Samuel 5:7 in connection with David's capture of Jerusalem from the Jebusites: "David captured the fortress of Zion—which is the City of David" (also 1 Chron. 11:5), implying that the fortress was known by that name prior to the capture and later received the popular name "city of David." "Mount Zion" is an alternate name, describing its topography. The name Zion is applied to the city of Jerusalem (e.g., Ps. 48:12; Isa. 1:27), at times called "the daughter of Zion" (Lam. 2:1) or described as the hill that David bought from Araunah for the temple site (Mount Zion, Ps. 42:6; see 2 Sam. 24:18–25). While Jerusalem was the political and geographical name of the city, the name Zion definitely had religious implications, most likely acquired after David's conquest, although the city of Salem had political associations even in Abraham's time (Gen. 14). Of the more than 150 times the word occurs in the Old Testament, over half of them are in Isaiah and the Psalms. Zion or Mount Zion is also used for the place where the Lord dwells (e.g., Ps. 9:11; 74:2), and sometimes for the place where Israel worships (Ps. 102:21–22). In the Prophets and Psalms restored Zion will be the place where Yahweh's kingdom will be centered (Jer. 30:17, 18), and from which Yahweh will reign. By the fourth century AD the name Mount Zion had mistakenly been given to the southwestern hill of Jerusalem, and even today Christians refer to that hill as Mount Zion.

[a] W. H. Bellinger Jr., "Zion," *NIDB* 5:895–96.

thoughts for them and puts them into his own words (called "irony of attribution"), and further, he breaks out into a prayer of affirmation, followed by instructions for Zion's pilgrims in the theme of the psalm. This gives us the following outline:

1. Mount Zion extolled as the "city of the Great King" (48:1–3)
2. Reaction of kings to Mount Zion's impregnability, told in the psalmist's own words (48:4–6)
3. Prayer in the temple affirming God's unfailing love (48:7–11)
   a. A flash of historical memory (48:7)

b. Prayerful meditation on God's unfailing love (48:8–11)
4. Admonition to Mount Zion's pilgrims (48:12–13)
5. Concluding benediction (48:14)

Historical and Cultural Background

See the sidebar "(Mount) Zion" and "Additional Insights" on Jerusalem following this unit.

Interpretive Insights

48:1 *Great is the LORD, and most worthy of praise . . . his holy mountain.* The Hebrew expression "most worthy of praise" is the Pual participle from the verb "praise" (*hll*), plus the adverb "very." The KJV combines accurate meaning and literary beauty in its translation: "Great is the LORD, and *greatly to be praised.*" The phrase "holy mountain" occurs in Isaiah 27:13 and 66:20.

48:2 *Beautiful in its loftiness, the joy of the whole earth.* The word translated as "loftiness" means "height." "The joy of the whole earth" means that the sight of Zion brings joy to the whole world. In Psalm 47:1 the peoples are summoned to acclaim the Lord's kingship "with cries of joy [*rinnah*]." "The joy of the whole earth" also occurs in Lamentations 2:15.

the heights of Zaphon . . . the city of the Great King. The general opinion is that the "heights of Zaphon" is a reference to a mountain north of Ugarit, near the present border between Syria and Turkey. It was known in Canaanite mythology as the dwelling place of the god Baal (see Exod. 14:2). The word "Zaphon" came to mean "north" in biblical Hebrew, thus the KJV "sides of the north." While the mythological interpretation is possible, it seems out of place here in a psalm where the God of Zion is being extolled. If the point is to compare the two mountains, the text as it stands does not accomplish this. Perhaps the better alternative is to view this as a generic reference to Mount Zion as the northernmost reaches of the city. The final expression, "city of the Great King," refers to a city that is fitting for a great king.[1]

48:3 *God is in her citadels.* "Citadels" (lit., "her palaces") may be a reference to the city's elevated fortifications, rather than residential palaces, as may also be the case in Lamentations 2:7.[2] The verse reads literally, "In her palaces/fortifications God is known as [her] fortress." This probably means that within the city proper God is recognized as the city's fortress. This would be a positive assessment of Jerusalem's faith at that moment in time.

48:4–5 *When the kings joined forces, when they advanced together.* This is a general description of the way kings perceived Zion with its fortifications: "They saw her and were astounded." The verb "astounded" occurs in Genesis 43:33 to describe the emotional reaction of Joseph's brothers to the way he was treating them (NIV: "in astonishment"). The kings come to Zion and see one thing, while the pilgrims come and see another (48:8–9), even

though it is the same sight.[3] The Hebrew particle *ken* ("thus") occurs between the two verbs to emphasize the second. Calvin says this word functions as a pointing finger.[4] We should understand it as follows: "They looked, (and that's the reason) they were astounded (at what they saw)."

48:6 *pain like that of a woman in labor.* The noun "pain" describes the would-be enemies of Zion as overcome by labor pains (Isa. 13:8 [NIV: "writhe"]; Jer. 22:23; Mic. 4:9). The sudden change in emotions seems to be the point of the simile.

48:7 *like ships of Tarshish.* These could be ships *from* Tarshish bringing their wares, or ships that were *seaworthy enough* to sail to Tarshish or to sail great distances (Isa. 2:16; see NIV footnote). There seem to have been two places called Tarshish: (1) in Asia Minor, which Genesis 10:4 suggests (Tarshish of "the sons of Javan"); (2) in the far west, in Spain, where the Phoenician colony of Tartessus was located. Another option would be North Africa.[5] See also Jonah 1:3.

48:8 *As we have heard, so we have seen . . . God makes her secure forever.* These are most likely the words of pilgrims who have come to Jerusalem and whose reaction is quite different from that of the kings (48:4–6)—the pilgrims react to what they have heard of God's promises, which have now become reality before their eyes. Calvin comments that

Even though the city was well fortified, it was God who provided the protection. In the ancient world, cities were surrounded by walls to create a place of refuge and defense. As the city of Jerusalem spread westward, its walls were also expanded. The remains of a wall from the eighth century BC are shown here.

this verse contains the rich doctrine "that God does not disappoint the hope which he produces in our minds by means of his word, and that it is not His way to be more liberal in promising than faithful in performing what he has promised."[6]

48:9 *Within your temple, O God, we meditate on your unfailing love.* This may be a second recognition that the pilgrims make: that God's "unfailing love" dwells in his temple.[7] This could allude to a specific ritual performed in the temple, or it could be merely a general description of the meaning of temple worship, God's unfailing love (*hesed*) being the central focus. The model service of Jehoshaphat's time laid out by the Chronicler informs us that the Kohathites and the Korahites "stood up and praised the LORD, the God of Israel"

(2 Chron. 20:19), which is close to the meaning of this verse.

48:10 *Like your name, O God.* On the first part of this verse, Calvin suggests that it means God's works correspond with his name.[8] Craigie suggests the English phrase "as good as one's word" as the sense in capsule form.[9]

48:12 *Walk about Zion, go around her, count her towers.* This is spoken to the pilgrims by a priest or officiant, suggesting either an actual or a mental tour of the city fortifications. It continues through verse 14. See Isaiah 33:18, where Jerusalem's towers are a spectacle for visitors. Hilber notes that Near Eastern city hymns feature an imaginary tour of the city.[10]

48:13 *consider well her ramparts, view her citadels, that you may tell of them to*

The psalmist encourages the people to "walk about Zion, . . . count her towers, . . . view her citadels" (48:12–13). The walls around the Old City of Jerusalem today are from the Ottoman Era and date to the sixteenth century AD. This section on the western side of the city provides a sense of the size and protection such city walls provided.

the next generation. The word translated as "ramparts" denotes some type of fortification, but the exact type is not clear.[11] The pilgrims are instructed to transmit this information to their children ("the next generation"). This is reminiscent of the charge in Deuteronomy 6:7 to "talk about them when you sit at home and when you walk along the road, when you lie down and when you get up." See Nehemiah 12:31–43 for Nehemiah's dedication of the Jerusalem wall.

48:14 *this God is our God for ever and ever; he will be our guide even to the end.* The sense seems to be that what the pilgrims see in Zion will convince them that "this God is our God for ever and ever." "He will be our guide" brings to mind the picture of the shepherd leading the way. The phrase "to the end" is the Hebrew *'al-mut*, which the Greek (LXX) takes as *'olamot*, "forever." Some scholars have proposed that it belongs to the beginning of Psalm 49, rather than the end of Psalm 48. See similar headings in Psalms 9 and 46.

Theological Insights

Sometimes ancient Israel had a strong sense of false security in their capital city and temple. It was partly because the temple, the dwelling place of God, was present in the city, and only in that truth was its invulnerability explainable. The point of Psalm 48 is that the Lord was the city's security (48:8), and "this God is our God for ever and ever" (48:14). There was nothing wrong with admiring the temple, as Jeremiah's compatriots did (Jer. 7:9–15), or, for that matter, admiring the great cathedrals and churches of the modern world, but the truth remains that the God of Scripture who is worshiped in those places (48:9) is the securing force.

Teaching the Text

Since we always want to have a sense of where we are as we work our way through the Psalms, we should point to the fact that Psalms 46, 47, and 48 pay tribute to Jerusalem. While Christianity has sometimes turned the names Zion and Jerusalem into symbols of the church, we need to take care that we not lose sight of the historical reality of this ancient city. So, resisting that temptation, we might build our lesson or sermon around three insights, built on textual observations.

The first is the difference between "hearing" and "seeing." Verse 8 highlights the emotion of anticipation that attends plans to make a pilgrimage to a holy site like Jerusalem. We know the disappointment of having our actual experience lag far behind the anticipation. But not so for these pilgrims who have heard of the city's beauty and upon arrival find that it is all they have anticipated. It is more than the discovery of sight, but it goes to the very heart of the city's theological reputation: "God makes her secure forever" (48:8c).

A second insight is laid out in the statement of verse 10: "As is Your name, O God, So is Your praise to the ends of the earth" (NASB). God's name is different from our modern names—God's name captures the essence of who he is. At this point we can beneficially talk about Moses's interchange with God at the burning bush: What should he tell the Israelites when they ask who sent him and when they ask him, "What is his name?" (Exod. 3:13). Rather than answering with a name as such, God answered with a character description: "I AM WHO I AM" (Exod. 3:14). It comes from the Hebrew verb "to be" (*hyh*) and evidently is intended to assure Israel that "God is with them" (cf. Isa. 7:14).[12] We may even make a short digression on the name of Jesus and refer to the angel's instructions to Joseph: "You are to give him the name Jesus, because he will save his people from their sins" (Matt. 1:21). This is good reason to treat God's name with great reverence (Exod. 20:7).

A third observation is that the Jerusalem pilgrims in the temple meditate on God's "unfailing love" [hesed] (48:9). This is as good a summary of worship as we have in the Old Testament. In fact, it is as good a summary of worship as we have anywhere in Scripture. The verb "meditate" here (dmh, "to be silent") can mean to be "struck dumb": "We are struck dumb [or

"awed"], O God, by your unfailing love" (author's trans.).

We may end the lesson with an emphasis on the idea of God as "Guide" at the end of the psalm (48:14). Yahweh as Guide is a prominent metaphor in the Psalms (e.g., Ps. 23:2, 3), and this metaphor becomes more than just a literary device as we find ourselves wandering in our own world with so many markers to point the way but so few that offer a Guide to lead us to our destination. In fact, in keeping with the theme that God's presence in Jerusalem is the securing force of the city, the final verse insists that our Guide is the most important aspect of the journey.

Illustrating the Text

There is a difference between hearing and seeing.

Personal Testimony: Drawing from your own life experiences, share a time you made a journey to a destination you had heard about but had never seen (for example, the Grand Canyon, the Pacific Ocean). Share with your listeners the sense of anticipation you had and how what you experienced when you arrived was far greater than anything you had imagined. This was the experience of the religious pilgrims who traveled from various cities to worship in the great city of Jerusalem (as talked about in this unit). This would also be a great opportunity to draw a parallel between hearing *about* God from others, as opposed to *seeing or*

God's name reaches to the ends of the earth. This twelfth- to thirteenth-century icon shows Moses removing his shoes as he stands in God's presence at the burning bush where God revealed his name as "I AM WHO I AM" (Exod. 3:14).

experiencing God firsthand. Just as experiencing the great city of Zion firsthand was better than simply hearing about it from others, so experiencing God for ourselves is better than simply hearing about him from others.

The uniqueness of the church

Quote: **William Temple.** The psalmist's description of the substance of worship is found in verse 9: "We meditate on your unfailing love." Archbishop of Canterbury William Temple (1942–44) expressed the essence of this statement on worship in an address he made to the people of the United States:

> I am disposed to begin by making what many people will feel to be a quite outrageous statement. This world can be saved from political chaos and collapse by one thing only, and that is worship. For to worship is to quicken the conscience by the holiness of God, to feed the mind with the truth of God, to purge the imagination by the beauty of God, to open up

the heart to the love of God, to devote the will to the purpose of God.[13]

The glory of God is awesome.

Church History: In John Calvin's commentary on the Psalms, he comments on Psalm 48:4:

> It is related of Caesar in ancient times, that when speaking of the ease with which he subdued Egypt, he made use of the laconic saying, "I came, I saw, I conquered"; but the prophet here states on the contrary, that the ungodly were struck with amazement at the mere sight of the city, as if God had dazzled their eyes with the splendour of his glory.[14]

We must be careful that we not underestimate the glory of God. It was because of God's glory that Moses was forced to hide his eyes (Exod. 3:5–6). And it is in the face of Jesus Christ that we have seen God's glory (John 1:14), a privilege Moses did not have, reserved for those who worship God in Jesus Christ.

Jerusalem and the Temple

The city of Jerusalem has a history of nearly four thousand years. "As the mountains surround Jerusalem, so the LORD surrounds his people" (Ps. 125:2). This geographical detail, describing the city as a natural fortress, is a simile for God's protecting care of his people and illustrates the fact that Jerusalem and Israel's religion are inseparable. Geographically, two mountain ridges running roughly north–south were surrounded by three valleys: the Kidron on the east, the Hinnom on the west, and the Tyropoean in the middle. There was no east–west highway that could accommodate armies or commercial traffic, contributing to Jerusalem's relative isolation. The most plausible route for invaders or traders was from the north.

Historically, Jerusalem is mentioned in Egyptian Execration texts of the nineteenth and eighteenth centuries BC as *urushalim*. Among the Amarna Letters from the fourteenth century BC, six are from Abdu-Heba, king of *urusalim*, then a city-state, to the Egyptian pharaoh.[1] In the Bible, Melchizedek, king of Salem (Jerusalem), provides the first introduction to the city, and he blesses Abraham (Gen. 14). Joshua had a military success against a coalition of five kings, including Adoni-Zedek of Jerusalem (Josh. 10:5–11), but it evidently fell short of a conquest of the city. That long-term success was achieved by David, who, sometime in the late eleventh or early tenth century, captured the city, which was then occupied by the Jebusites, and made it the political and religious capital of his kingdom (2 Sam. 5:6–16; 6). Part of that achievement was based on his purchase of the threshing floor of Araunah the Jebusite for the purpose of building the sanctuary there (2 Sam. 24:18–25). That fact also suggests that David did not drive out all the Jebusites when he captured Jerusalem.

David's plan to build the temple on the site of the threshing floor was thwarted by God's instructions through the prophet Nathan (2 Sam. 7), leaving the task to David's son and successor Solomon (1 Kings 6–9). Solomon's construction of the temple

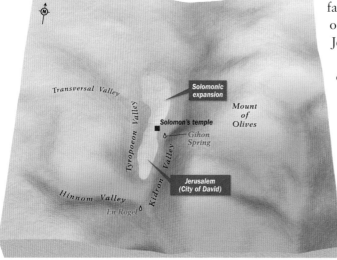

Transversal Valley

Tyropoeon Valley

Solomon's temple

Solomonic expansion

Mount of Olives

Gihon Spring

Kidron Valley

Jerusalem (City of David)

Hinnom Valley

En Rogel

The three valleys that encircle Jerusalem on the east, south, and west acted as a natural fortress providing protection for the city.

inaugurated the First Temple period. The city of Jerusalem remained the political and religious capital until it was conquered by Nebuchadnezzar in 586 BC, at which time he destroyed Solomon's temple.

The Second Temple period was inaugurated by the reconstruction of the temple during the years 520–516 BC under the Persian-appointed governor Zerubbabel, but that temple was not completed until the fifth century (Ezra 6:15). For a long period of time the city's political fortunes shifted from one conquering nation to another, with quasi independence from time to time, except for a century of independence during the Hasmonean period (ca. 160–63 BC). The Romans took control under Pompey in 63 BC, and in the last part of that century Herod the Great rebuilt the temple as a favor to the Jews. In the eighteenth year of his reign, Herod proposed this colossal project, promising the Jews that he would not demolish the old temple until all things were ready for the new construction (Josephus, *Antiquities* 15.389). To allay the Jews' fears, the main temple building was constructed in one and a half years. The porticoes, however, took an additional eight years, and the full project was not completed until around AD 63 (see John 2:20–21). The Romans destroyed the city and the temple in AD 70 as part of their effort to suppress the First Jewish Revolt.[2]

The Jewish temple that was in operation from the time of Jesus until its destruction in AD 70 was built by Herod the Great. This 50:1 scale reconstruction of the first-century AD city of Jerusalem, looking west, shows the temple complex at its eastern edge as the city spreads around it.

"No One Can Redeem the Life of Another or Give to God a Ransom for Them"

Big Idea *In the face of death, wealth cannot buy God off, but he can and does redeem (spare) our lives from the power of death at his own will.*

Understanding the Text

Psalm 49 has typically been classified as a wisdom psalm and dated anywhere from the tenth to the second century BC (see the sidebar "Wisdom Psalms" in the unit on Ps. 37). Kraus prefers the category of didactic poem because this psalm, like Psalms 73 and 139, aims to reflect on a problem.[1] In the same frame of thought, Craigie imagines that this psalm was the product of a question brought to a wise sage, a "counseling situation," no less.[2] Like Psalm 47, the audience is the wide sphere of humanity, addressed to "all you peoples," "all who live in this world" (49:1), and further defined as "both low and high, rich and poor alike" (49:2).

The Text in Context

Psalms 37, 49, and 73 deal with the question of the prosperity of the wicked and the suffering of the righteous (see "Additional Insights: Wealth and Wickedness in Psalms 37, 49, and 73" after the unit on Ps. 37). Like Psalm 47, Psalm 49 begins by addressing "all peoples," but in content, the two have little in common.

Outline/Structure

Psalm 49 consists of the musings of the poet. No other voices are heard. In fact, God is mentioned only twice (49:7, 15). The addressees and the literary method are set forth in 49:1–4, and the problem is posed in question form in 49:5–6: "Why should I fear when evil days come, when wicked deceivers surround me—those who trust in their wealth and boast of their great riches?" The question is enlarged in 49:7–11. A refrain that captures the essence of the "solution" closes the second and third stanzas (49:12, 20).

1. Introduction, addressed to a universal audience (49:1–4)
   a. The audience (49:1–2)
   b. The literary method (49:3–4)

2. The question introduced and reflected on (49:5–12)
   a. The question: "Why should I fear . . . ?" (49:5–6)
   b. Reflection (49:7–11)
   c. Refrain (49:12)
3. The "solution" introduced and reflected on (49:13–20)
   a. A summary of the "solution": "This is the fate . . ." (49:13)
   b. Death is the "shepherd" of the wicked (49:14)
   c. The contrasting destiny of the psalmist: "*But* God . . . will take" him from the realm of the dead (49:15)
   d. Self-admonition/answer to the question of 49:5: "Do not fear" (NIV: "Do not be overawed") (49:16–19)
   e. Refrain (49:20)

Historical and Cultural Background

While we do not have a definitive doctrine of immortality in the Old Testament, we have, especially in the Psalms, a theme of living in God's presence, a theme of life (see Ps. 16), and a theme of death, which is often expressed in terms of Sheol (see the sidebar "Sheol" in the unit on Ps. 6). Psalm 49 and other psalmic texts (e.g., Ps. 16:9–11) delineate the doctrinal platform on which the doctrine of eternal life is laid down for us in the New Testament. The problem of life's brevity, longing for permanence, and the desire to

The psalmist states that he will accompany his words of wisdom with the music of a harp or lyre. This Assyrian relief depicts two musicians from the court of Ashurbanipal. The one on the left carries a vertical harp and the other a lyre (645–635 BC).

Key Themes of Psalm 49

- Wealth cannot buy off death.
- Redemption has a cost.

be in God's presence, both before and after death, are the gridirons of the platform.

Interpretive Insights

49:1 *Hear this, all you peoples; listen, all who live in this world.* Compare this opening with the opening of Psalm 47:1. These imperatives signal that a speech or some important word is to follow. The word for "world" (*heled*) means "temporal life" and occurs in Psalm 17:14.

49:2 *both low and high, rich and poor alike.* "Low" (*bᵉne 'adam*, "sons of humankind") and "high" (*bᵉne 'ish*, "sons of a man") seem to refer to the common people and the more influential, respectively (see the comments on Ps. 4:2).[3]

49:3 *My mouth will speak words of wisdom.* The Hebrew word for "wisdom" is

Psalm 49

plural here, as is also the word for "understanding," suggesting the weighty importance of the terms. They are virtually synonymous. "Meditation" includes both thought and speech (Pss. 1:2; 19:14).

49:4 *with the harp I will expound my riddle.* For "harp" (*kinnor*), see the sidebar "Musical Instruments in Psalm 33" in the unit on Psalm 33 and the sidebar "Three Musical Instruments" in the unit on Psalm 92. The Hebrew word for "riddle" may refer to a "saying," "allegory" (Ezek. 17:2), "riddle" (Judg. 14:12–13), or a perplexing question (1 Kings 10:1; Ps. 78:2 [NIV: "hidden things"]).[4] Here, "riddle" is parallel to "parable" and is synonymous with it.

49:5 *wicked deceivers.* The phrase is difficult (lit., "[the] iniquity of the deceivers"). The Greek text (LXX) translates it "iniquity of my heels," perhaps implying iniquity that pursues.

49:6 *those who trust in their wealth.* These people compose the psalmist's secondary audience, but his primary hearers are those who are troubled by the activities of the wealthy and powerful.

49:7–8 *No one can redeem the life of another.* Literally, the sentence may read: "As for a brother, a person can absolutely not redeem him." There are some legal cases in Israelite law when a person can avoid capital punishment by paying a ransom (Exod. 21:29–30; Num. 35:31; Prov. 6:35; 13:8). But faced with the ultimate reality of death, there is no one who can pay that kind of price, which is in fact incalculable. Some take verse 8 as a gloss, but it reinforces the thought in the previous verse, suggesting the incalculable worth of a human being.

49:9 *so that they should live on forever.* Literally, "so that they should live again

forever." The idea is to continue living in this life without experiencing death. The Hebrew word for "decay" is used in other places as a synonym of Sheol (also translated as "pit" or "dungeon"; see Pss. 16:10; 30:9; Isa. 38:17; 51:14). Here it means death.

49:10 *the foolish and the senseless also perish.* The "foolish" one "is not a half-wit" but someone who "deliberately rejects the wisdom."[5] The "senseless" one is someone who lacks understanding (Prov. 30:2). These two terms occur in parallel in Psalm 92:6.

49:11 *Their tombs will remain their houses forever.* "Their tombs" is singular in Hebrew. The Greek text (LXX), Syriac, and Targum read the word as "tomb/grave" (*qibram*) rather than the Hebrew *qirbam* ("their inward thought"), transposing the middle letters. This emendation is recognized in the Talmud (*Mo'ed Qatan* 9b).

49:12 *People, despite their wealth, do not endure; they are like the beasts that perish.* The word "wealth" picks up on the verb "to be costly" in 49:8: "The ransom for a life is costly." This suggests that their wealth, however much it is, cannot suffice to ransom their life from death. The comparison with the beasts is repeated in 49:20. The simile "like the beasts that perish" makes the rich appear all the more irrational.

49:13 *This is the fate of those.* This verse is difficult. Hakham judges it to be "among the most obscure verses in the Book of Psalms."[6] The RSV seems to catch the sense while staying pretty close to the Hebrew text: "This is the fate of those who have foolish confidence, the end of those who are pleased with their portion." Then follows the description of death in 49:14.

49:14 *death will be their shepherd (but the upright will prevail over them in the* *morning).* This verse forms quite a contrast to Psalm 23, where the Lord is the psalmist's Shepherd and leads him safely through the "valley of the shadow of death" (23:4; see NIV footnote)! Here death conducts the psalmist to the other world or in the other world. Kidner points out that in the Old Testament it is unusual to find death personified and calls attention to the striking metaphor in Jeremiah 9:21, where death climbs into Zion's windows, captures its inhabitants, and carts them away.[7] Goldingay, as does the NIV, takes the parenthetical statement to refer to the situation between "the upright" and the fool in this world. It speaks of a reversal, when "in the morning" of that new day, those who have experienced trouble will experience a great deliverance.[8]

49:15 *But God will redeem me . . . he will surely take me to himself.* This is the climax of the psalm, even though its meaning is not absolutely clear.[9] It recalls the occurrence of the idea of redemption from 49:7 and 8 and seems to be the alternative result of faith to the end of a life of trust in wealth and power. Kidner calls this "one of the mountain tops of Old Testament hope."[10] The adversative particle translated as "but" (*'ak*) indicates the change of thought. Schaefer comments: "The lengthy description of inescapable death suddenly stumbles on the disjunctive *'ak*, 'but,' and the surprising

declaration, 'But God will ransom my soul, [he will take me] from the power of Sheol' (49:15)."[11] The verb "take" may be an allusion to Enoch ("God took him," Gen. 5:24). The phrase "to himself" is not in the Hebrew text. This is in stark contrast to 49:8: one cannot ransom one's own life, but God can "take" him from the power of Sheol (or save him from the power of death), as God took Enoch (cf. Ps. 73:24). Kidner, in his usual way, takes the historical sense of Scripture very seriously without muffling the eschatological hope that lies within it: "Whether this vision reached as far as resurrection or not, it tells us the first thing that matters beyond death, that nothing can separate the servant from his Master, whose concern for him is loving and active."[12]

49:16 *Do not be overawed when others grow rich.* The second-person singular verb might imply that the psalmist is speaking to himself, especially in view of his potential fear expressed in 49:5, or he may be speaking to his audience collectively.

49:17 *for they will take nothing with them when they die.* See Ecclesiastes 5:15 and 1 Timothy 6:7.

49:20 *People who have wealth but lack understanding are like the beasts that perish.* The first half of the verse is a repetition of 12a with slight differences. The word for "wealth" involves more than material riches. As is obvious in this psalm, it involves an attitude toward wealth that magnifies the material and depreciates the spiritual.

Theological Insights

There are few realities in life that bring the individual face-to-face with God as does the reality of death. Yet death has its detractors, two of which are the subject of this psalm: wealth and power. The psalmist feels threatened by the power that accompanies wealth. The dark clouds of an "evil day" have gathered, created by "those who trust in their wealth and boast of their great riches" (49:5–6). In the stark reality of the threat, the sage eludes the fear that these days could bring by appealing to the cost of a ransom from death and of paying God off—too costly (49:7–9)! Incalculable! The truth of the matter is that death shows no discrimination, coming to the wise and foolish alike (49:10). And wealth, despite its powerful influence during life, falls to others, and the cycle is repeated (49:16–19). Yet there is one redeeming factor, God, since only he can "redeem" one's life from death (49:15). In view of this shocking dilemma,

The psalmist tells his listeners not to be "overawed when others grow rich" (49:16). The pharaohs thought their wealth would provide a comfortable afterlife, but these riches have remained behind while their bodies have decayed. This photo taken in 1923 shows the antechamber to King Tutankhamen's tomb with all the funerary objects that the Egyptians thought would be useful in the afterlife.

from which there is no escape, except through God, the question hangs in the air: "Why should I fear?" (49:5). And the sage answers his own question as he turns to himself, or perhaps to his audience, and reprovingly admonishes: "Do not fear when one becomes rich" (author's trans.) because the wealthy will die and leave their riches and fame behind them (49:16–17).

Psalm 49 employs one of the Old Testament verbs for "redeem" (*pdh*). In Exodus 13:13, 15 it refers to the redemption of the firstborn male that otherwise belonged to the Lord, releasing him from the Lord's service to his family's service. The idea was to provide an equivalent value for the thing or person redeemed,[13] a value that, as in our psalm (49:7–8, 15), is not always specified. But the meaning is clear, that the life of an individual is too precious to provide an equivalent value: "The ransom for a life is costly, no payment is ever enough" (49:8). In the psalm's argument, the adversive particle that begins 49:15 ('*ak*) marks a decisive turn in the argument. No one can redeem a life from death but God, and that is precisely what God has done for the psalmist. It is an Old Testament alert to God's intervention into human history, in this case, into personal history. And it is hard to believe that the psalmist did not have in mind the story of Genesis 3. Regardless, he certainly was conscious of the threatening power of death, and even more conscious of the overwhelming power of God to loose its bonds on human life.

Teaching the Text

We may begin our lesson with the basic observation that Psalm 49 deals with wealth and power—they seem to go together. In fact, this psalm deals with the false security that wealth gives. The message, as with Psalms 47 and 48, is addressed to the whole world, not just Israel (49:1)—it is a universal problem. We may also observe that this is a message we all need to hear, whether we are rich or poor.

First, we may deal with the problem as Psalm 49 lays it out:

> Why should I fear when evil days come,
> when wicked deceivers surround me—
> those who trust in their wealth
> and boast of their great riches? (49:5–6)

Two things are involved here: the security that wealth brings to its patrons, and the fear and insecurity it causes for its non-patrons. Then the supplicant considers the false premise articulated in verses 8–9 that money can buy anything—death is one thing we cannot buy off (49:10). The psalm drives home this point by a refrain that occurs in verses 12 and 20: "People, despite their wealth, do not endure; they are like the beasts that perish" (49:12). To theologize a bit, we may observe that in the biblical story death was not God's doing—it was humankind's. But God put death to good use, just like he does with many of the evils of this world, making it *his* servant, until, of course, he finishes with it, and then death will be swallowed up in victory (1 Cor. 15:54). God makes death work for him in that it is a reminder that there is one boundary we cannot cross and that we are ultimately not in control—God is. In this sense it turns us toward God.

After dealing with the problem, we may then consider the "solution," which Psalm 49 announces in two ways. The first is in the refrain of verses 12 and 20, which captures the essence of the solution and closes the second and third stanzas of the psalm with the announcement that "people, despite their wealth, do not endure; they are like the beasts that perish" (49:12). We might call that the downside of the solution. The second part of the announcement comes in verse 15 with the declaration that "God will redeem me from the realm of the dead [from the power of Sheol, or death]; he will surely take me to himself." This is the upside of the solution. Perhaps it would be helpful to explain that the idea of redemption was to provide an equivalent value for the thing or person redeemed,[14] a value that, as in our psalm (49:7–8, 15), is not always specified. But the meaning is clear, that the life of an individual is too precious to provide an equivalent value for: "The ransom for a life is costly, no payment is ever enough" (49:8). That is, we have no ability to provide redemption for anyone, but God does, and God will. We might use the metaphor that the expression "but" (*'ak*, 49:15) is the fulcrum on which life's uncertainties, indeed, impossibilities, turn. Yet the idea that this pivot would turn in the direction of the New Testament drama of redemption is a bit surprising, at least in the context of this psalm. But we are thankfully reminded that God is in control—we are not—and only God can provide the equivalent value of human life, and that transaction is called *redemption*.

Illustrating the Text

The reality of death

Quote: Artur Weiser. German scholar Artur Weiser comments on the inevitability of death: "For in death man inevitably encounters the power of God, no matter how often he may have tried in other respects to evade that power and rely exclusively on his own strength. And because it is the power of God, all human power that is opposed to it is on that account bound to prove unavailing."[15] What we know as Christians is that not only is death inevitable, but every person who ever lived will encounter the power of God and fall to his or her knees before him in complete submission. Regardless of our perceptions of God while we are living in this world, the truth will be revealed, in no uncertain terms, at death. Understanding this reality should not only encourage those who put their trust in the Lord but also move them with a sense of desperation to proclaim the truth about the Lord to every person!

Wealth can't buy off death—but God can.

News Story: In 2013, the thirtieth anniversary of PNC Wealth Management's annual (tongue-in-cheek) Christmas Price Index (CPI), the *St. Louis Post-Dispatch* published the cost of the 364 items listed in the song "The Twelve Days of Christmas," according to their current prices. The CPI for buying just one set of each verse in the song would cost $24,263, and buying all 364 items would amount to $101,119.[16] Although money, and the power that often goes with it, can get us a lot of things, Psalm 49 reminds us that death is one thing money can't buy off (49:8–10). Yet God can: "God will redeem me from the realm of the dead, he will surely take me to himself" (49:15). And God did! That truth prompts Paul in his hymnic exultation in Romans 8 to ask, "Who shall separate us from the love of Christ?" and triumphantly to declare that "neither death nor life, neither angels nor demons, neither the present nor the future, nor any powers, neither height nor depth, nor anything else in all creation, will be able to separate us from the love of God that is in Christ Jesus our Lord" (Rom. 8:35, 38–39).

Invest in eternity.

Bible: Psalm 49 provides a great connection to the parable of the rich fool (Luke 12:16–21). In this parable Jesus tells the story of a rich man who plans to "take life easy; eat, drink, and be merry." But God says to the rich man, "You fool! This very night your life will be demanded from you. Then who will get what

In Matthew 6 Jesus teaches that treasures in heaven last forever. Treasures accumulated on earth only rust and decay, like this commemorative sword from AD 15.

you have prepared for yourself?" Jesus explains, "This is how it will be with whoever stores up things for themselves but is not rich toward God." You might also want to mention Matthew 6:19–21, where Jesus teaches the principle of treasures in heaven that last forever as opposed to earthly treasures that last only a lifetime.

The Afterlife and Immortality in the Old Testament

The Old Testament, and especially the Psalms, is full of hope, hope for a better life, politically, spiritually, socially, and materially. For the most part this hope is confined to this world, but hope, both ancient and modern, is characterized by an inner force that sometimes breaks out of bounds and makes forced entry into another sphere. That is one aspect, hope that rises from the human heart. And if the Old Testament writers only *hoped* for an existence after death, then that is the category in which we must consider many if not all of the references in the Old Testament to a postmortem existence, whether physical or spiritual. Yet, the question is whether there is such a thing in the Old Testament as *hope of immortality revealed*. Most students of the Old Testament will admit that the doctrine of immortality is not strong in this Testament, and even those texts that seem to advocate such an idea are controversial. In the Psalms such passages as 16:10; 23:6; 49:15; and 73:24–25 have been viewed as containing some degree of belief in the afterlife, especially for the righteous. Proponents of *immortality revealed* point to Job 19:25–27 as a wisdom text that affirms the afterlife. And Enoch (Gen. 5:24) and Elijah (2 Kings 2), some would insist, were "taken" out of the earthly life, with the implication that they entered another sphere of existence. We may make the following observations.

First, in Israel's world the doctrine of the afterlife is well attested, from the robust belief of Egypt to the rather anemic view of Mesopotamia and Canaan. Israel should not be expected to copy such a doctrine, but in view of the emphasis on life's brevity and its attendant plethora of troubles, it would be strange to find no remnants of such a doctrine in the Old Testament. So our natural inclination, especially with New Testament encouragement, is to look for them.

Second, it is a valid question whether those Old Testament texts we are concerned about, especially in the Psalms and Job, are more *human longings* than *expectations* and so do not fall in the category of revealed truth. David J. A. Clines proposes, for example, that Job 19:25 belongs in the category of Job's *desires* rather than his *knowledge*.[1] I am inclined, however, to believe that the opening verb "I know" governs the rest of the text (Job 19:25–27). Although Job looks enviously at a tree and laments that it has a much stronger hope of living again than does a person (Job 14:7–17), Job's experience in the dialogue is dynamic, not static, and thus his understanding undergoes change and development. What may be a *desire* in Job 14:7–17 has become a confident confession in 19:25–27 ("I know") or at least has moved into the category of hopeful

Of all of Israel's neighbors, Egypt had the most sophisticated view of the afterlife. For example, in the interior of the coffin of Gua, shown here, a map was painted on the bottom to guide the deceased to the afterlife. Pictures of items that would be needed in the afterlife and spells to provide help on the journey were included on the sides (Deir el-Bersha, Egypt, Twelfth Dynasty, 1985–1795 BC).

"thinking") is the bodily resurrection, embraced later in Judaism (2 Macc. 7).

Third, the New Testament witness is the final piece of our evidence, which, admittedly, some would not list in the category of "evidence." Yet when Peter quotes Psalm 16:8–11 (15:8–11 LXX) in Acts 2:22–33 and applies it to Christ's resurrection (also Paul, in Acts 13:35–37), he speaks authoritatively. While some may consider Peter's and Paul's use of this text more in the category of the Jewish hermeneutical method of *remez* ("hint"), these apostles seem to understand the text as revelation, just as Matthew does Hosea 11:1 (Matt. 2:15).

The conclusion to the matter is that the New Testament acts like a magnet that attracts these Old Testament texts to its doctrines of immortality and the resurrection, suggesting that the texts themselves were not devoid of the doctrine, even though they awaited the magnetic force of the New Testament, especially the resurrection of Christ, to activate this attraction.

confession. Even though the truth of the postmortem vindication is quite clear, I believe, the nature of his existence in that state is pivoted on the prepositional phrase "in my flesh" (19:26), which can mean "from my flesh" (implying bodily existence) or "without my flesh" (implying a spiritual existence). The fact that Isaiah 26:19 and Daniel 12:2 speak of a bodily resurrection does not, unfortunately, answer the question for us. Certainly the end product of this line of revelation (some would prefer

"If I Were Hungry I Would Not Tell You, for the World Is Mine, and All That Is in It"

Big Idea *One of the great dissimilarities between humanity and God is that we are needy people, but God needs nothing.*

Understanding the Text

Psalm 50 is a perfect example of the kind of liturgical piece that might be recited in the seventh year when the Torah was read at the Feast of Tabernacles (Deut. 31:9–13).[1] Yet when the Book of the Covenant was discovered in the temple during Josiah's reign (622–609 BC), it seems that this practice had not been observed for some time (2 Kings 23:1–3). In form-critical mode, Wilson considers the psalm a *covenant lawsuit*, in which Yahweh presents a legal indictment against Israel, the kind that one would expect in a court of law (e.g., Hosea 4:1).[2] As a rule this form is identified by the term "dispute" (*rib*), which does not appear in this psalm. Further, the psalm is more a corrective to Israel's understanding of sacrifice than an indictment.

The psalm is the first of the Asaph psalms and the only one in Book 2, separated from the other eleven that are located in Book 3 (Pss.

Psalm 50 recalls God's revelation of himself from the mountains of Sinai. Shown here is a view of the rugged terrain that Moses hiked to meet with God while the Israelites waited in the plain below watching the fiery display of God's presence.

73–83). Like other Asaph psalms, it exhibits a prophetic character in its inclusion of what appear to be prophetic "oracles" (50:7–15, 16b–23; two other Asaph psalms exhibit brief "oracles" also [75:4–5; 81:6–16]; 95:8–11 does as well, but it is not an Asaph psalm).[3]

The Text in Context

The historical and theological template on which Psalm 50 is written is the revelation on Sinai. The Sinai event is reflected in at least five ways in the psalm. First, the name of the people of Israel, "this consecrated people" (50:5, *hasidai*; lit., "my faithful ones"; see ESV), is a noun/adjective (*hasid*) that derives from one of the key covenant terms, *hesed* ("love, lovingkindness, unfailing love"), and it also describes Israel in another Asaph psalm (Ps. 79:2; NIV: "your own people"). More than any other term, the word *hesed*, like the word "love" (*agapē*) in the New Testament, characterizes God's relationship to Israel and the world. Second, these people have sealed their covenant with Yahweh by sacrifice (50:5), a detail that is accounted for in Exodus 24:5–8. Third, the psalm also recalls the picture of the fire that announced Yahweh's appearance on Mount Sinai ("Devouring fire preceded Him; it stormed around Him fiercely," 50:3 NJPS), a detail recorded in the Torah (Exod. 19:18; 24:17; Deut. 4:11). Fourth, the psalm deals with two topics of the Sinai revelation, in reverse order: sacrifice (see Exod. 20:24–26; Ps. 50:8–15) and the Ten Commandments (Exod. 20:2–17; Ps. 50:16–21—seventh, eighth, and ninth commandments). Fifth, the preface to the Ten Commandments, couched in its Elohistic form, occurs in

Key Themes of Psalm 50

- The true meaning of sacrifice is a relationship with God.
- The law and the commandments remind us of the ethical life, which is the essence of a life of faith.

The Divine Names in Psalm 50

The use of the divine names in the psalm is instructive. The psalm uses four names for Israel's God. It begins by piling up three divine names together: "The Mighty One ['el], God ['elohim], the LORD [YHWH]" (50:1). The Hebrew word 'el ("God"; NIV: "the Mighty One") is the shortened form of "God," associated with the patriarchs and Canaanite culture. The word 'elohim ("God") is the generic term for the deity, and the preferred name in the Elohistic Psalter, while YHWH ("LORD") is God's covenant name, reaffirmed to Israel in Exodus 3. The summons to "the earth from the rising of the sun to its setting" (50:1 ESV) is appropriately validated by these three divine names that span Israel's history as a covenant people and shows that God is Lord of the world. Two other names for God appear in the psalm, 'elyon ("Most High," 50:14), the name applied to Melchizedek's God (Gen. 14), whom Abraham equates with Yahweh (Gen. 14:22); and finally the name 'eloah (50:22), which is a poetic name for 'el and 'elohim. With the tetragrammaton (YHWH, "LORD"), Asaph, a Levitical singer, removes any doubt about the deity's identity—this is the covenant God. Moreover, God addresses the earth from the vantage point of Zion and in that context calls the heavens and the earth to witness this moment of divine judgment (50:4). It is more a corrective than a reproof (50:8), a corrective to Israel's way of thinking about sacrifice and God's relationship to it. The meaning of sacrifice is found not in God's need for food but in his desire to be in relationship with his people.

50:7c ("I am God, your God," substituting "God" for "Yahweh/LORD": "I am the LORD your God"; see Exod. 20:2/Deut. 5:6). Written, therefore, on the grid of the Sinai revelation, this prophet's message carries the gravity and urgency of the Torah. In fact, it may be considered an early example of the interpretation of the Torah—in this instance, of sacrifice—a practice that became a major function of the Levitical priests (Neh. 8:7–8). In view of the parody on the introduction to the Decalogue in 50:7a, and the selection of commandments that follows (50:18–20; see "Teaching the Text"), the author may be using the Decalogue as his model for the poem.

Like Psalm 49, this psalm addresses only the people, never God. And like other brief portions of the Psalms (e.g., 40:6–8; 51:16–17; 69:31), it deals with the ethical implications of the law.

Psalm 50 is one of twelve Asaph psalms (50; 73–83).[4] The Chronicler informs us that David appointed "some of the sons of Asaph, Heman and Jeduthun for the ministry of prophesying, accompanied by harps, lyres and cymbals" (1 Chron. 25:1). The fact that Psalm 50 is separated from the other Asaph psalms is a bit perplexing. Goldingay suggests that an editor recognized the prophetic similarity between Psalm 50 and the Asaph psalms and gave the psalm the same title.[5] Another explanation, just as plausible, is that the compiler of Books 2 and 3 saw the link between "adulterers" in 50:18 and David's adultery in Psalm 51 and, given his thematic criterion of sorting, made Psalm 50 the prelude to Psalm 51. Even though the term "adulterers" does not appear in Psalm 51,[6] the occasion for that psalm was, according to the superscription, David's adultery with Bathsheba. It is quite possible that the editor worded the title in such a way as to make the connection with Psalm 50. Moreover, the common theme of sacrifice shared by Psalms 50 and 51 is an additional magnetic attraction. Psalm 50 declares that the Lord does not need sacrifice, insisting that a right relationship to God is the most important factor (50:14–15), and Psalm 51 indicates that David understands this doctrinal point very well: "You do not delight in sacrifice, or I would bring it; you do not take pleasure in burnt offerings. My sacrifice, O God, is a broken spirit; a broken and contrite heart you, God, will not despise" (51:16–17).

Outline/Structure

God's words are the center of this psalm, as the earth is summoned to Zion to hear God's accusations against his people. After the summons and the announcement of the theophany in terms of the Sinai revelation, the main body of the psalm can be structured along the lines of two indictments:[7]

1. The Judge's summons to the earth as witness of God's judgment (50:1–4)
   a. The summons (50:1)
   b. The theophany (50:2–4)
2. The summons to Israel as witness of God's judgment (50:5–6)
3. The first accusation, regarding sacrifice (50:7–15)
   a. God's exhortation about sacrifice (50:7–13)
   b. God's injunction to sacrifice (50:14–15)
4. The second accusation, regarding ethical behavior (50:16–23)
   a. God's exhortation about the commandments and ethical behavior (50:16–21)
   b. God's final warning and admonition (50:22–23)

Historical and Cultural Background

The law court was one of Israel's basic institutions, assuring justice to God's people according to the divine laws set forth in the Torah. It typically convened in the morning inside the city gate and was composed of the city elders (Ruth 4:1–12), who served as both judge and jury. This was an analogy that the prophets sometimes used to portray Israel's pending judgment (e.g., Isa. 1:2; Hosea 5:1). In this psalm the Levitical prophet summons the heavens and earth as witnesses of God's judgment of Israel, whose false assumption is that sacrifice is something God needs in order to survive (suggested by Lev. 3:11, 16; Num. 28:2; Judg. 9:13). This assumption undergirded the Mesopotamian understanding of sacrifice, that it was a means of supplying the gods with food. Israel's God, on the contrary, had no need of sacrifice—if indeed he were ever hungry—and if he did get hungry, he still had no need of Israel's sacrifices, because he owned "the cattle on a thousand hills" (50:10).

Interpretive Insights

50:1 *The Mighty One, God, the* LORD *. . . from the rising of the sun to where it sets.* For the use of the three divine names, see the sidebar. The summons is to the whole earth, from east to west. The fact that God can summon the earth, just as he

can summon his own people (50:5), implies his lordship over it.

50:2 *From Zion, perfect in beauty, God shines forth.* "Perfect in beauty" is reminiscent of Psalm 48:2 in its description of Zion as "beautiful in its loftiness" (cf. Lam. 2:15). The Blessing of Moses describes the theophany on Sinai with this same verb, "shines forth" (Deut. 33:2).

50:3 *Our God comes and will not be silent; a fire devours before him . . . a tempest rages.* The statement that God will not be silent is, in essence, an announcement of the theophany (on Sinai), which comes, not in silence, but with thunder and God's voice. The theophany was preceded and followed by fire (Exod. 19:18; 24:17; Deut. 4:11; 1 Kings 19:12; Ezek. 1:4). Exodus 24:17 describes Yahweh's appearance on Sinai thus: "The appearance of the glory of the LORD was like a devouring fire" (ESV). The raging tempest is a description of the fire that follows or accompanies Yahweh's appearance.

50:4 *the heavens above, and the earth.* Calling the heavens and earth as witnesses

> The city gate was the location of the court where petitions for justice were heard. Here is the interior of a gate chamber at Beersheba showing the benches where the important men of the community would gather to hear legal cases.

is attested both in the Torah (Deut. 32:1) and in the prophets (e.g., Isa. 1:2). They are enduring witnesses to Yahweh's judgment on Israel.

50:5 *Gather to me this consecrated people, who made a covenant with me by sacrifice.* These are God's words. "This consecrated people" (*hasiday*; lit., "my consecrated ones") is the people of Israel, and the covenantal setting is suggested by the root of the word, which comes from *hesed* ("love, loving-kindness"), a key term

Unlike the gods of the ancient Near East who needed ritual offerings to provide them with food, Israel's God says, "I have no need of a bull from your stall" (50:9). This relief from the end of the fifth century BC shows a ram and a bull as sacrificial offerings.

of the Mosaic covenant (see "The Text in Context"). "To make a covenant" is literally "to cut a covenant," perhaps alluding to the practice in Genesis 15:7–21. The connection of the covenant and sacrifice is confirmed by Exodus 24:5–8.

50:6 *And the heavens proclaim his righteousness.* The imperfect with *waw* consecutive means this has already happened—the heavens proclaimed his righteousness at the time of the Sinai covenant—and probably implies that they still do.

50:7 *Listen, my people, and I will speak . . . I am God, your God.* Wilson calls this a "parody of the Shema" ("Hear, O Israel: The Lord our God, the Lord is one," Deut. 6:4). The final declaration is the Elohistic Psalter's version of "I am the Lord your God," which introduces the Ten Commandments in Exodus 20:2. Given the Elohistic Psalter's preference for *'elohim* ("God") rather than *YHWH* ("Lord"), *'elohim* replaces the tetragrammaton. The rest of the psalm, like the Ten Commandments, is composed of God's words.

50:8 *I bring no charges against you concerning your sacrifices . . . ever before me.* Yahweh has no problem with their sacrifices or their burnt offerings. The "continual burnt offerings" were those sacrifices made in the morning and afternoon services (see Lev. 1 and 3). The word "continual," or "ever" (*tamid*), gives the sacrifice its name, *tamid*.

50:9–11 *I have no need of a bull from your stall.* Yahweh explains why he has no need of the sacrifices: he owns all the animals and birds of the forests, and the cattle "on a thousand hills." So he has a sufficient supply, if indeed this is what he needs. The "insects of the fields" is a difficult phrase. The term occurs also in Psalm 80:13.

50:12 *If I were hungry I would not tell you.* The "if" here is the Hebrew *'im*, rather than *lu*. The former (*'im*) implies that the hypothetical statement is possible in either the past, present, or future, while the latter (*lu*) implies it is not possible.[8] Compared to Isaiah's argument against the hypocritical trampling of the temple courts with guilt-stained hands (Isa. 1:10–15), the argument here is against the pagan idea that God actually needs the animal sacrifices to sustain him.

50:13 *Do I eat the flesh of bulls or drink the blood of goats?* The question appeals to the perception of the audience: "Do you really think I eat the flesh of bulls . . . ?"

50:14 *Sacrifice thank offerings to God, fulfill your vows to the Most High.* This is the "thanksgiving offering" (*todah*, Lev. 7:12–15). The vows are those made when one is in trouble and promises to make a sacrifice to God when the trouble passes.

50:16 *But to the wicked person, God says.* The previous verses were spoken to the whole people of God. Now the psalmist turns to the "wicked" who fall within the bounds of the covenant but have no regard for it.

50:17 *You hate my instruction and cast my words behind you.* "Instruction" (*musar*) is in the sense of reproof or discipline, as in Proverbs 5:12–13. The picture of "casting behind" is that of a person walking along carrying a burden, and to get rid of it, the person casts it behind.

50:18 *When you see a thief, you join with him; you throw in your lot with adulterers.* This concerns the eighth (Exod. 20:15) and the seventh (Exod. 20:14) commandments.

50:20 *You sit and testify against your brother.* This concerns the ninth commandment (Exod. 20:16).

50:21 *When you did these things and I kept silent, you thought I was exactly like you.* One of the great human misperceptions about God is that he is like human beings, and mistakenly people read human intentions and ways of thinking into their view of God.

50:22 *Consider this, you who forget God.* Now the address is to a certain segment of the community, those who violate the covenant by disobeying his commandments.

50:23 *Those who sacrifice thank offerings honor me.* This refers back to those in 50:14 who are commanded to "sacrifice thank offerings to God." Note that the verb "honor" (*kbd*) occurs in 50:15 to describe those who are obedient to God's law, as it does here.

Theological Insights

The sacrificial system was central to Israelite religion, practiced routinely every day, at special religious festivals, and on other national and personal occasions. There was never a day when sacrifice was not being made in the Jerusalem temple. Yet, as happens with the principal features of any religious faith, sacrifices can become routine and devoid of meaning, and, of course, they can also be misunderstood. Although the Torah borders on the notion that sacrifice is "food" for God (see "Historical and Cultural Background"), this psalm corrects that understanding of sacrifice and distinguishes Israel's faith from that of her neighbors (see the sidebar "The Moral Law and Sacrifice in the Psalms" in the unit on Ps. 40). The psalm is not a condemnation of the sacrificial system of the classical prophetic strain, and it even distances itself from a general condemnation (50:8). Verse 23, in fact, commends sacrifice ("thank offerings") as a way of honoring God. Despite that, however, God has no need of Israel's sacrifices to satisfy his hunger, if indeed he ever feels famished, because he owns all the animals of the forest and the cattle on a thousand hills (50:9–13). The people can conduct their sacrifices, pay their vows, and pray to God, and, says God, "I will deliver you" (50:14–15b). In response to divine deliverance, Israel will honor God (50:15c, 23). In fact, the meaning of sacrifice is to be found in that relationship.

In this regard, there are some within the bounds of God's covenant with Israel whom God addresses as "wicked" and who have broken the commandments by saying one thing and doing another. They recite the statutes and pay lip service to the covenant (50:16), but they really hate God's

instruction (50:17). This is illustrated by their violation of the eighth ("you shall not steal," Exod. 20:15), seventh ("you shall not commit adultery," Exod. 20:14), and ninth ("you shall not bear false witness against your neighbor," Exod. 20:16 ESV) commandments. Rather than keeping the commandments, the wicked fall in line with thieves and adulterers (50:18) and "sit and testify against" their brother (50:20). In a general way, the two tablets of the Torah are represented in this psalm. Israel's relationship to God is the theme of the first tablet (commandments 1–4/5), represented here by 50:14–15, and interpersonal relationships, the theme of the second tablet (commandments 5/6–10), are represented in 50:16–20.

God's words, as we have proposed, are the centerpiece of this psalm. Six imperatives punctuate these words: "gather" (50:5), "listen" (50:7), "sacrifice" (50:14), "fulfill" (50:14), "call" (50:15), and "consider" (50:22). The span of these commands encompasses Israel's worship experience, which includes gathering, listening, sacrificing, fulfilling vows, calling on God, and considering the

Because the cattle on a thousand hills belong to the Lord, he would not need sacrifices if he were ever hungry. In ancient Israel, Bashan was known for its cows. This herd is from the same region, now called the Golan, where beef and dairy cattle are raised.

Lord's demands on them. The audience of the first imperative is not specific, perhaps the priests, but the second through sixth imperatives are obviously spoken to the people ("Listen, my people," 50:7)—even the final imperative, addressed in verse 16 to the "wicked" who have broken the commandments. That, of course, implies that the commandments were incumbent upon them and puts them within the covenant bounds.

Teaching the Text

We may begin our sermon/lesson by pointing out that one of the greatest aspects of true religion is knowing who God is. That is the thrust of this psalm, and the purpose of verses 7–15 as God identifies himself in relation to the sacrificial system and Israel's misunderstanding of it. In fact, the most important fact is that "I am God, your God" (50:7; see the comments on this verse, above). God is a covenant God, and that means a relational God, and this is our first point.

This leads into the second point, that the institutions of worship can often be misunderstood and misdirected so that their intent is not real worship but negotiation with God—the more we give to him, the more we get from him. Unfortunately, Israel had come to practice sacrifice under a false assumption, that sacrifice was something God needed, part of the popular theology of the day, growing out of their misperception about God: "You thought I was exactly like you" (50:21b). We need to clear up some of the false assumptions we have about God. Although we do not practice sacrifice, we nevertheless bring him our tithes and gifts, sometimes with the motive of getting some

return from him, or even the assumption, false indeed, that he needs them. But what God really wants is a relationship with us. The psalmist lays out this theme in two ways. In the first place, he says in effect, *I am not hungry, so I do not need your sacrifices if that is the reason you are bringing them. Furthermore, "If I were hungry, I would not tell you, for the whole world is mine"* (50:12). *In point of fact, I would not need to tell you, "for every animal of the forest is mine, and the cattle on a thousand hills"* (50:10). *Really, do you believe that "I eat the flesh of bulls" and "drink the blood of goats?"* (50:13). In the second place—and this is the truth of the matter—"I am God, your God" (50:7). Once we understand this, we are well on our way to healing our relationship with God and clearing up the misunderstanding of God that so often impairs our relationship.

Third, the psalmist presents an outline of true worship that consists not in sacrifice alone, although that is certainly part of it (50:14–15), but also in personal and corporate behavior. The anatomy of corporate worship is visible: "gather" (50:5), "listen" (50:7), "sacrifice" (50:14), "fulfill your vows" (50:14), and "call on me" (50:15). In the prophetic strain of thought, the psalmist insists that this is one side of worship, with its benefit ("I will deliver you," 50:15b), but there is another, an obedient life ("and you will honor me," 50:15b). Worship is a time to consider the life of obedience, and in Israel's case, they have broken the seventh, eighth, and ninth commandments: they have stolen, committed adultery, and borne false witness against their neighbor (50:18–21). In essence the Lord says, "When you worship me but do not keep my commandments, what does that mean about our relationship?" It is a natural connection to Jesus's teaching that if we love him we will keep his commandments (John 14:15).

Illustrating the Text

Know who God is.

Personal Testimony: The Psalms and the Prophets put knowing God at the center of theology. And sometimes, as this psalm attests, we know God through the witness and the actions of others. In one of my pastorates, a sweet little girl in my congregation, about two or three years old, passed through the narthex one Sunday morning after worship and said to her father, "Is he God?" When I heard the question, I responded, "No, darling, but thank you for the compliment." Her perceptive father reassured her likewise. Then on another Sunday as my wife was sitting near her and her parents before worship began, my wife overheard my admirer say, "Is he God?" Evidently the parents reassured her that I was not, and then she remonstrated, "Yes, he is!" I have thought about that a lot. The obvious is true: I am not God! But that little girl, in her innocence and growing faith, made up her mind that I was God. But what if I stumbled or misstepped and did or said something that gave her a distorted picture of God? With time, of course, she might outgrow it, but who knows what a lasting impression that could make on her, and how long it would take to convince her that God is not like that? So from that point, my prayer and my actions were intentionally to the effect that through me she would come to know truly who God is.

The Ten Commandments backwards

Quote: Martin Luther. Speaking of his books and the fact that he did not seek to earn money from them, nor did he ask the prince elector of Saxony for assistance, Martin Luther said: "The world is nothing but a reversed Decalogue, or the Ten Commandments backwards, a mask and picture of the devil, all contemners of God, all blasphemers, all disobedient; harlotry, pride, theft, murder, etc. are now almost ripe for the slaughter."[9] Luther's image of "a reversed Decalogue" is a striking way to describe what had gone wrong with Asaph's world, and with ours. The "not/no" of the commandments has been erased, and people are engaging in the activities that the commandments forbid

(vv. 18–20)—"the Ten Commandments backwards." In Psalm 46 David describes this reversal as the mountains receding into the primordial waters from which they, at God's command, had emerged in creation (see "Theological Insights" in the unit on Ps. 46).

Worship is a lifestyle.

Contrasting Concept: When we talk about worship with our listeners, most will immediately think about music or the church gathered for a service. But worship is much more than a service or even music. Actually, everything we do, when done for the Lord and in his name, is an act of worship (see Rom. 12:1). Worship is an act of the heart that leads to a response. In this way, worship involves all we do and think, our attitudes and motivations. There should be no difference in our motivations or attitudes, in how we treat people, whether we are in church or outside church—what we are when we are at church should be consistent with how we live and act when we are not. For example, challenge your listeners to consider how they might act differently if they performed the following activities as an act of worship (in the name of Jesus): waking up in the morning, responding to their families, doing their jobs (inside and outside the home).

"Create in Me a Pure Heart, O God, and Renew a Steadfast Spirit within Me"

Big Idea *God delights in the spiritual transaction of repentance that begins in the human heart.*

Understanding the Text

Bernhard W. Anderson calls Psalm 51 "one of the pearls of the Psalter."[1] Among the seven penitential psalms,[2] this one, in Weiser's estimation, is the most important because it "demonstrates the essence of true penitence."[3] This psalm falls generally under the classification of the individual lament, and more specifically, to use Kraus's subcategory, "Songs of the Sick and Anguished."[4] As a confession of sin, it is unparalleled in the Psalter, with only a few brief comparisons in Psalms 32:5; 38:18; 41:4; 69:5; and 130:1–8.

The Text in Context

Both Psalms 50 and 51 have an eye on the sacrificial system, but the focus is different. Psalm 50 raises no objections to sacrifices, even though God does not need them (50:8–15), while Psalm 51 insists that God takes no pleasure in sacrifices, but he has great regard for "a broken and contrite heart" (51:17). Despite the ostensible contradiction, they may in effect be complementary (see below). See "The Text in Context" in the unit on Psalm 50.

The psalmist commits himself to the duty of teaching others God's ways (51:13), having learned them from God himself, while the supplicant of Psalm 25 (25:4, 9, 12), without explicitly committing himself

After David's sin with Bathsheba, God pronounces judgment on David through the prophet Nathan. Psalm 51 records David's response. This illustration from the Queen Mary Psalter (1310–20) shows Nathan reproving the kneeling king.

personally to the task, prays that the Lord himself will execute the didactic function.

The poetic neighborhood in which Psalm 51 is located gives evidence that the formation of the Psalter utilized minicollections that were at the editors' disposal. After a long series of Korah psalms (Pss. 42–49), followed by the insertion of a single Asaph psalm (Ps. 50), the editor introduces a rather lengthy cadre of Davidic psalms (Pss. 51–65; 68–70; see the sidebar).

In Romans 3:4 the apostle Paul quotes the second half of Psalm 51:4 from the Greek translation (LXX) to show that God is just, even when some of the covenant people have been unfaithful. Even though David was unfaithful, God did not withdraw his faithfulness from him, anymore than he withdrew his faithfulness from unfaithful Israel.[5] In other words, God's faithfulness is not contingent on human faithfulness.

Outline/Structure

This psalm is difficult to outline. Schaefer provides a helpful way to look at it in three movements:

1. First Movement: Prayer for personal cleansing (51:1–9)
   a. The metaphors of forgiveness (51:1–2) [These verbs occur in reverse order in 51:7 and 9.]
      i. "blot out"
      ii. "wash"
      iii. "cleanse"
   b. Confession of sin (51:3–6)
   c. Prayer for cleansing (51:7–9)
2. Second Movement: Prayer for personal renewal and right sacrifice (51:10–17) [framed by repetition of "heart" and "spirit," 51:10, 17]

   a. Prayer for spiritual restoration (51:10–12)
   b. A vow to praise and public contrition (51:13–17)
3. Third Movement: Prayer for restoring the city and God's pleasure with Israel's worship (51:18–19)[6]

Historical and Cultural Background

The title of the psalm identifies the prophet Nathan's rebuke of David after his

---

Key Themes of Psalm 51

- While sin is against ourselves, others, and our world, it still offends God the most.
- David charts the path from our old creation to our new creation.
- "Where sin increased, grace increased all the more."

The Davidic Collection in Psalms 51–70

Psalms 51–70, primarily a collection of Davidic psalms, are subdivided into minicollections by the type of psalm (*mizmor, maskil, miktam, shir*), with the exception of Psalms 61; 69; and 70, which are all simply titled "Of David" (*le dawid*), and two psalms that have no Davidic attribution (Pss. 66 and 67). While the editorial criteria are not exactly clear, that these psalms comprise a "Davidic" collection is obvious, and the type of psalm (*mizmor*, etc.) seems to bear some significance, with each group of psalms perhaps belonging to a minicollection that bears that title.

- "A psalm of David" (*mizmor le dawid*): 51; 62; 63; 64
- "A maskil of David" (*maskil le dawid*): 52; 53; 54; 55
- "Of David. A miktam" (*le dawid miktam*): 56; 57; 58; 59; "A miktam of David" (*miktam le dawid*): 60
- "Of David" (*le dawid*): 61; 69; 70
- "A psalm of David. A song" (*mizmor le dawid shir*): 65; "Of David. A psalm. A song" (*le dawid mizmor shir*): 68
- "A song. A psalm" (*shir mizmor*; no Davidic connection): 66; "A song. A psalm" (*mizmor shir*): 67

adulterous relationship with Bathsheba as the event that has elicited this moving confession (2 Sam. 11–12). Adultery, prohibited by the seventh commandment (Exod. 20:14/Deut. 5:18; also 50:18b), was a moral violation that carried the death penalty for both partners (Deut. 22:22). It was recognized generally in Israel's world as such a serious offense that it was sometimes called the "Great Sin."

David prays that the Lord will cleanse him with hyssop (51:7a). There are several subspecies of this plant; one has white flowers and may suggest the result of the cleansing mentioned in 51:7b: "and I will be whiter than snow."[7] It is also mentioned as the applicator of the lamb's blood on the doorpost as a sign of God's favor to the Israelite family awaiting the exodus from Egypt (Exod. 12:22) and as an herb in the cleansing of the leper (Lev. 14:4).

Interpretive Insights

Title *after David had committed adultery.* See "Historical and Cultural Background."

51:1 *Have mercy on me, O God, according to your unfailing love . . . blot out my transgressions.* God's "unfailing love" (*hesed*) is the basis of God's mercy. Note the structure of the verse, which involves a chiasm, the verbal clauses (A and A′) and the adverbial modifiers (B and B′) appearing in crisscross positions:

A Have mercy on me, O God,
    B according to your unfailing
       love;
    B′ according to your great
       compassion
A′ blot out my transgressions.

51:2 *Wash away all my iniquity and cleanse me from my sin.* The verb translated as "wash away" is used of washing clothing and denotes the "treading" that one would do when washing laundry (cf. Jer. 2:22). More often in the Old Testament it refers to sacramental cleansing (Lev. 15). "Cleanse" refers to a sacramental cleansing that turns something defiled into something pure, usually accomplished by ritual washing and/or sacrifice. The three verbs of forgiveness in verses 1 and 2 ("blot out," "wash," and "cleanse") are repeated in reverse order in verses 7 and 9.

51:3 *For I know my transgressions.* Repentance involves a consciousness and admission of sin, made possible by Yahweh's revelation in the Torah. Other cultures of David's world recognized some sins as wrong, such as adultery and murder, but were unaware of other moral aberrations, since they had no such revelation from their deities.

51:4 *Against you, you only, have I sinned.* Wilson explains: "The measure of the psalmist's sin in this case is 'what is evil in [God's] sight' (51:4)—a much higher standard than the world holds."[8]

51:5 *sinful at birth.* While the doctrine of original sin may not be in mind here—nor is it a doctrine in Judaism—David may be thinking of the sinful nature and sinful tendencies of humanity, from the very beginning of the biblical story. In truth, this affects human beings "at birth," inclining them in the direction of sin.[9]

51:6 *Yet you desired faithfulness even in the womb; you taught me wisdom in that secret place.* "Faithfulness" ("truth," *'emet*) is parallel to "wisdom" (*hokmah*), and "womb" (lit., "the inner parts") is parallel to "secret place," so the entire verse is speaking about God's prenatal care of David, much like Jeremiah's awareness of both Yahweh's knowledge of him before he was conceived and his special mission before he was born (Jer. 1:5). The Hebrew word that the NIV translates as "womb" occurs only here and in Job 38:36 (NJPS: "hidden parts"). The last phrase of the verse suggests that the matter of repentance does not come naturally but is inspired by God.[10]

51:7 *Cleanse me with hyssop.* This is a figure of speech that is drawn from certain rituals prescribed in the Torah. Generally the hyssop plant was used as an applicator, while at the same time yielding its medicinal qualities in the process (Exod. 12:22; Lev. 14:4, 6, 49, etc.). See "Historical and Cultural Insights."

51:9 *Hide your face from my sins.* God's hiding his face from

The psalmist prays, "Cleanse me with hyssop" (51:7). This plant is most likely *Origanum syriacum*, shown here.

the worshiper's sins implies that God will not take them into account.

51:10 *Create in me a pure heart, O God, and renew a steadfast spirit within me.* The language of 51:10–12 is suggestive of the Genesis narrative. In addition to the verb "create," the second half of the verse picks up the noun "spirit," reminiscent of Genesis 1:2 (see also Gen. 6:17). Thus the psalmist prays that God will re-create him. The "spirit" (*ruah*) of the human person is the dynamic force that animates humans and resonates with the divine.

51:11 *Do not cast me from your presence.* The supplicant prays not to be "cast" out of God's presence, the place where he can be in communion with God. God's presence may be the sanctuary, or a spiritual relationship with God, certainly not apart from the sanctuary. Note the allusion to Genesis 3:23–24, where we have verbal synonyms for "cast."

51:13 *Then I will teach transgressors your ways.* First the supplicant needs to have his own life re-created, and then he can teach others God's ways.

51:14 *Deliver me from the guilt of bloodshed, O God.* The idea here resonates with David's story in 2 Samuel 11–12 and implicates him in the death of Uriah. It could, however, be a prayer that God will deliver him from having his own blood spilled, perhaps in revenge (lit., "deliver me from blood/bloodshed"). In light of the allusions to the Genesis narrative, we might also raise the question whether "you do not delight in sacrifice" (51:16) is an allusion to God's rejection of Cain's sacrifice, and "bloodshed" to Cain's murder of Abel, his brother (Gen. 4);[11] so serious is his sin that the psalmist may be casting himself in the role of Cain.

51:15 *Open my lips, Lord.* Note that the fact that "Lord" does not use small caps indicates that the name of the deity here is not *YHWH* but *'adonay*. The divine name *YHWH* is not used in this psalm.

51:16 *You do not delight in sacrifice.* This is not a rejection of sacrifice (see 51:19) but an admission that God has other preferences, in this case, "a broken and contrite heart" (51:17). Some take it to imply that no sacrifice would be effective in removing his sin, particularly since the sacrificial system did not provide atonement for the sins of adultery and murder. "Sacrifice" (*zebah*) may refer to a thanksgiving offering or to sacrifices in general, as is often the case with this word.[12]

51:17 *a broken spirit; a broken and a contrite heart.* In this case the Lord regards the psalmist's broken spirit as a sacrifice, compensating, perhaps, for the lack of provision for the atonement of intentional sin.[13] "Contrite" is an interpretation of the word *nidkeh* ("crushed"). It is less likely that David is admitting that his spirit has been broken by his sin. That would not fit well the penitent spirit of the psalm.

51:18 *May it please you to prosper Zion.* Verses 18 and 19 may be a response by a later, perhaps postexilic, community.[14] Yet, while it may seem like an alien thought in the psalm, the suppliant is so emotionally related to Zion that a restoration of his relationship to Yahweh will leave his aspirations only partially fulfilled. His inner cleansing and restoration to the joy of God's salvation require the restoration

If Psalm 51 reflects David's repentance of the sin of adultery and murder, verse 14 may allude to his ploy to have Uriah killed. By positioning Uriah in the front lines of the army, he became an easy target for the enemy archers, which resulted in his death. This Assyrian relief shows a city under siege with archers on the walls (from the palace at Nimrud, 728 BC).

of Zion. Not only does the psalmist's fulfillment require the welfare of Zion, but God's own full delight in the offerings made in Zion's sanctuary is also contingent on the welfare of Jerusalem. "May it please you" translates a prepositional phrase "in your endearing pleasure," the noun *ratson* ("pleasure") being a term of endearment rather than willingness.[15]

51:19 *Then you will delight in the sacrifices of the righteous, in burnt offerings.* The word *'olah* ("burnt offering") denotes a sacrifice that was totally burned on the altar (Lev. 6:8–9/Heb. 6:1–2). The two words for sacrifice, however, are not to be distinguished, but are used for sacrifice in general. It is only when David is restored to the joy of God's salvation and the walls of Jerusalem are in good repair that the pleasing combination will have transpired to bring God the greatest delight in the sacrifices that Israel offers. Sacrifices alone do not delight him, but the renewal of the people's hearts and the good welfare of their beloved city are circumstances attendant to God's delight.

Theological Insights

Long before Paul spoke about a "new creation" (2 Cor. 5:17), David recalled the language and imagery of the first creation and prayed for a "new creation" to take place in his life. Psalm 51:10–12 is reminiscent of the language of the early Genesis narrative (Gen. 1–11). The verb "create" (51:10) reflects the idea of a miraculous transaction, as Calvin comments,[16] reminiscent of the original creation (Gen. 1:1, etc.), and the second half of the line picks up the noun "spirit," that also occurs in the creation narrative (*ruah*, Gen. 1:2, "spirit" of God; Gen. 6:17, etc., "spirit of life"). While this may be merely coincidental, the fact that David prays, "Do not cast me from your presence" (root, *shlk*, v. 11a), brings to mind the expulsion of the first human couple from the garden of Eden (root, *shlh*, Gen. 3:23). Even though two different verbs are used, the effect is the same—the psalmist is praying that God will "re-create" him and transform him into a new person so that he will not be cast out of God's presence.

Nor is the psalmist far from Paul's theological truth that "where sin increased, grace increased all the more" (Rom. 5:20). That is indeed the faith that underlies the psalm. Schaefer makes the interesting observation that the word for sin and its cognates occur six times in the first movement and once in the last movement. At the same time, and in reverse proportion, the name God (*'elohim*) occurs once in the first movement and six times in the remainder of the psalm. Schaefer comments: "Sin disappears in the second half in the same ratio that God appears."[17]

Teaching the Text

To begin our study, we may observe that, while the historical titles sometimes seem to be loosely related to their psalm, Psalm 51 fits perfectly the story of David's adulterous relationship with Bathsheba (2 Sam. 11–12). Although the Samuel narrative does not give an account of David's repentance, his admission of sin (2 Sam. 12:13) and the emotional trauma associated with the death of his and Bathsheba's infant son certainly implies the spirit of repentance that permeates Psalm 51. We might build the lesson around the anatomy of repentance that this psalm lays out for its audience.

First, repentance means we are conscious of our sin, and David begins the psalm with a plea for God's mercy (51:1–2). In this prayer David describes God's forgiveness with three metaphors: "blot out" (which means to "wipe clean"), "wash away," and "cleanse." Following the literary pattern of double-tracking, these three verbs of forgiveness are repeated in verses 7 and 9, and in reverse order, so as to call attention to these transactions in a slightly different way.

The second step is confession, and that is what David does in verses 3–6. David describes the condition of this stage of repentance as "a broken and contrite heart"

(51:17), recognizing that ultimately his sin is against God and God only (51:4), which expresses the gravity of his sin. Others have been hurt in the process, but his sin has affected God most severely, because it was an infraction of his moral law.

The third stage of repentance is restoration. That is what David prays for when he has acknowledged his sins and laid them out before God (51:10, 12).

Note also that if we listen to the language of verses 10–12, we begin to hear overtones from the creation/Eden narrative: "create," "spirit," "do not cast me from your presence." Calvin says this language is reminiscent of the original creation and reflects the idea of a miraculous transaction,[18] reminding us also of Paul's statement about God's re-creative work in Christ. The work of transforming grace is reflected in the structure of the psalm, as Schaefer has observed (for the comments by both Calvin and Schaefer, see "Theological Insights").

The fourth step in repentance is one that we do not often associate with that process, at least as a vital part of repentance, and that is witnessing to others about God's grace. David commits himself to that task, to "teach transgressors your [God's] ways," "sing of your righteousness," and "declare your praise" (51:13–15). Further, we might say that repentance has an evangelistic edge: "and sinners will turn back to you" (51:13). While repentance for this suppliant is a very personal matter, its larger effect is the restoration of Zion, an indication that personal piety in the Psalms has corporate implications (51:18). One of the marvels of repentance is that it stretches from the individual to the community, and while it might be overreaching to suggest that repentance is not complete until it affects the community to which the repentant belongs, true repentance has the power to overflow the individual and spill over into the community of faith. That is, community repentance must certainly be personal, and personal repentance should be predictably communal.

Illustrating the Text

"Wash me, and I will be whiter than snow."

Hymn: "Whiter Than Snow," by James Nicholson. The hymn "Whiter Than Snow,"

The opening verses of Psalm 51 record David pleading for God's mercy. This illumination from a prayer book shows David kneeling reverently surrounded by pictures that illustrate his sin; the dead Uriah, the bathing Bathsheba, and the last judgment. The words from Psalm 6:1 convey his attitude of penitence, "Lord, do not rebuke me in your anger" (Book of Hours used in Lisieux, Normandy, France, ca. 1460–70).

written by Nicholson in 1872, is based on Psalm 51. The first verse is a prayer, inviting God both to reveal and to rid us of our sin (51:1–4). In the second verse we are confessing our desire to sacrifice our will and all we are to the Lord (51:16–17). In verse 3 we are confessing our faith in the sacrifice of Jesus on the cross to deal completely with our sin (51:7). Finally, the last verse is a prayer, asking God to create a new heart in us that we may live in a new way (51:10). Each verse ends with the petition, "Now wash me, and I shall be whiter than snow!"[19] We should recognize, however, that the hymn and the psalm deal with two different spiritual conditions. The hymn is concerned with how one deals with one's sinful condition in order to come to faith in Christ. The psalm is concerned with how one, already within the faith, deals with one's sinful condition.

A picture of a snow-covered mountain with the sun highlighting the white snow could complement this illustration well. Also, it would be good to have your listeners sing this song after you explain the meaning and its connection to the text.

David the prodigal

Bible: David's view of God is equivalent to the image of the father in the parable of the prodigal son (Luke 15). Like the prodigal, David has engaged in "wild living" (Ps. 51 title; Luke 15:13, 30), is obsessed by his sinful condition (51:3; Luke 15:17), and is aware that his sin is basically against God (51:4a; Luke 15:18–19). In both instances God is justified in the verdict (51:4b; Luke 15:19), and God is responsive to a broken and contrite heart (51:17; Luke 15:21–24). The story

of the prodigal is not designed to duplicate the story of Psalm 51, but it is a match for its spiritual character. This psalm, as well as the parable of the prodigal, sums up the teaching of Scripture about God's forgiveness. There is another story, said to be found in the Talmud, that wraps up this truth in a real-life action. Like the prodigal, a certain son left his father's house and went away. The father sent his servant to ask the boy to come home, and the boy sent back word, "It is too far. I cannot come back." Then the father returned word to his son, "Come as far as you can, and I will meet you there."

The power of God's grace

Christian Allegory: *Pilgrim's Progress*, by **John Bunyan.** Bunyan's book is a great picture of the sufficiency of God's amazing grace (see Rom. 5:20), or in the words of our psalm, the sufficiency of God's unfailing love (v. 1). As Christian is on his way to the Eternal City, Interpreter leads him to a place where there is a fire burning against a wall. And there at the wall is someone continually throwing water on the fire, trying to put it out, while the fire just burns higher and hotter. When Christian asks the meaning of what he sees, Interpreter leads him around to the other side of the wall, where he sees a man with a vessel of oil in his hand, which he is continually throwing into the fire. Interpreter explains: "This is Christ, who continually, with the oil of His grace, maintains the work already begun in the heart; by the means of which, notwithstanding what the devil can do, the souls of His people prove gracious still."[20]

"Why Do You Boast of Evil, You Mighty Hero?"

Big Idea *Those who live by wealth and power sometimes employ the power of speech as their weapon, but God's unfailing love is more powerful.*

Understanding the Text

Psalms 52–55 are each classified as a *maskil*. Psalm 32 is the first of thirteen psalms that have this term (see the comments on the title for Ps. 32). While its meaning is not known for certain, the basic meaning of the term, "to be skilled" / "to teach," makes a lot of sense here, since Psalm 52 seeks to teach the lesson that wealth, and the arrogant abuse that often goes along with it, will meet with God's judgment and be known by the epitaph of 52:7.

The type of Psalm 52 is elusive. Goldingay suggests that it is a "variant on a psalm of trust."[1] The verb "trust" describes the hero's reliance on his abundant wealth (52:7), in contrast to the psalmist, who trusts in God's unfailing love (52:8). Actually, the psalm does not fall into any one category, although it shares some features of the psalms of trust and the psalms of lament.

The Text in Context

The language of Psalm 52 reminds one of the concern of Old Testament wisdom for dealing with the arrogant prosperity of the wicked and the plight of the righteous. It shares this concern with Psalm 49:6–20 (see also 62:10), where the arrogance of the wicked and their reliance on wealth rather than God is the point of condemnation.

Outline/Structure

The poem is framed by a single concept, God's "unfailing love" (*hesed*, 52:1 [see ESV], 8; see "Teaching the Text"), translated into its cognate, the "faithful people" (*hasidim*, 52:9), producing a fourfold outline, as is reflected in the subjects of the poem.

1. You, the mighty hero (52:1–4)
2. He, the God of judgment (52:5)
3. They, the righteous (52:6–7)
4. I, the psalmist, confident in God's unfailing love (52:8–9)

Historical and Cultural Background

The title is the second in a row that associates the psalm with David's life. The story behind the title is told in 1 Samuel 22. If Psalm 52 is David's response to these events, the "mighty man" (52:1 ESV), whose "tongue plots destruction" (52:2), could be Doeg, who put eighty-five priests and their families to death at Saul's behest. While some doubt the Davidic connection, it nevertheless could very well be that it is genuine and that this is David's response to the atrocious crimes committed by Doeg, who may have been a member of Saul's "mighty men" (1 Sam. 14:52).

In contrast to the violent disruption of the wicked (52:5), the psalmist is like an "olive tree" (52:8; see the sidebar) growing in the house of God and worshiping in the presence of God's people (*hasidim*, 52:8–9). See also Psalm 1:3 and Jeremiah 17:8 for the symbol of the righteous as a flourishing tree.

Interpretive Insights

Title *A* maskil *of David. . . . Doeg the Edomite.* On the term *maskil*, see the discussion above. On David and Doeg, see "Historical and Cultural Background."

52:1 *Why do you boast of evil, you mighty hero?* The "mighty hero" is the addressee rather than God. For the addressee as Doeg, see "Historical and Cultural Background." The verb "boast" is from the same verbal root as "praise" (*hll*), but the object is "evil" rather than "God," thus changing the sense

of the verb and forming a wordplay. The contrary terms "evil" (*ra'ah*) and "unfailing love" (*hesed*) as the objects of "boast" certainly introduce a problem that translators have dealt with in various ways. The literal reading is possible. In that case, the second half of the sentence describes the counterforce ("unfailing love") to the boasting of evil. This is the sense of the ESV: "Why do you boast of evil, O mighty man? The steadfast love of God endures all the day." On the other hand, following the use of *hesed* in Leviticus 20:17 as "blasphemy," the second line would read: "all day long is blasphemy against God." The NIV seems to be dependent on the Septuagint, which has "lawlessness all day long" (*anomian holēn tēn hēmeran*). Evidently the Septuagint translator read the Hebrew *hesed* ("unfailing love") as *hamas* ("violence").[2]

52:2 *your tongue plots destruction; it is like a sharpened razor.* The RSV makes the last phrase of verse 1, "all day long," the beginning of this verse, although it makes sense where it stands in 52:1 if we understand the sentence as suggested above. The word "destruction" appears again in verse 7 (see

> Just like a sharp razor can slit the throat, a deceitful tongue "plots destruction" (52:2). This razor with a bronze blade and wooden handle is from Thebes (Eighteenth Dynasty, 1150–1069 BC).

Olive Trees

The olive tree was the most important tree in Israel's world. An evergreen, with leaves that are grayish green with a silver underside, it can live for centuries. Even when this tree is snarled and gruesomely knotty, it can produce abundant fruit and renew itself with numerous sprouts (Ps. 128:3). The fruit of the olive tree was used as food and was processed for cooking oil (1 Kings 17:12), oil for household lamps (Matt. 25:1–13), ointment for the skin (Ps. 104:15), medicine (Luke 10:34), cosmetics (Eccles. 9:7–8), and ritual anointing oil (Ps. 23:5; Exod. 30:22–33, etc.), and it was used in its purest form as the oil for the lamps that lit the sanctuary (Lev. 24:2–4). The fruit was the source of one of the three staples of the ancient Near Eastern diet: grain, wine, and oil (Deut. 7:13). The products of the olive tree, especially oil, were among ancient Israel's major exports (1 Kings 5:11; Ezra 3:7). The fruit of the tree, gathered in the fall, was pressed by heavy millstones, and the oil was caught in a vat and processed for its various uses.[a]

[a] F. Nigel Hepper, "Olive, Olive Tree," *NIDB* 3:325–26; Tate, *Psalms 51–100*, 38.

the comments on 52:6–7, below). Like a "sharpened razor," the tongue has the power to do evil or to do good.

52:3 *You love evil rather than good.* The hero's ethic is turned upside down (see Ps. 53:3). In Hebrew thought "goodness" (*tob*), that which is beautiful and helpful, is the opposite of "evil" (*ra'*).

52:5 *He will snatch you up and pluck you from your tent; he will uproot you.* The language of destruction predicts divine judgment that will befall the wicked ("He" = God). For more on the verbs in this verse, see the discussion of verse 8 below. See also James 1:26 and 1 Peter 3:10.

52:6–7 *The righteous will see and fear . . . "Here now is the man."* The verbs "see" and "fear" are in their present forms homonyms, *weyir'u . . . weyira'u* ("and they will see . . . and they will fear"), sounding the same but saying quite different things. (See 40:3b [Heb. 4b] for the same play on

words.) The NEB translates: "The righteous will look on, awestruck." These verses portray both divine judgment and the triumph of righteousness, two sides of one coin. The "mighty hero" of verse 1 (*gibbor*) has become the mere "man" (*geber*, from the same root, *gbr*) of verse 7. How are the mighty fallen!

grew strong by destroying others! Literally, "he grows strong by his destruction." "Destruction" occurs also in 52:2. Rather than "in his destruction," the Syriac and Aramaic versions have "in his wealth," which the RSV and NRSV follow.

52:8 *But I am like an olive tree flourishing in the house of God.* Compare the bird in Psalm 84:3 that has found a home in the sanctuary. Symbolically, there is no richer "soil" for nurturing God's people than "the house of God." In contrast to the wicked, whom God "brings down" like an old house ("snatches" from their dwelling, "plucks from" their tent, and "uproots" from their land in 52:5—total devastation), the psalmist is like an "olive tree" that is firmly planted and flourishing in God's house (see the sidebar). On "unfailing love," see the comments on 52:1 and "Teaching the Text."

52:9 *I will always praise you in the presence of your faithful people. And I will hope in your name.* Here we have a vow to worship in the temple. On "faithful people," see "Teaching the Text." The name YHWH does not occur in this psalm of the Elohistic Psalter. The short form of "God," *'el*, occurs twice (52:1, 5), and the longer form, *'elohim*, occurs three times (52:7, 8). David hopes in God's name, for God has manifested his goodness in what he has done.

According to the psalmist, the judgment for those with deceitful tongues is that God will pluck them from their tents and uproot them from the land of the living. This tent is in flames and its occupants dead in this Assyrian relief from the palace at Nineveh, 645–635 BC.

Theological Insights

Over against the wicked who use their power of speech like a weapon, the righteous are observant and will be awestruck by their laughter-producing observation that the wicked have arrogantly and falsely assumed that their wealth and power will bring them security. When laughter is the response, God is generally the subject (Pss. 2:4; 37:13; 59:8),[3] for laughter at the pretentious actions of the wicked is God's prerogative alone. Yet the righteous, by their observant and awestruck reaction to God's justice, might join in collateral activity with the divine and enjoy the unblemished laughter of heaven, elicited by heavenly justice. It is not so much hilarity over the wicked's destruction as joy over heaven's triumph.

Teaching the Text

We can begin our sermon/lesson by recognizing that the modern era is not the first to realize the power of language, for weal *and* for woe. Psalm 52 deals with this problem and articulates it in the following ways: "your tongue plots destruction" (52:2a); "[your tongue] is like a sharpened razor" (52:2b); "you love every harmful word" (52:4). This last statement is somewhat of a conclusion to the first section of the psalm (52:1–4). Using the literary device of synecdoche (the part for the whole), the psalmist uses the tongue to represent the whole person, the point being that the mighty hero is such a "man of his word" that he has become synonymous with his tongue (his word), and sadly a tongue of ill reputation.

This poem brings into focus the potential of human speech to become a lethal weapon, in this case, a "sharpened razor" (52:2), and the one who brandishes this dangerous weapon is exercised by an inverted ethic (52:3, 4), loving evil more than good. This "mighty hero" has worn his title audaciously, and his biography of destruction (52:2) seals his reputation as the one who grows strong by destruction (52:7). He becomes what he says (52:2, 4). This is a reminder that our speech is a projection of our personality and, more than that, a projection of our person. If we are not what we say, eventually the pattern of evil talk becomes retrojective in its effect and has the power to shape us into its foul image. Thankfully the righteous, faced with the powerful and wealthy, are encouraged by the hope of divine intervention.

While the supplicant is very much conscious of the power of evil, he is also quite aware that his trust in God has made him like an "olive tree flourishing in the house of God" (52:8)—that is the contrast between him and the evil person he indicts. In this confidence, the psalmist can write that person's epitaph in those terms: "Here now is the man who did not make God his stronghold but trusted in his great wealth and grew strong by destroying others!" (52:7).

A second and most important observation is that the poem is framed by a single concept, God's "unfailing love" (*hesed*, 52:1 and 8; see the comments on 52:1), translated into its cognate, the "faithful people" (*hasidim*, 52:9). This frame produces a fourfold outline, as is reflected in the "Outline/Structure" above. As is the case with God's covenant with Israel, and so often in the Psalms, grace is the framing concept of life and faith, and the people of Israel—thankfully, we too—live and believe within that frame. As difficult as it is, the psalmist—and we are his spiritual heirs—has to deal with the one who loves "evil rather than good" (52:3) within that context. Amazing grace!

Illustrating the Text

The danger of the tongue

News Story: On March 28, 1979, the nuclear reactor on Three Mile Island in Pennsylvania experienced a partial meltdown. To date, this has been the most serious accident in United States commercial nuclear power plant operating history. This potentially catastrophic event began when either a relatively minor mechanical or electrical failure prevented the main feedwater pumps from sending water to the steam generators that remove heat from the reactor core. This relatively minor incident that led to the reactor core meltdown could have been deadly.[4] One lesson learned from this event is that small missteps can create a chain of catastrophic events. This is certainly true with regard to the tongue (vv. 2–4). The tongue is one of the smallest organs in the human body, and yet it can be very destructive. A careless word can create hurt in others. An angry word can lead to wars between countries and conflict between people. A thoughtless word can spread gossip that destroys a person's reputation. We need to understand the potential of our words and discipline ourselves to be careful with the words we choose. It is not surprising that the ninth commandment regulates one's speech ("You shall not give false testimony against your neighbor," Exod. 20:16). It would be helpful to share an instance where you have experienced the destructive power of the tongue.

The positive power of words

History: Calvin said the only person who listened to his sermons was Denis Raguenier, his appointed recorder of sermons. Thanks to Raguenier's respect for the power of words and his shorthand skills, we have about 2,300 of the approximately 5,000 sermons Calvin preached.[5] A similar story is that of Gertrude Hobbs Chambers, who faithfully took down her husband's talks in shorthand and thus gave us Oswald Chambers's popular devotional, *My Utmost for His Highest*.[6]

Trust in the Lord is the path to a blessed life.

Contrasting Concept: Show a picture of a tree that has been uprooted by a storm. The tree is dead, and all it has to offer is the wood from its dead branches. Now, in contrast, show a picture of a healthy olive tree. These trees are not only beautiful, but their fruit can be used for food, olive oil, or even medicinal purposes. The olive tree is very hardy, fire resistant, drought resistant, and disease resistant. Because its root system is strong, it can actually regenerate the tree if the aboveground structure is destroyed. For these reasons, the trees can live to an old age. The contrast David makes in verses 5 (uprooted tree to describe the wicked) and 8 (olive tree to describe the righteous) is the difference between rejecting God and putting your trust in God.

David compares himself to a flourishing olive tree, one of the most valuable plants in the Middle East.

Psalm 52

"God Looks Down from Heaven . . . to See If There Are Any Who Understand"

Big Idea *History repeats itself in periodic unbelief, and God's judgment falls upon humankind, as it did in the generation of the flood.*

Understanding the Text

Psalm 53, an adaptive version of Psalm 14, is considered by some to be an individual lament, even though it is one of those genre-defying psalms that enjoy a noble company in the Psalter.

The Text in Context

Psalm 52:1 addresses the "mighty hero," who, in his arrogant boasts, is much like the "fool" of Psalm 53. Descriptively they look very much alike, for the mighty hero loves evil rather than good (52:3), while in Psalm 53 "there is no one who does good" (53:1, 3). If their moral degeneration is not equivalent, the difference between them is negligible.

As an adaptation of Psalm 14, Psalm 53 has been used as virtual evidence for the existence of an Elohistic Psalter (Pss. 42–83), which shows a preference for the divine name *'elohim* over the tetragrammaton *YHWH*.[1] Yet, the editor of Book 2 did not edit Psalm 14 merely to adapt it to his Elohistic preference but adapted it for a new historical setting, perhaps an event like that of Sennacherib's invasion in 701 BC (2 Kings 18–19).[2] The enemy attacked, but God scattered their bones and put them to shame through Israel. While the evildoers

Psalm 53 begins, "The fool says in his heart, 'There is no God.'" A historiated initial, showing the king and a fool, opens this psalm in a fifteenth- to sixteenth-century psalter from France.

(Israel) assailed the poor in Psalm 14 (14:6), the assailants of Psalm 53 (evildoers) are a foreign enemy.

Outline/Structure

In light of a new setting for Psalm 53, the outline reflects the unfounded dread that Israel has experienced, followed by God's judgment on their enemies, proving that they have nothing to dread.

1. The fool's perspective (53:1)
2. God's perspective (53:2–4)
   a. God's search for "any who seek God" (53:2)
   b. No one does good (53:3)
   c. The moral havoc of doing evil (53:4)
3. Dread and judgment (53:5)
   a. The unfounded dread of the righteous (53:5a–b)
   b. God's judgment as evidence of his presence (53:5c–d)
4. Hope for Israel's salvation (53:6)

Interpretive Insights

While the grammatical and orthographical differences between Psalms 14 and 53 are minor, the addition of verse 5b–d in Psalm 53 is significant and sheds light on the adaptive setting for Psalm 53. Table 1 offers a visual comparison of the two psalms, corresponding to the comments on each verse below. For additional comments on the verses, see the unit on Psalm 14.

Title *According to* mahalath. *A maskil of David.* The term *mahalath* may be a musical term, possibly the name of the tune for singing the psalm, or even a musical

Key Themes of Psalm 53

- The psalmist perceives a vacuum of faith.
- God is found in the "company of the righteous."

instrument. *Maskil* appears in the titles of Psalms 52–55 and in nine other titles. It may suggest a skilled way of presenting the song.[3]

53:1 *They are corrupt, and their ways are vile.* Instead of "deeds" (*'alilah*, 14:1), 53:1 reads "ways" (*'awel*), but both nuances suggest "evil deeds." Note the absence of "and" in 14:1 (see table 1).

53:2 *God looks down from heaven.* Typically the Elohistic Psalter prefers *'elohim* for God instead of *YHWH*, and three substitutions are made in Psalm 53 (vv. 2, 4, 6). *YHWH* does not appear at all in Psalm 53.

53:3 *Everyone has turned away.* There is a slight difference between the expressions "all" (*hakkol*, "the whole" [of mankind], 14:3) and "everyone" (*kullo*, "all of it [or "them"]," 53:3), although the meaning is the same. "Turned away" (*sar*, 14:3) and "turned away" (*sag*, 53:3) have two different roots; *sag* ("turn away" in disloyalty) is a clarification of *sar* ("turn away"), thus making the motive clear. That is, Psalm 53 tries to clarify the evil intent of the wrongdoers. But the Targum, perhaps viewing the change as a misreading, restores the 14:3 reading to *sar*.

53:4 *Do all these evildoers know nothing? . . . they never call on God.* Psalm 14:4 has "all," but 53:4 does not, a negligible difference. The NIV restores "all" in 53:4. Note the preference of *'elohim* in 53:4 rather than *YHWH* (14:4) (see the comments on 53:2). The God-deniers have no spiritual perception.

53:5 *But there they are, overwhelmed with dread, where there was nothing to dread. God scattered the bones of those who attacked you.* The first part of this verse and its duplicate (Ps. 14:5a) may speak of the evildoers, who are "overwhelmed with dread," even though "God is present in the company of the righteous"—the evildoers did not perceive it ("where there was nothing to dread"). Then in Psalm 53, to prove his presence, God has routed their enemies. It is possible also that in 14:5 it is Israel that is "overwhelmed with dread," not their enemies, even though "God is present in the company of the righteous" (14:5b)—they did not perceive it—and in 53:5a it is the evildoers, both audiences unaware of God's presence. Thus in 53:5b God has given Israel tangible proof of his presence as he has "scattered the bones of those who attacked you." My preference is the latter, since the writer/editor of Psalm 53 is drawing a contrast between the two generations.

53:6 *salvation for Israel . . . When God restores his people.* Psalm 14:7 has "salvation" (sg.) and 53:6 has "salvations" (pl.), but the plural rather than the singular is a common occurrence to emphasize the quality as well as the quantity (of God's salvation). Note also the use of *'elohim* in 53:6 rather than *YHWH* (14:7) (see the comments on 53:2).

Table 1. A Comparison of Psalms 14 and 53

Psalm 14	Psalm 53
For the director of music.	For the director of music. (According to *mahalath*.)
Of David.	(A *maskil*) of David.
14:1 The fool says in his heart, "There is no God." They are corrupt, their deeds are vile; there is no one who does good.	**53:1** The fool says in his heart, "There is no God." They are corrupt, (and) their <u>ways</u> are vile; there is no one who does good.
14:2 The LORD looks down from heaven on all mankind to see if there are any who understand, any who seek God.	**53:2** <u>God</u> looks down from heaven on all mankind to see if there are any who understand, any who seek God.
14:3 All have turned away [verb = *sar*], all have become corrupt; there is no one who does good, not even one.	**53:3** <u>Everyone has turned away</u> [verb = *sag*], all have become corrupt; there is no one who does good, not even one.
14:4 Do all these evildoers know nothing? They devour my people as though eating bread; they never call on the LORD.	**53:4** Do <u>all</u> [not in Heb. text] these evildoers know nothing? They devour my people as though eating bread; they never call on <u>God</u>.
14:5 But there they are, overwhelmed with dread, for God is present in the company of the righteous.	**53:5** But there they are, overwhelmed with dread, (where there was nothing to dread. God scattered the bones of those who attacked you; you put them to shame, for God despised them).
14:6 You evildoers frustrate the plans of the poor, but the LORD is their refuge. [This statement, which is absent from Psalm 53, suggests that the evildoers have been particularly hard on the poor.]	
14:7 Oh, that salvation [sg.] for Israel would come out of Zion! When the LORD restores his people, let Jacob rejoice and Israel be glad!	**53:6** Oh, that salvation [pl.] for Israel would come out of Zion! When <u>God</u> restores his people, let Jacob rejoice and Israel be glad!

Note: In the table, underlining indicates changed words in Psalm 53, and parentheses indicate additions.

Theological Insights

Psalms 14 and 53 provide an opportunity to think about the way God deals with two generations. While their historical perspectives are different (see "Teaching the Text" in this unit), God's way of dealing with them is virtually the same, even though it can be described in different ways. But we need not conclude that the difference in description, at least in the present case, implies that God's care for his people has changed. In one generation (Ps. 14) the evildoers are overwhelmed because of God's presence with his people (14:45b). Whether the evildoers recognize God's presence is not clear, but the effect is the same. In another generation (Ps. 53) God's presence is obvious, at least to his people, because "God scattered the bones of those who attacked you" (53:5b). The point is that God's presence is manifested to different generations in different ways, and sometimes the manifestation is less obvious to one generation than to another. And the critical center of consciousness is in God's people, not in the evildoers. See "Illustrating the Text."

Teaching the Text

Preaching duplicate psalms individually is possible,[4] but I think the better approach is to combine them into one sermon/lesson. Perhaps this would be easier in a classroom setting than the pulpit. However, it could be an instructive experience to deal with Psalm 53 separate from Psalm 14 and focus on the adaptation of Psalm 14 to the new situation faced by the writer of Psalm 53.

In addition to the feature of different divine names, perhaps to adapt to a new liturgical situation (see the sidebar, "The Divine Names and the Elohistic Psalter," in the unit on Pss. 42–43), we want to point out both what is added in Psalm 53 that Psalm 14 does not contain and what is left out of Psalm 53 that is included in Psalm 14 (see table 1). Both will open up the different perspectives of the two psalms. The additional words in Psalm 53:5 are in parentheses: "But there they are, overwhelmed with dread, where there was nothing to dread. God scattered the bones of those who attacked you; you put them to shame, for God despised them." Obviously the editor of Psalm 53 has observed that some terrible disaster has happened in Israel, and the fear of judgment has seized Israel's enemies when they did not expect

God scatters the bones of the evildoers, pronouncing his judgment by not allowing the corpses to be buried. So important was it to follow correct burial procedures that this inscription was placed above the seventh-century BC tomb of a royal steward found outside Jerusalem in the Arab community of Silwan. It curses the one who opens the tomb, most likely to prevent the bones from being disturbed.

it. Two occasions have been suggested as the historical setting, Jehoshaphat's defeat of the Moabites (2 Chron. 20:22–24) and the defeat of Sennacherib in 701 BC (2 Kings 18–19).[5] As reassurance to Israel, the language of verse 5b turns to a direct address ("you"), assuring them that this is what happens to fools who say there is no God. We can make the point that here is an example of the application of Scripture to the interpreter's situation—in Scripture itself—a principle that marks the interpretation of the Psalms. We can assure our listeners that God's regard for his people is always one of his top priorities.

The second key difference in the two psalms is 14:6, which regards the evildoers' frustration of the plans of the poor. In Psalm 14 the evildoers have turned against the poor, but in Psalm 53 God has turned against the evildoers. Instead of the direct assurance of God's presence with Israel ("God is present in the company of the righteous," 14:5b), Psalm 53 turns God's judgment personal by addressing Israel in the second person (53:5b). The point we can make is that God's judgment aims at the evildoers in both situations, and in both situations he acts on behalf of his own people, the poor in one case (Ps. 14), the congregation in the other (Ps. 53).

Illustrating the Text

God's work is perceptible only to those who believe.

Quote: As the Iron Curtain was crumbling in 1989, the *Manchester Guardian* carried an editorial about the fall of the Iron Curtain and the collapse of communism. The article observed that George Orwell, in

The historical setting referenced in Psalm 53 may have been the defeat of Sennacherib's army at the hand of the Lord during its siege of Jerusalem in 701 BC. Sennacherib is depicted on this Assyrian relief from the throne room at Khorsabad (721–705 BC).

his book *Nineteen Eighty-Four*, forgot the Christian message and the power of Christ to overturn kingdoms and dethrone rulers and upset the systems of philosophers and politicians. The editorialist wrote:

> He forgot the power of Christ the King. Stalin was right. The Pope has no divisions. In that respect he is as naked as the babe born in a manger all those centuries ago. Ceausescu had countless divisions, as did Honecker, Jaruzelski and all. But the events of recent months have once again demonstrated that God's mysterious ways are more than a match for even the most ruthless of men.
>
> . . . The notion that communism might be brought low not by armies and fleets, the almighty dollar, the CIA and so on, but by a God long since pronounced dead, never entered their heads. But it has come to pass and this Christmas, all over the world, wise men will be less inclined to mock, and more inclined to worship—as happened at the first Christmas.[6]

And so the church has a living Lord, who sometimes, perhaps more often than not, works in ways that only those who believe can perceive.

Respectable sins

Human Experience: In Psalm 53:1–3 we see that the fool's attitude regarding the nonexistence of God leads to sinful behavior. The Lord looks upon the earth to see if there are any who seek God, as evidenced by their behavior. What would God see in your life? How would you categorize yourself: as the fool or as the one who seeks God? It is our human tendency to compare our lives with others and therefore to see ourselves as being relatively good. But there are sins that we accept as normative, or respectable, that are still sins. Examples of these could be gossip, a critical spirit, "white" lies, an unforgiving heart, "justified" revenge, and so on. What do these sins say about your heart for the Lord? From God's perspective there really is no such thing as a "respectable sin." We must acknowledge our own sinful nature and seek the Lord with our heart, soul, and mind.

Is sin exclusively a religious thing?

Quote: *The Seven Deadly Sins*, **by Solomon Schimmel.** The subjects of Psalm 53 have practically or intellectually cut themselves off from God ("There is no God," 53:1), but the psalmist knows that denying God does not remove him from the equation—God still "looks down from heaven on all mankind" (53:2). The God deniers of this psalm celebrate their morally vacuous world by indulging in their corrupt and vile ways (53:1). A denial of God is a denial of good and an espousal of evil. Schimmel addresses the issue of making sin an exclusively religious matter:

> Because sin is associated with religion, secularists think that it is irrelevant to them. But many of the sins of tradition, and particularly the seven deadly ones, are primarily concerned with what it means to be human and humane and the responsibilities that we have to fulfill if we want to be considered as such. The theologians and moralists believed, rightly, that in the long run those who are moral and ethical are also happier. Conversely, by succumbing to immediate gratification of our impulses, usually injuring others in the process, we may experience pleasure. But in due time the pleasure will give way to unhappiness because it alone cannot sustain us spiritually.[7]

"I Will Praise Your Name, LORD, for It Is Good"

Big Idea *Faith affirms God and worships, and in that context confronts the ongoing conflict between truth and evil.*

Understanding the Text

Psalm 54 contains most of the characteristics of an individual lament, including an address to God, petition, lament/complaint, confession of trust, vow to praise, and assurance of being heard.[1] It is another of the thirteen psalms that have historical titles (see the sidebar).

The Text in Context

Psalm 54 belongs to a minicollection (Pss. 52–55) that is joined together by the phrase "A *maskil* of David." See "The Text in Context" in the unit on Psalm 52.

Outline/Structure

The following outline moves along the lines of the components of the individual lament:

1. Address (54:1)
2. Petition that God will hear (54:2)
3. Lament/complaint of the psalmist (54:3)
4. Confession of trust (54:4)
5. Prayer for revenge (54:5)
6. Vow to praise the Lord (54:6)
7. Assurance of having been heard (54:7)

The historical event connected to this psalm is the Ziphites' visit to Saul with information about David's hiding place. David had fled to the Desert of Ziph, a hilly region south of Hebron, in the Judean wilderness near the town of Ziph. This photo shows the region near Tell Zif, which may correspond to the ancient village.

Historical and Cultural Background

The present title of the psalm is so closely tied to the story connected to the psalm that an exact quotation is drawn from 1 Samuel 23:19: "Is not David hiding among us?" (also in 1 Sam. 26:1, without "among us"). The story referred to in the title is found in 1 Samuel 23:19–29 and 26:1–25. While fleeing from Saul, David and his men hide in the Wilderness of Ziph, the region around the town of Ziph (located about three miles south of Hebron; cf. Josh. 15:55). When the pro-Saul Ziphites report that David is hiding in the region and they can deliver him into Saul's hands, the king launches a search for the fleeing David. The outcome, however, turns in David's favor when he and his nephew Abishai sneak into Saul's camp at night, steal his spear and water jar, and escape to safety. When Saul and his army realize that David could have killed the king as he slept but refused to put forth his hand against the Lord's anointed, Saul acclaims David's integrity and his future success (1 Sam. 26:21–25). The portrait of the "arrogant foes" (54:3), "ruthless people" (54:3), and "those who slander" (54:5) harmonizes well with the story of the Ziphites who sought to betray David.

Interpretive Insights

Title *With stringed instruments.* This phrase (*binᵉginot*) appears in the titles of Psalms 4; 6; 54; 55; 67; and 76, with a variant form in Psalm 61 (see the comments on the title for Ps. 4). See also "Historical and Cultural Background" for the historical superscription.

54:1 *Save me, O God, by your name.* The phrase "your name" in reference to

Key Themes of Psalm 54

- The power and goodness of God's name work in harmony.
- God is our helper.
- Evil has a built-in quality that causes it to recoil on itself.
- We should have the proper disposition when our enemies are defeated.

Psalms with Historical Titles

Thirteen psalms have historical titles: Psalms 3; 7; 18; 34; 51; 52; 54; 56; 57; 59; 60; 63; 142. Regardless of when the historical titles became a part of the psalms, the psalmist or the editor saw something that connected the event and the psalm. It was not careless editing, but the problem is quite possibly a difference in the way the ancient mind and the modern connect events and ideas. One only has to read the midrashic literature to find a myriad of illustrations that represent the classical example of this way of thinking. Sometimes the midrashic method makes connections with the text in a way that we have difficulty understanding. In all the psalms with historical titles except Psalm 142, the authorial, musical, and literary terms occur first, followed by the historical note. This might imply that the latter information was added, or it may simply suggest a proper order of introductory information, the historical coming last.

The book of Psalms represents a long tradition of Scripture interpreting Scripture. In this regard, the significance of the historical perspective, quite evident in these titles, provides contrary evidence to any hermeneutical method that would downplay the significance of history in interpreting the Psalms. While other methods are extremely productive (e.g., the form-critical method), the historical perspective cannot be neglected.

God virtually forms an *inclusio* in the psalm, appearing in 54:1 and 6.

54:3 *Arrogant foes are attacking me; ruthless people . . . people without regard for God.* The NIV omits the conjunction "for/because" (*ki*), which begins the sentence and gives the reason for the psalmist's petition. The terms "arrogant foes" (*zarim*; also "strangers" or "foreigners") and "ruthless people" (*'aritsim*) are often parallel companions (Isa. 25:5; Ezek. 28:7;

31:12) and describe those who induce fear in others.[2] The phrase "people without regard for God" literally reads, "they have not set God before them." This description is similar to the one in 53:4, "they never call on God." These people belong in the same category as the "fool" of 53:1 and are the opposite of the righteous. Compare "I have set the Lord always before me" (Ps. 16:8 ESV).

54:4 *God is my help.* Here the psalmist introduces the underlying reason that generates his request: God is his helper. It is a turning point in the psalm, with *selah* (see NIV footnote) at the end of verse 3 probably alerting the reader to the change. While it is quite possible that *selah* was not original to the text of the Psalms but was a later liturgical note, this is one place where the term indicates a change in the tone of the psalm.[3]

54:5 *Let evil recoil on those who slander me; in your faithfulness destroy them.* In the margin, the Masoretes corrected the verb "to return" (*yashub*) to read "to cause to return" (*yashib*, Hiphil imperfect), implying that God has a causal relationship to this recoil action: "May he cause evil to recoil on my slanderers." The word "faithfulness" (*'emet*) may also be translated "truth," so that the phrase would mean, "by your truth destroy them" (see "Teaching the Text").

54:6 *I will sacrifice a freewill offering to you; I will praise your name, Lord, for it is good.* Sacrifice appears in neighboring psalms (50:7–15, 23; 51:16–17, 19) but here with no consideration of its appropriateness or God's desire for it (cf. 50:7–15). The "freewill offering" (*nᵉdabah*) was made voluntarily (Exod. 35:29; Lev. 7:16). Note that Psalm 52:9 also says that God's name is good. "Your name" also appears in verse 1.

54:7 *You have delivered me.* The Hebrew reads, "He delivered me." The NIV changes the person to "you" to make it more appropriate for the prayer, but the prayer is confined to verses 5 and 6. The JPS reads, "for it delivered me," referring to "name," which seems to be the intent.

my eyes have looked in triumph on my foes. The NIV interprets the literal statement, "my eyes have looked on my foes," in the context of the psalm that implies rejoicing, thus the added phrase "in triumph." Most English translations do the same.

Theological Insights

Accompanying the two references to God's name (54:1, 6) are two terms that identify God's character. In verse 1 the invocation calls on God to save the suppliant "by your might." The rabbis have commented that when *'elohim* occurs, it implies the power of God, as compared to the tetragrammaton, *YHWH*, which implies his mercy and compassion. While this is a generalization, it nevertheless is helpful to remember that context generally determines the choice of divine names in the Psalter, except in the Elohistic Psalter, where *'elohim* is probably an accommodation to a non-Jerusalemite setting for Books 2 and 3.[4] The point, however, is that the psalm is framed by God's name ("your name") and is defined by the accompanying phrases "by your might" (54:1) and "it is good" (54:6). The portrait of a powerful and good God is typical of the Psalter.

In that context, the affirmation of God as "my help" (54:4) is quite in agreement with David's general experience with God during his troubled life (e.g., Pss. 30:10; 46:5). To be helped by a powerful God, who is able, and a good God, who is willing, is David's testimony of triumph.

Teaching the Text

Drawing upon the "Big Idea," we may emphasize the fact that the psalmist prays for deliverance (54:1) and concludes by attesting that it has indeed come (54:7). Yet, in the midst of his worship he acknowledges the reality of the evil that stalks his personal life (54:3) and over which he triumphs through God's power. That is, the psalmist sets the evil of his personal world in the context of worship, and that calls forth the tone of triumph at the end of the psalm. To reinforce this point, we may stress the fact that evil, at least in the biblical sense, can never be studied apart from worship of the sovereign Lord, for from the beginning to the end of Scripture, God is in the process of triumphing over evil. Thankfully not many of us can say "ruthless people are trying to kill me" (54:3), but we encounter evil in other ways: social evils, personal slander, injustice in various venues, and more. And for the psalmist it is a very personal matter, and when we join Paul's victory cry, "Thanks be to God, who gives us the victory through our Lord Jesus Christ" (1 Cor. 15:57 ESV), the psalmist can join with us in that triumphant cry, because that is the gist of his poem.

To further develop the idea that, biblically speaking, evil must always be studied in the context of our sovereign God, we may observe that the psalm pits "truth" (*'emet*; NIV: "faithfulness") against "evil" (54:5). While evil and truth do not at first glance appear to be opposites, it is evil that is the enemy of truth, for evil always aims to distort truth. In fact, the psalmist recognizes an inherent quality of evil—or at least God's power to make it so—that evil will recoil on itself (54:5).

Another point we may make is that the Old Testament, and especially the Psalms, tends to deal not so much with the "problem" of evil as with the "problems" of evil, thus putting the issue in its practical settings. Usually they are personal, sometimes personal, sometimes political, and rarely theoretical. Only in the context of the sovereign Lord can we bring its many dissonant voices under his conquering control and proclaim with Paul, "We are more than conquerors through him who loved us" (Rom. 8:37).

Illustrating the Text

Hear my prayer, O God!

Personal Testimony: A consistent theme of the psalms is looking to the Lord for help in times of trouble and fear. We see this theme again in Psalm 54:1–2. Here David comes to the Lord with a plea, "Save me, O God, by your name" (v. 1a). Share with your

listeners a time when you came before God in need, crying out to him for deliverance, help, and intervention. Be vulnerable and open about the circumstances so they can identify with your heart. It is important that the audience hears from you that you have put your trust in the Lord and that you look to him in times of need.

Give thanks!

Quote: *Faded Denim: Color Me Trapped*, **by Melody Carlson.** Carlson writes in her novel about our human tendency to complain to God rather than to give thanks. When we focus on our hardships we tend to be blind to our blessings. The Psalms often reveal that thanksgiving and praise were close to the heart and lips of the psalmists, even while they were going through difficult times (e.g., Ps. 54:6–7). While at camp the

A frequent plea voiced by the psalmist is for God to hear his voice (27:7), hear his cry (28:2), hear his prayer (54:2), and listen to him (55:1). Ear tablets such as these were created to remind Egyptians that their gods heard all. Sometimes ears were added to paintings to remind the god to listen to a particular request.

main character, Emily, reflects on her own propensity to complain:

> Instead of thanking God for my two strong legs that are able to run and jump and climb, I whined about my "thunder thighs" and "thick" ankles. . . . I have been totally and unbelievably ungrateful for everything. Like a completely spoiled brat, I took my healthy body for granted. I criticized it and despised it. With crystal clarity, I know that I do not deserve the good health that God has mysteriously blessed me with. . . . As I watch these kids with their less-than-perfect bodies, I feel so thoroughly ashamed of myself. I mean, how could I have been so stupid and shallow and self-centered?[5]

Maintain godliness in an unjust world.

History: At times, as in Psalm 54, we see anger rise up in the heart of the psalmists with regard to injustice in the world. This is particularly true when the psalmist is personally the victim of injustice, betrayal, and attacks. Rather than permit those who have no regard for God to set his agenda (v. 3), he leaves vengeance to God (v. 5a) and acknowledges him as judge (v. 1). We can learn from the example of Anne Frank, who sought not to allow the evil of her world to taint her soul. Frank was just fifteen years old when she became a Holocaust victim at the hands of the Nazis during World War II. Her "crime" was simply that she was Jewish. Her story was told through her diary, which was published after her death. In it she writes: "And finally I twist my heart round again, so that the bad is on the outside and the good is on the inside, and keep on trying to find a way of becoming what I would so like to be, and could be, if there weren't any other people living in the world."[6] This provides a challenge to each of us to fight the tendency to allow bitterness and vengeance to tarnish our soul.

"Cast Your Cares on the Lord and He Will Sustain You"

Big Idea *When our trusted friends have betrayed us and the moral substructure has eroded, we can cast our cares on the Lord.*

Understanding the Text

Psalm 55 is generally considered an individual lament. The supplicant has suffered slander and threats from his enemies and, worst of all, betrayal by his trusted friend. We have observed previously that often the Psalms do not propose ultimate solutions to human problems but prescribe ways of coping with them, and this psalm is an excellent example of that principle: "Cast your cares on the LORD . . ." (55:22). For this speaker, as the king, supposedly has access to resources that the common people do not. But in a crisis situation like that described in Psalm 55, his resources are greatly reduced by the personal threats and the general lack of public sympathy that his city has exhibited. Yet this psalm does not capitalize on the privileges and powers of kingship but presents the problem of betrayal as a common crisis that many people encounter in life, probably no greater in the ancient world than in our own. In fact, one of the timeless features of the Psalms is that they deal with human issues on a level that all readers can access.

The Text in Context

This is the fourth psalm in a minicollection (Pss. 52–55) that is attributed to David and also called by the peculiar term "A *maskil* of David." Psalm 55 considers faithfulness in the context of a social covenant that has been broken—in fact, broken by one who has been the supplicant's bosom friend. The lesson the supplicant has learned from this bitter disappointment is to throw his burden on the Lord, and the Lord will sustain him.

While Psalm 55 is not an imprecatory psalm as such,[1] it does show a tendency to move into that mode of passion (55:15, 23). In light, however, of the strong faith imperative and declaration of trust (55:23), the psalmist does not yield to the temptation.

In his letter to the "exiles" of the faith, Peter quotes verse 22 as an imperative of faith and encouragement: "Cast all your anxiety on him because he cares for you" (1 Pet. 5:7). Peter's counsel to the young is that they humble themselves "under God's mighty hand, that he may lift [them] up in due time" (1 Pet. 5:6). In that context of humility, he quotes the first part of verse 22, "Cast all your anxiety on him," and then adds to this his understanding of the character of God, "because he cares for you" (1 Pet. 5:7). Whether he learned this from the great literature of the Torah (e.g., Exod. 34:6–7), the Psalms were a rich resource for recognizing the character of the Lord's unfailing love (*hesed*, not used in this psalm but implied), and this counsel was still appropriate for the Jews of the Diaspora, who were looking to the chief Shepherd's appearance (1 Pet. 5:4). These

people, like the psalmist, had been victims of their enemies too, yet gratefully were objects of divine love.

Outline/Structure

Some consider Psalm 55 to be composed of two psalms: verses 1–18 and verses 19–23. It seems very likely, however, as A. A. Anderson asserts, that the emotional stress of this author, persecuted by his enemies and betrayed by his friend, can

David is distraught (55:2), and his "heart is in anguish" (55:4). As his son Absalom plotted against him and his advisor Ahithophel betrayed him, he was forced to flee. Shown here is the Kidron Valley and the slopes up the Mount of Olives, the route David took as he left the city of Jerusalem, weeping and barefoot, with his head covered in sorrow (2 Sam. 15:30).

account for the emotional swings.[2] The following outline reflects the mood swings as well as the subject shifts.

1. Invocation (55:1–3)
2. Lament/complaint (55:4–8)
3. Petition and review (55:9–15)
   a. Petition against the enemy (55:9a; the wicked [pl.])
   b. Description of the evil city (55:9b–11)
   c. Review of betrayal (55:12–14; betrayer [sg.])
   d. Petition against the enemy (55:15; the wicked [pl.])
4. The psalmist's prayerful piety (55:16–17)
5. God's response to the psalmist's piety (55:18–19)
6. Betrayal revisited (55:20–21)
7. The lesson learned and commended (55:22–23)
   a. The lesson of justice for the righteous: "Cast your cares on the LORD" (55:22)
   b. The lesson of justice for the wicked: "God will bring down the wicked" (55:23a–b)
   c. The capstone of trust (55:23c)

Historical and Cultural Background

Historically speaking, Psalm 55 has been associated with David's betrayal by his trusted advisor Ahithophel, who turned against him and joined Absalom's political coup. While the prayer of David against Ahithophel in 2 Samuel 15:31 ("LORD, turn Ahithophel's counsel into foolishness") is different from the prayer of verse 15, it is not all that different from verse 9, where David prays that the Lord will "confuse the wicked, confound their words." The emotional tone of Psalm 55, in fact, is quite in line with David's emotional state as he and his supporters left Jerusalem weeping, with their heads covered (2 Sam. 15:30).

This psalm uses two metaphors to describe the easy talk of David's friend-turned-betrayer, "smooth as butter" and "more soothing than oil" (55:21). This window into the ancient world tells us something about the ancient diet and medicinal practice. The smooth taste of butter and the soothing effect of oil applied to the body

Words from a friend that should soothe, like oil on the skin, become like drawn swords in the mouth of a betrayer. Ointments with oils as their base were used to soothe and refresh skin that was exposed to the heat and dryness of the ancient Near East. The backrest of this royal throne shows Queen Anchesenamun applying ointment to the arm of her husband, King Tutankhamen (fourteenth century BC).

are fitting metaphors for speech that sounds good but is designed to destroy character. It is the latter motive that calls forth the two corresponding metaphors of "war" and "drawn swords."

Interpretive Insights

55:1 *do not ignore my plea*. The verb "ignore" (lit., "hide oneself") occurs in Deuteronomy 22:4 (RSV): "You shall not see your brother's ass or his ox fallen down by the way, and *withhold your help*" (i.e., "hide yourself"). The "plea" is a prayer for God's favor.

55:2 *My thoughts trouble me and I am distraught*. The meaning of this second half of the verse is difficult. Hakham translates the first verb as "I sob" and the second as "cry out," resulting in this rendering: "I sob in my complaint and I cry out."[3]

55:3 *because of what my enemy is saying*. The enemy is singular here, as in verses 12–13 and 20–21, but plural in 3b, 9, 15, 18, and 23. Goldingay suggests that the singular may individualize the group,[4] and Dahood explains that switching grammatical number is characteristic of Northwest Semitic curses,[5] perhaps for the purpose of individualization.

55:4 *My heart is in anguish*. The verb "to be in anguish" describes a woman in labor pains (Isa. 26:17; NIV: "writhes").

55:6 *Oh, that I had the wings of a dove!* Enviously, he thinks of the dove that can fly away from danger and find safety in the crevice of the rocks (Jer. 48:28). See Psalm 11:1.

55:9 *Lord, confuse the wicked, confound their words*. In the Hebrew the verb "confuse" has no object. The NIV has supplied "the wicked" (see 55:3), and the RSV "their plans." However, the final term in the sentence, "their language," may be taken as the object of both verbs, "confuse" and "confound": "Confuse, Lord, confound their language" (cf. ESV, NRSV). The text produces a picture of Babel (Gen. 11:5–9). In fact, the verb "confound" (*plg*) evokes the context of the Babel story, in which the birth of Peleg prefaces the story, and the comment follows: "because in his time the earth was divided [Niphal of *plg*]" (Gen. 10:25).

55:10–11 *Destructive forces are at work in the city; threats and lies never leave its streets*. Note the wickedness of the city: malice, abuse, destructive forces, threats, and lies. "Day and night" suggests the perpetual nature of wickedness, and "walls" and "streets" its full physical scope. There were only two places in the ancient city with room enough for large crowds to gather, the marketplace at the city gate and the court of the sanctuary. The ESV ("marketplace") and NJPS ("square") are among those translations that understand "its streets" to suggest a large area. It likely refers to the narrow lanes of the ancient city (not streets in the modern sense of the word) that were filled with "threats and lies," suggesting the complete corruption of the city. The term "destructive forces" (*hawwot*) implies criminal actions. The "city" is probably Jerusalem, implied by the phrase "house of God" (55:14).

55:12 *If an enemy were insulting me, I could endure it*. The Septuagint introduces the sentence with the conjunction "if" (*ei*), and the Hebrew allows for that with the conjunction *ki*, that can introduce a clause contrary to fact. This is the psalmist's great disappointment, that his trusted friend, with whom he once "enjoyed sweet fellowship" (55:14), has betrayed him. The fact that this companionship was enjoyed with those on their way to the "house of God" (55:14) only exacerbates the pain.

55:13 *But it is you, a man like myself.* It sounds like the supplicant is addressing his "friend" directly, but most likely it is a literary device to suggest, like the apostrophe, that the addressee is not present. Note the piling up of terms to "express the severity of the accusation":[6] "a man like myself, my companion, my close friend."

55:14 *as we walked about among the worshipers.* Psalm 42:4 describes the joy of the assembly on the way to the sanctuary.

55:15 *Let death take my enemies by surprise.* This sounds a bit like the curses that are prayed against the psalmist's enemies in the imprecatory psalms (Pss. 35; 69; 109).[7]

55:16 *As for me.* This phrase renders well the introductory pronoun "I," which functions as a pending case (*casus pendens*) and has the effect of drawing a contrast with the oppressors. The same grammatical effect can be seen in verse 13 ("but it is you"), in reference to the friend-betrayer, and verse 23 ("but as for me"), in reference to the psalmist.

55:17 *Evening, morning and noon.* This may reflect the Genesis notion that the day begins with evening and also suggest times of prayer (Dan. 6:10).

55:18 *He rescues me unharmed from the battle waged against me, even though many oppose me.* This is a difficult verse. However, with the occurrence of *shalom* ("peace") in the first colon of the verse, "he rescues me *unharmed*" (*bᵉshalom*, "in peace"), most likely the NIV's "from the battle waged against me" in the second colon is the proper sense. The Hebrew of the third colon is obscure. The NIV translates it: "even though many oppose me" (ESV: "for many are arrayed against me"). The Septuagint seems inclined toward the same sense, "for they were with me in many cases," referencing the psalmist's enemies. However, it could have the opposite meaning, and then it becomes a comment on God's great rescue, as reflected in the NJPS: "He redeems me unharmed from the battle against me; *it is as though many are on my side.*"

55:19 *God, who is enthroned from of old, who does not change.* In verse 16 the supplicant says that he, in contrast to his enemies, calls on God (*'elohim*), and the Lᴏʀᴅ (*YHWH*) saves him. Here God (*'el*) continues to be the subject and the evildoers the object. The defining clause, "who is enthroned from of old," is rendered in the Septuagint as "who exists from eternity." The clause "who does not change" is a difficult one. The word "change" is the word for changing garments (Gen. 45:22; see ESV).[8] The NIV understands the word to refer to God (but it is fem. pl.), while other versions understand it as a reference to the evildoers. The JB translates: "But God will hear me. Sovereign from the first, he will humble them; no change of heart for them, since they do not fear God."

55:20 *My companion attacks his friends; he violates his covenant.* This is the second description of the friend-turned-betrayer

(55:12–14 and 20–21). The subject "my companion" is supplied, for the subject is not specified; literally it reads, "he puts forth his hands against his friends." This is undoubtedly a reference back to the friend who has betrayed him. "Violates" also means "profanes." Perhaps this was a legal agreement, a contract, involving the psalmist, or more likely a social covenant (1 Sam. 18:3).

David describes his friend's words as being "smooth as butter" (55:21). But they were hypocritical words, full of deceit. Churns were used to agitate milk to separate out the butterfat from which butter was processed. The churn shown here was found at Beersheba, Israel, and is dated to the fourth millennium BC.

55:21 *smooth as butter . . . more soothing than oil.* The comparison is between words and actions. "Smooth as butter" and "more soothing than oil" (cf. Prov. 5:3) are parallel expressions that suggest charming speech whose purpose is deceit. See "Historical and Cultural Background."

55:22 *Cast your cares on the LORD.* This verse, considered by some to be an oracle of salvation spoken by a temple prophet,[9] is a parenthesis in the psalm, a self-instruction of the psalmist, and intended for other worshipers, bidding them turn to Yahweh and he will sustain them in this difficult situation of betrayal. The word "care(s)" means "burden," from the verb "to give, place" (*yhb*, used only in the Qal imperative). The Septuagint translates "anxiety, care" (*merimna*).

55:23 *will bring down the wicked into the pit of decay . . . But as for me, I trust in you.* This verse contrasts the fate of the wicked with the blessing of the righteous in verse 22. The "pit" suggests Sheol or the grave (55:15). This verse speaks confidently of God's judgment that the psalmist prays for in verse 15. The life of the wicked will be cut short ("will not live out half their days"), whereas the sign of God's favor is a long life (Pss. 21:4; 91:16). In the final declaration, it is the second time the psalmist has referenced himself personally. As in verse 16, he contrasts himself to the "bloodthirsty and deceitful" (see 55:12–14), whose lives will be cut short, although he does not specify the outcome of his trust. Perhaps it is sufficient to say, "I trust in you," without stipulating the outcome. God is enough.

Theological Insights

At certain turns in his thought, the psalmist falls into the temptation of "cursing" his enemies (55:15, 23), but he finally falls back on the real substance of his heart and instructs himself and his compatriots to "cast your cares on the LORD and he will sustain you" (55:22). The noun "cares" may imply that these are "burdens" that God has placed on the psalmist. In the theology of the Old Testament, at least until the postexilic era, God was understood to be the source/cause of everything,

David wishes he could fly like a dove and flee to the desert. This dove is leaving its perch on the Western Wall in Jerusalem.

even evil, so it is not surprising to find this kind of inference. Verse 22 of this psalm is among the great affirmations of faith in the Psalter. It comes close to Jesus's own assurance that his yoke is easy and his burden light (Matt. 11:30).

Among the emotional traumas of human frailties, the betrayal of a friend is one of the most painful. The New Testament story that looms above all other stories of betrayal is Judas's betrayal of Jesus with a kiss (Matt. 26:47–49). The Gospel story tells both sides of the betrayal: the crucifixion of Jesus and the guilt of Judas that leads to his suicide. In Psalm 55, we see only one side of the story, the story of the betrayed. The other side remains untold, unless, of course, the friend is Ahithophel, and his story ends in suicide also (2 Sam. 17:23). On the one side of the story, betrayal causes indescribable mental anguish because it breaks a covenant of friendship (55:20), a covenant between two persons of like nature ("a man like myself," 55:13). In this case the betrayal has been exacerbated by the fact that the two men shared not only friendship but faith. They have enjoyed fellowship in the sanctuary and made pilgrimage with other worshipers (55:14). Most betrayals have multiple layers, and this one is an instructive example.

The pain of David's betrayal has been deepened by what he has seen in the city of Jerusalem. The city's walls are the place of political intrigues, its streets filled with threats and lies, and malice and abuse are the substance of city life (55:9–11). In Genesis the city is a symbol of human depravity, built by Cain's son (Gen. 4:17). But that picture of urban life undergoes a redemptive transformation with God's choice of Jerusalem, where he sets up his residence, making it the city of God (Ps. 48:1). The picture of the city (we assume it is Jerusalem) that the psalmist paints is one of a city in the iron grip of evil. For David, to see the city he captured from the Jebusites, where he has established the sanctuary, in the grip of evil is equivalent to betrayal by his trusted friend, although less personal. In his weaker moments he wants to fly away like a dove and be at rest, "far from the tempest and storm" (55:6–8). In the New Testament the ultimate redemption of humanity comes to be expressed in the metaphor of a city (Rev. 21–22). The journey there is not an easy one, but it has been made by a list of noteworthies, the most prominent of them Abraham, who transitioned "by faith" from his nomadic life to "the city with foundations, whose architect and builder is God" (Heb. 11:10).

Teaching the Text

We may begin our sermon/lesson by observing that few of us have escaped the bitter problem of being betrayed by someone, and some of us have had the even more bitter problem of being betrayed by a friend. David, whom the Christian church has historically considered to be a prototype of Christ, has experienced this same kind of betrayal (55:13–14), much like Judas's betrayal of Jesus. It is so disturbing a situation that David just wants to take the "wings of a dove" and fly away (55:6–8). To escape is a common emotional reaction to betrayal.

Now, having spoken of the problem, we can look at the psalm as a model for dealing with betrayal. To accomplish this we should first of all look more closely at the nature of the betrayal David has experienced, betrayal by a very close friend (55:12–14, 20). Exacerbating the pain, he recalls that the friend's talk is "smooth as butter, yet war is in his heart" (55:21). And when David looks around the city, it is pretty much a blown-up model of his betrayer (55:9b–11). This observation has the effect of further emotional isolation: its walls are the place of political intrigues, and its streets are filled with threats and lies. If this is a picture of the city of Jerusalem, which it likely is, the idea of Jerusalem as the city of God (Ps. 48:1) has degenerated (55:11a; also Isa. 1:21–23). It is a picture of isolation and betrayal linking arms to make

the psalmist's situation all but hopeless, were it not for the greatest friendship of all, with the Lord, in whom he trusts (55:23). This, of course, is the point we must stress as the antidote to betrayal—discovering that God is our trusted Friend.

Second, to discover further how the psalm models a way of dealing with betrayal, we should observe that Psalm 55 has a view of the secular city that has arisen out of the love of the world, replete with immorality (55:9b–11), and contrasts that with a glimpse of another relational sphere, which we might compare to the city of God that has arisen out of love for God (see "Illustrating the Text"). In that "city" one calls on God, and he answers; one casts one's cares on God, and he sustains; one trusts in God, and no outcome need be defined, for in that trust, with God alone as its object, the dove that flies away from the city of this secular world finds a place of security in the ark of God's rest (55:6). Although David has been betrayed by his close friend and finds no respite for his pain in the city he loves, he nevertheless finds it in the Lord: "Cast your cares on the LORD and he will sustain you; he will never let the righteous be shaken" (55:22). This invitation is a welcome to grow deeper into God's grace, an equivalent summons to enter into Christ's rest, for in his own words, "my yoke is easy and my burden is light" (Matt. 11:30). See also 1 Peter 5:7 (see also "The Text in Context").

Illustrating the Text

The betrayal of a friend

Testimony: Ask someone in the church to share a story about a time he or she was betrayed by a friend. Choose the best avenue for the testimony, either through video or live testimony. Encourage the person to be vulnerable, to share the emotion associated with the betrayal. Also, remind the volunteer to avoid naming names and giving too many details about the betrayal itself. It is best to be general about the circumstances but very specific about the emotional price that was paid. After the testimony, connect the person's story to Psalm 55 (especially vv. 12–14). You may also want to connect the passage and the testimony to the betrayal of Jesus by Judas in Matthew 26.

God will always be faithful.

Applying the Text: The sense of betrayal is not an uncommon human experience.

If we live in this world for any length of time, chances are we will experience what we feel is a betrayal from someone we believed was trustworthy. Maybe it is a friend who turned his or her back on us. It could be a friend who pursued our spouse or partner. Possibly it is a parent who abandoned or mistreated us. Maybe it is a business partner who worked against our best interests. It could be an employee who left our business and took some of our customers. Betrayal is a common human experience. The question is, how do we respond when we feel betrayed? The Bible gives us some

> Jesus knew the emotions of being betrayed because of the actions of Judas, one of his disciples. When Jesus was condemned to death by crucifixion, Judas, filled with remorse, hanged himself, cutting his own life short. This ivory plaque from around AD 425 illustrates this event.

direction with regard to this question: pray that the Lord would confuse the betrayer's effort to be successful in his or her betrayal (55:9); share our pain with God in prayer and ask for help to deal with the disappointment of the betrayal (55:16–23); ask the Lord for the strength and ability to forgive the betrayer (Matt. 6:12).

There is hope for the world.

Church History: Augustine wrote one of the great books of Christian theology, called *The City of God*. In it he metaphorically traces two cities of human history back to Cain and Abel. Cain's city represents the secular city of humankind, characterized by evil, while Abel's city is the eternal city of God, known by truth and peace. The two cities arise out of two loves, the love of the world and the love of God. Psalm 55 has a view of the secular city that has arisen out of the love of the world, replete with immorality (55:9b–11). Yet the psalm also gives us a glimpse of the city of God that has arisen out of love for God. In that city one calls upon God and has a relationship with the Lord. Seeing our own world as the secular city described in Psalm 55, and the church as the eternal city of God, we must consider how we might minister to that "city of Cain." How can we impact our world through our relationship with God?

"In God I Trust and Am Not Afraid. What Can Mere Mortals Do to Me?"

Big Idea *To ask God to store our tears "in his bottle" is to affirm our trust in God's attentive care to the detail of our miseries.*

Understanding the Text

Psalm 56 is an individual lament that, suggested by the Greek and Aramaic translations of "A Dove on Distant Oaks," came to be used as a community lament (see the comments on the title below). As is often the case with laments, the psalm is tempered by statements of trust (56:3, 4, 11), so much so that we would not go entirely wrong if we called it an individual psalm of trust.

A lament typically contains the lament proper and the reason for the lament,

although the reason is not always given in a lot of detail. Here, however, there is some detail. The lament, found in verses 1b–c, 2, and 5–6, informs us that the suppliant's enemies have launched both physical (56:2, 6) and verbal assaults (56:5) against him. Saul's pursuit of David certainly constituted a physical threat to his life, and the report about David's popularity compared to Saul's constituted a verbal attack (1 Sam. 21:10–14), causing Achish, the king of Gath, to question David's motive for fleeing to Gath. Like Psalm 55:15, it even contains an imprecation against the psalmist's enemies (56:7).

Psalm 56 is historically connected to the seizure of David by the Philistines in Gath. This is an aerial view of Tell es-Safi, biblical Gath, one of the five cities that made up the Philistine pentapolis.

The Text in Context

Thirteen psalms, all of them Davidic, contain some historical information in their titles (see table 1).[1] While the link between the historical circumstances and the psalm is not always transparent, there are, as indicated above, some pretty firm links between Psalm 56 and the chapter of David's life that is recorded in the book of 1 Samuel (see "Historical and Cultural Background").

Psalm 34 links that poem to David's feigned insanity, while Psalm 56 makes no reference to this detail but rather mentions David's "arrest" by the Philistines of Gath.

Outline/Structure

As a rule, this psalm is thought to be composed of two parts plus a vow to thanks-

giving. Schaefer thinks of it in terms of three movements, and I have adjusted his outline to reflect the presence of the almost identical refrain.[2]

1. First movement (56:1–4)
   a. Initial plea (56:1)
   b. Complaint (56:2)
   c. Affirmation of trust (56:3–4a)
   d. Refrain (56:4b–c)
2. Second movement (56:5–11)
   a. Complaint (56:5–6)

Table 1. Title Comparisons of Psalms 56–60

Term	Psalm 56	Psalm 57	Psalm 58	Psalm 59	Psalm 60
"For the director of music"[a]	X[b]	X	X	X	X
Tune name	"A Dove on Distant Oaks"	"Do Not Destroy"[c]	"Do Not Destroy"	"Do Not Destroy"	"The Lily of the Covenant"[d]
"Of David"	X	X	X	X	X
"A miktam"[e]	X	X	X	X	X ("A miktam of David")
Historical note	"When the Philistines had seized him in Gath"	"When he had fled from Saul into the cave"		"When Saul had sent men to watch David's house in order to kill him"	"When he fought Aram Naharaim and Aram Zobah, and when Joab returned and struck down twelve thousand Edomites in the Valley of Salt"

[a] Occurs in the titles of fifty-five psalms and also Habakkuk 3:19.

[b] X = occurs in psalm.

[c] Besides Psalms 58 and 59, also Psalm 75.

[d] Also Psalm 80, "The Lilies of the Covenant," and Psalm 45, "Lilies."

[e] Also Psalm 16.

b. Imprecation (56:7)
c. Affirmation of trust (56:8–10)
d. Refrain (56:11)
3. Third movement (56:12–13)
   a. Vow of thanksgiving (56:12)
   b. Petition answered (56:13)

Historical and Cultural Background

The title of the psalm connects it to David's years of fleeing from Saul, and particularly "when the Philistines had seized him in Gath" (see 1 Sam. 21:10–22:1; 27:1–28:2). The writer of 1 Samuel does not give any specific information about this Philistine arrest. However, when informants approach the king about David's public popularity and Saul's declining approval, David acts like a madman "in their hands" (1 Sam. 21:13), which may imply that they take him into custody to control or manage his behavior.

Interpretive Insights

Title *A Dove on Distant Oaks.* This is probably a tune name to which the psalm was sung. The Greek text (LXX) has "concerning the people that were removed from the sanctuary," perhaps implying a postexilic perspective on the psalm. The Targum lends support to this view, commenting, "at the time when they are far from their cities, and they return and sing to the Lord of the World, like David the humble and blameless one."[3] These comments are evidence of the use of this individual lament as a community lament in a later era.

A miktam. Psalms 16 and 56–60 are described by this word. Eerdmans proposes that, in view of the peril that these psalms

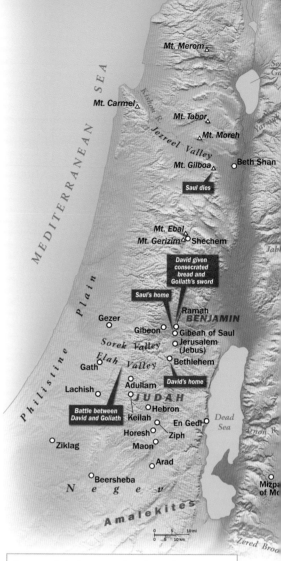

In many of the lament psalms, the psalmist is asking the Lord for deliverance from enemies who are oppressing him. Some of these psalms have titles that may connect the composition to specific historical events in the life of David such as his flight from Saul. This map shows significant places and events during the time of David's interaction with Saul.

expose, it might be a "silent prayer" that David prayed, understanding the noun to come from the verb *ktm*, "to cover" (the lips), thus suggesting a gesture of silence.[4] Others take their cue from its sense of "golden," which Luther took as a suggestion that it was a "golden psalm," putting forth Christ.[5]

56:1 *Be merciful to me, my God . . . in hot pursuit . . . they press their attack.* The invocation here is found also in Psalms 51:1 and 57:1 and internally in other psalms. The verb behind the phrase "in hot pursuit" means "trample" (*sh'p*). See Genesis 3:15, where *shup* ("crush"/"strike") is a variation of the root *sh'p* (see also Amos 2:7). Wilson sees the imagery of the dog pursuing its prey and snapping at the heels of its victims, taking the verb *sh'p* in the sense of "pant or gasp (for breath)" (Job 7:2; see NASB).[6]

56:2 *My adversaries pursue me . . . in their pride.* The verb "pursue" (*sh'p*) is the same as that in 56:1, "are in hot pursuit." The term for "pride" (lit., "high, exalted") is a difficult term in this context. It stands at the end of the sentence, outside the metrical pattern, and some exegetes delete it for that reason. It may, however, be rendered as an adverb, meaning "proudly," as the ESV does (equivalent to NIV's "in their pride").

56:3 *When I am afraid, I put my trust in you.* Trust is the antidote for fear. Verse 4b clarifies this: "In God I trust and am not afraid."

56:4 *In God, whose word I praise . . . What can mere mortals do to me?* Verses 4 and 10–11 comprise a refrain, almost verbally identical. Verse 10b, however, repeats 10a but inserts "Lord" for God, thus identifying God by his covenant name. It is most likely the intention of the psalmist and not an editorial change imposed on the Elohistic Psalter (compare with Psalm 55:22). The final question is a rhetorical one with the implied answer "Nothing."

Verse 11b is virtually synonymous with 4b, with *'adam* ("humankind," rather than *basar*, "flesh," as here) as the word for "man."

56:6 *they lurk.* The verb means "to lie in wait" (Prov. 1:11; NIV: "ambush").

56:7 *Because of their wickedness do not let them escape . . . bring the nations down.* This is similar to the curses that are found in the imprecatory psalms (e.g., Ps. 109; see also 55:15, which is not an imprecatory psalm as such). Some take the phrase "bring the nations down" to imply a postexilic setting,[7] but the peoples of David's world were definitely among his troublemakers. In 57:9 he also vows to praise God among the "nations" (*'ammim*) and among the "peoples" (*'ummim*).

56:8 *list my tears on your scroll . . . in your record.* The two repositories are "your bottle [*no'd*]" and "your scroll [*seper*]." In other contexts (Josh. 9:4; Judg. 4:19; 1 Sam. 16:20; Ps. 119:83), the word *no'd* means "bottle" or "leather container" (for wine, milk, etc.), so we should assume the same meaning here (see NIV footnote). The ESV reads: "Put my tears in your bottle. Are they not in your book?" The language is metaphorical, speaking of God's careful attention to his people's sorrow, so much so that he keeps a record of it and fills a bottle with their tears. See the associate metaphor, "golden bowls," in Revelation 5:8, which hold the prayers of the saints. For God's record book, see Psalms 69:28; 139:16; and Exodus 32:32–33.

56:9 *Then my enemies will turn back. . . . By this I will know that God is for me.* The significance of God's careful accounting of sorrow will have the effect of turning back the psalmist's enemies when he calls on God, and the result is help that is roused by God's solicitous care. The preposition "by" is not in the text, and the statement may simply be an affirmation of God's careful concern, meaning, "This I know: God is for me." This affirmation is only a step away from "God is with us" (cf. Isa. 7:14).

56:11 *What can man do to me?* There are three terms for humanity in the psalm: *'enosh* ("man," 56:1; NIV: "they"), *basar* ("flesh," 56:4; NIV: "mere mortals"), *'adam* ("man," 56:11), emphasizing mortality over against the immortal God. In comparison, "God" (*'elohim*) appears nine times, and "LORD" (*YHWH*) once (56:10), very likely to stress the overpowering presence of God against human nature, which is so responsive to human threats and the human attribute of fear.

56:12 *I am under vows to you, my God; I will present my thank offerings.* In the Mishnah, "under" vows is a common way to express the obligation of vows (*Menahot* 12.2).[8] The type of offering suggested here is the "peace offering" that was voluntary, part of

God is so concerned about the misery of his people that he is said to record and collect their tears. In the ancient Near East liquids were often held in leather containers similar to this wineskin or waterskin carried by a servant depicted on this relief from Persepolis, Iran, 358–338 BC.

which was eaten by the worshiper (Lev. 3:1–17; 7:11–21; 1 Sam. 11:15). See Psalm 22:25.

56:13 *you have delivered . . . my feet from stumbling.* The word for "stumbling" means a misplaced step.[9] A chiasm stresses the terms of the statement and highlights the contrast by the use of antithetic terms in the corresponding positions:

A For you have delivered me from death
  B and my feet from stumbling,
  B′ that I may walk before God
A′ in the light of life.

Theological Insights

Sometimes silence is more powerful than the spoken word. Psalm 56 offers a classic example in the repeated question, "What can mere mortals do to me?" (56:4c), and "What can man do to me?" (56:11b). The implied answer, perhaps more powerful because it is a silent answer, is "Nothing!" This is an illustration of the effectiveness of the rhetorical question. The psalm, of course, does not leave the implied answer entirely undefended, for the psalmist's experience is that when he calls for help, his enemies turn back, confirming his knowledge that "God is for [him]" (56:9).

On occasion the Psalms provide insight into the precious details of God's solicitous care for his people. In verse 8 the psalmist notes that God has recorded his misery. The NIV makes it imperative, "Record my misery," but it is actually a declarative clause with the emphatic "you": "As for my misery, *you yourself* have recorded it." This fact is the lead affirmation in the verse, so the imperative in the center is merely a detail of celestial knowledge that the psalmist is confident God will carry out, given his attention to keeping a record of human misery. We may compare Jesus's words that our heavenly Father is aware of every sparrow that falls to the ground and that "the very hairs of your head are all numbered" (Matt. 10:29–30).

The impression that the refrain and other details leave with the reader is that the opposition is relentless ("all day long," 56:1c, 5a), and while the psalmist's faith is generally firm and strong, it sometimes relapses into a need for confirmation. The repeated confession of trust (see "Outline/Structure") is not merely a literary device but indicative of the suppliant's spiritual depth. Yet out of this pattern of relapse and renewal comes his grateful vow to present thank offerings to God. The underlying sentiment of the prayer is the psalmist's confidence that God has heard him (56:9), a disposition of faith that enables him to pray confidently.[10] The writer to the Hebrews comments on this spirit of confidence: "Now faith is confidence in what we hope for and assurance about what we do not see" (Heb. 11:1).

While trust and fear may not be absolute opposites, they in no sense enjoy open communion. Where there is trust, there is generally a tinge of fear, which in effect is part of a larger dynamic. Trust unalloyed with fear falls outside the realm of human affections. Indeed, it is the presence of fear, suggests Weiser, that causes the psalmist "to throw himself into the arms of God at the very moment when he is in danger of succumbing to his fear. . . . Trust in God robs fear of its quality of terror; the fear of men is mastered by the fear of God."[11]

Fear	Balanced by Trust
A When I am afraid, (56:3a)	
	B I put my trust in you. In God, whose word I praise—in God I trust (56:3b–4a)
A′ and am not afraid. What can mere mortals do to me? (56:4b–4c)	
	B′ In God, whose word I praise, in the LORD, whose word I praise—in God I trust (56:10–11a)
A″ and am not afraid. What can man do to me? (56:11b)	

Teaching the Text

This psalm gives us an opportunity to deal with the deepest sorrows that grow out of life's detrimental circumstances and, at the same time, offers us an occasion to make the tender request of God that he would store up our tears.

As we begin our preparation (and this can be part of our presentation), we should note that this psalm has a refrain (56:4, 11), virtually identical, in which the suppliant's trust in God is concentrated and his fear dispelled. We may suggest that this represents two sides of the same coin: trust in God diminishes fear of human machinations against us. The purpose of a refrain is to stress the theme of the psalm or give support to some major theme in the poem.

One of the obstacles we meet in faith and prayer is the doubt that God hears our prayers, and that he even cares. Thankfully, this is the underlying sentiment of the prayer, that God has heard him (56:9)—a disposition of faith that enables him to pray confidently.[12] The psalmist is confident because he knows that God has recorded his misery (56:8). It is on this basis that he can confidently enjoin God, "Put my tears in your bottle," and then rhetorically ask, "Are they not in your book?" (ESV).

No emotional expression is more tender and intimate than tears, and here the supplicant expresses that in his request that God would store them in a bottle. Weiser comments: "Sleepless nights and many hours spent in torment and weeping are not endured in vain as far as God is concerned. Suffering, as it were, is capital invested with God, booked by him (cf. Mal. 3:16; Job 19:23) and collected by him."[13] A Jewish saying captures well the sentiment of verse 8: "There is no door through which tears do not pass" (see "Illustrating the Text").[14] In another place Isaiah says—and John repeats this twice in the book of Revelation—that God will wipe away the tears from all faces (Isa. 25:8; Rev. 7:17; 21:4), a metaphor to suggest the abolition of sorrow. The terms of the psalmist's prayer suggest that God gives attentive detail to our misery.

Since the refrain is a key to interpretation, we may explain that the reason the psalmist can exclaim "What can mortal man do to me?" is that he knows two things. The first is that *God is with him*—God has delivered him from death (56:13; see also 56:9b), not in absentia, but God was there in the situation to save him. At this point we can emphasize that God is not a God in absentia. In fact, one of the most reverberating declarations the Scriptures ever make is from Isaiah 7:14: God is with us (*Immanuel*). And the Lord incorporates that idea in the covenant formula that marks out his special relationship with Israel: "I will be

As Christians were put to death for their faith, they could cling to the words from Psalm 56:4: "In God I trust and am not afraid. What can mere mortals do to me?" Justin Martyr, depicted in this mosaic from the Church of the Beatitudes, was beheaded for his faith in AD 165.

your God, and you shall be my people, *and I will dwell in your midst*" (author's summary; see Lev. 26:12–13). This metaphor is a way to describe this idea in a picture that we can understand. God keeps our tears to remind himself of the misery we have endured in life (see also Isa. 49:16). Isaiah's vision of the day of salvation when God wipes our tears away (Isa. 25:8; cf. Rev. 7:17; 21:4) is another metaphor that informs us that our misery that God has remembered will be obliterated.

In light of his confident faith, David can ask rhetorically "What can man do to me?" because he knows *God is for him* (56:9). This declaration of God's favor is essentially equivalent to Paul's assertion in Romans 8:31: "If God is for us, who can be against us?" This simply means that God is so great and so powerful that if God is for us, then it makes no difference who may be against us, because God can overcome every opposition (Rom. 8:38–39; see also 1 John 4:4).

Illustrating the Text

"What can mere mortals do to me?"

Church History: On average, over one hundred thousand Christians worldwide were martyred for their faith per year in the first decade of the twenty-first century.[15] In many cases these Christians have gone to their death without fear, reflecting the heart of the psalmist: "What can mere mortals do to me?" (Ps. 56:4). Jesus similarly tells his followers, "Do not be afraid of those who kill the body and after that can do no more. . . . Fear him who, after your body has been killed, has authority to throw you into hell" (Luke 12:4–5). Christian martyrs over the centuries have echoed this sentiment. Justin Martyr (AD 165) said, "You can kill us, but you cannot do us any real harm."[16] Similarly, Offrus Greizinger (AD 1538) is quoted as saying, "You can take from me no more than my life."[17] Challenge your listeners to reflect on this bravery and this willingness to disregard what humans can do to us—even to the point of death. In the face of persecution, would we also be able to declare, "In God I trust and am not afraid" (Ps. 56:4)?

Tears in a bottle

Human Experience: A Jewish saying states that there are three kinds of prayers, each loftier than the preceding: "Prayer, crying, and tears. Prayer is made in silence; crying with raised voice; but tears overcome all things ['there is no door through which tears do not pass']" (see "Teaching the Text").[18] Those tears are so precious to God that he would store them in a bottle. It is a metaphor to inform us that God will not forget our sorrow, and that sense depicts the beautiful relationship we have with our God. Any parent or caregiver understands how a child's tears affect you. You have wiped them away many times and taken up the child in your arms to provide comfort. In a similar metaphor Isaiah says that the Lord has engraved Jerusalem's name on the palms of his hands so he will not forget her (Isa. 49:16). Paul Gerhardt sums up the sense of this metaphor in one of his hymns:

> Thou count'st how oft'n a Christian
>   weeps,
> And where his grief may lie;
> No silent tear can be too small,
> Thou tak'st and lay'st it by.[19]

Even the world knows

Classic Sermon: Stanislav Svec was a Baptist preacher in Czechoslovakia, and in one of his sermons ("Abide with Us!"), he tells about being incarcerated in a Nazi concentration camp during World War II: "During the last war, I was taken along with a number of my school-chums to a labour camp in Nazi Germany. All my friends knew that I was a Christian, and sometimes they mocked me, good-naturedly. But when the air raids came and we were in danger and fear, they all tried to be close to me as if I could make them safer."[20] The psalmist had put his trust in God, and he knew that the damage "mere mortals" could do to him was limited (v. 4). Our suppliant had his "mockers" too, just watching his every step (v. 5). People do mock, but God takes note of his children's sorrows (v. 8).

"Be Exalted, O God, above the Heavens; Let Your Glory Be over All the Earth"

Big Idea *In our deepest conflicts God's emissaries of love and truth will guide us into safe harbor.*

Understanding the Text

Psalm 57 is generally recognized as an individual lament. Some commentators, including Dahood, also see a royal element, and he calls it a "lament of a king."[1] This view is largely based on the title's association of David with the psalm and the description of persecution that could easily be applied to a national leader.

We should also note that the psalm is a prayer with intermittent reflective comments (see "Outline/Structure"). While it is not unusual for a psalmist to reference God in the third-person singular ("he") during a prayer when he normally would be using the second-person singular ("you"), the exceptions in this psalm are too long to be considered as belonging to the fabric of the prayer. This prayer/reflection pattern is very common in the Psalms.[2] In Psalm 57, the reflections are verses 2–4, 6 (or verse 6 could be part of the report), and 8. The reflective portions often expand on the problem that exercises the suppliant, or they fill in gaps where information is missing or employ some other form of literary device. In verse 8, the psalmist even speaks to himself ("Awake, my soul!"), as in the refrain of Psalms 42:5, 11; 43:5.

The Text in Context

The psalmic neighborhood shares some common elements. First, Psalms 54–56, like Psalm 57, are prayers that God will deliver the psalmist from enemies who have utilized slanderous speech as one of their major weapons of destruction (54:5; 55:3a, 9a, 12a; 56:2a; 57:4).[3] Second, Psalms 57; 58; and 59 are all sung to the tune of "Do Not Destroy," all attributed to David, and, along with Psalms 56 and 60, are all called a *miktam*.[4] Third, Psalms 56 and 57 have a duplicate beginning: "Be merciful to me, my God" (*hanneni 'elohim*). Fourth, Psalm 57 shares two terms with the preceding psalm: "pursue" (*sh'p*, also means "pant," 57:3b; 56:1, 2) and "on high" (the same verbal root, *rum*, but translated by the NIV as "be exalted" in 57:5a and "in their pride" in 56:2).[5] Fifth, both Psalms 56 and 57 have a refrain that expresses praise of God's universal sovereignty (56:4b–c, 11; 57:5, 11).

Psalm 57:7–11 is duplicated with only minor differences in Psalm 108:1–5, there introducing a psalm of praise, compared to its use here, where it concludes a lament (see discussion of Psalm 108).

Psalm 18:49, which Paul quotes in Romans 15:9, is a close equivalent of 57:9. Paul hears in this verse a confirmation of the promise made to the patriarchs that the nations have been included in God's saving plan (Gen. 12:3).

Outline/Structure

The psalm, composed of prayer and reflection, consists of two stanzas:

1. Prayer for mercy and reflection on God's answer (57:1–5)
   a. Prayer for mercy (57:1)
   b. Reflection on God's answer (57:2–3)

   c. Reflection on the reason for lament (57:4)
   d. *Refrain: exalting God above the heavens and earth (57:5)*
2. Lament of psalmist's plight and vow to give thanks (57:6–11)
   a. Reflection on the reason for lament (57:6)
   b. Prayer of steadfastness and vow to sing God's praise (57:7–9)
   c. Prayer affirming God's love and faithfulness (57:10)
   d. *Refrain: exalting God above the heavens and earth (57:11)*

Historical and Cultural Background

The title associates the psalm with David and identifies more specifically an occasion when "he had fled from Saul into the cave." The book of 1 Samuel relates two incidents when David is in a cave. The first is the cave of Adullam (1 Sam. 22:1), and the second, the cave at En Gedi (1 Sam. 24:3). Further, some take the *'al-tashhet* ("Do Not Destroy") as an allusion to David's directive to Abishai not to kill Saul (1 Sam. 26:9). The thirteenth-century rabbinic commentator David Kimhi makes this connection in his commentary on the Psalms.[6] However, these stories appear to be three distinct incidents, and the

The title of Psalm 57 links it to the time when David hid in caves as he fled from Saul. First Samuel 22 records that he hid in the cave of Adullam after leaving Gath. The near-central hill in this photo is Tel Adullam.

last one, where David gives instructions not to kill Saul, is in King Saul's camp, not in a cave at all.

The Psalms often provide information about the flora and fauna of the ancient world, and that is the case with Psalm 57. The presence of lions in David's world is well attested (1 Sam. 17:34–36), although eventually hunting and deforestation eliminated lions from the dense forests of the Jordan River. Quite appropriately, the imagery of hunting appears in 57:6, where the hunters spread a net over a pit to trap the animal (in this case, David), but David's enemies, who are in hot pursuit of him (57:3), fall into it themselves.

Interpretive Insights

Title *To the tune of "Do Not Destroy."* *... When he had fled from Saul*. In Deuteronomy 9:26 Moses prays: "Do not destroy [*'al-tashhet*] your people." The same phrase is used here (*'al-tashhet*) to describe the type of tune. Hakham suggests it was customary to sing Moses's prayer before this one, just as scriptural verses are recited in the synagogue before the *Selihot*.[7] Four psalms are to be sung to this tune, or this tune is sung before these four psalms, if we accept Hakham's interpretation: Psalms 57; 58; 59 (Davidic); and 75 (Asaph). For the phrase "When he had fled from Saul into the cave," see "Historical and Cultural Background."

57:1 *Have mercy on me, my God, have mercy on me*. The repetition of "have mercy on me" strengthens the request for mercy. See also Psalm 123:3. The same link between a prayer for mercy and seeking refuge is found in Psalm 16:1.

> When the psalmist takes refuge in the shadow of God's wings, he is depending on God for his safety. The Egyptian goddess Nekhbet appears frequently as a vulture on temple reliefs above the door lintel with wings outstretched to indicate her role as protector.

Tate calls this literary device the "pivot pattern," which employs a central word and uses it to pivot the ideas on either side, giving the pattern AB C AB.[8] Goldingay speaks of this phenomenon as a word doing double duty (57:5, 7a–b, 9, 11),[9] meaning that it occurs in one colon but applies to the following colon too, as in the following examples:

Have mercy (A) on me (B),
my God (C),
have mercy (A) on me (B). (57:1)

Steadfast (A) is my heart (B),
O God (C),
steadfast (A) is my heart (B). (57:7; this
  is the Hebrew word order)[10]

This method serves to emphasize the ideas on either side of the direct address and to put God, in this case, in the middle of the invocation, surrounded by the voice of the psalmist. It is the merger of art and theology.

I will take refuge in the shadow of your wings until the disaster has passed. The unusual verb form of "take refuge" is a past tense bearing a present-tense meaning.[11] The metaphor "shadow of your wings" appears several times in the Psalter (17:8; 36:7; 57:1; 63:7). The image is that of a bird gathering its chicks under its wings (Isa. 34:15; Matt. 23:37; Luke 13:34). Also, there are many instances of ancient deities with expansive wings, indicating the extensive use of this imagery. The same word for "disaster" (*hawwot*) appears in Psalm 91:3 ("deadly pestilence"). Note Psalm 91:4, which says, as here in 57:1c, "and under his wings you will find refuge."

57:2 *to God Most High, to God, who vindicates me.* Abraham knew God as *'el 'elyon* (Gen. 14:22). The article is never used with *'elyon*, just as it is never used with *YHWH*. Kidner makes two significant observations on "God Most High": (1) it "does not make Him remote: only unhampered in sending help—a fact which the opening of the Lord's Prayer should also bring to mind"; (2) it does not mean so much that he is all-powerful but that he is all-important.[12]

57:3 *God sends forth his love and his faithfulness.* God's "love and faithfulness" occur together in other places (e.g., Ps. 138:2), and it means that God fulfills the promise incumbent on him as a covenant partner.[13] "Love/mercy" (*hesed*) and "faithfulness/truth" (*'emet*) are personified as God's emissaries to save the psalmist from the impending disaster. While the NIV has translated *'emet* as "faithfulness," "truth" is a better translation for God's personified attribute, as we explained in Psalm 54 (see the comments on Ps. 54:5).

57:4 *men whose teeth are spears and arrows, whose tongues are sharp swords.* This metaphor compares the psalmist's enemies to vicious animals who tear their prey apart with their sharp teeth. This verse makes it clear that the supplicant has not escaped trouble but has found refuge *in the midst of* trouble. The Hebrew text has a beautiful alliterative effect, with four words that begin with the letter *heth* (close in sound to English "h" in "how" or German "ch"): *hanit* ("spear[s]"), *hitsim* ("arrows"), *hereb haddah* ("sharp sword[s]").

The Hebrew of this verse has the word *napshi* ("my soul, life") as the first word, which most English versions ignore—it seems to be extraneous. But the Greek (LXX) supplies a verb: "*he has delivered my soul.*" If we feel compelled to retain the word in translation, we may consider it as a pending case (*casus pendens*) and render it, "As for my life, I lie in the midst of lions."

57:5 *Be exalted, O God, above the heavens.* This refrain is repeated in 57:11.

57:6 *a net for my feet.* Psalm 35:7 is similar. The Hebrew word for "my steps" (see ESV) means "my feet," as it does in Isaiah 26:6 (NIV: "footsteps").

57:7 *My heart, O God, is steadfast.* "Steadfast" comes first in the Hebrew sentence for emphasis. The verbless clause (the verb "is" is implied) begins and ends the first half of the verse: "Steadfast [is] my heart, O God, steadfast [is] my heart." See Psalm 78:37.

57:8 *Awake, my soul! . . . I will awaken the dawn.* The word rendered "soul" is *kabod* ("honor") and parallels "heart." Also Psalm 16:9: "Therefore my heart is glad, and my soul [*kabod*] rejoices" (NRSV). The original meaning of *kabod* ("heavy, honor, glory") is "liver," since the liver was a heavy organ of the body. The phrase "I will awaken the dawn" is either some powerful music or a powerful metaphor—the latter, I am sure. Using personification (see also 57:3), the speaker imagines himself waking before the dawn, and as he begins to play his "harp and lyre," the sun begins to open its sleepy eyes and stretch its rested arms across the sky to lighten the world for another day (see Ps. 19:4–6).[14] See the sidebar "Three Musical Instruments" in the unit on Psalm 92.

57:9 *I will praise you, Lord, among the nations.* The musical nature of this psalm, both instrumental and vocal, is obvious. In 57:7, the psalmist says he will "sing and make music." In 57:8, he figuratively addresses the "harp and lyre," and in 57:9, he declares, "I will sing of you among the peoples." Also the hymn tune is provided in the title.

57:10 *reaching to the heavens.* Verbally this verse corresponds to 57:3, "He sends from heaven." Further, the combination of "love" and "truth/faithfulness" is duplicated. See Psalm 36:5 for similar language.

57:11 *let your glory be over all the earth.* The refrain expresses a universal theme (also 57:5), which is picked up in 57:9, where the supplicant intends to praise the Lord among the nations and sing of him among the peoples.

Theological Insights

The psalm personifies God's "love" (*hesed*) and "truth/faithfulness" (*'emet*), which God sends forth (57:3) in response to the supplicant's cry for help in 57:2. The psalmist does not describe their mission further, as Psalm 43:3 does with regard to "light" and "truth" ("faithful care"), which God sends forth to guide the supplicant to the sanctuary. But 57:10 describes those divine attributes as reaching the heavens and thus pervading the world where God's servant is threatened by "lions" (57:4), who, by their ravenous words (57:4, 6), have driven him to take refuge in the shadow of God's wings (57:1). And it is of some significance that he takes refuge in the very midst of the crises ("I am in the midst of lions," 57:4), evidently finding protection under the Lord's "wings" until the disaster has passed (57:1), barely escaping it. Phillips comments on Paul's well-known statement in Romans 8:37: "We often think that eventually all will be well (and so it will), but Paul's point is that in the midst of cold and hunger, of danger to life and limb, we are more than conquerors."[15]

In 57:2, the ESV has "to God who fulfills his purpose for me." The psalm may represent an early version of the theological notion of Israel as a "light to the Gentiles" (see also Ps. 96:3), a doctrine that reaches its summit in Isaiah's understanding of Israel's historic purpose (Isa. 42:6–7). In fact, the suppliant is in agreement with that purpose, which we see him fulfilling in 57:9–10 as he praises the Lord among the nations and sings of him among the peoples. This indeed seems to be the undefined design of God's emissaries of "love and faithfulness" whom he sends forth (57:3). As with the incipient notion of Israel as a light to the nations, we may also see the forming lines of Isaiah's quite well-developed view that the word of God goes forth to accomplish a purpose, for which it cannot fail (Isa. 31:2; 40:8; 45:23; 55:11). Mission accomplished!

companions, and one supports the other. So right off we should recognize that this psalm has a refrain (57:5, 11), as have many others, which highlights some idea that the poet wants to emphasize. It is not mere ornamentation. The contents of Psalm 57 are intended to bring us to the point of praising God's majesty: his saving and sheltering acts are so phenomenally great that he should be exalted above all humans and powers of the earth.

Yet we should point out that our exalted God is not so high that he cannot reach us, nor so exalted that he cannot understand our plight. Here we have one of the theological wonders of the Hebrew Scriptures: they bring together the transcendent and immanent portraits of God, holding them in delicate and affectionate balance (compare Gen. 1, God is transcendent, and Gen. 2–3, God is immanent; this comparison sets the stage for this wonderful

Teaching the Text

We want to remain faithful to the biblical text as we seek to hear the message of the Psalms and share that with our listeners. To do so, we need to know not just what a psalm says but how it is structured. Structure and meaning are

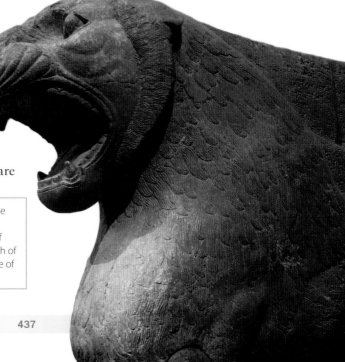

The legendary ferocity of sharp-toothed lions made them an apt metaphor for slanderous enemies and models for guardian statues at the entrance of temples and palaces. Notice the teeth in the mouth of this fifteen-ton lion statue that guarded the temple of Ishtar at Nimrud, 865–860 BC.

understanding of God). David says that God is highly exalted above the heavens (transcendent), and that is the reason we can "take refuge in the shadow" of his wings (immanent). Moreover, he is highly exalted because "he sends from heaven and saves me, rebuking those who hotly pursue me [transcendant/immanent]; God sends his love and his truth [immanent]" (57:3, author's trans.). That is, he can send his love and truth to save us because he is transcendently exalted in the heavens.

This is an appropriate stage in the lesson or sermon to observe that, poetically speaking, God dispatches his two emissaries, love and truth, to help us (57:3). We have met this literary figure of personification before (see Ps. 43:3, "light" and "truth"), and it is a way to personalize God's work. People in David's world were familiar with the image of international emissaries, and immediately they understood the purpose of God's emissaries of "love" and "truth," received by their earthly audience. As application, we may speak about the relationship between love and truth—part of love is truthfulness. These two divine emissaries are inseparable—where one goes the other must be present, or the one is impaired. It is an infraction against love if we do not tell those we love the truth. Without truth, love *hobbles*. The Western church has often, and sadly, opted for *love* to the neglect of *truth*, and that has led to a denigration of the Word of God and the distortion of the gospel (see "Illustrating the Text"). Psalm 57 tells us that God sends *love* and *truth* from heaven to save us, and we cannot be saved by love alone. Love and truth sum up the gospel. They are God's coambassadors.

Illustrating the Text

Half-truths

Statistics: In January 2013, National Public Radio listed twelve common "half-truths" that most of us accept as fact. In truth, Subway sandwich chain's footlong sandwich often measures closer to eleven inches than twelve inches; some scientists claim that pink is not actually a color; it may be that a palm tree is not technically a tree but a form of grass; and a two-by-four at a lumberyard is not two inches by four inches.[16] Although these "half-truths," or partial truths, are rather benign, that is not always the case. As Benjamin Franklin said, "Half a truth is often a great lie."[17] Sadly, we have become accustomed as a culture to stretching or even reshaping the truth as a means to promote our own agenda. But the reality is that we make decisions in light of what we believe to be true. As Christians, we must be committed to the truth, both in what we choose to believe and in how we relate to others.

Love and truth

Cultural Institution: The personification of "love" and "truth" (NIV: "faithfulness"; 57:3) as God's emissaries is a political metaphor.[18] In our world, and in David's too, one country sends its ambassadors to another country to represent the sending country's interests. In that world and in ours, the ambassadors must be received by the host country. The host country could claim, of course, that the credentials of the ambassador are not in order and refuse to receive him or her. That is precisely what some branches of the mainline church have done in recent years. They have decided that the credentials of God's ambassador, love, are quite in order, but the credentials of his other ambassador, truth, do not meet scrutiny. So truth goes a-begging. But love without truth is a cripple. Weiser comments, "When truth and reality, which ultimately belong together, come to differ from each other, then the foundations of human social life are shaken."[19] That is the dilemma of the world we live in, and tragically sometimes the sad dilemma of God's church.

In the shadow of his wings

Nature: A common metaphor in the psalms is God as a mother bird, sheltering her young under her wings. This is a powerful image that provides comfort for God's people. But what does it really mean? Perhaps it is best to look to nature for this answer. For example, consider the wood storks that spread their wings out to keep the sun off their young. Birds also use their wings to hide their young and protect them when danger is near. The spreading of a bird's wings over its babies is also done to provide warmth. This is the picture the Bible gives of God's care for us! (For "eagle's wings," see "The Text in Context" in the unit on Ps. 91.) As William O. Cushing proclaims in his hymn *Under His Wings*,

> Under His wings I am safely abiding;
> Tho' the night deepens and tempests
>   are wild.
> Still I can trust Him; I know He will
>   keep me;
> He has redeemed me, and I am His
>   child.[20]

Adult birds may spread their wings over their young to provide protection from sun, cold, and danger. Shown here is an adult stork with outstretched wings standing over the young in the nest.

"In Your Heart You Devise Injustice"

Big Idea *As one thinks in one's heart, so one does, and that explains many of the tragedies of history.*

Understanding the Text

Psalm 58 is usually identified as a community lament, although Gerstenberger is probably more accurate when he says it is "neither complaint nor thanksgiving nor hymn" but closer to the prophetic invective against the ruling classes.[1]

The Text in Context

Except for the historical note in the title of Psalm 57, the terms of the title of Psalm 58 are the same. Further, the two psalms share the metaphor of the "teeth" of lions to describe the wicked, warranting Wilcock's comment that they are sung to the same tune,[2] both musically (title) and theologically (57:4; 58:6).

Psalms 58 and 82 share similar contents in that they both issue a moral and social challenge to those who judge others unjustly (see "Teaching the Text" in the unit on Ps. 82). Psalm 58, however, addresses active perpetrators of evil deeds, while Psalm 82 addresses those who have neglected doing the right things regarding the poor and needy.

One can hardly read Psalm 58 without recalling the story of humanity's primordial sin in Genesis 3. The "sons of Adam" ("sons of man"; NIV: "people"; 58:1), "Adam" ("man"; NIV "people"; 58:11), and the snake (58:4) may be allusions to the story of the fall, as well might also the note that "even from birth the wicked go astray" (58:3), alluding to the fall and Cain's sin in Genesis 4. While the latter allusion may be a stretch, if we accept the allusions to Genesis 3, it may help to explain the moral straying of the wicked "from birth" (58:3), since that pattern has been obvious from the beginning of the human story.

The graphic picture of the righteous washing their feet (58:10; NIV: "dip") in the blood of the wicked is found also in Psalm 68:21–23. These are the victims of evil who now find respite in the wake of God's judgment. In Isaiah 63:3 we see a different picture of the Victor (Yahweh) emerging from the battle against evil, with his garments stained with blood.

Outline/Structure

The psalm falls basically into three parts:

1. The evil influence of the wicked (58:1–5)
2. Prayer for God's judgment (58:6–9)
3. Attestation to the two-pronged principle of divine justice: God rewards the righteous and judges the wicked (58:10–11)

Historical and Cultural Background

Traditionally this psalm has been generally dated during David's flight from Saul or Absalom, in the latter case taking the cue from the concern of the psalm for the administration of justice. That was the key piece in Absalom's political platform, at least as he presented his case to the public (compare Absalom's political platform by which he "stole the hearts of the people of Israel," 2 Sam. 15:1–6).

As the psalmist calls on God to act against the wicked, he once again uses lion imagery. He asks God to "tear out the fangs of those lions" (58:6), thereby preventing their vicious speech from continuing. This bronze lion was one of a pair found in a temple in Mari, second millennium BC. The statue once had teeth made of bone, but without them the lion does not look very ferocious.

Key Themes of Psalm 58

- Evil demands that we have a long view of history.
- The perpetrators of evil eventually become its victims.

This psalm contains seven "curses" (in condensed form) that provide a window into the ancient world. First is the cobra that cannot be charmed because it "has stopped its ears" (58:4). Second, the wicked are compared to the "teeth" of lions (see also 57:4), as the singer prays that God will "break the teeth in their mouths" (58:6). Third, the wicked are "like water that flows away" (58:7a; compare the wadi that is only a seasonal stream). Fourth, the wicked are warriors who "draw their bow" (58:7b), and the psalmist's prayer is that the arrows will fall short of their target. Fifth, the prayer is to the effect that they will be "like a slug that melts away as it moves along" (58:8a). The snail leaves its shell and makes its tiny trail as it seems to disappear. Sixth, the sad picture of a "still-born child that never sees the sun" (58:8b) moves the metaphors into the category of humanity. And seventh, another picture of human habitation appears as the wind sweeps away the thorns that are intended to fire up the cooking pots and leaves the hungry unsatisfied (58:9). Thus we have a few snapshots of life in Israel's world. The sevenfold curse might imply that it will indeed be effective. Yet it is not black magic that is involved here but prayer to the God who effects the curse (58:6).

Interpretive Insights

58:1 *Do you rulers indeed speak justly? Do you judge . . . ?* The word translated "rulers" (*'elem*) occurs in Exodus 15:11, where it has different vowels (*'elim*) and means "gods." Its meaning here is uncertain. The ESV renders it "gods," and in light of the closing verse, which declares "surely there is a God who judges the earth," this contrast between the "gods" who do not speak justly and the God who judges the earth (an *inclusio*), seems to capture the meaning of the psalm. The rhetorical questions anticipate a negative answer: "No, it is *not* true that you speak justly."

58:2 *you devise injustice.* The verb "devise" (*p'l*) means to "practice," and the parallel verb in the second half of the verse suggests that it is the "gods" who "make way for violence"[3] (Piel of *pls*) in the earth. Or if we take *'elem* to be "rulers," they are the perpetrators, and their subjects are the transfer agents who become the victims of their own evil deeds. Perowne translates the verb (*p'l*) as "weigh out," sarcastically intended. See Job 31:6; Psalm 62:9; Proverbs 16:2, and so on for "weighing/scales" as a metaphor for dispensing justice.[4]

58:3 *Even from birth the wicked go astray.* From this point the psalmist, having addressed the wicked in the second person, now speaks of them in the third person until 58:9, where he returns to the second person (see "Teaching the Text"). The meaning here is that their whole life has been devoted to evil (cf. Ps. 51:5; Isa. 48:8).[5] Ibn Ezra renders the verb "go astray" as "estranged" and translates, "The wicked are estranged from the womb," meaning "the wicked are different in nature at birth from other newborn children."[6] This forms

a perfect parallel with the last part of the sentence: "from the womb they are wayward, spreading lies."

58:4 *the venom of a snake . . . a cobra that has stopped its ears.* The word for "venom" also occurs in Deuteronomy 32:33 with that meaning. "Snake" (*nahash*) is a general term for various types of snakes. On stopping the ears, see Proverbs 21:13.

58:5 *the charmer.* The "charmer(s)" (*melahashim*) may be onomatopoetic, suggesting the "whispering" or "hissing" sounds the charmer emits to draw the serpents out in the open.[7] "Serpent charmers" are mentioned in Jeremiah 8:17 and Ecclesiastes 10:11. Ancient Near Eastern texts give special incantations that were supposed to ward off lethal attacks of snakes.[8] It is generally agreed that snakes are deaf, and they respond to the movements of the charmer, not the sounds of the charmer's pipe.[9] Coverdale's beautiful translation of the last colon of this verse picks up on the participle at the end of the line ("be or make wise") and renders it "charm he never so wisely."[10]

58:6 *Break the teeth.* This is the core verse of the psalm,[11] chiastically calling on God with both the generic *'elohim* and the covenant name *YHWH*:

> A   Break the teeth in their mouths,
>   B   O God;
>   B′   LORD,
> A′ tear out the fangs of those lions!

This is the first of seven curses, in a shortened form (see "Historical and Cultural Background"; also the "Additional Insights: Imprecatory Psalms" and "Additional Insights: Cursing or Loving Our Enemies" before and after the unit on Ps. 35). The effect of the curse, at least in the eyes of

The psalmist compares the speech of the wicked, who are continually spreading lies, to poisonous venom from a snake that cannot be controlled by a charmer. This painting of a charmer holding a snake is from the coffin of the chantress Amun Ta-ahuty, Egypt, tenth century BC.

so their evil will never materialize (58:8b); (5) let the wicked "be swept away" like thorns that have been gathered to fire up the oven for cooking and thus not produce the result intended (58:9).

The expression "draw the bow" literally means "tread [*drk*] the bow." See the comments on Psalm 7:12. Also, the phrase "let their arrows fall short" literally means "let them disintegrate."[12] The NIV seems to understand the verb to be from the root "to circumcise" (*mul*), but Koehler and Baumgartner identify it as "to dry up" (*mll*), thus "disintegrate."[13] See Psalm 90:6.

58:9 *Before your pots can feel the heat of the thorns.* Delitzsch hears an allusion to the time of Absalom, the meat in the pots being the new kingship of Absalom.[14] This certainly reads a lot into the text, but it is possible that the psalm was written against some troubled time of David's life.

58:10 *when they dip their feet in the blood of the wicked.* Along with Psalm 137:9, this statement is at the top of the charts for the spirit of vengeance that sometimes infiltrates the Psalms. It may be worth noting, however, that the righteous are passive here (lit., "when he sees the vengeance"). Generally speaking, the imprecatory psalms leave vengeance to God. Dahood's rendering of the preposition *beth* (NIV: "in") as "of" ("He will wash his feet *of* the blood of the wicked")[15] is not convincing. The Greek text (LXX) has "hands" rather than "feet."

58:11 *people will say, ". . . surely there is a God who judges the earth."* In this verse, we have the use of the generic term for humanity (*'adam*) and a plural participle ("who judges") that modifies "God"

the makers, may have depended somewhat on its literary beauty. These seven curses in 58:4–9 pass the test easily.

58:7–8 *Let them vanish like water . . . when they draw the bow, let their arrows fall short.* In a series of seven similes and metaphors (curses; see "Historical and Cultural Background" for all seven), the poet describes the destruction he wishes to come on his enemies: (1) let them vanish "like water that flows away" and is useless (58:7a); (2) "let their arrows fall short" and thus not hit their target (58:7b); (3) "may they be like a slug that melts away," thus wasting away (58:8a); (4) let them be "like a stillborn child that never sees the sun," and (*'elohim*).[16] The judgments the psalmist prays for will elicit the confession, evidently by humankind generally ("and mankind [*'adam*] will say"), that God's two-pronged justice is a reality: God rewards the righteous and judges the wicked.

Theological Insights

Although the psalmist may be personally under attack by his enemies, he nevertheless has a long view of human history. It is not only the wicked of his generation (or we would prefer the "gods" as the subject; see comments on 58:1) whose "hands mete out [lit., "weigh out," *pls*] violence on the earth" (58:2), using their own rigged scales, but their lying behavior seems to represent the history of human conduct ("even from birth," "from the womb," 58:3). Sadly, their evil inclination has been generated in their inner being (58:2), leaving little hope that their social behavior is only a temporary departure from the ethical norm.

If we understand the subject of 58:1 to be the "gods," then the wicked of verse 3 are the earthlings who carry on the evil work of the gods. This poem thus moves from the idea of the gods who activate injustice in the world, to the human wicked who carry out the gods' designs, to the victims of God's judgment in verse 10b, precisely what the prayer of verses 6–9 (the sevenfold curse) hopes for. Note the literary method of *word repetition*. For example, the "gods" of 58:1 become the objects of God's (the true God's) judgment in 58:11. This literary feature is employed to reiterate, reinforce, enlarge, contrast, or shift the meaning of ideas in another direction. Table 1 illustrates how our psalmist uses this device for reiteration and contrast.

Table 1. Reiteration and Contrast in Psalm 58

"Justly" (58:1a)	"The righteous" (58:11b)	Reiteration [from same root]
You rulers "judge" people (58:1b)	God "judges" the earth (58:11c)	Contrast
"People" ("sons of man"; 58:1b)	"People" (58:11a)	Reiteration
You mete out violence "on the earth" (58:2)	There is a God who judges "[on] the earth" (58:11c)	Contrast
Even from birth "the wicked" go astray (58:3a)	In the blood of "the wicked" (58:10b)	Reiteration, but the perpetrators become the victims

Vengeance is God's ("when they are avenged" = "when they [lit., "he"] see[s] vengeance"), and when it comes, the "righteous will be glad" (58:10a). Out of the knowledge of justice done comes the confession, evidently made by the whole world (*'adam*), that God rewards the righteous and judges the earth (58:11). In light of the world confession that Isaiah predicts (Isa. 45:23; cf. Rom. 14:11; Phil. 2:10), which seems to be a saving confession, we can at least hope that this too is a saving confession.

The victims of the twisted rules of law made by those who "weighed out" injustice to the rest of the world ("people," *bᵉne 'adam*, 58:1b) at last will "dip their feet in the blood of the wicked" (58:10b). The picture is ugly. While some religious traditions will not even permit Psalm 58 to be read in public because of the offensive imagery of 58:10, the idea of the righteous washing their feet in the blood of the wicked makes the picture of divine justice very real, albeit too real for some readers. Nevertheless, the graphic nature of this picture—call it

"The righteous will be glad when they are avenged, when they dip their feet in the blood of the wicked" (58:10). This basin for foot washing is from Lachish, Israel (eighth century BC).

vengeance if you like—draws out the gravity of evil and the urgency of justice. The blood of the righteous can never be silenced until God weighs out justice on his own scale, measured by the standard weights of his character.

Teaching the Text

The Psalms are a compendium of Old Testament moral teachings, on which Christianity is based, and Psalm 58 puts forward one of those basic teachings. In fact, this principle, already buried in the subconscious mind of the psalmist's community of faith, takes the form of a confession, even if begrudgingly, when the world sees that God does indeed reward the righteous and judge the world (58:11). If the climate of our world remonstrates against this principle, especially the principle of divine judgment, we must insist that this is nonetheless the ethical principle by which the Western world operates. As believers committed to the authority of Scripture, we cannot affirm the first part of verse 11 and disaffirm the second. If we do not accept the reality of

evil, the whole idea of good begins to diminish.

There is so much injustice in the world that we sometimes pessimistically begin thinking, like some of the patrons of the psalmists' world, that God, even if he is aware of it, does not really care. Yet Psalm 58 is a reminder that God still operates in his world as he always has: God rewards the righteous, and he punishes the wicked (58:10–11). The skepticism of our world regarding God's role in human affairs is merely the recurrence of the cynicism of our evil hearts.

The Swiss theologian Karl Barth has said that humankind is constantly under the grace of God's "yes," while at the same time it is under the judgment of God's "no."[17] It is not the "yes" (in the case of Psalm 58, the reward of the righteous) we mind so much but rather the "no" of God's judgment.

David took a long view of history and observed that human beings have a reputation for devising injustice and meting out violence on the earth (58:2). Sometimes we ourselves have been the hapless victims. We do not have to search history's archives exhaustively to realize that we ourselves have lived through some of the greatest atrocities and human tragedies in the history of the human race—the list gets long before we have worked through the annals of one or two recent generations. The question is, why do human beings devise injustice in their hearts? Why do they commit such atrocities against their fellow human beings? As Wilcock puts it, if we should "arraign the villains of history, we should not simply express our horror at their deeds; what really appalls us, we should tell them, is that coldly, deliberately, *in your heart you devise* such things" (cf. 58:2).[18] Jesus spells out this lamentable reality in Luke 6:45 (see also Gen. 6:5).

Judaism generally explains these verses in the sense that they describe the inclination to sin, which is an inclination from our birth. In comparison, the Christian doctrine of original sin insists that all sinned in Adam, and all must be redeemed in the second Adam, Christ (Rom. 5:12).

We may observe that when the church devalues the seriousness of sin, the corollary is that the church is likely to devalue the wonder of grace. Not only does the psalmist take a long view of history as he insists on the injustice of the human heart, but more importantly, he also emphasizes that God takes a long view of history as regards the reward of the righteous. This psalm takes sin seriously (see also 51:1), laying out the problem as well as God's way of dealing with it: God takes the righteous seriously and rewards them, and he also deals with sin appropriately and judges the earth (58:11).

If we want to take this Old Testament doctrine into the New Testament stratosphere of grace, we may stress the New Testament doctrine that Christ took our judgment and became sin for us (2 Cor. 5:21), taking grace to a new level of absolute triumph over sin.

Illustrating the Text

A long view of history

History: A long view of history provides a catalogue of tragic events that illustrate the reality of humanity's evil nature. Consider the following examples:

The psalmist calls on God to judge the evildoers when he says, "Let them vanish like water that flows away" (58:7). Wadis are dry streambeds most of the year, for when the rains come, the water quickly flows downstream leaving the wadis dry once more. Here is a section of the Wadi Qilt near Jericho.

- The "Holodomor" is the Ukranian word for "killing by hunger" and is used to describe Josef Stalin's genocide against the Ukraine by forced starvation (1932–33). Scholars believe that 4 to 5 million Ukrainians were killed.[19]

- The Khmer Rouge were members of the Communist Party who from 1975 to 1979 led a reign of terror in Cambodia that included the murder of an estimated 2.5 to 3 million Cambodians, or 21 percent of the population.[20]

- In 2014, the U.N. Commission of Inquiry on Human Rights accused the Pyongyang regime in North Korea of "crimes against humanity." Specifically, an estimated 80,000 to 100,000 North Koreans are being held in camps and are being systematically killed by starvation, neglect, forced labor, disease, and execution.[21]

A long view of history reveals the sinful and evil nature of humans. But God's long view of history encompasses his eternal justice, which rewards the righteous and judges the evils of humanity (58:11).

Turn to the Lord for salvation.

Story: Richard Mouw tells the story of a conference he attended where he overheard a group of young pastors discussing the atonement, a topic the conference speaker had just addressed. One of the men said he seldom talked about the substitutionary atonement in his sermons, but he talked about how Christ encountered "the power" of consumerism, militarism, racism, superpatriotism, and so forth. Mouw says he resisted the temptation to join the discussion. And then when he returned to his car, he turned on his car radio and just happened to get a local Christian station, and he heard a man tell a story about a successful businessman who had become a heavy drinker, unfaithful to his wife, distant from his children, and headed toward a divorce. Then one Saturday evening his ten-year-old daughter pleaded with him to go to church with them the next morning because she was singing in the service. He reluctantly agreed, and the next morning he wished he had not promised, because

he had a hangover. But he kept his promise. In the service he heard for the first time that he was a guilty sinner and that Jesus had taken his sin upon himself on the cross. The man wept as he heard the sermon, and he pleaded with the Lord Jesus to take away his burden of sin. From that moment his life began moving in a new direction. While Psalm 58 does not deal specifically with the topic of forgiveness, it does raise the reader's consciousness of the power of sin and God's determined plan to reward the righteous (58:10). Behind that word (*tsedeq* = salvation, well-being) lies the power of God's forgiving grace that makes us righteous.[22]

Reward and judgment are found in God's character.

Bible: In Ephesians 6:12 Paul describes the battle that believers are involved in. Wilcock remarks that the singer of this psalm is a participant in the battle, not a spectator.[23] God has a system of justice, and all actions are to be measured by the standards of that system, which are in reality two: the righteous are rewarded, and the wicked are judged (v. 11; of course, there are also many degrees in between). The explanation for this is found in the character of God, who is "righteous," and he rewards those who seek to be like him. Or to take a slightly different perspective, we reap what we sow (Gal. 6:7; also Job 4:8; Ps. 128:2; Isa. 3:10–11). Derek Kidner reminds us that this psalm warns the reader that he or she "faces a mirror, not only a portrait."[24]

"You Laugh at Them, LORD; You Scoff at All Those Nations"

Big Idea *Although the enemies of our personal world—sickness, slander, uncertainty, and so on— may roam as scavengers of the night, in faithful trust we will sing God's morning song of love.*

Understanding the Text

In terms of traditional categories, this psalm is an individual lament, for the suppliant's character has been maligned by his enemies, to which he attests his innocence and confesses his faith in the loving God.

The Text in Context

Judging from the titles of Psalms 56–60, we see literary threads that connect these psalms as a group (see table 1 in the unit on Ps. 56). Psalms 58 (58:3–5) and 59 (59:3–4, 6–7, 14–15) deal with the wicked who use the power of speech to destroy the objects of their malicious motivations.

Outline/Structure

Psalm 59 falls into two parts, each ending with a refrain affirming the psalmist's faith in "my faithful God" (NIV: "my God on whom I can rely"; 59:9–10a and 59:17). Within each of those parts is a double refrain (see "Teaching the Text"; Ps. 107 also has a double refrain).

1. Prayer for deliverance (59:1–10)
   a. Plea for deliverance (59:1–2)
   b. Protest of innocence (59:3–5)
   c. Enemies like snarling dogs (59:6–7)
      i. Negative refrain: *They return at evening, snarling like dogs* (59:6)
      ii. Enemies' arrogance against Israel and God (59:7)
   d. God's derisive response (59:8)
   e. Affirmative refrain: *You are my strength* (59:9–10a)
   f. Confidence in God's actions (59:10b–c)
2. The dynamics of defeat (59:11–17)
   a. Prayer that their defeat will be a witness of God's rule (59:11–13)
   b. Negative refrain: *They return at evening, snarling like dogs* (59:14)
   c. Enemies humiliated by defeat and hunger (59:15)

d. Psalmist's song of triumph
(59:16–17)
   i. The song of victory (59:16)
   ii. Affirmative refrain: *You are
   my strength* (59:17)

Historical and Cultural Background

The historical reference in the title refers to the incident mentioned in 1 Samuel 19:11, when Saul sends his men to David's house to kill him, and David's wife Michal (Saul's daughter) assists his escape.

Generally in the Old Testament dogs carry a negative connotation (e.g., Isa. 56:10–11). They were known as wild, vicious animals and were a danger to humans. In Psalm 59:6, 14–15, dogs are depicted as scavengers (see also 1 Kings 14:11; Ps. 22:16, 20). Verse 7 transitions from the metaphor of dogs to the psalmist's enemies, describing their words as "swords" (see also Ps. 57:4; Prov. 30:14). But the other side of the metaphor, not used here, is affirmed in the art of the ancient Near East, depicting dogs on hunting expeditions and as sheep herders (Job 30:1), attesting their domestication, probably in prehistoric times (see also Tob. 5:16; 11:4).[1]

Interpretive Insights

Title *To the tune of "Do Not Destroy."* For the title of Psalm 59,

> The title connects Psalm 59 to David's escape through a window after being warned by his wife about Saul's men gathering around his house with the intent to kill him. This illumination from the Biblia Pauperum, ca. AD 1405, illustrates this event.

Key Themes of Psalm 59

- God's laughter is balanced against his grief.
- Because of divine love, we can rely on God.

see table 1 in the unit on Psalm 56. The phrase "Do Not Destroy" is probably a tune name (see the comments on the title for Ps. 57).

59:1 *Deliver me from my enemies, O God . . . those who are attacking me.* Notice the parallel occurrence of the imperative "deliver me" in 59:1 and 2. Those "who are attacking" David are likely people whom he views as perennially and persistently "evildoers."

59:2 *those who are after my blood.* Literally, "men of blood," or "murderers."

59:3 *See how they lie in wait for me! . . . for no offense or sin of mine, LORD.* Perhaps

David repeatedly affirms that God is his fortress, his place of refuge and safety. In the ancient world, cities were fortified not only to defend strategic locations but also to provide a place of security and protection for the local population. Strong walls and gate systems were constructed. In the tenth century BC, King Solomon fortified the city of Hazor with a casemate wall and a six-chambered gate, the remains of which are shown in this aerial view.

this alludes to Saul's henchmen who came at night to kill David (1 Sam. 19:11). The psalmist is innocent (see David's protest of innocence before Saul, 1 Sam. 24:11), a point he reiterates in 59:4a. The divine name here virtually constitutes an oath to confirm his innocence.[2]

59:4 *I have done no wrong.* The description of divine attributes in Exodus 34:6–7 contains three words for "sin," which are also used here in 59:3 and 4: "wrong" (*'awon*, 59:4), "offense" (*pesha'*, 59:3), and "sin" (*hatta'at*, 59:3). See the sidebar "The Language of Forgiveness" in the unit on Psalm 32.

59:5 LORD *God Almighty . . . the God of Israel, rouse yourself.* The imperative translated "rouse yourself" literally means "wake up." It is parallel to the verb "arise" in 59:4b. The same two verbs occur together in Psalm 44:23 (see also 35:23). Four names of God reinforce the importance of the occasion. The divine name "LORD of Hosts" (*YHWH ts^eba'ot*) is more frequent than "God of Hosts," although here the name is literally "God Hosts" (*'elohim ts^eba'ot*; NIV consistently translates "LORD of Hosts" as "God Almighty"), lacking the construct form *'elohe*, as is also the case in

Psalms 80:4, 19 and 84:8 (see also "Teaching the Text").

59:6 *snarling like dogs.* This verse forms a subrefrain (59:14). See "Historical and Cultural Background."

59:7 *Who can hear us?* This is the only time in the psalm when we hear the words of David's enemies, although this is probably irony of attribution, as we sometimes have in the Prophets (e.g., Amos 8:5–6). That is, the psalmist is attributing these words, drawn from his observation of their actions and attitudes, to his enemies. In effect, their actions have spoken these words, scorning the possibility of God's retributive justice. See Psalms 55:21 and 57:4.

59:8 *But you laugh at them,* LORD; *you scoff at all those nations.* The parallel verb "scoff" tinges the verb "laugh" with derision. See the comments on Psalm 2:4 (see also Ps. 37:13; Prov. 1:26).

59:9–10 *my strength . . . my fortress.* The Greek text (LXX), and also the NIV, has "my strength" (psalmist's) for the Hebrew "his strength" (enemies'). In view of the last half of the verse (lit., "for God is my fortress") and the Masoretic correction of "his faithful God" (*'elohe hasdo*) to "my faithful God" (*'elohe hasdi*; NIV: "my God whom I can rely") in 59:10 (59:11 MT), the Septuagint reading is preferable. On *hesed*, see "Theological Insights."

God will go before me and will let me gloat. God will go before the psalmist in the sense of the vanguard who leads the way and protects the front flank. The Hebrew equivalent of "will let me gloat" is literally "he will show me my enemies," while a similar expression in Psalms 92:11 and 118:7 implies the "downfall" of the psalmist's enemies.

59:11 *do not kill them . . . or my people will forget.* As long as his enemies are humiliated and still alive, Israel ("my people") will not likely forget what God has done, just as verse 13 affirms that this humiliation of Israel's enemies will also be a witness "to the ends of the earth that God rules over Jacob." That God's people might forget what he has done is one of the passionate concerns of Deuteronomy (Deut. 8:8–11; see also Pss. 78; 106). The use of the expression "my people" here suggests that the king is speaking.

59:12 *For the sins of their mouths . . . For the curses and lies.* The "sins of their mouths," "words of their lips," and the "curses and lies" constitute the enemies' transgressions against Israel, and "pride" is their consummate sin. The description of "curses and lies" specifically defines their speech. The powerful human attribute of "pride" is used both negatively and positively in the Old Testament. In a good sense, Israel is called the "pride of Jacob," whom the Lord loves (Ps. 47:4; cf. Isa. 60:15). In the negative sense, "pride" is a spirit of superiority and independence from God (perhaps implied by the rhetorical question

of 59:7c, "Who can hear us?") that becomes a trap for its patrons (see also Prov. 16:18).

59:13 *consume them in your wrath . . . Then it will be known to the ends of the earth.* The enemies' defeat carries a double meaning: it means that Israel will not forget (59:11), and the world will know that God is sovereign. David's words to Goliath parallel the sense of the last clause: "and the whole world will know that there is a God in Israel" (1 Sam. 17:46b).

59:14 *They return . . . and prowl around the city.* This is verse 6 verbatim, but the meaning has changed. In verse 6, the psalmist's enemies are represented as canine scavengers who take advantage of the city, but here in their humiliation they are like hungry dogs that scavenge the city, not to ravage, but to survive.

59:17 *I sing praise to you.* Kidner observes that both the negative (59:6–7, 14–15) and the affirmative refrains (59:9–10a, 17) have a different meaning in their second occurrences. In verse 9 the theme was patient waiting: "I watch for you." In verse 17, David has experienced answered prayer (59:16b) and changes the previous "I watch for you" to "I sing praise to you."[3]

Theological Insights

The title positions the psalm in the time of Saul's pursuit of David's life. But even when David's opposition is clearly Saul (or Absalom, etc.), his psalms tend to enlarge the sphere to include two further categories of adversaries: David's personal enemies in general—and he had many of them (59:1–4)—and his international foes (59:5, 13). Once he moves to the nations in verse 5, his enemies seem to be international (59:13). From our contemporary understanding, we could all too easily accuse David of having a persecution complex, but the reality of his situation, as was true with many ancient monarchs, was that he was surrounded by enemies, both personal and international.

We have already discussed the unique, if not disturbing, theme of divine laughter (see the sidebar "The Laughter of God" in the unit on Ps. 2). But here is a good place to point out, as does Kidner,[4] that God's laughter has to be balanced over against his grief. God's laughter stems from his sovereign rule over the world, for which there are no credible competitors, regardless of the impression the pretenders might try to foist on their world. On the other hand, his grief grows out of his love (*hesed*) for his creation. In fact, the Genesis narrative informs us of God's primordial grief at the sin of humanity: "And the LORD was sorry that he had made man on the earth, and it grieved him to his heart" (Gen. 6:6 RSV). One could say quite accurately that this divine grief became one of the "controls" of divine redemption. When he contemplated Israel's destruction, whether theoretically or historically, he was overwhelmed with the thought of giving Israel up to exile: "How can I give you up, Ephraim? How can I hand you over, Israel? . . . My heart is changed within me; all my compassion is aroused" (Hosea 11:8). One of the most dramatic moments in the story of redemption, much like God's grief in Hosea, is Luke's description of the Savior's weeping over Jerusalem (Luke 19:41). The picture of God's derisive laughter over the defeat of his foes in this psalm (see also Pss. 2:4; 37:13) needs the complementary portrait of his tears over Israel and the world he created, but a people and a world that did not recognize him when he came (John 1:10–11).

We have often pointed out in our hermeneutical discussions the strategic placement of words, phrases, and refrains in the Psalms. Psalm 59 provides an example of the positioning of the Hebrew word *hesed*, incorporated in the refrain of verses 9–10a and 17 (the NIV translates *hesed* as "on whom I can rely"). This word is translated variously in the English versions as "love" or "unfailing love" (NIV), "lovingkindness," "mercy," "steadfast love," or "faithfulness." This term expresses the essence of God's character more frequently than any other term in the Old Testament and describes the vital nature of God's covenant relationship. Psalm 59 places the term strategically in the heart of the poem and thus strategically in the heart of God. In a world where all other relationships could quickly fall into shambles, as in Israel's world and in our world too, the poet positions the concept at the middle and end of the poem to indicate the centrality and finality of God's love. So critical is this that even God's judgment has been designed so that Israel ("my people," 59:11) and the nations (59:13) should never forget his sovereign reign. In the same strand of thought, Deuteronomy reminds the people of Israel not to forget the Lord their God (Deut. 8:11–20), lest forgetting his commandments leads them to destruction.

Teaching the Text

If we are building lessons or sermons on the Psalms in their canonical order, we should draw attention to the fact that both Psalms 58 (58:3–5) and 59 (59:3–4, 6–7, 14–15) are concerned about evil people who use the power of speech to destroy the objects of their malicious schemes. Despite our sometimes glib assertion that words do not hurt us, they in fact can damage our self-image and our public image and harm us at the core of our being. David describes them as "swords" (59:7) and the "snarling" of dogs (59:6).

To get into the substance of the psalm, we should draw attention to the double refrain of Psalm 59, one negative and one positive. The negative refrain (59:6 and 14) functions in the psalm to sound the theme of the harm that evil can do. In fact, David suggests that the enemies snarl and growl at their prey, daring God to do anything about it ("Who can hear us?" 59:7c). The positive refrain (59:9–10a, 17), however, carries the weight of the psalm's message: "You are my strength, I watch for you; you, God, are my fortress, my God on whom I can rely" (with a slight deviation in v. 17).

To build on the positive refrain, we may call the terms of the psalm that advocate this statement "friends of the refrain" (like "friends of the court"). The first "friend" is God's identity as expressed by his *names*: *'elohim* occurs nine times and God's covenant name (*YHWH*) three, with *'elohim* framing the psalm (59:1, 17). But it is the heaping up of terms in verse 5 that calls for special attention: Lord (*YHWH*), God Almighty (*'elohim tseba'ot*), God of Israel (*'elohe yisra'el*). As one reads the psalm, the effect of this conglomerate becomes rather obvious, especially when we observe that it is surrounded on both sides with a passionate appeal to God for help (59:4c and 5b). The multiuse of God's names

David describes his enemies as "snarling like dogs" (59:6, 14). This Assyrian relief shows handlers with their large, ferocious dogs lined up to prevent lions from escaping the arena (645–635 BC, Nineveh).

augments the passion of the suppliant's plea.

The second "friend" of the refrain is the force of God's *actions*. Even though God's voice is never heard in the psalm, his actions are nevertheless real, and that is the way he speaks: "Consume them in wrath, consume them till they are no more. Then it will be known to the ends of the earth that God rules over Jacob" (59:13). Most of us hear God's voice through the events of our lives, and in this sense we are like the psalmist.

The third "friend" of the refrain is God's *time*. Dogs range freely at night, scavenging for food (59:6, 14), while God's "love" (*hesed*) brings relief in the morning (59:16; cf. 30:5). The psalmist watches for God, evidently at night, when watchmen typically carry out their duty, hoping that, as morning breaks, God will wake up and help him (59:4b, 5b, 9). Then after their defeat, David's enemies, under the metaphor of dogs, prowl about the city, looking desperately for food, while the psalmist sings God's praise when morning comes (59:6).[5]

God's sense of renewal in the morning brings new life and a time of worship, as the psalmist joins the fourth "friend" of the refrain, God's *love*, which undergirds the psalm: "You are my strength, I sing praise to you; you, God, are my fortress, *my God on whom I can rely*" (59:17; see "Theological Insights"). The psalmist's morning song is a song of love, and unquestionably we can rely on God.

Illustrating the Text

The Lord is our shield.

Applying the Text: The psalmists often speak of the Lord in metaphors drawn from their everyday world, as in Psalm 59. That is the case, for example, with the terms "fortress" (59:1) and "shield" (59:11), which come from the military conflicts of David's world. The reality is that we tend, and rightly so, to experience God in terms of our world. The shield was a protector in battle, while a fortress was a place where one was safe and secure. It might be beneficial to think of offices or situations in our own lives that might be used as epithets for God. For example, to the sick God is "healer," to the conflicted he is "reconciler," to those torn apart by strife he is "tailor," and so forth.

Watching for God

Christian Literature: *A Quiet Neighborhood*, **by George MacDonald.** In MacDonald's novel, members of the church have gathered in the vicarage for a Christmas party, and the pastor of the country church reads to the guests two or three of Wordsworth's ballads between dances with this purpose:

> For I thought if I could get them to like poetry and beautiful things in words, it would not only do them good, but would help them to see what is in the Bible, and therefore to love it more. For I never could believe that a man who did not find God in other places, as well as in the Bible, would ever find Him there at all. And I have always thought that to find God in other books enables us to see clearly that He is more in the Bible than in any other book, or all other books put together.[6]

If we can find God in other places in the world, whether in metaphors, nature, or poetry, it can connect us more personally to him.

Words have the power to destroy.

Human Experience: Many of us are familiar with the children's rhyme, "Sticks and stones may break my bones, but words will never hurt me." This phrase has become a stock response to verbal bullying in playgrounds throughout the English-speaking world. But most of us have learned, over time, that this phrase really is not true. Broken bones heal, but an unkind word can stick for a lifetime. It would be helpful if you shared from your own experience how an unkind word brought pain to your life. In the Psalms we often see the psalmists struggling not only from physical attacks but from emotional attacks through words as well (e.g., 59:10, 12). It appears that these were often lies spoken and spread concerning the psalmist. David's response in Psalm 59 is to look to the Lord for help not only to deal with his enemies but to disempower the effect of their slander. Challenge your listeners to consider following the example of David when others use their words to hurt or destroy them.

God's presence at the point of the pen

Quote: Pierre Teilhard de Chardin. Teilhard de Chardin was a French philosopher and Jesuit priest who was also trained as a naturalist. He was well known for his keen powers of observation, and his thoughts about God were deeply influenced by insights gained from the world around him. He wrote, "We know we are Christians when we are attuned to God's presence 'at the point of my pen, my pick, my paint-brush, my needle—and my heart and my thought.'"[7] And David would add, "my fortress" (59:1) and "our shield" (59:11).

"Human Help Is Worthless"

Big Idea *When life's defeats have no explanation, we must affirm victory by God's help, for all human help, without God, is worthless.*

Understanding the Text

Psalm 60, judging from the first-person plural pronouns ("us," "our," "we"), is a community lament, prayed by the congregation after Israel's daunting defeat in battle, perhaps by the Edomites (60:8b). In the psalms of lament, the complaint can take one of three directions, or any combination: against God, against oneself, and against one's enemies.[1] Here the complaint is against God (60:1–3, 10). Like the Asaph psalms (Pss. 50; 73–83), which sometimes contain a direct word from God (50:7–15, 16b–23; 75:2–5; 81:6–16), Psalm 60 also contains such a word, spoken by a prophet or priest, or perhaps even the king, who is the psalmist, giving assurance that God's claim on Canaan still applies and that his intention to make the conquest complete is still in effect (60:6–9).

The Text in Context

This cadre of *miktam* psalms (Pss. 56–60) concerns the psalmist's enemies, both personal and national, and is written out of the conviction of innocence, whether implied or explicit (57:2; 58:10; 59:3–4). At the same time these psalms either declare God's righteousness and justice or praise God for his vindication.

Psalm 60:5–12 (60:7–14 MT) is duplicated, with slight variations, in Psalm

God raises a banner in Psalm 60:4. In a military context banners and standards were often carried by fighting forces. In this Assyrian relief, the war chariots of Ashurnasirpal II carry standards with depictions of warrior gods whom the Assyrians believed would protect them in battle.

108:6–13 (108:7–14 MT), giving us a good example of how the same material can be reapplied to a different setting. In both instances, however, the effect is virtually the same, for the oracle of Psalm 60 affirms God's promise to give Israel the land of Canaan, despite their recent loss, whereas Psalm 108 praises God for his faithfulness, which exceeds the heavens and now (the reader may assume) has been affirmed by the fact that the conquest is an accomplished reality. That is, in Psalm 60 the promise has not yet been fully realized, but in Psalm 108 it has been.

In terms of content and situation, Psalm 44 shares much in common with Psalm 60. The former poem is set in a time of defeat, like the latter, and Israel is innocent of moral blame, an explicit fact in Psalm 44 (44:17–18) but implied in Psalm 60.

Outline/Structure

Psalm 60 falls into three sections, with the oracle occupying the middle of the psalm:

1. Complaint and intercession (60:1–5; see the sidebar)
2. Oracle of salvation and closing lament (60:6–10)
   a. Oracle of salvation, echoing God's promise of Canaan (60:6–8)
   b. Closing complaint (60:9–10)
3. Final prayer for God's help (60:11–12)

Historical and Cultural Background

There are discrepancies between the items in the psalm's title and the historical

Key Themes of Psalm 60

- Reminding God of our faithfulness can be, in effect, a rehearsal of his promises.
- God's word of promise is ultimately fulfilled.

witnesses, attributable, at least in part, to scribal error: (1) twelve thousand Edomites slain (title); eighteen thousand according to 2 Samuel 8:13 and 1 Chronicles 18:12; (2) Edomites were the victims (title, and LXX of 1 Chron. 18:12), whereas the book of 2 Samuel has the Aramaeans (see the NIV footnote to 2 Sam. 8:13); (3) victory ascribed to Joab (title), but to Abishai by the Chronicler, and to David in 2 Samuel 8 (Joab was the commander of the army, and David was the commander in chief over him, so the victory was won by Abishai on Joab and David's behalf).[2]

The battle lamented in Psalm 60 was most likely against the Edomites, attested both in the title and verse 8b, alluding to a military defeat prior to the victory celebrated by the title and the books of Samuel and Chronicles. Hakham, taking a historical rather than a cultic interpretation of the psalm, proposes that after Israel's defeat by its neighboring nations, this psalm was recited as a prayer in the preparations being made for a new assault.[3]

Interpretive Insights

Title *The Lily of the Covenant*. See the comments for the title of Psalm 45.

Aram Naharaim and Aram Zobah . . . in the Valley of Salt. The name "Aram Naharaim" means "Aram of the Two Rivers" and designates northern Mesopotamia, the region where the patriarchs lived (Gen. 24:10). "Aram Zobah" is the Aramaean kingdom north of Damascus. Also, the "Valley of Salt" probably refers to the area south of the Dead Sea, and not the wadi by that name east of Beersheba.[4] On Joab and the Edomites, see "Historical and Cultural Background."

60:1 *you have been angry.* The Hebrew verb meaning "to be angry" is a denominative verb, deriving from the noun "nose," and suggests "snorting" of the nose in anger.[5]

60:2 *You have shaken the land.* The Targum interprets this correctly as "the land of Israel." The verbs describe an earthquake in terms of the shaking and fracture of the earth.

60:3 *wine.* See Isaiah 51:17; Jeremiah 25:15.

60:4 *raised a banner to be unfurled against the bow.* See Isaiah 30:17: "Till you are left like a flagstaff on a mountaintop, like a banner on a hill." After the exodus, Moses declared that Yahweh was Israel's "banner" (Exod. 17:15). Quite significantly, then, this is an allusion to Yahweh's choice of Israel as his people. Mesopotamian military standards had the deity's symbol on them.[6] Israel also carried banners into battle (Isa. 13:2–3; 31:9), but they probably bore no symbol of Yahweh, since such representations were forbidden (Exod. 20:4). The Hebrew noun "bow" (*qeshet*) is here represented by the Aramaic noun (*qoshet*). Aramaisms are very common in the Psalms.

60:5 *help us with your right hand, that those you love may be delivered.* The Hebrew verb that the NIV renders as "help us" should, according to the marginal note in the Masoretic Text, be read, "Help (answer) me." The difference is the pronoun. Perhaps the way the text is written ("us," rather than the way the text should be read, "me") suggests a use of the psalm by the

God as triumphal warrior is able to give Israel the land he promised it. God refers to Shechem, shown here as the modern city of Nablus, between Mount Gerizim on the left and Mount Ebal on the right.

congregation. On the "right hand," see Psalms 20:6 and 118:15–16. "Those you love" refers to the people of Israel. This is what the Lord calls Israel in the Song of the Vineyard (Isa. 5:1). We may assume, especially based on Deuteronomy 7, that this alludes to the Lord's election of Israel.

60:6 *God has spoken from his sanctuary.* Verses 6–8 give an oracle, not one that offers a new promise, but one that reaffirms a promise God made centuries ago to Israel (see Josh. 8:30–35). The phrase "from his sanctuary," in Hebrew, is "in his holiness" and could mean "sanctuary" or imply an oath, in the sense of sworn "by his holiness."[7] Psalm 89:35 and Amos 4:2 use the term like this.[8] In Psalm 150:1 it means "in his sanctuary," and Jerome and the Targum understand it thus.[9]

In triumph I will parcel out Shechem. Goldingay translates the verb "parcel out" as "allocate," suggesting that this was the moment described in Joshua 8:30–35 when the conquest was completed and Joshua "allocated" the land.[10] It was in the area of Shechem that the tribes positioned themselves on Mount Ebal and Mount Gerizim and pronounced the blessings and curses (Deut. 27:11–13). The psalmist recalls two cities, Sukkoth and Shechem, which are mentioned in the narrative of Jacob's return to Israel (Gen. 33:17–18). By this allusion to the promise of the land to Jacob, he in effect says that it is now to be fulfilled and that Israel will conquer both sides of the Jordan (Shechem is on the west, and Sukkoth is on the east).[11] The "Valley of Sukkoth" was located in Transjordan, north of the Jabbok River (Josh. 13:27).

60:7 *Gilead is mine, and Manasseh is mine . . . Judah is my scepter.* God is the

Complaint and Intercession in Psalm 60

The alternation between *complaint* and *intercession* gives a particular literary effect.

"You have rejected us, God, and burst upon us; you have been angry—" (60:1)	Complaint
"Now restore us!" (60:1)	Intercession
"You have shaken the land and torn it open;" (60:2)	Complaint
"Mend its fractures." (60:2)	Intercession
"You have shown your people desperate times; you have given us wine that makes us stagger." (60:3)	Complaint
["But for those who fear you, you have raised a banner to be unfurled against the bow."] (60:4)	[Belongs more to following intercession]
"Save us and help us with your right hand, that those you love may be delivered." (60:5)	Intercession

speaker, even though the king or the temple messenger is speaking on God's behalf. Gilead, located east of the Sea of Galilee, was the tribal inheritance of the half tribe of Manasseh. The phrase "my helmet" literally reads, "the strength of my head." "'My head' is the poetic equivalent of 'I, myself,' the head representing the whole person (synecdoche)."[12] Also, the phrase "Judah is my scepter" literally translates, "Judah is my lawgiver" (KJV), probably a veiled allusion to Jacob's blessing (Gen. 49:10). "Scepter" in the Hebrew means "command giver," or "lawgiver" (KJV).[13]

60:8 *Moab is my washbasin, on Edom I toss my sandal; over Philistia I shout in triumph.* "Washbasin" suggests menial service, to which Moab is destined. The meaning of the idiom "I toss my sandal" is still under discussion. It may symbolize forced possession of something.[14] In Ruth 4:7–10, Boaz's removal of his shoe symbolizes a legal transaction. Hakham takes it to suggest merely a tossing of one's muddy shoes into a dump,[15] perhaps here implying the menial future of Moab. These three countries (Moab, Edom, Philistia) bordered Israel, and this oracle declares that even their territories are included in Israel's legal claim to the land (see Exod. 15:14–15). The verb "shout in triumph" (root *r'*) leaves the reader with the sound of soldiers rushing into battle or celebrating a victory (cf. Ps. 65:13 [NIV: "shout for joy"]).

60:9 *Who will bring me to the fortified city?* This is a rhetorical question, whose implied answer is "God." In verses 6–8 God is speaking, and it is an oracle delivered by a prophet or priest or even recited by the king, or just beautifully created by the psalmist. Then in verse 9 the "I" of verses 6–8 transitions to the royal speaker. It seems obvious that the king is making plans for the next attack on the "fortified city," probably Petra.[16]

60:10 *Is it not you, God, you who have now rejected us . . . ?* The psalm returns to the language of verse 1, forming an *inclusio*.

60:11–12 *for human help is worthless.* The KJV translation is etched in the minds of many Bible readers: "for vain is the help of man." This memorable declaration of verse 11b is what Weiser calls "the bold venture of a genuine faith."[17] Here, and quite plausibly, David renounces all human efforts to bring God's promise about, for with the promise comes the divine assurance of fulfillment.[18] That human help is "vain" or "worthless" does not mean that all human effort is worthless but rather that it is worthless without God's enablement. The following statement in verse 12a

clarifies that: "With God we will gain the victory."

Theological Insights

Judging from Israel's defeat by their enemies, the conclusion, wrongly drawn from mere circumstances, is that God has rejected them. Yet the psalmist has a deeper knowledge of and confidence in God's love for Israel. As noted above, they are still "your people" and "your beloved," by Yahweh's election, and "those who fear you," by Israel's response. The outward circumstances are only one index of God's faithfulness to his people and, as Job discovered, not always the most reliable one.

Teaching the Text

In our modern war-torn world, we can connect to Psalm 60 because it grows out of a military situation. Israel has suffered defeat in battle, even though they cannot identify any moral infraction as its cause. So they go to God in prayer about it. The tragic times are described with the metaphors of the land "torn open" (60:2), and God giving Israel wine "that makes us stagger" (60:3). These pictures stand in contrast to the remnant of those who fear the Lord (60:4), known to the Lord as his "beloved" (60:5b; NIV: "those you love").

We may make the heart of our lesson or sermon David's reaction to this setback of giant proportions, making two observations. The first is that David uses the language of faith as he prays for God's intervention, speaking of those "who fear" God (60:4) and God's "beloved" (60:5b). He further speaks of God's "banner" unfurled on the field of battle to represent his presence there (60:4) and God's "right hand," which can save and deliver (60:5a). These are friendly reminders to God that they, Israel, have been faithful, reminders that God welcomes.

The second observation is that David remembers God's promise to give Israel the land: "God has spoken from his sanctuary" (lit., "his holiness"; 60:6). Verses 6–8 are one of the most beautiful passages in the Psalms. At first these verses seem cryptic and perplexing, but when we remember that Joshua conquered Canaan and parceled out the land to the tribes of Israel, we begin to see the details of this charming oracle. In other words, this is the picture behind the picture, the picture of God's parceling out the land, an enactment of his promise to give the land to Israel, a dress rehearsal of the event. Joshua's allotment of the land was done on God's behalf. This picture is found nowhere else in the Bible but is the psalmist's artistic creation of God, as it were, standing in the land of Canaan, saying, "In triumph I will parcel out Shechem." That is, he is, metaphorically speaking, running his finger over the map as he says, "Here's Shechem—I am giving it to you, Israel. And here's the Valley of Sukkoth—it's yours now, Israel. As for Gilead and Manasseh, they are mine, so here they are—all yours. And Ephraim—that's a big one, in fact, so big that you could call it the major portion ["my head"]—it's yours now. And Judah—it's not as big as Ephraim, but it is actually more important, because it is 'my scepter' ["my lawgiver"]—Jacob gave Judah a special blessing—so my darling Israel, take this one too. And Moab—it is my washbasin. The Moabites have not been

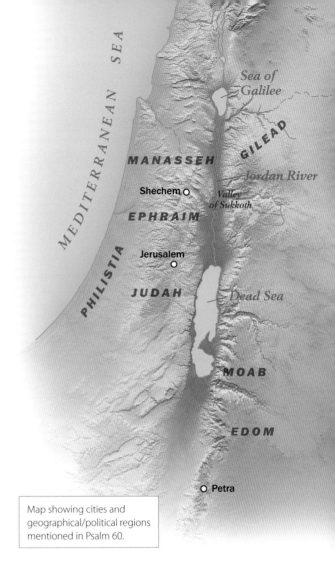

Map showing cities and geographical/political regions mentioned in Psalm 60.

too nice to you, so they are actually going to be your servants—take them too. And Edom—they are your distant cousins, but they have not acted like kinsmen ought, so when I toss my shoe over them, that is a symbol that they are mine too, and now they are all yours. And last of all, Philistia—they have been a thorn in the flesh for you, but not anymore—so take them too. That is a triumph, to be sure!"

This paraphrase is intended to give the picture of what is taking place here. *God had to give the land to Israel* ("With God

With God (who will once again go out with our armies) "we will gain the victory, and he will trample down our enemies" (60:12). This concept is nicely illustrated by this relief, which depicts the Assyrian god Ashur (winged figure at top left) fighting with Ashurnasirpal II, who has run over an enemy with the wheels of his chariot (from the palace at Nimrud, 865–860 BC).

we will gain the victory," 60:12a), and Israel has learned the hard way, by defeat, that "human help is worthless" (60:11b). But they should not forget that God promised the land to Abraham's descendants, and the psalmist creates this moving "video" of the transaction. It is a prophetic oracle in animation. This memorable declaration of verse 11b is quite plausibly David's renunciation of all human efforts to bring God's promise about.

We may conclude that it is not a renunciation of human effort as such—the Psalms, in fact, affirm and command the need of human effort—but it is the refutation of a belief system that would put human effort in the place of God's action. And with the promise comes the assurance of fulfillment,[19] or as the theological adage goes, "God's commandments are his enablements." The following statement in verse 12a puts it in perspective: "With God we will gain the victory." Without him, we cannot. In the absence of moral infraction, perhaps Israel has been simply overconfident.

Illustrating the Text

Whose Credit?

History: There are many examples in history of inventions that have often been credited to the wrong person. Consider the following:

- Henry Ford is sometimes given credit for inventing the automobile. Actually, the German Karl Benz invented the modern automobile, powered by his own four-stroke-cycle gasoline engine, in 1885. He was granted a patent in January 1886.

- Thomas Edison is often credited with inventing moving pictures. Actually, the Frenchman Louis Le Prince recorded the first moving picture at twelve frames per second in 1888, one or two years before Edison.

- The Wright brothers are generally regarded as the first to make a powered and sustained airplane flight. However, nine months prior to the Kitty Hawk flight there was a successful flight by a New Zealander, Richard Pearse.[20]

Before we become too judgmental about these examples of people claiming or being given credit for the accomplishments of others, we need to remember that we do the same thing each time we take credit for what God has done. In Psalm 60 we are reminded that the battles of life belong to the Lord and we need to depend on him and not ourselves (60:5, 11).

Abandoned!

History: During the American Civil War, the Confederates (southern states) courted support from both Great Britain and France. It seemed like a perfect fit with Europe in need of cotton for their textile industry and the South needing weapons and military support. But help was not to come, and this was a major factor leading to the Union's victory. The reason given for the lack of support for the South was Europe's recent rejection of the slave trade.[21] The people of Israel at the time of David felt much like the Confederates, in that a lack of support led to their military defeat. But unlike Europe during the American Civil War, the Lord had made a promise (of the land) to the people, and he would be faithful to that promise. Victory for Israel would come! One of the most effective things we can do in times of trouble is to focus our attention on the promises of God rather than on our circumstances. God will always be faithful, and hope comes as we live in light of his promises. This would be a good opportunity to share with your listeners some of the amazing biblical promises.

The Lord is sufficient.

Bible: Philippians 4:13. In this well-known passage, Paul writes about the provision and the contentment that come from God, both in times of abundance and in times of need: "I can do all this through him who gives me strength."[22] This New Testament verse is a reminder of the faith of Psalm 60. Through the work of God in us and through us there is nothing we cannot accomplish. There is no enemy that can defeat us when the Lord gives us strength. Ask your listeners to consider this promise in light of the enemies they face. For example, the enemy might be a broken relationship, an addiction, or an emotional battle. Indeed, we can do all things through him who gives us strength!

"You Have Given Me the Heritage of Those Who Fear Your Name"

Big Idea *In prayer we are led to God our Rock, and to a higher plane of faith and trust.*

Understanding the Text

Psalm 61 is an individual lament.[1] The reader is not informed about the problem, except that it is evidently, like the occasion for Psalms 42–43, related to the psalmist's "foe" (61:3b). Not generally included in the royal psalms, it nevertheless contains the beautiful prayer on the king's behalf in verses 6–7, or a prayer prayed by the king.

The Text in Context

A backward glance at Psalm 60 and a forward glance at Psalm 62 reveal shared terms. Both Psalms 60 and 61 refer to the faithful as those who "fear" God (60:4; 61:5). Facing forward, Psalm 62 (62:2, 6–7) calls God "my rock," in the same sense as 61:2, and both refer to God as "refuge" (61:3a; 62:7, 8). While these common terms may be coincidental, the editors of the book of Psalms had an eye for such connecting links.

Both geographically and metaphorically, this psalm is recited by one who feels distant from God and his sanctuary, much like the suppliant of Psalms 42–43 (there it is

unmistakably a geographical distance). The psalmist once mentions "the foe" (61:3), who is evidently the source of his problem and likely the cause of his remoteness from the sanctuary (61:4), although we do not know the enemy's identity.

Outline/Structure

The psalm falls into two parts, and interestingly the word *selah* at the end of 61:4 marks the center point:

1. Lament and intercession (61:1–4)
   a. Prayer for safety (61:1–2)
   b. Confession of faith (61:3–4)
2. Testimony and intercession (61:5–8)
   a. Testimony to answered prayer (61:5)
   b. Prayer for the king (61:6–7)
   c. Promise to fulfill vows (61:8)

Historical and Cultural Background

The prayer for the king in Psalm 61:6–7 seems a bit abrupt, but Kraus observes that prayers for the king occur quite spontaneously in Mesopotamian prayers also, so this prayer, however abrupt it seems to be, may not be an anomaly.[2] Another way to look at this prayer is to consider it an expression of ancient Israel's unity of personality. The supplicant's prayer and subsequent answer were incomplete without God's blessing on the king, an association in which his self-identity was tied up. So having received God's answer regarding his own situation (61:5), the psalmist prays also for the king, asking that love and faithfulness, attendants at God's throne (89:14), would protect the king.

In verse 8 the supplicant promises to fulfill his vows, using a verb that means "to offer a peace offering" (*shalem*, infinitive construct Piel).[3] The peace offering was shared together in a communal meal, and it signified that all was well between Yahweh and the worshiper.[4] This would be an appropriate conclusion to the lament and the crisis the psalmist faced.

Interpretive Insights

Title *With stringed instruments.* The designation "with stringed instruments"

Psalm 61 contains a prayer for the king in which long life and God's protection are requested. The Nabonidus Cylinder, shown here, records the reconstruction of several temples and includes a petition by Nabonidus in which one of his requests is a long life (Ur, 555–539 BC).

- Live and worship as resident aliens.
- God is the Protector manifested in life's institutions and activities.

(*'al-n⁰ginat*), a variation of the phrase that appears in the title of a number of other psalms (see the comments on the title for Ps. 4), may mean a prayer sung to the accompaniment of stringed instruments.[5]

61:1 *Hear my cry, O God.* The word "cry" (*rinnah*) is a synonym of "prayer," as it is in Solomon's prayer in 1 Kings 8:28,[6] and a common way to begin a lament (e.g., Ps. 17:1).

61:2 *From the ends of the earth . . . I call as my heart grows faint; lead me to the rock.* The phrase "from the ends of the earth" designates the remotest parts of the earth. The verb translated "grows faint" is used to describe the fainting caused by emotional distress or physical fatigue, or when death is near (Pss. 102 title; 107:5; 143:4; Lam. 2:11, 19; Jon. 2:7; also translated as "grows weak" or "life ebbs away"). The psalmist's refuge is a remote rock, high above the battlefield, where he is safe from danger.

61:3 *a strong tower.* In Proverbs 18:10, the name of Yahweh is the strong tower, and the righteous run to it. See also Judges 9:51.

61:4 *I long to dwell in your tent forever . . . in the shelter of your wings.* The verb "to dwell" (*gur*) has the nuance of dwelling in a foreign land as a resident alien (see "Theological Insights"). The phrase "in the shelter of your wings" suggests the bird sheltering its young under its wings. The word "shelter" is synonymous with "shadow" in the phrase "shadow of

over a long period of time, and the Targum is an illustration of a Jewish interpretive era that partially overlaps early Christianity.

61:7 *appoint your love and faithfulness to protect him*. God assigns his personified "love and faithfulness" (*hesed* and *'emet*) to keep the psalmist. See Psalm 89:14.

61:8 *fulfill my vows*. This usually implies a public act of worship accompanied by a sacrifice and, in this case, accompanied by music. The verb translated "fulfill" (*shlm*) means to offer a peace offering (see "Historical and Cultural Background").[7]

Theological Insights

The verb "to dwell" (*gur*) in verse 4 carries the nuance of dwelling as a "resident alien" (or "sojourner"). In the ancient world this class of residents included those who had been settled in their adopted country for some time and as a result received certain privileges,[8] even though they were not full citizens. Abraham was a resident alien in Hebron (Gen. 23:4), Moses in Midian (Exod. 2:22), and Elimelek in Moab (Ruth 1:1), as were the Israelites in Egypt (Exod. 22:21). On the one hand, the worshiper's desire to "dwell" in God's house forever sounds very much like Psalm 23:6, where the verb (*yshb*) may imply a more permanent dwelling. While it may be inappropriate to stress the difference too much, Psalm 23 speaks of dwelling in the Lord's house after the psalmist has

your wings." The two terms occur parallel in Psalm 91:1. "Shelter" suggests a hidden place, thus a safe one. See also Ruth 2:12.

61:6 *the king's life*. As it often does, the Targum interprets the king as the Messiah. The messianic interpretation of the Psalms represents a later period of interpretive history, especially the early Christian era, evident in their New Testament usage. The dimensions of that, of course, developed passed through the "valley of the shadow of death" (23:4; see NIV footnote) and been triumphant over his enemies, which sounds a bit more final than Psalm 61. In our psalm the suppliant seems still to be in the midst of the crisis, calling to God from the "ends of the earth" (61:2), even though he is assured that God has heard his vows (61:5). It is in this confidence that he sojourns as a resident alien and registers his determination to fulfill his vows in the future ("day after day," 61:8). Peter uses this same metaphor for Christians living in the Roman Empire, who are aliens of that culture but citizens of another country (1 Pet. 1:1, 17). Similarly, the Epistle to the Hebrews describes the patriarchs as aliens in their land of sojourn, looking for a better country (Heb. 11:13).

Teaching the Text

While the two verbs for "dwell" mentioned above (*gur* and *yshb*; see "Theological Insights") may at times function as synonyms, when we hear the psalmist crying to God "from the ends of the earth" (61:2a), we get the sense that the psalmist is geographically or emotionally distant, or both. In this case we might surmise that he is thinking of his restoration to the sanctuary as that of a "resident alien," if not officially, then emotionally. Maybe it is because he is in the midst of the crisis, as he certainly is, that he uses this verb (*gur*) and gives his "dwelling" in God's house a different nuance. Indeed, he feels faint because the crisis is so intense (61:2b), and the thought of being in God's house as a guest is enough at this point. He is so distant from God that he can hardly think of being a bona fide resident! As we

determine the place and value of worship for our own lives, this is a helpful question to ask: "How much at home are we in the Lord's house?" It is not necessarily negative to feel like a sojourner so long as we are *on our way* to becoming bona fide citizens.

The language of the psalm alerts us to an important dynamic of its message. For example, the intensity of the suppliant's spiritual plight can be inferred from the prayer expressions: "my cry" (61:1a), "my prayer" (61:1b), and "I call" (61:2a, 2b). Even though we know that he is in a crisis, he evidently does not want that to become center stage. In fact, he refers to the enemy only one time ("the foe," 61:3). Rather, he wants God and his trust in God to be the focus of the psalm and the focus of his life. At this point we can see that the psalmist is on a journey to becoming the worshiper he aims to be.

To that end the psalmist associates himself with God's power, strength, and refuge, which is the substance of the psalm. When we look at a psalm, we must pay close attention to metaphors, language, and word pictures. In fact, the psalmist uses four different word pictures. First, David prays that the Lord will lead him to "the rock that is higher than I" (61:2; see Exod. 33:17–34:7), a reminder that there is a refuge "above" us, a place outside ourselves, where God protects his children. It may be an echo of the rock where Moses, having asked to see Yahweh's glory, took refuge and saw only the deity's "back" and not his face (Exod. 33:17–34:7). It is particularly vivid when viewed over against the fainting heart that is debilitated and battle fatigued by life's constraints (61:3). Second, the psalmist calls the Lord his "strong tower against the foe," which is a word snapshot of the ancient city wall (61:3; see Judg. 9:51), where the watchman was stationed to look out for approaching danger. Third, the sanctuary, "your tent" (61:4a), was also a place where individuals might take refuge and find protection in those sacred precincts (1 Kings 2:28). Fourth, the word picture of the Lord as a bird with its young under the protection of its wings (61:4b) is a tender portrait of taking refuge in God. These four metaphors convey the idea of security, strength, worship, and parental care, all combined to give the picture of a faith that undergirds the whole of life and its demands.

A subtle literary feature occurs at the end of the psalm: the psalmist prays for the king, that God's "love and faithfulness" will protect him (61:6–7). This is a particularly beautiful picture of the power of prayer, suggesting the spiritual lesson that prayer has a widening effect. The psalmist has prayed for himself, and now he broadens his prayer to intercede for the king. Prayer is an opportunity to take our own personal concerns to God, but one of the many beautiful things about it is that, when we pray for ourselves, we discover that our prayers widen to include others whom we love, and even others whom we do not care that much about. We are transformed by the power of prayer.

With this completed picture of the psalmist's world, secured by God his Rock, with love and faithfulness as divine attendants, and sheltered under the Almighty's wings, the psalmist can sing and pay his vows to God. The journey of God's people is laced with dangers of all kinds: physical, emotional, political, relational. But our psalmist informs us that God is our perfect security and strength, which we are likely to find in the several dimensions of our lives, both institutional and behavioral.

Illustrating the Text

The power and regimen of prayer

Biography: **John Calvin.** The psalmist had experienced effective prayer (v. 5). Herman J. Selderhuis describes John Calvin's practice of prayer:

> If Calvin was not always battling someone, what did he do during the day? What did a typical day look like for him? Calvin began each day with prayer. He prayed a

God is described as "a strong tower against the foe" (61:3). Towers were built as part of a city's defenses, like this partially restored one at Hazor. It was constructed to protect the western side of the city as the Assyrians invaded Israel in the eighth century BC.

lot because he expected so much from it. Thus a fact unknown to many also speaks for itself: the longest chapter by far of the *Institutes* is devoted to prayer. The Bible calls us to pray continually, but in Calvin's opinion nothing would come of this if you did not establish a regular regimen. Prayer too ought to be done in good order and, as with so many other things, with moderation and directly from the heart. Calvin thus established what was virtually a monastic rule: "We pray when we get up in the morning before we begin our daily work, when we come to the table to eat, after we have eaten under God's blessing and when we get ready to go back to bed again." The worldwide Reformed practice of praying before and after every meal, at home and elsewhere, had its origin in Calvin.[9]

Pray for "the king."

Quote: Abraham Lincoln. In Psalm 61:6–7, the psalmist prays specifically for the king.

This is a good reminder to us of the importance of prayer for those in authority over us, whether we agree with their policies or not. God commands that we pray for those in authority, and in Psalm 61 we see a great example of this. We need to pray for the Lord's work in and through the lives of our presidents. As Abraham Lincoln understood, the Lord's blessing is central to the success of any nation: "It is the duty of nations as well as men, to own their dependence upon the overruling power of God . . . and to recognize the sublime truth, announced in the Holy Scriptures and proven by all history, that those nations only are blessed whose God is the Lord."[10] Depending on the size of your group, either pray for the nation's president on behalf of the congregation or invite people to lift up prayers for their leader.

"Truly My Soul Finds Rest in God"

Big Idea *God is our "all in all," and that truth prompts us to invite others into our faith.*

Understanding the Text

Psalm 62 is an individual psalm of trust.[1] (See sidebar "Psalms of Trust" in the unit on Ps. 16.) The crisis that has called forth this marvelous expression of faith is not clear. However, we can be confident of this much: David has been assaulted by the unscrupulous attacks of his enemies, who flattered him with their words but cursed him in their hearts (62:3–4). Their erroneous

David may be using military imagery again when he affirms that God is his fortress but then views himself as a "leaning wall" and a "tottering fence" (62:3). In this Assyrian relief, the Assyrian army is attacking a well-fortified city, using sappers and a battering ram to weaken the city wall (Nimrud, 865–860 BC).

assessment of his character is that he is a "leaning wall" and "tottering fence" just waiting to be brought down by their devious schemes.

The Text in Context

There are both verbal and conceptual correspondences between Psalms 61 and 62. The verbal are "rock" (*tsur*, 61:2; 62:2); "love" (*hesed*, 61:7; 62:12); to "fulfill" vows (61:8; 62:12 [NIV: "You reward"]). The conceptual is God as the psalmist's "strong tower" / "fortress" (61:3; 62:2).[2]

In terms of language, Psalm 62 has striking similarities with Psalm 39, with almost identical titles. They share the restrictive use

Table 1. Similarities
between Psalms 62 and 39

Terms	Psalm 62	Psalm 39
"Only, surely, truly" (*'ak*)	62:1, 2, 4, 5, 6, 9	39:5c, 6a, 6b, 11c
"Breath" (*hebel*) / "to put vain hopes in" (*hbl*)	62:9a and d; 62:10b	39:5a, 6b, 11c
"Silence/rest" (*dumiyyah*) / "To be silent" (*dmm*)	62:1 (NIV: "finds rest"); 62:5 (NIV: "finds rest")	39:2
"Mankind" (*'adam*)	62:9a and b (*bᵉne 'adam*; lit., "sons of man"; NIV: "lowborn")	39:5c, 11c (*kol-'adam*; lit., "all mankind"; NIV: "everyone")
"Man" (*'ish*)	62:9 (*bᵉne 'ish*; lit., "sons of a man"; NIV: "highborn")	39:6a, 11a (NIV: "everyone"; "anyone")

of the word "only" (*'ak*; for these terms, see table 1), suggesting a stylistic comparison; the metaphor "breath" (*hebel*, 62:9; 39:5; etc.); and the "silence" of the psalmist (62:1; 39:2), leading some scholars to propose the same author for both psalms. Indeed, they both are associated with David, and they very well could have been written by him. The two psalms, with their similarities of language and difference of content, illustrate how language can be used to convey very different messages (see the sidebar).

Outline/Structure

The psalm has two parts, with a refrain focusing on the psalmist's trust in God (62:2 and 6). If we take the word *selah* at the end of 62:4 as the midpoint of the psalm, similar to Psalm 61:4, then the second stanza begins with a reaffirmation of the opening declaration of trust, with slight variations, the main one being

Key Themes of Psalm 62

- The psalmist sets the tone for a life totally dependent on God.
- Life based on social status and wealth will come up "weightless."

Psalms 39 and 62: Same Language but Different Meaning

The circumstances that prompted both Psalms 39 and 62 were similar; in Psalm 39 they were more likely the evil deeds of the wicked (39:6), while in Psalm 62 they were deceitful words (62:4), though evil deeds were not excluded (62:10). The response of the psalmist in each instance is one of the basic differences between the poems. In Psalm 39 the worshiper breaks his self-imposed silence when he realizes that it is counterproductive, and the lesson he draws from his enemies' evil deeds is that "everyone is but a breath" (39:5). Even wealth cannot give humanity substance. In contrast, the worshiper of Psalm 62 finds God to be the spiritual source of silence and peace (62:1), and the lesson he draws is that trust in God is the only source of peace and hope (62:5). Even wealth and social status cannot give human beings substance. Indeed, human life, when weighed on the scales, is "weightless" without God. The meaning of life is in God, and in God alone.

"my *salvation* comes from him" (62:1b) and "my *hope* comes from him" (62:5b). Our outline would then take the following form:

1. Trust in God alone (62:1–4)
   a. Trust and refrain (62:1–2):
      Truly my soul finds rest in God;
      my salvation comes from him.
      Truly he is my rock and my salvation; he is my fortress, I will never be shaken.
   b. The crisis alluded to (62:3–4)
2. Trust in God alone as compared to wealth and status (62:5–12)
   a. Trust and refrain (62:5–6):
      Truly my soul finds rest in God;

my hope comes from him. Truly he is my rock and my salvation; he is my fortress, I will never be shaken.

b. God as "my mighty rock, my refuge" (62:7)

c. Invitation to trust in God rather than social status (62:8–9)

d. Admonition *not* to trust in wealth or illegal gains (62:10)

e. A final word from God (62:11–12)

   i. One thing: Power belongs to God, who dispenses it with unfailing love (62:11–12a)

   ii. Two things: God rewards human deeds fairly (62:12b)

Historical and Cultural Background

God is "rock" and "fortress" (62:2), terms taken from David's military code book, and as Kidner observes, the Davidic psalms "are seldom free from some shadow of an enemy."[3]

The deceptive approach of the psalmist's enemies is described as blessing with their mouths but cursing in their hearts (62:4). In the ancient world of Israel, curses were very common (see Exod. 21:17). They did not employ profanity, as we use the word "curse" colloquially, but involved the pronouncement of catastrophes on one's enemies. This, of course, brought the gods into the picture, because curses were made in the name of the gods, who were thought to make the curses effective on their victims.[4]

Interpretive Insights

Title *For Jeduthun.* The designation "For Jeduthun" is also found in Psalms 39 and 77 (lit., "according to Jeduthun" here and in Ps. 77). See 1 Chronicles 16:41. Hakham mentions favorably the proposal that "Jeduthun" is a musical instrument named after the family of Jeduthun that either made it or played it.[5]

62:1 *Truly my soul finds rest in God.* God alone is the source of rest. See "Theological Insights" for the translation of "truly/alone" (*'ak*). "Rest" signifies faith, as it does in Psalm 37:7 ("*Be still [dmm; see 62:5] before the* LORD").

62:2 *Truly he is my rock and my salvation.* "Rock" and "salvation" form a hendiadys, which is equivalent to "the rock of my salvation" (Ps. 89:26 ESV; cf. Deut. 32:15).[6] At the end of 62:2 is a word (*rabbah*, "very") that seems extraneous. In verse 6 the text has the same expression ("I will not be shaken") but without this extra word. Perhaps it is a scribal error.

62:3 *How long will you assault me?* Now David turns to his enemies with this rhetorical question. The verb "assault" (Polel of *hut*) does not occur anywhere else in the Hebrew Bible and has the object "man" (NIV: "me"), which may refer to the psalmist.

62:4 *Surely they intend to topple me.* Note the third person, referring to the wicked. After they lift him up, either initiated by the suppliant's trust in them or their deceptive offer of help, they "topple" him.

62:5 *Yes, my soul, find rest in God; my hope comes from him.* The verb "find rest / be silent" (*dmm*) shares the same root with the noun "rest/silence" (*dumiyyah*) in 62:1. A few manuscripts have the noun of 62:1 here rather than this verbal form.

62:7 *my honor.* "Honor" (*kabod*) in Hebrew carries the basic sense of "heavy." Contrast the "honor" of David's character with the metaphor of "breath" as a disqualifier of the value of humanity without God (62:9).

62:8 *Trust in him at all times, you people . . . for God is our refuge.* Now the psalmist turns to the "people" (*'am*). The verbs are plural. These are the people of Israel or, if this is a liturgy, the worshiping congregation in the temple.

62:9 *Surely the lowborn are but a breath . . . If weighed on a balance, they are nothing.* Some identify the "lowborn" (*bᵉne 'adam* = "sons of man") as ordinary people, and the second term, "highborn" (*bᵉne 'ish* = "sons of a man"), as the privileged class (see the comments on Ps. 4:2). The metaphor of weighing them on a balance seems to confirm their relative importance. We should also observe that this metaphor refers to God's judgment of our lives in this world, not in the world to come.[7] All human beings are a "breath," and when taken together and weighed on the scales, they still add up to nothing. The NJPS translates: "Men are mere breath; mortals, illusion; placed on a scale all together, they weigh even less than a breath."

62:10 *Do not trust in extortion or put vain hopes in stolen goods.* "Extortion" refers to property obtained unlawfully. This may be a warning against depending on any property, especially one gained illegally, particularly in view of the reference to wealth, or "riches," in the second half of the verse. The verbal idea behind "put vain hopes in" is a single word in Hebrew (root *hbl*) and derives from the noun "breath" (*hebel*) used in the last part of the previous verse. Wealth is not wrong in itself but becomes wrong when one sets one's heart on it; only God can give security and hope (1 Tim. 6:17 may allude to this verse).

62:11–12 *One thing . . . two things.* This is a poetic way to say "a few" times (e.g., Prov. 30:15, 18, 21).[8] Usually the last figure ("two") is the one that determines the exact number. The two things that God has spoken (this is the only time God speaks in the psalm) are (1) that power belongs to God and (2) that God rewards everyone according to what he or she has done. God

The psalmist tells his listeners not to hope in stolen goods or set their hearts on riches. The owner never retrieved this hoard of silver ingots that he had perhaps hidden for safety. They were found during excavations at Tel Goren in En Gedi.

Psalm 62

is just, and rewarding each one according to his or her deeds is an expression of his fairness, included in God's "unfailing love." This is the baseline of divine justice. Mercy exceeds the baseline.

Theological Insights

The structure of a psalm generally arises out of the sentiments of the psalmist. That is, subject matter demands the service of structure and literary style. Often the main idea of a psalm is found in the first verse or two, as it is here: "Truly my soul finds rest in God" (62:1). This sets the tone for the entire poem and calls literary structure into service by the use of the Hebrew particle 'ak, translated in the NIV as "truly, surely, yes." This word is the first word in six verses (62:1, 2, 4, 5, 6, 9) and often applies to the second part of the verse as well. The NIV's affirmative translation of the word is certainly permissible but, in my view, not preferable. Rather, the restrictive sense, "only/alone," is to be preferred. That is the basic meaning of the poem: *only* God gives rest and provides refuge and salvation. Wealth or status are inadequate. The word can carry three nuances: (1) the affirmative, rendered "truly, surely, yes" (thus NIV's translation); (2) the restrictive, often translated "only, alone" (ESV); (3) the antithetic, rendered "however, but."[9] Verses 11–12 function as a concluding affirmation of this theological point: only God can provide rest, refuge, and salvation, because "power belongs to . . . God." Furthermore—and this is crucial to the psalmist's theology—power is not ar-

"If weighed on a balance, they are nothing" (62:9). Scales with balance pans, similar to this one from the Roman period, were used with standardized weights to determine the weight of objects.

bitrary but is governed by God's "unfailing love" (62:12a). Who could not find refuge in such a God as this!

The speaker makes the point that everything in life is nonsubstantive, weightless (*hebel*), outside of God (62:9, 10), and this is the central idea of the psalm. He even uses a verb constructed out of the noun "breath" (do not "put vain hope in," 62:10b; see the comments on this verse above) to reinforce the point. While he does not develop the idea in the same frame as does Qoheleth, the speaker in Ecclesiastes (e.g., Eccles. 1:2), the idea of the "meaninglessness" of life outside of God is quite the same, with one critical difference, as I will explain. In this psalm, the suppliant knows God as his rock, fortress, and salvation, who manifests himself most graciously in his unfailing love (*hesed*)—an allusion to the covenant relationship—and in his just dealings with his people (62:12). Qoheleth, too, finds his meandering way to a similar conclusion when he acclaims the fear of God and keeping his commandments as the "conclusion of the matter" (Eccles. 12:13), even though he is not as confident about God's fair dealings with humanity as he is about God's judgment of all human deeds, good or evil (Eccles. 12:14). Nor is his theology governed by the view that "God alone" is his hope, but he knows rather that "God alone" is the only thing left when he has considered all his options. His "God alone" position is a faith of desperation rather than our psalmist's faith of affirmation. But the quality of such a faith, whether it grows out of desperation or affirmation, is of substantive value when it matures to trust in God alone. Only the path that leads to it is different. Thus, Psalm 62 may not strike the theme of "vanity of vanities" (Eccles. 1:2 KJV) with the same force as Ecclesiastes, because the psalm's theology is much more positive than Qoheleth's, but the speaker knows the "weightless" value of status (62:9) and things (62:10).

Teaching the Text

We may begin our sermon or lesson by recognizing that Psalm 62 introduces the subject very early: "Truly my soul finds rest in God" (62:1). It is important that we understand "rest" (*dumiyyah*) as more than physical inactivity; basically it is rest from one's troubles and cares. David hints at that in verses 1 and 5.

Once we have clarified and defined the subject of the psalm, we may point out that the subject is served by the structure of the poem (see "Theological Insights"), with basically two literary features functioning in service to the subject matter. First, David uses a single word to introduce verses 1, 2, 4, 5, 6, and 9, the word "alone" or "only" (*'ak*; NIV: "truly," 62:1, 2, 6; "surely," 62:4,

9; "yes," 62:5). Second, there is a refrain in verses 1–2 and 5–6, with only a slight variation in the second refrain. Thus we get the following pattern (author's trans.), in which I have positioned the word "alone" at the beginning of the sentence as it occurs in the Hebrew:

Refrain	*Alone* my soul rests in God (60:1) *Alone* is he my rock and my salvation (60:2)
	Alone they will topple him from his lofty place [in the sense that their *only* goal is to topple him] (60:4)
Refrain	*Alone* my soul rests in God (60:5) *Alone* is he my rock and my salvation (60:6)
	Alone are lowborn men a breath, [*alone*] are the highborn a lie ["lowborn men" are *nothing but* (*alone*) a breath," etc.] (60:9)

This one qualifying word (*'ak*) that stands out in front of these six verses strips away all other sources of hope and salvation and asserts with clarity that our rest is in God *alone*.

Now having established the subject of the psalm, we may consider the rejected alternatives (62:5–12). The first is that of *social status*, and the psalmist speaks of the opposite ends of the spectrum, "lowborn" and "highborn" (62:9). That, contends David, has nothing to commend it to the world: "Surely the lowborn are but a breath" (62:9a). The same can be said for the other end of the social spectrum: "The highborn are but a lie" (62:9b). Both are to be viewed in contrast to God, who is a rock and fortress, and in whom David has found rest.

The second object of comparison is *riches* (62:10), which probably include both illegal money and that which is honestly earned. "Do not trust" them; "do not set your heart on" them (Matt. 6:21; 1 Tim. 6:17–19).

The conclusion of the psalm brings together a pair of thoughts. First is the dual thought of God's power and love: God exercises his power by the standard of love (*hesed*), within the compass of his covenant. We can trust a God like that. The second concluding truth is that God will reward each person "according to what they have done" (62:12b).

By way of application, we may observe the expansive use of language in the psalm. First, the psalm moves from "I"/"my" ("my rock and my salvation," "my fortress," "I will never be shaken," 62:2) to the more inclusive "our" (lit., "refuge *for us*"; 62:8), concluding with the all-inclusive "sons of Adam" and "sons of man" (see the comments on 62:9). It is clear that all are included in the message of this psalm. Second, the psalmist moves from the generic use of God (*'elohim*), which occurs six times, to the more intimate "Lord" (not the tetragrammaton but its substitute, *'adonay*). In fact, the final two sayings transition the reader from the robust imagery of power, represented by "rock" and "fortress," to the tender image of God's "unfailing love" (*hesed*) that issues in his just dispensation of reward for human deeds (62:12). Third, the psalmist's faith in God's power advances from "my rock" (62:2a) to "my mighty rock" (62:7b). The quality of his faith deepens and finally heightens into the description of God's unfailing love (62:12a).

According to Augustine's *Confessions*, his autobiography, his early years were restless ones until, like the psalmist, his soul found its rest in God. The painting of Augustine shown here is by Antonello da Messina (1472–73).

Illustrating the Text

Rest in the Lord.

Church History: Saint Augustine, the Bishop of Hippo, was a skilled orator and writer who made a great impact on the Christian church in his generation and subsequent generations as well. In AD 391, after a long struggle in which he renounced his early philosophical beliefs and embraced the Christian faith, he was ordained a priest. In *Confessions*, Augustine writes this amazing statement that captures the heart of Psalm 62: "You stimulate him to take pleasure in praising you, because you have made us for yourself, and our hearts are restless until they can find peace in you."[10]

Bible: Matthew 11:28–30. In this well-known passage, Jesus holds out the offer of rest to those who will come to him.

Trusting in God alone

Applying the Text: In 2010 researchers at Vanderbilt University, the University of Kentucky, and the University of Pittsburgh did a study of lottery winners. They concluded that the big winners were more likely to go bankrupt.[11] For many of them, the money was a trap. But we don't have to be rich to trust in our possessions. We can build a false trust in what we have no matter how much or how little it is, even though more wealth offers a much bigger attraction. The important question is how we use what we have. Are we good stewards of our resources? Do we give God his part? If we don't, we probably wouldn't if our income were a million dollars a year. I have known a lot of people who haven't had great wealth—modest would be the right word, some even impoverished—but who have had generous hearts. I think those people could be trusted with riches. But only God knows whether that is true. How we deal with possessions certainly says something about where our trust is.

David was a man of great wealth and privilege, at least in his later years, and he had learned that *rest in God alone* was the only position he could live by.

Paul seems to be reflecting this psalm in 1 Timothy 6:17–19: "Command those who are rich in this present world not to be arrogant nor to put their hope in wealth, which is so uncertain, but to put their hope in God, who richly provides us with everything for our enjoyment" (v. 17).

Relentless pursuit

Poetry: One night in 1917, a group of people gathered in the back room of a bar known as the Hell Hole. Among the group were the famous playwright Eugene O'Neill and journalist Dorothy Day. O'Neill began to quote Francis Thompson's poem "The Hound of Heaven," which talks about our tendency to run from the God who pursues us. Day was deeply moved by this poem, and sometime later she surrendered her life to the Lord, choosing to live a life of poverty and care for the homeless. Day later wrote in her autobiography about Thompson's poem: "It is one of those poems that awakens the soul, recalls to it the fact that God is its destiny."[12] David writes in the Psalms about the relentless pursuit of a loving God. It is this God who provides the rest for our souls that we all long for and deeply need.

"Your Love Is Better Than Life"

Big Idea *Even in the "dry and parched land" of our problems, God's love is still better than life.*

Understanding the Text

Psalm 63 is an individual lament,[1] which Kraus puts into his subcategory of "the prayer song of the persecuted and the accused,"[2] for which the psalm certainly qualifies in view of "those who want to kill" him (63:9). It also contains elements of thanksgiving (63:3–7) and confidence (63:8–10),[3] which is not unusual for lament psalms.

The Text in Context

The psalmist, in a "parched land where there is no water" (63:1), recounts his previous experience in the sanctuary (63:2), just as the thirsty soul of Psalm 42, isolated in a foreign land, remembers going to the house of God (42:4). In the more immediate context, Psalms 61 and 63, both attributed to David, have affinities that may be more coincidental than intentional, but the similarities are of value in the broad scope of Book 2, especially the prayer for the king (61:6–7; 63:11) and the longing for the sanctuary (61:4; 63:2; see table 1). The longing for God's presence, which began Book 2 (see "The Text in Context" in the unit on Psalms 42–43)—there a levitical longing—now is the king's passion, matching up with David's passion for God's presence in Book 1 (see Pss. 16; 23; 26; 27).

Table 1. Shared Terms and Concepts between Psalms 61 and 63

Terms and Concepts	Psalm 61	Psalm 63
David	Title: "Of/ for David"	Title: "A psalm of/for David"
God's name	61:5, 8	63:4
Shelter under God's "wings"	61:4	63:7
Longing for the sanctuary	61:4	63:2
Vow to endless praise	61:8	63:4
Third-person reference to the king	61:6–7	63:11

Outline/Structure

The psalm moves along the lines of thirst for God, praise that arises from the vision of God in the sanctuary, and lament over enemies, which was evidently the occasion for the psalm.

1. Thirst for God in a dry and parched land (63:1)
   a. Confession (63:1a–b)
   b. Thirst for God (63:1c–f)
2. Vision of God in the sanctuary and life (63:2–8)

a. David's vision of God in the sanctuary (63:2)

b. Vow to praise God because his love is better than life (63:3–5)

c. Night contemplation of God (63:6)

d. David's worship in the sanctuary (63:7)

e. David's faith and God's support (63:8)

3. Complaint against David's enemies (63:9–10)

a. His enemies' intention to kill him (63:9a)

b. His assurance of their end (63:9b–10)

4. The king's and Israel's rejoicing and the silencing of the enemies (63:11)

Historical and Cultural Background

Delitzsch gives convincing reasons to assign Psalm 63 to the time of Absalom's rebellion. His reasons are the following: (1) during Saul's pursuit, David could not easily call himself "king"; (2) during his flight from Absalom he spent one or two days in the "fords in the wilderness" (2 Sam. 15:23, 28; 17:16), that is, the wilderness of Judah; (3) he was called "weary" (2 Sam. 16:2, 14; NIV: "exhausted"); and (4) he longs for the sanctuary (Ps. 63:2), which was not established, at least in Jerusalem, until his reign.[4] Yet, in view of the "Desert of Judah" in the title and the allusion to "a dry and parched land" (the Negev) in verse 1, the time could very well be David's wilderness period.

The horror of war can be seen in the word pictures of verse 10: "the sword," where the expression is literally, "they

will pour him out [*ngr*, "to pour"; cf. 2 Sam. 14:14] on the handles [lit., "hands of"] the sword"; and "food for jackals," a picture of the scavengers of the wilderness devouring their carnage.

Interpretive Insights

Title *When he was in the Desert of Judah.* While David was fleeing from Saul, he spent time in several places in the Judean wilderness (1 Sam. 23:14, 24; 24:1; 25:1; see also "Historical and Cultural Background"). The "Desert of Judah" lies between the Judean hill country and the Dead Sea. Rainfall is so minimal, and thus some regions so arid, especially in the eastern part, that the area is called "desert,"[5] but not "desert" in the sense of sand and sand dunes. "Wilderness" is probably a good compromise.

63:1 *earnestly I seek you; I thirst for you, my whole being longs for you.* The word for "seek" (*shhr*) is different from the one used in a worship setting (*bqsh*). A. A. Anderson says the verb *shhr* belongs

Psalm 63 is connected to a time when David was in the "Desert of Judah." This is an arid, rugged region.

to wisdom language (Job 7:21; 8:5; 24:5; Prov. 1:28; 7:15; 8:17).[6] Whether or not it is a denominative verb from the word for "dawn" (*shahar*), verse 6 nevertheless looks back on the night, and the Septuagint has "I cry to thee early" (*orthrizō*; thus KJV, "early will I seek thee"). For "I thirst for you," compare Psalm 42:2. The verb translated "longs" occurs nowhere else in the Old Testament. However, in parallel with the verb "thirst" in the previous colon of the verse, the meaning seems to be "to yearn."[7] The memory of the Israelites' thirst during the wilderness sojourn (Exod. 15:22–27; Deut. 8:15) may be in the psalmist's mind, a crisis whose remedy is mentioned explicitly in Psalm 78:15–20.

63:2 *I have seen you in the sanctuary.* The verb "to see" (*hzh*) sometimes means "to have a vision" ("*to gaze* on the beauty of the LORD," Ps. 27:4). The same root forms the noun "vision" (*hazon*) that describes a prophet's oracle (e.g., Isa. 1:1), and it also forms the noun "seer" (*hozeh*). It appears that the psalmist is writing from the perspective of already having seen Yahweh in the sanctuary. Verses 2 and 4 (MT 63:3, 5) begin with "thus, so" (*ken*), which the NIV has not translated. But this word can have a resultant meaning, "for this reason," which seems to be appropriate here. That is, the psalmist's longing of verse 1 was a result, at least in part, of his experience in the sanctuary (63:2): "Thus I have seen you in the sanctuary and beheld your power and glory." In parallel manner, the "thus, so" that begins verse 4 is a result of the vision of God in the sanctuary: (As a result of the fact that I have seen you in the sanctuary,) "thus I will praise you as long as I live."

beheld your power and your glory. Psalms 78:61 and 132:8 speak of the ark

of the covenant as God's "power" (NIV: "might"). Psalm 96:6 also describes God's "power [NIV: "strength"] and glory" in the sanctuary. It would logically follow that the suppliant's singing "in the shadow of your wings" (63:7) is an allusion to the ark of the covenant with its winged cherubim on either end.

63:3 *Because your love is better than life, my lips will glorify you.* The psalmist is convinced, most likely by his vision of God in the sanctuary, that life without God's "love" (*hesed*) is not worth living. The verb "glorify," or "extol" (*shbh*), occurs parallel to "praise" (*hll*) in Psalm 117:1, attesting to its other five occurrences in the Psalter as "praise."[8]

63:4 *I will lift up my hands.* This gesture of worship was a symbol of reaching up to God, much like the expression "lift up my soul" (Ps. 25:1 ESV). It occurs in Psalms 28:2; 119:48; and 134:2, as well as here.

63:5 *with the richest of foods.* Literally, "my soul is satisfied as *with marrow and fat*." This verse continues the thought of verse 4, "I will praise you as long as I live . . . just like my soul is satisfied with marrow and fat." The "fat" of animals was reserved for the Lord (Lev. 3:16; 7:23), thus the idea of "choicest [or "richest"] of foods." Quite marvelously the murderous plans of his enemies would fail, and they would become "food for jackals" (63:10), while he was eating "the richest of foods."

63:6 *I think of you through the watches of the night.* The verb "think" (*hgh*) is the same verb translated "meditate" in Psalm 1:2. The night was divided into several "watches" (Judg. 7:19; 1 Sam. 11:11). In later Judaism there were three.

63:7 *in the shadow of your wings.* This metaphor occurs also in Psalms 17:8 and 36:7 (see also 61:4; 91:4). This may be a veiled reference to the wings of the two cherubim that flanked either end of the ark of the covenant. But more intimately, it is a description of the psalmist's relationship to God and his protective presence.

63:8 *I cling to you; your right hand upholds me.* In Deuteronomy the verb translated here as "cling" describes Israel's intimate relationship to God (Deut. 4:4; 10:20; 11:22; 13:4; 30:20; NIV: "hold fast"). The "right hand" usually being the stronger hand denotes God's strength or God himself. This is an instance of synecdoche, the "right hand" meaning God's whole being.

63:9 *the depths of the earth.* The idea is that the human spirit descends below the subterranean waters to the deep recesses of the earth (Job 26:5; Ps. 139:8). While the nature of that world after death is not very clear, there are arguably Old Testament texts that suggest hope of a better life (Pss. 16:10; 49:15; 139:8; Job 19:26), even a bodily resurrection (Isa. 26:19; Dan. 12:2).[9] Here, sadly, the picture is one of doom for the psalmist's enemies.

63:10 *food for jackals.* The slain would be eaten by these omnivorous scavengers and not be given a proper burial, something that was greatly feared in ancient Israel (see 2 Sam.

21:10–14; 2 Kings 9:10). On "the sword," see "Historical and Cultural Background."

63:11 *all who swear by God . . . the mouths of liars.* The phrase "all who swear by God" literally reads, "all who swear by him," where the NIV has interpreted "him" as God. While this may well be, there is evidence that the people sometimes swore by God *and* the king (1 Sam. 17:55; 25:26; 2 Sam. 11:11; 15:21),[10] even though the Israelites were commanded to swear by the name Yahweh and no other (Deut. 6:13). The "liars" are evidently those who want to kill the psalmist (63:9). If the background is David's flight from Saul, then he is likely alluding to Saul and his men, or if Absalom's rebellion, they are the supporters of Absalom.

Theological Insights

Kidner observes: "Once more the worst has brought out David's best, in words as it did in deeds."[11] The suppliant's experience in the wilderness, most likely brought about by those who want to kill him (63:9), has caused him all the more to "thirst" for God (cf. 42:1). Furthermore, the hardship created by their murderous and lying designs has resulted not in his destruction but in the praise of God; and quite contrary to his enemies' intentions, it has resulted in their own destruction—a boomerang effect.

At the same time, the psalmist's experience in the sanctuary, where he has gazed on God's power and glory (63:2), has taught him the real value of God's love (*hesed*)—it

Those who seek to kill David will themselves be killed and their corpses left for the scavenging jackals to devour. Here a jackal stands over what remains of the carcass it has been eating.

"is better than life" (63:3; see "Teaching the Text"). With that settled value, the psalmist seeks God with his "whole being" (63:1). While David can never forget his enemies (63:9–10), his suffering in the wilderness of life and worship in God's sanctuary combine to produce, as Paul has said of the Christian's experience, "a far more exceeding and eternal weight of glory" (2 Cor. 4:17 KJV).

Teaching the Text

When a psalm presents us with a memorable saying such as verse 3, we should try to determine what role that saying plays in the total message of the psalm: Is the saying the centerpiece of the message and every other piece fits around it? Or is it an auxiliary message that is just one component of a larger message complex? To determine that, we need to examine the context of the saying. In our present case, David begins by declaring that he has seen God "in the sanctuary," where he has beheld his power and glory (63:2). Verse 3 then says something more about what he has learned there: "Your love [hesed] is better than life," and because of that, he will praise the Lord. He would prefer to die rather than to live

without God's love (cf. Phil. 1:21). In the totality of biblical revelation, the love of God is the sine qua non for understanding God, so much so that John can equate God with love and write: "God is love" (1 John 4:8).

Then begins a section of praise (63:4–6) that flows naturally out of the statement of verse 3, thus suggesting that the statement of verse 3 is the fulcrum on which these two pieces move. That leads us to seek the theological ramifications of this saying, especially in the verses that follow it. The first, as already suggested, is that it leads the supplicant into praise ("Because . . . , I will praise you" 63:3–4). The more we learn about God, the more we will love him.

The second ramification is the satisfaction this conviction brings him. God's love has been laid before him as a feast of the "richest of foods" (lit., "marrow and fat"; 63:5), reserved only for God but laid on the banquet table of the psalmist's life. It is not overstating biblical theology to say that when God gives us his best, he gives us himself: "He who did not spare his own Son, but gave him up for us all—how will he not also, along with him, graciously give us all things?" (Rom. 8:32).

Third, the truth of verse 3 has infused the psalmist's whole life to the extent that he thinks about God not just in his waking hours but also in the "watches of the night" (63:6). This gives his statement in verse 1 ("my whole being longs for you") a ring of authenticity.

Fourth, the truth of verse 3 means that the psalmist "clings" to God, and God's "right hand upholds" him (63:8). That is another way to express the truth of verse 1. The psalmist's relationship to God— and ours should imitate this model—is encompassing, and he has come to the recognition that God is everything, his all in all.

Illustrating the Text

"My whole being longs for you."

Personal Stories: Eugene Peterson tells the story of the beginnings of the church he and his wife, Jan, planted in Maryland in the 1960s in his book *The Pastor: A Memoir*. After meeting for two and a half years in the basement of their home, they built a sanctuary, encouraged and enabled by much enthusiasm and excitement in the congregation. After the dedication, Peterson noticed that attendance began to drop off. Even some of the people who had been most enthusiastic and involved in the project began to miss church. This caused him a lot of anguish, and he visited them, one by one, hoping to understand what was happening, only to discover that the enthusiasm evidently could not be sustained once the project was accomplished. Even the chairman of the building committee was going fishing on Sunday mornings rather than going to church. He explained that there were other things in life that he realized he was missing, and just to be out with a fishing rod in his hand and the quiet peace of nature all around was something he was newly discovering. Without judging people like these, we can admit that many of us need to adopt and learn to live by the motto "my whole being longs for you" (v. 1). When we live under that banner, and only then, will we come to confess that "your love is better than life" (v. 3).

An expectation for worship

Science: Many people have a very low expectation for worship. They just show up at church out of tradition or to "put in their time." This was not the case for David (see 63:2). Science journalist Chris Berdik has argued, based on science, that expectation matters. Discussing the power of the "placebo effect" in medicine, Berdik argues that this same principle can be applied broadly to all areas of life. For instance, Berdik writes, "brain scans reveal that expectations about a wine's quality (based on price or a critic's review) actually change the level of activity in the brain's reward centers when a person takes a sip. Highly-trained weight lifters can out-do their personal bests when they believe they've taken a performance booster."[12] In other words, expectations matter. What might happen in worship if every Christian came with the expectation that they were going to see the power and glory of God? Choose to prepare for worship by expecting to meet the Lord!

Desire God.

Theological Book: *When I Don't Desire God: How I Fight for Joy*, **by John Piper.** Piper writes about fasting as a way to deepen our hunger for God. He quotes William Law: "If you don't feel strong desires for the manifestation of the glory of God, it is not because you have drunk deeply and are satisfied. It is because you have nibbled so long at the table of the world. Your soul is stuffed with small things, and there is no room for the great."[13] Almost everyone longs to say with integrity, "You, God, are my God, earnestly I seek you; I thirst for you" (63:1). If you do not hunger for God, it is not because God does not satisfy. Rather, it is because your heart is divided between the Lord and the desires of the world.

"They Will Proclaim the Works of God and Ponder What He Has Done"

Big Idea *God outstrategizes evil and its perpetrators and exhausts their arsenal of weapons.*

Understanding the Text

Psalm 64 is an individual lament, identifying the problem that stimulated the psalmist as the "threat of the enemy," the "conspiracy of the wicked," and the "plots of evildoers" (64:1–2). It sums up with the aphoristic commentary of verse 6c: "Surely the human mind and heart are cunning" (lit., "the inward person and heart are deep"). In addition to this detailed description of the problem (the malicious speech of the wicked [64:3] and the strategy of the wicked [64:4–6]), which is not always the case with the laments, the psalmist presents God's response to the evil machinations of David's enemies (64:7–8), followed by the human reaction to God's work (64:9) and the proper response of the righteous (64:10).

The Text in Context

Psalm 64 is a complement to Psalm 63 in two ways. First, verses 7–8 provide a different description of the punishment of the wicked, who in 63:10 are "poured out" on the handles of the sword and now, with a change of metaphor, are the objects of God's arrows. The sword they were "poured out" on in 63:10 is the sword they wield so cruelly against David in 64:3. Second, the Responder to the onslaught of the wicked in Psalm 63 is implied to be God by the reference to "your right hand" (63:8) and the king's rejoicing in God (63:11), whereas Psalm 64 unmistakably identifies God as the Warrior who shoots his arrows at the wicked (64:7)—nothing implied here. In fact, Psalm 64 goes a step further and uses God's covenant name, Yahweh, to identify him as the source of the rejoicing of the righteous. While in 63:11 the king is rejoicing in God, the picture is completed in 64:10, adding all of God's people to the king's rejoicing. Wilson suggests that Psalms 56–68 form a group of poems that have an increasingly expansive emphasis on God's subjection of the nations (67:3–4, 7) and their acknowledgment of his power, with the effect that the nations join in the universal chorus of praise (66:1, 4, 8; 67:3–5; 68).[1]

Outline/Structure

Psalm 64 is composed of essentially four parts:

1. Petition (64:1–2)
2. Scheming enemies (64:3–6)
   a. Description of the evildoers' actions (64:3)
   b. Description of the evildoers' moral strategy (64:4–6)
3. God's actions on behalf of the righteous (64:7–8)
4. Response of all people and the righteous (64:9–10)
   a. The general human reaction to God's works (64:9)
   b. The call to the righteous to rejoice in the Lord (64:10)

The wicked are punished in different ways in Psalms 63 and 64. In 63:10, they are "given over to the sword." With weapons drawn, these two Assyrian soldiers are about to bring the lives of two enemy warriors to an end. This section of a larger Assyrian relief battle scene is from the Northwest Palace, Nimrud, 865–860 BC.

Key Themes of Psalm 64

- Words can be turned into weapons.
- Evil has a boomerang effect.

Historical and Cultural Background

The *Midrash on the Psalms* interprets Psalm 64 as referring to the Persian officials who plotted against Daniel and caused him to be thrown into the lions' den.[2] The reason for this connection seems to be the principle of *gezerah shavah* (inference from identical expressions). That is, the Hebrew word for the NIV's "plots" (*rigshah*, 64:2) occurs in its verbal form in Daniel 6:7, 12, and 16, thus suggesting the connection to the Jewish interpreters.[3] While there is certainly the possibility that the psalm was applied to later historical situations, it seems to fit comfortably into the life of David and his many conflicts, especially with Absalom, since words were so important in that conflict (2 Sam. 15:1–6).

Interpretive Insights

64:1 *I voice my complaint; protect my life from the threat of the enemy.* The act of complaining is a grievance expressed in

words. See 1 Samuel 1:16, where the word for "complaint" is translated as "anguish." The word "threat" (*pahad*) means "fear" (a terrifying fear) and may refer to the enemies' secret plotting.[4]

64:2 *from the conspiracy of the wicked.* The "wicked" are those who do evil things against the righteous (also Ps. 28:3). The word for "conspiracy" (*sod*) means "assembly" in Genesis 49:6 (NIV: "council") and "evil plot" in Psalm 83:3 (NIV: "conspire").[5] Either sense is possible.

64:3 *They sharpen their tongues . . . aim cruel words like deadly arrows.* The verb "sharpen" has this meaning in Deuteronomy 32:41. See also Psalm 57:4. Some understand the final phrase of the Hebrew verse (*dabar mar*, "cruel words") to mean "poison." See Job 6:4.

64:4 *at the innocent . . . without fear.* The victims are "innocent" in two ways: morally innocent and unaware of the danger. So the offense is doubled. The attitude "without fear" implies without fear of God or man. Assonance, which emphasizes the vowel sounds more than the consonants, marks the enemies' volley of arrows, *yoruhu w^elo' yira'u,* "they shoot . . . without fear" (note the repeated "u" sound). The Hebrew verbs "shoot" (*yrh*) and "fear" (*yr'*) sound very much alike in Hebrew (homonyms).

64:5 *They encourage each other in evil plans . . . hiding their snares . . . "Who will see it?"* The first part of the verse literally reads: "They harden themselves (for) their evil deed(s)." The hiding of "snares" is a hunting metaphor, referring to the nets used for trapping animals and humans (see Ps. 9:15–16). The evildoers believe either God is not involved in the moral world or he is not interested (see Ps. 10:4, 11, 13). This is why their question ("Who will see it?") is obviously a rhetorical one, whose implied answer is "no one." But with God it is not rhetorical.

64:6 *They plot . . . "We have devised a perfect plan!"* The Hebrew root *hps* ("search" or "complete") is used three times in the first half of this verse (NIV: "plot," "devised," "plan"), suggesting intensity and aurally producing a beautiful example of alliteration (emphasis on the consonants): "We have completed a diligent search" (*yahp^esu . . . hepes m^ehupas*). Dahood renders it: "Who can investigate our perfect crime!"[6]

64:7 *But God will shoot them with his arrows.* The evil design is turned on the evildoers. The conjunction (*waw*) that begins the verse has an adversative meaning, "but," and suggests that this is not what the evildoers expected (64:6b).

64:8 *He will turn their own tongues against them.* Literally, "their tongue(s) will trip on themselves."

64:9 *All people will fear.* In contrast to the wicked who have no fear of anyone (64:4), now the fear of God falls on "all people" (*kol-'adam*). Verses 8b–9 contain a theme summed up in Isaiah 26:9: "When your judgments come upon the earth, the people of the world learn righteousness."

64:10 *The righteous will rejoice.* The term "righteous" is parallel with "the upright in heart." This recalls the final verse of Psalm 63: "But the king will rejoice in God" (63:11).

Theological Insights

In Psalm 64 God turns the evildoers' metaphorical instruments of war ("tongues like swords," "cruel words like deadly arrows," 64:3) against them. In fact, God becomes the opposing warrior, shooting them with his arrows and making them trip on their own tongues (or words; 64:8a). The response is both universal and particular: first, from "all people" (*kol-'adam*), whose appropriate reaction is to fear God and to proclaim his works (64:9), even to "ponder" them; and second, from the "righteous" and the "upright in heart" (synonyms), who rejoice in the Lord and take refuge in him (64:10).

Both the evildoers and the righteous—the evildoers by observation, and the righteous by faith—are sure that God is up to the challenge of evil.[7] He will not stand by and watch his people destroyed by malicious words, but he will exhaust the enemies' own arsenal of destructive weapons to defend his own people. Some may doubt his resolve, but when they see it acted out in reality, they will "ponder anew what the Almighty can do," and others will rejoice because their faith in him has been vindicated. Divine judgment is always a match for evil machinations.

The way the psalmist puts his poem together affirms that. Weiser helpfully puts the two sides of the poem together:[8]

Evildoers	God
They "aim cruel words like deadly arrows" (64:3b)	"God will shoot them with his arrows" (64:7a)
"They shoot suddenly, without fear" (64:4b)	"They will suddenly be struck down" by God (64:7b)
They lay the "traps" (NIV: "plots"; 64:2b)	God will cause their tongues to trap them (64:8a)
They plan their secret ambush (64:4a)	God will expose them publicly (64:8c)
They do their unscrupulous work with no fear (64:4b)	God does his work so that people fear him (64:9a)

Teaching the Text

Psalm 64 formulates a message about how God turns the plans and weapons of evildoers against them. Although they are heavily armed and well strategized (64:2–3) and are brashly overconfident (64:6), God outstrategizes them and exhausts their deadly arsenal in his favor (64:7, 8). Quite effectively the poet turns the "tongues" of evildoers into weapons and gives the audience a sense of the lethal power of words. This psalm provides an opportunity for the teacher or preacher to speak about the power of words, especially when we, metaphorically speaking, turn them into weapons (64:3), which, sadly enough, we often do.

Further, this psalm gives us one of those fascinating pictures of God in the Hebrew Scriptures, an "archer" shooting arrows at his enemies (64:7). Some would say that is not a worthy picture of God. Admittedly, it is pretty bold. However, there is a perspective on this picture of God as "archer" that is quite reassuring. It gives us a picture of God entering the fray of human conflict. When the psalmist is threatened by evildoers who use their tongues as weapons against him, he has the assurance that he is not in the battle by himself: God is there with him. In fact, God is not only *there*, but he is a participant in the conflict. And if God be for us, who can be against us (Rom. 8:31)!

The psalm uses the imagery of war to describe David's personal conflict—his enemies have used their tongues as weapons to destroy him (64:8a). The imagery is switched from the psalmist's enemies to God, who takes up the role of warrior and aims his arrows at the psalmist's foes. While this image may make us a bit uncomfortable, the idea of God's participation in our human conflict is most reassuring (see "Our sharpshooter God" in "Illustrating the Text").

While it is a very different message from that of the incarnation—God's taking on our humanity in Jesus of Nazareth—it is still the message of God's identification with us in our need and participation with us in the conflict of our struggles. So this picture of our "sharpshooter" God should

not be all that surprising, aiming his sure-fire arrows at the evildoers of this world and hitting his target every time.[9] It is not vengeance but justice.

The Christian church has interpreted this psalm to have its ultimate meaning in Christ. It was very common in the New Testament, and even more common in the early church, to view David as the "Christ" figure (Heb. *mashiah*, "anointed one") and his enemies as the enemies of Christ and the cross. In this hermeneutical mode, Psalm 64:1–6 is interpreted not only as historical but also as a prophetic vision of the suffering of Christ. So we should not turn the biblical message of justice into a story of Christ dying for the principles of justice as established by our society. Rather, he died for our sins that have violated God and our neighbor, and a good starting place for understanding what that means is the Ten Commandments. It is God's standard of justice, not ours, for which Christ has given his life, although the two standards overlap at significant points.

Illustrating the Text

Our sharpshooter God

Bible: Psalm 64 gives us one of those fascinating pictures of God as an "archer" (v. 7). We're not at all bothered when the Scriptures describe God as a "Shepherd," but an "archer," poised with his bow and arrow to shoot his enemies, is pretty bold. However, this snapshot of God has another perspective. God enters into the fray of human conflict. In fact, God was not only *there*, but he was a participant in the conflict. This psalm does not deal with war, not in the real sense of the word, but uses the imagery of war to describe the conflict David is involved in (v. 8a), even though other psalms do describe the real carnage of the battlefield. This psalm then is a good reminder that when we are struggling with life's issues, when we are struggling with those who oppose us and oppose God, there is every reason to believe that God is in the struggle with us, and in this case, he is described as one of the archers taking aim at his enemies: "The battles is not yours, but God's" (2 Chron. 20:15). Charles Spurgeon has described God this way: "They shoot, and shall be shot. A greater archer than they shall take sure aim at their heart. One of his arrows shall be enough, for he never misses his aim."[10] It is not vengeance—it is justice. It is a way of saying that God is engaged in the battle against our foes, which implies that he is present when our conflicts and troubles are in progress, and he is there, on our side, participating in the conflict, and because of this, "we are more than conquerors" (Rom. 8:37).

"Ponder anew what the Almighty can do"

Hymn: "Praise to the Lord, the Almighty," by Joachim Neander. Neander was a German Lutheran minister in the seventeenth century. One of the stanzas of this beautiful hymn enjoins worshipers, "Ponder anew what the Almighty can do," which is a close proximity to Psalm 64:9: "All people will fear; they will proclaim the works of God and ponder [*hiskil*] what he has done" (lit., "his work"). Another stanza celebrates God's marvelous work of subduing evil and turning the warring factions of human life into peace. It is in pondering anew that fresh insights about God's work in the world come into view. This is an activity both for individuals and for the corporate church. God's resources and his as-yet-unrevealed strategies are incalculable.

Praise to the Lord, who doth prosper
    thy work and defend thee;
Surely His goodness and mercy here
    daily attend thee.
Ponder anew what the Almighty can
    do,
If with His love He befriend thee.

Praise to the Lord, who, when tempests
    their warfare are waging,
Who, when the elements madly around
    thee are raging,
Biddeth them cease, turneth their fury
    to peace,
Whirlwinds and waters assuaging.[11]

"But God will shoot them with his arrows" (64:7). Gods were often depicted as warriors in the ancient world. In this Assyrian palace relief, the god Ashur is pictured with an arrow ready to fly from his bow as he precedes King Ashurnasirpal in battle (Nimrud, 865–860 BC).

"When We Were Overwhelmed by Our Sins, You Forgave Our Transgressions"

Big Idea *Nature's wonders and God's forgiveness come together as dual witnesses of grace.*

Understanding the Text

Psalm 65 is a community psalm of thanksgiving,[1] grammatically indicated by the plural pronouns ("we" and "our") in verses 1–5. (See the sidebar "Psalms of Thanksgiving" in the unit on Pss. 9–10.) The psalm of thanksgiving includes two essential elements: a report of the crisis that generated the thanksgiving ("we were overwhelmed by sins," 65:3a) and the acknowledgment of deliverance ("you forgave our transgressions," 65:3b). The account of an abundant harvest (65:9–13) leads some scholars to connect this psalm to one of the agricultural festivals (Passover / Unleavened Bread—barley harvest; Feast of Weeks—wheat harvest; Feast of Tabernacles [Sukkot]—grape harvest). It certainly sounds like a harvest hymn, whose beauty, says Kidner, "puts every harvest hymn to shame as plodding and contrived."[2]

The Text in Context

Psalms 65–68 are grouped together by two common words in their titles: "song" (*shir*) and "psalm" (*mizmor*). The editor of Book 2 probably had

The Feast of Tabernacles, also called Sukkot, is one harvest festival that may have been connected to Psalm 65. Ancient Israelites built booths that may have been like this as they remembered the wilderness wanderings and celebrated the final harvest period of the agricultural cycle.

this minicollection at hand as he put the larger collection together, or he provided links to connect these four psalms, two of which are not attributed to David (Pss. 66 and 67).

Outline/Structure

The psalm falls into two parts, part 1 dealing with the forgiveness of sins (65:1–5), transitioning into part 2 (65:6–13) by the reference to the "ends of the earth and of the farthest seas" in verse 5c. Part 2 begins with two successive Hebrew participles to describe God's creation of the world ("who formed" and "who stilled," 65:6, 7), and then moves into the Creator's care of his world (65:9–13). This psalm of thanksgiving is phrased in terms of the praise of God.

Part 1 (65:1–5)
  a. Praise of God, who forgives sins (65:1–4)
  b. Praise of God, who is the hope of the world (65:5)
Part 2 (65:6–13)
  a. Praise of God, who created the world (65:6–7)
  b. Praise of God, who calls forth songs of joy by the wonders of his creation (65:8)
  c. Praise of the Sustainer of the earth and Giver of bountiful harvests (65:9–13)

Historical and Cultural Background

The historical setting is uncertain. However, Sennacherib's invasion of Judah in 701 BC and the abundant harvest that Isaiah promised in the "third year" (Isa.

Key Themes of Psalm 65

- God's grace is both a centrifugal and a centripetal force.
- The DNA of redemption is written in the story of creation.

37:30) present this general time frame as a possibility.[3] Even if one retains the right of Davidic authorship, the psalm could have been reused in that context, as often happened.

Culturally speaking, this poem points to the agrarian nature of Israelite society, so dependent on rainfall, agriculture, and husbandry. In the ancient Near East agriculture and husbandry were the foundation of society.

Interpretive Insights

65:1 *Praise awaits you, our God, in Zion; to you our vows will be fulfilled.* The word rendered "awaits" (*dumiyyah*) occurs also in Psalm 62:1. It can be translated as "silence," and rendered literally, "Silence is praise." Fulfilling a vow involved a peace offering and singing praise to God. In fact, the verb "to pay a vow" and the noun "peace offerings" have the same root (*shlm*; see the comments on Ps. 61:8).[4]

65:2 *all people.* The Hebrew phrase *kol-basar* (lit., "all flesh"; NIV: "all people") refers to all human beings, including gentiles. The use of this phrase in Genesis 6–9 includes animals too.

65:3 *When we were overwhelmed by sins, you forgave.* Literally, "our transgressions were too strong for me; you forgave them." This psalm knows the acuteness of our sins but, thanks to forgiveness, not its despair, because it is "precisely to you" (the sense of the preposition *'ad* ["to"] rather than *l^e* ["to"] of 65:1b) that all people will come (65:2). That is the power of grace that calls one and all to the forgiving God.

65:4 *those you choose . . . filled with the good things of your house.* This verse may have been a prayer the pilgrims recited as they passed through the gates of the temple.[5] "Those you choose" is a singular reference in Hebrew and could point to a king or priest. The latter officiant is the one who is "brought near" to the altar, alluding to the priest's approach to the sacrificial altar (e.g., Exod. 40:12, 14, 32; Lev. 7:35).[6] However, it could also have a collective meaning, as the NIV translates it. Whether "all people" of verse 2 are among "those you choose" is not certain, but Isaiah pictures the day when the gentiles will come to Yahweh's "holy mountain in Jerusalem" and become "priests and Levites" (Isa. 66:18–24). The "good things of your house" may refer to the peace offerings that the worshipers shared. See Psalm 22:26: "The poor will eat and be satisfied."

65:5 *You answer us with awesome and righteous deeds.* Literally, "you answer with awesome deeds, in righteousness." The latter phrase, "in righteousness," is the standard by which God performs his awesome deeds. In Psalm 65:5–8, the message seems to be that the God who kept the primordial waters in their place can certainly keep the "nations" (65:7) in bounds.

65:6 *who formed the mountains . . . having armed yourself with strength.* The verb translated "formed" is the equivalent of "creates." The image of one having armed himself with strength is that of a man tightening his belt to augment his strength before engaging in a strenuous task (cf. Job 40:7).

65:7 *who stilled the roaring of the seas . . . the turmoil of the nations.* See also Psalm 89:9. The idea seems to be that God rules over the seas to keep them from flooding the dry land. See Psalms 29 and 46 for the idea that God, in the beginning, stilled the roaring of the seas. Note that the Hebrew participle ("who stilled") governs three objects: "the roaring of the seas, the roaring of their waves, and the turmoil of the nations." The latter phrase, occurring at the end of the verse, carries the sense, "This, too, he stills."[7]

65:8 *awe at your wonders.* "Wonders" is the same word that designates God's miraculous "signs" in Egypt ("signs and wonders," 135:9; cf. 78:43; 105:27). This verse can be rendered literally: "The inhabitants of the remotest regions fear because of your signs; you cause them to sing for joy at the outgoings of the morning and the evening."

65:9 *You care for the land and water it . . . The streams of God are filled.* The verb translated "water" means "to overflow" (Joel 2:24). The use of 'elohim (in "streams of God") suggests "the largest streams." See the comments on Psalm 36:6; see also Jonah 3:3.

65:10 *You drench its furrows and level its ridges.* This is a description of the early rains that soften the ground for plowing.

65:11 *You crown the year with your bounty.* This is a reference to the harvest.

65:12–13 *the hills are clothed with gladness. The meadows are covered with flocks.* These lovely metaphors (vv. 8–13) are a descriptive way to say, "The *earth* declares the glory of God" (see Ps. 19:1; also 30:11).

One way that the psalmist sees God enriching the land is that "the meadows are covered with flocks" (65:13). Here flocks graze in the fields of Israel.

Theological Insights

The book of Psalms, more than any other book of Scripture, creates in its readers a consciousness of sin and, just as starkly, the overwhelming power of forgiveness. Paul's statement about sin and grace in Romans 5:20 could easily be designated as the caption of this topic in the Psalter: "Where sin abounded, grace did much more abound" (KJV). Sometimes this awareness became so acute for the psalmists that they would have sunk into despair had it not been for the power of forgiveness.

Verses 2 and 3 imply that forgiveness has a centripetal power that pulls "all flesh" (NIV: "all people") to the center of grace. This, as every Israelite knew, was represented by the temple that was "filled with the good things" of God (65:4). The language of verse 4, to "choose," to "bring near," and to "dwell" (NIV: to "live"), may allude to the priests, Aaron's family, whom God "chose" to "come near" the altar for sacrifice and to "dwell" in the temple. Yet it could as easily allude to the people of Israel, the people of God, chosen as a "kingdom of priests" (Exod. 19:6) and "brought near" to the altar, where forgiveness becomes a reality, a reality to which "all people will come" (in Heb. 4:16, note the priestly language: "approach God's throne of grace with confidence"). Isaiah foresees the day when even the gentiles will be able to approach God's sanctuary and offer their sacrifices, and his house "will be called a house of prayer for all nations" (Isa. 56:7).

Quite clearly, God is not the exclusive deity of Israel, but his wonders attract the attention of "the whole earth" (lit., "the inhabitants of the ends" [of the earth]; 65:8). Nor do his wonders end with the marvels of creation, but they extend to the meadows "covered with flocks" and the valleys "mantled with grain" (65:13). Here God becomes the Valet of Israel's rocky landscape and clothes the wilderness with grass, dons the hills with gladness, covers the meadows with flocks, and throws a mantle of grain over the valleys. Israel's topography was never so beautifully adorned.

Teaching the Text

Sometimes a psalm is so theologically inclusive that, if we look carefully, we can see the outline of biblical doctrines and sometimes the broader outline of biblical theology. We have to train our eyes to look for the clues, and when we have found them, we will have received the answer to the psalmist's prayer in Psalm 119:18: "Open my eyes that I may see wonderful things in your law."

As we peruse the psalm, we will notice that the doctrines of both creation and redemption come into view, but in reverse order. In a sense we could say that all other biblical doctrines fall under these two.

Redemption:
When we were overwhelmed by sins,
    you forgave our transgressions.
        (65:3)

We may make the observation that the doctrine of redemption, seen on its macrocosmic scale as the redemption of Israel from Egypt, reduces in many biblical contexts to the personal transaction of God's forgiveness, as it does here. Redemption is never theoretical.

Then the psalm moves to the topic of creation in verse 6 and stretches that subject out to the beautiful metaphors and language of the remainder of the psalm.

Creation:
Who formed the mountains by your
        power,
    having armed yourself with
        strength,

who stilled the roaring of the seas,
    the roaring of their waves,
    and the turmoil of the nations.
        (65:6–7)

We should inform our audience that, in the Psalms, creation and redemption are closely linked. The reason, at least in part, is that only the Creator can redeem. So when the Redeemer steps onto the stage of a biblical text, the Creator is waiting backstage to step forth at the proper time, and vice versa.

For New Testament believers, it is always appropriate to ask what the connections of this text are to the faith of the New Testament. That was a question the apostles always had in mind, and it is appropriate for us as well. The expansive plan God had before he created the world included redemption, or we might say God's eternal plan of redemption included creation. There is a Jewish saying that one should carry two stones in one's pocket. On one stone should be written, "I am but dust and ashes," and on the other, "For my sake was the world created," and one should use each stone as one needs it. In a sense, our psalmist, by beginning with redemption and proceeding to creation, is expressing a similar thought. God's forgiveness of his sins has triggered a powerfully beautiful essay on God's creation of the world.

This relationship became a major feature of New Testament theology. Paul says that God has chosen us in Christ "before the foundation of the world, that we should be holy and without blame before him in love" (Eph. 1:4 KJV). He has this mystery in mind as he admonishes his young disciple Timothy not to be ashamed of the testimony about the Lord but to "share in the suffering of the gospel by the power of God, who saved us and called us to a holy calling, not because of our works *but because of his own purpose and grace, which he gave us in Christ Jesus before the ages began*" (2 Tim. 1:8b–9 ESV, emphasis added). And Peter declares that God made provision for our redemption through Christ's precious blood "before the creation of the world" (1 Pet. 1:19–20). John also speaks of "the Lamb slain from the foundation of the world" (Rev. 13:8 KJV; see also 17:8). That means that *grace* or *redemption* was an eternal reality, and it also means that creation presupposes redemption. Or to put it another way, when we meet the Creator of the world in Genesis 1 and 2, we are meeting the Redeemer of the world, the one who forgives our sins. Indeed, the fact that God has redemption in mind is already evident in Genesis 3:15, when the Lord promises that the woman's offspring will crush the serpent's head. This has long been seen as a messianic prophecy that Christ fulfilled. Truly this world is incredibly beautiful and marvelously designed, but the wonder of wonders is grace.

Creation is something we all have in common, and if we understand that grace is built into the order of creation, then we are confronted anew with the God of the universe, who is not only Creator but also Redeemer, who not only formed the mountains but forgives our sins. David can begin Psalm 65 by talking about grace and then, without apology, transition to the topic of creation. While the suppliant did not have the advantage of the wide biblical understanding that we gratefully have, he understood that grace and creation belong together. That link helped to set the stage for the New Testament attestation of God's eternal decree of redemption.

God's wonders are extolled by reflecting on his creative power in the past as well as his current abundant provision. The "valleys are mantled with grain" (65:13) in this photo of wheat fields in Israel.

Illustrating the Text

Overwhelmed by sin

Church History: The Reformer Martin Luther struggled greatly with his sins before "discovering" grace in the book of Romans. Luther would sometimes confess his sins for as long as six hours at a time, and still he was frightened that he had more sins to confess. It appears, at that time, Luther could relate to David's words in Psalm 65:3, "When we were overwhelmed by sins . . ." Luther reflected on discovering grace in Romans:

> Night and day I pondered until I saw the connection between the justice of God and the statement that "the just shall live by his faith." Then I grasped that the justice of God is that righteousness by which through grace and sheer mercy God justifies us through faith. Thereupon I felt myself to be reborn and to have gone through open doors into paradise.[8]

Both David and Luther provide instruction to us about the importance of understanding the gravity and scope of our sin, and this understanding underlies the marvel of grace.

"When we were overwhelmed by sins, you forgave our transgressions" (65:3). Martin Luther came to realize this truth as he spent hours in prayers of confession and studying God's Word. This portrait of Luther is a reproduction of a painting by Lucas Cranach the Elder (AD 1525).

The centripetal power of grace

Bible: There are basically two models of missionary activity in the Psalms and the Prophets: (1) the centrifugal, which portrays Israel as radiating its light to the nations (Isa. 42:6) and dispatching its emissaries with the good news of salvation (Isa. 52:7–10); and (2) the centripetal, which portrays the nations of the world drawn to Israel by the sheer magnetic force of her God and the good news of salvation (Isa. 66:22–24; Ps. 47:9). The Christian church, basically answering the Great Commission to "go and make disciples of all nations" (Matt. 28:19–20), has generally emphasized the first model over the second. But the second has its merits and its prominence in the Psalms, as here in 65:2: "To you all people will come." The attraction seems to be the overpowering grace of forgiveness demonstrated in Israel's history (65:3), perhaps linking to the saving news of 64:9. God's works on Israel's behalf benefit the world as well, pointing certainly in the direction of the cross and its universal saving power. The church's task is to engage both models of grace, recognizing that the dynamics of each are different.

God's grace is sovereign.

News Story: In 1992, a cargo ship hit rough seas, and several shipping containers were washed overboard. One container holding twenty-eight thousand plastic bath toys broke open, and the toys began to float in the Pacific; some of them found their way to Alaska, South America, and even the Arctic. About two thousand toys were caught in a vortex of currents, creating a floating, plastic trash heap. Some of the toys periodically break away and end up finding a shore. But the rubber toys do not just break themselves free. Rather, it takes an event of nature—a storm, a shift in winds, or an act of marine life—to enable the toys to break free of the vortex.[9] This story provides a picture of God's sovereign grace and the connection with creation. Left to ourselves, we would be forever caught in the consequences of our sin. But the sovereign God who created the universe does for us what we could never do for ourselves, not leaving us to founder helplessly in our despair but breaking us free from our bondage. We are set free from the power of sin and death through the eternal power of the cross of Jesus Christ. The psalmist exults in this power of grace, "When we were overwhelmed by sins, you forgave our transgressions" (v. 3).

"Come and See What God Has Done"

Big Idea *God's redeeming work in our lives is the extension of his great redeeming acts in history.*

Understanding the Text

This psalm appears to be a hybrid of a hymn, a community psalm of thanksgiving, and an individual psalm of thanksgiving.[1] It only hints at the adversity that has prompted the psalmist to make and pay his vows of thanksgiving to God in the temple ("when I was in trouble," 66:14). This hint, though nothing more than that, takes its place parallel to Israel's trial in Egypt, which he likens to "prison" and going through "fire and water" (66:11–12).

Some believe the psalm is composed of two independent psalms (66:1–12 and 66:13–20). A. A. Anderson resolves the problem by proposing that the second part of the poem is spoken by the king and that the entire psalm is a national thanksgiving after some unspecified victory.[2]

The Text in Context

In a collection of Davidic psalms (with the exception of Psalms 50; 66; 67; and 71), the editor of Book 2 evidently sees thematic reasons for including Psalms 66 and 67 in the collection. To make the connection smoother, he grouped them in a minicollection of psalms that became Psalms 65–68, all now sharing the two terms "a psalm" (*mizmor*) and "a song" (*shir*) in their titles.[3] There are verbal links between Psalms 65 and 66, which may have assisted the editor in his decision:

Links	Psalm 65	Psalm 66
"Your house/temple"	65:4	66:13
Fulfill vows	65:1	66:13
Prayers	65:2	66:18–20
Awesome deeds	65:5	66:3, 5
Universal perspective	65:2	66:1, 4, 8

Within the context of the Hebrew Bible, Psalm 66 radiates the blessing to the world that God promised through Abraham (Gen. 12:2–3). Even though it begins with a universal perspective, the summons to "come and see what God has done" (66:5) is a call to see the awesome deeds he performed when he brought Israel out of Egypt and gave them the land of Canaan (66:6). Just as God has been faithful to Israel during their "prison" era and brought them "through fire and water" (66:11–12), he continues to be faithful to the psalmist, whose prayer God has not rejected, nor has God withheld his love from the psalmist (66:19–20).

Outline/Structure

One can make a case for three psalms within a psalm: a hymn (66:1–4), a community psalm of thanksgiving (66:5–12), and an individual psalm of thanksgiving (66:13–20). Both thanksgiving psalms contain reports of the crisis and the deliverance as an accomplished fact:

1. Hymn of praise (66:1–4)
2. Community psalm of thanksgiving (66:5–12)
   - Crisis: "You brought us into prison" (66:11–12b)
   - Deliverance: "You brought us to a place of abundance" (66:12c)
3. Individual psalm of thanksgiving (66:13–20)
   - Crisis: "When I was in trouble" (66:14b)
   - Deliverance: "But God has surely listened and has heard my prayer" (66:19–20)

It is my opinion that the three poems, however, rather than being independent, radiate with blessing from the center of God's covenant with Israel: to the world (66:1–4, 8), to Israel (66:11–12), and to the psalmist (66:16–20). Not mentioned as such, the covenant is attested in the redemptive events of the exodus and the entrance into Canaan (66:6). If the poems were originally independent, they are now artfully integrated into a whole.

Historical and Cultural Background

The historical setting of Psalm 66 is not at all clear. A. A. Anderson suggests that it could have been composed to celebrate a great military victory, but the military language is missing.[4] There is also the possibility that, like Psalm 65, it celebrated one of the agricultural festivals, and that

In this psalm of thanksgiving, the listeners are told to "come and see what God has done" (66:5). It then recounts when God parted the waters so that the Israelites could walk on dry ground. This may allude to the crossing of the Red Sea, which is depicted in this illumination from a *machzor* (AD 1466), a Jewish prayer book used during the major Jewish festivals.

Psalms 65 and 66 were considered complementary. That is, Psalm 65 celebrates God's creation of the world, and Psalm 66 God's redemption of Israel, with both of them in a complementary relationship celebrating God's faithfulness to his people, Israel, and to the world he promised to bless through Abraham's offspring.

Verse 11 contains a gem of a metaphor, obscured by the NIV's "and laid burdens on our backs." It is literally "and laid afflictions on our loins," which suggests the practice of captors who would tie ropes around their prisoners' loins to minimize their mobility.

The psalm gives some clarity to another picture, that of temple sacrifice: whole burnt offerings, rams, bulls, and goats (66:13–15). The list is not intended to be complete but most probably to represent the sacrificial system generally.

Interpretive Insights

Title *A song. A psalm.* See Psalm 65 for the same designations "song" and "psalm" in the title.

66:1 *Shout for joy to God, all the earth!* The call to worship is duplicated in Psalms 98:4 and 100:1, except for the use in those later instances of the divine name (*YHWH*).

66:3 *How awesome are your deeds! . . . your enemies cringe before you.* The word "how" (*mah*) is an exclamation (Ps. 8:1, 9) and implies, in this case, intensity. Here, and in Psalms 18:44 (= 2 Sam. 22:45; NIV: "cower") and 81:15, the verb "cringe" (Piel, *khsh*) denotes "unwilling homage."[5] The idea is that God's enemies are aware of his power, and just to escape its grip, they feign obedience (see NASB). In that

spirit, the earth's obeisance in 66:4 may also have a tinge of hypocrisy. Paul's quotation of Isaiah 45:23 in Romans 14:11 implies, as does Isaiah, that not all knees that bow to God in ultimate submission are bowing in believing faith, but some bow in forced surrender to the omnipotent God.

66:4 *they sing praise to you.* The verb "sing praise" (*zmr*) can mean to make music or sing to the accompaniment of an instrument.

66:5 *Come and see what God has done.* Having addressed the whole world, the psalmist now turns to his more immediate audience, Israel, before he again addresses "all people" in verse 8.

66:6 *He turned the sea into dry land.* The crossings of the Red Sea (Exod. 14:21–22; 15:19) and the Jordan River (Josh. 3:14–17) are in mind here, since he mentions both the "sea" and the "river" (NIV: "waters"). The details of dry land and passing over on foot are the same in both accounts. These are the only incidents from God's "awesome deeds" that our writer mentions, but it is enough. The final clause of the verse begins with the adverb "there" (*sham*), which might suggest that the event was celebrated at that place or perhaps reactualized in the sanctuary. Yet the idea of reactualization is difficult to demonstrate from the psalmic literature, even though it has become a rather firm piece of the form-critical picture of worship.

66:7 *He rules forever by his power.* This may be an allusion to the last verse of the Song of the Sea: "The LORD reigns for ever and ever" (Exod. 15:18).

66:8–9 *Praise our God, all peoples.* Note the change to "our"/"us"/"we." This begins the community psalm of thanksgiving

(66:5–12). Verse 9 gives the reason that "all peoples" are justified in praising God, even though it relates to Israel's own history. It is out of that historical context that "all peoples" are called to praise God, and out of that context that they are blessed.

66:10 *For you, God, tested us; you refined us.* God's "testing" (*bhn*) is an allusion to the Egyptian bondage. Israel's four-hundred-year slavery in Egypt had the purpose of "refining" (*tsrp*), not punishing, them. The analogy is the metallurgical process of refining silver (see the comments on Ps. 26:2). The purpose of the refining process was to remove the impurities, a common metaphor used by the prophets (e.g., Isa. 48:10; Jer. 6:29; Zech. 13:9).

66:11 *You brought us into prison.* This is a further allusion to the Egyptian bondage.

66:12 *You let people ride over our heads . . . you brought us to a place of abundance.* The metaphor of "riding over" suggests that their enemies rode them like a horse ("over our heads").[6] The Hebrew word for "abundance" denotes rest,[7] here most likely used as an allusion to Canaan. The psalmist has skipped from Egypt to Canaan, having already alluded to the Red Sea and the Jordan River in 66:6.

66:14 *vows my lips promised.* This continues the promise of 66:13 to fulfill his vows and provides a brief commentary on vow making, which is often done in a time of trouble.

66:15 *I will sacrifice fat animals to you and an offering of rams . . . bulls and goats.* Here the person changes from "you" (God) to "I" (the psalmist or the king). The word for "goats" can mean male sheep or goats (Gen. 31:10). If the speaker is the king, then this abundance of animal sacrifices would

The Hebrew Oath

In the Old Testament an oath consists of the *condition*, introduced by "if" ('*im*), followed by the *curse* that should result if the oath is not kept. Psalm 137:5 contains the full form of the oath, both condition and curse:

- Condition: "If I forget you, Jerusalem,"
- Curse: "may my right hand forget its skill."

Generally, Old Testament oaths have the condition but not the curse. This means the condition, if positive, has to be translated as a negative, and, if negative, as a positive. When David calls Uriah from the battlefield and orders him to go home and enjoy his wife on this brief furlough, Uriah refuses and takes an oath, which reads literally: "If I do this thing." From the form one can see that the curse is missing, which means that this positive condition must be translated: [I swear that] "I will not do this thing" (2 Sam. 11:11).

The Israelites knew the consequences of invading armies. Rushing into battle, troops with their horses and chariots could trample those who opposed them. On this Neo-Hittite orthostat from Carchemish, an archer in a chariot rides "over the head" (cf. 66:12) of his enemy (950–850 BC).

Psalm 66

pose no problem, for he had large flocks. It could also be a general reference to the sacrificial system.

66:16 *all you who fear God*. The psalmist is addressing the congregation, or Israel in general.

66:17 *I cried out to him*. The Hebrew begins with "to him" to emphasize that it is to the Lord, and to no one else, that he cries. Goldingay observes that in the Old Testament, calling on God when one is in trouble is a form of praise.[8] That is, the parallel lines in verse 17 bring together the experiences of petition and praise. The suppliant has "cried out" to God from his distress, and in the parallel line he asserts that this was praise. These acts of prayer appear to be not in succession but in synonymy. It indicates a recognition that God is the one to look to for help, not other deities or foreign allies.

66:18 *If I had cherished sin*. The verse reads literally, "As for iniquity, if I had seen (it) in my heart, the Lord would not hear (me)." The psalmist is somewhat self-reflective and has not detected sinful motives in his heart. This is an oath that he has sworn to establish his innocence.

66:19 *but God has surely listened*. Here is the answer as an accomplished fact, a typical feature of the psalms of thanksgiving. Compare this to the affirmation that in the historical perspective of the Egyptian bondage, God has preserved their lives (66:9). In view of that, God's attention to the psalmist's prayer is a repetition of his saving action in Israel's history.

66:20 *Praise be to God, who has not rejected my prayer or withheld his love from me!* Unanswered prayer was believed to be a sign of God's displeasure. The main verb

governs both "my prayer" and "his love," giving us the sense: "who has not turned aside my prayer and his love from me."

Theological Insights

In its call to "all the earth" (66:1, 4) and "all peoples" (66:8), this psalm exhibits a universal offer of relationship with Israel's God. It is not a theology that has a legitimacy of its own apart from Israel's, but rather it is tied to God's covenant with Israel, enunciated in the redemptive events of the exodus from Egypt and the entrance into the promised land. Behind the story of Israel in miniature is the blessing of the nations that God promised through Abraham and his descendants (Gen. 12:2–3).

Psalm 66 is a psalm of thanksgiving made when sacrifices were brought to fulfill a vow made during adversity (66:14).[9] The historical review of the Red Sea and the Jordan River (66:6) and the Egyptian bondage (66:10–12) is intended to say that just as God was faithful in those circumstances to deliver Israel, he will be faithful again in the present circumstance,[10] extending to Israel and the individual psalmist.

When our psalmist prays, "If I had cherished sin in my heart, the Lord would not have listened" (66:18), he immediately follows with the declaration that God has indeed listened and answered his prayer (66:19). This raises the question of whether God answers the prayers of sinners. Calvin quips that those are the only kind of prayers God answers, because we are all sinners. What the psalmist refers to is the condition of his heart, or we might say, the sincerity of his heart, his outward conduct as it corresponds to his inner motives.[11] This seems to be the gist of Paul's statement in

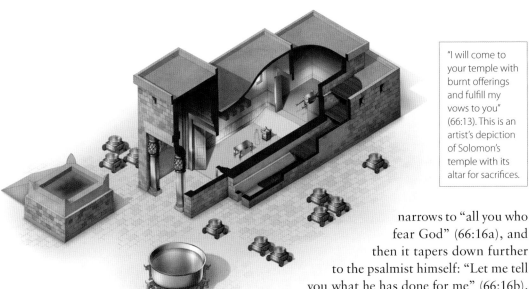

2 Timothy 2:19: "Everyone who confesses the name of the Lord must turn away from wickedness."

Teaching the Text

This psalm provides a pattern of faith that is laid out in the canonical Hebrew Scriptures. They begin with all humankind, narrow down to the elect family of Abraham and his descendants, and eventually generate a personal piety represented by the Psalms. Psalm 66 lays out that order of development, which is not to suggest that the psalmist was a historian; rather, this pattern was a reflection of his understanding of God's work in history. This detail will be no problem as we build our lesson, nor should it be a problem in the development of a sermon, if the point is to assist our listeners in seeing God's work of grace in the spectrum of history.

The poem begins wide—"all the earth" (66:1) and "all peoples" (66:8)—and narrows to "all you who fear God" (66:16a), and then it tapers down further to the psalmist himself: "Let me tell you what he has done for me" (66:16b). To further support this observation, we may draw attention to the grammatical persons. First, the second-person plural imperative occurs ten times (66:1, 2 [2x], 3, 5 [2x], 8 [2x], 16 [2x]), addressing "all the earth" (66:1–3), "all peoples" (66:8), "all you who fear God" (66:16), and perhaps both the universal audience and Israel in verse 5, with one instance of the first-person plural cohortative ("let us rejoice," 66:6c). Second, these imperatives are interspersed with the second person, "you," applied to God (66:3–4, 10–15). Three times God is addressed directly, once by "all the earth" (66:3–4), once by Israel (66:10–12), and once by the psalmist (66:13–15), again illustrating the pattern. Third, the last movement of the poem (66:13–20) is dominated by the first person, "I." As noted, the audience is wide at first and then narrows to Israel and finally to the worshiper himself. This pattern helps us see how we personally fit into God's larger program of grace, and how God is concerned with the whole world and with individuals too.

A second phase of the lesson or sermon may follow the lines of the imperative

Psalm 66

"come," issuing two invitations. First, "*Come* and see *what God has done, his awesome deeds for mankind!*" (66:5) evidently is addressed to the widest audience, all humankind. Immediately then the psalmist rehearses the miracle at the Red Sea (66:6). While we should not read too much Christian theology into this text, it certainly seems to suggest that this event, though peculiar to Israel's history, was in the larger divine plan also performed on behalf of the whole of humanity (*b^ene 'adam*, "mankind," 66:5). Second, after rehearsing God's wonderful deeds in Israel's history (66:5–12), the psalmist moves into personal thanksgiving and reissues his invitation, rehearsing his own personal story, "*Come* and hear, all you who fear God; let me tell you *what he has done for me*" (66:16). The nation's story has become the psalmist's own story. It is quite appropriate by way of application to draw a parallel and say that in Christianity, the church's story must become the individual's story. Moreover, we can make the observation that the last step in this architectural design is God's actions on the individual's behalf, representing a personal faith that is attested by Psalm 1 and many subsequent witnesses.

Illustrating the Text

All the earth bows down to the Lord.

Nature: In Psalm 66:4, the psalmist proclaims that "all the earth bows down to you; they sing praise to you, they sing the praises of your name." Notice that this is a statement and not a command. In other words, this is an observation the psalmist makes with regard to nature. For example, consider the oak tree, of which there are approximately six hundred species. Oak trees typically have spirally arranged leaves, but some have serrated leaves, and still others have leaves with smooth margins. Many of the species do not drop dead leaves until the spring, as opposed to the fall. The flowers are produced in the spring, and the fruit is a nut called an acorn.[12] Imagine the creativity of the God who made each species of oak tree and each individual tree. These trees bow to the Lord and worship him by being everything God created them to be. As you observe nature, look carefully to see how everything he made praises him. In the same way, God created each individual person different and unique. And we praise him by being what God created us to be as we live in obedience to his design and purpose.

God's care of the world and of each person at the same time

Quote: Augustine. It is difficult for us to understand how God can care for the world he made and care as passionately for each individual who makes up that world. While

Augustine provides no explanation for this phenomenon, he recognizes the truth when he prays: "O omnipotent Good, you who care for each one of us as though he was your only care and who cares for all of us as though we were all just one person."[13] This truth touches on the mystery of God's love and the mystery of God. Psalm 66 summons corporate Israel to "come and see what God has done" *for humanity* (v. 5) and then issues a call to "come and hear, all you who fear God; let me tell you what he has done *for me*" (v. 16).

Vows are important.

Cultural Institution: According to divorce statistics from 2013, the actual rate of divorce in America approaches 50 percent of all marriages.[14] Add to this statistic that it is estimated that between 30 and 60 percent of all married men in the United States will engage in infidelity at some point during their marriage. With women the infidelity rate is between 20 and 50 percent.[15] However, in almost every wedding ceremony the couple makes a commitment, a vow, to be faithful to each other for life. The state of the institution of marriage in America is an indication of the reality that many people do not take their vows seriously. Rather, many utter these vows while at the same time thinking, "as long as something better doesn't come along." It is important that we reclaim the seriousness of vows. As we read in Numbers 30:2, "When a man makes a vow to the LORD or takes an oath to obligate himself by a pledge, he must not break his word but must do everything he said." We see the seriousness of vows in Psalm 66:13–14. While marriage vows and religious vows are different, the former made between spouses before God and the latter made directly to God the gravity of both is essentially the same—they are to be kept, for ultimately God is the one we are accountable to.

"May All the Peoples Praise You"

Big Idea As the nations see God's equitable judgment and guidance in the life of Israel, they will come to acknowledge his sovereignty.

Understanding the Text

Judging from its first-person plural pronouns ("us"), this psalm is a community psalm of thanksgiving.[1] Hakham calls it a psalm of thanksgiving for an abundant harvest.[2] Israel acknowledges God's blessings and prays for their extension, even salvation to the nations of the world (67:2, 7).

The Text in Context

Psalm 66 ends with a word of blessing ("Blessed [*baruk*] be God"; NIV: "Praise be to God"; 66:20), and Psalm 67 begins with a prayer of blessing in language akin to the priestly benediction. While the priestly benediction (Num. 6:24–26) was given to Israel by a priest ("The LORD make his face shine on *you* and be gracious to *you*"), here it is transferred to the lips of the people ("May God be gracious to *us* and bless *us* and make his face shine on *us*," 67:1). The people are praying for themselves and the nations, acting in the priestly role of a "kingdom of priests" (Exod. 19:6) that Yahweh assigned them at Sinai. Yet, unlike the prophets, they never address the nations directly, but they refer to the nations only indirectly ("the peoples," "the nations"),

for in their priestly (not prophetic) role they are praying *for* the nations.

This prayer of blessing belongs to two strands of Old Testament theology. One is the blessing God gives to the world through Abraham and his descendants (Gen. 12:2–3), and the other is Yahweh's deliverance of Israel from exile, which becomes a witness to the world that God reigns (Isa. 40–55).[3] Note how God's blessing on Israel ("us") becomes a literary *inclusio*, occurring at the beginning of the psalm (67:1) and at the end (67:6–7). It is in this context of blessing that the nations will come to salvation (see Gen. 12:2–3).

Wilson draws attention to the developing theme of universal salvation that stretches through Psalms 56–68 (61:2; 65:5) and reaches a climax in Psalm 67 with the salvation of the nations (67:2, 7), positioning the reader for the celebration observed in Psalm 68.[4]

Outline/Structure

Psalm 67 has a well-balanced structure, with the refrain (67:3 and 5) and the middle verse (67:4) bearing the thematic weight. The refrain highlights the universal theme of the psalm, that "all the peoples" praise God, and verse 4 as the center verse (excluding the title) gives the reason why the nations can and ought to sing God's praise so joyfully: God rules the peoples justly and guides them like a shepherd, just as he does Israel. This is a virtual admittance to the covenant family. Excluding the title, the outline forms a chiasm, with verses 3–5 constituting the main theme of the psalm.[5]

A Israel's prayer for blessing that leads the nations to salvation (67:1–2)
    B Refrain (67:3)
        C Reason for nations' praising God (67:4)
    B′ Refrain (67:5)
A′ Israel's acknowledgment of blessing that leads the nations to salvation (67:6–7)

Historical and Cultural Background

Some interpreters insist that this psalm is postexilic because of the universal perspective that the nations will come to saving faith (67:2, 7). However, the salvation of the nations is not necessarily a postexilic idea in the Old Testament. Israel, in the Babylonian exile and early postexile, came to see salvation's new dimensions and possibilities and embraced the salvation of the nations as part of their theological platform, but it was, to some extent, woven into the fabric of Old Testament theology prior to that.

Interpretive Insights

Title *With stringed instruments.* The phrase "with stringed instruments"

(*bin⁽ᵉ⁾ginot*) occurs in the titles of Psalms 4; 6; 54; 55; 67; and 76, with a variant form in Psalm 61 (see the comments on the title for Ps. 4).

67:1 *May God . . . make his face shine on us.* This verse is a hint of the priestly benediction (Num. 6:24–25). The shining of God's "face" is associated with God's favor, manifested in deliverance, redemption, and salvation (Pss. 31:16; 80:1, 3, 7, 19; 118:27).[6] The priestly benediction became a stylized way of reiterating God's blessings on Israel. It is certainly not necessary to date the psalm in the postexilic era, as some do, based on the assumption that the priestly benediction was a later literary development. Quite to the contrary, the priestly benediction was discovered on a silver amulet in Ketef Hinnom in Jerusalem, dated in the seventh–sixth centuries BC.[7]

67:2 *so that your ways may be known on earth,*

The language of the priestly blessing in Numbers 6:25 is used when the people sing, may God "make his face shine on us" (67:1). This tiny silver scroll, seventh to sixth century BC, found at Ketef Hinnom in Jerusalem contains the same phrase from Aaron's benediction.

your salvation among all nations. God's blessing on Israel will result in his ways becoming known to the world. This is another way to phrase the Abrahamic blessing: "I will bless those who bless you, and whoever curses you I will curse; and all peoples on earth will be blessed through you" (Gen. 12:3). Psalm 66 calls the nations to praise God because of what he has done for Israel. Now Psalm 67 goes a step further and announces God's salvation for the nations (see also 1 Chron. 16:23; Pss. 74:12; 98:3; Isa. 26:18; 45:8; 49:6; 52:10).

67:3 *May the peoples praise you, God.* The verb "praise" (= "to give thanks") has a double meaning, to praise and to accept God's authority.[8] Three words are used for the nations, quite synonymously: "nations" (*goyim*, 67:2), "peoples" (*'ammim*, 67:3, 4, 5), and "countries" (*le'ummim*, 67:4; NIV: "nations"). However,

in the Old Testament generally the preferred word for Israel is *'am*, and for the nations, *goyim*. The clear distinction is found in Numbers 23:9, yet the two terms sometimes interchange (e.g., Isa. 1:4).

67:4 *for you rule the peoples . . . and guide the nations of the earth.* Verse 4, sandwiched between the two occurrences of the refrain (67:3 and 5), gives reasons that all the peoples should praise the Lord—God judges (NIV: "rules") the peoples equitably and "guides" (*nhh*) them, just as he does Israel (a shepherd's guidance; see Ps. 23:3b: "he leads [*nhh*] me in paths of righteousness" [ESV]).

67:5 *may all the peoples praise you.* The word "all," occurring in the second half of the verse, reinforces and strengthens the first half, "May the peoples praise you, God." After verse 4, with its explanation of God's just rule in the world and his guidance of the nations as he guides Israel, the refrain of verse 5, being reinforced by those benefits, has all the more power and validation.

Theological Insights

Psalm 67 focuses the reader's attention on the broad horizons of the world, calling the nations not merely to submit to God's power but to acknowledge his grace. While we cannot be certain that the international aspects of Psalm 66 have a saving connotation, there is no

This psalm of thanksgiving and call to praise was to be accompanied by stringed instruments. The harp, lute, and lyre were some of the stringed instruments used. These plaques from Mesopotamia show two different styles of harp and a lute being played.

doubt that Psalm 67 foresees the salvation of the nations (67:2, 7). Knowing God's ways is the sure path to salvation, or better, the two are the same. We do not see the nations gathering in Jerusalem to acknowledge Yahweh as God, but the prayer is to that effect. The appeal is not to them but to God, who makes known his salvation to the nations (67:2).

With God's shining face ("make his face shine on us," 67:1), this psalm illuminates the landscape of grace and, like a sudden flash of lightning, exposes its extremities. One, of course, is "salvation" (67:2), which is the highest peak of the topography of grace, and in this case, all the more "amazing" grace because it is the salvation of the nations. At the other end of the landscape the shining face of God lights up the harvest (67:6), which, in Old Testament theology, is one of the most important manifestations of God's blessing. When Amos, for example, wants to describe the eschatological day of grace, he paints the picture of a harvest that is so abundant that it can hardly be gathered before the plowman breaks the ground for a new planting (Amos 9:13). One harvest overtakes another. Weiser sees the eschatological significance of the "harvest" in verse 6 and comments: "The temporal things become the promise of the things that are eternal."[9] This cosmic transaction that God effects among the nations causes them to break into joyful singing (67:4). "Salvation" is God's grace more absolutely, while the "harvest" is only a manifestation of it, but both appear under the illuminating face of God.

Teaching the Text

Perhaps we ought to begin this sermon/lesson by observing that the world of nations has become, in our world, a community of peoples, and the church is called to speak to this community. We might also observe the international perspective of the Old Testament faith by citing God's promise that Abraham's descendants would be a blessing to all peoples on earth (Gen. 12:2–3) and Isaiah's summary phrase of that role, "a light to the nations" (Isa. 42:6 RSV).

As we speak about the message of this psalm, we can utilize our international knowledge and connectedness to our advantage in order to bring our audience into the international context of the psalm. In our concern for the salvation of the nations, we should observe the perspective of this psalm: God does not expect them to acknowledge his lordship blindly, but he gives historical and visible evidence that he is Lord and worthy to be worshiped. That is the sense of verse 2: "so that your ways may be known on earth, your salvation among all nations." As we observed in Psalm 66, it is the historical evidence of God's deliverance of Israel from Egypt, particularly the triumphs at the Red Sea and the Jordan River (66:6–12), that provides the basis for the call for "all the earth" to acknowledge Yahweh's lordship ("Come and see what God has done," 66:5). This theme is struck also among the Canaanites after the miracle at the Jordan River (Josh. 5:1), even though it is not a saving fear of God. This is ultimately, however, what the psalmist prays for, "that all the ends of the earth *will fear him*" (67:7).

Expository preaching/teaching often requires an application of other texts of Scripture that support the one we are dealing with. This, however, must be done carefully and discreetly, lest we engage in mere proof-texting rather than sound exposition. In this regard, we may mention that in Isaiah 40–55 the nations see Yahweh's miraculous rescue of Judah from the Babylonian exile, and they acknowledge that he is in control of the world. These were the invisible footprints of God in history (Ps. 77:19). They saw the physical manifestations but did not see God. Yet that was enough, at least enough to recognize God's ruling sovereignty. His saving sovereignty is another matter. Paul's quotation of Isaiah 45:23 in Romans 14:11 and in Philippians 2:10–11, "that at the name of Jesus every knee should bow, in heaven and on earth and under the earth, and every tongue acknowledge that Jesus Christ is Lord, to the glory of God the Father," may involve confessions of both God's ruling sovereignty and his saving sovereignty.

Psalm 67 presents us with two ways by which God makes himself known to the world and proves that the nations can trust him: (1) his miraculous ways manifested in history (exodus, etc.), and (2) the blessing of the harvest. They obviously fall into two different categories, one miraculous and the other natural. First, God proclaims Israel's "salvation [exodus] among all nations" (67:2), by which the world is to know his "ways." Second, he blesses with an abundant harvest (67:6).

It is imperative that we seek to recognize God both in his miraculous revelations in history (the exodus, the return from exile, the cross, and the resurrection) and in the natural blessings of our lives. These are God's "professional credentials." We sometimes call this "providence," and theologically we can say that God manifests his eternal reality of grace in the harvest. Yet we should not claim that the two manifestations of grace are qualitatively equal, but they are *God's* grace, and that is the mark of identification that makes all the difference.

Illustrating the Text

Ministry for the world

Christian Organization: There are many organizations that exist to bring the message of salvation through faith in Jesus Christ to the ends of the earth. One such organization is Wycliffe Bible Translators. The organization was founded by William Townsend, a missionary to the Cakehiquel Indians of Guatemala. Townsend caught the vision for his organization when the men of the tribe expressed their concern and surprise that God did not speak their language. Wycliffe's vision is to make "God's word accessible to all people in the language of their hearts." The organization has completed more than seven hundred translations, and hundreds more are in process. Wycliffe is just one of many organizations committed to bringing the gospel to the ends of the earth.[10] This would be a great opportunity to share with your listeners what your church is doing to fulfill the Great Commission (Matt. 28:18–20).

The idolatry of the human spirit

Cultural Trends: Our world poses a great challenge as the church prays with the psalmist, "so that your ways may be known on earth" (v. 2). On August 22, 2012, the *Chicago Tribune* published an article on people who want to have faith but do not want any of the traditional teachings of Judaism and Christianity. "The idea of god in their home is not the Holy Trinity or the Jewish God of Abraham, Isaac and Jacob. Instead, it resides in the concepts of home and community, and a transcendence of the human spirit."[11] Some polls are saying that America is becoming less religious. A WIN-Gallup International poll claims that the number of people who are "religious" (an interesting term in itself) dropped from 73 percent in 2005 to 60 percent in 2012. The poll also found that 5 percent of Americans say they are atheists, which is up from 1 percent in 2005.[12] What is happening is a human inclination that is as old as Adam and Eve. It seeks to replace God with the human spirit. In one sense, we shouldn't be surprised to see people trying to invent their own religion—that's what humans have been doing since the beginning of time. Nor should we be surprised, by the power of grace, when "all the ends of the earth will fear him" (v. 7; Rev. 19:6).

It's not about us!

Story: The *Parable of the Life-Saving Station*, by Theodore Wedel (1953), was written to remind Christians not to lose their purpose. It would be helpful to read the story to your listeners or share it in your own words. The story is about a lifesaving station on a coast where there are a lot of shipwrecks. At first the little station is very effective in its mission to save those who have been shipwrecked. But over time, the crew members lose their vision and begin to exist simply for themselves. They think it would be better if they existed as just a club for themselves rather than to serve and save others. Some, still believing in the original purpose, go down the coast to build another lifesaving station. The parable ends with these words: "History continued to repeat itself, and if you visit that sea coast today, you will find a number of exclusive clubs along that shore. Shipwrecks are frequent in those waters, but most of the people drown."[13] Based on Psalm 67, it is hard to know to what extent Israel had developed a practical witness to the world of nations, but it is quite obvious that they had a vision of the world's salvation.

"When You Ascended on High, You Took Many Captives"

Big Idea *The story of God's redeeming grace gives us the sense of being present on the journey.*

Understanding the Text

There is no virtue in trying to make a difficult psalm sound easy. It is widely agreed that Psalm 68 is textually and theologically one of the most difficult psalms in the Psalter. Yet most scholars agree that there is a story line that stretches through the psalm, a condensed history of Israel—or we should probably say, of Yahweh's presence with Israel—from Egypt to Zion. The action on the stage is a divine drama, with only shadow figures of biblical persons playing their minor roles in the drama of victory, while Yahweh is the attested star of the drama.

The psalm does not fit any of the genre classifications that we use. Some have called it a song of victory, and others just refuse

Psalm 68 begins, "May God arise, . . . may his foes flee before him." This understanding that the gods fought on behalf of their people was common in the ancient world. This Assyrian relief shows enemy soldiers fleeing before Ashurnasirpal's chariot and his god Ashur, who is fighting alongside him (Nimrud, 865–860 BC).

to apply a genre label, which is probably the best approach. Hossfeld and Zenger suggest that it is composed of nine strophes, formed over a long period of time. To demonstrate the composite nature of the poem, they point to other Old Testament texts that have contributed to its formation: the ark saying in Numbers 10:35–36 (Ps. 68:1), the Song of Deborah in Judges 5 (Ps. 68:26, 35), Psalm 29, and the psalm of Deuteronomy 33:25, 26–29 that frames the Deuteronomy text.[1] Given the hints of a composite nature, the story line nevertheless has produced a succinct and quite beautiful narrative of salvation history.

The Text in Context

Wilson makes a case for Psalm 68 as the climax in a series of psalms (Pss. 65–68) sharing a call to praise God and a universal motif. The latter theme comes to its climax in Psalm 68 as we see Yahweh striding majestically from exodus out of Egypt to Jerusalem, sending his foes in flight, and finally taking up residence on Mount Zion.[2]

Paul quotes verse 18 in Ephesians 4:8, changing (1) the subject from God to Christ; (2) the collective "man" to "men"; and (3) the verb "received" to "gave":[3] "When he [Christ] ascended on high, he took many captives and gave gifts to his people" (Eph. 4:8). Whereas the psalm says God *took/received gifts* (evidently tribute from the conquered nations), in Ephesians Christ is the subject, and he *gave gifts* to human beings. What probably lies behind Paul's adaptation of the text is the tradition that produced the Targum of this psalm. While the *Targum of the Psalms* may likely fall somewhere between the fourth and sixth centuries AD,[4] the Babylonian

- God's presence in Israel's history and ours is pervasive.
- God's promenade of redemption begins in Egypt and ends in Jerusalem.

Talmud (*Megillah* 21b) mentions an Aramaic translation of the Psalms, thus suggesting an earlier Aramaic tradition. In any event, Paul's changes may reflect the Aramaic tradition that came to be encrypted in the extant *Targum of the Psalms*. This tradition (or some would say Paul himself) changed the Hebrew verb "took" to the Aramaic "gave" and interpreted Psalm 68:18 in terms of Moses's ascension to heaven to receive the Torah, which he then gave to Israel. In Paul's theology, the Receiver of gifts (God) has become the Giver of gifts (Christ; Eph. 4:11–13). David summons the "kings of the earth" to join in Israel's song: "Sing to God, you kingdoms of the earth, sing praise to the Lord, to him who rides across the highest heavens, the ancient heavens [lit., "heavens of the ancient heavens"]" (68:32–33). The Jewish reader of the first century could hardly miss the messianic clue contained in the "heavens of the ancient heavens," and Paul echoes this idea when he describes Christ as the one "who ascended higher than all the heavens" (Eph. 4:10).

Outline/Structure

The heart of Psalm 68 is the compact salvation history found in verses 7–35, a quick series of snapshots from the exodus to the establishment of the sanctuary on Mount Zion in Jerusalem. There are three strophes (enclosed in brackets below) in the psalm that sound like a commentary on Israel's present situation, evidently a military crisis, and apply Yahweh's saving story to it. We may divide the psalm into two parts (these are larger than the strophes):

1. An appeal for God's power against Israel's enemies, inspired by the words of Moses in Numbers 10:35 (68:1–6)
    a. Appeal (68:1–3)
    b. Summons to praise that identifies God as the Lord (*yah*), perhaps alluding to Moses's experience at the burning bush in Exodus 3:15 (68:4)
    c. The Lord further identified in terms of his social justice (68:5)
    d. The Lord further identified in terms of the historic justice of the exodus (68:6)
2. A brief history of Israel from Egypt to Jerusalem (68:7–35)
    a. Exodus and wilderness (68:7)
    b. Sinai (68:8)
    c. Settlement of Canaan (68:9–10)
    d. Celebration at the Red Sea (68:11)
    e. Israelite conquest (68:12–14)
    f. Mount Bashan jealous of Mount Zion as Israel marches toward the sanctuary in Jerusalem (68:15–16)
    g. The Lord's sweeping victory through Canaan on his way to the Jerusalem sanctuary (68:17–18)
    h. [Praise of God for bearing Israel's burdens and giving victory over his enemies (68:19–23)]
    i. God's victory procession into the Jerusalem sanctuary (68:24–27)
    j. [Prayer that God will repeat this victory march and defeat Israel's enemies (68:28–31)]
    k. [Summons to the nations to sing and proclaim the power of God (68:32–35)]

Historical and Cultural Background

Hakham suggests that the psalm was composed for a victory celebration and that the ark was carried in the procession. This would account for the opening words that are Moses's prayer in Numbers 10:35, when the ark was moved from one place to another.[5] The procession described in the psalm is reminiscent of David's procession that brought the ark from the house of Obed-Edom to Jerusalem with much rejoicing (2 Sam. 6:12).[6]

Interpretive Insights

68:1 *May God arise.* Except for the name *'elohim* ("God") and the pronouns "his" instead of "your," this is a virtual duplication of the ark saying in Numbers 10:35.

68:3–4 *may the righteous be glad . . . who rides on the clouds . . . his name is the* Lord. Four verbs for rejoice reinforce the idea: "be glad," "rejoice" (*'lts*), "be happy," and "rejoice" (*'lz*). There are also three verbs for "sing" in verse 4 ("sing," "sing in praise," "raise your voice" [NIV: "extol"]), adding up to seven verbs in all for making joyful worship, and that is the tone of the psalm. The descriptive clause "who rides in the clouds" suggests God's majesty and control of nature. A shortened form of the divine name Yahweh (*yah*) appears here, which is elsewhere attached to the praise verb "hallelujah" (ending "-jah" = *yah*). It also appears in Exodus 15:2 and Psalm 150:6 (twice) and is the final word in the Psalter.

68:5 *A father to the fatherless, a defender of widows, is God in his holy dwelling.* God is Father to those who have none, and the Judge who defends the claims of their widowed mothers. Since the verse describes God's work on behalf of the helpless in this world, we might assume "his holy dwelling" is the temple in Jerusalem.

68:6 *God sets the lonely in families.* "Lonely" (lit., "solitary ones") probably alludes to the Israelites in Egypt, and "in families" literally means "at home," a likely reference to Canaan.[7] Thus it is the story of the exodus and Canaan in miniature, as the rest of this verse and verses 7–14 attest: "He leads out the prisoners with singing."

68:7 *When you, God, went out before your people, when you marched through the wilderness.* The exodus is in view here, using words similar to Exodus 13:21–22. The verb "marched" may carry the nuance of Habakkuk 3:12, "to march vigorously" (NIV: "strode").[8]

68:7–35 Verses 7–35 are a virtual history of Israel from Egypt to the establishment of the sanctuary on Mount Zion. See "Outline/Structure."

68:8 *the earth shook, the heavens poured down rain.* The sheer weight of the Almighty as he walks through the land makes the earth shake. See Isaiah 64:1 for the imagery of the mountains shaking at God's presence. Perhaps the imagery of the rain is that the shaking of the earth caused the heavens to "drip" (*ntp*) rain.

68:9 *your weary inheritance.* The "inheritance" is the land of Canaan. The word "weary" is probably an allusion to Israel's forty years in the wilderness, after which the Lord refreshed them in Canaan with abundant showers.

The Lord led the Israelites out of Egypt and through the wilderness to the promised land. Shown here is the Wilderness of Zin, one of the locations for the Israelite wilderness wanderings recorded in Numbers.

68:10 *Your people settled in it . . . you provided for the poor.* In 2 Samuel 23:11, 13, the Hebrew word for "people" (*ḥayyah*) is used for a "group" (NIV: "band"). A better rendering here would be "your community." The "poor" (*'ani*) is likely a synonym for the "righteous," as in Zechariah 9:9 ("righteous and victorious, lowly [*'ani*] and riding on a donkey").

68:11 *The Lord announces the word, and the women who proclaim it.* The announcing of the word probably refers to God's decrees on Sinai. Isaiah 40:9 speaks of those who "bring good tidings" (*mᵉbasseret*; see NKJV) about the return of the exiles. Here the good news applies to the exodus. The NIV translates the feminine participle (*mᵉbassᵉrot*) as "women who proclaim," but in Isaiah 40:9 it is also feminine and may simply suggest their office as "announcers" of good tidings, just as the noun *qohelet* in Ecclesiastes 1:1 uses the feminine of office (cf. Ezra 2:55; Neh. 7:57). In that case, it may merely refer to the company of people in general who announce the good news.

68:12 *Kings and armies flee in haste; the women at home divide the plunder.* In the context, the "kings" are likely those whom Joshua defeated in the conquest. It is out of character for women to divide the spoil, a job that men normally do. Isaiah 3:12 depicts women ruling over Israel to suggest the unusual or for shock effect, which may be the sense here.

68:13 *while you sleep . . . sheathed with silver . . . with shining gold.* This difficult verse may be part of the speech of those who bear the good tidings: "After you return from battle, you will rest in peace among the sheepfolds."[9] The reference to wings of "silver" and feathers of "gold" may be part of the spoil.

68:14 *the Almighty scattered . . . it was like snow fallen on Mount Zalmon.* God's name "Almighty" (*shadday*), used by the patriarchs, appears in the Psalter only here and in Psalm 91:1. According to Judges 9:48, there was a Mount Zalmon near Shechem. Albright proposes that it is Jebel Druze, on the border of Bashan.[10] The region is known for its black volcanic basalt, perhaps connecting with the root of the word (*tslm*), which means "black."

68:15 *Mount Bashan.* Compared to Mounts Zalmon and Bashan, Zion is a little hill, but this is precisely where the Lord has chosen to dwell.

68:16 *why gaze in envy, you rugged mountain . . . ?* Israel marches toward Mount Zion, "the mountain where God chooses to reign," with God and his chariots leading the way and a retinue in accompaniment. I consider this to be an envious glance of Mount Bashan toward Zion, although some understand verse 15a to be a deriding rhetorical question: "Do you think Mount Bashan is the mountain of God!"[11] The question "why gaze in envy?" is answered by the last part of the verse. This is the place "where the LORD himself will dwell forever." Note the use of the divine name associated with his dwelling place (see Deut. 12).

68:17 *the Lord has come from Sinai into his sanctuary.* God's presence that once encircled Sinai has now moved to Mount Zion.

68:18 *ascended on high . . . received gifts . . . that you, LORD God, might dwell there.* The "ascended" probably refers to the ascending of the mountainous fortresses to take enemies captive as God made his way to Mount Zion in the promised land. The "gifts" are an act of submission on the part of the nations that God has taken captive. The trail of conquest that took the rebellious captive was for the purpose that God (*yah 'elohim*) might dwell on Mount Zion. See also "The Text in Context."

68:19 *Praise be to the Lord . . . who daily bears our burdens.* The Masoretic punctuation of the verse puts a major break after "day by day," connecting it with "Praise be to the Lord," rather than with the final clause as does the NIV ("who *daily* bears our burdens"), which would be literally: "the God of our salvation will load us generously" (with blessing).[12]

68:21 *the hairy crowns of those who go on in their sins.* This is a reference to Israel's enemies.

68:22 *I will bring them from the depths of the sea.* This is similar to Amos 9:3: "Though they hide themselves on the top of Carmel, there I will hunt them down and seize them. Though they hide from my eyes at the bottom of the sea, there I will command the serpent

to bite them." See Psalm 139:7–11 for another picture of people trying to escape from God.

68:23 *that your feet may wade in the blood of your foes.* See Psalm 58:10.

68:24 *Your procession, God.* This alludes back to verse 7, where God goes out before his people. It is the triumphal march from Egypt to Mount Zion.

68:25 *In front are the singers.* The procession is led by the choir in front, followed by the instrumentalists, and surrounded by girls beating drums or timbrels.

68:26 *Praise God in the great congregation.* These words appear to be those of the leader of the procession.

68:27 *the little tribe of Benjamin . . . Judah's princes . . . of Zebulun and of Naphtali.* "Benjamin" is the name of both the last son of Jacob (and Rachel) and the tribe that produced Israel's first king, Saul. Although no longer the "royal" tribe, this tribe still has the honor of leading the procession, perhaps because the city of Jerusalem was located in its tribal claim. The Davidic monarchy came from the tribe of Judah. The "princes" of Judah are the leaders of the tribe. Zebulun and Naphtali were located in

Captive nations present God with gifts. Five different nations are depicted bringing tribute to Shalmaneser III on this monument known as the Black Obelisk, which highlights his military accomplishments (858–824 BC).

the north. The mention of two northern and two southern tribes may be intended to suggest the whole of Israel.

68:28–30 *Summon your power, God . . . Rebuke the beast among the reeds.* This prayer grows out of Israel's historical experience and petitions God to repeat the work he has done in the past. It continues through verse 30 and anchors the homage of the kings in the importance of the temple in Jerusalem, where God has chosen to dwell (68:16). The animals here ("beast among the reeds") are symbols of God's and Israel's enemies. See Psalm 22:12 for "bulls of Bashan" (cf. 68:15, 22).

68:31 *Envoys will come from Egypt; Cush will submit herself to God.* The word for "envoys" occurs nowhere else in the Old Testament, and thus its meaning is in doubt. Other suggested meanings include "gifts," "noblemen," and "chariots."[13] Cush's submission to God is a further explication of verse 30 and the salvation of the nations predicted in Psalm 67:2. "Cush" is Egypt (Gen. 10:6; Isa. 20:3–5; 43:3).

68:33 *who rides across the highest heavens.* Similar to verse 4. Also see Psalms 18:9–10; 104:3.

68:35 *You, God, are awesome in your sanctuary.* The concluding picture of the psalm is God dwelling in his sanctuary in Jerusalem, his ultimate destination from the time he "went out before" his people from Egypt (68:7).

Theological Insights

Psalm 68 asserts the pervasive presence of God in two ways: first, in God's stride across the expanse of Israel's journey from Egypt to Mount Zion (see "Teaching the Text"); second, in the forty-two occurrences of God's names, including virtually all the significant names: God (*'elohim* and *'el*), Lord (*YHWH*), Lord (*'adonay*), Yah (shortened form of *YHWH*), and Almighty (*shadday*). In this way our artful writer tells us that God was with Israel all along their journey; in fact, it was basically *his* journey.

The occurrence of the divine names is not a literary coincidence but is code language to inform the reader that God is in Israel's history from the beginning to the end—he pervades it. Not only is God pervasive in Israel's history, connoted by his names, but he holds salvation history together in a pattern of victory, putting kings to flight (68:12) and taking bounty in his wake (68:18). This is further indicated by the initial prayer that is virtually lifted from Numbers 10:35, except that the name of the deity is *'elohim* rather than Yahweh, in keeping with the practice of the Elohistic Psalter. But we should make no mistake about it, "his name is the Lord [*yah*]" (68:4; see the comments on this verse, above). The prayer of Numbers both directs the ark's transfer and asks for the defeat of Israel's enemies. Both events are in view in the psalm, and both are necessary for the victory that is celebrated on Mount Zion at the end of God's victory march from Egypt to Mount Zion (68:24–27). While the ark is never mentioned in the psalm, it does seem to be in the mind's eye of the psalmist as he describes the procession to Mount Zion and Yahweh's dwelling in his sanctuary (68:1, 35). The two extremities of God's saving activities are the exodus and the establishment of the sanctuary on Mount Zion.

Teaching the Text

Sometimes we need to look more at the story line of our lives than at the individual episodes. John Newton was evidently looking at that long perspective when he wrote: "'Tis grace hath brought me safe thus far, And grace will lead me home."[14] Indeed, at times it is hard to understand the individual episodes of life in isolation without looking at the long perspective. We know this in many facets of our lives—business, education, marriage, and so on—because we are able to see the parts in light of the whole.

In a similar way, in Psalm 68 the journey across the geographical expanse is a story across the years. We may point out that the biblical faith is a historical faith that has geographical milestones representing God's landmarks for Israel. Here the psalmist maps out God's victory march of grace, the milestone markers being Egypt, Sinai, and Canaan, concluding with Zion (68:35a).

An important thing that the psalmist accomplishes is to carry the believer along the journey of grace. It is a log that reminds us of Luke's story of Christ's journey toward the cross (Luke 9:51–19:44). This grand tour of redemption is both beautiful and evocative, evoking sights of women proclaiming the word, armies fleeing in fear, singers and musicians celebrating the steady march to Zion, and the tribes in their appointed places. While the picture out of the suppliants' social world may be the triumphal procession, the psalm is a

Young women playing timbrels are part of the procession as God enters the sanctuary. These figurines from Achzib, eighth to seventh century BC, hold hand drum–style instruments.

review of Israel's salvation history, which the Christian church has, on the witness of Jesus and the apostles, adopted as its own. The readers have the sense of being carried along on this journey of grace, or, in another sense, of being grandstand observers of the redemptive events, and of taking a front-row-seat position in Zion's sanctuary. And the ultimate victory cry is "Praise be to God!" (68:35), while later saints rejoice in "so great a salvation" (Heb. 2:3). See "Illustrating the Text."

Illustrating the Text

"Tell me the old, old, story."

Quote: *Christ in the Psalms*, by Patrick Henry Reardon. In Christian interpretation,

Psalm 68 is commonly identified as strongly messianic. It is the "old, old story," [15] the church's history claimed and reclaimed from its Hebrew forebears. Reardon sums it up very well:

> Here we have the deeper, more authentic sense of the psalm: Jesus, the author and perfecter of our faith, arising from the dead ["May God arise," v. 1], triumphant over sin and death ["may his enemies be scattered," v. 1], bringing His saints from the demonic depths of Hades ["I will bring them from Bashan; I will bring them from the depths of the sea," v. 22], leading the Church in her journey through history ["When you, God, went out before your people," v. 7].[16]

The church has seen itself as ancient Israel, coming out of Egypt, trekking through the wilderness, and making its ascent to Zion, primarily in Jesus Christ (Matt. 2:13–15), and historically in its corporate witness as Christ's representative in the world (see "Teaching the Text" in the unit on Psalm 67).

Amazing grace!

Hymn: "Amazing Grace," by John Newton. From television coverage of the Olympic Games to the funeral of President Ronald Reagan, we hear references to Newton's song "Amazing Grace."[17] Take your listeners line by line through the lyrics of verses 2, 3, and 4 of this hymn. Explain the meaning of each verse and connect them to Psalm 68, which tells the story of God's grace in human history. The song tells the story of a gracious and good God who has done marvelous things for nations

God is described as a "father to the fatherless, a defender of widows" (68:5). In this Assyrian relief three women, one with her child, hold their hands over their heads in mourning as they are led into captivity after a military defeat (Nimrud palace relief, 865–860 BC).

and individuals. God's story of life with us is a story of amazing grace. Do you see the grace of God in the events of history? Do you see the grace of God in your own life journey? If not, maybe you have not opened your heart to God. Or possibly you are not opening your eyes to see what he is doing.

God of the fatherless

Statistics: In Psalm 68:5, David makes a powerful statement about the heart and character of God: "A father to the fatherless, a defender of widows, is God in his holy dwelling." The Lord has compassion and is the defender of those in need. And he often uses us in the process of caring for the orphan and the widow. There are orphan children throughout the world in desperate need of protection and homes. Consider these statistics:

- In 2013, over seven million children were in institutional care worldwide.
- HIV/AIDS has orphaned 17.9 million children in the world.
- There were 123,000 orphans in the United States as of the end of 2008.[18]

God wants to use us to minister to the fatherless. He has a heart for them. Do you? This would be a good opportunity to help people know how to get involved in alleviating this worldwide problem.

"Zeal for Your House Consumes Me"

Big Idea *Our passion for worship and for God may evoke misunderstanding from others.*

Understanding the Text

Psalm 69 is an individual lament that has grown out of the worshiper's persecution and assaults by those who hate him. The psalmist is ill (69:29) and falsely accused (69:4). Often these two conditions are combined, as with Job, to create an intolerable situation for the psalmists.

Psalm 69 belongs to a subcategory of psalms sometimes called imprecatory psalms, because they contain "curses" against the psalmist's enemies (see "Additional Insights: Imprecatory Psalms," before the unit on Ps. 35). They take the form, however, of prayers that God will curse their enemies, or the impersonal "may they be . . . " Typically, vengeance is left in God's hands.

The Text in Context

Psalm 69 is almost the opposite of Psalm 68. In Psalm 68 Israel celebrated Yahweh's triumphal and saving march from Egypt to Zion, leaving the reader with a picture of God at last in his sanctuary in Zion. In Psalm 69, David is in great distress, almost drowned by the engulfing waters of trouble (69:2) but suffering vicariously for God's sake (69:7). Driven by a zeal for God's house, which has warranted

John's Gospel records that Jesus said, "I am thirsty" (John 19:28) to fulfill the Scriptures, perhaps Psalm 69:21. Shown here is an eleventh-century ivory carving that depicts the sponge of vinegar being lifted toward the lips of Jesus.

insults from those who do not share his passion (69:9), he summons the whole creation (heaven, earth, and seas) to join in summative praise of God's salvation of Zion (69:34–35). The climax of salvation history—that is, Israel's salvation represented by God's taking up his dwelling in Zion, taught by Psalm 68—is celebrated again, along with hopes of rebuilding the cities of Judah. Even though very different from Psalm 68, Psalm 69 may be viewed as a complement to that psalm, especially when we recognize that the Lord, after a long march of redemption, has taken up his permanent residence in Zion's sanctuary. If that does not justify the psalmist's zeal for God's house, then nothing could.

In addition to the contrast between the two psalms, there are verbal expressions that link them together in order to draw a frame for the contrast described above:[1]

Psalm 68	Psalm 69
"May his foes [lit., "those who hate him"] flee before him" (68:1b)	"Those who hate me without reason" (69:4a)
"May the righteous be glad" (68:3a)	"The poor will see and be glad" (69:32a)
"Our God is a God who saves" (68:20a)	"Save me, O God" (69:1a)
"That you, LORD God [yah 'elohim], might dwell there" (68:18e)	"Those who love his name will dwell there" (69:36b)

Outline/Structure

The psalm has a three-part structure composed of lament, petition, and praise:

1. Lament (69:1–12)
   a. A metaphorical description of the psalmist's troubles (69:1–4)
   b. Review of the opposition (69:5–12)

Key Themes of Psalm 69

- A defining passion for God's house sometimes is misunderstood.
- The compelling interest in God's kingdom is our highest priority.

Psalm 69 in the New Testament

Psalm 69 (along with Pss. 22 and 110) is one of the most quoted psalms in the New Testament. The assaults on the psalmist, his vicarious suffering, and unjustified accusations point in a messianic direction and have found their fulfillment in Jesus's life and teachings, especially his passion. Jesus himself applies the words of verse 4a to those who see his works but still hate him "without reason" (John 15:25; Ps. 69:4; cf. also Ps. 35:19). After Christ had cleansed the temple, his disciples remembered the psalmist's words in verse 9a, "zeal for your house consumes me" (John 2:17; Ps. 69:9a). John alludes to verse 21 when the soldiers bring Jesus vinegar to drink in response to his plea, "I thirst" (John 19:29; Ps. 69:21; cf. Matt. 27:34). Paul twice quotes Psalm 69 in his Letter to the Romans, the first time to explain how David prophesied the rejection of Christ by his own people (Rom. 11:9–10; Ps. 69:22–23), and the second time to reinforce his teaching that we ought to bear the failings of the weak (Rom. 15:3; Ps. 69:9b). Luke writes that Judas's death, which vacated his apostolic office, later filled by Matthias, was a fulfillment of verse 25 (Acts 1:20; Ps. 69:25). Even if modern interpreters tend to feel uncomfortable with the content and tone of Psalm 69, the New Testament writers heard its prophetic voice foretelling the Savior's actions and suffering, and we should listen carefully too.

[Note that each of the "review" sections begins with "You (God) know" (see 69:5 and 19a).]

2. Petition (69:13–29)
   a. Plea that God will answer him (69:13–18)
   [Three times the suppliant prays: "answer me" (69:13b, 16a, 17b).]

b. Review of the opposition
(69:19–21)
[Begins with "You know"
(69:19a)]
c. Prayer for judgment (69:22–29)
3. Praise (69:30–36)
a. The psalmist's vow to praise
God (69:30–33)
b. Creation's praise and the
people's settlement in the land
(69:34–36)

Historical and Cultural Background

Hakham suggests that Psalm 69 may have been intended as a lament over Zion after the destruction of the first temple.[2] It is, of course, possible that David himself wrote this psalm (all three imprecatory psalms are titled "for/of David"), and it was later used to lament Zion's destruction and the Babylonian seizure of the land of Judah in 586 BC. The temple in Israel was the focal point of religious life and the place where life and faith came together.

The climax of the "curses" in verses 22–28 contains a prayer that the wicked may be "blotted out of the book of life" (69:28). Such a notion is also found in the religious literature of Mesopotamia.[3]

Interpretive Insights

Title *To the tune of "Lilies."* Literally, "on lilies" (*'al-shoshannim*). Probably a tune name, this phrase occurs in the titles of Psalms 45 and 69, while variants occur in the titles of Psalms 60 (*'al-shushan 'edut*, "according to the lily of the covenant") and 80 (*'el-shoshannim 'edut*, "to the lilies of the covenant").

69:1 *Save me, O God, for the waters have come up to my neck.* The same metaphor of waters is also used in Isaiah 8:7–8. Note that the first part of the psalm (69:1–4) is centered on "me," the psalmist, a figure of the Suffering Servant (see "your servant," 69:17).

69:2 *I sink in the miry depths . . . the floods engulf me.* These are metaphors descriptive of the assaults of David's enemies, whereas the physical suffering of verse 3 seems to be literal.

69:4 *I am forced to restore what I did not steal.* We do not know what situation this refers to, but there were either legal or social pressures, or perhaps both, to make reparations for something he did not steal or plunder.

69:5 *You, God, know my folly.* Calvin takes this as irony.[4] It is not a confession as such but, to use Tate's phrase, a "protestation of innocence" (also Pss. 7:4–5; 17:3–5; 139:1–24).[5] The psalmist can hardly confess his wrong and claim innocence too (note "without cause," 69:4).

69:6 *Lord, the LORD Almighty, may those who hope in you not be disgraced.* The use of three names for God reinforces the prayer. The lesson here is that an individual failing has consequences for the wider community. Wilson draws attention to the shared concern of Psalms 69 and 70–71 for disgrace and shame as a result of enemy attacks (69:6–7, 19; 70:2; 71:1, 13).[6]

69:7 *I endure scorn for your sake.* The Hebrew word for "scorn" bears social consequences of rejection and rebuke. Note that it is for God's sake that he bears reproach.

69:9 *zeal for your house consumes me.* See 2 Samuel 7 and 1 Chronicles 28:11–29:5

"Those who sit at the gate mock me" (69:12). The city gate area, with its gate chambers and nearby plaza, was where the influential people of the city gathered to conduct business transactions and legal proceedings. Shown here are excavated and partially restored benches in one of the gate chambers at the city of Arad.

69:17 *Do not hide your face from your servant.* God's hiding his face was a sign of rejection, and the prayer itself suggests that this was one of David's fears, perhaps exacerbated by the many conflicts he faced during his reign.

69:18 *Come near and rescue me; deliver me because of my foes.* Three imperatives form this request: "come near" (*qrb*), "rescue" (*g'l*), and "deliver" (*pdh*). In social life, the verb "rescue" meant to "redeem" one from enslavement for a debt, while the verb "deliver" was used in a very similar way. In Zechariah 10:3–12 (esp. 10:8), this verb is used in the eschatological sense of delivering Israel from enslavement to a foreign power.[7]

69:21 *gall . . . vinegar.* His enemies give him this instead of comfort.

69:22 *May the table set before them become a snare.* The principle is that they should be dealt with as they themselves have dealt with the psalmist. See also verse 27. The five "curses" reiterated in verses 22–28, if they became effective, would deprive the victim of the basic needs of life and make life hardly worth living.[8]

69:26 *For they persecute those you wound.* The psalmist's hurt is attributed to God. While some think this is a mistaken notion on the suppliant's part, it is an Old Testament idea that God is the cause of illness and misdeeds (e.g., Ps. 38:3). See "Theological Insights" in the unit on Psalm 71.

69:28 *May they be blotted out of the book of life.* To be blotted out of the "book of life" is to be considered dead.[9]

69:29 *But as for me.* Suddenly the psalmist shines the spotlight on himself. See the

for David's preparations for building the temple. David had a great passion for building the temple, and while the story in the books of Samuel and Chronicles is clear on this matter, the idea that he was misunderstood for it seems to be an additional insight to the story.

69:12 *Those who sit at the gate.* These are probably the judges who convene the law court at the gate.

69:13 *in the time of your favor.* This could mean one of two things, either a favorable time for God to answer or a favorable time for the worshiper to make his petition. In Isaiah 49:8, the time of favor is the Lord's time of salvation.

69:16 *out of the goodness of your love; in your great mercy.* Two parallel phrases indicate the strong favor and mercy of God. The phrase "goodness of your love" brings together God's goodness (*tob*) and love (*hesed*), mutually defining each other. The phrase "in your great mercy [*rahamim*]" brings the perspective of a mother's love (the singular noun *rehem* means "womb").

same turn of focus on the psalmist in verse 13 ("But [as for me,] I pray to you, LORD").

69:30 *I will praise God's name in song.* This is a vow, even though it is not called by that name, and it suggests the musical manner in which the psalmist fulfills it.

69:31 *a bull with its horns and hooves.* An acceptable animal sacrifice was required to have a cloven hoof (Lev. 11:3). The nouns "ox" and "bull" are synonyms. A similar idea occurs in Psalm 51:16–17, where God prefers a "broken and contrite heart" to sacrifice.

69:34 *Let heaven and earth praise him, the seas and all that move in them.* The whole creation, in triadic terms of heaven, earth, and seas, is called on to praise God. Kidner suggests this concluding praise "is yet another reminder that the most desperate of prayers can end, and rightly so, in doxology."[10]

69:35 *the cities of Judah.* This may suggest a date later than David, since Israel was the name of the united empire, and Judah the name of the southern kingdom after the division of the kingdom under Solomon's

son and successor, Rehoboam. However, David reigned over Judah alone for seven and a half years before he became king of both political entities, Judah and Israel.

69:36 *the children of his servants will inherit it.* "His servants" may be a reference to the patriarchs, for Abraham, Isaac, and Jacob are called God's servants in Exodus 32:13. This renewal of God's people and land is couched in terms of the settlement of Canaan. Isaiah 65:9 predicts such a return to Zion and repossession of the land.

Theological Insights

The psalmist's faith is defined by his zeal for God's house, which has evidently been misinterpreted by those who do not share it. The fact that God's house, most likely the temple (some suggest the whole of the people of God), is his passion means that

> The "children of his servants" (69:36) who will inherit Zion may be referring to the descendants of the patriarchs, Abraham, Isaac, and Jacob. Underground tombs, which may be the burial place of Abraham and Isaac, lie beneath this structure built by Herod the Great in the first century BC.

David is the secondary object of the insults that are really intended for God (69:9). As God's representative, the king is responsible for the people, and some of his detractors have interpreted his zeal for God's house as fanaticism. David expended much expense to collect materials for the construction of the temple. Yet only those who have invested their whole lot in God ever reach the pinnacle of faith. And moreover, it is only those who attain to this kind of concern for the kingdom who make all other interests secondary, even tertiary.

Teaching the Text

One of David's concerns is that he, because of his own behavior and example, might not bring disgrace on those who hope in God (69:6). This mark of theological integrity is an attribute that ought to create great respect for the psalmist, regardless of his less noble traits. In our theological context we might put it like this: the kingdom of God is so important that it should be the most compelling interest in our lives. If we define the kingdom by the Lord's Prayer ("Thy kingdom come, *thy will be done on earth, as it is in heaven*"), we will not be far from the kingdom concept of the Old Testament as well as the New. God's kingdom is both *now* and *not yet*. The conflict that is carried on to bring about the kingdom is like a civil war, where certain regions have fallen into kingdom hands, yet the battle still goes on until all enemy forces have surrendered unconditionally.

It may be helpful to distinguish briefly between the church and the kingdom—they are not exactly synonymous. The church is the institution that Christ has established in the world to bring about the kingdom of God, or the loyalist force that is conducting the battle against the powers of evil. The kingdom is the realm where God reigns and his will is established ("Thy Kingdom come, thy will be done"). In Revelation 11:15 John announces the time when the church and the kingdom become synonymous, the time when the will of God has preempted the will of the kingdom of this world.

Psalm 69, although it never uses the phrase, has a lot to say about the kingdom of God. With the suppliant, in fact, it becomes a personal matter. He prays that his behavior will not bring shame on those who hope in God and seek him. Indeed, his passion for the temple (69:9a) is nothing less than a passion for God and for his kingdom. It is this passion that has produced a willingness to endure insults, scorn, and social isolation, knowing that he does so for God's sake (69:7). He evidently accepts this as part of his believing life, not a part he enjoys nor a part that he has invited—he is not a masochist. But he realizes that suffering for God or for the kingdom—they are synonymous—is part of the faith he professes. When his enemies insult God, they insult him, and that is an index to his intimate relationship with God.

It is, of course, only those who have invested their whole lot in God who would ever experience this kind of effect ("zeal for your house consumes me," v. 9). This suffering turns our eyes away from ourselves to God and puts our lives in the larger perspective of God's kingdom. It is in fact the kind of suffering that makes us participants in Christ's suffering and makes us *like him*. God is remaking us in his image, and part of the re-creative process is to bring us into his suffering. Paul declares to the Philippian church that God has granted them "on behalf of Christ not only to believe in him, but also *to suffer for him*" (Phil. 1:29). The apostle picks up this idea of compelling interest in the kingdom of God again in Philippians 3: "Whatever were gains to me I now consider loss for the sake of Christ. . . . I want to know Christ—yes, to know the power of his resurrection and *participation in his sufferings*, becoming like him in his death" (Phil. 3:7, 10; see also 2 Thess. 1:5; Heb. 13:13). As the Western world becomes more secular, we discover that our religious convictions are less respected and subject to subtle, even blatant, attacks. David's steadfastness can help us restore our equilibrium and maintain the courage of our faith convictions.

This compelling interest in God's kingdom, taken as a spiritual discipline, will make us less critical of "those who hope" in God and more self-critical, less self-centered and more God-centered, less compelled by our own comforts and conveniences and more constrained by the kingdom's interest: "Thy kingdom come, thy will be done on earth, as it is in heaven."

A passion for the kingdom of God should help believers stand firm in the face of suffering and even advance the cause of Christ, much like soldiers, in the face of battle, can perform deeds of bravery because of their belief in their cause. The courageous soldiers who fought at the Battle of Gettysburg under the command of Colonel Joshua L. Chamberlain, shown here, can provide such an example.

Illustrating the Text

No surrender!

History: On July 2, 1863, in the American Civil War, the Union's Colonel Chamberlain was given instructions during the battle at Gettysburg to hold the ground on Little Round Top at all costs. Outnumbered ten to one, Chamberlain's men held until they were almost out of ammunition. Instead of retreating, Chamberlain ordered a bayonet charge. The Confederate army was so caught off guard that many surrendered, while the remainder of the troops fled. Colonel Chamberlain's heroism on that day saved the left flank of the Northern army and possibly the Battle of Gettysburg.[11] Imagine if all Christians had that same sense of commitment to the kingdom of God. That is, no matter what obstacles, temptations, or sufferings we faced, we would not give ground but would hold firm for the Lord. Ask your listeners to consider where they might be compromising the kingdom of God. Where are they giving into temptation? Where have they lost heart and are no longer standing for the Lord?

Integrity

True Story: *A Traveler's Guide to the Kingdom,* **by James Emery White.** In his book, White tells the story about his visit to the pub where C. S. Lewis and his friends used to meet to discuss their latest works. While he was there, the manager complained about Christians who came to the famous pub and stole menus, utensils, and even pictures from the walls. After his conversation, White made the following observation: "The irony is bitter; the manager of The Eagle and Child pub holds Christians and, one would surmise, Christianity itself, in disdain because of the behavior of the Christians who flock to pay homage to Lewis. Many wouldn't dare drink a pint (of beer), but they will gladly steal."[12] For better or for worse, we are witnesses for Christ. The world is watching, and our actions either draw people to Christ or repel them. David cared about his witness, as we see in Psalm 69:6. How careful are you to ensure that your witness does not bring scorn to God's name?

A compelling commitment to the kingdom of God

Film: *Chariots of Fire.* The 1981 movie *Chariots of Fire* is based on the story of two athletes in the 1924 Olympics, Eric Liddell and Harold Abrahams. Liddell was a committed Christian who refused to compromise his commitment to God even when it meant that he would be scratched from his Olympic event. The issue at stake was Liddell's refusal to compete on the Sabbath. Pressure was placed on him by members of the British royal family and government. At one point the Prince of Wales says to Liddell, "There are times when we are asked to make sacrifices in the name of that loyalty. And without them our allegiance is worthless. As I see it, for you, this is such a time." But Liddell would not compromise, saying, "God made countries, God makes kings, and the rules by which they govern. And those rules say that the Sabbath is His. And I for one intend to keep it that way." What we see in this movie is Liddell's perspective that his first allegiance is to the kingdom of God.

"The LORD Is Great!"

Big Idea *The message of this psalm, applied to the waiting community in exile, is that "the LORD is great!" proclaimed as a word of hope and deliverance not yet realized, even as they pray, "Come quickly, LORD."*

Understanding the Text

Psalm 70 is a duplicate of Psalm 40:13–17, with minor variations (see the unit on Ps. 40), and has features of a psalm of lament.

The Text in Context

Psalms 69 and 70 have common linguistic links (see table 1). It is quite possible that Psalm 69 was written with Psalm 40:13–17 in view in order to make the transition from the lament of Psalm 69 to the hope of Psalm 70. Goldingay observes that the terms of Psalm 70 both reiterate and reinforce the terms of Psalm 69, and he suggests that this reinforcement is the reason for the duplication here of Psalm 40:13–17.[1] It seems to me that the weight represented by these two psalms is more broadly distributed, stretched out over the cadre of Psalms 69–71. Like Psalm 40–41, that together comprise a conclusion to Book 1, this trilogy of psalms comprises a conclusion to Book 2, and in combination with Psalm 72, provides a transition to Book 3, whose historical setting is the

Table 1. Linguistic Links between Psalms 69 and 70

Similar and Duplicate Terms	Psalm 69	Psalm 70
Theme of shame	"May those who hope in you not be disgraced because of me" (in favor of Israel; 69:6)	"May those who want to take my life be put to shame" (against enemies; 70:2)
Petition of hurry	"Answer me quickly" (69:17)	"Come quickly, LORD, to help me" (70:1; cf. v. 5)
Those who seek God	"May those who seek you" (69:6)	"May all who seek you" (70:4)
Poor and needy	"The poor will see" (69:32) "The LORD hears the needy" (69:33)	"But as for me, I am poor and needy" (70:5)
Need for rejoicing	"The poor will see and be glad" (69:32)	"May all who seek you rejoice and be glad" (70:4)
Those who love God's name/ salvation	"Those who love his name will dwell there" (69:36)	"May those who long for your saving help always say, 'The LORD is great!'" (70:4)

■ God is great!

■ We identify with the poor and needy.

The plea for God to "come quickly" (70:5) and "hasten . . . to save" (70:1) is taken up by the Israelites as they face deportation and exile following the successful Babylonian invasion. This is not the first time that they have faced exile. This Assyrian wall relief shows Israelites being deported from Lachish by the victorious army of Sennacherib (Nineveh palace, 700–692 BC).

71:13, 24), and now the psalmist presumably represents Israel, whose enemies are now the Babylonians. The second webbing theme is the prayerful motif that the psalmist not be put to shame ("shame," 69:6; 70:2, 3; 71:3, 13, 24), with corporate Israel the object and their enemies the perpetrators. The third webbing theme is the urgency that God act hurriedly ("urgency," 69:17; 70:1; 71:12), the circumstances which generate the haste being that of the humiliation of exile. The theme transitioning to the new era that produced Book 3 was that of the poor and needy ("humiliation," 69:32; 70:5), corporately the humiliated community, and personally the figure of David, who identified with the poor and needy, and is, in a rhetorical sense, their representative (see the sidebar, "The Editing of Book 2").

Babylonian exile. Three themes (see "Additional Insights: Corresponding Verbal and Thematic Connections in Psalms 69–72," following the unit on Ps. 72) incorporated in those psalms weave a strategic webbing for the conclusion/transition to the new era, and a fourth theme leads from this cadre of psalms into the hope-filled Psalm 72. The first webbing theme is the recognition that there are those who seek the psalmist's hurt ("enemies," 69:4, 7, 10–12, 17–21; 70:21;

It is no coincidence that three of these themes are excerpted from the conclusion of Book 1 (40:13–17), and the editor/

Table 2. A Comparison of Psalm 40:13–17 and Psalm 70

Psalm 40:13–17	Psalm 70
Title For the director of music. Of David. *A psalm*.	**Title** For the director of music. Of David. *A petition*.
40:13 *Be pleased* to save me, LORD; come quickly, LORD, to help me.	**70:1** *Hasten, O God*, to save me; come quickly, LORD, to help me.
40:14 May *all* who want *to take* my life be put to shame and confusion; may all who desire my ruin be turned back in disgrace.	**70:2** May *those* who want *to take* (omitted) my life be put to shame and confusion; may all who desire my ruin be turned back in disgrace.
40:15 May those who say to me, "Aha! Aha!" *be appalled* at their own shame.	**70:3** May those who say to me, "Aha! Aha!" *turn back* because of their shame.
40:16 But may all who seek you rejoice and be glad in you; may those who long for your saving help always say, "The LORD is great!"	**70:4** But may all who seek you rejoice and be glad in you; may those who long for your saving help always say, "The LORD is great!"
40:17 But as for me, I am poor and needy; *may the Lord think of me*. You are my help and my deliverer; you are my *God*, do not delay.	**70:5** But as for me, I am poor and needy; *come quickly to me, O God*. You are my help and my deliverer; *LORD*, do not delay.

The Editing of Book 2

Hossfeld and Zenger speak of a "theology of the poor" that pervades Psalms 70–72 (see table 3), concluding the Second Davidic Psalter (Psalms 51–72).[a] Psalms 70–72 correspond in several ways to the conclusion of the First Davidic Psalter (which Hossfeld and Zenger define as Pss. 3–41). Psalm 70 is, with minor variations, a duplicate of Psalm 40:13–17, forming a corresponding psalm "of David" that portrays him as the prototype of the poor and needy, not just their defender. Psalms 40 and 41 portray David as the prototype of the righteous person, and now in Psalms 70–72, in a rhetorical way, he has taken his place in the company of the poor and needy, a condescension, to be sure, but only in the sense that he has joined this company as the righteous individual who is now synonymous with the "poor and needy," their royal representative. The equation was already made at the end of Psalm 40: "But as for me, I am poor and needy" (40:17). David, or the editor of Book 2, has again affirmed that portrait by including the words of Psalm 40:13–17 in the conclusion to the Second Davidic Psalter (70:5a). Indeed, Psalm 41 begins with the pronouncement, "Blessed are those who have regard for the weak [dal]" (41:1a), and the portrait of the ideal king drawn in Psalm 72 includes this character trait as critical to his royal position: "He [the king] will take pity on the weak [dal] and the needy ['ebyon]" (72:13a).

This editorial ordering of the psalms to present this Davidic portrait may be explained as a product of the time in which the Second Davidic Psalter was shaped. Wilson points out that the seams of Books 1–3 are marked by the presence of three royal psalms, Psalms 2; 41; and 72.[b] The obvious interest in the monarchy marks the end of Book 3 when Psalm 89 concludes with its probing inquiry into the failure of the Davidic dynasty. So the "final" editing of Books 1–3 must take place in the Babylonian exile, when Israel was a captive people (69:33; note also the prayer to "rebuild the cities of Judah," 69:35). In this political context, David's identification with this humiliated and captive people as the "poor and needy" (70:5) would provide a dimension of great comfort—their ideal king identifies with them and has entered their condition of humiliation.

[a] Hossfeld and Zenger, *Psalms 2*, 188.
[b] Wilson, *Hebrew Psalter*, 211.

compiler of Book 2 obviously picked up those verses intentionally because they carried the weight of his historic burdens as one era was slipping away and another was pressing into reality: *urgency* (40:13), *shame* (40:14–15), and *humiliation* (poor and needy, 40:17). Here we have a good illustration of how duplicate psalms adapt the same words for their distinctive settings.

Outline/Structure

1. Prayer that God will hasten to save the psalmist (70:1)
2. Prayer against the psalmist's enemies (70:2–3)
3. Prayer for all who seek God (70:4)
4. Prayer for the psalmist himself (70:5)

Interpretive Insights

The textual differences between Psalm 40:13–17 and Psalm 70 are minor. Table 2 offers a visual comparison of the two psalms (in the table, italics indicate textual differences). For additional comments on the verses, see the unit on Psalm 40.

Title *A petition.* Instead of "A psalm," as in the title for Psalm 40, Psalm 70 reads, "A petition" (*lᵉhazkir*), a term that appears also in Psalm 38 (see the comments on the title for Ps. 38).

70:1 *Hasten, O God.* As is typical in the Elohistic Psalter, twice Psalm 70 substitutes the name "God" (*'elohim*) for "LORD" (*YHWH*; 70:1, 4; see also the changes in 70:5). Verse 1 opens with *'elohim*, in place of "Be pleased, LORD" from Psalm 40:13. The NIV prefixes "Hasten," evidently taking it from the end of the verse (as does also the NASB). The problem is that the first half of the verse has no main verb, with only an infinitive, "to save (me)," at the end of the clause. On the basis of the analogy with 40:13, which is a duplicate verse (except it employs an initial verb, "be pleased"), the NRSV renders it, "Be pleased, O God, to deliver me!"

Table 3. The "Poor and Needy" toward the End of Book 2

Psalm 40	"But as for me, I am *poor* ['*ani*] and *needy* ['*ebyon*]" (40:17)
Psalm 68	"From your bounty, God, you provided for the *poor* ['*ani*]" (68:10)
Psalm 69	"But as for me, *afflicted* ['*ani*] and *in pain* [*k'b*]" (69:29) "The LORD hears the *needy* ['*ebyon*]" (69:33)
Psalm 70	"But as for me, I am *poor* ['*ani*] and *needy* ['*ebyon*]" (70:5)
Psalm 71	[The terms do not occur in this psalm]
Psalm 72	"May he judge . . . your *afflicted ones* ['*ani*] with justice" (72:2) "May he defend the *afflicted* ['*ani*] among the people and save the children of the *needy* ['*ebyon*]" (72:4) "For he will deliver the *needy* ['*ebyon*] who cry out, the *afflicted* ['*ani*] who have no one to help" (72:12) "He will take pity on the *weak* [*dal*] and the *needy* ['*ebyon*] and save the *needy* ['*ebyon*]" (72:13)

70:2 *May those who want to take my life.* Psalm 70 omits two words from Psalm 40:14, "all" (*yahad*, "together") and "to take" (*sph*). In 70:2 the NIV translates "those" in place of the missing "all" and also supplies the verb "to take." The Hebrew reads literally, "May those who seek my life be ashamed and be confused" (cf. ESV).

70:3 *those who say to me . . . turn back because of their shame.* Psalm 70:3 omits "to me" from 40:15, although it has been restored by the NIV (cf. ESV). In 70:3 the

verse opens with the verb *shub* ("turn back") in place of *shmm* ("be appalled") in 40:15.

70:4 *The LORD is great!* Although obscured by the NIV's translation, 70:4 is one of the occasions where Psalm 70 replaces the name "LORD" (*YHWH*) with "God" ('*elohim*) (see the comments on 70:1). The Hebrew therefore reads, "God is great!"

70:5 *come quickly to me, O God . . . LORD, do not delay.* Twice in this verse, the divine name is changed from the name used in 40:17: "Lord" ('*adonay*) is changed to "God" ('*elohim*), and in reverse of the typical pattern of Book 2, "God" ('*elohim*) is changed to "LORD" (*YHWH*). The verb accompanying the first divine name is also different in 70:5, *hush* ("come quickly," repeating 70:1), in place of *hshb* ("think," 40:17).

Theological Insights

This psalm begins with a petition that God will "come quickly" (*hushah*, 70:1) to

The proclamation "The LORD is great!" (70:4) seems to be the central message of the psalm while the Israelites wait for God's deliverance from their Babylonian captivity. Under King Nebuchadnezzar, the Babylonian army was God's instrument of judgment on the Israelites. This Babylonian cuneiform tablet chronicles the first eleven years (605–595 BC) of Nebuchadnezzar's reign, including the conquest of Jerusalem.

533   Psalm 70

save the psalmist, and ends with the same request, though turned into the negative "do not delay" (70:5d), thus forming an *inclusio*.

The proclamation "God is great!" (70:4b ESV) seems to be the central message of the psalm while the community in their captivity (69:33) waits for God's deliverance. In fact, it appears from the nature of the psalms in Book 2 that Israel was in captivity (see "The Structure and Composition of the Psalter" in the introduction), and that is an idea we need to take into account as we interpret this psalm, especially in its present context. If David is the author of the psalm, then the editor is using his words to identify him as one of the captives. That is, David identifies with the "poor and needy," the latter being a designation of those who are in exile.

Teaching the Text

If the preacher or teacher has already exposited Psalm 40, then this might be a reason to skip Psalm 70, since it is a virtual duplicate of Psalm 40:13–17. Yet the challenge to deal with this psalm from Book 1 in its new setting is one that should be considered very seriously. As I have explained above (in the sidebar "The Editing of Book 2"), these verses now serve the function of providing a partial conclusion to Book 2. The setting is the world of the Babylonian exile, and the editor of Book 2 is putting the psalms together in a pattern that both reflects that historical setting and injects hope into it. Here the presenter may take the kind of interpretive liberty that Psalms expositors have assumed for centuries, John Calvin being one of the best examples. Calvin moved easily between the historical circumstances and his own life and world. His precedent was the Psalms themselves, for there is evidence that the psalmists took the earlier biblical texts and applied them to their own circumstances and world. So the Psalms have set the hermeneutical pattern for us.

In view of that method, the preacher or teacher can draw parallels between the community of faith of Psalm 70, confused and troubled, and our own contemporary community of faith, the church. This poem paints a picture of an unbelieving world—and that's where we live—that posed a challenge to Israel's survival. Its unbelief is described in terms of its opposition to the people of God, who were now in exile, humiliated, politically defeated, and spiritually deflated. In Scripture there is no more caustic condemnation of evildoers than those who are described by their conflict with God's people.

The editor who put Book 2 of the Psalms together (Psalms 42–72) positions this psalm here at the end of the collection to tell us something about the desperation of the time. And he prays what we might call a "prayer of hurry," asking the Lord to hurry and help him: "Come quickly, Lord, to help me" (v. 1b). David's prayer in Psalm 40 was one of personal distress, but here it is prayed over the national distress of Israel, in a foreign land, humbled by defeat, demeaned by their mocking captors (see Ps. 137). The situation was urgent, and the circumstances critical: "Come quickly, Lord, to help me." When David wrote this prayer, he was praying on his own behalf. When the editor reused the prayer in Book 2, he represented the voice of David praying for the nation.

One may stress the desperation of the exile, and draw a parallel between the urgency of our own time, rising out of a growing skepticism and unbelief. Out of that context, David prayed, and the editor reinstalled this prayer on the nation's behalf, imploring God to come quickly to his help or all would be lost. The desperation of the psalm is reinforced by the fact that it ends with the same prayer of hurry: "Come quickly to me, O God" (v. 5b).

But there is another feature of the psalm that should reinforce the sermon or lesson, which is the declaration at the end of verse 4, and this may be considered the heart of the poem:

> May those who love your salvation
> say evermore, "God is great!" (70:4
> ESV)

Here the community of faith, "those who love your salvation," is offering a word of hope amidst their despair. They may easily be compared to the church today, and this clause appropriately describes God's people in any age. The latter clause of verse 4 is the message David wanted to proclaim in the time of his own personal distress, and the message proclaimed to a languishing people in despair in the exile: "God is great!" This powerful word of praise runs counter to the hopelessness of the exile and of our own time of unbelief. God's greatness countermands despair, puts new sinews on the dead bones in the charnel house of a defeated world. Acknowledging God's greatness is to lay claim on hope and new life. When God is exalted, the world is right side up. When man is exalted, the world is upside down. "God is great!" is a mighty force toward uprighting the upside-down world of any age.

All of us have personal moments when we want to pray, "Come quickly, Lord, to help me." And as we look at our desperate world, we want to pray that prayer of hurry that is prayed at the end of the canonical Scriptures with new zest and urgency. It is not a coincidence that at the end of John's book about Christ and his church, we hear the word of promise, "Yes, I am coming soon," and the church responds, "Amen. Come, Lord Jesus!" (Rev. 22:20). In a sense John is providing the Savior's response to the psalmist's prayer, "Come quickly." This is, or ought to be, the prayer of the church in every age: "Come quickly, Lord Jesus." Come quickly before our strength is gone and we are overcome by the oncoming darkness of evil. Come quickly before the church loses its will to survive, and becomes, like Samson, deprived of its power and blinded to the truth. "Amen. Come, Lord Jesus!"

Illustrating the Text

Redemptive suffering

Quote: *Letters to a Diminished Church*, by Dorothy Sayers. Even if David's identification with the poor and needy is not an Old Testament instance of vicarious suffering, or suffering in the place of the poor and needy, his portrait here is certainly an instance of suffering *with* them, and that is only a step away from suffering in their place. There have been many attempts to offer analogies that help us understand why God in Christ suffered in our place. Dorothy Sayers offers the following:

> He was not a kind of demon pretending to be human; he was in every respect a genuine living man. He was not merely

a man so good as to be "like God"—he was God.

Now, this is not just a pious commonplace; it is not a commonplace at all. For what it means is this, among other things: that for whatever reason God chose to make man as he is—limited and suffering and subject to sorrows and death—he [God] had the honesty and the courage to take his own medicine. Whatever game he is playing with his creation, he has kept his own rules and played fair. He can exact nothing from man that he has not exacted from himself.[2]

Bloom where you are planted.

Christian Organization: Prison Fellowship Ministries was founded by Chuck Colson to evangelize prisoners and restore families through faith-based programs that facilitate their reentry into society. Colson had been named as one of the "Watergate Seven" and pleaded guilty to the charge of obstruction of justice in the Watergate scandal. Just prior to his sentencing, Colson committed his life to Jesus Christ. In 1974 he served seven months in a federal prison. It was while Colson was in prison that God gave him a vision for Prison Fellowship Ministries. Colson could have seen his incarceration as simply a "negative" in his life and

focused his attention on getting this time in his life behind him. Rather, he opened his heart to the Lord, and God used him in mighty ways.[3] Too often, when we are in challenging circumstances, our only focus is, "How do I get out of this?" Rather, we need to be open to the Lord at all times. Just as Israel exalted God's greatness even in their captivity, we too can bring praise to God even as we experience suffering and long for deliverance.

For such a time as this

Bible: The story of Joseph in the book of Genesis provides great insight into how to live well for the Lord amid suffering, and a vivid reminder of God's care for those in need. Having been sold into slavery by his brothers, falsely accused by Potiphar's wife, and sent to prison, Joseph easily could have become bitter toward God. But throughout

Joseph trusted in God for help and deliverance, so he could say to his brothers, "You intended to harm me, but God intended it for good to accomplish what is now being done, the saving of many lives" (Gen. 50:20). This illumination from the fourteenth-century AD Golden Haggadah shows scenes from the life of Joseph.

Joseph's story we see that he seeks to honor the Lord. After he has finally been released from prison, his brothers, in the midst of a time of great need, come to Egypt, where he is now in a position of power. Joseph has come through great struggles and been elevated to the second place of leadership in Egypt, and now it is his brothers and his whole family who are suffering. Once Joseph reveals his identity, his brothers are terrified. But Joseph, with his perspective on the providence of God, proclaims, "You intended to harm me, but God intended it for good to accomplish what is now being done, the saving of many lives" (Gen. 50:20). Joseph exemplified great faithfulness to God amid suffering and uncertainty, and through him God demonstrates his loving care for the hungry and hurting, both for the people of Egypt, who are spared the worst suffering of the famine, and especially for Jacob and his family.

"Even When I Am Old and Gray, Do Not Forsake Me, My God"

Big Idea *When our strength ebbs with age, our spiritual inclination is to pray that God will not forsake us.*

Understanding the Text

Psalm 71 has no title, evoking the idea that Psalms 70 and 71 might be viewed as a single unit. In view of their verbal affinities (see "Additional Insights: Corresponding Verbal and Thematic Connections in Psalms 69–72," following the unit on Ps. 72), the latter psalm, perhaps composed by David himself in his old age, was likely adapted by the compiler of Book 2 to provide a transition to the new era of exile (69:33) that, according to Psalm 89, introduced some spiritual introspection about the failed Davidic dynasty and Israel's future in the covenant. David's kingship (or more generally, the monarchy), alongside the sanctuary, is the central institution of the Psalter, and the compiler of Book 2 sought to provide a transition from David the king to David the prophet, the latter "office" being a much more useful figure in the exile. Verse 17 assumes a prophetic tone, sounding, in fact, like Jeremiah, whom God called in his youth (Jer. 1:6). Here David steps into that intermediary role and, with the didactic voice of a prophet, speaks to a nation

that remembers its youthful days and prays that God will not forsake them now.

Since Book 3 concludes with the lament over the end of David's dynasty, we assume that Book 3 (Pss. 73–89) was compiled during the exile (see "The Structure and Composition of the Psalter" in the introduction) or in the early postexilic period. For the sake of this afflicted and needy people, the compiler positions David at the door of the new era, speaking to the people in exile and praying for them in the "old age" of their history. The individual voice of David has become the corporate voice of the nation, the "I" of Psalm 70 (see "The Text in Context" in the unit on Ps. 70; and "I" as the corporate voice of Israel in "Historical and Cultural Background" in the unit on Ps. 116). The compiler of Book 4 (Pss. 90–106) also introduces a similar rhetorical device by positioning Moses, Israel's greatest prophet, at the door of the new era of exile, and installing the prayer of Moses, the man of God, at the beginning of the collection (Ps. 90). Like Moses of Psalm 90, David prays in a prophetic voice (see the comments on

71:17) for this God-forsaken community (71:11). In view of the awesome challenge of this new era, David, as his strength is failing, prays one last prayer for the next generation (71:18), rehearsing God's mighty deeds on behalf of his people, much like Moses prays a final prayer for Israel (Deut. 33).

Psalm 72 then becomes the fulfillment of his intent to pray for the next generation (71:18). Having become the "poor and needy" incarnate (70:5), David prays that God will make Solomon the defender of the afflicted and savior of the needy (72:4). So the stage is set for the community's most trying era, the Babylonian exile, when they were reshaped into the people of God through suffering and humiliation.

The Text in Context

Psalms 69–72 share some similar and duplicate terms that suggest these psalms constitute a cadre of poems intended to form an appropriate conclusion to Book 2.

Key Themes of Psalm 71

- The power of shame can have a healing effect.
- In the Hebrew Bible God is the author of weal and woe.
- A mature faith is characterized by its constancy.

See "Additional Insights" following the unit on Psalm 72; see also the sidebar in the unit on Psalm 70.

Outline/Structure

The following outline treats Psalms 70 and 71 as a single unit:

1. Prayer for salvation (70:1–71:13)
   a. Prayer that God will hasten to save the psalmist (70:1)
   b. Prayer against the psalmist's enemies (70:2–3)
   c. Prayer for all who seek God (70:4)
   d. Prayer for the psalmist himself (70:5)
   e. Prayer to God as refuge and fortress (71:1–4)
   f. Prayer to the God of life from birth to old age (71:5–9)
   g. Prayer to God against the psalmist's accusers (71:10–13)
2. Praise for God's salvation (71:14–24)
   a. Vow to praise God (71:14–16)
   b. Vow to tell of God's wonders to the next generation (71:17–18)

The words of Psalm 71 may have been used as a prayer by the Israelites in exile. There were two mass deportations of the residents of Judah to Babylon during Nebuchadnezzar's military campaigns. The first occurred in 597 BC and the second after the destruction of Jerusalem in 586 BC. In Babylon, the exiles would have seen the beautiful Ishtar Gate, shown here as a partial reconstruction, which directed the processional way to the great temple of Marduk.

c. Acclamation of God's greatness (71:19–21)
d. Vow to praise God with voice and instruments (71:22–24)

Historical and Cultural Background

It appears that the psalm was adapted for the exilic community; in fact, it represents the exilic community praying in David's voice. The *Midrash on the Psalms* interprets verse 9 as the nation praying in exile: "I have become old in my exile."[1] We have already observed that the historical context in which a psalm was composed may not be the context for which it was adapted in the editorial process, in the present case, the Babylonian exile. Some, for example, believe that Psalm 71 was written by David at the time of Absalom's rebellion, which many commentators insist took place in the later years of David's life.[2]

Interpretive Insights

71:1 *let me never be put to shame.* This contrasts with 70:2, where the psalmist prays that those who seek his life be put to shame (see the "Additional Insights" section following the unit on Ps. 72).

71:2 *In your righteousness.* God's "righteousness" is the standard of justice by which he acts. It can also mean "righteous deed(s)" (71:15–16) in the sense of God's saving actions in history, like the exodus and the miracle at the Red Sea, although these are not mentioned in the psalm.

71:3 *you are my rock and my fortress.* A "fortress" is a high place of safety. Here "rock" and "fortress" are parallel and suggest that it is a place of refuge situated on the rock.

71:6 *From birth I have relied on you.* The verb translated as "relied" means "leaned." In Judges 16:29, it describes how Samson "leaned," or "braced himself," on the two pillars of the Philistine temple.

71:7 *I have become a sign to many.* The "sign" could be positive or negative, but in the context of God's goodness to the psalmist, it is probably a positive sign. The Lord made Ezekiel a negative "sign" to Israel (Ezek. 12:6).

71:9 *Do not cast me away when I am old.* Having reviewed his reliance on God from birth (71:6), our suppliant now prays that God not abandon him in old age. He speaks out of a lifetime of relationship with God and further hints at his declining strength because of his advancing years: "when my strength is gone." Note the emphasis on age: "since my youth" (71:5b, 17a), "from birth" (71:6a), "from my mother's womb" (71:6b), "when I am old" (71:9a), "when I am old and gray" (71:18a). See also Psalm 37:25.

71:10–11 *my enemies speak against me.* Their opposition seems to focus on the speaker's advancing years and declining strength. Their words, or the speaker's representation of their words, and their strategy to deal with the suppliant's problem as they perceive it are given in verse 11.

71:13 *May my accusers . . . be covered with scorn and disgrace.* The root of the word "accusers" is the same as the word *satan* (Job 1:6), which means "adversary." The verb "be covered" suggests that they are dressed in scorn and disgrace as one would put on a garment. Job, using a different but synonymous verb, speaks about being clothed in "righteousness," quite a preferable alternative (Job 29:14).

71:14 *As for me, I will always have hope.* The expression "as for me" (lit., "but I") draws a contrast with what was just said, calling attention to his hopeful disposition as compared to the shame of his opponents. The use of the adverb "always/continually" (*tamid*, 71:3, 6, 14; see the "Additional Insights" following the unit on Ps. 72) strengthens the psalmist's constancy. Crenshaw says it underlies his vow, and he renders it, "But I keep on hoping."[3]

71:16 *I will come.* He does not say where, but we assume he comes to the temple, where he rehearses God's mighty acts, which are so many he could never relate them all (71:15).

71:17 *Since my youth, God, you have taught me.* This sounds a bit like Jeremiah, whom God calls to prophesy in his youth (Jer. 1:6), and the fact that the psalmist's word comes directly from God ("God, you have taught me") places it in that prophetic disposition. We may assume that God's "marvelous deeds" (*nipla'ot*), that is, his great works in redemptive history, are the content of God's instruction. In verse 16, the psalmist speaks of God's "mighty acts" (*geburot*), and in verse 19, of the "great things" (*gedolot*) God has done, which causes the psalmist to break out into an exclamation of praise: "Who is like you, God?" (71:19). The psalm closes with a vow to "meditate" (see the comments on 71:24) on God's "righteous acts" (simply "your righteousness," 71:24; cf. 71:2, 15, 16, 19; see the "Additional Insights" following the unit on Ps. 72).

71:18 *till I declare your power to the next generation.* This would be a very appropriate motive for David, if he is the speaker, in preparation for Psalm 72, which David dedicates to Solomon, the next generation. This vow is based on the instruction in Exodus 10:2 and Deuteronomy 32:7.

71:19 *Your righteousness, God, reaches to the heavens.* In verse 15, he vows to tell of God's "righteous deeds" (simply "righteousness").

71:20 *you have made me see troubles.* Deuteronomy 32:39 expresses the idea that God is totally sovereign, causing both weal and woe. The following expression, "you will restore my life again," is conveyed by the same verb in the Deuteronomy text ("bring to life").

71:21 *You will increase my honor.* "My honor" is literally "my greatness" and suggests that the psalmist holds a high office, probably the office of king.

71:24 *My tongue will tell of your righteous acts all day long.* The verb "tell" is "meditate" (*hgh*; see Ps. 1:2). One might expect a reference to the Torah to follow, and the word "your righteousness" does occur in Psalm 119 as a designation of the Torah.

Theological Insights

A theme that ties Psalms 69–71 together is that of shame (69:6–7; 70:2–3; 71:1, 13, 24; see the "Additional Insights" following the unit on Ps. 72). In the modern Western world, where shame has become virtually a discredited emotion, we have some difficulty understanding this theme, which occurs here and in many places in the Psalter. In Israel's world people were tied together by familial bonds that had implications for social life. If one member of the family fell into disrepute, the whole family shared in the dishonor (see Gen. 34:25–31). Next to death itself, to be "covered with scorn and disgrace" (71:13) was the worst curse that could befall a person.[4]

The psalmist articulates another concept that is often expressed in the Old Testament, that God causes weal and woe: "Though you have made me see troubles, many and bitter" (71:20a). In the Old Testament, God is the ultimate cause of everything. This theological position builds a fence, so to speak, around the idea of God's sovereignty. Evil is no threat to God, because it too comes under his control. In fact, it probably was not until the exilic or postexilic age that Old Testament theology came to distinguish between God as the source of good and Satan as the source of evil. The clearest illustration of this is in the parallel stories of David's numbering of Israel. According to 2 Samuel, the Lord was angry with Israel and incited David to take a census (2 Sam. 24:1), whereas 1 Chronicles, written either in the exile or postexile, and obviously with a different theological perspective on the event, substitutes "Satan" for the Lord as the inciter of the census (1 Chron. 21:1). It was not until Israel had become very confident in their monotheistic faith, which happened in the Babylonian exile, that the Old Testament began to distinguish the causes of good and evil.

Teaching the Text

The subject of this psalm is very personal for the suppliant, evidenced by the pronouns "I," "me," and "my," as it is also for many who read this commentary: the emotional expressions, as well as the physical maladies, of advancing age. Yet those circumstances cannot overpower the integrity and constancy that have produced a unique portrait of mature faith, a model for us to contemplate and hopefully emulate.

First, mature faith is characterized by *constancy*, expressed here with the chronological term "always" or "continually" (*tamid*, 71:3, 6, and 14; see the "Additional Insights" following the unit on Ps. 72). While some unevenness characterizes every individual's faith, the suppliant's faith, for the most part, was not an on-and-off pattern but a steady movement. Other expressions emphasize David's faith as a continuing disposition by telling us that he has relied on God "from birth" (71:6), that he has related God's "marvelous deeds" from his youth (71:17), and that he is in the stage of advancing age (71:18).

Second, faith is a *public matter*, for whether we want to be or not, we are "signs" of faith to other people (71:7), and we proclaim God's righteous deeds to others (71:15–17). We might mention that Paul calls our life a "letter of recommendation" (2 Cor. 3:1b–3). So how are we writing our letter, a recommendation that other people are depending on?

Third, faith is a *proclamation to the next generation*. David has been entrusted with the good news of what God has done, and he vows to declare God's power to the next generation (71:18). Every generation of believers, indeed every individual believer, needs to ask the question, "What is the spiritual legacy we are (or, I am) leaving to the next generation?" (see Deut. 6:4–9).

Illustrating the Text

Finish the race.

Sports: In 2012, Meghan Vogel was a junior runner for West Liberty–Salem High School in Ohio. At the Division III state meet in Columbus, Vogel won the 1,600-meter title. Later that day, with little energy left, she was struggling to finish the 3,200-meter race. With twenty meters to go in the race, Arden McMath, a sophomore from Arlington High School, collapsed in front of Vogel. Rather than run by her, Vogel stopped and helped McMath finish the race, making sure to keep McMath ahead of her at the finish line, even though that put Vogel in last place. For Vogel, it was about finishing the race.[5] The apostle Paul writes, at the end of his life, "I have fought the good fight, I have finished the race, I have kept the faith" (2 Tim. 4:7). This is the goal for all Christians. In Psalm 71, David makes a vow to the Lord, "As for me, I will always have hope; I will praise you more and more" (71:14). David understood the need to be committed to the Lord to the very end of his life.

A sign to many

Cultural Institution: The Statue of Liberty has stood for over a century as one of the world's most recognizable symbols. It has provided the inspiration for various stories, poems, and songs because of its powerful message of democracy, particularly to the countless people who have immigrated to the United States. The shackles at the feet of the statue represent America's breaking the chains of tyranny and accepting democracy. The twenty-five windows symbolize heaven's rays shining through to the world.[6] As the Statue of Liberty has come to be a sign of freedom and hope for the world, the cross has become a sign

of hope and liberty for people all over the world. And the life of each Christian has the potential to become a sign to the world of a great, loving, and powerful God. But this will happen only if we are willing to represent the Lord to the world. As the psalmist writes, with confidence, "I have become a sign to many" (Ps. 71:7).

"I have become a sign."

Personal Testimony: On a Sunday in May 1993, as my wife and I were saying goodbye to friends we had met at our church in Marburg, Germany, while on sabbatical, a young lady came up to my wife, Rhonda, and told her this story. During ProChrist, the Billy Graham meetings held across Europe in March, Rhonda had boarded the bus one evening on her way to the meeting, and she sat down and smiled at the young woman. This young woman was feeling very bad after having an argument with her parents, and Rhonda's smile was just what she needed. The young woman had been wanting to tell her this, so she made it a point that morning to come to Rhonda and relate this personal word. Rhonda had become a "sign" of faith (71:7) without speaking a single word.

The Statue of Liberty, pictured here, has become a symbol of liberty, providing hope to those who come to the shores of the United States. How much more should believers, with the psalmist, proclaim God's righteous deeds and mighty acts to a world in need of deliverance.

"Endow the King with Your Justice, O God"

Big Idea *Prayer for the blessing of the nations is also a prayer for the poor and needy of the world.*

Understanding the Text

Psalm 72 is generally classified as a royal psalm. This means its focus is on the king and his kingdom. Some commentators view it as a coronation psalm, which is a little difficult to see because it does not have the same references to the establishment of the kingship as does Psalm 2:7. However, it could have been used in some capacity when Israelite kings were crowned.

It is one of only two psalms associated with Solomon (the other is Ps. 127), and it certainly resonates with Solomon's prayer for a "discerning heart" to govern Israel in 1 Kings 3:6–14. The content of the psalm, however, leaves the matter indecisive as to whether the psalm was written *by* Solomon or by David *for* Solomon. Calvin posits that it was originally a psalm by David, later adapted by Solomon.[1] Our interpretation assumes the position that David wrote the psalm as a prayer for Solomon.

Psalm 72 is unique in the Psalter in that it has a postscript: "This concludes the prayers of David son of Jesse" (72:20). Job has a similar colophon: "The words of Job are ended" (Job 31:40b).

The Text in Context

Psalm 72 is set in the broad context of God's promises to Abraham (Gen. 12:1–3), and, of course, the covenant with David (2 Sam. 7). The second half of verse 17, in fact, uses two verbs for "blessed." First, the psalmist says of the king: "Then all nations will be blessed [*brk*] through him," reminding the reader of the blessing of Abraham (Gen. 22:18; 26:4). Second, the text reads: "and they will call him blessed [*'shr*]," using a verb that is related to the plural noun used to pronounce one "blessed" (see Ps. 1:1; etc.). While this noun is used more frequently than the verb, the latter occurs in Proverbs 31:28 to describe the "good wife's" blessing by her children. The noun "blessed" (*'ashre*), which begins the Psalter (Ps. 1:1) and also begins the last psalm of Book 1 ("Blessed [*'ashre*] are those who have regard for the weak," 41:1), occurs internally in two other psalms that come at the end of Books 3 and 4: Psalms 89:15 ("Blessed ['*ashre*] are those who have learned to acclaim you") and 106:3 ("Blessed ['*ashre*] are those who act justly").

Psalm 72 is not quoted in the New Testament, but its messianic tones are in line with those of prophetic texts like Isaiah 11:1–5 and Zechariah 9:9–10.

Outline/Structure

Aside from the opening entreaty and the concluding doxology and colophon, the psalm falls into five parts:

Opening entreaty (72:1)
Part 1: Hope for a just rule (72:2–4)
"People" are mentioned three times and not mentioned again in the poem. The monarch's responsibility for the "afflicted" and "needy" is acknowledged.
Part 2: Desire for an enduring reign (72:5–7)
The length of his reign is compared to the sun and moon, and its success to the rain that nourishes the earth, causing righteousness to flourish until the moon no longer exists.
Part 3: Pleas for worldwide dominion (72:8–11)
These verses are a prayer that the king will rule universally ("from sea to sea," 72:8) and that his reign will be universally acknowledged.
Part 4: Prayer for compassionate justice (72:12–14)
This section is introduced by "yes, indeed" (*ki*; NIV: "for"), and the discussion returns to justice

for the "needy," "afflicted," and "weak," the topic of part 1 (72:2–4) and verse 7 ("righteous" = the afflicted and the needy).
Part 5: Desire for a prosperous kingdom (72:15–17)
Begins with "and" (*we*) and the jussive "Long may he live!" (72:15). The king's wealth (gold), spiritual benefit (prayer and blessing), and abundant harvest are the focus, and the psalmist prays that his name will continue "as long as the sun" (72:17).
Concluding doxology (72:18–19)
Colophon (72:20)

Historical and Cultural Background

The prayer that God would "endow the king with justice" (72:1) is in keeping

The psalmist prays, "Endow the king with your justice" (72:1). In the ancient world, kings were charged by the gods to administer justice as they ruled. The basalt stele that contains the legal sayings of Hammurabi includes a relief at the top that shows Hammurabi, king of Babylon, standing before Shamash, the god of justice (eighteenth century BC).

Psalm 72

with other ancient Near Eastern documents, one of the best known being Hammurabi's Law Code (eighteenth century BC).[2] The connection of king and justice was a common feature of kingship in the biblical world.

The historical context of the psalm is not clear, except that it definitely arises out of Israel's monarchy. If it is written by David *for* Solomon, as we have suggested, then it probably comes toward the end of David's reign in the first half of the tenth century BC. The hopes in the psalm expressed for Solomon's reign are quite in keeping with the historical data of the book of 1 Kings. His reign was one of prosperity and peace (Ps. 72:3–7, 16; 1 Kings 4:21b–23, 26–28), and his realm extended all the way from the Euphrates River to the border of Egypt (Ps. 72:8; 1 Kings 4:21). The writer of 1 Kings even mentions the gold and gifts brought by the Queen of Sheba to Solomon (Ps. 72:10b, 15; 1 Kings 10:1–10).

Interpretive Insights

Title *Of Solomon.* The Hebrew "to/for [l^e] Solomon" is rendered in the Greek text (LXX) as "for/concerning Solomon" (*eis Salōmōn*), while the Targum has "by the hand of Solomon" and interprets the psalm messianically. Although some commentators consider the superscription to suggest that Solomon is the author (Ps. 127 is also ascribed to him), the king (= Solomon) is referenced in the third-person singular, rather than the first person. This in itself would not, of course, mandate that Solomon could not be the author, but it seems more appropriate that David should pray this prayer on Solomon's behalf (see the introduction to "Understanding the Text").

72:1 *Endow the king with your justice, O God.* The petition in this verse is the only direct address to God in the psalm and the only time the king is mentioned.

72:2 *your afflicted ones.* While these are the socially and legally oppressed, in light of the political situation of the Babylonian exile, which we are assuming for the period when Book 2 was edited, they are likely the exiles themselves (see the sidebar in the unit on Ps. 70). The editor is reapplying this royal psalm to his own time.

72:3 *May the mountains bring prosperity to the people.* The "mountains" and "hills" are representatives of creation that bring forth peace (lit., "May the mountains raise up peace to the people"; NIV translates *shalom*, "peace," in 72:3, 7 as "prosperity"). If these are the mountains around Jerusalem, then they form part of the defensive system and in that respect contribute to peace. Compare Psalm 1:3, where the person who meditates on the Torah is like a "tree planted by streams of water, which yields its fruit in season."

72:4 *the afflicted among the people . . . the children of the needy.* The "afflicted" and the "needy" are parallel terms that have already been introduced in Psalms 69:29, 33; 70:5 (see table 3 in the unit on Ps. 70). See also 72:2, 12, 13.

72:6 *May he be like rain falling on a mown field.* In Hebrew, the subject of the verb is unexpressed. The NIV interprets it as the king, but it could be the king's words, like Deuteronomy 32:2: "Let my teaching fall like rain and my words descend like dew, like showers on new grass, like abundant rain on tender plants." See also Job 29:22–23.

72:7 *In his days may the righteous flourish.* The opposition faced by the righteous

throughout their history, as represented by Books 1 and 2, has now turned in the direction of victory. The "righteous" are likely synonymous with the "afflicted" and "needy."

72:8 *May he rule from sea to sea and from the River to the ends of the earth.* The verb translated "rule" is the same as that in Genesis 1:26, where all humankind is given authority over creation. The realm of the king's rule is worldwide. Wilson draws attention to the theme of God's kingdom that begins in Psalm 56 and continues to the end of Book 2.[3] The word "River" normally refers to the Euphrates River and is one of the farthest borders of David's kingdom (see comments on 72:9–11).

72:9–11 The description of the king's global rule is broken down into (1) "the desert tribes" (72:9a), likely those nomadic groups east of the Jordan River in present-day Jordan; (2) "his enemies" (72:9b), a general term for his international enemies; (3) "the kings of Tarshish" (72:10a), perhaps in Spain or North Africa (Jon. 1); (4) "kings of . . . distant shores" (72:10a), another general geographical term

describing distant nations; (5) "kings of Sheba and Seba" (72:10b), kingdoms located in the southern Arabian peninsula (Gen. 10:7; Isa. 43:3); (6) "all kings" and "all nations" (72:11), general terms summing up the above.

72:9 *lick the dust.* A metaphor of humiliation and defeat. See Isaiah 49:23 and Micah 7:17.

72:10 *bring tribute.* The word "tribute" signifies a tax that conquered nations would pay the conquering king.[4] The writer of 1 Kings describes both Solomon's extensive realm and the tribute he has received: "And Solomon ruled over all the kingdoms from the Euphrates River to the land of the Philistines, as far as the border of Egypt. These countries brought tribute and were Solomon's subjects all his life" (1 Kings 4:21).

72:12–13 *he will deliver the needy . . . He will take pity on the weak and the needy.* The worldwide reign of the king is not impressive if the day-to-day and person-to-person nature of his rule is not charged with compassion, which is a reflection of God's own compassion. The king was God's representative in the world, and this verse contains an expression of God's compassion channeled through the king. See table 3 in the unit on Psalm 70 for the terms related to "weak" and "needy" in the surrounding psalms.

72:14 *He will rescue them from oppression and violence.* The word for "oppression" suggests deceit and lies (Ps. 55:11; NIV: "threats").[5] The two nouns "oppression" and "violence" form a hendiadys meaning "wicked deceit."[6] The idea of "rescue" (*g'l*, "to redeem") is to avenge the blood of someone, especially a family member.

72:15 *Long may he live!* This acclamation of a long life for the king is made at his coronation or at other times of affirmation. The verse begins with "and" (which the NIV has left untranslated), followed by the acclamation for a long life, which is a blessing for his faithful service to the needy and afflicted (72:12–14).

72:17 *Then all nations will be blessed through him, and they will call him blessed.* The verb "be blessed" (*brk*) occurs in Genesis 12:1–3 in the Niphal conjugation (with either a passive or reflexive meaning), but it also occurs in the Hitpael stem (reflexive) concerning Abraham, when he has obeyed the Lord in carrying out the "sacrifice" of Isaac (Gen. 22:18). It further occurs in this reflexive stem in Genesis 26:4, the reaffirmation of Abraham's blessing to Isaac: "through your offspring all nations on earth will be blessed [or "bless themselves"].[7] The second half of the sentence uses a different verb for "call him blessed," *'shr*, which is used also by the children of the "good wife" in Proverbs 31:28 to bless their mother ("Her children arise and call her blessed"). See "The Text in Context."

72:18–19 *Praise be to the Lord God . . . Amen and Amen.* This doxology is the most elaborate of the five doxologies that conclude the five books of the Psalter, except, of course, the extended doxology of Psalms 146–50 that concludes Book 5, or the completed Psalter. See "Trends in Psalms Studies" in the introduction.

72:20 *This concludes the prayers of David son of Jesse.* Even though there are Davidic psalms in Books 3, 4, and 5, Hakham expresses the view that this was not removed when the book was enlarged because it marked the end of one of the five sections, and because it was perceived to be part of the psalm to which it was attached.[8]

Theological Insights

It is easy to see how interpreters have read the theme of the universal reign of the Messiah King from this psalm. Even though the New Testament does not quote the psalm, it falls in the New Testament range of the universality of Christ's reign. If we pay close attention to the terms of the psalm, such as "May all kings bow down to him" (72:11a) and "May he endure as long as the sun" (72:5a), then we can certainly not claim the fulfillment of these terms through the Israelite kings, at least, if we press these two descriptors of that age. So a *fuller sense* (*sensus plenior*) interpretation is helpful, and that comes only in the universal reign of the Messiah that the

All the kings of Israel and Judah fell short of the ideal king described in Psalm 72. Although Solomon began well by asking God for a discerning heart and wisdom to govern (depicted here), he failed in the task of ruling in justice and righteousness. This illumination is from the French Bible translation and commentary known as *La Bible historiale complétée* by Guyart des Moulins (1357).

of the "ideal" king, which David prays that Solomon will become. In fact, Solomon began well (1 Kings 3), but as with so many other kings, his reign took a downward spiral from which it never recovered. The "afflicted" and "needy" were to be the kings' concern because they were economically helpless and socially vulnerable. The prophets identify this category of citizens as the special object of the monarchy's and the society's care (e.g., Isa. 1:17; Jer. 21:12; Amos 8:4). In the Beatitudes, Jesus takes the material qualities of this group of people and turns them into the spiritual values of the kingdom of God (Matt. 5:1–12).

Teaching the Text

To begin our lesson or sermon, we may observe that David, in his prophetic voice (cf. Ps. 71), prays for his son Solomon, asking God to make him the ideal king who will defend the afflicted and needy (72:2–4, 12–14) and have a long and prosperous reign (72:5–11, 15–17a). As the man of war, David is not permitted to build the temple, but his son, he prays, will reign over an era of peace (*shalom*; see the comments on 72:3). Perhaps this is even a wordplay on Solomon's name, *sheʾlomoh*, which is a virtual homonym of the word *shalom*. We might apply this lesson by recognizing that this kind of prayer should characterize all those who, due to age and nature, are conscious that it is time to think about their own legacy and how they will transfer it to the coming generation (see "Teaching the Text" in the unit on Ps. 71). If, as we have explained in our discussion of Psalm 71 (see the introduction to "Understanding the Text" in that unit), this conclusion to

prophets proclaim (e.g., Isa. 66:18–23) and that Christ ultimately fulfills (Rev. 11:15).

The defense of the afflicted and needy was one of the monarchy's major responsibilities and, unfortunately, one of its major failures. In Psalm 69:32–33, we already have the notion that the Lord hears the "needy," and David confesses his identity with the "poor and needy" in Psalm 70:5, anticipating the prayer of Psalm 72 that the king will "deliver the needy" (72:12) and "save the children of the needy" (72:4). This psalm, of course, presents a picture

Book 2 is at the same time a "foreword" to Book 3, reflecting the political and social conditions of the Babylonian exile, then this is all the more reason to stress the need of the older generation to transfer a proper social and spiritual perspective to the coming generation, to encourage and inspire them.

While the defense of the afflicted and needy falls within the king's responsibilities, we may speak also of the message of the prophets who, while not denying the monarch's obligation toward the disadvantaged and oppressed, emphasize the duty of the society to fulfill this role (see "Theological Insights"). This gives good precedent for our role in the care of the oppressed, which, in our world, is quite a diverse category, ranging all the way from those who suffer political oppression, to children who are neglected and abused, and to parents who shirk their responsibilities to their families, to name only some of the most evident examples of oppression in the modern world. We should not be as much afraid of becoming dominated by the "social gospel" as we should be of neglecting

the social aspects of the gospel. There is no way we can preach an authentic gospel of grace and at the same time ignore the social responsibility of the church to show that grace in human relationships.

We may also stress Jesus's own emphasis on fulfilling the social needs of society in his discourse in Matthew 25. There he includes—in fact, assumes the identity of—the hungry, thirsty, stranger, naked, sick, and imprisoned (Matt. 25:34–40). In addition, we may speak about the issue of *faith* and *works* as they are considered by James (James 2:14–26) and his definition of true religion (James 1:27).

Illustrating the Text

Nationalism and the Christian worldview

History: We do not have to look very far to see the frightening evidence of the mix of nationalism and religion. It is not only apparent in the world today but was a major ingredient in Adolf Hitler's ability to control the German masses during World War II. History writer Milton Mayer documents the slow progression of anti-Semitism and its role in blinding the populace to the atrocities of the government: "Ordinary people— and ordinary Germans—cannot be expected to tolerate activities which outrage the ordinary sense

The defense and care of the needy and afflicted are also the responsibility of God's people. Jesus spoke about caring for the stranger and those who are hungry, thirsty (shown here), naked, sick, or imprisoned (Matt. 25:34–40). In this Assyrian relief from a palace in Nineveh, 640–620 BC, one of the women prisoners holds a waterskin for a small child despite the presence of a soldier with an upraised arm wielding a stick.

of ordinary decency unless the victims are, in advance, successfully stigmatized as enemies of the people, of the nation, the race, the religion."[9] Religion, or specifically, the "German Christian" movement, was driven largely by nationalism. While each of us identifies with a nation, we must always remember that our primary allegiance is not to state but to the Lord. We are Christians first, people of the Bible first and foremost. When our nation turns its back on justice and God's way, then we need all the more to speak loudly and boldly for kingdom principles. We are to have passion not just for "our people" but for the people of the world.

A commitment to the poor

Statistics: At any given time in history, there will be people in need. There will always be victims of injustice, orphans, and the poor among us. And in every generation, Christians are to be committed to expressing the heart of God for the hurting people of the world in their time. For example, in the United States as of July 2013, "four out of five U.S. adults struggle with joblessness, near-poverty or reliance on welfare for at least parts of their lives, a sign of deteriorating economic security and an elusive American dream."[10] And it is estimated that in 2010–12, 870 million people in the world did not have enough to eat, a number representing more than the populations of the United States and the European Union combined.[11]

The reign of the eternal King

Children's Book: *The Last Battle*, **by C. S. Lewis.** In Psalm 72, David writes of the rule of the king, a passage many read from the perspective of the eternal rule of Jesus. In *The Last Battle*, Lewis writes about the return of Aslan (representing Christ) and the eternal reign of the King. Lewis summarizes the end of life in this world for the children by saying,

> But for them it was only the beginning of the real story. All their life in this world and all their adventures in Narnia had only been the cover and the title page: now at last they were beginning Chapter One of the Great Story which no one on earth has read: which goes on forever: in which every chapter is better than the one before.[12]

With a similar meaning, Psalm 72 leaves us poised on the verge of God's future kingdom, waiting breathlessly for the next chapter to begin: "May the whole earth be filled with his glory" (72:19b), and that is where all who hope in God must remain.

Corresponding Verbal and Thematic Connections in Psalms 69–72

Psalms 69–72 form a conclusion to Book 2, and the following table is intended to show the verbal and thematic connections between these Davidic psalms. Psalms 71 and 72 do not have "to/for/by David" in their titles, but Psalm 71 seems to be a continuation of Psalm 70, while Psalm 72 is the prayer that David, now "old and gray" (71:18), prayed for Solomon, his successor son, with the intent to "declare your power to the next generation, your mighty acts to all who are to come" (71:18).

Hossfeld describes the internal relationships of these psalms, 69 to 70, 70 to 71, and 71 to 72, as they build in emotional and theological momentum to form this concluding word of David,[1] matching the strong David collection represented by Book 1. If we should wonder why Book 3 has only one Davidic psalm and Book 4 only two, the reason is likely found in the fact that Book 3 represents the soul-searching mood of the exile and the tragic end of the Davidic dynasty (the theological adjustments that had to be made in light of the exile are contemplated in Ps. 89). So David had only a single and minimal representative in Psalm 86. In view of the depressive mood over David's dynasty in Psalm 89, the community of faith needed a robust voice of comfort, so the editor(s) stations Moses at the "gate" of Book 3 to bring a word of comfort and reassurance to this languishing community, and Psalms 101 and 103 (and perhaps also the lament of 102, although not assigned to David) are the meager (in number, not in content) David representatives in Book 3. Once the reputation and hope of the Davidic dynasty had recovered, Book 5 was poised to celebrate its revival.

In the following table the reader will see the connections between and among the last four psalms of Book 2, which may suggest more an editorial viewpoint than an authorial one. The reuse of Psalm 40:14–16 as Psalm 70 is an illustration of the reprocessing style at work in the Psalter as a whole.

Corresponding Verbal and Thematic Connections	Psalm 69	Psalm 70	Psalm 71	Psalm 72
1. Praise of God	69:18, 30–31, 34	70:4b, 5b	71:5–8, 14–17, 18b–19, 22–24	72:18–19
2. Seek my life/hurt (*bqsh*)		70:2	71:13, 23	
3. Those who seek God (*bqsh/drsh*)	69:6 (*bqsh*), 32 (*drsh*)	70:4		
4. Shame / be ashamed / be put to shame (n. *boshet*; v. *bush*)	69:6 (v.)—do not let God's people be ashamed	70:2 (v.), 3 (n.)—let the enemies be ashamed	71:1 (*bush*), 13 (*bush*)—let the accusers be ashamed	
5. Reproach (n. *herpah*; v. *hrp*)	69:7 (n.), 9 (n. pl.), 10 (n. pl.), 19 (n.), 20 (n.)	70:2 (v.)	71:13 (n., "scorn")	
6. Dishonor (n. *kelimmah*; v. *klm*—Niphal)	69:6, 7	70:2	71:13 ("disgrace")	
7. (Coming) generation(s)			71:18	72:5
8. Hurry / hasten / make haste (*mhr*; *hush*)	69:17 (*mhr*)	70:1 (*hush*), 5 (*hush*)	71:12 (*hush*)	
9. Poor and needy ('*ani*; '*ebyon*; pl. '*ebyonim*)	69:29 ('*ani*, "afflicted"), 33 (pl. '*ebyonim*)	70:5		72:4 ('*ebyon*), 12 ('*ebyon* and pl. '*ebyonim*)
10. Afflicted ('*anawim*; *aniyyim*)	69:32 ("humble")			72:2 ("poor"), 4 ("poor")
11. Rejoice / be glad (*smh*; *sis*)	69:32 (*smh*)	70:4 (*sis* and *smh*)		
12. Those who love God's name/ salvation ('*hb*)	69:36 ("name")	70:4 ("salvation")		
13. (God's) name (*shem*)	69:36			72:17
14. Redeem/ransom (*g'l*; *pdh*)	69:18 (*g'l*, "ransom")		71:23 (*pdh*)	72:14 (*g'l*)
15. Deliver (*ntsl*, Niphal and Hiphil)	69:14 (2x)			
16. Save/rescue (*ysh'*; *plt*)	69:1 (*ysh'*), 35 (*ysh'*)	70:5 (*plt*, "deliverer")	71:2 (*plt*), 3, 4 (*plt*)	72:4 ("give deliverance"), 13 (*ysh'*)
17. Continually (*tamid*)	69:23	70:4 ("evermore")	71:3, 6, 14	72:15
18. All day long (*kol hayyom*)			71:8, 15, 24	72:15
19. (God's/people's) righteous/ righteousness (*tsedeq/tsedaqah*)	69:28 (pl. "righteous"—the people of God)		71:2 (God's righteousness), 15 (God's "righteous acts"), 16 (Yahweh's "mighty deeds"), 19 (God's "righteousness"), 24 (God's "righteous help")	72:1, 2, 3 (God's righteousness), 7 (pl. "righteous"—the people of God)
20. Wait/hope (*yhl*)	69:3		71:14 (*yhl*)	
21. Wait/hope (n., *tiqwah*; v. *qwh*)	69:6 ("looked for," part., *qwh*), 20 (v. *qwh*)		71:5 (n. *tiqwah*)	

Note: I have used the English Standard Version for this table because the translation of terms is more consistent and thus easier to follow from psalm to psalm, and I have added numbers for ease of reference.

Connections in Psalms 69–72

Notes

Introduction to the Psalms

1. See Bullock, *Encountering*, chapters 7–14, on which the definitions in this commentary are dependent.

2. Westminster Shorter Catechism, Q & A 1.

3. Lewis, *Psalms*, 94–95.

4. Lewis, *Psalms*, 96.

5. Bullock, *Encountering*, 136.

6. Witvliet, *Biblical Psalms*, 32.

7. See Card, *Sacred Sorrow*.

8. Westermann, *Praise and Lament*, 55–61.

9. See Wilson, *Psalms,* 1:31–57, for his excellent discussion of Hebrew poetry, and Hrushovski, "Prosody, Hebrew," for a discussion of Hebrew poetry from biblical times to modern.

10. Calvin, *Psalms*, 1:xxxvii.

11. Luther, "Psalter," 254.

12. Gunkel, *Introduction to Psalms*.

13. Wilson, *Hebrew Psalter*.

14. See Zenger, "Composition and Theology."

15. Hossfeld and Zenger, *Psalms 2*, 1.

16. See the discussion of Psalms 89 and 90.

17. The "macrostructure," according to our usage, is a collection of psalms that comprises one of the five books, or a combination of them. There are many "microstructures" or minicollections that comprise each book.

18. Hossfeld and Zenger, *Psalms 2*, 2.

19. McCann, "Books I–III," 100.

20. Wilson, "Royal Psalms," 85–94.

21. Hossfeld and Zenger, *Psalms 3*, 1.

22. Bullock, *Encountering*, 66.

23. Hossfeld and Zenger, *Psalms 2*, 7.

24. Hossfeld and Zenger, *Psalms 3*, 2, 5.

25. Hossfeld and Zenger, *Psalms 3*, 5.

26. Bullock, "Shape of the Torah."

27. The metaphor "the shadow of your wings" occurs in Deuteronomy 32:11, but the wording varies a bit from the phrase in Psalm 17:8.

28. See Witvliet, *Biblical Psalms*.

Psalm 1

1. Jonathan Edwards, "Nothing upon Earth Can Represent the Glories of Heaven," in *Sermons and Discourses 1723–1729*, vol. 14 of *The Works of Jonathan Edwards*, ed. Kenneth P. Minkema (New Haven: Yale University Press, 1997), 145–46.

2. N. T. Wright, *The Case for the Psalms: Why They Are Essential* (New York: HarperCollins, 2013), 7, 26.

Psalm 2

1. Hilber, *Cultic Prophecy*, 89–101.

2. See "The Structure and Composition of the Psalter" in the introduction.

3. Wenham, *Psalms as Torah*, 81, observes that the verb *hgh* ("meditate"/"plot") involves the use of the tongue, mouth, and throat. It does not describe "silent" meditation. It is used of lions roaring (Isa. 31:4), pigeons cooing (Isa. 59:11), and nations plotting.

4. Mowinckel, *He That Cometh*, 156.

5. Kraus, *Psalms 1–59*, 130.

6. Keel, *Symbolism*, 248.

7. This alternative reading is provided in the NIV footnote.

8. Michael Scott Horton, *Putting Amazing Back into Grace: An Introduction to Reformed Theology* (Nashville: Thomas Nelson, 1991), 25–26; quoting Robert Rosenblatt, "What Really Matters?" *Time* (October 1983): 24–27.

9. Robert L. Scott Jr., *God Is My Co-Pilot: A True Story of Inspiration* (Broomfield, CO: Summa Iru Specialty Publishing, 2011).

Psalm 3

1. Bullock, *Encountering*, 137.

2. Terrien, *Psalms*, 91.

3. Delitzsch, *Psalms*, 1:136.

4. Schaefer, *Psalms*, 12.

5. If you want to sing the Psalms, you may use the *Scottish Psalter*, the *Genevan Psalter,* the *Psalter Hymnal* (Grand

Rapids: CRC Publications, 1987), *The Book of Psalms for Singing* (Pittsburgh: Board of Education and Publication, Reformed Presbyterian Church of North America, 1998), and *The Psalms for All Seasons* (Grand Rapids: Brazos, 2011), or other resources.

6. Peter Wehrwein, "Astounding Increase in Antidepressent Use by Americans," Harvard Health Blog, October 20, 2011, http://www.health.harvard.edu/blog/astounding -increase-in-antidepressant-use-by-americans.

7. P. T. Forsyth, *The Soul of Prayer* (London: Independent Press, 1916), 17; also available online at http://www.ccel .org/ccel/forsyth/prayer/files/soul_of_prayer03.htm.

Psalm 4

1. Craigie, *Psalms 1–50*, 80.
2. Bullock, *Encountering*, 29.
3. Bullock, *Encountering*, 29; Kraus, *Psalms 1–59*, 26.
4. Terrien, *Psalms*, 101.
5. Terrien, *Psalms*, 102.
6. "Lincoln to Hodges," *New York Daily Tribune*, April 29, 1864. See also http://housedivided.dickinson.edu/sites /lincoln/letter-to-albert-hodges-april-4-1864.
7. Rick Reilly, "The Lessons of Nathaniel Jones," ESPN .com, last modified April 28, 2011, http://sports.espn.go.com /espn/news/story?id=6436820.

Psalm 5

1. Kidner, *Psalms 1–72*, 57.
2. Briggs and Briggs, *Psalms*, 41.
3. See figures 304 and 306 (*magen*) in Keel, *Symbolism*, 222.
4. Some consider Job to be an exception, but that book deals with unjust suffering, which is certainly a subset of the problem of evil but is not the problem itself.
5. Horatius Bonar, *Hymns of Faith and Hope* (London: James Nisbet, 1857), 237.
6. Although this quote is commonly attributed to Edmund Burke, many scholars believe that while it is true to, and possibly derived from, his writings, Burke himself never actually wrote or spoke these words. See Paul F. Boller and John George, *They Never Said It* (Oxford: Oxford University Press, 1989).
7. Selderhuis, *John Calvin*, 161.

Psalm 6

1. A. A. Anderson gives these correspondences: Psalm 6:1/Psalm 38:1; Psalm 6:2/Psalm 41:4; Psalm 6:4/Psalm 109:26; Psalm 6:6/Jeremiah 45:3; Psalm 6:7/Psalm 31:10; Psalm 6:8/Psalm 119:115; Psalm 6:10/Psalms 35:4, 26; 83:13 (A. A. Anderson, *Psalms 1–72*, 87).
2. Craigie, *Psalms 1–50*, 92.
3. Snaith, *Distinctive Ideas*, 128.
4. A. B. Davidson, *Theology*, 31.
5. Delitzsch, *Psalms*, 1:172.
6. Craigie, *Psalms 1–50*, 90–91.
7. Kidner, *Psalms 1–72*, 61.
8. These are the words of my revered professor Rabbi Sheldon A. Blank, Hebrew Union College–Jewish Institute of Religion.
9. Kidner, *Psalms 1–72*, 61.

10. Craigie, *Psalms 1–50*, 93–94.
11. Irving Stone, *The Agony and the Ecstasy: A Biographical Novel of Michelangelo* (New York: Doubleday, 1961), 90.
12. Augustine, *Confessions* 1.4 (trans. R. Warner), in W. Edgar and K. S. Oliphint, eds., *Christian Apologetics Past and Present: A Primary Source Reader* (Wheaton: Crossway, 2009), 1:211.

Psalm 7

1. Bullock, *Encountering*, 136–38; see also the discussion of psalms of lament in the introduction.
2. *Selah* does not function as a strophe divider, except in certain instances, and in those psalms the position of *selah* probably has a liturgical function (see, e.g., Ps. 24; see also the sidebar "Selah" in the unit on Ps. 3).
3. Craigie, *Psalms 1–50*, 99.
4. Kraus, *Psalms 1–59*, 26. See also Bullock, *Encountering*, 28.
5. Calvin, *Psalms*, 1:70.
6. Calvin, *Psalms*, 1:80.
7. Perowne, *Psalms*, 1:141.
8. A. A. Anderson, *Psalms 1–72*, 96.
9. Craigie, *Psalms 1–50*, 99.
10. Calvin, *Psalms*, 1:92.
11. Terrien, *Psalms*, 118–19.
12. Psalm 97:9 brings the two appellations together, but with a disjunctive accent between them, giving the meaning, "For you, LORD, are the Most High over all the earth."
13. The major disjunctive accent ('*atnah*) provides the clue that we have a general statement, followed by two particulars.
14. Michael Reynolds, "Massacre at Malmédy during the Battle of the Bulge," *World War II Magazine*, February 2003; available online at http://www.historynet.com /massacre-at-malmedy-during-the-battle-of-the-bulge.htm.
15. Alison Auld, "Most Sexual Abuse Victims Have Little Faith in Justice System: Survey," *Globe and Mail*, May 5, 2013.
16. *Iron Man*, directed by Jon Favreau (Hollywood, CA: Paramount Pictures, 2008), DVD.

Psalm 8

1. Delitzsch, *Psalms*, 1:189.
2. Terrien, *Psalms*, 131.
3. Bullock, *Encountering*, 30.
4. Spurgeon, *Psalms*, 21–22.
5. Spurgeon, *Psalms*, 24.
6. Kraus, *Psalms 1–59*, 82.
7. See Schaefer, *Psalms*, 25.
8. Delitzsch, *Psalms*, 1:200.
9. Kidner, *Psalms 1–72*, 67.
10. Augustine, *Confessions* 1.1.
11. Westminster Shorter Catechism, Q & A 1 (emphasis added).
12. George Carey, *Why I Believe in a Personal God: The Credibility of Faith in a Doubting Culture* (Wheaton: Harold Shaw, 1989), 29.
13. C. S. Lewis, *Letters to an American Lady*, ed. Clyde S. Kilby (Grand Rapids: Eerdmans, 1967), 18.

14. "Joachim Neander," Hymnary.org, http://www.hymnary.org/person/Neander_Joachim.

Additional Insights, pages 66–67

1. Augustine, *On the Psalms.*
2. Sabourin, *Psalms,* 157.
3. Craigie, *Psalms 1–50,* 68, 110, etc.
4. See Walter C. Kaiser Jr.'s treatment of the Psalms and their messianic witness, *The Messiah in the Old Testament.*
5. With the exception of Psalm 89, this is Hermann Gunkel's list. See Bullock, *Encountering,* 178–80.
6. Kirkpatrick, *Psalms,* 1:lxxix.
7. Derek Kidner (*Psalms,* 2:18–25) emphasizes that the NT quotations from the Psalms are a guide to determining the messianic psalms, and points out that the messiah is represented under these aspects: (a) the anointed King (e.g., Ps. 2/Acts 4:25–29; Ps. 45:7/Heb. 1:8); (b) God's Son (e.g., Ps. 2:7/Acts 13:33); (c) Son of man (Ps. 8:4/Heb. 2:5–9); (d) Priest (Ps. 110:4/Heb. 5:6); (e) Stone (Ps. 118:22/Luke 20:17–18); (f) God (Ps. 45:7/Heb. 1:8).

Psalms 9–10

1. A. A. Anderson points to Psalms 22; 52; and 77 as examples of mixed types (*Psalms 1–72,* 104).
2. For a study of this order in the Psalms, see Villanueva, *Uncertainty of a Hearing,* 102–13.
3. The partial acrostic seems suspicious, however, and it could be unintentional that we have seventeen letters of the Hebrew alphabet in this psalm, with five missing.
4. A.A. Anderson, *Psalms 1–72,* 104.
5. The sequence of the letters is as follows: *aleph* (9:1–2), *beth* (9:3–4), *gimel* (9:5–6), *he* (9:7–8), *waw* (9:9–10), *zayin* (9:11–12), *heth* (9:13–14), *teth* (9:15–16), *yod* (9:17), *kaph* (9:18–20), *lamed* (10:1–6), *pe* (10:7–8), *ayin* (10:9–11), *qoph* (10:12–13), *resh* (10:14), *shin* (10:15–16), *taw* (10:17–18). The letters *daleth, mem, nun, samekh,* and *tsade* are missing. The letter *shin* serves as both *shin* and *sin.*
6. See the comments on the title for Psalm 4.
7. Kidner, *Psalms 1–72,* 69.
8. A. A. Anderson, *Psalms 1–72,* 108.
9. Craigie, *Psalms 1–50,* 115.
10. Hakham, *Psalms,* 1:53.
11. Psalms 3:7; 7:6; 9:19; 10:12; 17:13; 74:22; 82:8; 132:8.
12. "2013 World Hunger and Poverty Facts and Statistics," World Hunger Education Service, http://www.worldhunger.org/articles/Learn/world%20hunger%20facts%202002.htm.
13. Westminster Shorter Catechism, Q & A 1.

Psalm 11

1. Hakham, *Psalms,* 1:67.
2. Hakham, *Psalms,* 1:68.
3. Hakham, *Psalms,* 1:69.
4. Hakham, *Psalms,* 1:70.
5. Kenneth W. Osbeck, *Amazing Grace: 366 Inspiring Hymn Stories for Daily Devotions* (Grand Rapids: Kregel, 1990), 287.
6. Max Lucado, *The Children of the King,* illustr. Sergio Martinez (Wheaton: Crossway, 2014).

Psalm 12

1. The Hebrew of verse 8 is very difficult. I have used the NIV's translation, which is a restatement of the gist of the psalm, while Hakham renders it, "When the downtrodden among the children of man arise" (Hakham, *Psalms,* 1:77), a virtual prophecy of the restoration of the righteous. Neither is certain, but both are in some accord with the psalm. For certain, however, is the *inclusio* formed by the occurrence of the expression "sons of man" (*bene 'adam*) in 12:1 and 8.
2. Goldingay, *Psalms,* 1:196.
3. Eveline J. Van der Steen, "Metallurgy," *NIDB* 4:68–70.
4. Hakham (*Psalms,* 1:75) is probably correct in translating the dual form of seven as "twice seven times," suggesting that the product was impeccably purified.
5. Adamson, *James,* 60.
6. Goldingay, *Psalms,* 1:198.
7. Hakham, *Psalms,* 1:73.
8. Hakham, *Psalms,* 1:74.
9. Hakham, *Psalms,* 1:75.
10. Goldingay, *Psalms,* 1:201.
11. Hakham, *Psalms,* 1:72.
12. Charles Dickens, *The Tale of Two Cities* (1859; Toronto: Bantam, 1981), 1.
13. Buber, *Right and Wrong,* 11.
14. "UMass Researcher Finds Most People Lie in Everyday Conversation," June 10, 2002, http://www.eurekalert.org/pub_releases/2002-06/uoma-urf061002.php.
15. Judith Aquino, "31% of People Lie on Resumes, and 9 Other Surprising Truths about Lying," Business Insider, March 7, 2011, http://www.businessinsider.com/75-of-women-lie-about-money-and-other-shocking-facts-2011-3?op=1.
16. John H. Sailhamer, *Introduction to Old Testament Theology: A Canonical Approach* (Grand Rapids: Zondervan, 1995), 203–4.

Psalm 13

1. Kidner, *Psalms 1–72,* 77. See 2 Samuel 15–19.
2. Delitzsch, *Psalms,* 1:252.
3. Schaefer, *Psalms,* 32.
4. See Blank's discussion (*Jeremiah,* 25–26, 183) of this word of hope.
5. Westermann, *Praise and Lament,* 74.
6. Kidner, *Psalms 1–72,* 78.
7. See Ferris, *Communal Lament.*
8. A. A. Anderson, *Psalms 1–72,* 128.
9. Hilber, "Psalms," 329.
10. Westermann, *Living Psalms,* 70.
11. Perowne, *Psalms,* 1:176.
12. See comments on Psalm 6:3.
13. Delitzsch, *Psalms,* 1:252.
14. Calvin, *Psalms,* 1:183.
15. Terrien, *Psalms,* 159.
16. Martha T. Moore and Linda Kanamin, "Pa. Town 'in a Daze' after Teens, Teachers Are Killed," *USA Today,* October 23, 1996, http://usatoday30.usatoday.com/news/index/crash/ncrash12.htm.

17. William R. White, *Stories for the Journey: A Source-book for Christian Storytellers* (Minneapolis: Augsburg, 1988), 47–49.

Psalm 14

1. A. A. Anderson, *Psalms 1–72*, 131.
2. Perowne, *Psalms*, 1:181.
3. Joash (2 Kings 12:4–16); Josiah (2 Kings 22:3–7).
4. Kidner, *Psalms 1–72*, 79.
5. Elmslie, *Jewish Proverbs*, 129. For an analysis of the biblical terms, see Perowne, *Psalms*, 1:182; Delitzsch, *Psalms*, 1:256–57.
6. Schaefer, *Psalms*, 33.
7. Psalm 5:9c (5:10c LXX); Psalm 5:9c (5:10d LXX); Psalm 140:3b (139:4b LXX); Psalm 10:7 (9:28 LXX); Isaiah 59:7a–b; Proverbs 1:16; Isaiah 59:7d; 59:8a; Psalm 36:1 (35:2 LXX). Taken from Beale and Carson, *Use of the Old Testament*, 616, 617.
8. Legend has it that Peter, encouraged by his supporters, fled from the city of Rome to escape execution and met the Master running in the opposite direction into the city. Peter asked him, "Where are you going [*Quo vadis*], Master?" And the Master replied that he was going into the city to be crucified again. Thus Peter turned on his heels and ran into the city of Rome, to be crucified upside down (see *The Acts of Peter*).
9. Jessica Pressler, "Matthew McConaughey: Leading Man of the Year 2013," *GQ*, December 2013, http://www.gq.com/moty/2013/matthew-mcconaughey-leading-men-of-the-year-leading-man.
10. Byard Duncan, "George Saunders: Life Coach of the Year 2013," *GQ*, December 2013, http://www.gq.com/moty/2013/george-saunders-men-of-the-year-life-coach.
11. Philip Yancey, "What Good Is God," *The Blog* (blog), *Huffington Post*, October 23, 2010, http://www.huffingtonpost.com/philip-yancey/what-good-is-god_b_772236.html.

Psalm 15

1. See Gerstenberger, *Psalms*, 86–88.
2. Mays, *Psalms*, 85.
3. See the sidebar "Wisdom Psalms" in the unit on Psalm 37.
4. E.g., VanGemeren, "Psalms," 147.
5. Terrien, *Psalms*, 170. The verb "dwell" (*gur*) can have the sense of "take refuge."
6. Delitzsch, *Psalms*, 1:265.
7. Delitzsch, *Psalms*, 1:265.
8. Terrien, *Psalms*, 70.
9. Delitzsch, *Psalms*, 1:268. One translation is "to trip over his tongue."
10. Hebrew Hiphil infinitive construct from the verb "to cause one's own hurt" (*r'*).
11. With a similar humanitarian motive, the Torah forbids taking a bribe, because it will confuse the motives of the receiver (Exod. 23:8; see also Deut. 16:19). The prophets also condemn this practice (Isa. 1:23; 5:23; Amos 5:11–15).
12. Schaefer, *Psalms*, 34.
13. The Babylonian Talmud identifies eleven character traits in this answer, while others find as many as twelve. We must remember that all these traits produce the full picture of the ethically enabled person who can enter the sanctuary. So the number is not as important as the content.
14. See Lewis's discussion of the modern practice of charging interest (*Mere Christianity*, 72–73).
15. "Regular Check-Ups Are Important," Centers for Disease Control and Prevention, last modified February 5, 2014, http://www.cdc.gov/family/checkup/.
16. Adrian Nocent, *The Liturgical Year*, 4 vols. (Collegeville, MN: Liturgical Press, 1977), 1:35.

Psalm 16

1. Bullock, *Encountering*, 166–76.
2. See the discussion in Beale and Carson, *Use of the Old Testament*, 536–39, and their side-by-side comparison of the translations of the Septuagint and Hebrew (537).
3. Perowne, *Psalms*, 1:190.
4. Gruber, *Rashi's Commentary*, 226.
5. Delitzsch, *Psalms*, 1:273–74. Isaiah 38:9 prefixes a similar word, *miktab* ("writing, inscription"), to the prayer of Hezekiah, but it probably should be read *miktam*.
6. Psalms 7:1; 11:1; 16:1; 25:20; 31:1; 71:1; 141:8; 144:2.
7. A. A. Anderson, *Psalms 1–72*, 142.
8. Perowne, *Psalms*, 1:188.
9. The Hebrew personal pronoun standing at the end of the clause, *hemmah* ("they"), sometimes is used where the connecting verb in English ("are") would occur. As for the word "nobles" (*'addire*), which is in construct with the phrase "all my desire," another instance of a noun in construct with a phrase is Ps. 90:14, "the years [*shenot*] when we have seen evil." See Hakham, *Psalms*, 1:93n3.
10. Delitzsch, *Psalms*, 1:280.
11. Delitzsch, *Psalms*, 1:284.
12. See Schaefer, *Psalms*, 37, for a list of the vocabulary shared by Psalms 16 and 17.
13. Calvin, *Psalms*, 1:229–30.
14. See the sidebar "Sheol" in the unit on Psalm 6. See also Johnston, "Psalm 16."
15. *Shahat* normally means "grave" or "pit" (Ps. 7:15; Prov. 26:27) but may mean "destruction" of the body (= death). See Perowne, *Psalms*, 1:196.
16. Beale and Carson, *Use of the Old Testament*, 537.
17. Delitzsch, *Psalms*, 1:286.
18. Perowne, *Psalms*, 1:191.
19. VanGemeren, "Psalms," 159.
20. Calvin, *Psalms*, 1:224.
21. Irene Ting-Ting Lai, "History of Hymns: 'Forth in Thy Name, O Lord,'" General Board of Discipleship of the United Methodist Church, http://www.gbod.org/lead-your-church/history-of-hymns/resource/history-of-hymns-forth-in-thy-name-o-lord.
22. Charles Wesley, "Forth in Thy Name, O Lord, I Go," in *The English Hymnal with Tunes* (London: Oxford University Press, 1933), no. 259.

Psalm 17

1. Schaefer, *Psalms*, 39; VanGemeren, "Psalms," 160. Psalms 7; 26; and 35 are other examples of the psalm of innocence.

2. A. A. Anderson, *Psalms 1–72*, 147; Schaefer, *Psalms*, 39.

3. E.g., A. A. Anderson, *Psalms 1–72*, 147.

4. Delitzsch, *Psalms*, 1:291.

5. Psalms 17:8; 36:7; 57:1; 61:4; 63:7; 91:4.

6. See Keel's brief discussion in *Symbolism*, 190–92.

7. Psalms 10:9–10 and 17:12 describe the lions lying in ambush and suddenly pouncing on their prey (see Keel, *Symbolism*, 85–86).

8. Hakham, *Psalms*, 1:100.

9. Hakham, *Psalms*, 1:100.

10. Delitzsch, *Psalms*, 1:289.

11. Hakham, *Psalms*, 1:102.

12. Calvin, *Psalms*, 1:241.

13. Kidner, *Psalms 1–72*, 187–88.

14. Hakham, *Psalms*, 1:103.

15. Hakham, *Psalms*, 1:104.

16. Hakham, *Psalms*, 1:104.

17. Perowne, *Psalms*, 1:201.

18. Kidner, *Psalms 1–72*, 89.

19. Marie Brenner, "American Nightmare: The Ballad of Richard Jewell," *Vanity Fair*, February 1997, http://www.vanityfair.com/magazine/archive/1997/02/brenner199702.

Psalm 18

1. A. A. Anderson, *Psalms 1–72*, 153; see also Bullock, *Encountering*, 151–58.

2. Waltner, *Psalms*, 101.

3. Delitzsch (*Psalms*, 1:334–44) discusses 2 Samuel 22 in relation to Psalm 18.

4. Deuteronomy 32:43; Psalm 117:1; and Isaiah 11:10.

5. Delitzsch, *Psalms*, 1:325.

6. Psalms 11:4–7; 22:3; 47:8; 68:5; 93:2; 123:1.

7. A. A. Anderson, *Psalms 1–72*, 157.

8. Delitzsch, *Psalms*, 1:323.

9. Delitzsch, *Psalms*, 1:330.

10. Waltner, *Psalms*, 104.

11. William A. Clebsch and Charles R. Jaekle, *Pastoral Care in Historical Perspective: An Essay with Exhibits* (Englewood Cliffs, NJ: Prentice-Hall, 1964), 22.

Psalm 19

1. Mays, "Torah-Psalms," 3–12.

2. Mays, "Torah-Psalms," 11. See also Bullock, *Encountering*, 213–26.

3. See Bullock, *Encountering*, 215.

4. Hakham, *Psalms*, 1:133.

5. Kidner, *Psalms 1–72*, 97–98.

6. Weiser, *Psalms*, 199.

7. Hakham, *Psalms*, 1:135.

8. Hakham translates "all of them" as "all of them, without exception" (Hakham, *Psalms*, 1:137).

9. Goldingay, *Psalms*, 1:293.

10. Mazar and Panitz-Cohen, "Land of Honey."

11. Goldingay, *Psalms*, 1:297.

12. Kidner, *Psalms 1–72*, 99.

13. Lewis, *Psalms*, 63.

14. "The Story of . . . How Great Thou Art," Manna Music, http://www.mannamusicinc.com/hgta.htm.

15. Voice of the Martyrs is one of many organizations that tracks the persecution of Christians and also seeks to aid and uplift those who face oppression and persecution and facilitate the distribution of God's Word, even when it is dangerous. For more information, see Voice of the Martyrs, *2014 Global Report on Where Christians Are Persecuted Today*, http://www.persecution.com/uploads/media/downloads/194_GlobalReport2014FinalLow.pdf.

16. "Pakistan: A Routine Faith," Voice of the Martyrs website, posted August 11, 2014, http://www.persecution.com/public/newsroom.aspx?story_ID==373030.

Psalm 20

1. See Bullock, *Encountering*, 178–82.

2. Craigie, *Psalms 1–50*, 185.

3. Goldingay, *Psalms*, 1:302.

4. Goldingay, *Psalms*, 1:302.

5. Hilber, "Psalms," 336.

6. Craigie, *Psalms 1–50*, 188.

7. Goldingay, *Psalms*, 1:306; but see the introductory comments in "Understanding the Text," above.

8. Goldingay, *Psalms*, 1:304.

9. "U.S. Government Response to the September 11 Attacks," *Wikipedia*, last modified June 2, 2014, http://en.wikipedia.org/wiki/U.S._government_response_to_the_September_11_attacks.

10. "History of 'In God We Trust,'" U.S. Department of the Treasury, last modified March 8, 2011, http://www.treasury.gov/about/education/Pages/in-god-we-trust.aspx.

Psalm 21

1. Craigie, *Psalms 1–50*, 190.

2. See the discussion of 2 Chronicles 20 in "Historical and Cultural Background."

3. Kidner, *Psalms 1–72*, 103.

4. Craigie, *Psalms 1–50*, 189.

5. Hakham, *Psalms*, 1:154.

6. Goldingay, *Psalms*, 1:314.

7. Calvin, *Psalms*, 1:349.

8. Craigie, *Psalms 1–50*, 192.

9. Hakham, *Psalms*, 1:152.

10. Hilber, "Psalms," 316.

11. Hakham, *Psalms*, 1:153.

12. Craigie, *Psalms 1–50*, 193.

13. On the problem of war in the Old Testament, see Craigie, *Problem of War*; Longman and Reid, *God Is a Warrior*. On the problem of genocide, see Gundry, *Show Them No Mercy*.

14. Schaefer, *Psalms*, 50.

15. G. K. Chesterton, *Orthodoxy* (Garden City, NY: Doubleday, 1959), 160.

16. Robert Lowry, "How Can I Keep from Singing," in *Psalms and Hymns, and Spiritual Songs* (Richmond, VA: Presbyterian Committee of Publication, 1882), no. 803.

Psalm 22

1. See my discussion of the lament psalms in Bullock, *Encountering*, 136–38.

2. The NIV reads, "To the tune of 'The Doe of the Morning,'" but the words "to the tune of" do not occur in the Hebrew text. See Bullock, *Encountering*, 30, for a brief definition.

3. See the comments on the title of Psalm 6 in that unit.

4. Psalms 2:1; 10:1; 11:3; 13:1; 15:1.

5. Schaefer, *Psalms*, 52.

6. Other multiple terms are "surround" (22:12 and 16, describing the enemies) and "bulls," "lions," and "dogs" (22:12, 13, 16), reversing these terms in 22:20–21.

7. See Tobit 5:16.

8. Craigie, *Psalms 1–50*, 200.

9. Goldingay, *Psalms*, 1:332.

10. Hakham, *Psalms*, 1:162.

11. Hakham, *Psalms*, 1:166. Also Hilber, "Psalms," 339.

12. Kidner, *Psalms 1–72*, 109.

13. Calvin, *Psalms*, 1:361.

14. Calvin, *Psalms*, 1:359.

15. Lewis, *Mere Christianity*, 106.

16. As we develop this idea, we might also describe the concept of "praise." It is joy expressing itself in words and deeds of gratitude, a joy that, says Lewis, has to be shared with others for its completion (see "The Anatomy of Praise" in the introduction).

17. Looking at this concept from another angle, in the prefatory clause, "Yet you are holy" (ESV), David recognizes God's presence in a world that seemed God-forsaken. If our audience has a philosophical interest, we might deal briefly with the question of why God demands praise. Does he *need* it? Is he an egotist? If God denied, or refused to acknowledge, or declined human expression that what he made was good, or that he was holy, knowing the contrary, it would be false, and thus a denial of his nature. Lewis's discussion of this question is helpful. This truth is borne out by the structure of the book of Psalms, with its doxologies at the conclusion of each book, and its summative expression of praise at the end (see "Trends in Psalms Studies" in the introduction).

18. Dietrich Bonhoeffer, *Psalms: The Prayer Book of the Bible* (Minneapolis: Augsburg Fortress, 1970), 49.

19. John Ortberg, *The Life You've Always Wanted* (Grand Rapids: Zondervan, 2002), 22–25.

20. Elizabeth Barrett Browning, "Cowper's Grave," *The Poetical Works of Elizabeth Barrett Browning* (London: John Murray, 1914), 143.

Psalm 23

1. See also Bullock, *Encountering*, 166–72.

2. Goldingay, *Psalms*, 1:345.

3. Knight, in his gem of a book, *The Song of Our Syrian Guest*, presents the metaphor of Shepherd and lamb consistently in both parts of the psalm.

4. Delitzsch, *Psalms*, 1:329.

5. The terms "house of the Lord" and "temple of the Lord" are used interchangeably in the Hannah story (1 Sam. 1:7, 9 ESV), and the temple is also called "the house of the Lord" in 1 Kings 7:12, 40, 45, 51 (ESV), and so on.

6. Hilber, "Psalms," 340.

7. Hakham, *Psalms*, 1:170.

8. Hakham, *Psalms*, 1:171.

9. Goldingay, *Psalms*, 1:352.

10. Hakham, *Psalms*, 1:172.

11. A slightly different spelling (*naweh* in Exod. 15:13; the pl. construct form in Ps. 23:2 includes an *aleph*), but the same word.

12. See further the use of the verb *nhh* of Israel's experience in the wilderness (e.g., Exod. 13:17, 21; 15:13; Deut. 32:12; Ps. 77:20).

13. See Bullock, "Shape of the Torah."

14. African American spiritual, "Were You There When They Crucified My Lord?"

15. Quoted by Alton H. McEachern, "Preaching from the Psalms," *Review and Expositor* 81 (1984): 458.

16. Billy Graham, *Facing Death and the Life After* (Waco: Word), 93–94.

17. Francis Thompson, "The Hound of Heaven," in *Selected Poems of Francis Thompson* (New York: John Lane, 1908), 51–56.

18. John Calvin, *Steward of God's Covenant: Selected Writings of John Calvin*, ed. by J. F. Thornton and S. B. Varenne (New York: Vintage, 2006), 170.

Psalm 24

1. Kidner, *Psalms 1–72*, 113.

2. See *m. Tamid* 7.4.

3. Hakham, *Psalms*, 176.

4. Although this was not Herod's temple, the mishnaic tractate *Middot* (3.7) helps us understand the massive dimensions of that building, and thus gives us perspective. According to *Middot* the entrance hall of the porch was forty cubits high and twenty cubits wide (60 ft. x 30 ft.). "Above it were five carved oak beams; the lowest one projected beyond the entrance one cubit [18 in.] to either side, the one above it projected beyond it one cubit to either side, [and so on]; thus the uppermost was thirty cubits long [40 ft.]. Between every two beams was a course of stones" (Danby's trans.).

5. Hakham, *Psalms*, 1:176.

6. Snaith, "Selah," 55.

7. Hakham, *Psalms*, 1:180.

8. Delitzsch, *Psalms*, 1:339.

9. Goldingay, *Psalms*, 1:356. Goldingay's "processional liturgy" is essentially the same as our term "entry liturgy," since the goal of the procession is entry into the Lord's house.

10. Wilson, *Psalms*, 1:450.

11. Robert Jastrow, *God and the Astronomers*, 2nd ed. (New York: William Morrow, 1993), 292.

12. Michele Johnson and J. D. Harrington, "NASA's Kepler Mission Announces a Planet Bonanza, 715 New Worlds," NASA, February 26, 2014, http://www.nasa.gov/ames/kepler/nasas-kepler-mission-announces-a-planet-bonanza/.

13. Ray Villard and Kailash Sahu, "The Milky Way Contains at Least 100 Billion Planets according to Survey," HubbleSite.org, January 11, 2012, http://hubblesite.org/newscenter/archive/releases/2012/07/full/.

14. "Universe," *Wikipedia*, last modified May 31, 2014, http://en.wikipedia.org/wiki/Universe. A light year is the distance light travels in one year. Light travels at a speed of approximately 186,000 miles per minute.

15. C. Michael Hawn, "History of Hymns: 'Lift Up Your Heads, Ye Mighty Gates,'" General Board of Discipleship of the United Methodist Church, http://www.gbod.org/lead-your-church/history-of-hymns/resource/history-of-hymns-lift-up-your-heads-ye-mighty-gates.

16. "Lift Up Your Heads, Ye Mighty Gates," in *Hymns for Praise and Worship* (Nappanee, IN: Evangel Press, 1984), no. 371.

Psalm 25

1. Goldingay, *Psalms*, 1:368.
2. Craigie, *Psalms 1–50*, 217.
3. Hakham, *Psalms*, 1:182.
4. Goldingay, *Psalms*, 1:368–69.
5. Philip J. Nel, "*bosh*," *NIDOTTE* 1:625.
6. Moule, *Hope*, 11, quoting Dr. M. A. C. Warren.
7. Goldingay, *Psalms*, 1:371.
8. Delitzsch, *Psalms*, 1:343.
9. Goldingay, *Psalms*, 1:373.
10. Gruber, *Rashi's Commentary*, 270.
11. Terrien, *Psalms*, 255.
12. Delitzsch, *Psalms*, 1:347.
13. Goldingay, *Psalms*, 1:377.
14. This type of "narrative" identity—that is, naming the person the writer has in mind by descriptive language but never mentioning the person's name—is illustrated in Job 28:28. In the dialogue of Job, nowhere is Job's name mentioned (until one comes to the speeches of Elihu, which fall outside the dialogue), but by "narrative" identity the writer of Job identifies him as the truly wise man in 28:28, as he remembers God's words (dramatic irony) in the prologue: "And he said to man, 'Behold, the fear of the Lord, that is wisdom, and to turn away from evil is understanding'" (ESV). This, of course, was precisely the way Job was described in the prologue, in both the writer's (Job 1:1b) and Yahweh's words (Job 1:8; 2:3). After the prologue, we do not hear God's voice again until the epilogue (Job 38–42), except in 28:28, when he identifies Job, without naming him, as the truly wise man. This has been part of the argument of the dialogue, the bantering back and forth between Job and his friends, offering their descriptions of the wise person. Finally the Lord himself settles the argument with Job's quotation of his words in 28:28, and the reader, by dramatic irony, makes the connection with the prologue.
15. "Types of Educational Opportunities Discrimination," United States Department of Justice, http://www.justice.gov/crt/about/edu/types.php.
16. Mark Goulston, "Why Men Don't Ask for Directions: A Self-Analysis," *Just Listen* (blog), *Psychology Today*, May 3, 2010, http://www.psychologytoday.com/blog/just-listen/201005/why-men-dont-ask-directions-self-analysis.
17. Donald R. Hands, "The Role of Shame in Clergy Misconduct: Toward Liberation from Shamed Sexuality," *Action Information* 17 (May/June 1991): 1–4.

Psalm 26

1. Craigie, *Psalms 1–50*, 224, following Vogt, "Psalm 226."
2. Gunkel, *Psalms*, 187n810.

3. Wilson, *Psalms*, 1:470–71. Psalm 25 of this group contains no explicit reference to the temple or God's dwelling, unless the question in 25:12 implies the temple.
4. Based on Hakham's outline (*Psalms*, 1:194).
5. Hilber cites evidence of ritual washings in ancient Near Eastern temples (Hilber, "Psalms," 343, citing Groenewoud, "Water"; and *ANEP*, no. 619).
6. Schaefer, *Psalms*, 65.
7. Goldingay, *Psalms*, 1:382.
8. Delitzsch, *Psalms*, 1:351.
9. Wilson, *Psalms*, 1:474–75.
10. Braude, *Midrash*, 359. See *m. Sukkah* 4.5.
11. See Paul A. Kruger, "*pl'*," *NIDOTTE* 3:616.
12. Hakham, *Psalms*, 1:197.
13. Hakham, *Psalms*, 1:197.
14. Hakham, *Psalms*, 1:197.
15. Albert Schweitzer, *The Light within Us* (New York: Philosophical Library, 1959), 4.

Psalm 27

1. Weiser, *Psalms*, 235.
2. Bullock, *Encountering*, 167.
3. Gerstenberger, *Psalms*, 124.
4. See the discussion on Psalms 9 and 10.
5. Goldingay, *Psalms*, 1:391.
6. R. Davidson, *Worship*, 95.
7. Craigie, *Psalms 1–50*, 231, 233–34.
8. Perowne, *Psalms*, 1:265, suggests that Psalms 26; 27; and 28 were composed at the time of Absalom's rebellion.
9. Perowne, *Psalms*, 1:268.
10. Weiser, *Psalms*, 249.
11. Hakham, *Psalms*, 1:203.
12. Craigie, *Psalms 1–50*, 233.
13. E.g., Perowne, *Psalms*, 1:268–69.
14. E.g., Hakham, *Psalms*, 1:206.
15. Weiser, *Psalms*, 252.
16. Weiser, *Psalms*, 252–53.
17. Hakham, *Psalms*, 1:204.
18. Hakham, *Psalms*, 1:204.
19. Schaefer, *Psalms*, 69.

Psalm 28

1. Gunkel, *Introduction*, 121. He lists thirty-nine psalms in this genre.
2. Gerstenberger, *Psalms*, 128.
3. Gunkel, *Introduction*, 122.
4. Bullock, *Encountering*, 136.
5. Kidner, *Psalms 1–72*, 122.
6. Craigie, *Psalms 1–50*, 237.
7. Perowne, *Psalms*, 1:271; Delitzsch, *Psalms*, 1:362.
8. Craigie, *Psalms 1–50*, 241.
9. Hilber, "Psalms," 344.
10. Hakham, *Psalms*, 1:208.
11. Craigie, *Psalms 1–50*, 238.
12. Hakham, *Psalms*, 1:208. See Keel, *Symbolism*, 67–68.
13. Hakham, *Psalms*, 1:208. After the Hebrew word *pen* ("lest"), the condition to avoid is expressed by the Hebrew imperfect verb, with the results that would follow taking the Hebrew perfect: "lest you do nothing for me [that is what

he wants to avoid], and I become like those who go down to the pit [that is, die—the results of the action]."

14. Hakham, *Psalms*, 1:210.

15. Wilson, *Psalms*, 1:496.

16. Wilson, *Psalms*, 1:497.

17. The Hebrew word for "shield" (*magen*) is the smaller protective device, while Psalm 5:12 uses the word that designates a shield that covers the full body (see the comments on that verse). See Keel, *Symbolism*, 222–23.

18. Hakham, *Psalms*, 1:211.

19. Hilber, "Psalms," 320–21.

20. Wilson, *Psalms*, 1:498.

21. Hakham, *Psalms*, 1:212.

22. Selderhuis, *John Calvin*, 193.

23. Calvin, *Psalms*, 1:467.

24. Halvor and Mirja Ronning, online letter, Home for Biblical Translators website, accessed July 17, 2014, http://mail .bibletranslators.org/display.php?M=8091&C=40544434 a75ea786653f76812feefa5a&S=98&L=15&N=81.

25. Corri B. Zoli, "The International Law of Diplomacy & U.S. Embassy Attacks," Institute for National Security and Counterterrorism, Syracuse University, September 20, 2012, http://insct.syr.edu/the-international-law-of-diplomacy -and-u-s-embassy-attacks-post-arab-spring-transitions/.

Psalm 29

1. Since Psalm 29 is contained in an earlier collection (Book 1), Psalm 96, which is contained in Book 3, a later collection, most likely quotes from Psalm 29.

2. The psalm has a literary beauty of its own, reminiscent of some of the earliest biblical poetry, like the Song of the Sea (Exod. 15), the Balaam oracles (Num. 23–24), and the Song of Deborah (Judg. 5). Kidner incisively observes that the "primitive vigour of the verse . . . wonderfully matches the theme" (Kidner, *Psalms 1–72*, 124).

3. Perowne, *Psalms*, 1:274.

4. Beyond the parallel verses shown here, the verbal duplication ends, but some thematic correspondence continues: the "waters" and the "sea" (29:3; 96:11b), and the "cedars" and "all the trees of the forest" (29:5; 96:12b).

5. Hakham, *Psalms*, 1:220n13.

6. Hilber prefers a northern site near Damascus known by the same name in a Ugaritic text, which, he insists, fits the other northern references better (Hermon/Sirion; see Hilber, "Psalms," 346–47). But given the literary balance of the psalm, focusing on the calamitous storm on the Levant, with the temple as the "eye" of the storm, concluding in the area of Kadesh Barnea, where the Israelites encamped for thirty-eight of their forty years in the wilderness (Num. 13:26), this reading seems preferable. It is certainly more memorable in Israel's history than the northern site, which played no role at all in Israelite history.

7. Occurs elsewhere in Psalm 89:6; Exodus 15:11; Job 41:25; and Daniel 11:36.

8. See Wilson's discussion of "Henotheism and Monotheism" (Wilson, *Psalms*, 1:507–9).

9. Hakham, *Psalms*, 1:215.

10. Perowne, *Psalms*, 1:274.

11. Perowne, *Psalms*, 1:274–75.

12. Perowne, *Psalms*, 1:276.

13. Delitzsch, *Psalms*, 1:369, prefers the "storm cloud" option.

14. Hilber, "Psalms," 346.

15. Kidner, *Psalms 1–72*, 127.

16. Psalms 93, 96, 99. See Bullock, *Encountering*, 187–97.

17. Delitzsch, *Psalms*, 1:373.

18. Goldingay, *Psalms*, 1:415.

19. Selderhuis, *John Calvin*, 215.

Psalm 30

1. Kraus, *Psalms 1–59*, 47–52.

2. See Bullock, *Encountering*, 136–45.

3. Bullock, *Encountering*, 136–45.

4. Kidner, *Psalms 1–72*, 128.

5. Craigie, *Psalms 1–50*, 252.

6. Wilson, *Psalms*, 1:514.

7. 1 Maccabees 4:52–58; 2 Maccabees 10:1–8; see the rabbinic tractate *Soferim* 18b.

8. By "reuse" of the psalm, we do not necessarily mean its "reinterpretation," the former suggesting a virtual application of the contents to another dedication or rededication of the temple. Regarding "reinterpretation," Rashi says the rabbis reapplied the psalm to the days of Mordecai, Esther, and Haman (Gruber, *Rashi's Commentary*, 291).

9. Wilson, *Psalms*, 1:515.

10. Gruber, *Rashi's Commentary*, 290.

11. Calvin, *Psalms*, 1:487.

12. Perowne, *Psalms*, 1:280.

13. Perowne, *Psalms*, 1:282.

14. R. Ficker, "*rnn*," *TLOT* 3:1241.

15. Perowne, *Psalms*, 1:280.

16. Kidner, *Psalms 1–72*, 129.

17. Wilson, *Psalms*, 1:518, citing Holladay, *Lexicon*, 34.

18. Perowne, *Psalms*, 1:280.

19. Wilson, *Psalms*, 1:519.

20. Wilson, *Psalms*, 1:519.

21. Wilson, *Psalms*, 1:517.

22. Kidner, *Psalms 1–72*, 128.

23. Natan Sharansky, *Fear No Evil* (New York: Random House, 1988), 403–4.

Psalm 31

1. Craigie, *Psalms 1–50*, 258; Bullock, *Encountering*, 136–44.

2. Bullock, *Encountering*, 168–69.

3. Craigie, *Psalms 1–50*, 259.

4. Mays, *Psalms*, 142.

5. Craigie, *Psalms 1–50*, 259.

6. Delitzsch, *Psalms*, 1:382.

7. Hakham, *Psalms*, 1:230.

8. Mays, *Psalms*, 143.

9. Delitzsch, *Psalms*, 1:386.

10. Hakham, *Psalms*, 1:232.

11. Hakham, *Psalms*, 1:233.

12. Hakham, *Psalms*, 1:234.

13. Delitzsch, *Psalms*, 1:387.

14. The summary statement is: "I will be your God" (part A), "and you will be my people" (part B), "and I will dwell in

your midst" (part C). Leviticus 26:12 has all three parts, but not in the same order: "I will walk among you [part C] and be your God [part A], and you will be my people [part B]."

15. Delitzsch, *Psalms*, 1:389.

16. Craigie, *Psalms 1–50*, 81.

17. Craigie, *Psalms 1–50*, 262.

18. Hakham, *Psalms*, 1:239.

19. Schaefer, *Psalms*, 76.

20. "Insanity—The Ride," Stratosphere Hotel, http://www.stratospherehotel.com/Activities/Thrill-Rides/Insanity.

21. James Strong and John McClintock, *Cyclopaedia of Biblical, Theological and Ecclesiastical Literature*, 12 vols. (New York: Harper, 1894), 4:159–61.

22. *Ecumenical Creeds and Reformed Confessions* (Grand Rapids: Christian Reformed Church Publications, 1988), 13.

23. "Last Words," *Wikiquote*, last modified June 1, 2014, http://en.wikiquote.org/wiki/Last_words.

Psalm 32

1. Bullock, *Encountering*, 152–56.

2. Bullock, *Encountering*, 206.

3. See the unit on Psalms 9–10.

4. This is an adaptation of Hakham's outline, *Psalms*, 1:242.

5. Delitzsch, *Psalms*, 1:393.

6. Hakham, *Psalms*, 1:242.

7. Kraus, *Psalms 1–59*, 25; Bullock, *Encountering*, 28.

8. Hakham, *Psalms*, 1:243.

9. Hakham, *Psalms*, 1:244, and n. 6.

10. Westminster Shorter Catechism, Q & A 14.

11. Rick Nauert, "Brain Scans Show Depression's Link to Guilt," *PsychCentral*, August 26, 2008, http://psychcentral.com/news/2008/08/26/brain-scans-show-depressions-link-to-guilt/2826.html.

12. This story is not contained in some of the ancient Greek manuscripts of the Gospel of John, but many scholars believe it is an authentic story about Jesus.

13. Karl Menninger, *Whatever Became of Sin?* (New York: Hawthorn, 1973), 1–2.

Psalm 33

1. Kidner, *Psalms 1–72*, 136. Gunkel has laid out the basic form and characteristics of the hymn, and, of course, included this psalm among the twenty-five hymns in his list (*Introduction to Psalms*, 22).

2. Wilson, *Psalms*, 1:556.

3. See the sidebar "The Relationship between Psalms 1 and 2" in the unit on Psalm 1.

4. Bullock, *Encountering*, 33.

5. Craigie, *Psalms 1–50*, 273.

6. Alter, *Psalms*, 114.

7. See Craigie, "Poetry."

8. Alter, *Psalms*, 115.

9. Alter, *Psalms*, 116n20.

10. Luther, *Table Talk*, no. 102, 72–73.

11. Frederick Buechner, *A Room Called Remember* (San Francisco: Harper & Row, 1984), 42.

12. Anne Graham Lotz, *Wounded by God's People* (Grand Rapids: Zondervan, 2013), 155–56.

13. Monthly unemployment statistics are available from the US Department of Labor, Bureau of Labor Statistics, at http://data.bls.gov/timeseries/LNS14000000.

14. US national debt statistics are available from the US Department of the Treasury, Bureau of the Fiscal Service, at http://www.treasurydirect.gov/govt/reports/pd/pd_debt tothepenny.htm.

Psalm 34

1. See the sidebar "The Alphabetic Acrostic Psalms" in the unit on Psalm 25.

2. Hakham, *Psalms*, 1:264.

3. Bullock, *Encountering*, 152–54.

4. Craigie hypothesizes that the first part, including the title, was an individual thanksgiving and was expanded by the wisdom composition, giving the new product an acrostic form and preserving the title (Craigie, *Psalms 1–50*, 278). While the two-genre theory is plausible, the psalmists do not always write exclusively within one genre. So the present version of the psalm could have been the original.

5. Hoerth, *Archaeology*, 260.

6. See Wilson, *Psalms*, 1:569.

7. Hakham, *Psalms*, 1:262.

8. See "Reading between the Lines" in the introduction.

9. The personal sense of David's portrait as a righteous man would come from the historical information about him, which we have largely in the books of Samuel and Kings, and there is information to support such a portrait (e.g., 1 Sam. 13:14). The rhetorical sense of David as a righteous man, however, is a literary convention, constituted of David's psalms and the way the editor (or editors) of the Psalter has put them together. We do not mean that the editors contrived this portrait, but rather we mean that they drew upon his historical virtues as their basis and then used literary sources to build their rhetorical portrait. In one sense, this portrait makes him out to be "bigger than life," but their purpose was not to enlarge David's portrait beyond its historical dimensions so much as it was to provide a picture of the ideal person who exemplified the virtues of a righteous individual.

10. Yet the books of 1–2 Samuel are replete with positive comments about David's spiritual and ethical character (e.g., 1 Sam. 13:14; 2 Sam. 24:10). So the editors of the book of Psalms have not invented ex nihilo this portrait of David.

11. Hosea 10:5 uses this word: "The people who live in Samaria *fear* for the calf-idol of Beth Aven." In this context, it could carry a double nuance, both worship and dread of Yahweh's judgment. For the most part, however, it seems to carry a negative tone, being used, for example, in the phrase "terror on every side" (see the comments on Ps. 31:13). See M. V. Van Pelt and W. C. Kaiser Jr., "*gur*," *NIDOTTE* 1:839–40.

12. "John Newton: Reformed Slave Trader," *Christian History*, August 8, 2008, http://www.christianitytoday.com/ch/131christians/pastorsandpreachers/newton.html.

13. C. S. Lewis, *The Lion, the Witch and the Wardrobe* (New York: Harper, 1950), 77.

Additional Insights, pages 260–61

1. Zenger, *God of Vengeance?*, 79.
2. Mowinckel, *Psalms in Israel's Worship*, 2:49.
3. See Bullock, *Old Testament Poetic Books*, 140–41.
4. This is a summary of my discussion of the imprecatory psalms in *Encountering*, 228–34.
5. Lewis, *Reflections*, 30.

Psalm 35

1. Craigie, *Psalms 1–50*, 285; Eaton, *Psalms*, 158.
2. The larger group includes Psalms 35; 55; 59; 69; 79; 109; and 137.
3. Compare Psalms 69:22–25, 27–28; 109:6–15.
4. E.g., Delitzsch, *Psalms*, 1:418–19; also Bullock, *Encountering*, 230–31.
5. The terms of this outline are Kidner's (*Psalms 1–72*, 142–45).
6. Delitzsch, *Psalms*, 1:418–19.
7. Dahood, *Psalms*, 1:210.
8. Wilson, *Psalms*, 1:586.
9. Wilson, *Psalms*, 1:581.
10. Craigie, *Psalms 1–50*, 287.
11. Wilson, *Psalms*, 1:578.
12. Wilson, *Psalms*, 1:583.
13. Wilson, *Psalms*, 1:346.
14. Holladay, *Psalms*, 305.

Additional Insights, pages 268–69

1. Bullock, *Encountering*, 227–38. See "Theological Insights" for the unit on Psalm 15.
2. John Walton, email correspondence with author, June 9, 2013.
3. See Craigie, *Problem of War*; Gundry, *Show Them No Mercy*; von Rad, *Holy War*.
4. Wilson, *Psalms*, 1:581.
5. Wilson remarks: "This is, then, not so much a case of wishing your enemy ill as it is a desire for righteousness and justice to prevail with all its necessary consequences" (Wilson, *Psalms*, 1:588). Even though I find Wilson's statement helpful, it still leaves much to be explained about the imprecatory psalms.

Psalm 36

1. Dahood, *Psalms*, 1:218.
2. Craigie, *Psalms 1–50*, 291.
3. Bullock, *Encountering*, 47–49.
4. Craigie, *Psalms 1–50*, 291.
5. Wilson, *Psalms*, 1:590.
6. The NIV makes the verbs and possessive pronouns plural, but the Hebrew is singular. The grammatical number does become plural in 36:7 and continues to the end of the psalm.
7. Compare the formulaic expression for life in Deuteronomy 6:7: "when you sit at home and when you walk along the road," or the alternate expression, "when you lie down and when you get up."
8. Hakham, *Psalms*, 1:277.

9. The Hebrew term for "heavens" has the definite article after the preposition *beth* (*bᵉhashamayim*), which is very unusual (also 2 Kings 7:12, *bᵉhasadeh*). In 2 Kings 7:12, the marginal correction eliminates the article, but here there is no Masoretic correction. The sense of the phrase, in any case, is not altered.
10. Hakham, *Psalms*, 1:276.
11. Hakham, *Psalms*, 1:276.
12. Schaefer, *Psalms*, 89.
13. Gregory the Great, *Moralia on Job* 31.87.
14. Bradley R. E. Wright, *Christians Are Hate-Filled Hypocrites . . . and Other Lies You've Been Told* (Minneapolis: Bethany House, 2010), 133.
15. "Custer's Last Stand," The Civil War (website), accessed July 21, 2014, http://www.sonofthesouth.net/union-generals/custer/custers-last-stand.htm.

Psalm 37

1. Bullock, *Encountering*, 204–6.
2. The NIV has paragraphed the psalm so that each of the twenty-two paragraphs represents a letter of the Hebrew alphabet.
3. Delitzsch, *Psalms*, 2:12.
4. Goldingay, *Psalms*, 1:532.
5. See Pippert, *Words from the Wise*, 25–30.
6. See the sidebar "The Laughter of God" in the unit on Psalm 2.
7. Delitzsch, *Psalms*, 2:15.
8. Stuck in Israel's historical memory was the insecurity of landlessness, first represented in the life of their ancestor Abraham, second by the wilderness period, and third by the experience of exile (Brueggemann, *Land*, 6–9). Although the Assyrians introduced that practice as a military policy of control and containment, and even if David, much before the Assyrian era, is the author of this psalm, displacement by war, famine, and marauding, on a smaller scale than exile, was a fearful reality.

Psalm 38

1. Westermann, *Praise and Lament*, 267; see also Westermann, "Role of the Lament"; and Bullock, *Encountering*, 140.
2. Weiser, *Psalms*, 323.
3. See "The Text in Context" for Psalm 6; see also Bullock, *Encountering*, 207.
4. For example, Kraus, *Psalms 1–59*, 414.
5. Beale and Carson, *Use of the Old Testament*, 400.
6. Hilber, "Psalms," 353.
7. Wilson, *Psalms*, 1:616.
8. Delitzsch, *Psalms*, 2:20.
9. Kidner, *Psalms 1–72*, 154.
10. Hakham, *Psalms*, 1:298.
11. Calvin, *Psalms*, 2:56.
12. Hakham, *Psalms*, 1:298.
13. Victor P. Hamilton, "*kesel*," NIDOTTE 1:680.
14. Hakham, *Psalms*, 1:300.
15. Delitzsch, *Psalms*, 2:23.
16. Calvin, *Psalms*, 2:63.
17. Calvin, *Psalms*, 2:55.

18. Quoted in C. S. Lewis, *A Year with Aslan: Daily Reflections from the Chronicles of Narnia*, ed. Julia L. Roller (New York: Harper Collins, 2010), 368.

19. Lisa Whelchel, "Creative Discipline Ideas," Focus on the Family (website), accessed July 21, 2014, http://www.focusonthefamily.com/parenting/effective_biblical_discipline/creative_discipline_ideas.aspx?p1143774. Material adapted from her book *Creative Correction: Extraordinary Ideas for Everyday Discipline* (Wheaton: Tyndale House, 2005), chap. 1, "Tools to Create a Work of Art."

Psalm 39

1. See Goldingay's list (*Psalms*, 1:554).

2. See "The Text in Context" for Psalm 62.

3. Goldingay, *Psalms*, 1:555.

4. See "Historical and Cultural Background" for Psalm 20.

5. Hakham, *Psalms*, 1:307.

6. Hakham, *Psalms*, 1:308.

7. Hakham, *Psalms*, 1:309.

8. Hakham, *Psalms*, 1:310.

9. A. H. Konkel, "*gur*," *NIDOTTE* 1:837.

10. A. H. Konkel, "*toshab*," *NIDOTTE* 4:284.

11. Wilson, *Psalms*, 1:630.

12. Malcolm Muggeridge, *Jesus Rediscovered* (London: Collins, 1969), 17–18.

13. George MacDonald, *What's Mine's Mine*, 3rd ed. (London: Kegan Paul, Trench, 1889), 245.

Psalm 40

1. See Bullock, *Encountering*, 153.

2. Both Weiser (*Psalms*, 333–34) and Craigie (*Psalms 1–50*, 314) vouch for the unity of the psalm.

3. See "The Text in Context" for Psalms 9–10.

4. Wilson, *Psalms*, 1:536.

5. Some Hebrew manuscripts have the tetragrammaton (*YHWH*) in 70:4b rather than *'elohim* (God).

6. One of the major differences between the Hebrew (MT) and the Greek (LXX) texts is the term "body" in the Septuagint for "dug-out ear" in the Masoretic Text in Psalm 40:6 (see NIV footnote: cf. Heb. 10:5). One way to look at this substitute term is to understand "ear" as a figure of speech for the whole body (Waltner, *Psalms*, 209). The NIV and other translations render the verb "dig" (*krh*) as "open," linking an "open ear" (ESV) to understanding and doing God's will (40:8).

7. For example, Waltner, *Psalms*, 207, considers the "new song" to be verses 5–10.

8. Craigie, *Psalms 1–50*, 315.

9. Delitzsch, *Psalms*, 2:42.

10. Calvin, *Psalms*, 2:89.

11. Delitzsch, *Psalms*, 2:35.

12. Hakham, *Psalms*, 1:313n1a.

13. Wilson, *Psalms*, 1:637.

14. Delitzsch, *Psalms*, 2:36.

15. Calvin, *Psalms*, 2:98.

16. Hakham, *Psalms*, 1:316. Hakham comments on the unusual pointing of the noun *hata'ah*, pointed with a *hatef patah* and without the expected *dagesh* under the tet, that it may be intentional, to intimate "that the verse is not referring to an actual sin-offering, in which case the *het* would be vocalized with a *patah* and the *tet* would have a *dagesh*" (316n5).

17. Delitzsch, *Psalms*, 2:41.

18. Wilson, *Psalms*, 1:636n5.

19. Three preceding psalms, Psalms 37:7, 34; 38:15; 39:7, speak of "waiting" or "hoping," and this was likely a factor that led to positioning Psalm 40 here in this collection (see table 2 in the unit on Ps. 39).

Psalm 41

1. Kraus, *Psalms 1–59*, 47–56. See also "Understanding the Text" in the unit on Psalm 30.

2. Craigie, *Psalms 1–50*, 319.

3. See "Theological Insights" for Psalm 25 and the note there; see also "The Text in Context" for Psalm 26.

4. Perowne, *Psalms*, 2:343.

5. Wilson, *Psalms*, 1:653n11.

6. Braude, *Midrash*, 1:438.

7. The meaning of the last phrase is difficult, but the terms are generally clear. The JB translates: "most carefully you make his bed when he is sick"; the NLT renders the entire verse in terms of Yahweh's "caretaking" role: "The LORD nurses them when they are sick and restores their health."

8. Kidner, *Psalms 1–72*, 161.

9. Wilson, *Psalms*, 1:658.

10. Hakham, *Psalms*, 1:322.

11. The revised NIV often, as here, makes singular pronouns plural in the interest of gender-inclusive language.

12. Hakham, *Psalms*, 1:323.

13. The practice of visiting the sick is attested by David's visit to his son Amnon, feigning illness (2 Sam. 13:5), and King Ahaziah's visit to the ailing King Joram of Israel (2 Kings 8:29).

14. Gaster, "Short Notes," 74.

15. Ryken, Wilhoit, and Longman, "Heel."

16. Kidner, *Psalms 1–72*, 163.

17. Wilson, *Psalms*, 1:662–63.

18. Hakham, *Psalms*, 1:326.

19. Georges Bernanos, *The Diary of a Country Priest* (New York: Carroll & Graf, 1965), 298.

20. Brennan Manning, *Abba's Child* (Colorado Springs: Navpress, 2002), 124–25.

Psalms 42–43

1. A. A. Anderson, *Psalms 1–72*, 328.

2. Goldingay, *Psalms*, 2:21.

3. Delitzsch, *Psalms*, 2:61.

4. In Book 2, the Davidic psalms (Pss. 51–65, 68–70) form the heart of the collection, whereas Book 3 contains only one Davidic psalm (Ps. 86). See Bullock, *Encountering*, 74.

5. See "The Structure and Composition of the Psalter" in the introduction.

6. For the designation "*maskil*," see also the comments on the title for Psalm 32.

7. Kraus, *Psalms 1–59*, 25.

8. Goldingay, *Psalms*, 2:23.

9. The phrase "my Savior and my God" literally reads, "Saviors [note the plural, perhaps the final letter (*tav*) should be read as a feminine singular construct form] of his countenance and my God." The Greek (LXX), Syriac, and Latin (Vulgate) use the personal pronoun "my," as in 42:11 and 43:5, rather than the Hebrew (MT) "his." In Hebrew writing the letter *waw* could easily be mistaken for the letter *yod*, making it "his countenance" rather than "my countenance." We probably should accept this slight textual change. In the Hebrew pointing, "my God" begins the next sentence, but it seems logical to follow the Greek and Syriac in joining it to verse 5 and its final phrase, "my Savior and my God."

10. Delitzsch, *Psalms*, 2:72.

11. Delitzsch, *Psalms*, 2:62.

12. Quoted by Alton H. McEachern, "Preaching from the Psalms," *Review and Expositor* 81 (1984): 458.

13. Quoted in Lloyd John Ogilvie, *The Essence of His Presence: How Christ Wants to Bless Your Life* (Nashville: Thomas Nelson, 2007), 77.

14. Richard J. Foster and James Bryan Smith, eds., *Devotional Classics* (San Francisco: HarperSanFrancisco, 1993), 119.

Psalm 44

1. Kidner, *Psalms 1–72*, 170.

2. Kidner, *Psalms 1–72*, 170.

3. Delitzsch, *Psalms*, 2:76–77.

4. Calvin, *Psalms*, 2:148.

5. Kidner, *Psalms 1–72*, 1:168; A. A. Anderson, *Psalms 1–72*, 1:337.

6. Craigie, *Psalms 1–50*, 332–33.

7. Hakham, *Psalms*, 1:342n2b.

8. Hakham, *Psalms*, 1:342.

9. Hakham, *Psalms*, 1:343.

10. A. A. Anderson, *Psalms 1–72*, 340.

11. Kidner, *Psalms 1–72*, 169–70.

12. Hakham, *Psalms*, 1:347.

13. A. A. Anderson, *Psalms 1–72*, 344.

14. Dahood, *Psalms*, 1:267.

15. Goldingay, *Psalms*, 2:46, says: "So God is able to go behind locked doors, for instance, and discover what religious practices people are undertaking in the apparent privacy of their own homes and to look into people's hearts to see where they are even more secretly appealing to strange deities."

16. Hakham, *Psalms*, 1:350.

17. Craigie, *Psalms 1–50*, 334.

18. Blank, *Prophetic Faith of Isaiah*, 125.

19. Isaiah 48:9; 49:7; 55:5; 66:5; Ezekiel 20; 36; Jeremiah 14:7, 21; Psalms 6:4; 23:3; 25:11; 106:8; 109:21; 143:11 (the phrase is sometimes translated "because of").

20. Kidner, *Psalms 1–72*, 168.

21. Charles Williams, a British journalist and theologian, says of the church: "There are always three degrees of consciousness, all infinitely divisible: (1) the old self on the old way; (2) the old self on the new way; (3) the new self on the new way. The second group is the largest, at all times and in all places" (*He Came Down From Heaven* [1938; reprint, Grand Rapids: Eerdmans, 1984], 119).

Psalm 45

1. Kidner, *Psalms 1–72*, 170.

2. Craigie, *Psalms 1–50*, 337.

3. Delitzsch, *Psalms*, 2:87.

4. Delitzsch, *Psalms*, 2:86.

5. Cited by Hakham, *Psalms*, 1:352n2.

6. See Hilber, "Psalms," 357, for acknowledgments from the ancient literature.

7. Hilber, "Psalms," 358.

8. Hakham, *Psalms*, 1:354.

9. Hakham, *Psalms*, 1:355–56.

10. Hakham, *Psalms*, 1:356.

11. Kidner, *Psalms 1–72*, 173.

12. Pictures made with the Polaroid cameras of a past generation were first faint and then gained clarity in a matter of minutes.

13. Timothy J. Keller, "Sex and the End of Loneliness," sermon preached February 25, 1996, http://sermons .redeemer.com/store/index.cfm?fuseaction=product.display &product_ID=18328. See also Roland E. Murphy's discussion of the Song of Songs and the biblical concept of marriage in *Song of Songs*, 100–105.

Psalm 46

1. Gunkel, *Introduction to Psalms*, 29, 56–57.

2. Goldingay, *Psalms*, 2:65.

3. See Bullock, *Encountering*, 174–76.

4. See Bullock, "Shape of the Torah."

5. Hakham, *Psalms*, 1:362.

6. Goldingay, *Psalms*, 2:66.

7. Snaith's explanation ("Selah," 43–56) probably comes closest to its meaning. According to his understanding it is a liturgical term used by the Levites to call for a congregational response. See the sidebar "*Selah*" in the unit on Psalm 3.

8. See the sidebar "'The LORD Reigns': The Kingship of Yahweh Psalms," in the unit on Psalm 93.

9. Craigie, *Psalms 1–50*, 343; Craigie, "Poetry"; Eissfeldt, *Kleine Schriften*, 4:10–11.

10. Craigie, *Psalms 1–50*, 345.

11. Kidner, *Psalms 1–72*, 176.

12. Amos's oracles against the nations in Amos 1:3–2:5 are an example.

13. Tim Challies, "Hymn Stories: A Mighty Fortress Is Our God," Challies.com, July 7, 2013, http://www.challies .com/articles/hymn-stories-a-mighty-fortress-is-our-god.

14. Emory M. Thomas, *Robert E. Lee: A Biography* (New York: Norton, 1995), 80.

Psalm 47

1. Mowinckel, *Israel's Worship*, 1:115, 122.

2. See the introduction to "Understanding the Text" in the unit on Psalm 45; see also Bullock, *Encountering*, 187–97. This hypothesis has come under suspicion in recent years, and it is better to speak of the psalms of the heavenly King, which unquestionably represent an emphasis

in certain psalms (Pss. 47; 93; 95–99). See also the sidebar "The LORD Reigns: Psalms of the Heavenly King" in the unit on Psalm 93.

3. See "The Nature of the Book" in the introduction.

4. An "apostrophe" is a literary term for an address to an inanimate object, or to an audience too distant to hear the speaker.

5. The issue in Malachi 1:2–3 and Deuteronomy 7 is Yahweh's love for *Jacob/Israel*, rather than his love for the "land" of Jacob.

6. Hakham, *Psalms*, 1:368.

7. See Hilber, "Psalms," 361; Keel, *Symbolism*, 297.

8. Goldingay, *Psalms*, 2:78.

9. See the comments on the title for Psalm 32.

10. Scott Hoezee, "How We See Things," *Perspectives: A Journal of Reformed Thought*, April 2007, http://www.rca.org/page.aspx?pid=2763.

11. J. I. Packer, *Revelations of the Cross* (Peabody, MA: Hendrickson, 1998), 181.

12. Eugene H. Peterson, *A Long Obedience in the Same Direction: Discipleship in an Instant Society*, rev. and exp. ed. (Downers Grove, IL: InterVarsity, 2000), 53.

13. Helmut Thielicke, *Encounter with Spurgeon* (Philadelphia: Fortress, 1963), 11, quoted in Eugene H. Peterson, *Long Obedience*, 53.

Psalm 48

1. Hakham, *Psalms*, 1:374.

2. Hakham, *Psalms*, 1:374.

3. Craigie, *Psalms 1–50*, 353.

4. Calvin, *Psalms*, 2:223.

5. Hakham, *Psalms*, 1:375.

6. Calvin, *Psalms*, 2:225–26.

7. Hakham, *Psalms*, 1:376.

8. Calvin, *Psalms*, 2:228–29.

9. Craigie, *Psalms 1–50*, 354.

10. Hilber, "Psalms," 364.

11. Hakham, *Psalms*, 1:377.

12. See Eichrodt's discussion of this text, *Theology of the Old Testament*, 1:187–92.

13. Gerald Kennedy, *The Parables: Sermons on the Stories Jesus Told* (New York: Harper & Brothers, 1960), 150.

14. Calvin, *Psalms*, 2:223.

Additional Insights, pp. 366–367

1. Jerome Murphy-O'Connor, "Jerusalem," *NIDB* 3:246, 248.

2. See Hoerth, *Archaeology*, 417–21; J. J. M. Roberts, "Temple, Jerusalem," *NIDB* 5:494–509.

Psalm 49

1. Kraus, *Psalms 1–59*, 480.

2. Craigie, *Psalms 1–50*, 358.

3. Hakham, *Psalms*, 1:381.

4. A. A. Anderson, *Psalms 1–72*, 375.

5. A. A. Anderson, *Psalms 1–72*, 377.

6. Hakham, *Psalms*, 1:386n1.

7. Kidner, *Psalms 1–72*, 184.

8. Goldingay, *Psalms*, 2:104.

9. A. A. Anderson, *Psalms 1–72*, 349.

10. Kidner, *Psalms 1–72*, 182.

11. Schaefer, *Psalms*, 123–24.

12. Kidner, *Psalms 1–72*, 184–85.

13. Robert L. Hubbard Jr., "*pdh*," *NIDOTTE* 3:578.

14. Hubbard, "*pdh*."

15. Weiser, *Psalms*, 388.

16. *St Louis Post-Dispatch*, November 28, 2011, A6.

Additional Insights, pp. 376–77

1. Clines, *Job 1–20*, 457–66, 470.

Psalm 50

1. Craigie, *Deuteronomy*, 370–71.

2. Wilson, *Psalms*, 1:766.

3. See Delitzsch's list of characteristics for the Asaph psalms (*Psalms*, 3:140–43).

4. See "The Nature of the Book" in the introduction and the sidebar "The Divine Names" in the unit on Psalm 4.

5. Goldingay, *Psalms*, 2:111.

6. Proposed by McFall, "Logical Arrangement."

7. This is basically Wilson's approach (*Psalms*, 1:759–66).

8. GKC, 159.

9. Luther, *Table Talk*, no. 144, 96.

Psalm 51

1. B. W. Anderson, *Out of the Depths*, 81.

2. See "The Text in Context" in the unit on Psalm 6; for a longer discussion, see B. W. Anderson, *Out of the Depths*, 77–96.

3. Weiser, *Psalms*, 401.

4. Kraus, *Psalms 1–59*, 47–56; Bullock, *Encountering*, 138–43.

5. Morris, *Romans*, 156.

6. This is an adaptation of Schaefer's outline (*Psalms*, 129).

7. Nareuveni, *Tree and Shrub*, 122.

8. Wilson, *Psalms*, 1:774.

9. See Hakham, *Psalms*, 1:406n8, for five different explanations.

10. See *y. Makkot* 2.6.

11. Suggestion by John Walton, email correspondence with author, June 8, 2013.

12. See Hakham, *Psalms*, 1:316, also n. 4.

13. Two categories of sins are described in the Pentateuch: sins of ignorance (*shegagah*, Lev. 4), or unintentional sins; and sins of a high hand (*beyad ramah*, Num. 15:30–31), or intentional (defiant) sins. The laws of the Pentateuch prescribe sacrifices for the unintentional sins but none for the intentional sins (adultery falls in this category). That raises the question of whether there is any atonement for those sins. Some scholars have pointed to the Day of Atonement (*yom kippur*) when the high priest sprinkled the blood of the goat (a sin offering) on the mercy seat "for all their sins" (Lev. 16:16, RSV), and have insisted that this sin offering atoned for intentional sins as well as unintentional. This is

based upon the phrase "their transgressions" (*pishe'hem*; NIV: "rebellion"), which connotes rebellious acts. Others, however, have understood this sacrifice to apply only to the impurities of the sanctuary. Even if we take the phrase "their transgressions" to mean intentional (defiant or rebellious) sins, it may very well be that David was praying that the Lord would grant forgiveness in view of David's sacrifice of "a broken and contrite heart" (51:17)—he could not wait for the Day of Atonement, even if the Israelites observed it in his day. The biblical Day of Atonement covered the sins of the year just passed, but in the Middle Ages, when Christians forced so many Jews to convert to Christianity on the pain of death, and under that compulsion, the prayers on the Day of Atonement were considered to apply to the sins of the coming year, so as to cover any such exigency.

14. Weiser, *Psalms*, 410.
15. Hakham, *Psalms*, 1:411.
16. Calvin, *Psalms*, 2:298.
17. Schaefer, *Psalms*, 129.
18. Calvin, *Psalms*, 2:298.
19. "Whiter Than Snow," HymnPod: Traditional Hymns Podcast, June 4, 2006, http://www.hymnpod.com/2009/06/04/whiter-than-snow/.
20. Homer B. Sprague, *Masterpieces in English Literature* (New York: J.W. Schermerhorn, 1874), 1:308.

Psalm 52

1. Goldingay, *Psalms*, 2:142.
2. The third line of the NIV ("you who are a disgrace in the eyes of God?") is a mystery to me, and there is no indication of its source.
3. See the sidebar "The Laughter of God" in the unit on Psalm 2.
4. "Three Mile Island Accident," World Nuclear Association, last modified January 2012, http://www.world-nuclear.org/info/safety-and-security/safety-of-plants/three-mile-island-accident/.
5. Selderhuis, *John Calvin*, 131.
6. "Bush's Inspiration: Scottish Preacher He Reads before Breakfast Every Day," *The Scotsman* website, updated March 3, 2003, http://www.scotsman.com/news/world/bush-s-inspiration-scottish-preacher-he-reads-before-breakfast-every-day-1-548463.

Psalm 53

1. See the sidebar "The Divine Names" in the unit on Psalm 4 and the sidebar "The Divine Names and the Elohistic Psalter" in the unit on Psalms 42–43.
2. Goldingay, *Psalms*, 2:150.
3. Kraus, *Psalms 1–59*, 25.
4. See the sidebar "Duplicate Psalms" in the unit on Psalm 14.
5. Delitzsch, *Psalms*, 2:148; Wilson, *Psalms*, 1:793.
6. "Tidings of Comfort and Joy in 1989," *Manchester Guardian*, December 1989.
7. Solomon Schimmel, *The Seven Deadly Sins: Jewish, Christian, and Classical Reflections on Human Nature* (New York: Free Press, 1992), 4.

Psalm 54

1. See Westermann's list of components (*Praise and Lament*, 73–80); see also Bullock, *Encountering*, 136–45.
2. Wilson, *Psalms*, 1:799.
3. See also Psalms 42–43 and the sidebar "*Selah*" in the unit on Psalm 3.
4. See the sidebar "The Divine Names and the Elohistic Psalter" in the unit on Psalms 42–43.
5. Melody Carlson, *Faded Denim: Color Me Trapped* (Colorado Springs: NavPress, 2006), 196.
6. *The Diary of Anne Frank: The Revised Critical Edition*, Netherlands Institute for War Documentation (New York: Doubleday, 2003), 721.

Psalm 55

1. Bullock, *Encountering*, 228–38. See also "Additional Insights: Imprecatory Psalms," after the unit on Psalm 34.
2. A. A. Anderson, *Psalms 1–72*, 412; also Weiser, *Psalms*, 419.
3. Hakham, *Psalms*, 1:431.
4. Goldingay, *Psalms*, 2:166.
5. Dahood, *Psalms*, 1:35.
6. A. A. Anderson, *Psalms 1–72*, 416.
7. The Masoretic Text (Hebrew) has a marginal correction here that separates the single word *yashshimawet* into two words, *yashshi mawet*. The root of the verb *yashshi* (*nsh'*) means "to exact interest" (*shw'*), and the literal sense is "let death exact/collect (its due)." Another root of *nsh'* means "to deceive," and the sense is "Let death surprise them" (Tate, *Psalms 51–100*, 50). The NIV seems to have opted for this meaning.
8. A. A. Anderson, *Psalms 1–72*, 418.
9. See A. A. Anderson, *Psalms 1–72*, 419.

Psalm 56

1. See the sidebar "Psalms with Historical Titles" in the unit on Psalm 54.
2. Schaefer, *Psalms*, 130.
3. Stec, *Targum of Psalms*, 113.
4. Eerdmans, *Psalms*, xx and 29.
5. Luther, *First Lectures*, 259.
6. Wilson, *Psalms*, 1:821n5.
7. Wilson, *Psalms*, 1:822.
8. Hakham, *Psalms*, 1:446.
9. Hakham, *Psalms*, 1:446.
10. Calvin, *Psalms*, 2:356.
11. Weiser, *Psalms*, 423.
12. Calvin, *Psalms*, 2:356.
13. Weiser, *Psalms*, 424.
14. Synopsis Sohar, ap. Schoettgen, ad loc.; quoted by Westcott, *Epistle to the Hebrews*, 128.
15. "Martyrs 2000–2010," World Christian Database, Center for the Study of Global Christianity, Gordon-Conwell Theological Seminary, http://www.worldchristiandatabase.org/wcd/news.asp?Article=45.
16. Kenneth Boa, *Passionate Living: Wisdom and Truth; A Devotional* (Colorado Springs: Authentic Books, 2007), 42.

17. "Inspirational Quotes from Martyrs Mirror," Martyrs Mirror of the Defenseless Christians, http://www.homecomers.org/mirror/quotes.htm.

18. Synopsis Sohar, ap. Schoettgen, ad loc.; quoted by Westcott, *Epistle to the Hebrews*, 128.

19. Weiser's translation (*Psalms*, 424). The hymn is found in *Evangelisches Kirchengesangbuch* (Darmstadt: Evangelische Kirche in Hessen und Nassau, 1951), no. 230.

20. Lewis A. Drummond, ed., *Here They Stand: Biblical Sermons from Eastern Europe* (Valley Forge, PA: Judson, 1978), 184.

Psalm 57

1. Dahood, *Psalms*, 1:50.
2. See, for example, the outlines for Psalms 12; 16; 25.
3. Wilson, *Psalms*, 1:830.
4. On *miktam*, see the comments on the title for Psalm 16.
5. Delitzsch gives a list of similarities in the psalms that he believes belonged to the time of Saul (*Psalms*, 2:173).
6. Kimhi, *Psalms (42–72)*, 376.
7. Hakham, *Psalms*, 1:448.
8. Tate, *Psalms 51–100*, 76.
9. Goldingay, *Psalms*, 2:193.
10. Tate, *Psalms 51–100*, 76.
11. Hakham, *Psalms*, 1:448n2.
12. Kidner, *Psalms 1–72*, 206.
13. Hakham, *Psalms*, 1:449.
14. For more information on the "lyre" (*kinnor*) and "harp" (*nebel*), see Braun, *Music*, 16–19 and 22–24, respectively.
15. Phillips, *Ring of Truth*, 27.
16. Linton Weeks, "12 Half-Truths We Live With," National Public Radio, January 19, 2013, http://www.npr.org/2013/01/19/169709740/12-half-truths-we-live-with.
17. "Benjamin Franklin Quotes," Thinkexist.com, http://en.thinkexist.com/quotation/half_a_truth_is_often_a_great_lie/146051.html.
18. In Psalms, the NIV almost consistently translates the Hebrew word *hesed* ("loving-kindness") as "love" or "unfailing love." But it is not the exact equivalent of the New Testament *agapē*, although both have a covenantal association, *hesed* with the Mosaic covenant, and *agapē* with the new covenant in Christ.
19. Weiser, *Psalms*, 159.
20. Quoted in Kenneth Osbeck, *Amazing Grace: 366 Inspiring Hymn Stories for Daily Devotions* (Grand Rapids: Kregel, 1990), July 17.

Psalm 58

1. For example, Hosea 4:4–11; 5:1–2; Amos 2:6–8; 4:1–3; 6:1–6; Micah 3:9–12; Jeremiah 22; Ezekiel 34; see Gerstenberger, *Psalms*, 233.
2. Wilcock, *Psalms 1–72*, 211.
3. Koehler and Baumgartner, *Lexicon*, 2:935.
4. Perowne, *Psalms*, 2:455.
5. Perowne, *Psalms*, 2:456.
6. Ibn Ezra, *Second Book of Psalms*, 98.
7. Perowne, *Psalms*, 2:456.
8. Hilber, "Psalms," 373.

9. Cansdale, *Animals*, 206–7.
10. Coverdale, *Psalter*.
11. Terrien, *Psalms*, 439.
12. Hakham, *Psalms*, 2:6.
13. Koehler and Baumgartner, *Lexicon*, 1:594.
14. Delitzsch, *Psalms*, 2:184.
15. Dahood, *Psalms*, 2:56, 63.
16. Normally the word *'elohim* ("God"), which is plural in form, takes the singular verb/participle when it refers to Israel's God and the plural when it refers to the "gods" of the world. Here the plural participle is used, suggesting that it may mean: "Surely there are gods who judge the earth." See Kidner, *Psalms 1–72*, 210.
17. Barth, *Church Dogmatics*, 4.1:591–92.
18. Wilcock, *Psalms 1–72*, 209.
19. "Holodomor Facts and History," http://www.holodomorct.org/history.html; "The History Place: Genocide in the 20th Century," http://www.historyplace.com/worldhistory/genocide/stalin.htm.
20. "Killing Fields," *Metapedia*, last modified January 2, 2012, http://en.metapedia.org/wiki/Killing_Fields.
21. "North Korea's Crimes against Humanity Have 'No Parallel' Today," *Washington Post*, WP Opinions, February 19, 2014, http://www.washingtonpost.com/opinions/north-koreas-crimes-against-humanity-have-no-parallel-today/2014/02/19/dafec350-99a7-11e3-b88d-f36c07223d88_story.html.
22. Richard Mouw, "Getting to the Crux of Calvary," *Christianity Today*, June 4, 2012, http://www.christianitytoday.com/ct/2012/may/getting-to-the-crux-of-calvary.html.
23. Wilcock, *Psalms*, 2:210.
24. Kidner, *Psalms*, 2:208–9.

Psalm 59

1. Hilber, "Psalms," 373.
2. Hakham, *Psalms*, 2:11.
3. Kidner, *Psalms 1–72*, 214.
4. Kidner, *Psalms 1–72*, 212; see also Wilson, *Psalms*, 1:855–56.
5. Schaefer, *Psalms*, 146.
6. George MacDonald, *A Quiet Neighborhood* (Colorado Springs: Victor Books, 1997), 74.
7. Jim Manney, *A Simple, Life-Changing Prayer: Discovering the Power of St. Ignatius Loyola's Examen* (Chicago: Loyola Press, 2011), 22.

Psalm 60

1. Bullock, *Encountering*, 136–38.
2. Delitzsch, *Psalms*, 2:193–94.
3. Hakham, *Psalms*, 2:26.
4. A. A. Anderson, *Psalms 1–72*, 442.
5. A. A. Anderson, *Psalms 1–72*, 442.
6. Hilber, "Psalms," 373.
7. Hakham, *Psalms*, 2:23n12.
8. Delitzsch, *Psalms*, 2:128.
9. Goldingay, *Psalms*, 2:231.
10. Goldingay, *Psalms*, 2:231.
11. Hakham, *Psalms*, 2:24.
12. Hakham, *Psalms*, 2:24.

13. Delitzsch, *Psalms*, 2:198.

14. Delitzsch, *Psalms*, 2:199.

15. Hakham, *Psalms*, 2:24.

16. Delitzsch, *Psalms*, 2:200.

17. Weiser, *Psalms*, 441.

18. Weiser, *Psalms*, 441–42.

19. Weiser, *Psalms*, 441–42.

20. "Top 10 Wrongly Attributed Inventions," List-Verse, April 10, 2009, http://listverse.com/2009/04/10/top-10-wrongly-attributed-inventions/.

21. "Milestones: 1861–1865, Preventing Diplomatic Recognition of the Confederacy," U.S. Department of State, Office of the Historian, https://history.state.gov/milestones/1861-1865/confederacy.

22. "Tim Tebow and Facial Evangelism," Contextual Criticism (blog), November 8, 2008, http://mythandhope.blogspot.com/2008/11/tim-tebow-linking-to-jesus.html.

Psalm 61

1. Tate, *Psalms 51–100*, 110.

2. Kraus, *Psalms 60–150*, 9–10.

3. Hakham, *Psalms*, 2:30.

4. Richard E. Averbeck, "*shelem*," *NIDOTTE* 4:135.

5. Bullock, *Encountering*, 29.

6. Hakham, *Psalms*, 2:28.

7. Hakham, *Psalms*, 2:30. See also Psalm 50:14; 2 Samuel 15:7–8.

8. They were poor and as a rule lived in service to an Israelite who was their master and protector (Lev. 19:10; 23:22; 25:6).

9. Selderhuis, *John Calvin*, 161.

10. William J. Federer, "Abraham Lincoln's Proclamation Appointing a National Fast Day," in *America's God and Country: Encyclopedia of Quotations* (St. Louis: Amerisearch, 2000), 170–71.

Psalm 62

1. Bullock, *Encountering*, 166–74.

2. Schaefer, *Psalms*, 149.

3. Kidner, *Psalms 1–72*, 221.

4. Hilber, "Psalms," 374, calls attention to the fact that in Mesopotamia and Ugarit, worshipers provided a defensive system against curses by their prayers and rituals.

5. Hakham, *Psalms*, 1:306, and n. 1.

6. Hakham, *Psalms*, 32.

7. A. A. Anderson, *Psalms 1–72*, 453.

8. Roth, *Numerical Sayings*, 55.

9. Koehler and Baumgartner, *Lexicon*, 1:45.

10. J. D. Childs with Robert Feduccia Jr., *Teaching Manual for Great Catholic Writings* (Winona, MN: St. Mary's Press, 2006), 106.

11. Alexander Eichler, "Mega Millions Lottery Could Make You More Likely to Go Bankrupt," *Huffington Post*, March 20, 2012, http://www.huffingtonpost.com/2012/03/30/mega-millions-lottery-bankrupt_n_1392414.html.

12. Ken Gire, *Relentless Pursuit: God's Love of Outsiders including the Outsider in All of Us* (Bloomington, MN: Bethany House, 2012), 24–25.

Psalm 63

1. Bullock, *Encountering*, 144.

2. Kraus, *Psalms 1–59*, 47–52.

3. A. A. Anderson, *Psalms 1–72*, 455.

4. Delitzsch, *Psalms*, 2:213.

5. Aharoni, *Land of the Bible*, 41.

6. A. A. Anderson, *Psalms 1–72*, 456.

7. Hakham, *Psalms*, 2:38.

8. A. A. Anderson, *Psalms 1–72*, 457–58.

9. See "Additional Insights: The Afterlife and Immortality in the Old Testament" following the unit on Psalm 49; see also the sidebar "Death and the Underworld," in Hilber, "Psalms," 348–49.

10. A. A. Anderson, *Psalms 1–72*, 460.

11. Kidner, *Psalms 1–72*, 224.

12. Chris Berdik, interview by Gareth Cook, "How the Power of Expectations Can Allow You to 'Bend Reality,'" *Scientific American*, October 16, 2012, http://www.scientificamerican.com/article/how-the-power-of-expectations-can-allow-you-to-bend-reality/.

13. John Piper, *When I Don't Desire God: How I Fight for Joy* (Wheaton: Crossway, 2004), 172.

Psalm 64

1. Wilson, *Psalms*, 1:898, 900.

2. Braude, *Midrash*, 1:526–29.

3. Hakham, *Psalms*, 2:49–50.

4. A. A. Anderson, *Psalms 1–72*, 461.

5. Hakham, *Psalms*, 2:45.

6. Dahood, *Psalms*, 2:103.

7. Schaefer, *Psalms*, 155.

8. Weiser, *Psalms*, 458. See also Schaefer's lineup (*Psalms*, 155).

9. Spurgeon, *Treasury of David*, 3:154.

10. Spurgeon, *Treasury of David*, 3:154.

11. Joachim Neander, "Praise to the Lord, the Almighty," trans. Catherine Winkworth, in *The Covenant Hymnal* (Chicago: Covenant Press, 1973), no. 29.

Psalm 65

1. Bullock, *Encountering*, 159–63.

2. Kidner, *Psalms 1–72*, 229.

3. Wilcock, *Psalms 1–72*, 228.

4. Hakham, *Psalms*, 2:51.

5. Hakham, *Psalms*, 2:57.

6. Goldingay, *Psalms*, 2:277.

7. Hakham, *Psalms*, 2:54.

8. Craig D. Atwood, *Always Reforming: A History of Christianity since 1300* (Macon, GA: Mercer University Press, 2001), 82.

9. Bryan Nelson, "What Can 28,000 Rubber Duckies Lost at Sea Teach Us about Our Oceans?," Mother Nature Network, March 1, 2011, http://www.mnn.com/earth-matters/wilderness-resources/stories/what-can-28000rubber-duckies-lost-at-sea-teach-us-about.

Psalm 66

1. Schaefer, *Psalms*, 160.

2. A. A. Anderson, *Psalms 1–72*, 472.

3. Wilson, *Hebrew Psalter*, 163–64; Wilson, *Psalms*, 1:915.

4. A. A. Anderson, *Psalms 1–72*, 472–73.

5. A. A. Anderson, *Psalms 1–72*, 473.

6. Hakham, *Psalms*, 2:62.

7. Hakham, *Psalms*, 2:62.

8. Goldingay, *Psalms*, 2:295.

9. Hakham, *Psalms*, 2:64.

10. Hakham, *Psalms*, 2:64.

11. Calvin, *Psalms*, 2:478.

12. "Oak Tree Facts," SoftSchools.com, http://www.softschools.com/facts/plants/oak_tree_facts/505/.

13. Augustine, *The Confessions of St. Augustine*, trans. Rex Warner (New York: New American Library, 1963), iii.11.

14. "Divorce in America," Daily Infographic, October 24, 2013, http://dailyinfographic.com/divorce-in-america -infographic: "41% of first marriages end in divorce; 60% of second marriages end in divorce, 73% of third marriages end in divorce."

15. David M. Buss and Todd K. Shackelford, "Susceptibility to Infidelity in the First Year of Marriage," *Journal of Research in Personality* 31 (1997): 194, http://www.todd kshackelford.com/downloads/Buss-Shackelford-JRP-1997 .pdf.

Psalm 67

1. Weiser, *Psalms*, 472.

2. Hakham, *Psalms*, 2:67.

3. Mays, *Psalms*, 224.

4. Wilson, *Psalms*, 1:928.

5. Alden, *Psalms*, 2:42, gives a chiastic outline of the psalm that is very similar to ours.

6. Wilson, *Psalms*, 1:927.

7. Barkay, "Amulets from Ketef Hinnom."

8. Hakham, *Psalms*, 2:66.

9. Weiser, *Psalms*, 477.

10. "About Wycliffe," Wycliffe Bible Translators, https://www.wycliffe.org/about.

11. Lisa Pevtzow, "They're on a Mission," *Chicago Tribune*, August 22, 2012.

12. William Hageman, "Keeping the Faith at Home," *Chicago Tribune*, August 22, 2012.

13. Tom Holladay and Kay Warren, *Foundations: 11 Core Truths to Build Your Life On; Teacher's Guide*, vol. 2 (Grand Rapids: Zondervan, 2003), 189–90.

Psalm 68

1. Hossfeld and Zenger, *Psalms 2*, 161.

2. Wilson, *Hebrew Psalter*, 190–91.

3. See Thielman, *Ephesians*, 265, and his general discussion of Paul's use of Psalm 68 (265–73).

4. Stec, *Targum of Psalms*, 2.

5. Hakham, *Psalms*, 2:88.

6. Kidner, *Psalms 1–72*, 238.

7. Dahood, *Psalms*, 2:137.

8. Hakham, *Psalms*, 2:73.

9. Hakham, *Psalms*, 2:76.

10. Albright, "Early Hebrew Lyric Poems," 23.

11. Hakham, *Psalms*, 2:77n24b.

12. Hakham, *Psalms*, 2:80.

13. Hakham, *Psalms*, 2:85n48.

14. John Newton, "Amazing Grace," *The Covenant Hymnal* (Chicago: Covenant Press, 1973), no. 305.

15. This phrase is from A. Catherine Hankey's hymn "Tell Me the Old, Old Story," but she does not rehearse Israel's history as the paradigm of the church's story.

16. Patrick Henry Reardon, *Christ in the Psalms* (Ben Lomond, CA: Conciliar Press, 2000), 134.

17. For more on the life of John Newton, see "Illustrating the Text" in the unit on Psalm 34.

18. "Children's Statistics," SOS Children's Villages USA, http://www.sos-usa.org/our-impact/childrens-statistics.

Psalm 69

1. Hakham, *Psalms*, 2:105.

2. Hakham, *Psalms*, 2:104.

3. Hilber, "Psalms," 377; Paul, "Heavenly Tablets."

4. Calvin, *Psalms*, 3:50.

5. Tate, *Psalms 51–100*, 196.

6. Wilson, *Psalms*, 1:951–52.

7. Hossfeld and Zenger, *Psalms 2*, 181.

8. Kidner, *Psalms 1–72*, 248.

9. Hakham, *Psalms*, 2:101.

10. Kidner, *Psalms 1–72*, 249.

11. "Joshua Lawrence Chamberlain," Civil War Trust, http://www.civilwar.org/education/history/biographies /joshua-lawrence-chamberlain.html.

12. James Emery White, *A Traveler's Guide to the Kingdom: Journeying through the Christian Life* (Downers Grove, IL: InterVarsity, 2012), 26–27.

Psalm 70

1. Goldingay, *Psalms*, 2:358.

2. Dorothy L. Sayers, *Letters to a Diminished Church: Passionate Arguments for the Relevance of Christian Doctrine* (Nashville: W Publishing Group, 2004), 2.

3. Charlene Israel, "Remembering Prison Fellowship's Chuck Colson," CBN News, April 23, 2012, https://www .cbn.com/cbnnews/us/2012/April/Chuck-Colson-Dies-at-80/.

Psalm 71

1. Braude, *Midrash*, 1:555.

2. Hakham, *Psalms*, 2:117.

3. Crenshaw, *Psalms*, 149.

4. See Crenshaw's discussion of this topic (*Psalms*, 145).

5. Doug Binder, "Prep Runner Carries Foe to Finish Line," June 5, 2012, http://espn.go.com/high-school/track -and-xc/story/_/id/8010251/high-school-runner-carries -fallen-opponent-finish-line.

6. Sarah Bigler, "What the Statue of Liberty Symbolizes," Travel Tips, *USA Today*, http://traveltips.usatoday .com/statue-liberty-symbolizes-29045.html.

Psalm 72

1. Calvin, *Psalms*, 3:100.

2. Hilber, "Psalms," 377.

3. Wilson, *Psalms*, 1:988.

4. Hakham, *Psalms*, 2:122.

5. Hakham, *Psalms*, 2:123.

6. Hakham, *Psalms*, 2:123.

7. Walton (*Genesis*, 393–94) offers an attractive interpretation of the two verbs for blessing in the Abraham story (e.g., Niphal [passive] in Gen. 12:3 et al.; and Hitpael [reflexive] in Gen. 22:18 et al.). He suggests that the writer nuanced his terms so that some contexts require the passive form ("be blessed"), meaning that the blessing will come through Abraham, while others require the reflexive ("bless themselves"), in that they will ingratiate themselves to God/king/Abraham's seed.

8. Hakham, *Psalms*, 2:127–28.

9. Milton Mayer, *They Thought They Were Free: The Germans, 1933–1945* (Chicago: University of Chicago Press, 1955), 55.

10. David Browne, *Family Preparedness for the New Millennium* (Bloomington, IN: iUniverse Books, 2013), 8.

11. "2013 World Hunger and Poverty Facts and Statistics," Hunger Notes, http://www.worldhunger.org/articles/Learn/world%20hunger%20facts%202002.htm.

12. Leland Ryken and Marjorie Lamp Mead, *A Reader's Guide through the Wardrobe: Exploring C. S. Lewis's Classic Story* (Downers Grove, IL: InterVarsity, 2005), 115.

Additional Insights, pp. 552–53

1. Hossfeld and Zenger, *Psalms*, 2:199–200.

Bibliography

Recommended Resources

Anderson, A. A. *Psalms 1–72.* Vol. 1 of *The Book of Psalms.* New Century Bible. Grand Rapids: Eerdmans, 1972.

Craigie, Peter C. *Psalms 1–50.* Word Biblical Commentary 19. Waco: Word, 1983.

Goldingay, John. *Psalms.* 3 vols. Baker Commentary on the Old Testament Wisdom and Psalms. Grand Rapids: Baker Academic, 2006.

Holladay, William L. *The Psalms through Three Thousand Years: Prayerbook of a Cloud of Witnesses.* Minneapolis: Fortress, 1993.

Kidner, Derek. *Psalms 1–72.* Tyndale Old Testament Commentaries. 14a. Downers Grove, IL: InterVarsity, 1973.

Select Bibliography

Adamson, James B. *The Epistle of James.* New International Commentary on the New Testament. Grand Rapids: Eerdmans, 1976.

Aharoni, Yohanan. *The Land of the Bible: A Historical Geography.* Translated by A. F. Rainey. Rev. ed. Philadelphia: Westminster, 1979.

Albright, W. F. "A Catalogue of Early Hebrew Lyric Poems." *Hebrew Union College Annual* 23 (1950–51): 1–39.

Alden, Robert. *Psalms: Songs of Dedication.* Vol. 2. Chicago: Moody, 1975.

Alter, Robert. *The Book of Psalms: A Translation with Commentary.* New York: Norton, 2007.

Anderson, Bernhard W. *Out of the Depths: The Psalms Speak for Us Today.* 3rd ed. Louisville: Westminster John Knox, 2000.

Augustine. *On the Psalms.* Translated by Dame Scholastical Hebgin and Dame Felicitas Corrigan. Ancient Christian Writers. Volume 1: Psalms 1–29; Volume 2: Psalms 30–37. New York: Paulist Press, 1960–61.

Bach, Johann Sebastian. "Cantata 31." In *Handbook to Bach's Sacred Cantata Texts: An Interlinear Translation with Reference Guide to Biblical Quotations and Allusions,* edited by Melvin P. Unger, 110. London: Scarecrow, 1996.

Bainton, Roland H. *Here I Stand: A Life of Martin Luther.* Nashville: Abingdon, 1950.

Barkay, G. "The Amulets from Ketef Hinnom: A New Edition and Evaluation." *Bulletin of the American Schools of Oriental Research* 334 (2004): 41–71.

Barth, Karl. *Church Dogmatics.* Vol. 4.1, *The Doctrine of Reconciliation,* translated by G. W. Bromiley. Edinburgh: T&T Clark, 1956.

Beale, G. K., and D. A. Carson, eds. *Commentary on the New Testament Use of the Old Testament.* Grand Rapids: Baker Academic, 2007.

Bernanos, George. *The Diary of a Country Priest.* Translated by Pamela Morris. New York: Macmillan, 1937.

Blank, Sheldon H. *Jeremiah, Man and Prophet.* Cincinnati: Hebrew Union College Press, 1961.

———. *The Prophetic Faith of Isaiah.* New York: Harper, 1958.

The Book of Common Worship. Presbyterian Church in the U.S.A. Philadelphia: Board of Christian Education of the Presbyterian Church in the United States of America, 1946.

Bouwsma, William J. *John Calvin: A Sixteenth-Century Portrait.* New York: Oxford, 1988.

Braude, William G. *The Midrash on Psalms.* Vol. 1. New Haven: Yale University Press, 1959.

Braun, Joachim. *Music in Ancient Israel/Palestine*. Translated by Douglas W. Stott. Grand Rapids: Eerdmans, 2002.

Briggs, Charles Augustus, and Emily Grace Briggs. *A Critical and Exegetical Commentary on the Book of Psalms*. 2 vols. International Critical Commentary. New York: Scribner's, 1907.

Brown, W. P. *Character in Crisis: A Fresh Approach to the Wisdom Literature of the Old Testament*. Grand Rapids: Eerdmans, 1996.

Brueggemann, Walter. *The Land*. Philadelphia: Fortress, 1977.

Buber, Martin. *Right and Wrong*. London: SCM, 1952.

Bullock, C. Hassell. *Encountering the Book of Psalms: A Literary and Theological Introduction*. Grand Rapids: Baker Academic, 2001.

———. "Ethics." In *Dictionary of the Old Testament: Wisdom, Poetry & Writings*, edited by Tremper Longman III and Peter Enns, 193–200. Downers Grove, IL: IVP Academic, 2008.

———. *An Introduction to the Old Testament Poetic Books*. Rev. ed. Chicago: Moody, 2007.

———. "The Shape of the Torah as Reflected in the Psalter, Book 1." In *From Creation to New Creation: Essays in Honor of G. K. Beale*, edited by Daniel M. Gurtner and Benjamin L. Gladd, 31–50. Peabody, MA: Hendrickson, 2013.

Calvin, John. *Commentaries on the Epistle of Paul the Apostle to the Romans*. Vol. 19 of *Calvin's Commentaries*. Translated by John Owen. Grand Rapids: Baker Books, 2003.

———. *Commentary on the Book of Psalms*. 5 vols. 1845–49. Reprint, Grand Rapids: Baker, 1979.

Cansdale, G. S. *Animals of Bible Lands*. Exeter: Paternoster, 1970.

Carasik, Michael. *The Commentators' Bible: Leviticus; The JPS Miqra'ot Gedolot*. Philadelphia: Jewish Publication Society, 2004.

Card, Michael. *A Sacred Sorrow Experience Guide: Reaching Out to God in the Lost Language of Lament*. Colorado Springs: NavPress, 2005.

Cheung, Chi Chung (Simon). *Wisdom Intoned: A Reappraisal of "Classifying Wisdom Psalms."* Thesis. St. Edmund's College, University of Cambridge, 2010.

Clines, David J. A. *Job 1–20*. Word Biblical Commentary. Dallas: Word, 1989.

Conomos, Dimitri E. *The Late Byzantine and Slavonic Communion Cycle: Liturgy and Music*. Dumbarton Oaks Studies 21. Washington, D.C.: Dumbarton Oaks Research Library and Collection, 1984.

Cottrill, Amy C. *Language, Power, and Identity in the Lament Psalms of the Individual*. New York: T&T Clark, 2008.

Coverdale, Miles. *The Psalter*, edited by W. S. Peterson and Valerie Macys. http://www.lutheransonline.com/lo/675/FSLO-1059011476-804675.pdf.

Craigie, Peter C. *The Book of Deuteronomy*. New International Commentary on the Old Testament. Grand Rapids: Eerdmans, 1976.

———. "The Poetry of Ugarit and Israel." *Tyndale Bulletin* 22 (1971): 3–31.

———. *The Problem of War in the Old Testament*. Grand Rapids: Eerdmans, 1978.

Crenshaw, James L. *The Psalms: An Introduction*. Grand Rapids: Eerdmans, 2001.

Culley, Robert C. *Oral Formulaic Language in the Biblical Psalms*. Near and Middle East Series 4. Toronto: University of Toronto Press, 1967.

Dahood, Mitchell J. *Psalms*. 3 vols. Anchor Bible 16, 17, 17A. Garden City, NY: Doubleday, 1966–70.

Davidson, A. B. *The Theology of the Old Testament*. Edinburgh: T&T Clark, 1904.

Davidson, Robert. *The Vitality of Worship: A Commentary on the Book of Psalms*. Grand Rapids: Eerdmans, 1998.

Davis, Ellen F. *Getting Involved with God*. Cambridge, MA: Cowley, 2001.

Delitzsch, Franz. *Biblical Commentary on the Psalms*. 3 vols. London: Hodder & Stoughton, 1888–94.

De Vaux, Roland. *Ancient Israel: Its Life and Institutions*. London: Darton Longman & Todd, 1961.

Eaton, John. *The Psalms*. London: T&T Clark, 2003.

Eerdmans, B. D. *The Book of Psalms*. Cambridge: Cambridge University Press, 1951.

Eichrodt, Walter. *Theology of the Old Testament*. 2 vols. Old Testament Library. Philadelphia: Westminster, 1961–67.

Eissfeldt, Otto. *Kleine Schriften*. 5 vols. Tübingen: Mohr, 1962–73.

Elmslie, W. A. L. *Studies in Life from Jewish Proverbs*. London: Clarke, 1917.

Ferris, Paul Wayne, Jr. *The Genre of Communal Lament in the Bible and the Ancient Near East*. Atlanta: Scholars Press, 1992.

Gaster, Theodor H. "Short Notes." *Vetus Testamentum* 4 (1954): 73–79.

Gerhardt, Paul. "If God Himself Be for Me." In *The Lutheran Book of Worship*, translated by Richard Massie, no. 454. Minneapolis: Augsburg, 1978.

Gerstenberger, Erhard S. *Psalms: Part 1 with an Introduction to Cultic Poetry*. Forms of the Old Testament Literature 14. Grand Rapids: Eerdmans, 1988.

Goulder, Michael D. *The Psalms of the Sons of Korah*. Journal for the Study of the Old Testament Supplement Series 20. Sheffield: JSOT Press, 1982.

Groenewoud, E. M. C. "Use of Water in Phoenician Sanctuaries." *Journal of the Ancient Near Eastern Society* 38 (2001): 149–50.

Gruber, Mayer I. *Rashi's Commentary on the Psalms*. Brill Reference Library of Judaism 18. Leiden: Brill, 2004.

Gundry, Stanley N., ed. *Show Them No Mercy: Four Views on God and Canaanite Genocide*. Grand Rapids: Zondervan, 2003.

Gunkel, Hermann. *Introduction to Psalms: The Genres of the Religious Lyric of Israel*. Translated by James D. Nogalski. Macon, GA: Mercer University Press, 1998.

———. *The Psalms: A Form-Critical Introduction*. Philadelphia: Fortress, 1967.

Hakham, Amos. *The Bible: Psalms with the Jerusalem Commentary*. 3 vols. Jerusalem Commentary. Jerusalem: Mosad Harav Kook, 2003.

Hengstenberg, E. W. *Commentary on the Psalms*. Translated by P. Fairbairn and J. Thomson. 3rd ed. 3 vols. Edinburgh: T&T Clark, 1851.

Hilber, John H. W. *Cultic Prophecy in the Psalms*. Berlin: De Gruyter, 2005.

———. "Psalms." In *Zondervan Illustrated Bible Backgrounds Commentary: Old Testament*, edited by John W. Walton, 5:316–463. Grand Rapids: Zondervan, 2009.

Hoerth, Alfred J. *Archaeology and the Old Testament*. Grand Rapids: Baker, 1998.

Holladay, William L., ed. *A Concise Hebrew and Aramaic Lexicon of the Old Testament*. Grand Rapids: Eerdmans, 1972.

Hossfeld, Frank-Lothar, and Erich Zenger. *Psalms 2: A Commentary on Psalms 51–100*. Hermeneia. Minneapolis: Fortress, 2005.

———. *Psalms 3: A Commentary on Psalms 101–151*. Hermeneia. Minneapolis: Fortress, 2011.

Hrushovski, Benjamin. "Prosody, Hebrew." In *Encyclopedia Judaica*, 2nd ed., edited by Michael Berenbaum and Fred Skolnik, 16:595–623. Detroit: MacMillan Reference, 2007.

Ibn Ezra, Abraham. *Commentary on the Second Book of Psalms: Chapters 42–72*. Translated by H. Norman Strickman. Boston: Academic Studies, 2009.

Jenni, Ernst, and Claus Westermann, eds. *Theological Lexicon of the Old Testament*. Translated by Mark E. Biddle. 3 vols. Peabody, MA: Hendrickson, 1997.

Johnston, Philip S. "'Left in Hell,' Psalm 16, Sheol and the Holy One." In *The Lord's Anointed: Interpretation of Old Testament Messianic Texts*, edited by Philip E. Satterthwaite, Richard S. Hess, and Gordon J. Wenham, 213–22. Grand Rapids: Baker, 1995.

———. *Shades of Sheol*. Downers Grove, IL: InterVarsity, 2002.

Kaiser, Otto. "The Law as Center of the Hebrew Bible." In *Sha'arei Talmon: Studies in the Bible, Qumran, and the Ancient Near East Presented to Shemaryahu Talmon*, edited by Michael Fishbane and Emanuel Tov with the assistance of Weston W. Fields, 93–103. Winona Lake, IN: Eisenbrauns, 1992.

Kautzsch, E., ed. *Gesenius' Hebrew Grammar*. Translated by A. E. Cowley. 2nd ed. Oxford: Clarendon, 1910.

Keel, Othmar. *The Symbolism of the Biblical World: Ancient Near Eastern Iconography and the Book of Psalms*. Translated by Timothy J. Hallett. 1978. Reprint, Winona Lake, IN: Eisenbrauns, 1997.

Kierkegaard, Søren. *Purity of Heart Is to Will One Thing*. Translated by Douglas V. Steere. New York: Harper & Row, 1938.

Kimhi, David. *The Commentary of Rabbi David Kimhi on Psalms (42–72)*. Edited by Sidney I. Esterson. PhD diss., Johns Hopkins University, 1931. Reprinted from the Hebrew Union College Annual. Cincinnati, 1935.

Kirkpatrick, Alexander Francis. The Book of Psalms. Cambridge Bible for Schools and Colleges. Repr., Cambridge: Cambridge University Press, 1910.

Knight, William Allen. *The Song of Our Syrian Guest*. Norwood, MA: Plimpton, 1904.

Koehler, Ludwig, and Walter Baumgartner. *The Hebrew and Aramaic Lexicon of the Old Testament*. Leiden: Brill, 2001.

Kraus, Hans-Joachim. *Psalms 1–59: A Continental Commentary*. Translated by Hilton C. Oswald. Minneapolis: Augsburg, 1988.

———. *Psalms 60–150: A Continental Commentary*. Translated by Hilton C. Oswald. Minneapolis: Augsburg, 1989.

Krinetzki, L. "Jahwe ist uns Zuflucht und Wehr: Eine stilistisch-theologische Auslegung von Psalm 46 (45)." *Bibel und Leben* 3 (1962): 26–42.

Larue, Gerald A. "Recent Studies in *Hesed*." In *Hesed in the Bible*, edited by Nelson Glueck, translated by Alfred Gottschalk, 1–32. Cincinnati: Hebrew Union College Press, 1967.

Lewis, C. S. *Mere Christianity*. Westwood, NJ: Barbour, 1952.

———. *Reflections on the Psalms*. London: Geoffrey Bles, 1958.

———. *The Weight of Glory and Other Addresses*. New York: HarperCollins, 2001.

Longman, Tremper, III, and Daniel G. Reid. *God Is a Warrior*. Grand Rapids: Zondervan, 1995.

Luther, Martin. *First Lectures on the Psalms I*. Edited by Hilton C. Oswald. Vol. 10 of *Luther's Works*. Edited by Jaroslav Jan Pelikan and Helmut T. Lechman. St. Louis: Concordia, 1974.

———. "Preface to the Psalter." In *Word and Sacrament I*, edited by E. Theodore Bachman, vol. 35 of *Luther's Works*, 253–57. Philadelphia: Muhlenberg, 1960.

———. *The Table Talk of Martin Luther*. Edited by Thomas S. Kepler. Translated by William Hazlitt. Reprint, Grand Rapids: Baker Books, 1995.

Mays, James Luther. "The Place of the Torah-Psalms in the Psalter." *Journal of Biblical Literature* 106 (1987): 3–12.

———. *Psalms*. Interpretation. Louisville: John Knox, 1994.

Mazar, Amihai, and Nava Panitz-Cohen. "It Is the Land of Honey: Beekeeping at Tel Rehov." *Near Eastern Archaeology* 70 (2007): 202–19.

McCann, J. Clinton, Jr. "Books I–III and the Editorial Purpose of the Hebrew Psalter." In *The Shape and Shaping of the Psalter*, edited by J. C. McCann Jr., 93–107. Journal for the Study of the Old Testament Supplement Series 159. Sheffield: JSOT Press, 1993.

McFall, Leslie. "The Evidence for a Logical Arrangement of the Psalter." *Westminster Theological Journal* 62 (2000): 223–56.

Milgrom, Jacob. *Leviticus: A Book of Ritual and Ethics*. A Continental Commentary. Minneapolis: Augsburg Fortress, 2004.

Morris, Leon. *The Epistle to the Romans*. Pillar New Testament Commentary. Grand Rapids: Eerdmans, 1988.

Moule, C. F. D. *The Meaning of Hope*. Philadelphia: Fortress, 1963.

Mowinckel, Sigmund. *He That Cometh*. Translated by G. W. Anderson. Oxford: Blackwell, 1959.

———. *The Psalms in Israel's Worship*. Translated by D. R. Ap-Thomas. 2 vols. Oxford: Blackwell, 1962.

Murphy, Roland. "A Consideration of the Classification 'Wisdom Psalms.'" In *Congress Volume: Bonn, 1962*, 156–67. Supplements to Vetus Testamentum 9. Leiden: Brill, 1963.

———. *The Song of Songs*. Hermeneia. Minneapolis: Fortress, 1990.

Nareuveni, Nogah. *Tree and Shrub in Our Biblical Heritage*. Translated by Helen Frenkley. Kiryat Ono, Israel: Neot Kedumim, 1984.

Neale, John M., and Richard F. Littledale. *A Commentary on the Psalms: From Primitive and Mediaeval Writers*. 4 vols. 1884. Reprint, Charleston, SC: Nabu, 2010.

Paul, S. M. "Heavenly Tablets and the Book of Life." *Journal of Near Eastern Studies* 5 (1973): 345–53.

Perowne, J. J. Stewart. *The Book of Psalms*. One-volume edition. London: George Bell, 1883.

Peters, John P. *The Psalms as Liturgies*. New York: Macmillan, 1922.

Phillips, J. B. *Ring of Truth: A Translator's Testimony*. New York: Macmillan, 1967.

Pippert, Wesley G. *Words from the Wise: An Arrangement by Word and Theme of the Entire Book of the Proverbs*. Longwood, FL: Xulon, 2003.

Prévost, Jean-Pierre. *A Short Dictionary of the Psalms*. Translated by Mary Misrahi. Collegeville, MN: Liturgical Press, 1997.

Pritchard, J. B, ed. *The Ancient Near East in Pictures relating to the Old Testament*. Princeton: Princeton University Press, 1954.

Roth, W. M. W. *Numerical Sayings in the Old Testament*. Vetus Testamentum Supplement 13. Leiden: Brill, 1965.

Ryken, Leland, James C. Wilhoit, and Tremper Longman III, eds. "Heel." In *Dictionary of Biblical Imagery*, 376. Downers Grove, IL: InterVarsity, 1998.

Sabourin, Leopold. *The Psalms: Their Origin and Meaning*. New York: Alba House, 1974.

Sakenfeld, Katharine Doob, ed. *The New Interpreter's Dictionary of the Bible*. 5 vols. Nashville: Abingdon, 2009.

Schaefer, Konrad. *Psalms*. Berit Olam: Studies in Hebrew Narrative and Poetry. Collegeville, MN: Liturgical Press, 2001.

Selderhuis, Herman J. *John Calvin: A Pilgrim's Life*. Downers Grove, IL: InterVarsity, 2009.

Snaith, Norman H. *The Distinctive Ideas of the Old Testament*. London: Epworth, 1944.

———. "Selah." *Vetus Testamentum* 2 (1952): 43–56.

Sperber, Alexander. *A Historical Grammar of Biblical Hebrew*. Leiden: Brill, 1966.

Spurgeon, C. H. *Psalms*. Vol. 1. Edited by Alister McGrath and J. I. Packer. Crossway Classic Commentaries. Wheaton: Crossway, 1993.

———. *The Treasury of David*. 3 vols. Reprint, Peabody, MA: Hendrickson, 2011.

Stec, David M. *The Targum of the Psalms*. Collegeville, MN: Liturgical Press, 2004.

Stewart, James S. *The Gates of New Life*. New York: Charles Scribner's Sons, 1940.

Tate, Marvin E. *Psalms 51–100*. Word Biblical Commentary 20. Dallas: Word, 1990.

Terrien, Samuel. *The Psalms: Strophic Structure and Theological Commentary*. Eerdmans Critical Commentary. Grand Rapids: Eerdmans, 2003.

Thielman, Frank. *Ephesians*. Baker Exegetical Commentary on the New Testament. Grand Rapids: Baker Academic, 2010.

VanGemeren, Willem, ed. *New International Dictionary of Old Testament Theology and Exegesis*. 5 vols. Grand Rapids: Zondervan, 1997.

———. "Psalms." In *The Expositor's Bible Commentary*, edited by Frank E. Gaebelein, 5:1–880. Grand Rapids: Zondervan, 1991.

Villanueva, Federico G. *The "Uncertainty of a Hearing": A Study of the Sudden Change of Mood in the Psalms of Lament*. Supplements to Vetus Testamentum 121. Leiden: Brill, 2008.

Vogt, E. "Psalm 226, ein Pilgergebet." *Biblica* 43 (1962): 328–37.

von Rad, Gerhard. *Holy War in Ancient Israel*. Translated by Marva J. Dawn. Grand Rapids: Eerdmans, 1991.

———. *Wisdom in Israel*. Nashville: Abingdon, 1972.

Waltner, James H. *Psalms*. Believers Church Bible Commentary. Scottdale, PA: Herald, 2006.

Walton, John W. *Genesis*. NIV Application Commentary. Grand Rapids: Zondervan, 2001.

Weatherhead, Leslie D. *A Shepherd Remembers*. London: Hodder & Stoughton, 1937.

Weiser, Artur. *The Psalms: A Commentary*. Old Testament Library. Philadelphia: Westminster, 1962.

Wenham, Gordon. *Psalms as Torah: Reading Biblical Song Ethically*. Grand Rapids: Baker Academic, 2012.

Westcott, Brooke Foss. *The Epistle to the Hebrews*. New York: Macmillan, 1906.

Westermann, Claus. *The Living Psalms*. Grand Rapids: Eerdmans, 1989.

————. *Praise and Lament in the Psalms*. Translated by Keith R. Crim and Richard N. Soulen. Edinburgh: T&T Clark, 1965.

————. *The Praise of God in the Psalms*. Translated by Keith R. Crim. Richmond, VA: John Knox, 1965.

————. "The Role of the Lament in the Theology of the Old Testament." *Interpretation* 28 (1974): 20–38.

White, Reginald E. O. *They Teach Us to Pray*. New York: Harper and Brothers, 1957.

Wilcock, Michael. *The Message of Psalms 1–72: Songs for the People of God*. The Bible Speaks Today. Downers Grove, IL: InterVarsity, 2001.

Wilson, Gerald Henry. *The Editing of the Hebrew Psalter*. Chico, CA: Scholars Press, 1985.

————. *Psalms*. Vol. 1. NIV Application Commentary. Grand Rapids: Zondervan, 2002.

————. "The Use of Royal Psalms at the 'Seams' of the Hebrew Psalter." *Journal for the Study of the Old Testament* 35 (1986): 85–94.

Witvliet, John D. *The Biblical Psalms in Christian Worship: A Brief Introduction and Guide to Resources*. Grand Rapids: Eerdmans, 2007.

Zenger, Eric. "The Composition and Theology of the Fifth Book of Psalms: Psalms 107–145." *Journal for the Study of the Old Testament* 80 (1998): 77–102.

————. *A God of Vengeance? Understanding the Psalms of Divine Wrath*. Translated by Linda M. Maloney. Louisville: Westminster John Knox, 1996.

Image Credits

Unless otherwise indicated, photos are copyright © Baker Publishing Group and Dr. James C. Martin. Unless otherwise indicated, illustrations and maps are copyright © Baker Publishing Group.

The Baker Photo Archive acknowledges the permission of the following institutions and individuals.

Photos on pages 89, 233 © Baker Publishing Group and Dr. James C. Martin. Courtesy of the Aegyptisches Museum, Berlin, Germany.

Photos on pages 156, 356 © Baker Publishing Group and Dr. James C. Martin. Courtesy of the Art Institute of Chicago.

Photos on pages 3, 9, 11, 18, 28, 48, 50, 68, 84, 114, 122, 126, 143, 145, 146, 160, 176, 183, 209, 218, 231, 236, 260, 262, 290, 340, 375, 392, 397, 399, 405, 454, 456, 465, 470, 474, 489, 517, 520, 531, 533 © Baker Publishing Group and Dr. James C. Martin. Courtesy of the British Museum, London, England.

Photos on pages 167, 168, 416 © Baker Publishing Group and Dr. James C. Martin. Courtesy of the Egyptian Ministry of Antiquities and the Museum of Egyptian Antiquities, Cairo, Egypt.

Photos on pages 22, 106, 223 © Baker Publishing Group and Dr. James C. Martin. Courtesy of the Eretz Museum, Tel Aviv, Israel.

Photos on pages 21, 54, 152, 245, 269, 284, 331, 336, 342, 367, 419, 445, 519 © Baker Publishing Group and Dr. James C. Martin. Collection of the Israel Museum, Jerusalem, and courtesy of the Israel Antiquities Authority, exhibited at the Israel Museum, Jerusalem.

Photo on page 207 © Baker Publishing Group and Dr. James C. Martin. Collection of the Israel Museum, Jerusalem, and courtesy of the Israel Antiquities Authority, exhibited at the Rockefeller Museum, Jerusalem.

Photos on pages 6, 507 © Baker Publishing Group and Dr. James C. Martin. Collection of the Israel Museum, Jerusalem, and courtesy of the Israel Antiquities Authority, exhibited at the Shrine of the Book, the Israel Museum, Jerusalem.

Photos on pages 184, 255, 428 © Baker Publishing Group and Dr. James C. Martin. Courtesy of the Metropolitan Museum of Art, New York.

Photos on pages 1, 71, 90, 113, 274, 338, 348, 545 © Baker Publishing Group and Dr. James C. Martin. Courtesy of the Musée du Louvre; Autorisation de photographer et de filmer. Louvre, Paris, France.

Photos on pages 81, 86, 196, 240, 271, 406, 508 © Baker Publishing Group and Dr. James C. Martin. Courtesy of the Oriental Institute Museum, Chicago.

Photos on pages 36, 539 © Baker Publishing Group and Dr. James C. Martin. Courtesy of the Pergamon Museum, Berlin.

Photo on page 8 © Baker Publishing Group and Dr. James C. Martin. Courtesy of the Skirball Museum, Hebrew Union College–Jewish Institute of Religion, 13 King David Street, Jerusalem 94101.

Photo on page 522 © Baker Publishing Group and Dr. James C. Martin. Courtesy of the Skulpturensammlung, Germany.

Photo on page 364 © Baker Publishing Group and Dr. James C. Martin. Courtesy of St. Catherine's Monastery, Sinai, Egypt.

Photos on pages 100, 170, 382 © Baker Publishing Group and Dr. James C. Martin. Courtesy of the Turkish

Ministry of Antiquities and the Istanbul Archaeological Museum.

Photo on page 501 © Baker Publishing Group and Dr. James C. Martin. Courtesy of the Turkish Ministry of Antiquities and the Museum of Anatolian Civilizations, Ankara, Turkey.

Photos on pages 24, 138, 249, 294 © Baker Publishing Group and Dr. James C. Martin. Courtesy of the Vatican Museum.

Additional image credits

Photo on page 504 © 3523studio / Shutterstock.com.

Photo on page 286 © AG-PHOTOS / Shutterstock.com.

Photo on page 227 © Albertus teolog / Wikimedia Commons.

Photo on page 327 © Bill Kennedy / Shutterstock.com.

Photo on page 48 © The British Library, London, UK / Bridgeman Images.

Photo on page 449 courtesy of The British Library, Creative Commons CC0 1.0 Universal Public Domain Dedication, http://www.bl.uk/catalogues/illuminated manuscripts/ILLUMIN.ASP?Size=mid&IllID=8730.

Photo on page 394 courtesy of The British Library, Creative Commons CC0 1.0 Universal Public Domain Dedication, http://www.bl.uk/catalogues/illuminated manuscripts/ILLUMIN.ASP?Size=mid&IllID=15711.

Photo on page 402 courtesy of The British Library, Creative Commons CC0 1.0 Universal Public Domain Dedication, http://www.bl.uk/catalogues/illuminated manuscripts/ILLUMIN.ASP?Size=mid&IllID=19732.

Photo on page 93 courtesy of The British Library, Creative Commons CC0 1.0 Universal Public Domain Dedication, http://www.bl.uk/catalogues/illuminated manuscripts/ILLUMIN.ASP?Size=mid&IllID=26233.

Photo on page 187 courtesy of The British Library, Creative Commons CC0 1.0 Universal Public Domain Dedication, http://www.bl.uk/catalogues/illuminated manuscripts/ILLUMIN.ASP?Size=mid&IllID=26234.

Photo on page 549 courtesy of The British Library, Creative Commons CC0 1.0 Universal Public Domain Dedication, http://www.bl.uk/catalogues/illuminated manuscripts/ILLUMIN.ASP?Size=mid&IllID=42209.

Photo on page 537 courtesy of The British Library, Creative Commons CC0 1.0 Universal Public Domain Dedication, http://www.bl.uk/catalogues/illuminated manuscripts/ILLUMIN.ASP?Size=mid&IllID=52150.

Photo on page 499 courtesy of The British Library, Creative Commons CC0 1.0 Universal Public Domain Dedication, http://www.bl.uk/catalogues/illuminated manuscripts/ILLUMIN.ASP?Size=mid&IllID=52888.

Photo on page 388 courtesy of The British Library, Creative Commons CC0 1.0 Universal Public Domain Dedication, http://www.bl.uk/catalogues/illuminated manuscripts/ILLUMIN.ASP?Size=mid&IllID=53825.

Photo on page 344 courtesy of The British Library, Creative Commons CC0 1.0 Universal Public Domain

Dedication, http://www.bl.uk/catalogues/illuminated manuscripts/ILLUMIN.ASP?Size=mid&IllID=57221.

Photo on page 251 © Dan Howell / Shutterstock.com.

Photo on page 212 © David P. Lewis.

Photo on page 59 © E. A. Wallis Budge (1857–1937) / Wikimedia Commons.

Photo on page 121 © Egyptian Museum, Turin, Italy / De Agostini Picture Library / The Bridgeman Art Library.

Photo on page 354 © Elzbieta Sekowska / Shutterstock .com.

Photo on page 56 courtesy of the Franklin D. Roosevelt Library and Museum, Hyde Park, New York.

Photos on pages 148, 410, 434 © Fred Mabie.

Photos on pages 13, 27, 33, 38, 96, 119, 299, 313 courtesy of the Getty's Open Content Program.

Photo on page 152 © Guillaume Piolle / Wikimedia Commons, CC-BY-3.0.

Photo on page 310 © Hill, W. E. (William Ely), 1887–1962, LC-DIG-ds-00175.

Photo on page 350 © J. Albert Cole. Prints & Photographs Division, Library of Congress, LC-USZ62-77142.

Photo on page 234 © karenfoleyphotography / Shutter stock.com.

Photo on page 179 © Kathryn Hooge.

Photo on page 62 © Kevin Key / Shutterstock.com.

Photos on pages 79, 133, 203, 229, 446, 468, 525 © Kim Walton.

Photos on pages 53, 64, 116, 193, 199, 201, 247, 281, 292, 304, 315, 332, 369, 371, 377, 422, 437, 443, 453, 462, 485, 512, 547, 550 © Kim Walton. Courtesy of the British Museum, London, England.

Photos on pages 210, 473 © Kim Walton. Collection of the Israel Museum, Jerusalem, and courtesy of the Israel Antiquities Authority, exhibited at the Israel Museum, Jerusalem.

Photos on pages 40, 45, 159, 267, 273, 316, 334, 386, 441 © Kim Walton. Courtesy of the Musée du Louvre; Autorisation de photographer et de filmer. Louvre, Paris, France.

Photos on pages 256, 289, 412, 508 © Kim Walton. Courtesy of the Oriental Institute Museum, Chicago.

Photo on page 30 © Kim Walton. Courtesy of the Pergamon Museum, Berlin.

Photo on page 83 © Kim Walton. Courtesy of The Reuben and Edith Hecht Museum at the University of Haifa, Israel.

Photo on page 75 courtesy of Laing Art Gallery, Newcastle-upon-Tyne, UK / © Tyne & Wear Archives & Museums / Bridgeman Images.

Photo on page 486 © Lenka Peacock, 2007.

Photo on page 124 © Leoncillo Sabino. The Metropolitan Museum of Art, CC-by-2.0.

Photo on page 258 © TheLeopards / Wikimedia Commons.

Photo on page 276 © Library of Congress, Prints & Photographs Division, Civil War Photographs, [reproduction number, LC-DIG-cwpbh-03110].

Contributors

General Editors
Mark. L. Strauss
John H. Walton

Associate Editors, Illustrating the Text
Kevin and Sherry Harney

Contributing Author, Illustrating the Text
Donald C. Porter

Series Development
Jack Kuhatschek
Brian Vos

Project Editor
James Korsmo

Interior Design
Brian Brunsting
William Overbeeke

Visual Content
Kim Walton

Cover Direction
Paula Gibson
Michael Cook

Index

evildoers, 40–42, 46, 48, 100, 192, 194, 196, 210–11, 264, 275, 280, 282, 284, 403–6, 453, 486–87
exalt, 223
exile, exiles, 172, 414, 506, 531, 534, 538
exodus, 169–71, 248, 345, 347, 499, 500, 502, 513, 515, 516, 518
extortion, 473
eye of faith, 92
eyes of the Lord, 253, 256

face of God, 34, 92, 256, 330, 507, 509
fainting, 465, 467
faith, 233, 282–83, 287
  as a journey, 326
  confirmation of, 429
  constancy of, 542
  and practice, 253
  as public matter, 542
  vacuum of, 101
  and works, 550
faithfulness, 82, 273, 391, 435
faithful people. *See* hasid, hasidim
fall, 440
false gods, 34, 180
falsehood, 341
false witness, 177, 179, 383, 384
fat, 122, 274
fatherless, 71, 515
fear of man, 127–30
fear of the Lord, 137, 139, 185, 254–55, 257–59, 272, 464, 487
Feast of Tabernacles, 378
feeble, 290–91
firmament, 135
flattery, 272
fleeing, 76, 78
flood, 218, 219
foes, 46, 90
fool, 96, 98–99, 402, 406, 410
foolishness, of the world, 115
foreigners and strangers, 296, 300–303
forever, 209–10, 317
forgiveness, 116, 224, 238, 240, 393, 491–92, 493
"for pipes," 39
"for the sake of your name," 169, 170, 184–85, 333–34
fortifications, 361
"fortified city," 460
fortress, 132, 212, 450, 472, 476, 540
foundations, 76, 77, 80, 86
fountain of life, 272, 274
freewill offering, 410
friends, betrayal by, 316
fuller sense (*sensus plenior*), 341, 548
future, 282

Gath, 59, 253, 254, 424, 425, 426
gentiles, 127, 355–56, 437, 493
Gilead, 459, 461
gloating, 451
glory, 217–18, 220, 225, 254, 287
God
  anger as short lived, 224
  answers prayer, 46, 502
  as archer, 486–88
  covenant faithfulness of, 46, 230, 233
  covenant with Israel, 35–36

  does not change, 418
  enduring love of, 10
  as exalted, 265
  faithfulness of, 184, 192, 275, 435–37, 466, 468, 498
  "flawless" word of, 80–81, 82, 83, 84, 131
  forsakes his Son, 162
  glory of, 63, 135–36, 138, 217–19, 220, 365, 480
  goodness of, 525
  greatness of, 533–35
  as guide, 364
  hands of, 230, 232, 234
  hatred of evil, 40–41, 76
  as help, 410, 411–12
  hiding his face, 225
  holiness of, 42, 459, 461
  intimacy with Israel, 123
  as judge, 443–44
  justice of, 56, 71, 275
  laughter of, 23, 24, 249, 280, 282, 399, 450, 452
  as light, 199–200, 202–3, 204
  looks down from heaven, 78, 99, 403
  love of, 125, 131, 184, 220, 275, 324, 326, 435–37, 454, 466, 468, 482
  majesty of, 60–61, 63–64
  as midwife, 163
  power of, 132, 151, 153, 220–21, 330, 411, 467, 476, 480
  presence of, 74, 114–16, 150, 347, 478, 518
  as refuge, 346, 359, 473
  rejects idolators, 231
  remoteness of, 157, 160
  restores his people, 99
  righteousness of, 33, 54, 55, 166, 275, 540, 541
  right hand of, 330
  as shepherd, 166, 168, 171, 488
  sovereignty of, 23, 41, 83, 161, 221, 248, 451, 542
  as strong tower, 465
  and suffering, 300
  transcendence and immanence of, 61–62, 139, 318, 437–38
  unfailing love of, 46, 47, 49, 150, 153, 192, 195, 196, 239, 244–45, 248–50, 274, 328, 333, 334, 362, 364, 390, 396, 400, 415, 474, 476, 569
  as with us, 430
  as warrior, 28, 51, 83, 152, 484
  wrath of, 290
God of Jacob, 347, 353
gold, 137
Goliath, 79, 451
good, 256
goodness and love, 169, 171–73, 174, 525
goodness and mercy, 325, 326
grace, 124, 131, 242, 317, 446, 495–97, 503, 508–9, 510, 519–20
grain, 33, 35
grass withers, 280
great assembly, 161, 308
groan, 83
guidance, 184, 186–87

habitation, 193
"Hallelujah" psalms, 11
Hammurabi's Law Code, 545–46
handbreadth, 297, 299
hard questions, 92
harp, 245, 369, 370, 436

harvest, 492, 509, 510

harvest hymn, 490

hasid, hasidim, 35, 82, 224, 228, 233, 239, 241, 379, 396, 400

heads, 178, 180

healing, 240, 317

hearing and seeing, 363

heart, 53

   secrets of, 332, 334

heaven, 349

heavenly beings, 216

heavenly temple, 134

heavenly throne, 76–77, 78, 355

heavens, 246, 273, 275, 436

   declare glory of God, 135–36, 138

Hebrew poetry, 4–5

helpless, 515

Heman the Ezrahite, 2

henotheism, 54, 215

herem, 152

Hermon, 324

hesed, 10–11, 35, 46, 47, 56, 153, 184, 186, 192, 220, 228, 233, 239, 244, 248, 271, 274, 325–26, 328, 379, 396, 397, 452, 474, 480, 481–82, 569

hiding place, 237, 239

historical titles, of psalms, 408, 409

holiness, 42, 216

holy life, 108

holy mountain, 29

holy of holies, 194

holy ones, 112

holy war, 152

honey, 137

honor, 472–73

hope, 183–84, 187, 248, 281, 282, 291, 298, 299, 304, 376, 540–41

horses, 142, 144, 146, 149, 297

house of mourning, 89

house of the Lord, 167, 171, 191, 198–99, 200, 203. *See also* dwelling place of God

"How long?," 46, 47, 89, 91

human effort, 460–62

humanity, 60, 72

human threats, 428

humility, 339, 341–42

hunting, 51, 75

hymn, 244, 352

hypocrites, hypocrisy, 192, 196, 210–11

hyssop, 390, 391

idolatry, 112, 177, 179, 511

image of God, 62

Immanuel, 430

immortality, 369, 376–77

imprecatory psalms, 67, 260–61, 262, 266, 269, 414, 418, 427, 522

incantations, 315

incarnation, 162, 164, 171

individual lament, 26, 44, 50, 74, 80, 88, 96, 118, 156, 182, 206, 222, 228, 262, 288, 296, 320, 414, 424, 432, 448, 464, 478, 484, 522

individual psalm of thanksgiving, 222, 236, 237, 253, 304, 498, 499

individual psalm of trust, 110, 166, 198, 228, 470

inhabiting praises of Israel, 159, 162, 164

inheritance, 112, 113–14, 115, 116, 209, 279, 280, 283, 515

injustice, 280, 284, 440–47

innocence, 191–92, 193, 194, 316, 486, 524

innocent suffering, 44

instruction, 186–87

instruments, 436

integrity, 53, 185, 195, 316

isolation, 328, 421

Israel

   faithful to covenant, 330, 332

   as God's inheritance, 209, 247

   in the wilderness, 480

jackals, 479, 481

Jacob, 178

javelin, 264

Jeduthun, 297, 472

Jehoshaphat, 329–30

Jerusalem, 167, 325, 326, 344, 348–49, 358, 363, 366–67, 420

Jesus Christ

   ascension of, 356–57

   betrayal of, 420

   death of, 161–62

   forsakenness of, 157

   as good shepherd, 171

   resurrection of, 111, 114

   as the way, and the truth, and the life, 109

Joab, 32

Job, 289, 300, 333, 556, 561

Joshua, 202, 203, 232, 234

joy, 153, 223, 224, 226–27, 326

   in God's presence, 191

   of the journey, 115–16

Judah, 459, 461, 517, 526

judgment, 17, 398

   on evildoers, 405–6

   of God, 194

justice, 70, 76–77, 120, 130, 152, 268–69, 273, 283, 339, 342, 444–45, 545–50

kidneys, 53

king

   coronation of, 354, 356

   prayer for, 142–43, 145

   See also royal psalms; psalms of the earthly king; psalms of the heavenly King

kingdom of God, 134, 161, 350, 356, 527–28

kingdom of priests, 493, 506

King of glory, 178–79, 180

King of kings, 341

kings, as shepherds, 167–68

kingship, 20, 336, 339, 544–50

kiss the son, 23

Korah psalms, 321–22, 358–59

labor pains, 361

lamb, psalmist as, 166

lament, 3–4, 26, 106, 198, 424

   of a king, 432

   and praise, 163–64

   See also community lament; individual lament

lamp, 199, 203

land of the living, 202

laughter of God, 23, 24, 249, 280, 282, 399, 450, 452

law, 121, 129
  in human hearts, 307, 309–10
law (*torah*), 136, 307
law court, 380–81
Lebanon, 219
lending money, 106
length of days, 149–50, 170
Levites, 110, 176, 322
liars, 81, 481
libations of blood, 112–13
lies and deceit, 53, 80, 82, 85, 86–87
life, 149–50, 161, 369
life after death, 122, 287
lifting up of hands, 480
lifting up the "soul," 182–83
light, 199, 202–3, 204, 325, 327
lightning, 129, 217, 219
lilies, 338, 457, 524
lions, 119, 122, 158, 159, 160, 255, 434, 436
liver, 436
lonely, 515
longing for God, 323, 325
Lord's Prayer, 527–28
Lord's Supper, 255
lot, 113, 115
love, 123, 132–33, 271, 273, 470
  for enemies, 107, 268–69
  for God, 127, 131–32, 260
  for God's name, 41
  for neighbor, 260, 269
  and truth, 438
loving-kindness, 35, 186
lyre, 436

mahalath, 403
malice, 208
Manasseh, 459, 461
mankind, 60–61, 72
maqef, 5
marriage, 136, 340–41, 343
martyrs, 431
maskil, 237, 323, 355, 396, 403, 408, 414
Masoretes, 4–5
meaninglessness, 299, 474
meditate, meditation, 364, 370, 480, 541
meek, 279, 280, 285
Melchizedek, 55, 150, 345, 347, 353, 354, 366
memorial sacrifice, 290
mercy, 44, 45, 390, 434, 474
Messiah, 21, 209, 261, 548–49
Messianic psalms, 66–67, 263, 557
metaphors, 75, 268
Michal, 449
mighty, 178
"mighty hero," 397–99, 402
mighty rulers, 216
miktam, 111, 426, 432, 456
military language, 130, 131–32, 199, 230
miracles, 510
mizmor, 27, 174, 490, 498
Moab, 459–60, 461
monotheism, 54, 116
moral law, and sacrifice, 307

morning sacrifice, 39
mortality, 71–72
Mosaic covenant, 36, 184, 186, 356, 381–82, 569
Moses, 1, 10, 72, 264–65, 466
Most High, 53, 54–55, 129, 150–51, 153, 345, 353, 354, 355, 435
mountain of the Lord, 174, 177, 191
mountains, 273, 275, 546
Mount Bashan, 516
Mount Mizar, 324
Mount Sinai, 208, 379
Mount Zalmon, 516
murder, 194
musical instruments, 245
musicality of the psalms, 246
muzzle, 297, 298
myrrh, 338, 339

Nabal, 99
name of God, 58, 333–34, 363–64
names of God, 34, 54–55, 97, 305, 322, 379, 453, 518
naming, 70
Naphtali, 517
nations, 21, 52, 71, 72, 355–56, 427, 436–37, 502, 506–10, 548
natural blessings, 510
nature, disordering of, 348–49
needy, 282, 312, 546–51
nepesh, 136, 161, 194, 230, 231, 264
new atheism, 102
new covenant, 36, 307, 309
new creation, 393
new song, 245, 305, 306
New Testament, quotation of psalms, 66–67, 287, 377, 488, 523, 557
new wine, 33, 35
next generation, 539, 541, 542
Noah, 106, 218, 219, 273
northern kingdom, 8, 320, 321

oaths, 52, 501
obedience, 36, 123, 310
offerings, 307, 309
oil, 209, 274, 416, 419
old age, 538–40
olive trees, 397, 398
only/alone, 474–75
"on the way," 197, 203
opposition, as relentless, 429
oppression, 548, 550
original sin, 391
other gods, 54
overcome, 91
ox, 217

pantheism, 98, 140
panting, 326
parallelism, 5
pastures, 167, 169
paths of life, 114–16, 166, 168, 184
patience, 286–87, 309
peace, 35, 216, 218, 219, 220, 256, 282
peace offering, 428, 465
penitential psalms, 44, 46–47, 388
persecution, 48, 160, 265
petition, 88, 288, 532

Philistia, 461
Philistines, 425
pierced hands and feet, 160
piety, 92
pilgrim prayer, 190
pit, 208, 224, 306, 370, 419
plea for help, 81
pleasures, 14
plunder, 83
poetry, 4–5
polytheism, 54, 61, 116
poor, 72–73, 81, 99, 101, 108, 282, 286, 312, 516
   and needy, 83–84, 531–33, 534
portion, 110, 112, 113, 115, 116
pottery, broken, 22, 231
practical atheism, 98, 101
praise, 2–3, 128, 161, 162–64, 209, 219, 491, 500–501, 502, 508, 526, 560
   of children and infants, 60
   of Israel, 159
   and lament, 163–64
prayer, 26, 91, 120, 211
   for enemies, 36
   of innocence, 118
"prayer of hurry," 534
prayer song of the sick, 222, 312
precepts, 136–37
presence of God, 114–16, 150, 347, 478, 518
pride, 276, 427, 451
pride of Jacob, 354, 451
problem of evil, 411, 556
processional liturgy, 179, 560
promised land, 168, 171, 203, 279, 301, 354, 502, 517
prophets, 308–9, 381
protection, 168
proud, 306
providence, 510
psalm of innocence, 190, 558
Psalms
   five books of, 8–11, 530–32, 538
   individual and corporate perspectives in, 206
   name, 1
   numbering of, 69, 70
   place in canon, 5–6
   reuse of, 223, 562
   structure and composition of, 7–11
psalms of anger, 260. See also imprecatory psalms
psalms of lament, 2, 3–4, 26, 325, 456. See also community lament; individual lament
psalms of praise, 2–3, 234, 355, 433. See also maskil
psalms of thanksgiving, 2, 69, 502. See also community psalm of thanksgiving; individual psalm of thanksgiving
psalms of the earthly king, 8, 20, 336, 337. See also royal psalms
psalms of the heavenly King, 157, 218, 330, 336, 337, 556. See also royal psalms
psalms of trust, 32, 111, 121, 166, 182, 344, 396
psalter, 1, 13
pure heart, 177, 180
"put to shame," 45, 183, 186, 230, 232, 233, 531, 540

queen, 340
question/answer format, 104, 108, 175, 177
quiet waters, 167, 169, 171

ramparts, 363
rebuke, 300
reconciliation, 34, 36
redeemer, 138
redemption, 247, 248, 252, 371, 372–74, 494–95, 500, 502
Red Sea, 248–49
refining, 501
reflective prayer, 111, 182, 432
refuge, 52, 76, 78, 112, 199, 255, 284, 435, 464, 468
reiteration and contrast, 444
rejoice, 240
remember, 184, 186, 288, 324
repentance, 53, 393–94
resident alien, 105, 466–67
rest, 168, 280, 472, 475, 501
restoration, 10, 317, 318, 392, 394
resurrection, 123, 371, 377
retribution, 282
riches, 475
riddle, 370
righteous, 99, 107, 282, 487, 516, 546–47
righteousness, 53, 100–101, 273, 492, 540
   of psalmist, 120, 123, 129, 130–31
righteous one, 17, 256, 313–14, 317, 532, 563
right hand, of God, 115, 121, 458–59, 481, 484
rise up. See arise/rise up
river, 345, 346–47, 349
rock, 132, 138, 464, 467, 468, 470, 472, 476, 540
   God as, 208, 213
rod and staff, 169
royal liturgy, 148, 198
royal psalms, 10, 20, 67, 126, 142, 148, 306, 336, 544. See also psalms of the earthly king; psalms of the heavenly King
ruin, 291
ruthless witnesses, 268

sackcloth, 225
sacrifice, sacrificial system, 34, 40, 144, 200, 307, 308–9, 379–80, 383–85, 388, 392–93, 500, 501, 502
safety, 35
saints, 112, 224, 229
salvation, 29, 90, 150, 291, 404, 472, 539
sanctuary, 191, 459, 461, 478, 480, 482
Satan, 542
Saul, 74, 111, 119, 254, 309, 424, 426, 433–34, 441, 449, 479
schemes, 194, 280, 291
scorn, 524
scribe, 338–39, 340
scroll, 307
sea, seas, 273, 345, 346, 492
security, 168, 208, 224
seeing God's face, 34, 78, 191
seeking God's face, 178, 201
selah, 28, 32, 50, 68, 178, 345–46, 410, 464, 556
self-examination, 124
self-image, of psalmist, 92–93
selfishness, 102
self-reliance, 146
Sennacherib, 491
Septuagint, 6, 7
servant of the Lord, 127–28, 135, 270–71
sevenfold curse, 441–43
shadow of death, 168

"shadow of your wings," 122, 124, 435, 439, 464–65, 481, 555
shaken, 106, 224
shalom, 546, 549
shame, 45, 183, 230, 540, 541
Shechem, 459, 461
sheep, as defenseless, 331
shelter, 465–66
Shema, 233, 382
sheminith, 45, 82
sheol, 46, 114, 128, 208, 224, 370, 374, 419
shepherd, 166, 168, 171, 209, 212, 371, 488
shield, 41, 51, 53, 209, 264, 348, 355, 562
shiggaion, 52
shir, 490, 498
shout, 354
sickbed, 314, 315
sickness, 298
    and sin, 288–92, 315
silent, silence, 208, 280, 298, 300, 428, 472, 491
silver, 82, 83, 85
sin, 44, 138–39, 188, 238, 450
    intentional and unintentional, 567–68
    recoils on sinner, 54
Sinai, 516
    theophany on, 381
singing praise, 70, 245–46, 298, 355, 500
slander, 106, 107, 315, 432, 435
snail, 441
snake, 442
snares, 486
social ostracism, 292
social status, 475
Sodom and Gomorrah, 75, 76
sojourner, sojourning, 105, 106, 466–67
Soli Deo Gloria, 163
Solomon, 1, 8, 21, 72, 338–39, 544, 546, 549
Song of Moses, 209, 331, 345
Song of Songs, 337, 339
song of the sick, 222
songs of deliverance, 239
son of man, 61, 67
sons of Adam, 81, 85, 440, 476
sons of Korah, 1, 321, 322–23, 330, 346
sorrow, 90, 429–30
soul, 46, 136, 161, 194, 264, 436
southern kingdom, 8, 526
speaking, 107
spear, 264
speech, 82, 123, 451, 453, 455
spirit, 230, 393
Spirit of God, 246–47
spiritual exercises, 29–30
statutes, 136
steadfast hearts, 436
steadfast love, 121
stealing, 194, 383, 384
still-born child, 441
still small voice, 216
storm, 214–18
straight path, 202
street, 229
strength, 208, 209, 220, 450
stringed instruments, 33, 409, 465, 507

stronghold, 199–200
strong tower, 465, 467
stumbling, 428
suffering, 41, 47, 48, 113, 185, 289, 292–93, 300, 309, 527–28
    of righteous, 368
Suffering Servant, 67, 524, 525
Sukkot, 215
Sukkoth, 459, 461
sword, 51, 160, 479
synonymous parallelism, 5

tabernacle, 39, 200, 224
Tarshish, 361
tasting and seeing the goodness of the Lord, 255, 257
teaching, 186–87
tearing down, 208–9
tears, 324
    in a bottle, 427, 430
teeth, 442
    of lions, 435, 440, 441
temple, 39, 76, 176–77, 178, 180, 191, 194, 200, 223, 362, 366–67, 500, 525
Ten Commandments, 127, 194, 379–80, 382, 386–87, 488
ten-stringed lyre, 245, 246
testimonies, 186
"test me," 191, 192
tetragrammaton, 54, 85, 97, 112, 305, 322, 379, 382, 402, 411, 476
thank offering, 383
thanksgiving psalms, 68, 69. *See also* community psalm of thanksgiving; individual psalm of thanksgiving
theodicy, 283
thief, 383
thirst for God, 323, 478–81
thunder, 129
tombs, 370
tongue, power of, 399–400, 486–88
Torah, 14, 15, 129, 138–39, 179. *See also* law (*torah*)
Torah psalms, 134, 135
trees, flourish and die, 280
tribute, 547
troubles, 308
truly/alone, 472, 474
trumpet, 354–55, 359
trust in the Lord, 76–78, 88, 91–94, 111, 159, 182–83, 190, 204, 234, 279, 282, 286, 470
    as antidote to fear, 127–30
    and blessing, 30
    in the name of the Lord, 144–45, 146–47
    in own resources, 146
truth, 81, 85–86, 325, 326, 339, 341, 411
    and love, 438
turn, turn back, 45
typology, 341
Tyre, 340

Ugaritic literature, 112–13
unbelief, 101
unfailing love. *See* God, unfailing love of
universal salvation, 506–10
untitled psalms, 68, 236, 244, 538
uprightness, 185

valley, 168
vanity, 299, 475